OXFORD STUDIES IN BYZANTIUM

Editorial Board

OXFORD STUDIES IN BYZANTIUM

Oxford Studies in Byzantium consists of scholarly monographs and editions on the history, literature, thought, and material culture of the Byzantine world.

BASIL II AND THE GOVERNANCE OF EMPIRE (976–1025)

Catherine Holmes

OXFORD
UNIVERSITY PRESS

OXFORD
UNIVERSITY PRESS

Great Clarendon Street, Oxford OX2 6DP

Oxford University Press is a department of the University of Oxford.
It furthers the University's objective of excellence in research, scholarship,
and education by publishing worldwide in

Oxford New York

Auckland Cape Town Dar es Salaam Hong Kong Karachi
Kuala Lumpur Madrid Melbourne Mexico City Nairobi
New Delhi Shanghai Taipei Toronto

With offices in

Argentina Austria Brazil Chile Czech Republic France Greece
Guatemala Hungary Italy Japan Poland Portugal Singapore
South Korea Switzerland Thailand Turkey Ukraine Vietnam

Oxford is a registered trade mark of Oxford University Press
in the UK and in certain other countries

Published in the United States
by Oxford University Press Inc., New York

British Library Cataloguing in Publication Data

Data available

Library of Congress Cataloging in Publication Data

Holmes, Catherine, 1968–
Basil II and the governance of Empire (976–1025) / Catherine Holmes.
p. cm. — (Oxford studies in Byzantium)
Includes bibliographical references and index.
1. Basil II, Emperor of the East, ca. 958–1025.
2. Emperors—Byzantine Empire—Biography. 3. Byzantine
Empire—History—Basil II Bulgaroctonus, 976–1025. 4. Scylitzes, John, fl. 1081.
Synopsis historiarum. I. Title. II. Series.

DF595.H65   2005   949.5 '02' 092—dc22

2005019532

Typeset by SPI Publisher Services, Pondicherry, India
Printed in Great Britain on acid-free paper
by Biddles Ltd, King's Lynn

ISBN 0–19–927968–3   978–0–19–927968–5

1 3 5 7 9 10 8 6 4 2

Preface

Some ten years ago, in the introduction to his *New Constantines* (Aldershot, 1994), Paul Magdalino pointed to a striking anomaly: that famous, long-lived, Byzantine warrior-emperors held little appeal for modern scholars. Perhaps, he suggested, it was the odour of autocracy that surrounded them that was so repellent. Few Byzantine emperors were more famous, more long-lived, more warlike, more autocratic, and more controversial than Basil II, the emperor who is most commonly known as the Bulgar-slayer. But when I started investigating Basil's reign in 1995 few emperors had been as comprehensively ignored. More recently scholarly interest in the emperor himself and the age in which he lived has revived; I now find myself with companions in the search for Basil II, above all Paul Magdalino and Paul Stephenson. While I have been working on this book their conversations and publications about Basil have been of immense help and encouragement.

This volume grew out of an Oxford D.Phil. thesis dealing with the same subject. In both my thesis and this book I have wrestled with the same problems. How does one write about a figure whose mythical status is so great, but whose reign has left such sparse and inconsistent evidence? How does one identify the right questions to ask of the reign, or the right contexts within which to make sense of the reign? Finally I decided that pursuing such an elusive figure would only be interesting if the difficulties inherent in the pursuit were made interesting; if difficulties could be turned into opportunities. Certainly it is true that we have to see Basil in distorting mirrors: in the writings of later Byzantine historians, especially John Skylitzes, and amidst the confused morass of 'voices off' from the empire's eastern borderlands. But I have found that identifying and making sense of those mirrors has proved a fascinating experience in its own right, and an immensely satisfying, if strangely disorientating, way of perceiving the emperor himself.

My explorations have taken roughly a decade. There are many people from that time I wish to thank. My principal appreciation must be for my D.Phil. supervisors James Howard-Johnston and Mark Whittow. I thank James for his scrupulous attention to detail, his unerring ability to detect a false argument, and his steadfast support over many years; I thank Mark for his willingness to supervise the final stages of the thesis, for enabling me to experience archaeology in Turkey, for acting as sub-editor to this book, and for his friendship. I would also like to thank Jonathan Shepard very heartily indeed for introducing me to Byzantine Studies when I was an undergraduate, and for reading a draft of this book. I should also like to acknowledge Feras Hamza, who at a crucial moment in 1997 helped me to understand some of the Arabic of Yahya ibn Sa'id.

My life as a graduate student of Byzantine Studies in Oxford was made a particular pleasure by all the members of the Byzantine Seminar and by the students and fellows at Balliol College. There are too many people to name who contributed to that wonderful life, but let me mention here Peter Frankopan, Peter Sarris, Julie Dickson, Jeyanthi John, Mathan Satchi and Maurice Keen. Among the institutions I wish to thank are the British Academy, which sponsored my graduate studies, and Balliol College, which awarded me a Jowett Senior Scholarship for the period 1995–7. Funding from the British Institute of Archaeology at Ankara enabled me to travel to Turkey in 1995. From 1998 until 2001 I was able to continue studying the history of Byzantium thanks to a research fellowship at Gonville and Caius College, Cambridge. Since 2001 my home has been University College, Oxford. Whether at Caius or Univ I have encountered extremely kind and intellectually stimulating communities of fellows and students. They have helped me to broaden my historical interests and enthusiasms while allowing me time to muse on the reign of Basil II. I would also like to thank all those Byzantinists who have encouraged me over the past ten years to keep working on Basil, in particular Judith Waring, Charlotte Roueché, Margaret Mullett, and Jean-Claude Cheynet.

There are also those whom I wish to thank for their support from older and newer times. From older times I would like to thank Ann Dyball, my Greek teacher at school, as well as those supervisors from Cambridge who kept faith with me when I was ill as an undergraduate, particularly Christine Carpenter, David Abulafia and Anna Abulafia. From newer times I would like to thank Matthew Grimley for bringing me the greatest happiness. Finally I would like to thank my family, especially my parents Patricia and George Holmes, and my brother Robert, for their love, support, encouragement, and imagination. It is to my parents that the book is dedicated.

Contents

List of Maps   xi

Abbreviations   xii

Note on Transliteration and Citation   xiv

Introduction   1

1. Basil's Reign in Modern and Medieval
   Historical Literature   16

2. Basil II and John Skylitzes: The Historian's
   Career and Working Methods   66

3. Basil II and the Testimony of John
   Skylitzes: Textual Analysis   120

4. Basil II and the Testimony of
   John Skylitzes: Contexts   171

5. The Revolts of Skleros and Phokas:
   Historiography and the Skleros Manifesto   240

6. Administration and Imperial Authority
   on the Eastern Frontier   299

7. Administration and Imperial Authority
   on Byzantium's Western Frontiers   392

8. The Reign of Basil II: A Reconstruction   448

Appendix A: Coverage of Basil's Reign in
                    John Skylitzes' *Synopsis Historion*   544
Appendix B: Translation of the *Prooimion*
                    to John Skylitzes' *Synopsis Historion*   548
Bibliography   551
Index   589

List of Maps

1. Anatolia 976–89: the revolts of Bardas
   Skleros and Bardas Phokas   244
2. The eastern frontier: Byzantium and its
   eastern neighbours c.950–1050   305
3. The Balkans c.971–1025   397
4. Byzantine southern Italy c.950–1025   431

Abbreviations

AB	*Analecta Bollandiana*
AASS	*Acta Sanctorum*
B	*Byzantion*
BCH	*Bulletin de Correspondance Hellénique*
BHG	*Bibliotheca Hagiographica Graeca*
BK	*Bedi Kartlisa*
BMGS	*Byzantine and Modern Greek Studies*
Byz Forsch	*Byzantinische Forschungen*
Byz Slav	*Byzantinoslavica*
BZ	*Byzantinische Zeitschrift*
Cah Arch	*Cahiers Archéologiques*
CCCM	Corpus Christianorum. Continuatio Medievalis
CCSG	Corpus Christianorum. Series Graeca
CFHB	Corpus Fontium Historiae Byzantinae
CSHB	Corpus Scriptorum Historiae Byzantinae
DAI	*De Administrando Imperio*; ed. G. Moravcsik and trans. R. J. H. Jenkins, CFHB I (Washington DC, 1967)
DMA	*Dictionary of the Middle Ages*
DOP	*Dumbarton Oaks Papers*
EEBS	*Epeteris Etaireias Byzantinon Spoudon*
EI	*Encyclopaedia of Islam*, New Edition (Leiden, 1960–)

HA	*Handes Amsorya*
HUS	*Harvard Ukrainian Studies*
JHS	*Journal of Hellenic Studies*
JÖB	*Jahrbuch der Österreichischen Byzantinistik*
MGH ss	*Monumenta Germaniae Historica, Scriptores*
NCMH	*New Cambridge Medieval History*
ODB	*Oxford Dictionary of Byzantium*
OMT	Oxford Medieval Texts
PG	*Patrilogiae Cursus Completus, Series Graeca-Latina*
PO	*Patrilogia Orientalis*
PP	*Past and Present*
REArm	*Revue des Études Arméniennes*
REB	*Revue des Études Byzantines*
RESEE	*Revue des Études Sud-Est Européennes*
SBS	*Studies in Byzantine Sigillography*
TIB	*Tabula Imperii Byzantini*
TM	*Travaux et Mémoires*
Viz Vrem	*Vizantijskij Vremminik*
ZRVI	*Zbornik Radova Vizantološkog Instituta*

Note on Transliteration and Citation

Greek names and place-names are transliterated with *k* and *os*, except in cases where a Latinate or Anglicized version is very familiar. Given the centrality of John Skylitzes' *Synopsis Historion* to my analysis, wherever possible I have tried to use the names of places and individuals as they appear in Skylitzes' text. Turkish place-names follow current Turkish usage. Arabic names and place-names follow the *Encyclopaedia of Islam*, New Edition (Leiden, 1960–), but in a simplified version so that diacritics are omitted. Armenian names and place-names follow the spelling adopted by Robert Thomson in *History of the House of the Artsrunik'* (Detroit, 1985); Georgian names and place-names follow the spelling adopted by Thomson in *Rewriting Caucasian History: The Georgian Chronicles* (Oxford, 1996). For first names with an obvious English analogue, I use the English version: thus, John, Michael, Constantine.

In footnotes I refer to original sources in full on the occasion of the first citation. Thereafter, I use abbreviations: thus, Skylitzes, *Synopsis*; Psellos, *Cronografia*; *DAI*; *Regesten*; *Life of John and Euthymios*.

Introduction

In the tenth and eleventh centuries the Byzantine Empire became the most formidable state in the Near East. Using a mixture of force and diplomacy the Byzantines pushed well beyond their long-established core territories in Anatolia and on the Aegean coasts. They annexed much of the Balkan landmass, the northern reaches of the Fertile Crescent, western Armenia and Georgia, and the islands of Crete and Cyprus.[1] In the same period Byzantium's cultural and religious influence spread even more widely, as missionaries, artists and architects bore the spiritual message and physical accoutrements of Orthodox Christianity far beyond the empire's territorial frontiers.[2] The reign of Basil II (976–1025) is usually regarded as the apogee of this period of

---

[1] For a narrative outline of this general period see G. Ostrogorsky, *History of the Byzantine State* (trans. J. Hussey), 2nd English edn. (Oxford, 1968), 210–98; W. Treadgold, *A History of the Byzantine State and Society* (Stanford, Calif., 1997), 446–583.

[2] For the cultural and religious expansion of Byzantium see e.g. D. Obolensky, *The Byzantine Commonwealth: Eastern Europe, 500–1453* (London, 1971); H. C. Evans and W. D. Wixom, *The Glory of Byzantium: Art and Culture of the Middle Byzantine Era, AD 843–1261* (New York, 1997).

expansion. The emperor's most conspicuous achievement
came in 1018 when Bulgaria was annexed after thirty years
of warfare, but territorial additions also occurred elsewhere.
In the east the Christian princedom of Tao in Georgia was
absorbed in 1000; twenty years later Vaspurakan in Armenia
was added. Towards the end of Basil's reign Byzantine forces
also became more active in the southern Italian sphere,
consolidating and expanding imperial authority in the face
of a variety of local and supra-regional powers including the
Ottonian emperors of Germany. By 1024 the emperor was
planning to invade Muslim Sicily. When Basil died in 1025
the empire's frontiers were at their most far-flung since the
seventh century. Nor was expansion purely territorial. By
the end of his life Basil's wealth was legendary: a labyrinthine
treasury was rumoured to extend under the Great Palace.[3]
One medieval historian alleged that Basil's riches were so
great that he remitted taxation for the final two years of his
reign.[4]

Basil died admired and feared by his contemporaries.
According to the eleventh-century Armenian historian Aristakes of Lastivert, when Basil went on procession through
the streets of Constantinople shortly before his death, his
subjects were too terrified to look him in the face and hid in
their houses.[5] Historians from the Muslim world described

[3] Psellos (Michael): *Michele Psello Imperatori di Bisanzio (Cronografia)*,
ed. S. Impellizzeri and trans. S. Ronchey, 2 vols. (Rome, 1984), i. 44–6.

[4] Skylitzes (John): *Ioannis Skylitzae Synopsis Historiarum*, ed. I. Thurn,
CFHB 5 (Berlin, 1973), 373.

[5] Aristakes of Lastivert, *Récit des malheurs de la nation arménienne*, trans.
M. Canard and H. Berbérian according to the edn. and trans. (Russian) by
K. Yuzbashian, (Brussels, 1973), 25.

him as having great political ability, sound judgement, and strength of mind.[6] Nor was this praise stilled by death. Instead as the decades passed his reputation continued to grow. In his remarkable pen-portrait of the emperor the mid-eleventh-century historian Michael Psellos claimed that Basil, 'purged the empire of barbarians and also completely subjugated his own people'.[7] According to Psellos, Basil was an emperor who had little time for high culture, and ruled his empire with plain speech and an iron fist. By the end of the twelfth century this reputation had hardened yet further. Now Basil was commonly known as Bulgar-slayer, the sobriquet by which he is still often identified.[8]

Yet Basil's success during life and after death seems all the more remarkable given the very inauspicious start to his reign. When he came to the throne in 976 the treasury was all but empty, exhausted by the military campaigns of his imperial predecessors Nikephoros Phokas (963–9) and John Tzimiskes (969–76). During the first thirteen years of his reign Basil and his younger brother Constantine, his co-emperor, faced two intense periods of civil war. The first was waged between 976 and 979 by the general Bardas Skleros; the second between 987 and 989 by another general, Bardas Phokas. At this time, Bardas Skleros also rebelled once again. These wars only ended with the death of Phokas

---

[6] al-Rudhrawari: *Eclipse of the Abbasid Caliphate*, ed. and trans. H. Amedroz and D. Margoliouth, 6 vols. (Oxford, 1920–1), vi. 119.

[7] Psellos, *Cronografia*, i. 42–3; translation into English, E. R. A. Sewter, *Michael Psellus: Fourteen Byzantine Rulers* (London, 1966), 44.

[8] For further discussion of Basil's posthumous reputation see Chapter 1, section 1. Henceforth such cross-references will be abbreviated to Arabic numerals; thus, see below 1.1.

on the field of battle in April 989, and the surrender of Skleros shortly afterwards. But victory had come at an immense price. Basil had only been able to achieve victory by allying himself with his pagan Rus neighbours to the north. In return for military assistance from the Rus, Basil's sister Anna had been dispatched as a bride to Vladimir, prince of Kiev, who at the same time converted to Orthodox Christianity. Military ignominy in these early years of Basil's reign extended yet further, above all when the emperor suffered a humiliating defeat against the Bulgarians in 986.

The scale of Basil's recovery after the early disasters of his reign and his subsequent military conquests persuaded later medieval Byzantine writers to claim that he was the greatest emperor since Herakleios.[9] Yet, viewed with detachment, it is clear that Basil's golden legacy was relatively short-lived. Within thirty years of his death the empire began to fragment amid Turkish attacks in the east, and Norman and nomad raids in the west. By the early 1040s the empire once again became prone to *coups d'état*. By the 1070s revolt became all-out civil war as leading aristocratic dynasties struggled to capture Constantinople, often enlisting in their armies those external foes who were threatening the territorial integrity of the empire.

Because of the position of Basil's reign between the expansion of the tenth century and the political and military disintegration of the later eleventh, its significance to any understanding of the history of medieval Byzantium in

---

[9] Choniates (Michael): *Michaelis Choniatae Epistulae*, ed. F. Kolovou, CFHB 41 (Berlin, 2001), 285.

particular, and the Near East in general, could hardly be clearer. If nothing else Basil's fearsome reputation among contemporaries and later generations seems worthy of detailed investigation. Yet, his is a reign strangely neglected by modern historians. The last detailed general overview was produced at the turn of the nineteenth century by Gustave Schlumberger.[10] For much of the twentieth century very little was published in connection with Basil. Re-engagement with the emperor in print has only begun to revive in the last decade.[11] But while this renewed scholarly interest is extremely encouraging, it has yet to make a substantial impact on the standard view of Basil's reign. According to that standard view, the reign falls into two distinct temporal and geographical phases. The first phase consists of thirteen years of internal civil unrest, when the emperor found himself threatened by the ambitions of the empire's leading aristocratic families, such as the Skleroi and the Phokades. These families are sometimes labelled the 'Powerful' (*Dynatoi*). Basil's military victory over these families in 989, and his issuing of draconian legislation in 996 against the Powerful, are usually seen as laying the foundations to the second, and much more glorious, phase of Basil's reign. This second period is usually characterized as an unbroken litany of armed conquests in Bulgaria, Armenia, Georgia, and southern Italy.

---

[10] G. Schlumberger, *L'Épopée byzantine à la fin du dixième siècle*, 3 vols. (Paris, 1896–1905). This three-volume work covers the period 969 to 1057. The sections dealing with Basil's reign are located in vol. i, 327–777; vol. ii, *passim*.

[11] See below 1.1.

Yet, there are grounds for thinking that Basil's reign deserves substantial reanalysis, not just because the model outlined above is too schematic and simplistic, but more importantly because of the direction that Byzantine Studies have taken in recent decades. Since the 1970s most historians have approached Byzantine history of the so-called Middle Period (ninth to twelfth centuries) primarily through analysis of the empire's socio-economic structures. The result has been substantial growth in knowledge about the empire's economy, its armed forces, its administration, its fiscal resources, and the personnel of its elites between the ninth and twelfth centuries. But while it has proved relatively straightforward to acquire knowledge about fundamental structures, it has proved more difficult to date crucial periods of change within those structures, and it is in this chronological sense that Basil's reign has taken on a special resonance. In the absence of firm datable evidence charting structural transformation, Basil's exceptionally obscure reign has often been used as a convenient black-hole period during which fundamental changes are assumed to have occurred. As a result Basil's reign has come to be seen as the time when a centrifugal polity, dominated by a struggle between a provincial, military aristocracy and imperial authority, was transformed into a more centripetal state focused on the person of the emperor in Constantinople. Yet, as we shall see in greater detail in later chapters, interpretations of Basil's reign as the crucible of structural revolution ultimately rest on rather shallow foundations: the allegations made by Michael Psellos that Basil's character underwent a profound mutation in response to the difficulties he experienced in his early years as emperor. According to Psellos, Basil turned from a wastrel, the lover of luxury, into an ascetic warrior, the lover of battle and privation. It is from this single medieval description of Basil's change in character that modern historians have extrapolated the incidence of more fundamental structural change in medieval Byzantine history.[12]

An important reason, then, for studying Basil's reign in much greater depth is to see whether historians have been correct to identify this period as central to long-term social and political structural changes in the Byzantine Empire. But how should such an inquiry be framed? A traditional approach would involve constructing a sustained analytical chronology of the reign which traces the development of internal politics and external relations. However, in the case of Basil's fifty-year hegemony a comprehensive narrative which deals evenly with the different chronological periods of the reign and with the various geographical regions, frontiers, and neighbours of the empire, is inhibited by an extremely fragmented source-base, a phenomenon familiar to historians of early medieval Europe and the Near East. Particularly problematic is the uneven and piecemeal record left by medieval historians. Surviving historical narratives of the reign are rare and often late in date. Even when all the available medieval narratives, in Greek and other languages, are collated, long chronological gaps and substantial geographical lacunae are frequent. The fragility of the historiographical record makes it difficult to integrate other written sources (such as saints' lives, military manuals, and

---

[12] See esp. the discussion below at 1.2.1.

Introduction

letters), many of which are of uncertain date, into any general analysis of the reign.

The obvious shortcomings of the written sources mean that the material record cannot be ignored. And here, indeed, there are real signs for hope. In the century since Schlumberger wrote his analysis of Basil's reign, many hundreds of lead seals and coins from the later tenth and early eleventh centuries have been discovered, analysed, and published. Recently archaeological excavations and surveys in many of the former provinces of the medieval Byzantine Empire have begun to expand in scale and ambition. Indeed, it is this material archive that has enabled scholars to begin to investigate the structures underpinning medieval Byzantine society in much greater depth, as recent research into Byzantine administration, the army, and the economy illustrate so clearly.[13] Yet, in order to maximize the potential of the material archive in reconstructing political and diplomatic history, the right questions must be asked of it. It is unrealistic to expect material evidence, which so often cannot be dated accurately, to plug geographical or chronological lacunae in the written sources. Nor should the material record be asked to provide answers to very specific political, administrative, or chronological problems about which the written texts are silent. Such an approach is either likely to founder through the lack of appropriate evidence, or may simply result in the selective use of material to support preconceived models.[14]

[13] See Chs. 6 and 7 for further analysis of this literature.
[14] See similar arguments made by P. Doimi de Frankopan, 'The Numismatic Evidence from the Danube Region, 971–1092', *BMGS* 21 (1997), 30–9;

Yet, if the medieval evidence is fraught with so many caveats, how *should* this reign be approached? In the time that has passed since Schlumberger's publications, no new substantial tenth- or eleventh-century history or chronicle has been uncovered which might provide the underpinning to a reworked narrative treatment. In these circumstances there seems little profit to be gained in writing a history of Basil's reign which simply synthesizes the extant written sources and adds ephemeral details from the material record. Such an undertaking is unlikely to expand significantly on Schlumberger's very competent analysis, which with great sensitivity integrated a heterogeneous array of sources into a narrative framework. In addition, a synthesis of this variety bristles with methodological difficulties. A linear narrative structured around the fragmented and piecemeal record provided by the medieval historians may simply replicate those historians' chronological, geographical, and prosopographical lacunae. Furthermore, an effort to integrate sources from outside the historical record may mean that those sources are read out of their most meaningful context. The result could be the creation of entirely false realities.

Instead, in order to develop an analysis which moves beyond a narrative based on what recent scholars have seen as plundered evidence,[15] we need to consider how to

idem, 'The Workings of the Byzantine Provincial Administration in the 10th–12th Centuries: The Example of Preslav', *B* 71 (2001), 73–97.

[15] M. Mullett, *Theophylact of Ochrid: Reading the Letters of a Byzantine Archbishop* (Aldershot, 1997), 4; A. Kaldellis, *The Argument of Psellos' Chronographia* (Leiden, 1999), 1–2.

turn the nature, limitations, and potential of our different sources to best use. This is an approach that involves investigating the internal structures of source materials and identifying those sources' most meaningful contexts. It is an approach that requires the exploration of contexts far beyond the geographical and chronological boundaries of Basil's reign. It is an approach that is inherently deconstructive. It is also an approach that is explicitly source-led. My reason for advocating such an approach is that it is only by understanding how the sources that reflect on Basil's reign actually work, that we can ever hope to construct a clear and reasonably accurate picture of the reign itself.

The most crucial sources in the study of Basil's long reign are the testimonies of the various medieval historians. Although these testimonies contain vast lacunae and serious flaws, they must be fundamental to an apprehension of political and diplomatic change during the reign. They are the only form of evidence which provides some sort of chronological spine; they are the only form of evidence which focuses specifically on the political and diplomatic history of the later tenth and early eleventh centuries. More to the point, until we have established how and why these medieval historians constructed their own chronologies and interpretations, we cannot hope to use *other* source materials to good effect. Modern historians, whether consciously or otherwise, always set their understanding of alternative sources of evidence, both written and material, against the background provided by medieval historians. Paradoxically, then, if eventually we want to use alternative materials to investigate Basil's empire, we need to have a solid grasp of the most obvious form of evidence, the historiographical record: and it is on this form of evidence that this book will focus.

The opening chapter has a very limited ambition: to lay bare the bones of the modern models and the medieval evidence relating to Basil's reign. It delineates how modern scholarship has shaped our understanding of Basil's hegemony by outlining the received view of the reign in the modern literature, by identifying where the focus of modern historiography concentrates, and by examining the relationship between modern analysis and medieval interpretation. Above all, this chapter demonstrates the extent to which a very narrow reading of Michael Psellos' account of Basil's reign dominates the modern historiography. The chapter then moves on to assemble and briefly discuss all the available medieval sources for the reign. In particular, it identifies those occasions where common ground is to be found between several medieval historical narratives, as well as those periods for which there is very little medieval testimony. Subsequent chapters explore further some of the most significant concentrations in the medieval evidence.

Chapters 2 to 4 look in greater detail at the main Greek narrative account of the reign composed by John Skylitzes at the end of the eleventh century. Despite the recent French translation of Skylitzes' text published by Bernard Flusin and Jean-Claude Cheynet, the *Synopsis* remains a relatively little-studied text.[16] In these circumstances, Chapter 2

---

[16] B. Flusin and J.-C. Cheynet, *Jean Skylitzès: Empereurs de Constantinople* (Paris, 2003).

summarizes and analyses the small, scattered body of scholarship which has been dedicated to this author and his text,
the *Synopsis Historion*. The chapter ends by indicating how
this research can help us understand Skylitzes' very idiosyncratic treatment of Basil II. Chapter 3 represents a detailed
textual analysis of Skylitzes' use of source materials. At the
end of the chapter, the principal implications of this analysis
for Skylitzes' presentation of the Byzantine past, including
the reign of Basil, are highlighted. Chapter 4 explores the
literary, social, and political contexts behind the *Synopsis
Historion*. It considers how these contexts influenced the
construction of Skylitzes' text as a whole and the author's
coverage of the reign of Basil in particular. The next chapter
continues to build out from earlier chapters, but takes us
beyond Skylitzes. It examines that period of Basil's reign
which is most fully represented by all the medieval historians of the reign: the revolts of Bardas Skleros and Bardas
Phokas which took place in the period 976 to 989. The
chapter compares Skylitzes' coverage of these events with
the rest of the medieval historical record, including those
texts originally written in Arabic, Armenian, and Georgian.
It identifies a hitherto unacknowledged manifesto in the
Greek tradition written in praise of Bardas Skleros.

Taken together, all these historiographical chapters demonstrate how the medieval narrative of Basil's reign in Greek,
as represented primarily by Skylitzes but also by Psellos, was
conditioned by the political and literary demands of history
writing in the later eleventh century. They also suggest that
the Greek historians' retrospective vision of the Byzantine
past has badly obfuscated our understanding of the nature

of and tensions within late tenth- and early eleventh-century Byzantine governance, especially relations between the constituent members of the Byzantine political elite. While Psellos and Skylitzes have persuaded modern historians that the ambition of powerful aristocratic families shaped the governance of the Byzantine Empire during Basil's reign, it will be argued that this interpretation in fact reflects much later eleventh-century preoccupations rather than political reality in the later tenth and early eleventh centuries.

Chapters 6 and 7 move on to use the historiographical analysis conducted in Chapters 1 to 5 to construct a picture of governance in Basil's Byzantium which more accurately reflects later tenth- and early eleventh-century political and administrative realities. These chapters are primarily concerned with the exercise of political authority in three frontier regions of Byzantium: the east, the Balkans, and southern Italy. These are regions where at least some sustained contemporary written narratives survive, in contrast to a region such as Anatolia where the historiographical record falls completely silent between 990 and 1021. In these two chapters frontier governance is discussed not only through scrutiny of the surviving medieval historiography, but also in relation to other extant evidence, especially contemporary lead seals owned by imperial officials. Chapter 6 deals with the empire's eastern territories, including those acquired by Basil's imperial predecessors in northern Syria and Mesopotamia, as well as those annexed by Basil himself in Armenia and Georgia. Chapter 7 investigates Byzantine governance of the Balkans and southern Italy during Basil's reign. Recently it has been suggested that

Basil II's wars in Bulgaria were on a rather smaller scale than has been traditionally thought, and that they may have been punctuated with long periods of peace. This chapter offers qualified support to the first of these suggestions, while at the same time adhering to the more traditional view that warfare was endemic in the Balkans for much of Basil's reign. More generally each of these chapters will argue that in regions where we have enough evidence to see imperial administration operating on the ground in real time, many of the stereotypes about Basil's harsh and repressive methods of governance prove incorrect. Direct oppression was used sparingly and with exemplary purposes in mind; indirect negotiation was Basil's preferred style of practical governance, at least in those localities of his empire where a reasonable amount of contemporary evidence survives.

The first seven chapters of this book demonstrate how we can only get closer to the contemporary realities of Basil's reign if we recognize the limitations and potential of the extant evidence, and are willing to work in ways which will allow that evidence to speak. The book is explicitly constructed around the contours of the evidence rather than around preordained temporal, geographical, or thematic categories. Its chapters do not constitute a comprehensive chronological and geographical treatment of the period 976–1025; the evidence is simply too uneven to support such a project. Nor are they systematically arranged to cover discrete themes: there is no separate chapter on Basil's relations with the Powerful, on art and literature, on administrative reforms, on Constantinople, on the separate provinces, or on Byzantium's different neighbours. This is not to say that these themes are ignored. Each surfaces throughout these seven chapters. My point is merely that questions about the chronology, geography, and grand themes of Basil's reign are only worth asking, and indeed answering, once the evidence-base has been soundly delineated and examined.

Yet, all is not caution. If much of this book is concerned with deconstructing evidence and showing the degree to which many apprehensions about Basil's reign are somewhat misplaced, the final chapter offers a short account of a reconstructed Basil. It is here that a new narrative of the reign is sketched out. It is here that new interpretations of old concerns are offered: Michael Psellos' treatment of the reign, the legislation of 996, and the startling and famous image of the soldier-emperor in the Psalter, now in Venice, which was commissioned by Basil himself. It is in the course of this discussion that the relationship between the emperor and the army, rather than that between emperor and great families, is identified as the crucial structural tension in Byzantine governance in the later tenth and eleventh centuries. It is here that the significance of Basil's reign for the later eleventh-century collapse of the Byzantine empire is assessed. It is here that Basil is rehabilitated as the central political figure of Byzantine history in the so-called Middle Period.

1

Basil's Reign in Modern and Medieval Historical Literature

1.1 BASIL II AND MODERN HISTORIANS

Basil II's reign last attracted substantial scholarly interest in print towards the end of the nineteenth century, when Gustave Schlumberger included his narrative treatment of the reign in his much longer three-volume work, *L'Épopée byzantine à la fin du dixième siècle,* which covered the period 971 to 1057.[1] In compiling his account of Basil's reign Schlumberger made considerable use of the work of the Russian scholar V. R. Rozen, who had drawn attention to the vast array of material relevant to the reign of Basil in the chronicle of the eleventh-century Arab historian, Yahya ibn Sa'id of Antioch.

---

[1] For Basil's reign see Schlumberger, *L'Épopée byzantine,* i. 327–777; ii. *passim.* V. R. Rozen, *Imperator Vasilij Bolgarobojca: Izvlechenija iz letopisi Jach-i Antiochijskago* (St Petersburg, 1883; repr. London, 1972). Schlumberger's study built on his earlier analysis of the reign of Nikephoros Phokas (963–9): *Un empereur au dixième siècle: Nicéphore Phocas* (Paris, 1890).

Since Schlumberger's publication, however, scholarship about Basil has been rather less ambitious and more narrowly focused. Most studies have taken the form of specialist investigations which trace the empire's relations with its geographical neighbours. In the case of the Balkans it has been the identity of the Kometopouloi, the dynasty who led the Bulgarian Empire in wars against Basil, which has attracted most detailed discussion. Byzantine administrative arrangements, particularly those developed on the Danube frontier during the reigns of Basil II and his imperial predecessor John Tzimiskes, have sporadically ignited interest. It has only been in the last five years that Paul Stephenson has presented a more rounded picture of how Byzantium approached warfare, diplomacy, and governance in the Balkans during Basil's reign, both before and after the conquest of the Bulgarian Empire in 1018.[2] Another favoured topic from the reign of Basil II has been the exact chronology of events surrounding the conversion to Christianity of Vladimir prince of Kiev in 988. Less frequent, however, have been attempts to set these events in the wider context of Byzantine–Rus relations in the later tenth and early eleventh centuries.[3] In Caucasia short articles have been devoted to

---

[2] On the identity of the Kometopouloi see: N. Adontz, 'Samuel l'Arménien roi des Bulgares', in *Études arméno-byzantines* (Lisbon, 1965), 347–407; W. Seibt, 'Untersuchungen zur Vor- und Frühgeschichte der "bulgarischen" Kometopulen', *HA* 89 (1975), 65–98. See most recently, P. Stephenson, *The Legend of Basil the Bulgar-Slayer* (Cambridge, 2003), chs. 2–3; for further discussion of the administration of the Balkan frontier and Stephenson's work see 7.1 below.

[3] See e.g. A. Poppe, 'The Political Background to the Baptism of the Rus', *DOP* 30 (1976), 196–244; D. Obolensky, 'Cherson and the Conversion of the Rus: An Anti-Revisionist View', *BMGS* 13 (1989), 244–56; the entirety of

the surrender of the Christian princedoms of Tao and Vas-purakan.[4] While more sustained attention has been paid to the empire's relations with its Muslim neighbours in the east, particularly by Forsyth and Farag, most of this research remains unpublished.[5]

Scholarship dedicated to Byzantium's relations with neighbouring powers during Basil's reign has been charac-terized by fragmentation. Frontiers and neighbours have been treated separately rather than in a connected sense. The same is true of the domestic history of the reign. While as we shall see in Chapter 5 the Skleros and Phokas revolts between 976 and 989 have attracted a relatively abundant literature, only two short studies deal with relations between emperor and internal elites during the reign as a whole.[6] As

HUS, 12–13 (1988–9); J. Shepard, 'Some Remarks on the Sources for the Conversion of Rus', in S. W. Swierkosz-Lenart (ed.), *Le origini e lo sviluppo della cristianità slavo-bizantina* (Rome, 1992), 59–95. For further discussion of the Rus during Basil's reign see below 8.7.

[4] Z. Avalichvili, 'La Succession du curopalate David d'Ibérie, dynaste de Tao', *B* 8 (1933), 177–202; W. Seibt, 'Die Eingliederung von Vaspurakan in das byzantinische Reich', *HA* 92 (1978), 49–66; for further discussion of Transcausia see below at 6.3.1, 6.3.4, and 8.4.

[5] J. H. Forsyth, 'The Chronicle of Yahya ibn Sa'id al-Antaki', Ph.D. thesis (Michigan, 1977). Another unpublished doctoral thesis dealing with the eastern frontier during the reign of Basil is that of W. A. Farag, 'Byzantium and its Muslim Neighbours during the Reign of Basil II (976–1025)', Ph.D. thesis (Birmingham, 1979). I would like to thank Professor John Haldon for drawing my attention to this thesis. The only published study is W. Felix, *Byzanz und die islamische Welt im früheren 11. Jahrhundert* (Vienna, 1981). However, this only begins in 1000 and thus omits the first half of Basil's reign.

[6] C. S. Sifonas, 'Basile II et l'aristocratie byzantine', *B* 64 (1994), 118–33; more recently, I have tried to approach this issue: C. Holmes, 'Political Elites in the Reign of Basil II', in P. Magdalino (ed.), *Byzantium in the Year 1000* (Leiden, 2003), 35–69: much of what appears in this book was initially worked out in the course of writing that article.

I shall discuss at greater length below, historians are now interested in how we should approach Michael Psellos' portrayal of Basil II as an irascible and austere emperor. But with the exception of Barbara Crostini's work on high culture, little of this research has suggested how we should rebuild a picture of the Byzantine empire in the later tenth and early eleventh centuries once Psellos has been decoded and deconstructed.[7] Indeed, it is only very recently that any sustained and truly innovative interest in the reign of Basil II has begun to emerge. Foremost among that interest has been Paul Stephenson's work on the exploitation of the emperor's posthumous reputation as 'Bulgar-slayer' by later generations of historians and politicians, including not only later Byzantine figures but also those from the nineteenth and twentieth centuries.[8] Also important for the historian of Basil's reign has been the publication by Paul Magdalino of *Byzantium in the Year 1000*. This is a volume of papers by several contemporary scholars about various aspects of Byzantine history and culture in Basil's reign. As a result new pictures of Basil's hegemony are now beginning to emerge from different angles; but nonetheless, a general sustained

[7] M. Arbagi, 'The Celibacy of Basil II', *Byzantine Studies/Études byzantines* 2(1) (1975), 41–5; L. Garland, 'Basil II as Humorist', *B* 67 (1999), 321–43; Kaldellis, *Argument of Psellos' Chronographia, passim*; B. Crostini, 'The Emperor Basil II's Cultural Life', *B* 64 (1996), 53–80. For further discussion of Psellos see below 1.2.1 and 8.3.

[8] D. Ricks and P. Magdalino (eds.), *Byzantium and the Modern Greek Identity* (Aldershot, 1998), 61, 106–8, 119–23; P. Stephenson, 'The Legend of Basil the Bulgar-slayer', *BMGS* 24 (2000), 102–32; idem, 'Images of the Bulgar-slayer: Three Art Historical Notes', *BMGS* 25 (2001), 44–68; idem, *Legend of Basil the Bulgar-Slayer, passim* but esp. chs. 5–8.

interpretation of the reign as a whole has yet to be produced.[9]

Yet, despite the modern historians' traditional reluctance to engage with Basil's reign in detail, this emperor's hegemony is routinely seen as having an exceptionally important position within long-term trends in Byzantine history. In part allegations of the importance of Basil's reign rest on the emperor's military conquests, particularly in Bulgaria. It is these triumphs which are said to represent the apogee of the medieval Byzantine world. But, in other respects too, Basil's reign is seen as seminal. It is often interpreted as a key transitional period within long-term changes to the nature and structure of Byzantine political society and governance. This approach is one that particularly typifies those modern historians with a strong interest in that series of tenth-century imperial novels which attack the so-called 'Powerful' (those individuals known in Byzantine Greek as the *Dynatoi*).

As is well known, such legislation was first promulgated in 934 by the emperor Romanos Lekapenos (920–44). Romanos was concerned that as a result of the famine of 927–8 and the harsh winter of 933–4 members of the Powerful were acquiring properties from those whom he identified as 'Poor' at prices significantly below market value. He tried to force these Powerful to return their recent acquisitions to the former owners.[10] The legislation was strengthened by his

[9] P. Magdalino (ed.), *Byzantium in the Year 1000* (Leiden, 2003).
[10] N. Svoronos, *Les Novelles des empereurs macédoniens concernant la terre et les stratiotes* (Athens, 1994), 82–92. *Theophanes Continuatus*, ed. I. Bekker, CSHB (Bonn, 1838), 443, 448–9; R. Morris, 'The Powerful and the Poor in

imperial successor Constantine Porphyrogenitus who not only lengthened the time period allowed for the Poor to repurchase their lands from the Powerful, but also ordered that no compensation was to be paid in instances where properties had been acquired by force.[11] In the 960s Nikephoros Phokas extended the restrictions on acquisitions by the Powerful to any free peasant village communities (*choria*) where they might already hold lands.[12] Finally in 996 Basil issued his own draconian version of the anti-Powerful legislation. His novel required that all property acquired by the Powerful from within free peasant *choria* since 927 should be restored to its former owners without compensation for either the original purchase price or for subsequent improvements. It also abolished the principle that property ownership was immune from judicial inquiry after forty years.[13]

Scholarly discussion of this legislation has produced highly conflicting pictures of the resources underpinning political authority, the identity of the Powerful, the relationship between the Powerful and the state, and the overlap between the private and public spheres during the whole of the tenth century. For George Ostrogorsky the legislation

---

Tenth-Century Byzantium: Law and Reality', *PP* 73 (1976), 8–10; P. Lemerle, *The Agrarian History of Byzantium from the Origins to the Twelfth Century: The Sources and Problems* (Galway, 1979), 94–7; M. Kaplan, *Les Hommes et la terre à Byzance du VIe au XIe siècle* (Paris, 1992), 421–6.

[11] Svoronos, *Novelles*, 98–100; Lemerle, *Agrarian History*, 97–8; Kaplan, *Les Hommes*, 426–7, 431–2.

[12] Svoronos, *Novelles*, 180–1; Lemerle, *Agrarian History*, 100–2; Kaplan, *Les Hommes*, 434–5.

[13] For further discussion of the 996 novel see below 8.3.

reflected a bitter struggle between the Macedonian imperial dynasty and a powerful landowning aristocracy which was greedy to siphon off the manpower and territorial resources of the Byzantine state. Paul Lemerle disagreed, arguing that the Powerful were rarely great families with independent resources, but instead the state's own functionaries. As a result, anti-Powerful legislation was more concerned with restraint of the servants of the state rather than the suppression of an independent magnate class. For Lemerle and his followers, however, imperial legislation was not really about the relationship between emperor and elites, but instead that between the state and the fisc. For these historians the main characteristic of the Byzantine fiscal system was the joint contribution of taxes paid by poor landowners living within the *chorion*. In this sense, the chief fear expressed by the novels was that lands from the *chorion* were becoming detached from the basic tax unit and consolidated into private estates, *idiostata*; as a result the state was becoming enfeebled.

As far as Basil II is concerned, these rather different readings of the Poor–Powerful legislation yield very different pictures of the nature of political authority and society during his reign. According to Ostrogorsky, Basil's victory in 989 over Skleros and Phokas and his promulgation of the 996 novel signalled a triumph for the emperor over an entire class of magnates with extensive estates, especially those whose family origins lay in central Anatolia. Once these magnates had been destroyed in battle, and emasculated through the confiscation of their estates as a result of the novel of 996, Basil II was able to take the helm of state alone and launch the empire into a period of glorious overseas conquest, a period Ostrogorsky termed the apogee of medieval Byzantium.[14] In contrast, while Lemerle, and more recently Kaplan, have been willing to acknowledge that the novel issued by Basil in 996 was deployed at a superficial level as a weapon to punish those who rebelled against the emperor in the pre-989 period, they would see its chief purpose as the traditional tenth-century imperative of protecting the fiscal integrity of the *chorion*.[15] In these terms this legislation has little resonance for relations within the political elite during Basil's reign or for the structures of internal governance. Thus, depending on whether one reads the tenth-century legislation according to the Ostrogorsky or the Lemerle model, Basil's reign can either be regarded as a crucial turning point in the political relationship between emperor and aristocracy, or as part of a long-running, ultimately unsuccessful, imperial effort to maintain the integrity of the state's fiscal base.

For those with an overriding interest in the novels of the tenth century, Basil's reign represents a highly significant coda to longstanding centrifugal political and fiscal processes. However, for other historians the reign represents an overture: the preface to a more centripetal

---

[14] Ostrogorsky, *History of the Byzantine State*, 305–7; idem, 'Agrarian Conditions in the Byzantine Empire in the Middle Ages', in M. Postan (ed.), *Cambridge Economic History of Europe*, i., *The Agrarian Life of the Middle Ages*, 2nd edn. (Cambridge, 1966), 216–21.

[15] Lemerle, *Agrarian History*, 85–115; Kaplan, *Les Hommes*, 414–43. For a summary of how these broad modern historiographical models affect our understanding of Basil's reign see also Sifonas, 'Basile II et l'aristocratie', 118–19.

eleventh-century Byzantium characterized by a greater political and administrative focus on Constantinople, and the ascendancy of a new urban and civilian aristocracy. This notion of a more centralized Byzantium taking shape in Basil's reign was first articulated in the 1970s by Hélène Ahrweiler and Nikolaos Oikonomides on the basis of their analysis of a variety of imperial administrative documents from the tenth and eleventh centuries. They both pointed to the centralization of administrative institutions during Basil's reign, above all those organs of government connected with revenue collection. Underpinning this model was the assumption that during Basil's reign the territorial and fiscal resources of the state were enormously enhanced by estates confiscated from those who rebelled with Skleros and Phokas and those who contravened the anti-Powerful legislation of 996.[16]

The greater centralization of Byzantium during Basil's reign has also been stressed in recent years by Jean-Claude Cheynet, but in political as well as administrative terms. Exhaustive analysis of an evidence-base which includes lead seals and medieval historical narratives has enabled Cheynet to develop many new ways of thinking about the resources and motivations of different political individuals and groups, the development of the administrative structures, and the evolution of the relationship between public and private power within Byzantium over a three-hundred

---

[16] H. Ahrweiler, 'Recherches sur la société byzantine au XIe siècle: Nouvelles hiérarchies et nouvelles solidarités', *TM* 6 (1976), 99–124; and in the same volume, N. Oikonomides, 'L'Évolution de l'organisation administrative de l'empire byzantin au XIe siècle', 125–52.

year period from 963 to 1210. The result is an indispensable
and unprecedented corpus of information about a political
elite whom Cheynet terms 'l'aristocratie'.[17] Although Cheynet's research is only now moving towards a direct analysis
of Basil's reign,[18] his existing prosopographical analysis of
the principal families and individuals of the later tenth and
early eleventh centuries has, nonetheless, enabled him to
hypothesize a transformation in the articulation of political
authority in Byzantium in the tenth and eleventh centuries.
Cheynet has suggested that during the middle years of the
tenth century public office and private estates, particularly
in central and eastern Anatolia, were beginninng to coalesce
in the hands of a small number of great families, including
the Phokades and Skleroi. However, after Skleros and Phokas were defeated in 989, Basil II ensured that the Byzantine
aristocracy ceased to hold public office in regions where they
were also estate owners and instead exercised official command in areas where they had no landed interest. Put
crudely, those who had estates in the eastern half of the
empire served in the west, and vice versa. As the geographical location of private resources and public authority bifur-
cated, Constantinople became the political fulcrum of
empire, with the Byzantine aristocracy choosing to be
absentee landowners and relocating their households to
the capital.[19]

---

[17] See in the first instance, J.-C. Cheynet, *Pouvoir et contestations à Byzance* (Paris, 1990).

[18] J.-C. Cheynet, 'Basil II and Asia Minor', in Magdalino (ed.), *Byzantium in the Year 1000*, 71–108.

[19] Cheynet, *Pouvoir et contestations*, 303–9, 333–6.

A yet more explicit articulation of a transformation in the presentation and exercise of political authority during Basil's reign has been provided by Michael Angold in a brief introductory chapter to his wide-ranging study of politics and society in eleventh- and twelfth-century Byzantium, *The Byzantine Empire 1025–1204*. Like Ostrogorsky, Angold sees Basil as a brake on those centrifugal forces which undermined the cohesion and integrity of the tenth-century Byzantine state. Like Ostrogorsky, he interprets Basil's victory in 989 over Skleros and Phokas and his promulgation of the 996 novel as the key stages in the destruction of an Anatolian magnate elite whose authority had threatened imperial power in Constantinople for much of the tenth century. Like Ahrweiler and Oikonomides, Angold regards Basil in the post-revolt period as a centralizing force. For Angold Basil is a complete autocrat who created a lean, idiosyncratic style of government focused on his own person and the capital city. Although he criticizes the methods of Jean Claude Cheynet, Angold nonetheless agrees that during Basil's reign aristocrats began to migrate away from their countryside estates to Constantinople.[20]

A more striking feature of Angold's representation of Basil's reign is the extent to which he departs from earlier historians' approbation for the autocracy of Basil II. Rather than the essential predicate of military triumph, for Angold

---

[20] M. Angold, *The Byzantine Empire 1025–1204*, 2nd edn. (New York, 1997), 19–20 (for his criticism of Cheynet); see, however, Angold (ed.), *Byzantine Aristocracy* (Oxford, 1984), 3, for ideas about centralization; idem, 'Autobiography and Identity: The Case of the Later Byzantine Empire', *Byz Slav* 60 (1999), 39.

Basil's personal rule was a blunt and malign instrument; it represented a poisonous legacy for his imperial successors. Basil was responsible for imposing a rigid and immobilizing structure of state control which sapped the energies of what would have otherwise been a flourishing polity and economy. Imperial attack on the great landowning magnates of Anatolia and support for peasant landowers achieved through the novel of 996 were retrograde steps. The provisions of the novel were exacerbated by later fiscal changes such as the *allelengyon*, a measure introduced during Basil II's wars with the Bulgarians which made the Powerful responsible for making up shortfalls in the taxes of the Poor; but also a measure which Basil refused to revoke once the Bulgaria wars were over. Such measures, Angold argues, inhibited major landowners, those who alone were able to produce a surplus that could be rechannelled into investment in agriculture or spent in the commercial market place. As a result the economic vitality of the tenth-century empire was dampened. Heavy taxation, particularly of the magnates, took coinage out of circulation and caused widespread deflation. In order to deprive the magnates of private retinues the armies of the provinces (or themes) were replaced by mercenary forces under Basil's direct control. Typical of such forces were the Varangian or Rus troops sent from Kiev to help Basil defeat Bardas Phokas in 988–9. Meanwhile, Basil's later overseas wars were not only expensive, but even when successful introduced a host of new problems. Annexation of Bulgaria, western Georgia (Iberia), and southern Armenia (Vaspurakan) destroyed long-established buffer zones between Byzantium and its principal neighbours. In addition, such conquests brought both non-Greek speaking, and in the case of the Armenians and Syrians, non-Chalcedonian Christian populations, within the empire. Finally Basil failed to provide an heir. When he died at the age of 70 in 1025 he was succeeded by his brother Constantine (1025–8), who was himself 67 years old. Constantine's daughters were all unmarried and in their forties, beyond child-bearing age. With Basil's death the pressures that built up within this rigorously controlled system proved too great to contain. Under pressure from the aristocracy emperors such as Romanos III (1028–34) eased fiscal demands. But soon without the immense revenues customary under Basil, the state rapidly ran into budgetary difficulties.[21]

Angold's vision of Basil is novel in the depth of its disparagement. Yet, like many other interpretations of this reign, Angold's analysis proves to be less about Basil himself, and more about how Basil's reign might help to explain much longer processes of political and social change. In the case of Angold, his principal concern is why an apparently economically and culturally buoyant tenth-century empire succumbed to internal and external collapse in the second half of the eleventh century. Potential answers to these questions have often included the idea that the empire was ill defended because of the demise of the theme armies; that the empire's army was the victim of disloyal mercenaries; that the empire had lost erstwhile buffer zones along its borders; that expenditure began to exceed income; that heterodox populations

---

[21] Angold, *Byzantine Empire*, 24–34.

could not live within an essentially orthodox empire.[22] It is striking that Angold's description of Basil's hegemony is primarily concerned with identifying the origins of these later eleventh-century malaises rather than with the detailed political and diplomatic realities of the reign itself.

1.2   BASIL II AND THE MEDIEVAL HISTORIANS

1.2.1   The impact of Michael Psellos' *Chronographia*

The ways which Basil's reign has been interpreted within *longue durée* models of tenth- and eleventh-century Byzantine history clearly differ according to the particular interests and methods of modern historians. However, while their approaches may vary, historians generally agree that the reign marked a crucial watershed in relationships within the political elite, in administrative practice, and in ties between centre and provinces. Only Lemerle and Kaplan,

---

[22] See e.g. S. Vryonis, *The Decline of Medieval Hellenism in Asia Minor and the Process of Islamization from the Eleventh through the Fifteenth Century* (Berkeley, 1971), 69–113; idem, 'Byzantium: The Social Basis of Decline in the Eleventh Century', in *Byzantium: Its Internal History and Relations with the Muslim World* (London: Variorum, 1971), no. II; J. V. A. Fine, 'Basil II and the Decline of the Theme System', *Studia Slavico-Byzantina et Medievalia Europaensia*, i (Sofia, 1989), 44–7. Some of these views have recently been endorsed by J. Haldon, although he locates the later 11th-c. decline within broader structural changes in 10th- and 11th-c. Byzantine society rather than attributing responsibility to Basil's hegemony alone (J. Haldon, 'Approaches to an Alternative Military History of the Period ca. 1025–1071' in V. N. Vlyssidou (ed.), *The Empire in Crisis (?): Byzantium in the 11th Century (1025–1081)* (Athens, 2003), 45–74); also see below 8.9.

with their vision of the ongoing enfeeblement of the fisc, would see Basil's reign as a period of continuity rather than change. Yet, it is striking that however diverse modern historians' interests in Basil's reign may be, their models of transformation are all shaped to a considerable degree by a single medieval text: Michael Psellos' well-known analysis of the reign in the *Chronographia*, his history of fourteen eleventh-century Byzantine emperors which he composed in the middle decades of the eleventh century, and which begins with a portrait of Basil himself.[23]

In his account of Basil's reign Psellos appears to argue that after defeating Bardas Skleros and Bardas Phokas, the emperor crushed the greater families of the empire, took civil and military affairs into his own hands, and appointed a series of less significant figures, 'neither brilliant in intellect, nor remarkable in lineage, nor excessively trained in public speaking' as his subordinates. According to Psellos, Basil then led his armies in ceaseless campaigning on the frontiers: 'he spent the greater part of his reign, serving as a soldier on guard at our frontiers and keeping the barbarian marauders at bay; not only did he draw nothing from his reserves of wealth but even multiplied his riches many times over.'[24]

Psellos' explanation for this transformation in governance has its origins in Basil's character or *ethos*.[25] Psellos suggests that the revolts of the early years of Basil's reign caused the

---

[23] Psellos, *Cronografia*, i. 8–55; for further discussion of the dating of Psellos' history see below 5.3.

[24] Psellos, *Cronografia*, i. 46–7; trans. Sewter, *Michael Psellus*, 46.

[25] See also, Kaldellis, *Argument of Psellos' Chronographia*, 23–8, 42–4, 49–51, 55, 85–7.

emperor to undergo such a profound alteration of character that he was turned from a sybaritic dilettante to an austere military man of steel.[26] He shunned ceremony. He stored jewels in his treasury rather than decking himself with them. Nor was it merely his character which became harsh and unforgiving; his highly personal style of governance was marked by the same traits: 'It is perfectly true that the great reputation he built up as a ruler was founded rather on terror than loyalty, for as he grew older and became more experienced, he relied less on the judgements of men wiser than himself. He alone introduced new measures, he alone disposed his military forces. As for the civil administration, he governed, not in accordance with the written laws, but following the unwritten dictates of his own intuition.'[27]

Although few historians today would explicitly identify the shifting sands of personality as the cause of deep-seated structural changes, it is clear that Psellos' bipartite model of the reign, and his allegations that the emperor was able to re-engineer the government of the empire after the early revolts, has exercised a very significant, if often unacknowledged influence, on most modern analyses of the reign.[28] Nowhere is this more visible than in the general text-book accounts of Byzantine history which divide Basil's reign into two distinct temporal and geographical phases: the first

---

[26] Psellos, *Cronografia*, i. 12–13, 28–9, 42–51.

[27] Psellos, *Cronografia*, i. 42–3; trans. Sewter, *Michael Psellus*, 43–4.

[28] e.g. in his discussion of Basil's reign, Michael Angold explicitly cites Psellos when arguing that Basil became a complete autocrat who created an idiosyncratic and personalized style of government which his 11th-c. imperial successors were unable to follow (Angold, *Byzantine Empire*, 28).

thirteen years as a period of endemic insurrection fomented by the great magnate families of the Anatolian plateau, the Skleroi and the Phokades; the next thirty-six years as a much more glorious phase of successful military campaigns and territorial acquisitions led by the emperor himself. The turning point in the reign is identified as 989, the year when both Phokas and Skleros were defeated. According to this model, these victories enabled Basil to emasculate the empire's land-owning aristocracy and to develop a highly centralized state focused on his own person.[29] Within such presentations of the reign relatively little attention is paid to the empire's external relations before 989 or to internal affairs after 989.

There are, of course, partial exceptions to this general rule, above all Schlumberger's long narrative appraisal of the reign, and Mark Whittow's more recent overview of Basil's hegemony. Both Schlumberger and Whittow stress the significance of the international context in the first two decades of the reign, as Basil's empire faced hostile neighbours on at least three frontiers: in western Macedonia from the Bulgarians under the leadership of the Kometopouloi; in southern Italy from the Muslims of Sicily and the Maghreb and the Ottonians of Germany; and in the east from the Fatimids of Egypt and the Buyids of Baghdad. Both Schlumberger and Whittow also mention the revolt of Nikephoros Phokas and Nikephoros Xiphias which disturbed the domestic equilibrium of the empire towards the end of the

---

[29] Ostrogorsky, *History of the Byzantine State*, 298–315; Treadgold, *Byzantine State and Society*, 513–33.

reign in 1021–2. Both understand the importance of the symbiotic relationship between internal and external affairs: that the domestic history of Byzantium cannot be studied without reference to the capacities, ambitions, and motivations of the empire's neighbours.[30] Nonetheless, it is significant that despite their willingness to expand the canvas of the reign to include the broader international context, both Schlumberger and Whittow follow the template of the reign laid out by Psellos. For both historians the defeat of Skleros and Phokas in 989, followed up by the promulgation of the novel of 996, remains the key moment of transformation within the reign.[31]

There are several reasons why the bipartite interpretation that Psellos appears to offer is so appealing. First, Psellos appears to provide a precise chronological context for structural change: the end of the revolts of Skleros and Phokas in 989. Second, he provides a superficial link between the internal and external history of the reign: once internal strife in the shape of the Skleros and Phokas revolts was crushed, external victory could begin. Finally, and most importantly, Psellos' model finds no rival among other medieval historians. As we shall see shortly, historians such as Yahya ibn Sa'id, Stephen of Taron, and John Skyliztes treat the events and personalities of the reign in greater detail than Psellos, offering a greater wealth of prosopographical, chronological, and toponymical data; yet they provide

---

[30] Schlumberger, *L'Épopée byzantine*, i. 327–777; ii. *passim*; M. Whittow, *The Making of Orthodox Byzantium* (London, 1996), 358–90.

[31] Schlumberger, *L'Épopée byzantine*, i. 745–6; ii. 40–2, 122–30; Whittow, *Making of Orthodox Byzantium*, 373–9.

no explicit analytical framework within which to interpret the reign.

Yet, it is important to question whether historians have been wise in subordinating their understanding of Basil's reign, either consciously or subconsciously, to Psellos' interpretation. Psellos' appraisal is of course far from being a comprehensive chronological narrative which pays detailed attention to Byzantium's different provinces, frontiers, and neighbours. It contains no dates. The only concrete episodes that he includes in his appraisal of a fifty-year reign are the revolts of Skleros and Phokas (976–89) and the deposition of the emperor's uncle and chief functionary at court, Basil Lekapenos, the *Parakoimomenos*. As Barbara Crostini has indicated, even these events are misordered; the deposition of the *Parakoimomenos*, which took place according to Yahya ibn Sa'id in 985, is placed in Psellos' account after the defeat of Phokas, dated by Yahya to April 989.[32] Most of Psellos' account, particularly the post-989 phase, constitutes an abstract description of Basil's physiognomy and his character in war and in peace. These passages are devoid of any factual substance. While Psellos asserts that Basil was a consistent campaigner, he makes no mention of Basil's wars with Bulgaria or his more occasional expeditions to the east.[33] Nor does he make reference to the revolt of Nikephoros Phokas and Nikephoros Xiphias in 1021–2, a rebellion which is mentioned by nearly all the remaining historical accounts of Basil's reign.[34] This

[32] Crostini, 'Emperor Basil II's Cultural Life', 57–60.
[33] Psellos, *Cronografia*, i. 42–55.
[34] See below 1.2.2 and 8.8 for further analysis of this revolt.

rebellion involving the son of Bardas Phokas, the famous rebel from earlier in the reign, must make us question the degree to which Basil subjugated the greater families of the empire after 989.

It is likely that the Xiphias–Phokas revolt receives little coverage in Psellos' account because to include it would be to disturb the literary harmony of his text, a harmony which demanded that internal feuding be followed by external success, and that Basil the dilettante emperor be followed by Basil the austere general. Such polarities cannot accommodate such a blip of domestic instability at the end of the reign. That Psellos was, in the final instance, primarily concerned with creating textual harmony rather than reporting a chronologically coherent chain of events may explain that other most striking characteristic of his account: the fact that he makes no mention of Byzantium's relations with the empire's neighbours in the first thirteen years of Basil's reign, and no mention of the empire's internal affairs after 989.

1.2.2   The other medieval historians

One might suppose that the most obvious way of assessing the validity of modern and medieval models of Basil's reign, and of escaping the interpretative straitjacket imposed by such models, would be to develop a sustained chronology of Byzantium's internal and external history in the later tenth and early eleventh centuries. However, in the case of Basil's reign an extremely problematic source-base makes it difficult to construct a comprehensive narrative which offers balanced geographical and chronological coverage.[35]

Let us take the Greek historiographical record first. It is perhaps surprising that despite the scale of the emperor's territorial conquests, the reign of Basil is sparsely covered by historians writing in Greek. Although Michael Psellos indicates that historians were at work during Basil's reign itself, the only extant contemporary account is that of Leo the Deacon.[36] A member of the palace clergy during the first two decades of Basil's reign, Leo wrote a detailed history of the reigns of Nikephoros Phokas (963–9) and John Tzimiskes (969–76). To this he appended a short summary of the revolts of Bardas Skleros and Phokas (976–89), as well as an eyewitness account of Basil's expedition against Bulgaria which came to grief in the Gates of Trajan near Sardica (Sofia) in 986. However Leo's testimony, written *c*.995,

---

[35] Schlumberger was fully aware of the difficulties presented by the paucity of sources for this period: 'le commun règne des deux fils de Romain est l'époque la plus obscure de l'histoire de l'empire byzantin'; 'les sources byzantines sont, hélas, d'une pauvreté peut-être plus extraordinaire, plus désespérante encore, que pour aucune autre période des siècles dixième et onzième sur lesquels nos informations sont si rares' (*L'Épopée byzantine*, i. 329, 586–7).

[36] Leo the Deacon: *Leonis Diaconi Caloënsis Historiae Libri Decem*, ed. C. B. Hase, CSHB (Bonn, 1828), 169–76. For references to other historians active during Basil's reign, see Psellos, *Cronografia*, i. 12–13. One of these historians may have been Theodore of Sebasteia (dicussed below at 2.4). It is possible that a chronicle of the reign of Basil II owned in the later Middle Ages by the library of the monastery of St John, Patmos, was written by another historian working in the later 10th or early 11th c. Mention of this chronicle is made in an unpublished early 14th-c. manuscript (K. Snipes, 'The "Chronographia" of Michael Psellos and the Textual Tradition and Transmission of the Byzantine Historians of the Eleventh and Twelfth Centuries', ZRVI 27–8 (1989), 57).

terminates with the defeat of Phokas in 989 and the earthquake which devastated Constantinople and its environs shortly afterwards.[37] While Michael Psellos' short and very general account in the *Chronographia*, written in the third quarter of the eleventh century, is the earliest extant description in Greek of the whole period of Basil's hegemony, the first extensive surviving Greek narrative of the reign is that compiled in the later eleventh century by John Skylitzes as part of a much longer historical synopsis.[38] Yet, as I shall explain more fully below and in the next chapter, Skylitzes' treatment is less than comprehensive. The first half of his testimony is dominated by the revolts of Skleros and Phokas, the second by Basil's campaigns in Bulgaria. He has relatively little to say about Constantinople, the eastern frontier, the north, or Italy. His account also contains many chronological confusions, particularly in relation to Bulgaria. Nor are these geographical lacunae or chronological difficulties eased by any subsequent historians writing in Greek. From the twelfth century onwards most accounts represent a paraphrase or a fusion of the pre-existing testimonies of Skylitzes and Psellos.

---

[37] The exact date when Leo wrote his history is not known. However, it is likely that he was writing after 995. Leo himself mentions that repairs to Hagia Sophia, which had been damaged in an earthquake, took six years to complete. According to both Leo and Yahya ibn Sa'id this earthquake happened in 989 (Leo the Deacon, *Historiae Libri Decem*, 175–6; Yahya ibn Sa'id al-Antaki, 'Histoire', ed. and trans. I. Kratchkovsky and A. Vasiliev, *PO 23* (1932), 429). The widespread belief among modern historians that Leo wrote some three years earlier *c*.992 is based on John Skylitzes' erroneous dating of the 989 earthquake to 986 (Skylitzes, *Synopsis*, 331–2).

[38] Psellos, *Cronografia*, i. 8–55; Skylitzes, *Synopsis*, 314–69.

In some senses historians writing in languages other than Greek can clarify the chronological outlines of Basil's reign, especially those at work in the east writing in Arabic, Armenian, Syriac, and Georgian. Of particular importance are the contemporary histories of Yahya ibn Sa'id and Stephen of Taron. Yahya was a Christian Arab doctor, who migrated to Antioch from Cairo during the second half of Basil's reign, a period when members of the indigenous Christian and Jewish administrative elite of Egypt were persecuted, and in some cases exiled, by al-Hakim, the Fatimid caliph. The extant version of his chronicle begins in 937/8 and ends with the reign of Emperor Romanos III (1028–34). His historical writings often display great chronological, patronymical, and toponymical accuracy, particularly in relation to events in the eastern half of the Byzantine Empire, but also on occasion in Constantinople, Anatolia, and the Balkans; they also range across most of the contemporary Near East from Egypt to Syria, Iraq, Byzantium, and various Christian Caucasian states. Moreover, Yahya's migration to Antioch allowed him to consult a variety of histories written in Greek which are no longer extant but which reflect on the internal history of Byzantium and, to an extremely limited extent, on warfare with Bulgaria. In addition, his use of local chronicle and hagiographical materials provides a unique view of events in Antioch during the later tenth and early eleventh centuries.[39]

---

[39] Yahya ibn Sa'id al-Antaki, 'Histoire', ed. and trans. (French) I. Kratchkovsky and A. Vasiliev, *PO 23* (1932), 372–520, contains coverage from 976 to 1013/4; the section covering 1013–34 appears as 'Histoire de Yahya ibn Sa'id d'Antioche', ed. I. Kratochkovsky, trans. (French) F. Micheau and

While the world chronicle of the Armenian monophysite historian Stephen of Taron is less finely honed than Yahya's testimony, it also contains an invaluable fusion of materials of significance for the history and prosopography of the reign of Basil. Although Stephen's principal concern is with the domestic histories of various Christian Caucasian princedoms in Armenia and Iberia (western Georgia), he also pays close attention to relations between these powers and the Byzantine Empire. Furthermore, he displays particular interest in the fates of those individuals from Caucasia who entered Byzantine service during Basil's reign, many of whom fought in imperial campaigns in the Balkans.[40] Moreover, although the extant version of Stephen's chronicle ends in 1004, a longer redaction of his historical writings may have been available to the later eleventh-century Armenian historian Aristakes of Lastivert. If this is true, then the material included in Aristakes' account of Basil's wars against Georgia at the end of his reign may be taken from the history of Stephen.[41]

G. Troupeau, *PO* 47 (1997), 373–559. For a translation into Italian, see also B. Pirone (trans.), *Yahya al-Antaki Cronache dell'Egitto fatimide e dell'impero Bizantino 937–1033* (Bari, 1998). For an assessment of Yahya's working methods, sources, and significance as a historian, see in the first instance the excellent unpublished Ph. D. thesis by Forsyth, 'The Chronicle of Yahya ibn Sa'id al-Antaki'.

[40] Stephen of Taron: *Des Stephanos von Taron armenische Geschichte*, trans. H. Gelzer and A. Burckhardt (Leipzig, 1909), 137–217. Schlumberger, *L'Épopée byzantine*, i. 362, 587, noted the dominance within Stephen's account of all matters Armenian.

[41] Aristakes of Lastivert, *Récit des malheurs*, 2–26; for references to his use of Stephen of Taron's extended history see Aristakes, *Récit des malheurs*, 8–9.

Apart from Yahya, Stephen, and Aristakes, several other historians writing in languages other than Greek can also illuminate the history of the Byzantine east in Basil's reign. Some of these writers were exact or near contemporaries such as Ibn Miskawayh at work in Buyid Baghdad,[42] Elias of Nisibis,[43] and a variety of historians and hagiographers writing in Georgian.[44] In addition, the accounts of later chroniclers, such as the Armenian histories of Matthew of

[42] Ibn Miskawayh: *Eclipse of the Abbasid Caliphate,* ed. and trans. H. Amedroz and D. Margoliouth, 6 vols. (Oxford, 1920–1), v. 424–5, 436–9. Ibn Miskawayh was a servant of Adud al-Daula, the Buyid emir, who ruled in Baghdad between 978 and 983 (see further discussion below 5.2.1).

[43] Elias of Nisibis: *La Chronographie de Mar Elie bar Sinaya, Métropolitain de Nisibe,* ed. and trans. L. J. Delaporte (Paris, 1910), 134–42. This text, composed in two columns (the first in Syriac and the second in Arabic), is mainly a short list of entries concerned with Mesopotamia under the rule of the Bedouin Uqalid dynasty. However, it was written by a contemporary of Basil's, and occasionally refers to events in Byzantium. It confirms, for example, that Basil annexed Bulgaria in 1018.

[44] The Life of John and Euthymios, composed *c.*1040, is perhaps the most valuable of the Georgian materials for the internal history of Byzantium, in particular the revolt of Bardas Skleros (Life of John and Euthymios: B. Martin-Hisard, 'La Vie de Jean et Euthyme: Le Statut du monastère des Ibères sur l'Athos', *REB* 49 (1991), 67–142); see below 5.2.1. The *Chronicle of K'art'li* composed in the 11th c. and included in the much longer text of the Georgian Royal Annals comments on relations between Byzantium, the Black Sea kingdom of Abasgia and various Caucasian princedoms (for the most recent translation see Georgian Royal Annals: *Rewriting Caucasian History: The Georgian Chronicles,* trans. R. Thomson (Oxford, 1996), 274–85). A history written rather earlier in the 11th c. (*c.*1030) by Sumbat Davit'isdze, which is included in only some versions of the Royal Annals (but *not* those translated by Thomson), includes more extensive coverage of the episodes in the *Chronicle of K'art'li*; see S. H. Rapp, 'Imagining History at the Crossroads: Persia, Byzantium and the Architects of the Written Georgian Past', Ph.D. thesis (Michigan, 1997), 492–3. I am grateful to Stephen Rapp for allowing me to see his unpublished translation of Sumbat's text.

Edessa[45] and the continuator of Thomas Artsruni,[46] the Syriac accounts of Michael the Syrian and Bar Hebraeus,[47] and the Arabic text of the late eleventh-century Seljuk historian, Abu Shudja al-Rudhrawari,[48] contain some highly significant contemporary materials from the later tenth and early eleventh centuries. These eastern materials will be analysed in greater depth in Chapters 5 and 6 of this book.

As one moves away from the eastern frontier, towards the north and west, historiographical material becomes exceptionally limited. From north of the Black Sea the only extant text is the *Russian Primary Chronicle* composed in the early decades of the twelfth century.[49] Narrative histories from the Balkans are equally sparse and late. The history of the Priest of Diokleia, composed in Slavonic (but surviving only in a sixteeth-century Latin translation), is customarily dated to the later twelfth century. However, it contains traces of some earlier materials, including an excerpt of a late eleventh-century life of St Vladimir, who earlier in the eleventh

---

[45] Matthew of Edessa: *Armenia and the Crusades in the Tenth to Twelfth Centuries: The Chronicle of Matthew of Edessa*, trans. A. E. Dostourian (Lanham and London, 1993), 34–50.

[46] Thomas Artsruni: *History of the House of the Artsrunik'*, trans. R. W. Thomson (Detroit, 1985), 368–71.

[47] Michael the Syrian: *Chronique de Michel le Syrien, Patriarche Jacobite d'Antioche (1169–99)*, ed. and trans. J. B. Chabot, (Paris, 1905–1910), 132–46; Bar Hebraeus: *The Chronography of Gregory Abu'l Faraj, the Son of Aaron, the Hebrew Physician, Commonly Known as Bar Hebraeus*, ed. and trans. E. A. Wallis Budge (London, 1932), 175–89.

[48] al-Rudhrawari: *Eclipse of the Abbasid Caliphate*, ed. and trans. H. Amedroz and D. Margoliouth, 6 vols. (Oxford, 1920–1), vi. 6–7, 23–35, 115–19. For more on documents from Buyid Iraq relevant to the domestic and external history of Byzantium in Basil's reign see below 5.1.

[49] *The Russian Primary Chronicle, Laurentian Text*, ed. and trans. S. H. Cross and O. P. Sherbowitz-Wetzor (Cambridge, Mass., 1953), 90–135.

century was ruler of Diokleia. This small Serb princedom was located to the north-west of Dyrrachion, that coastal port on the Adriatic which oscillated between Byzantine and Bulgar control throughout Basil's reign. The life included in the Priest of Diokleia sheds some occasional light on Bulgarian–Byzantine relations in the later tenth and early eleventh centuries, offering a partial check to two of Skylitzes' more important Balkan narratives: the rise of Samuel Kometopoulos (the tsar of the Bulgars) in the early decades of Basil's reign; and the collapse of the Bulgarian state in the period 1017–18.[50] However, beyond the Priest of Diokleia, few other narratives from the Balkans reflect on Basil's reign.[51]

In Italy narrative histories are slightly more plentiful. There are three rather laconic redactions of the Annals of Bari.[52] But despite their brevity they occasionally provide

[50] Priest of Diokleia: *Letopis Popa Dukljanina*, ed. F. Šišić (Belgrade and Zagreb, 1928), 292–375; J. Ferluga 'Die Chronik des Priesters von Diokleia als Quelle für byzantinische Geschichte', *Vyzantina* 10 (1980), 431–60; P. Stephenson, *Byzantium's Balkan Frontier* (Cambridge, 2000), 73 n. 87, 119; idem, *Legend of Basil the Bulgar-Slayer*, 27–8, 73.

[51] Allusions to the reign in the chronicle of Thomas of Split and Hungarian chronicles are exceptionally rare: *Thomae Archidiaconi Spalatensis. Historia Salonitanorum pontificum atque Spalatensium a S. Domnis usque ad Rogerium (d.1266)*, ed. Fr. Rački (Zagreb, 1894), 43; *Scriptores rerum Hungaricarum tempore ducum regumque stirpis arpadienae gestarum*, ed. E. Szentpétery (Budapest, 1937–8).

[52] Annals of Bari: *Annales Barenses*, ed. G. H. Pertz, MGH ss 5 (Hanover, 1844), 51–6; *Lupus Protospatharius*, ed. G. H. Pertz, MGH ss 5 (Hanover, 1844), 51–63. See below 7.2 for the use of these texts in reconstructing the southern Italian experience. There is a third version of the text, the *Anonymi Barensis Chronicon*; however, the manuscript of this version is now lost: see V. von Falkenhausen, 'Between Two Empires: Italy in the Reign of Basil II', in Magdalino (ed.), *Byzantium in the Year 1000*, 138 n. 14.

useful information about the fate of Byzantine officials dispatched from Constantinople to Apulia and Calabria, the two regions of southern Italy under direct Byzantine authority in Basil's reign. Annals also survive from those areas which neighboured the Byzantine territories but which were controlled by local Lombard princes. However, such texts rarely mention the Byzantine Empire, focusing instead on politics within the Lombard princedoms themselves and relations with the Ottonian (and later Salian) emperors of Germany.[53] Slightly more rewarding are the narratives of William of Apulia and Amatus of Montecassino composed towards the end of the eleventh century, which record the penetration of the Normans into Byzantine southern Italy in the final decade of Basil's reign.[54] However, the most sustained and contemporary history of relations between Byzantium and Italy comes from northern Italy, where the contemporary history of John the Deacon, written in Venice, makes frequent references to trading and strategic contacts between Venice and Constantinople, thus providing a key background context to the Adriatic dimension of the

[53] e.g. Annals of Benevento: *Annales Beneventani 788–1130*, ed. G. H. Pertz, MGH ss 3 (Hanover, 1839), 176. The fullest treatment is afforded by the version of the 'Chronicle of Montecassino' by Leo Marsicanus (Leo of Ostia), written in the later 11th or early 12th century (Leo Marsicanus: *Chronica Monasterii Casinensis (Die Chronik von Montecassino)*, ed. H. Hoffmann, MGH ss 34 (Hanover, 1980), 236–43, 261, 275–6).

[54] Amatus of Monte Cassino: *Storia de' Normanni di Amato di Montecassino volgarizzata in antico francese*, ed. V. de Bartholomaeis (Rome, 1935), 24–40. This is a 14th-c. French version of Amatus' 11th-c. original text that is now lost. A paraphrase of this text in Latin is also to be found in Leo Marsicanus' chronicle. See also William of Apulia: *Guillaume de Pouille, La Geste de Robert Guiscard*, ed. and trans. M. Mathieu (Palermo, 1961): 98–108; cf. B. Kreutz, *Before the Normans* (Philadelphia, 1991), pp. xxviii–xxx.

conflict between Byzantium and Bulgaria. Unfortunately, John's account ends in 1008, long before the denouement of the conflict between Basil and the Bulgarians.[55] The rather terser *Chronicon Venetum* and the fourteenth-century chronicle of Andrea Dandolo add little to John's account.[56]

Further western perspectives on Basil's reign are rare, limited to occasional references in historical narratives written north of the Alps. Despite the recent history of strong competition between Byzantium and Otto I for the loyalties of the Lombard princes of southern Italy, and the marriage between Otto II and the Byzantine princess Theophanu in 972 which resolved that conflict, histories produced within the Ottonian milieu have very little to say about Byzantium in the post-972 period. Thietmar of Merseburg, a contemporary writing around 1018, is aware of Byzantine diplomatic contacts with Italy, Germany, Poland, and the Rus of Kiev, but he rarely explores such ties in detail; his only extensive coverage of relations between the Ottonians and Byzantines is limited to Otto II's invasion of southern Italy

---

[55] John the Deacon: 'La cronaca Veneziana del Giovanni Diacono', in G. Monticolo (ed.), *Chronache Veneziane* (Rome, 1890), 139–71; see below 8.6 for further discussion of Byzantine–Venetian relations.

[56] *Chronicon Venetum quod vulgo dicunt Altinate*, ed. H. Simonsfeld, MGH ss 14 (Hanover, 1883), 60–6. This chronicle contains a 13th-c. necrologium that lists the tombs of Byzantine emperors, including that of Basil. This Latin text represents a translation from a Greek original; the underlying Greek text may have been an updated version of chapter 42 of the 10th-c. ceremonial handbook, *De Cerimoniis* (P. Grierson, 'Tombs and Obits of Byzantine Emperors', *DOP* 16 (1962), 58); Andrea Dandolo: *Chronicon Venetum: Andreae Danduli ducis Venetiarum chronica per extensum descriptum aa. 46–1280*, ed. E. Pastorello (Bologna, 1938), 179–206.

in the early 980s.[57] More intriguing are a handful of asides about Byzantium in the histories of Ralph Glaber and Ademar of Chabannes, both written in France in the first half of the eleventh century. Both historians allude to the rise in the number of pilgrims taking ship in Byzantine southern Italy for Jerusalem, a context they both use to explain the arrival of the Normans in this region towards the end of Basil's reign.[58] Both comment using pilgrims' eyewitness testimony on the destruction of the shrine of the Holy Sepulchre in Jerusalem by al-Hakim, the Fatimid caliph, in 1009.[59] Ademar of Chabannes also makes an explicit link between Basil's Balkan wars and his fabled austerity, claiming that the emperor took an oath to become a monk if he defeated the Bulgars.[60] Meanwhile Ralph points to a debate between the papacy and Constantinople towards the end of Basil's reign

---

[57] Thietmar of Merseburg: *Thietmar Meresburgensis Episcopi Chronicon*, ed. R. Holtzmann, *MGH* SrG n. s. 9 (Berlin, 1935), 76–7, 123–8, 142, 167 ff., 488, 532; T. Reuter, *Germany in the Early Middle Ages 800–1056* (London, 1991), 175; Schlumberger, *L'Épopée byzantine*, ii. 611–14. See also *Annales Quedlingburgenses*, ed. G. H. Pertz, *MGH ss* 3 (Hanover, 1839), 74–5.

[58] Ralph Glaber: *Rodulfi Glaber Historiarum Libri Quinque*, ed. and trans. J. France (Oxford, 1989), 97–8, 132–6, 202–4; Ademar of Chabannes: *Ademari Cabannensis Chronicon*, ed. P. Bourgain et al. (Brepols, 1999), 173–4, 182; for more on western pilgrims travelling eastwards via Byzantium in Basil's reign and shortly afterwards, see *Gesta Normannorum Ducum*, ed. and trans. E. M. C. van Houts, 2 vols. (Oxford, 1992–5), i. 80, 118–19; Orderic Vitalis: *The Ecclesiastical History of Orderic Vitalis*, ed. M. Chibnall, 6 vols. (Oxford, 1980), ii. 78–85.

[59] Ademar of Chabannes, *Chronicon*, 166–7; Ralph Glaber, *Historiarum Libri Quinque*, 132–6; see also M. Biddle, *The Tomb of Christ* (Stroud, 1999), 72–3.

[60] Ademar of Chabannes, *Chronicon*, 154. It was this brief episode that persuaded Arbagi that Basil II never married (Arbagi, 'Celibacy of Basil II', 41–5); see also Stephenson, *Legend of Basil the Bulgar-Slayer*, 73.

about church jurisdiction, a debate not recorded by any other source.[61] Yet, it is important to note that while these asides may be fascinating, they are usually undated and lack detail.

Taken together the non-Greek narratives can add important new dimensions to our understanding of Basil's reign. Narratives from the east, and to a lesser extent from Italy, can add chronological backbone. Even where non-Greek narratives are relatively insensitive to chronology they can shed light on regions often ignored by the Greek materials. Yet it is striking that when all the historical narratives are aggregated, large chronological and regional gaps are still very conspicuous. A brief chronological and regional survey of the reign as represented in the historical narrative record makes this point with greatest clarity.

The reign begins positively enough. All the historical narratives produced in Greek and in the east are liberal in their coverage of the Skleros and Phokas revolts that dominated the first thirteen years of the reign.[62] Meanwhile, Leo the Deacon, Yahya, Psellos, and Skylitzes all comment on contemporary events at court. They allude to the tensions that developed between Basil and his great uncle Basil the *Parakoimomenos* which led in 985 to the deposition of the older Basil.[63] A close-up of this relationship is provided by

[61] Ralph Glaber, *Historiarum Libri Quinque*, 173; K. Leyser, 'Ritual, Ceremony and Gesture: Ottonian Germany', in T. Reuter (ed.). *Communications and Power in Medieval Europe: The Carolingian and Ottonian Centuries* (London and Rio Grande, 1994), 227–8.

[62] See below 5.1 for further discussion of these narratives and these revolts.

[63] Psellos, *Cronografia*, i. 8–33; Skylitzes, *Synopsis*, 314–35; Yahya, *PO* 23, p. 417.

Ibn Shahram, an Arab envoy sent to the court of Constantinople from Baghdad in 981–2. An edited version of his diplomatic report is preserved in the testimony of the Seljuk historian al-Rudhrawari.[64] Byzantium's position in the east during the first thirteen years of Basil's reign, above all its rather troubled relations with Fatimid Egypt in northern Syria and relations with the local client state of Aleppo, are described in detail by Yahya, while some useful snapshots of key armed engagements are preserved by some other historians writing in Arabic such as Ibn al-Kalanisi, who wrote in Damascus in the mid-twelfth century;[65] meanwhile western histories offer some material about Otto II's invasion of southern Italy in 981–2;[66] and Skylitzes begins his exceptionally confused account of Byzantium's relationship with the Balkans with a summary of the rise of the Kometopoulos family, which prefaces a rather longer account of Basil II's disastrous campaign in Bulgaria in 986.[67]

However, once we move to the post-989 period this relatively thick historiographical picture becomes much thinner and more fragmented. During the decade following the civil wars, the only area of the Byzantine world that receives close attention is the east: the Armenian and Arabic records, above all Stephen of Taron and Yahya, reflect on

[64] al-Rudhrawari, *Eclipse*, vi. 23–34.

[65] Yahya, *PO 23*, pp. 372–429. Ibn al-Kalanisi, for example, includes a detailed description of a brutal Byzantine raid on the Syrian town of Hims, which was then in Fatimid hands (M. Canard, 'Les Sources arabes de l'histoire byzantine aux confins des Xe et XIe siècles', *REB* 19 (1961), 296–7).

[66] Thietmar of Merseburg, 123–8; *Lupus Protospatharius*, 55; Leo Marsicanus, *Chronica Monasterii Casinensis*, 186–7.

[67] Skylitzes, *Synopsis*, 328–31.

Byzantine warfare with the Fatimids and Aleppo, and on the absorption of the Iberian (Georgian) princedom of Tao in 1000–1.[68] Coverage of the Balkans is much less impressive during the same period. Skylitzes' treatment of warfare with the Bulgars is sporadic and confused: a mélange of bald summary passages and a rather longer narrative of Tsar Samuel's defeat at the hands of Nikephoros Ouranos, Basil II's most senior general, at the battle of the River Spercheios in 997.[69] Nor can his picture be substantially enhanced from the testimonies of Yahya or Stephen. As both Schlumberger and Runciman pointed out long ago, neither Yahya nor Stephen can answer very many crucial chronological or topographical questions about the Balkans.[70] Yahya's Bulgarian testimony is meagre, vague, repetitive, uncertain about prosopography, and undated; only at the very end of the reign does it offer some reliable information about administrative changes at the time of Basil's conquest of

---

[68] Yahya, *PO* 23, pp. 432–63; Stephen of Taron, *Armenische Geschichte*, 192–213; for Byzantine warfare in northern Syria reported by the rather later historians Ibn al-Kalanisi, al-Rudhrawari, and Bar Hebraeus, see Canard, 'Les Sources arabes de l'histoire byzantine', 297–300; al-Rudhrawari, *Eclipse*, vi. 219–43; Bar Hebraeus, *Chronography*, 179–82.

[69] Skylitzes, *Synopsis*, 339–43; for further analysis of Skylitzes' Balkan material see below 2.4 and 3.3.2.

[70] Schlumberger, *L'Épopée byzantine*, i. 586–7; S. Runciman, *History of the First Bulgarian Empire* (London, 1930), 269–70. It should be noted, however, that other historians have been less wary about the relatively insubstantial nature of Yahya and Stephen's Bulgarian testimony, and have used these historians to support their own hypotheses about the prosopography and chronology of the Balkan conflict between Basil and Samuel: Adontz, 'Samuel l'arménien', 347–407. More caution about the potential of the Balkan evidence contained in eastern sources has been exhibited by Whittow, *Making of Orthodox Byzantium*, 389, 423.

Bulgaria in 1018.[71] While Stephen offers some detailed snap-shots of armed engagements in the Balkans, his narrow and exclusive focus on the Armenian dramatis personae of Basil's armies means that he offers relatively little sense of Byzantium's overall strategic position in this region.[72] More-over, neither historian demonstrates any strong sense of the exact nature of the relationship between the Bulgarian royal family, represented by the princes Boris and Romanos, whose seat of power before 971 was Preslav in eastern Bulgaria, and the members of the Kometopoulos family, who came to rule Bulgaria when the kingdom's geopolitical centre of gravity shifted to western Macedonia after 975.[73] Some indirect hints of the wider diplomatic context within which Byzantium's conflict with Samuel of Bulgaria played out in the 990s are provided by the Venetian narratives of John the Deacon and Andrea Dandolo. Both historians describe the agreement struck in 992 through which the Venetians secured trading concessions in return for provid-ing naval assistance to the Byzantines; the chrysobull describing this agreement only survives in a Latin transla-tion.[74] Nonetheless, while documentary evidence from the

[71] Yahya's coverage of Basil's Balkan wars between 991 and the Bulgarians' final surrender of 1018 is limited to two short passages of text, both of which are devoid of chronological or topographical detail. Moreover, both passages claim, with what looks like a suspicious degree of repetition, that the emperor achieved a final victory after a four-year period of fighting (Yahya, *PO* 23, pp. 431, 461–2). For Yahya's more precise coverage of the 1018 surrender see Yahya, *PO* 47, pp. 407–8; the surrender is also discussed below at 7.1.

[72] For references to Armenian protagonists in Basil's Balkan campaigns see Stephen of Taron, *Armenische Geschichte*, 147, 185, 198.

[73] See below 8.5 for further discussion.

[74] John the Deacon, 'La cronaca Veneziana', 148–9; Andrea Dandolo, *Chronicon Venetum*, 187; A. Pertusi, 'Venezia e Bisanzio nel secolo XI', rpr.

monastic archives on Mount Athos confirms that Basil II was actively looking for allies in the Adriatic in his struggle with Samuel of Bulgaria during the 990s, especially among the Serbs, it should be noted that neither John the Deacon nor Andrea Dandolo link the 992 treaty directly to Basil's Bulgarian wars.[75]

The historiographical record thins out even further after 1000. Between the early 1000s and 1014 there is almost complete silence about Asia Minor, the eastern frontier, and Constantinople itself. Stephen of Taron's world history ends in 1004. At the same time Yahya falls almost silent, concerning himself merely with a description of the idiosyncratic and erratic behaviour of al-Hakim, the Fatimid caliph of Egypt.[76] Indeed, it is the destruction of the Church of the Holy Sepulchre in Jerusalem by al-Hakim in 1009 that proves to be the only event in the eastern half of the empire to attract attention from historians across the geographical spectrum, including from Ralph Glaber in Burgundy, during this fifteen-year period.[77] Meanwhile, in the Balkans Skylitzes' coverage is reduced to a series of exceptionally terse, highly generalized accounts of campaigns, some of

---

in V. Branca (ed.), *Storia della civiltà veneziana*, 3 vols. (Florence, 1979), i. 195–8.

[75] e.g. a document from the Lavra relates details of a Serbian embassy to Basil in 992: *Actes de Lavra I: Des origines à 1204*, Archives de l'Athos V, eds. P. Lemerle *et al.* (Paris, 1970), no. 10; G. Ostrogorsky, 'Une ambassade serbe auprès de l'empereur Basile II', *B* 19 (1949), 187–94.

[76] Yahya, *PO* 23, pp. 463–520.

[77] Yahya, *PO* 23, p. 492, Skylitzes, *Synopsis*, 347; Bar Hebraeus, *Chronography*, 184; Elias of Nisibis, *Chronographie*, 140–1; Ralph Glaber, *Historiarum Libri Quinque*, 132–6.

which are dated, some of which are not.[78] The fact that no event in Skylitzes' account of Basil's wars in Bulgaria can be dated with certainty to the period between 1005 and 1014 has led some recent historians to suggest that Samuel and Basil struck a peace accord in 1005 which endured for nearly ten years. This argument, which I do not find completely convincing, will be analysed further at the end of the next chapter and in Chapter 8.[79] Notwithstanding my scepticism about the 1005 truce, it is true that very little is said about the Balkans by any historical text during the first fifteen years of the eleventh century. And indeed, only slightly more can be said in the same period about Byzantium's westernmost provinces. The arrival of Byzantine officials in southern Italy continues to be recorded by local annalists. The Annals of Bari and *Lupus Protospatharius* also record the incidence of Arab attack on southern Italy in this period, a picture confirmed by the Venetian record.[80] The outbreak of a major tax revolt in Apulia in 1010–11 led by a local notable from Bari, Meles, which is recorded by the Annals of Bari, also registers in Skylitzes' bald narrative of this period.[81] Meanwhile, the only historiographical tradition to provide any genuine sense of narrative continuity is that

[78] For Skylitzes' terse treatment of many Balkan events see further discussion below: 2.4, 3.3.2, and 7.1.

[79] Skylitzes, *Synopsis*, 343–8; Stephenson, *Byzantium's Balkan Frontier*, 69–71; see also Whittow, *Making of Orthodox Byzantium*, 389. See below 2.4 and 8.5.

[80] Annals of Bari, 52; *Lupus Protospatharius*, 56–7; John the Deacon, 'La cronaca Veneziana', 166–7; Andrea Dandolo, *Chronicon Venetum*, 202.

[81] Annals of Bari, 52; Skylitzes, *Synopsis*, 348; J. Gay, *L'Italie méridionale et l'empire byzantin depuis l'avènement de Basil I jusqu'à la prise de Bari par les Normands (867–1071)* (Paris, 1904), 399–403.

from Venice: both John the Deacon and Andrea Dandolo describe diplomatic and strategic relations between Venice and Constantinople; these culminated in the marriage of Doge Peter Orseleo's son John to Maria Argyrina *c.*1004.[82]

It is only after 1014 that the historiographical gloom hanging over the reign really begins to lift. At this point Yahya includes some rather parochial material on northern Syria, sketching out the relationship between Byzantium, Aleppo, and the Fatimids.[83] Meanwhile Skylitzes' historical *Synopsis* contains some detailed snapshots of the military and diplomatic actions preceding and following the annexation of Bulgaria. These include an account of the battle of Kleidion in 1014, the Byzantine victory that Skylitzes alleges caused the death of Basil II's long-term adversary Samuel; negotiations with Samuel's nephew John Vladislav; a long account of the surrender of the chief members of the Bulgarian royal family and their senior military commanders in 1018; and a series of episodes describing the post-1018 situation in the north-west Balkans, the most vivid of which is the entrapment of the Bulgarian dissident commander Ibatzes by one of Basil's generals, Eustathios Daphnomeles.[84] Across the Adriatic many historians, from both north and south of the Alps, concern themselves with the second outbreak of Meles' rebellion in Apulia in 1017 and the suppression of this revolt by the Byzantine *katepano* of

---

[82] John the Deacon, 'La cronaca Veneziana', 155–170; Andrea Dandolo, *Chronicon Venetum* 197–203.

[83] Yahya, *PO* 47, pp. 373–408.

[84] Skylitzes, *Synopsis*, 348–66; the Ibatzes–Daphnomales episode is discussed further below at 4.2.2.

Italy, Basil Boiannes.[85] As we enter the final five years of the reign, the historiographical light begins to shine even more intensely, as most of the Greek and eastern narratives comment on a series of closely interlinked events: the absorption of the southern Armenian princedom of Vaspurakan (at some point between 1015 and 1021); the bequest to Basil of the northern Armenian kingdom of Ani (which was only finally realized in 1042); Basil II's campaigns against George of Abasgia and Iberia in 1021/2; and the domestic revolt against imperial authority in central Anatolia led by Nikephoros Phokas and Nikephoros Xiphias.[86]

So long did Basil rule and so extensive was his empire that it is clearly unrealistic for a historian to hope that the medieval historiographical record will offer uniformly even coverage of all periods and regions within the reign. Some unevenness is only to be expected. However, what I hope this detailed survey of the historiography relevant to Basil's reign reveals is the degree to which the surviving historiographical record leaves large periods and regions of Basil's hegemony almost completely undocumented. Instead the testimonies of medieval historians cluster around two periods, at the beginning and end of the reign; between

---

[85] *Lupus Protospatharius*, 57; Ralph Glaber, *Historiarum Libri Quinque*, 97–8; Ademar of Chabannes, *Chronicon*, 173–4; William of Apulia, 98–104; Amatus of Monte Cassino, *Storia de'Normanni*, 24–40; Leo Marsicanus, *Chronica Monasterii Casinensis*, 236–43, 261; see below 7.2 and 8.6 for more on these events.

[86] Skylitzes, *Synopsis*, 366–7; Yahya, *PO* 47, pp. 459–69; Aristakes of Lastivert, *Récit des malheurs*, 11–25; Matthew of Edessa, *Armenia and the Crusades*, 44–9; Georgian Royal Annals, 281–4; see below 8.8 for further discussion of these events.

989 and 1014 coverage is extremely thin. In terms of region, the east is relatively well served by the extant historiographical record; the Balkans and Italy are partially but more sporadically covered; Constantinople, Anatolia, and relations with the regions north of the Black Sea receive exiguous coverage after 989.

1.3   OTHER WRITTEN SOURCE MATERIALS

One could, of course, argue that rather than relying on the medieval historiography to construct a sustained narrative of Basil's reign, the modern historian should attempt to use non-historiographical written sources from the later tenth and early eleventh centuries more actively and creatively. Such a proposal has some merit to it, not least because some material of this sort does survive, both in Greek and in other languages. To take Greek first, there are several relevant extant sources from the eastern half of the empire. A few anecdotes in the *Miracles of Saint Eugenios of Trebizond* certainly enhance our picture of the eastern dimension of the Phokas and Skleros revolts as well as Basil's expedition to Iberia (Georgia) in the twilight years of his reign.[87] A handful of letters from Philetos Synadenos (the judge, or *krites*, of Tarsos) and the general Nikephoros Ouranos, as

---

[87] *Miracles of St Eugenios:* for a new edition of the material relating to Basil's reign see N. M. Panagiotakes, 'Fragments of a Lost Eleventh-Century Byzantine Historical Work', in C. Constantinides *et al.* (eds.), *Φιλέλλην*, *Studies in Honour of Robert Browning* (Venice, 1996), 321–57.

well as a few chapters from Ouranos' own military manual, are useful in rather different ways, not least in the insight they provide into military and administrative practices on Byzantium's eastern frontier with the Muslim world.[88] Meanwhile, descriptions of the travels of St Lazarus and his eventual establishment of a monastic foundation on Mount Galesion in western Asia Minor yield hints about everyday life in the eastern half of the Byzantine empire in the later tenth and early eleventh centuries.[89]

In the Balkans an anonymous military manual, the *Taktikon Vári*, usually dated to the later tenth century, sheds some light on the strategies and tactics developed by Byzantine armies during warfare against the Bulgars.[90] Some miscellaneous reflections about Basil's reign and his campaigns in the Balkans are also recorded in the later eleventh-century advice book of Kekaumenos.[91] Further snippets of information about the revolts of the early years of Basil's reign and

[88] For Synadenos' and Ouranos' letters see J. Darrouzès (ed.), *Épistoliers byzantins du Xe siècle* (Paris, 1960), 217–59; for Ouranos' *Taktika* see, J. A. de Foucault, 'Douze chapitres inédits de la "Tactique" de Nicéphore Ouranos', *TM* 5 (1973), 281–310; also E. McGeer, *Sowing the Dragon's Teeth: Byzantine Warfare in the 10th Century* (Washington DC, 1995), 88–162. See also below 6.4.

[89] St Lazaros of Mount Galesion: *AASS*, Nov. 3:508–88 (Brussels, 1910), 508–88 (*BHG* 979); see also the new translation by R. P. H. Greenfield, *The Life of Lazaros of Mt Galesion: An Eleventh-Century Pillar Saint* (Washington, DC, 2000).

[90] G. T. Dennis, *Three Byzantine Military Treatises* (Washington DC, 1985), 246–326. This military manual is known as the *Taktikon Vári* in honour of its first editor, R. Vári. Dennis chooses to call it 'Campaign Organisation and Tactics'.

[91] Kekaumenos: *Cecaumeni Consilia et Narrationes*, ed. and trans. (Russian) G. Litavrin (Moscow, 1972).

his dealings with the Balkans can be gleaned from a small number of documents in the archives of the monasteries on Mount Athos, as well as from saints' lives which reflect on contemporary Greece and Macedonia.[92] This hagiographical material includes the lives of Saint Nikon Metanoeite of Sparta, Saint Athanasios founder of the Lavra monastery on Mount Athos, and Saint Phantinos the Younger, as well as a panegyric of Saint Photios of Thessalonika.[93] If one turns to non-literary texts, then one could add to the list of available written evidence at least four inscriptions. The first, found at Dyrrachion on the Adriatic coast, refers to the political vicissitudes experienced by that city during Basil's reign; the second, found at Dristra on the Lower Danube, to the rebuilding of a church; the third, to the building of a fortress at Megale Gephyra in Thessaly in 1015; and the fourth, inscribed in Cyrillic rather than Greek letters, to the strengthening of another fortress, this time at Bitola in

---

[92] The contents of the relevant Athos documents are explored further in 7.1.

[93] St Nikon: *The Life of St. Nikon,* ed. and trans. D. F. Sullivan (Brookline, Mass., 1987); St Athanasios: *Vitae Duae Antiquae Sancti Athanasii Athonitae,* ed. J. Noret, CCSG 9 (Brepols, 1982). Saint Phantinos was born in Calabria in southern Italy, but spent the last eight years of his life in Thessalonika; he died in 973 shortly before the reign of Basil began: *La vita di San Fantino il Giovane,* ed. and trans. E. Follieri (Brussels, 1993). Saint Photios was the spiritual adviser to Basil II during the emperor's Balkan campaigns (Crostini, 'The Emperor Basil II's Cultural Life', 78). The panegyric celebrating his life was written by an anonymous author (*BHG* 1545). The existence of this text, contained in a manuscript from the Synodal Library in Moscow, was first signalled at the end of the 19th c. by V. G. Vasilievskij in *Žurnal Ministerstva Narodnago Prosveščenija* (1886). Schlumberger cites occasional references from the panegyric, while noting the unedited state of the text (*L'Épopée byzantine,* i. 645–6; ii. 47–8). Today the text still appears to be unpublished in full. It is not well-known to scholars, and is rarely cited.

western Macedonia by John Vladislav, the Bulgarian tsar, also dated, although with rather less certainty, to 1015.[94] Apart from the testimony provided by Skylitzes and the Priest of Diokleia little is known about the history of Bulgaria *after* Basil's conquest of 1018, although three charters produced before May 1020 give some idea of the ecclesiastical arrangements that followed annexation.[95]

Turning away from the Balkans, provincial life on Crete is partially illuminated by the rarely studied will of the hermit John Xenos of Crete (987–1027).[96] Further west the letters of Leo, Metropolitan of Synada, the envoy who was sent to Italy to negotiate a marriage alliance between Basil II and Otto III in the later 990s, shed light on Byzantine diplomacy with the emperors of Germany and the influence that both imperial powers sought to exercise over the Papacy and the

[94] Dyrrachion: C. A. Mango, 'A Byzantine Inscription relating to Dyrrachium', *Archaëologischer Anzeiger* 3 (1966), 410–14; Lower Danube: I. Ševčenko, 'A Byzantine Inscription from Silistra Reinterpreted', *RESEE* 7 (1969), 591–8; M. Salamon, 'Some Notes on an Inscription from Medieval Silistra', *RESEE* 9 (1971), 487–96; Thessaly: reference from J.-C. Cheynet, 'Grandeur et decadence des Diogénai', in V. N. Vlyssidou, *The Empire in Crisis (?): Byzantium in the 11ᵗʰ Century (1025–1081)* (Athens, 2003), 125; Bitola: references from Stephenson, *Legend of Basil the Bulgar-Slayer*, 29–30; these inscriptions contribute to the reconstruction of Basil's engagement with the Balkans offered in Ch. 8 below.

[95] *Regesten*: F. Dölger, *Regesten der Kaiserurkunden des öströmischen Reiches von 565–1453*, 3 vols. (Munich, 1925), i. 103–4; H. Gelzer, 'Ungedruckte und wenig bekannte Bistumsverzeichnisse der orientalischen Kirche', *BZ* 2 (1893), 42–6; J. Zepos and P. Zepos (eds.), *Ius Graecoromanum*, 8 vols (Athens, 1931), i. 272–3; Stephenson, *Byzantium's Balkan Frontier*, 75.

[96] See in the first instance, M. Angold, 'The Autobiographical Impulse in Byzantium', *DOP* 52 (1998), 228–9; M. Hinterberger, *Autobiographische Traditionen in Byzanz* (Vienna, 1999), 246–9.

internal politics of the city of Rome.[97] Otto III's interest in southern Italy is also refracted through the *Vita* of St Neilos, a Byzantine hermit from Rossano in Calabria, whom the German emperor sought out as a spiritual adviser.[98] Other hagiographical materials illuminate the Byzantine presence in southern Italy, including the life of St Sabas the Younger written by Orestes, the patriarch of Jerusalem (d.1005).[99] Finally a large number of archive documents reflecting the activities of various Byzantine regional commanders survive in southern Italy.[100]

[97] Leo of Synada: *The Correspondence of Leo, Metropolitan of Synada and Syncellus,* ed. M. P. Vinson (Washington DC, 1985): letters 1–13, which were written while Leo was in Italy and Germany in 997–8. Other letters within Leo's collection are useful for shedding some light on the agriculture and economic life of the upland region of western Anatolia where his see of Synada was situated: see especially Leo of Synada, *Correspondence,* letters 43, 54; L. Robert, 'Sur les lettres d'un métropolite de Phrygie au Xe siècle', *Journal des Savants* (1961), 97–166; (1962), 1–74.

[98] St Neilos the Younger: G. Giovanelli, *Bios kai politeia tou hosiou patros hemon Neilou tou Neou* (Grottaferrata, 1972); see also von Falkenhausen, 'Byzantine Italy in the Reign of Basil II', 138, 145, 151.

[99] St Sabas: *Historia et laudes SS. Sabae et Macarii iuniorum e Sicilia auctore Oreste patriarcha Hieroslymitani,* ed. G. Cozza Luzi (Rome, 1893); A. Guillou, 'La Lucanie byzantine', *B* 35 (1965), 134; V. von Falkenhausen, *Untersuchungen über die byzantinische Herrschaft in Süditalien vom 9. bis ins 11. Jahrhundert* (Wiesbaden, 1967), 67, 88. For a fuller list of hagiographical materials of interest from southern Italy in this period see von Falkenhausen, 'Byzantine Italy in the Reign of Basil II', 138–9. Orestes was not simply patriarch of Jerusalem. He was also a very close associate and blood relative of the Fatimid caliph al-Aziz. He was sent to Constantinople by al-Aziz's son, al-Hakim, to negotiate the truce that in 1001 brought peace between Egypt and Byzantium. Orestes died in Constantinople (Yahya, *PO* 18, pp. 802–3; *PO* 23, pp. 415, 460, 462, 481–4; Ralph Glaber, *Historiarum Libri Quinque,* 136–7; Biddle, *Tomb of Christ,* 74; for the truce see below 8.4); for further discussion of the hermit saints of southern Italy see Kreutz, *Before the Normans,* pp. xxix, 126–7.

[100] See below 7.2 for further discussion.

Meanwhile in Constantinople itself, an assortment of other materials may prove useful for understanding the articulation and exercise of imperial power. Expressions of centralized authority include an administrative list known as the *Escorial Taktikon*, produced in the final quarter of the tenth century, shortly before Basil came to the throne.[101] Equally important statements of imperial authority are the two great novels of the reign: first, legislation from 988 which in the context of raising support and resources for the emperors during the revolt of Bardas Phokas temporarily reversed existing prohibitions on the foundation of new monasteries; and second, the long, draconian novel of 996 which attacked the Powerful.[102] To such legislation can be added a handful of texts which refract the concerns of Basil's patriarchs.[103] Court rhetoric is represented by a contemporary encomium delivered by Leo the Deacon to a young Basil II.[104] Imperial propaganda can be identified in many other locations: the epitaph on Basil II's tomb;[105] the emperor's coins and seals;[106] repairs to monuments in the vicinity of

[101] See below 6.1 and 7.1.

[102] Svonoros, *Novelles*, 184–217, 231–2. On the 996 novel see above 1.1 and below 8.3.

[103] See in the first instance V. Grumel, *Les Régestes des actes du patriarcat de Constantinople Régestes*, vol. i, fascs. II–III, *Les Régestes de 715–1206*, 2nd edn., J. Darrouzès, (Paris, 1989), 310–38.

[104] I. Sykutres, 'Λέοντος τοῦ Διακόνου ἀνέκδοτον ἐγκώμιον Βασιλείου Bʹ, *EEBS* 10 (1932), 425–34. For another contemporary reference to the making of speeches before Basil II by the *didaskalos* John Sikeliotes see below 3.1.

[105] S. G. Mercati, 'Sull' Epigrafio di Basilio II Bulgaroctonos', *Collectanea Bizantina*, 2 vols. (Rome, 1970), i. 230. See also M. D. Lauxtermann, *Byzantine Poetry from Pisides to Geometres: Texts and Contexts* (Vienna, 2003), 236–8.

[106] The images on the gold and silver coinage of Basil II are discussed in their political context by P. Grierson, *Catalogue of the Byzantine Coins in the*

Constantinople;[107] luxury silks sent abroad as diplomatic gifts.[108] As well as materials that represent an official celebratory imperial line, other texts from the capital survive that cast a more critical slant on the reign. The poems of John Geometres written in the 980s and 990s convey some sense of contemporary concern about Basil's rule during the

Dumbarton Oaks Collection and in the Whittemore Collection, 5 vols. (Washington DC, 1966–99), iii. 599–633. For discussion of the iconography of Basil's seals, including the significance of those instances when he appears without his brother and co-emperor, Constantine VIII, see W. Seibt, *Die byzantinischen Bleisiegel in Österreich I: Kaiserhof* (Vienna, 1978), 85–8; also more recently the *Zacos Collection of Byzantine Lead Seals*, 2 (1999), nos. 198–9.

[107]   There are two such inscriptions on the Theodosian land walls and one on the sea walls (R. Janin, *Constantinople byzantine: développement urbain et répertoire topographique*, 2nd edn. (Paris, 1964), 268, 276, 297); Schlumberger, *L'Épopée byzantine*, ii. 537, 593; see also H. Maguire, 'The Beauty of Castles: A Tenth-Century Description of a Tower at Constantinople', Δελτιον της Χριστιανικης 'Αρχαιολογικης Εταιρειας 17 (1993–4), 21–4. See also an inscription found in the vicinity of the Long Walls of Thrace which is believed to relate to a repair carried out during Basil's reign on the aqueduct system feeding Constantinople: G. Seure, 'Antiquités thraces de la Propontide', *BCH* 36 (1912), 568–71. I would like to thank Jim Crow for drawing my attention to these inscriptions. This inscription has been more recently discussed but its location misidentified as Derkos rather than the Anastasian Walls (C. Ashdracha, 'Inscriptions Byzantines de la Thrace orientale (VIIIe– XI siècles)', Αρχαιολογικὸν Δελτίον 44–46 (1989–91), no. 89, 306–9).

[108]   For the two lion silks, now found in Cologne and Berlin, bearing inscriptions that refer to Basil and his brother Constantine see A. Muthesius, *Byzantine Silk Weaving AD 400 to AD 1200* (Vienna, 1997), 34–7; Schlumberger, *L'Épopée byzantine*, ii. 293, 629. It is also possible that a silk from Bamburg showing an imperial triumph may represent Basil II's entry into Athens in 1018 after the annexation of Bulgaria (G. Prinzing, 'Die Bamberger Guntertuch in neuer Sicht', *Byz Slav* 54 (1993), 218–31; J.Kirmeier, *Kaiser Heinrich II. 1002–1024* (Augsburg, 2002), no. 183, pp. 355–6). An alternative context has recently been suggested for the Bamberg silk: a commemoration not of Basil's victory over the Bulgarians, as is so often alleged, but instead of John Tzimiskes' conquest in 971 (Stephenson, 'Images of the Bulgar-slayer', 57–63; idem, *Legend of Basil the Bulgar-Slayer*, 62–5).

early decades of his reign.[109] The life of Saint Symeon the New Theologian written *c.*1040 offers a window into disputes during the first decade of the eleventh century between the imperial court and Symeon the troublesome *hegoumenos* of the monastery of St Mamas.[110] Meanwhile a miracle collection connected to the Hospital of Sampson illuminates the organization of the household of one of the most important court figures of Basil's reign: Leo, *patrikios, praepositos, droungarios* of the fleet and *logothetes* of the *dromos,* who was sent eastwards in 977 with plenipotentiary powers to put an end to the first revolt of Bardas Skleros, a mission that he failed to achieve.[111] Further evidence for what Constantino-politans thought of their city, their empire, and their own times may also be present in other less obvious forms of contemporary literature, such as the *Apocalypse of Anasta-sia,*[112] as well as the great encyclopaedic enterprises of the later tenth century: the *Souda,* a vast compendium of useful knowledge;[113] the collection of some one hundred and twenty

[109] M. D. Lauxtermann, 'John Geometres – Poet and Soldier', *B* 58 (1999), 356–80; idem, 'Byzantine Poetry and the Paradox of Basil's Reign', in Magda-lino (ed.), *Byzantium in the Year 1000,* 199–216; idem, *Byzantine Poetry,* esp. 234–5; also see below 5.2.1 and 7.1.

[110] P. I. Hausherr, ed. and trans., *Vie de Syméon le Nouveau Théologien (949–1022) par Nicétas Stéthatos* (Rome, 1928); B. Krivocheine, *Symeon the New Theologian (949–1022)* (New York, 1986); J. McGuckin, 'Symeon the New Theologian and Byzantine Monasticism', in A. Bryer and M. Cunningham (eds.), *Mount Athos and Byzantine Monasticism* (Aldershot, 1996), 17–35.

[111] The *Miracles of Sampson: PG* 115, cols. 278–308; Skylitzes, *Synopsis,* 295, 303, 320–2; I am grateful to Professor Cyril Mango for these references.

[112] J. Baun, *Tales from Another Byzantium: Celestial Journey and Local Community in the Medieval Greek Apocrypha* (Cambridge, forthcoming).

[113] *Souda: Suidae Lexicon,* ed. A. Adler, 5 vols. (Leipzig, 1928–38); P. Lemerle, *Le Premier Humanisme byzantin: Notes et remarques sur enseigne-ment et culture à Byzance des origins au Xe siècle* (Paris, 1971), 297–9.

saints' lives collated by Symeon Metaphrastes' team of hagiographers;[114] or the *Patria of Constantinople*, an antiquarian
guide to the city's capital compiled from much older materials in the final decade of the tenth century.[115] Paul Magdalino's recent investigations of contemporary astrological texts
suggest that modern historians interested in the later tenth
and early eleventh centuries should also find a context for
interest in and fear of the millennium in the second and third
decades of Basil's reign.[116]

To the list of Greek written materials can be added sources
of written and material evidence from non-Greek language
backgrounds. If we look only at the field of Byzantium's
diplomatic relations with its neighbours, several isolated
items immediately seem relevant. There is a letter written
in 988, in the epistolary collection of Gerbert of Aurillac, the
Archbishop of Rheims who later became Pope Sylvester II,
requesting a Byzantine bride for Robert, the son of the new
king of France, Hugh Capet.[117] Another letter from a western

[114] See in the first instance on the Metaphrastic tradition: C. Høgel, 'Hagiography under the Macedonians: The Two Recensions of the Metaphrastic
Menologion', in Magdalino (ed.), *Byzantium in the Year 1000*, 217–32.

[115] *Patria*: T. Preger, *Scriptores Originum Constantinopolitanarum*, 2 vols
(Leipzig, 1901–7; repr. 1989); see also G. Dagron, *Constantinople imaginaire*
(Paris, 1984), 21–2; *ODB*, iii. 1598.

[116] P. Magdalino, 'The Year 1000 in Byzantium', in Magdalino (ed.), *Byzantium in the Year 1000*, 233–70; on millennial gloom see also below 5.2.1.

[117] Gerbert of Aurillac: *Correspondance: Gerbert d'Aurillac*, eds. P. Riché
and J.-P. Callu, 2 vols. (Paris, 1993), i. 268–71. This letter seems to have been
sent by Gerbert on behalf of King Hugh, although some historians have
doubted the letter's authenticity, or have argued that it was actually sent by
Hugh rather than Gerbert (K. Ciggaar, *Western Travellers to Constantinople:
The West and Byzantium, 962–1204* (Leiden, 1996), 164). Letter 47, sent to
Rome in 984 asking for contemporary diplomatic news of the Byzantines,
Fatimids, and Italy, is also of interest.

cleric which throws interesting light on east–west relations in Basil's reign is that from Fulbert of Chartres written to the Bishop of Pecs offering his best wishes to King Stephen of Hungary. This evidence, read in conjunction with material in Ralph Glaber's chronicle, helps to show how after King Stephen's conversion to Christianity at the turn of the millennium, western European pilgrims were more easily able to travel eastwards to regions like Byzantium by land.[118] Meanwhile, further south, Latin archive documents offer an important window onto Byzantium's diplomatic relations with the Lombard princes of southern Italy and various local notables in Croatia, Serbia, and Dalmatia.[119] The employment of Armenian forces within Byzantine armies in the Balkans is attested by the survival of an Armenian Gospel Book commissioned in Adrianople in 1007.[120] Much further west, Ibn al-Kardabus and Ibn Bassam refer to the arrival of embassies sent from Constantinople at the courts of the Umayyad rulers of Islamic Spain in the first decade of the eleventh century.[121] Meanwhile, a list of gifts

[118] Fulbert of Chartres: *The Letters and Poems of Fulbert of Chartres,* ed. and trans. F. Behrends, OMT (Oxford, 1976), 148–9; see also Ralph Glaber, *Historiarum Libri Quinque,* 97–8; see above 1.2.2 for evidence from Glaber and Ademar of Chabannes on western pilgrim traffic which went eastwards by sea.

[119] *Codex Diplomaticus Cavensis,* eds. M. Morcaldi *et al.,* 8 vols (Naples, Milan, and Pisa, 1873–93); *Codice Diplomatico Amalfitano,* I, ed. R. Filangieri di Candida (Naples, 1917): both discussed by Kreutz, *Before the Normans,* pp. xxix–xx; see also Schlumberger, *L'Épopée byzantine,* i. 536–8; *Codex Diplomaticus Regni Croatiae, Dalmatiae et Slavoniae,* 1, ed. M. Kostrenčic (Zagreb, 1967), 44–64.

[120] V. Nersessian, *Treasures from the Ark: 1700 Years of Armenian Christian Art* (London, 2001), 182–3; this artefact is also discussed below in 7.1.

[121] Ibn al-Kardabus: *Historia de al-Andalus (Kitab al-Iktifa),* trans. F. Maíllo Salgado (Madrid, 1986), 85; D. Wasserstein, *The Rise and Fall of the Party Kings* (Princeton, 1985), 135.

exchanged between Byzantine and Islamic courts refers to embassies between Basil II and al-Hakim, the Fatimid caliph of Egypt, as well as to imperial contacts with Muslim rulers of Sicily.[122] As we shall see in Chapter 5, diplomatic relations between Byzantium and Muslims further east, especially the Buyid court of Baghdad, can be tracked in a variety of literary deposits including letters, propaganda bulletins, and guides to diplomatic behaviour.[123]

Yet, despite this rich and varied vein of later tenth- and early eleventh-century evidence, such sources from outside the boundaries of historical narrative are, nonetheless, extremely difficult to use in the composition of a sustained narrative of the political and diplomatic developments in Basil's reign. Paradoxically the very thinness of the narrative provided by the medieval historians makes deploying materials from outside the historiographical record highly problematic. This is because without a strong political and diplomatic chronology in place, knowing how or where to locate details from other written sources becomes almost impossible. Indeed, this absence of a viable narrative may explain why so many of the literary sources described above have received only sporadic attention from Byzantine literary scholars as well as from historians. It may also be the reason for the relative neglect of the artistic productions of Basil's court, such as the Psalter now found in Venice, which

---

[122]   The *Kitab al daha'ir wa-l-tuhaf* was probably composed in late 11th- or early 12th-c. Fatimid Egypt from much earlier materials; see M. Hamidullah, 'Nouveaux documents sur les rapports de l'Europe avec l'Orient musulman au moyen âge', *Arabica* 7 (1960), 291, 296.

[123]   See below 5.1.

bears a frontispiece illustration of the emperor in military dress, and the illustrated *synaxarion,* known as the *Menologion* of Basil II.[124] In the final chapter of this book we will consider what to make of some of these items, particularly of their propaganda value. But before we can move on to that, we need to begin a new interpretation of Basil's reign by looking afresh at the historiographical record, above all at the main narrative text in Greek, John Skylitzes' *Synopsis Historion.*

---

[124] A lack of background narrative context is a problem which surfaces in recent attempts to date and interpret many of the texts I have described above including the literary works of Nikephoros Ouranos, the correspondence of Leo of Synada, and Basil's psalter: E. McGeer, 'Tradition and Reality in the *Taktika* of Nikephoros Ouranos', *DOP* 45 (1991), 129–40; Vinson, *The Correspondence of Leo, passim*; A. Cutler, 'The Psalter of Basil II', in *Imagery and Ideology in Byzantine Art* (Aldershot: Variorum, 1992), no. III. Very little research has been published on the *Menologion* since S. Der Nersessian, 'Remarks on the Date of the Menologium and the Psalter written for Basil II', *B* 15 (1940–1), 104–25, and I. Ševčenko, 'The Illuminators of the Menologium of Basil II', *DOP* 16 (1962), 243–76. As Barbara Crostini ('The Emperor Basil II's Cultural Life', 53–80) has so appositely pointed out, the other reason why the arts and literature of the later 10th and early 11th c. have been so widely neglected, is the naïve belief on the part of many modern scholars that since Michael Psellos alleged that Basil himself had no interest in the arts, there were no arts at all. Only with Paul Stephenson's interest in the legend of Basil the Bulgar-slayer has there been some renewed research into the visual imagery emanating from Basil's court (Stephenson, 'Images of the Bulgar-slayer', 44–68; idem, *Legend of Basil the Bulgar-Slayer*, ch. 4; for a brief discussion of the Psalter see below 8.3).

2

Basil II and John Skylitzes: The Historian's Career and Working Methods

2.1 SCOPE AND PROBLEMS OF THE *SYNOPSIS HISTORION*

The importance of the *Synopsis Historion* of John Skylitzes to any understanding of the political, military, and diplomatic history of the Byzantine Empire during the reign of Basil II cannot be overstated. Skylitzes' account of Basil's hegemony written towards the end of the eleventh century is the earliest surviving connected narrative of the reign in Greek. It is the principal source for several of the most politically significant events of the reign, including the revolts of the generals Bardas Skleros and Bardas Phokas as well as Byzantium's long war of attrition against the First Bulgarian Empire. It is the primary source which most later historians, both medieval and modern, have used to construct a chronology of the later tenth and early eleventh centuries.[1]

---

[1] Those medieval historians who based their accounts of Basil's reign on Skylitzes' narrative include George Kedrenos and John Zonaras: *Georgius*

Yet Skylitzes' account also presents considerable problems to the historian of Basil's reign. In the first place it is relatively late, composed nearly three-quarters of a century after the emperor's death. It is not an eye-witness account of the later tenth and early eleventh centuries. Instead it is a fusion of the writings of other earlier historians, and indeed one of the most significant problems presented by the *Synopsis* is the relationship between Skylitzes' narrative and the different source materials which underpin it. Furthermore, the *Synopsis* represents a highly abbreviated account of two-and-a-half centuries of the Byzantine past. All versions of Skylitzes' *Synopsis Historion* run from 811 to 1057, and if the author of the Continuation of Skylitzes (*Skylitzes Continuatus*) can be identified with Skylitzes himself, the account

Cedrenus, ed. I. Bekker, 2 vols., CSHB (Bonn, 1938–9), ii. 416–80; *Ioannis Zonarae Epitomae Historiarum Libri XIII–XVIII*, ed. T. Büttner-Wobst, CSHB (Bonn, 1897), 538–69; those historians who either used Skylitzes' testimony directly or indirectly through Zonaras include Constantine Manasses and Michael Glykas: *Constantini Manassis Breviarum Chronicum*, ed. O. Lampsidis, CFHB 36 (Athens, 1996), 314–21; *Annales (Biblos Chronike)*, ed. I. Bekker, CSHB (Bonn, 1836), 575–9. Among modern historians Skylitzes' account provides the main template for Ostrogorsky, *History of the Byzantine State*, 298–315; Treadgold, *Byzantine State and Society*, 513–33. Schlumberger, *L'Épopée byzantine*, i. 327–777, and ii. *passim*, adopts a more complex chronological structure which integrates the narrative outline provided by Yahya ibn Sa'id as well as that of Skylitzes. This is an approach also followed by Whittow, *Making of Orthodox Byzantium*, 358–90. The result of integrating Yahya into the narrative means that Schlumberger and more recently Whittow pay much greater attention to Byzantium's eastern frontier during Basil's reign than those historians who rely solely on Skylitzes. For more on how Yahya's testimony can be used to unravel the history of the Byzantine east in this period see above 1.2.2 and below 6.3.3. For further discussion about later Byzantine historians who use the *Synopsis* in their own works, see Flusin and Cheynet, *Jean Skylitzès*, p. xxiii.

continues to 1079.[2] The abbreviated nature of Skylitzes' account means that the amount of text dedicated to individual reigns is slim. Within the five hundred pages of I. Thurn's critical edition of the *Synopsis*, Basil's fifty-year reign is covered in only fifty-five pages.[3]

Another important consequence of the text's brevity is that its geographical and chronological coverage is extremely uneven. In the case of Basil's reign, the first half of Skylitzes' account is dominated by the Skleros and Phokas revolts, the second half by warfare against Bulgaria. As far as the first half of the reign is concerned, chapters 1 to 10 of the *Synopsis Historion* (more than twenty per cent of the forty-seven chapters Skylitzes dedicates to Basil) are concerned with the first three years of the reign and the revolt of the general Bardas Skleros (976–9).[4] The next two chapters deviate briefly from the theme of internal revolt by dealing with warfare between Byzantium and Bulgaria in the first decade of the reign, concentrating on Basil II's defeat in the Gates of Trajan in 986 against the army of Tsar Samuel.[5]

---

[2] The Continuation of the *Synopsis* has been published by E. T. Tsolakes, *Skylitzes Continuatus*: Ἡ Συνέχεια τῆς χρονογραφίας τοῦ Ἰωάννου Σκυλίτζη (Thessalonika, 1968). For a summary of the arguments about whether *Skylitzes Continuatus* should be identified with Skylitzes see below 2.3. Because it is mutilated at the start the only manuscript of the main text of the *Synopsis* (as opposed to the Continuation) which does not begin in 811 is U [*Vind. Hist. Gr. 74*]. This manuscript begins with the reign of Basil II (Skylitzes, *Synopsis*, p. xxvi).

[3] Skylitzes (John): *Ioannis Scylitzae Synopsis Historiarum*, ed. I. Thurn, CFHB 5 contains Skylitzes' narrative to 1057. The coverage of the reign of Basil is to be found between pages 314 and 369.

[4] Skylitzes, *Synopsis*, 314–328. See Appendix A for a chapter-by-chapter breakdown of Skylitzes' coverage of Basil's reign.

[5] Ibid. 328–31.

However, this deviation is short. Chapters 14 to 19 return to the theme of internal insurrection, and cover the second revolt of Bardas Skleros and the contemporaneous rebellion of Bardas Phokas, events which lasted a little over two years, between 987 and 989.[6] With the death of Phokas and the surrender of Skleros, the second half of Skylitzes' testimony for the reign is almost exclusively concerned with the Bulgarian wars. Seventeen of the twenty-eight post-989 chapters are concerned with conflict in the Balkans.[7] Many of these are very short, compressed chapters; only on rare occasions, such as the Battle of the River Spercheios, a victory for Basil's senior general Nikephoros Ouranos in 997, and the Battle of Kleidion, a victory for Byzantine forces led by Basil himself in 1014, is narrative coverage more extensive.[8] Equally striking is the fact that of those chapters dealing with Bulgaria, three-quarters are concerned with the period 1014 to 1018.[9] Meanwhile, most chapters dedicated to matters other than the Balkans are extremely terse, often comprising little more than a handful of lines.[10] It is also noteworthy that there is very little accurately dated material at all which deals with the period between 1005 and 1014 in any part of the empire.

[6] Ibid. 332–9.

[7] The Bulgarian testimony is to be found between p. 341 and p. 366 of Skylitzes' account of the reign (the major part of chs. 23 to 44).

[8] Skylitzes, *Synopsis*, 341–2, 348–50.

[9] All of chs. 35 to 44 except for ch. 39 (Skylitzes, *Synopsis*, 348–66).

[10] e.g. ch. 33 dealing with the destruction of the Church of the Holy Sepulchre in Jerusalem by Fatimid forces in 1009 extends to only seven lines (Skylitzes, *Synopsis*, 347).

The net result of Skylitzes' twin focus on early internal strife and the final stages of warfare in the Balkans is that large regions of the internal Byzantine world and the empire's relations with its neighbours are rarely touched upon. For example, Skylitzes' coverage of events within Constantinople itself is limited to short notices concerning natural disasters, the accessions and deaths of patriarchs, and occasional urban improvements, such as the rebuilding of Hagia Sophia after the earthquake of 989 and the restoration of the Aqueduct of Valens towards the end of the reign.[11] After the emperor's victories over Skleros and Phokas in 989 relations within the political elite of the empire are treated brusquely. Basil II's novel of 996 against the Powerful is cited in the same short, undated chapter (chapter 21) which deals with the emperor's decision to imprison Eustathios Maleinos, one of the rebels who supported the insurgency of Bardas Phokas in 987.[12] At the end of his account of the reign, Skylitzes includes a cursory survey of the 1021–2 revolt of Nikephoros Phokas and Nikephoros Xiphias in Cappadocia.[13] Virtually no mention is made of Basil II's fiscal policy, beyond two short references to the emperor's imposition of a measure known as the *allelengyon*. The first reference notes that this decree, issued *c*.1002, ordered that the taxes of those poor landowners who defaulted should be paid by their powerful neighbours. The second reports that the emperor

---

[11] Skylitzes, *Synopsis*, 331–2, 340–1, 347–8, 366, 369.
[12] Ibid. 340; for further discussion about the imprisonment of Eustathios Maleinos see below 8.3.
[13] Skylitzes, *Synopsis*, 366–7.

refused a request by Patriarch Sergios that the tax should be lifted after the end of the Bulgarian wars in 1018.[14]

Further afield, references to the empire's dealings with its neighbours, especially those outside the Balkans, are extremely cursory and confused. For example relations between the empire and its eastern neighbours from 990 to 1022 are described in a garbled account which is less than a page long (chapter 20).[15] The surrender of the Armenian princedom of Vaspurakan in the final decade of the reign is to be found in a compressed chapter, which also contains a notice dealing with a joint Byzantino-Rus expedition against the north coast of the Black Sea (chapter 39).[16] Still in the north, the events surrounding the alliance between Basil and Vladimir prince of Kiev in 988–9 are summarized in a two-line parenthesis inserted into Skylitzes' coverage of the revolt of Bardas Phokas. Skylitzes merely mentions that Basil's armies included Russian troops, which had been dispatched after the emperor had married his sister Anna to Vladimir *archon* of the Rus. He makes no reference to the conversion of the Rus to Christianity which accompanied the Byzantien-Rus alliance, nor to the mysterious siege of Cherson conducted by the Rus after the agreement had been reached.[17] Meanwhile, Skylitzes' coverage of Byzantine

---

[14] Skylitzes, *Synopsis*, 347, 365.

[15] Ibid. 339–40; a passage also discussed below in 2.4.

[16] Skylitzes, *Synopsis*, 354–5; see below 8.4 for the difficulties associated with using Skylitzes' testimony to date the surrender of Vaspurakan; also see below 2.4 for further discussion of the incidence and impact of Skyiltzes' use of compressed narratives.

[17] Ibid. 336; for more on Basil's relations with the Rus and medieval historiographical interest in these developments, see below 8.7.

relations with western Europe is exiguous. A few lines inserted at the end of chapter 34 mention a revolt against imperial rule in southern Italy during the second decade of the eleventh century, organized by a local notable from Bari called Meles.[18] Finally, just before Skylitzes reaches the end of his testimony of the reign, he refers to the advance expedition to Sicily led by the eunuch Orestes, which was intended to prepare the way for Basil's own invasion of the island, a campaign which was brought to a premature end by the emperor's death in 1025.[19] Apart from these brief references, Skylitzes makes no reference at all to the empire's dealings with the other western powers such as the Ottonian emperors of Germany, the Capetian kings of France, or the pope.

Yet, despite its obvious chronological and geographical deficiencies, Skylitzes' account of the reign of Basil II is the principal text with which the historian of Byzantine political and military history in the later tenth and early eleventh centuries must engage. The important question is how this engagement is to be achieved profitably. The most obvious way of approaching Basil's reign through Skylitzes' text is to compare the material in his account with information and interpretation contained in other written sources which also report on the same period. As we shall see later in this chapter, this is an approach which Jonathan Shepard has used to great profit when looking at Skylitzes' post-Basil, mid-eleventh-century coverage.[20] However, this method is less useful for looking at Basil's reign. No substantial

---

[18] Skylitzes, *Synopsis*, 348.   [19] Ibid. 368.   [20] See below 2.4.

alternative histories covering the later tenth or early eleventh centuries composed in Greek survive against which Skylitzes' account of the reign as a whole can be assessed. Those appraisals of the reign written in other languages, such as the histories of Yahya ibn Sa'id and Stephen of Taron, focus predominantly on the eastern frontier, a region which Skylitzes himself barely mentions.[21] Indeed, the only section of the reign where a direct comparison between Skylitzes' account and other historical narratives is possible is the first thirteen years of the reign, when the revolts of Bardas Skleros and Bardas Phokas attract the attention of a variety of historians writing both in Greek and in other languages. Such a direct comparison will be undertaken in Chapter 5 of this volume.

However, even if information and interpretation in Skylitzes' account of the first thirteen years of revolts can be compared with other historical records, one still needs to ask how the *rest* of his testimony for the post-989 period is to be read. In the next four chapters it will be argued that the most fruitful method of approaching Skylitzes' treatment of Basil II lies less in trying to improve upon his factual accuracy by comparing his account with other texts, and more in understanding the principles of selection, presentation, and interpretation which underpin his own text. In this sense the key questions to be asked are: how and why does Skylitzes offer his reader this particular text? Behind these questions lies the explicit acknowledgement that all of the historical writing about the ninth to eleventh centuries contained in

[21] For these historians see above 1.2.2.

Skylitzes' *Synopsis* is conditioned to a greater or lesser extent by the fact that this material was recopied, reshaped, and rewritten by Skylitzes himself in the later eleventh century. The vital precondition to analysing the history of earlier periods described in Skylitzes' account, such as the reign of Basil II, is establishing the nature of those later eleventh-century filters.

An investigation of this nature means looking at Skylitzes' composition from a variety of directions: at his working methods, his relationship with his sources, the genre within which he wrote, his competence as a historian, his purpose in writing and his anticipated audience. Investigation of such variables should proceed at two different but related levels: one which looks closely at the text itself; the other which sets the text in its wider contexts of the time at which it was written. The next chapter (Chapter 3) is predominantly concerned with the first of these levels. It represents a detailed textual analysis of a small section of the *Synopsis* designed to elucidate Skylitzes' working methods and the relationship of his text to his underlying sources. In the following chapter (Chapter 4) this textual analysis will provide the foundation for a broader discussion of how Skylitzes and his narrative relate to the wider literary, social, and indeed, political contexts of the period in which the *Synopsis* was compiled. But since Skylitzes' text is often cited, but rarely studied in detail by modern scholars, this current chapter will present a brief overview of the present state of Skylitzes scholarship, including an outline of what is known about the author's own biography. Greatest attention will be paid to existing research into Skylitzes' sources and working methods, particularly Jonathan Shepard's work on Skylitzes' mid-eleventh-century material. The implications of Shepard's analysis for a better understanding of Skylitzes' coverage of Basil II's reign will also be discussed, particularly in relation to the vexed Balkan testimony in the *Synopsis Historion*. Some initial caveats, however, need to be made explicit. Although reference to the Continuation of Skylitzes' testimony will be made where relevant, the principal engagement will be with the main 811–1057 section of the *Synopsis*.

2.2   SKYLITZES SCHOLARSHIP FROM DE BOOR TO THURN

2.2.1   Before the critical edition

It is only in the past thirty years that John Skylitzes has come to be widely recognized as an independent historian. Before I. Thurn published a critical edition of the main body of the *Synopsis Historion* (811 to 1057) in 1973, shortly after E. T. Tsolakes had produced an edition of the Continuation (1057–79) in 1968, most modern scholars only had access to Skylitzes through the world chronicle of George Kedrenos. This twelfth-century text was published in a Bonn Corpus edition of 1838/9. It includes a verbatim copy of Skylitzes' testimony from 811 to 1057.[22]

---

[22] John Skylitzes: Skylitzes, *Synopsis*; Skylitzes Continuatus: ῾Η Συνέχεια τῆς χρονογραφίας τοῦ Ἰωάννου Σκυλίτζη ed. Tsolakes; George Kedrenos: *Georgius Cedrenus,* Bekker, vol. ii.

The obscurity of the *Synopsis Historion* has until very recently resulted in a lack of scholarly interest in Skylitzes and his text. In general appraisals of Byzantine historiography Skylitzes has traditionally been identified as a world chronicler whose unsophisticated literary production was intended for an audience of credulous monks.[23] Further comment has tended to come primarily from those historians interested in the early history of Bulgaria, with attention focusing in this case on a fourteenth-century manuscript of the text, [U] [*Vindob. Hist. Gr. 74*], which contains some information about the western Balkans during the reigns of Basil II and Michael IV not found in other manuscripts. It has sometimes been argued that this extra material represents a fuller form of the *Synopsis* closer to Skylitzes' original account. The more widespread scholarly view, however, is that most of this material was interpolated into a copy of the *Synopsis* by the Macedonian bishop Michael of Devol in the early twelfth century.[24]

---

[23] F. Hirsch, *Byzantinische Studien* (Leipzig, 1876), 358–76; K. Krumbacher, *Geschichte der byzantinischen Literatur von Justinien bis zum Ende des oströmischen Reiches, (527–1453),* 2 vols., (New York, repr. 1970 of 1897 edn.), i. 365–8; G. Moravcsik, *Byzantinoturcica: Die Byzantinischen Quellen der Geschichte der Türkvölker,* 2nd edn. (Berlin, 1958), 335–41.

[24] The most sustained research was conducted by C. de Boor, 'Zu Johannes Skylitzes', *BZ* 13 (1904), 356–69 and 'Weiteres zur Chronik des Skylitzes', *BZ* 14 (1905), 409–67. His interests centred on the manuscripts of the text and the relationship between the *Synopsis* and the Continuation. The most detailed study of manuscript [U] was undertaken by B. Prokic, *Die Zusätze des Johannes Skylitzes* (Munich, 1906). H. Grégoire's view ('Du Nouveau sur l'histoire bulgaro-byzantine: Nicétas Pegonitès, vainqueur du roi Bulgare, Jean Vladislav', *B* 12 (1937), 289–91) that manuscript [U] represented the fullest version of the *Synopsis* has been challenged by J. Ferluga, 'John Scylitzes and Michael of Devol', *ZRVI* 10 (1967), 163–70.

It was only when critical editions of the main text and its Continuation appeared in the late 1960s and early 1970s that the *Synopsis* began to be more widely investigated, although scholarly interest has still been somewhat sporadic. Skylitzes and his text have not been as closely examined as the writers of other historical synopses in Greek, such as John Malalas or Theophanes the Confessor.[25] An unpublished Ph.D. thesis by Stamatina McGrath uses Skylitzes' text for prosopographical evidence about the Byzantine aristocracy of the ninth to eleventh centuries, but does not investigate the text itself in great depth.[26] Only the Madrid manuscript [M],

Ferluga supported the idea that Michael of Devol was responsible for the additional material in [U], a position adopted by most recent historians of the history, literature, and culture of western Macedonia: G. Prinzing, 'Entstehung und Rezeption der Justiana-Prima-Theorie im Mittelalter, *Byzantinobulgarica* 5 (1978), 272; Mullett, *Theophylact of Ochrid*, 238–9; Stephenson, *Byzantium's Balkan Frontier*, 72, n. 83; Flusin and Cheynet, *Jean Skylitzès*, pp. xxi–ii.

[25] E. Jeffreys *et al.* (trans.), *The Chronicle of John Malalas* (Melbourne, 1986); E. Jeffreys *et al.* (eds.), *Studies in John Malalas* (Sydney, 1990); C. A. Mango and R. Scott (trans.), *The Chronicle of Theophanes Confessor* (Oxford, 1997); J. N. Ljubarskij, 'Concerning the Literary Technique of Theophanes the Confessor', *Byz Slav* 56 (1995), 317–22; P. Speck, 'Der "Zweite Theophanes": Eine These zur Chronographie des Theophanes', Ποικίλα Βυζαντ ινα, 13 (1975), 431–75. E. Jeffreys, 'The Attitudes of Byzantine Chroniclers towards Ancient History', *B* 49 (1979), 199–238, discusses both Malalas and Constantine Manasses; R. Macrides and P. Magdalino, 'The Fourth Kingdom and the Rhetoric of Hellenism', in P. Magdalino (ed.), *The Perception of the Past in Twelfth-Century Europe* (London, 1992), 120–39, discusses 11th- and 12th-c. synoptic historical writing, but only deals with Constantine Manasses, Michael Glykas, and John Zonaras in detail. The standard summary of Skylitzes and the *Synopsis* is found in H. Hunger, *Die hochsprachliche profane Literatur der Byzantiner*, 2 vols. (Munich, 1978), ii. 389–93.

[26] S. McGrath, 'A Study of the Social Structure of the Byzantine Aristocracy as seen through Ioannis Skylitzes' "Synopsis Historiarum"', Ph.D. Thesis (Washington: Catholic University of America, 1996).

which was copied and illustrated in the twelfth-century kingdom of Sicily, has attracted any consistent attention in the secondary literature, and this has tended to come from art historians interested in the miniatures of this version of the *Synopsis*. Relatively little work has been done on the relationship between this manuscript and the other copies of the *Synopsis*. Work on the Madrid manuscript has not focused on the more general question of how Skylitzes' *Synopsis* was produced in the eleventh century and disseminated in the centuries after the text was written.[27] It is possible that Skylitzes' relative obscurity has been reinforced by the absence of a modern language translation of his text. This situation has been rectified only very recently with the publication of a French translation of the *Synopsis* up to 1057 by Bernard Flusin and Jean-Claude Cheynet.[28] But while this translation with its accompanying commentary and brief introduction is highly welcome, it remains the case that a full monograph treatment of Skylitzes has yet to appear.

[27] See e.g. A. Grabar and M. I. Manousacas, *L'Illustration du manuscrit de Skylitzès de la Bibliothèque Nationale de Madrid* (Venice, 1979); J. C. Estapanan, *Skylitzes matritensis, I: reproducciones y miniaturas* (Madrid, 1965). Analysis of the textual content of this manuscript has been confined to a study of the poems about Byzantine emperors which appear in this version of the *Synopsis* alone: I. Ševčenko, 'Poems on the Deaths of Leo VI and Constantine VII in the Madrid Manuscript of Skylitzes', *DOP* 23–4 *(1969–70)*, 185–228. Recently, important new work on the illustrations has appeared: V. Tsamakda, *The Illustrated Chronicle of Ioannes Skylitzes in Madrid* (Leiden, 2002).

[28] B. Flusin and J.-C. Cheynet, *Jean Skylitzès: Empereurs de Constantinople* (Paris, 2003).

2.2.2   Manuscript tradition

When I. Thurn published his critical edition of the *Synopsis Historion* the text's complicated manuscript history was finally elucidated. Thurn listed nine twelfth- to fourteenth-century manuscripts containing the narrative from 811 to 1057. Although he acknowledged that later manuscripts also existed, it was from the medieval manuscripts that he compiled his edition.[29] Of the manuscripts in question, none is a contemporary autograph, although four [A, C, M, and O] are datable to the twelfth century and were thus copied within a century of the author's own lifetime.[30] Of the four twelfth-century manuscripts, [A] is probably the oldest.[31] Thurn also suggested that the surviving medieval manuscripts fell into three main families: [ACE], [VBO], and [MNU]. It was to this final family that the version of the text contained in the world chronicle of Kedrenos was

[29] Skylitzes, *Synopsis*, pp. xx–xxviii: A (*Vind. Hist. Gr. 35*); C (*Coisl. 136*); E (*Scorial. T. III. 9*); O (*Achrid. 79*); V (*Vat. Gr. 161*); B (*Ambr. C 279*); M (*Matr. II*); N (*Neap. III. B. 24*); U (*Vind. Hist. Gr. 74*). In this elucidation of the manuscript history of the text Thurn built on the earlier work of de Boor, 'Zu Johannes Skylitzes' and 'Weiteres zur Chronik des Skylitzes'.

[30] For evidence that Skylitzes was at work at the end of the 11th c. see below 2.3.

[31] Skylitzes, *Synopsis*, p. xx; Thurn also assumed that the Madrid manuscript [M] should be dated to the 13th or 14th century (ibid., p. xxiv). Subsequently Nigel Wilson, 'The Madrid Scylitzes', *Scrittura e Civiltà*, 2 (1978), 209–19, proved that it was probably copied in the mid-12th c., a view which gained support from I. Ševčenko, 'The Madrid Manuscript of the Chronicle of Scylitzes in the Light of its New Dating', in I. Hütter (ed.), *Byzanz und der Westen* (Vienna, 1984), 117–30. While Wilson argued that this manuscript was copied in the royal scriptorium in Palermo, more recent research suggests that it was copied at the monastery of San Salvatore in Messina (Tsamakda, *The Illustrated Chronicle of Ioannes Skylitzes*, 329–41).

connected.[32] Thurn also produced a summary of the interpolations to be found within the medieval manuscripts. Apart from registering the additional Bulgarian material in manuscript [U], he drew attention to the insertions included in the other manuscripts, such as a eulogy to Emperor John Tzimiskes (969–76) in the [ACE] family, and eleven poems describing the deaths of several tenth-century emperors in the Madrid Skylitzes.[33] Recently manuscript [O], which was known to Thurn but which he had not seen for himself, was rediscovered in Sofia. The fact that this manuscript also contains the Continuation increases to five the number of manuscripts known to continue Skylitzes' testimony as far as 1079.[34]

2.3 CONSTRUCTING SKYLITZES' BIOGRAPHY

At the same time as critical editions of the *Synopsis* and the Continuation were published, several scholars were at work on the biography of John Skylitzes. By synthesizing the research of various earlier generations of scholars, W. Seibt provided the most coherent model of Skylitzes' curriculum vitae.[35] Three sources of evidence were integral to his outline

---

[32] Skylitzes, *Synopsis*, p. xxvii.   [33] Ibid. pp. xxix–xxxii.

[34] J.-M. Olivier, 'Le "Scylitzès" d'Ochrid retrouvé', *BZ* 89 (1996), 417–19; Thurn, *Synopsis*, pp. xxii discusses manuscript [O]. Thurn himself had suggested that only four texts included the Continuation. These other four manuscripts are [A, V, B and U].

[35] W. Seibt, 'Ioannes Skylitzes: Zur Person des Chronisten', *JÖB* 25 (1976), 81–6. The introduction to Thurn's edition relates a very short biography of Skylitzes (Skylitzes, *Synopsis*, pp. vii–viii); see also S. Antoljak 'Wer könnte eigentlich Joannes Skylitzes sein?' *Acts of the 14th International Congress 1971* (Bucharest, 1974), 677–82; Flusin and Cheynet, *Jean Skylitzès*, pp. v–vi.

of Skylitzes' career: an array of prosopographical details presented in the title sequence to one of the manuscripts; circumstantial evidence contained in imperial and patriarchal documents of the later eleventh century; and allusions in other Byzantine historical writings to the compiler of the *Synopsis*. Seibt began his analysis with the biographical information contained in the title at the head of the text in the oldest manuscript [A] [*Vind. Hist. Gr. 35*]: that the author of the *Synopsis Historion* was one John Skylitzes, *kouropalates*, and former [*megas*] *droungarios* of the *Bigla*.[36] Turning to a variety of archival materials from the later eleventh century, Seibt argued that the John Skylitzes identified in the manuscript title to the *Synopsis* was almost certainly the same person as John the Thrakesian, *kouropalates* and *megas droungarios* of the *Bigla*, who was involved in 1092 in a series of communications with Emperor Alexios Komnenos (1081–1118) about marriage legislation.[37] Seibt saw the same John the Thrakesian behind the John *megas droungarios* of the *Bigla* who was recorded as a participant at a patriarchal synod, also in 1092. Moving backwards in time he identified

[36] The title sequence to the *Synopsis* in manuscript [A] [*Vind. Hist. Gr. 35*] has a lacuna where the word *megas* was once inscribed. In the title sequence contained in manuscript [C] [*Coisl. 136*] Skylitzes is also called the *megas droungarios* (Skylitzes, *Synopsis*, 3). The prefix *megas* was added to the office of *droungarios* of the *Bigla* in the second half of the 11th c. (R. Guilland, *Recherches sur les institutions byzantines*, 2 vols. (Amsterdam, 1967), ii. 573).

[37] For the memorandum (*hypomnesis*) sent by John and the reply (*lysis*) sent by the emperor see Zepos, and Zepos, *Ius Graecoromanum*, i. 319–25. Note that John the Thrakesian not only corresponded with Alexios on this subject of marriage legislation, he also composed a commentary against the tome of the patriarch Sisinnios issued *c*.997 on the same subject (A. Laiou, 'Imperial Marriages and their Critics in the Eleventh Century: the Case of Skylitzes', *DOP* 46 (1992), 166–7).

John the Thrakesian at a slightly earlier stage in his career. According to a novel dated to June 1090, one John *proedros* and *droungarios* of the *Bigla* was also *eparch* of Constantinople. Seibt believed this figure was John the Thrakesian before he was promoted to the title of *kouropalates*. Finally, Seibt suggested a *terminus post quem* for Skylitzes' appointment as *droungarios*. Since Nicholas Skleros was *droungarios* in 1084, Seibt concluded that Skylitzes must have been appointed in the second half of the 1080s. Taking all these materials together, Seibt concluded that the author of the *Synopsis Historion* was, by the 1090s, a high-ranking government official, who as *megas droungarios* of the *Bigla,* occupied the most senior position within the Byzantine judiciary.[38]

For Seibt the fact that other Byzantine historians knew the author of the *Synopsis Historion* as John the Thrakesian was additional proof that the John Skylitzes cited in the manuscript title-sequences was the same individual as John the Thrakesian, the high-ranking Komnenian official. One of these other historians was George Kedrenos, who referred to the synoptic historian John the Thrakesian in the preface to his own world chronicle. Since he copied the *Synopsis* of Skylitzes verbatim into his own text, it can be safely assumed that Kedrenos equated John the Thrakesian with Skylitzes.[39]

---

[38] Seibt, 'Zur Person', 81–3, and *Die Skleroi* (Vienna, 1976), 96–7. In the 9th and 10th c. the occupant of the senior position at the *Bigla* was the emperor's military chief of palace security. By the end of the 11th c. this official had become the senior judicial officer within the Byzantine empire (Oikonomides, 'L'Évolution de l'organisation administrative', 133–4). Guilland, *Recherches*, ii. 573, lists the *droungarioi* of the *Bigla* during the latter part of the 11th c. but does not mention Skylitzes.

[39] Kedrenos, i. 5.

In addition, Seibt noticed that the twelfth-century historian John Zonaras also knew Skylitzes as 'the Thrakesian'. In his coverage of the death of Isaac Komnenos, Zonaras mentions that one story of the emperor's demise is to be found in the testimony of 'the Thrakesian'. This particular story, that Emperor Isaac I fell while hunting near Nikaia, proves to be the account conveyed in the Continuation of the *Synopsis Historion*.[40] With this observation Seibt also provided the most convincing evidence that the author of the 811–1057 *Synopsis* was responsible for the composition of the Continuation as well.[41]

[40] Seibt, 'Zur Person', 81.

[41] Seibt's conclusion brought to an end a long-standing debate over the relationship between the two texts. The arguments *against* seeing a single author were first put by de Boor, 'Weiteres zur Chronik', 460–7. The case was restated by Moravcsik, *Byzantinoturcica*, 340–1. Moravcsik, argued that since Kedrenos, who copied Skylitzes so slavishly, only included the 811–1057 section of the *Synopsis* in his text, the Continuation must have been written by another author at a different time. Moravcsik saw support for the idea of different and later authorship for the Continuation in the fact that Michael Attaleiates, whose *Historia* was the principal source of the Continuation, was not named as one of Skylitzes' sources in the preface to the original *Synopsis*. Tsolakes countered Moravcsik's case by arguing that the list of historians in the preface to the *Synopsis* is not an exhaustive enumeration of Skylitzes' sources. He believed that the similarities in working methods, vocabulary, and phraseology between the two texts pointed to a common author. Back references within the Continuation to events included in the main text of the *Synopsis* and a concentration on Balkan and Italian matters in both compositions also suggested a single author (*Skylitzes Continuatus*, 76–99). See also M. Hicks, 'The Life and Historical Writings of Michael Attaleiates', M.Litt. thesis (Oxford, 1987), 60–7. However, as J. Shepard, 'A Suspected Source of Scylitzes' *Synopsis Historiarum*: The Great Catacalon Cecaumenus', *BMGS* 16 (1992), 180–1 n. 28, points out, it is Zonaras' reference to the Thrakesian which provides the most convincing evidence that a single author wrote both the *Synopsis* and the Continuation. The common identity of Skylitzes and the Continuator has recently also been accepted by the French translators of his text (Flusin and Cheynet, *Jean Skylitzès*, pp. vi, xxi–xxii).

Seibt's neat fusion of the manuscript title-sequences, the evidence from the imperial and patriarchal documents, and the information conveyed by other Byzantine historians, was however, subject to one difficulty: George Kedrenos identified John the Thrakesian not as a *kouropalates,* but instead as a *protovestiarios,* a position which by the later eleventh century was almost always held by a member of the ruling imperial dynasty.[42] Seibt's solution was to argue that Kedrenos had made a transcription error, and that rather than *protovestiarios* he meant to write *protovestes* or *protovestarches.* Armed with this emendation, Seibt suggested that John Skylitzes, also known as John the Thrakesian, wrote the main 811–1057 section of the *Synopsis* in the 1070s when he held the relatively lowly title of *protovestarches* or *protovestes.* Shortly after this date his 811–1057 text was incorporated into the world chronicle of Kedrenos. By 1090 Skylitzes was *proedros, megas droungarios* of the *Bigla* and *eparch.* Two years later he was a *kouropalates.* But by 1094–5 he had retired, since according to the list of participants at the Synod of Blachernai held in this year, it was Nicholas Mermentoulos rather than Skylitzes who was now the *megas droungarios* of the *Bigla.*[43] Seibt concluded that it was in his retirement in the later 1090s that Skylitzes added the

---

[42] Oikonomides, 'L'Évolution de l'organisation administrative', 129–30.

[43] While he held the position of *droungarios* of the *Bigla* Mermentoulos was a regular correspondent of Archbishop Theophylact of Ochrid (*Théophylacte d'Achrida Lettres,* ed. and trans. P. Gautier, CFHB 16/2 (Thessalonika, 1986), letters 25, 29, 33, 47, 76; Mullett, *Theophylact of Ochrid,* 101, 103, 118, 121, 183, 271, 275; see also *Zacos Collection of Byzantine Lead Seals,* 3 (Auction 135, Spinks catalogue, 6 October 1999), no. 253. Later in his career he became *praitor* of Thrace and Macedonia. His last known position was as eparch of Constantinople (*Zacos Collection of Byzantine Lead Seals,* 2, (1999), no. 219).

1057–79 Continuation to the 811–1057 narrative he had compiled some twenty years earlier.

Since Seibt constructed his biography, some of his conclusions have been confirmed. For instance, his identification of John Skylitzes with John the Thrakesian is now certain. Attention has recently been drawn to the fact that an anonymous commentary on the twelfth-century canon lawyer Balsamon explicitly names John Skylitzes as 'the Thrakesian'.[44] However, other elements of Seibt's reconstruction of Skylitzes' career seem less secure, in particular his assertion that Skylitzes must have worked on the main 811–1057 section of his text during the 1070s. This assertion rests on nothing more than the reinterpretation of what is assumed to be Kedrenos' misreading of *protovestarches* or *protovestes* as *protovestiario*s. In fact, Seibt provided no corroborating evidence for this emendation, and beyond this extremely problematic reference no other evidence has emerged which suggests that Skylitzes composed the *Synopsis* in the 1070s. Indeed, one could argue that all the circumstantial evidence points in a rather different direction, not towards a 1070s date of composition but instead towards a rather later date sometime during the reign of Alexios Komnenos (1081–1118).[45]

---

[44] τοῦ τηνικαῦτα κουροπαλάτου καὶ μεγάλου δρουγγαρίου τῆς Βίγλας κυροῦ Ἰωάννου τοῦ Σκυλίτζη τοῦ καὶ Θρᾳκησίου: V. Tiftixoglu, 'Zur Genese der Kommentare des Balsamon', in N. Oikonomides (ed.), *Byzantium in the Twelfth Century* (Athens, 1991), 528–9. I am grateful to Paul Magdalino for this reference.

[45] This is a position adopted by Flusin and Cheynet, although their reasons for favouring a date of composition in the reign of Alexios are not stated (Flusin and Cheynet, *Jean Skylitzès*, p. xxii).

One reason for preferring to attach the text's composition to this rather later date is the fact that all the manuscripts that include a title sequence identify Skylitzes in terms of the position that he held during Alexios' reign, either as *megas droungarios* of the *Bigla* or as former *megas droungarios*.[46] This would suggest that Skylitzes either worked on his text while he was *megas droungarios*, thus at some point in the decade between 1084 and 1094 when he held this position, or after he had been replaced as *megas droungarios*, in which case he was writing at some point after 1094. In either case Skylitzes would have been at work during the reign of Alexios Komnenos. Of course, it could be argued that select-ing a composition date on the basis of information conveyed in the title sequences of manuscripts themselves copied long after Skylitzes was active is no more secure than Seibt's decision to challenge and change the information conveyed by Kedrenos. But there is another reason for accepting a later composition date, a reason which removes the need to amend Kedrenos' labelling of Skylitzes as *protovestarios*. For while Seibt rejected Skylitzes as a *protovestarios* on the grounds that this rank was reserved to the imperial family in the later eleventh century, it is becoming increasingly clear that during the reign of Alexios many ranks once assumed to be the preserve of relatives of the emperor were also held by other senior political figures, particularly those who were close supporters of the imperial regime. For example, during the first half of Alexios' reign the Doge of Venice, who became a close Byzantine strategic ally in this period, was

---

[46] See above p. 81 n. 36.

appointed to the office of *protosebastos*, one of those ranks sometimes thought to be the monopoly of the imperial family.[47]

The Doge of Venice was, of course, a vital overseas supporter. However, it is likely that senior internal supporters of the Komnenian regime were rewarded with very privileged titles in the same way. That Skylitzes may fit into this particular context is suggested by those ranks and offices that we know for certain that he held during Alexios' reign in the period between 1090 and 1092. The positions of *eparch*, *droungarios* of the *Bigla*, and *kouropalates* all indicate that he was one of the Komnenian party's chief domestic apparatchiks and a very close associate of the emperor himself. The importance of the title of *kouropalates*, for example, becomes manifest when one looks at the list of imperial officials present at the Synod of Blachernai held in 1094–5; at this time only seventeen laymen held titles of superior rank, most of whom were members of aristocratic families related to the ruling dynasty[48] Moreover, while

---

[47] Angold, *Byzantine Empire*, 128, 168; D. Nicol, *Byzantium and Venice: A Study in Diplomatic and Cultural Relations* (Cambridge, 1988), 60.

[48] For discussion of the Synod of Blachernai see P. Magdalino, *The Empire of Manuel I Komnenos (1143–1180)* (Cambridge, 1993), appendix 2, pp. 501–3. The title of *kouropalates* was denigrated by the author of the late 11th-/early 12th-c. *Historia Syntomos* as, 'common now and borne by many people' (Pseudo-Psellos: *Michaeli Pselli Historia Syntomos*, ed. and trans. W. Aerts, CFHB 30 (Berlin, 1990), 100). Yet this comment occurs in the context of a discussion of the prominence of the title in the 10th c. when it carried even greater cachet. Leo Phokas, the brother of Emperor Nikephoros Phokas (963–9), held this title, as did Bardas Skleros after he surrendered to Basil II in 989. When Skleros was *kouropalates* he was described as second in rank only to the emperor (Skylitzes, *Synopsis*, 339; Psellos, *Cronografia*, i. 38–9). R. Guilland, 'Curopalate', in *Titres et fonctions de l'empire byzantin* (London,

Skylitzes' tenure of the position of *megas droungarios* of the *Bigla* indicates that he was a trained lawyer, evidence from the twelfth-century *Ecloga Basilicorum* suggests that important officers of the Komnenian judiciary were appointed primarily for their political loyalty rather than their skill as lawyers.[49] Another sign of Skylitzes' political importance to the Komnenian regime was his exercise of the office of *eparch* of Constantinople during the early 1090s, the period when the emperor was under constant threat from internal rivals as well as external foes at a time when he often had to be absent from Constantinople on military campaigns.[50] At such a sensitive time the *eparch*, responsible for public order and the administration of justice within the capital city of the empire, had to be a servant of the utmost loyalty and discretion. Indeed, the seniority of the offices that Skylitzes held in the first half of the reign of Alexios Komnenos makes it likely that he was of one of the most important of Alexios Komnenos' household men, or as they came to be known

1976), no. III, 190–2, discusses the relative decline in the title's prestige during the 11th c.; he recognizes that Skylitzes and John Thrakesios held the title *kouropalates* but does not seem to realize that they were the same man.

[49] They were appointed, 'not because of their legal knowledge but because of their rank and their loyalty...to the emperor.' (Cited by Magdalino, *Manuel Komnenos*, 262–3).

[50] Cheynet, *Pouvoir et contestations*, 96–9, 361–7, argues that by the 1090s Alexios' regime was widely criticized. Despite enjoying some respite from Norman attack after the death of Robert Guiscard in 1085, and defeating the Pechenegs in 1091/2 at Levounion, domestic discontent was rife. Opposition ranged from criticisms contained in the 1090–1 speeches of John the Oxite, the rebellion of the general Humbertopoulos in the same year, and the conspiracy of Nikephoros Diogenes in 1094; for further discussion of this political uncertainty see below 4.2.2.

later in the Komnenian period, *vestiaritai*. As Michael Angold has argued, such men were simultaneously, 'the most difficult group to place in the hierarchical scheme of the Byzantine court', and yet personal servants of the emperor who, 'were treated as honorary members of the imperial family'. [51] From what we know of Skylitzes' career, it seems to me that he was one of the earliest examples of a senior Komnenian household official of the utmost discretion and loyalty, who simultaneously possessed some of the most important offices of state, as *eparch* and *megas droungarios*, while at the same time serving as the head (or one of the heads) of the emperor's household, endowed with the position of *protovestarios*.

Interpreting the available prosopographical details for Skylitzes' career is clearly difficult. None of the details concerning his career can be tied with final certainty to the chronology of his textual output. Nonetheless, I would argue that the weight of the evidence strongly suggests that Skylitzes wrote the main section 811–1057 of his narrative in the first half of the reign of Alexios Komnenos rather than in the 1070s. The narrative of 811–1057 was probably finished by the end of the eleventh century. The most likely *terminus ante quem* of his work is the end of the reign of Alexios Komnenos in 1118, the year when Michael of Devol added his interpolations to the *Synopsis Historion*.[52]

---

[51] Angold, *Byzantine Empire*, 244; a member of the imperial court coterie central to Komnenian government, and a figure comparable with Skylitzes, seems to have been Theodore Senaecherim, an *oikeios* of Alexios Komnenos (discussed below in 4.2.1).

[52] See above p. 76 n. 24.

Nonetheless, an important point to make at this stage is that without additional circumstantial evidence from later eleventh- and twelfth-century literary or sigillographical sources, little more can be said about the biography of Skylitzes.[53] This is because it is unlikely that more information about the person of the author will come from either the main narrative of the *Synopsis* or the Continuation. Apart from the prosopographical nuggets contained in the title sequences, the texts themselves provide virtually no biographical data. The only hint of personal detail occurs in the preface to the *Synopsis*, where the author indicates that he was a contemporary of the historian Michael Psellos.[54] But since the chronology of Psellos' career is uncertain, this reference does little more than confirm that Skylitzes was active in the second half of the eleventh century.[55] Yet such a dearth of biographical details in the text of the *Synopsis* itself is not surprising. As a synoptic history, Skylitzes' text was an entirely derivative production, a synthesis wrought from other written testimonies. Little overt information about the career of the compiler can be expected from such a literary production, and modern scholarly attempts to amplify Skylitzes' curriculum vitae by isolating biographical clues from within the text have not been convincing. It has

[53] It is possible that a seal in the Zacos collection may have belonged to Skylitzes. According to the Greek text, seal 504 belonged to a John *kouropalates* and *droungarios* of the *Bigla* (G. Zacos, *Byzantine Lead Seals II*, compiled by J. Nesbitt (Berne, 1985), pl. 51). It should be noted that the English description of the owner of this seal is printed by mistake with seal 508.

[54] Skylitzes, *Synopsis*, 4; the preface and its contents are discussed further in 3.1.

[55] Dating of Psellos' historiographical output is discussed further in 5.3.

been argued, for example, that a reference in the Continuation to the Serb leader Bodin, who died in 1101, as if he were still alive, offers a *terminus ante quem* to Skylitzes' historical writings.[56] However, rather than demonstrating that Skylitzes was writing before 1101, this passage merely indicates that it was the author of Skylitzes' *source* who was active before this date. Comparable evidence from his coverage of the reign of Michael VI indicates that Skylitzes' most likely contribution to such an apparently biographical allusion was his verbatim copying of an underlying source rather than personal reflection. At one point in his testimony he copies his root source, the biography of Katakalon Kekaumenos, so closely that he implies that Michael VI was still alive. In fact Michael VI died before August 1059. Quite clearly Skylitzes was not at work before 1059; instead this reference indicates that it was his source, Katakalon Kekaumenos, who was writing before the death of Michael VI.[57]

2.4 SKYLITZES' SOURCES AND WORKING METHODS

Given the difficulties of making further progress with a biography of Skylitzes, those scholars who have studied

[56] Antoljak, 'Johannes Skylitzes', 679, following the example given by Tsolakes in Skylitzes Continuatus: ‘Η Συνέχεια τῆς χρονογραφίας τοῦ Ἰωάννου Σκυλίτζη, 75–6.

[57] Shepard, 'A Suspected Source', 178; idem, 'Isaac Comnenus' Coronation Day', *Byz Slav* 38 (1977), 24; for more on Skylitzes' use of a biography of Katakalon Kekaumenos see below 2.4; for the author's verbatim copying see below 3.2.

this historian since the publication of the critical edition of his text have tended to concentrate on Skylitzes' source materials, his working methods, and the ways in which he used and abused his underlying texts. In the case of those sections of the *Synopsis Historion* dealing with the ninth and early tenth centuries many of Skylitzes' source materials are still extant; in the case of the second half of the tenth century and the first half of the eleventh century virtually none of his sources survive. However, it should be stressed that modern scholarly investigations into Skylitzes' treatment of his underlying texts are rare and usually very limited in ambition.[58] For example, there is only one examination of Skylitzes' ninth- and early tenth-century testimony. Conducted by D. Polemis in 1975, this analysis was concerned with the rather narrow issue of why the earliest sections of Skylitzes' narrative contained patronymical information absent from his main sources, the Logothete, Genesios, and Book Six of the Continuation of Theophanes (also known as *Theophanes Continuatus*), texts which are all still extant. Polemis concluded that these prosopographical additions, often connected to the Argyros or Doukas families, did not reflect Skylitzes' access to alternative lost sources, but instead represented the author's flawed attempts to create internal coherence within his text. That is to say Skylitzes habitually extracted family names from one source and matched them with first names from another regardless of context.[59]

---

[58] A detailed study of Skylitzes' sources is being conducted in Ioannina according to Flusin and Cheynet, *Jean Skylitzès*, p. xii.

[59] D. Polemis, 'Some Cases of Erroneous Identification in the Chronicle of Scylitzes', *Byz Slav* 26 (1975), 74–81.

Investigations of Skylitzes' tenth-century testimony have been equally short, limited in scope, and generally inconclusive. In one study Markopoulos considered the *Synopsis Historion* in relation to the widespread claim that Theodore Daphnopates, *protoasekretis* at the court of Romanos II (959–63), was the author of the Continuation of Theophanes (*Theophanes Continuatus*). This claim is of interest to the student of Skylitzes for two related reasons. First, because in the preface to the *Synopsis Historion* Skylitzes lists Theodore Daphnopates as one of his sources; second, because Skylitzes clearly draws on material from Book Six of *Theophanes Continuatus* for his coverage of the pre-948 period. However, since Markopoulos could find no secure evidence to link Daphnopates to the Continuation of Theophanes, he concluded that it was impossible to identify any solid relationship between the literary productions of Theodore Daphnopates and John Skylitzes.[60]

In another short study by Frei a different and more substantial relationship between Skylitzes and Theodore Daphnopates has been suggested. On the basis of a comparison between Skylitzes' text and a sermon by Daphnopates, Frei has argued that Theodore Daphnopates was responsible *not* for the sixth book of *Theophanes Continuatus*, but instead for a lost history of the reigns of Constantine VII (945–59) and Romanos II (959–63) which was then used much later by Skylitzes. His argument is based on certain similarities in narrative structure, vocabulary, and word

---

[60] A. Markopoulos, 'Théodore Daphnopatès et la Continuation de Théophane', *JÖB* 35 (1985), 171–82; Markopoulos is supported by Flusin and Cheynet, *Jean Skylitzès*, p. x.

order between Skylitzes' account of the arrival of the relic of the hand of John the Baptist in Constantinople during the reign of Constantine VII and a homily composed by Theodore Daphnopates to celebrate the first anniversary of this event. It was Frei's belief that Daphnopates used his own speeches as primary sources in the compilation of a history, and that it was from this intermediate Daphnopates' history that Skylitzes in turn compiled his own testimony for the period 948–63.[61] However, the fact that Frei only dealt with one episode, covering less than six lines of Greek in Skylitzes' *Synopsis Historion*, in which only the most general parallels of vocabulary and content with the sermon of Theodore Daphnopates are visible, leaves his conclusions resting on rather narrow foundations.

Nonetheless Frei's study of Skylitzes' mid-tenth-century testimony highlights the more general problem with which the historian interested in post-948 sections of the *Synopsis* has to wrestle, namely that none of the sources Skylitzes used in composing his mid-tenth- to mid-eleventh-century narrative survive. In these circumstances, students of the material in the *Synopsis* covering the second third of the tenth century and first quarter of the eleventh century have scoured the content and structure of the text in order to find hints of Skylitzes' lost sources. Skylitzes' rather schizophrenic analysis of Emperor Nikephoros Phokas (963–9), at one point favourable, at another violently hostile, has been

---

[61] P. Frei, 'Das Geschichtswerk des Theodoros Daphnopates als Quelle der *Synopsis Historiarum* des Johannes Skylitzes', in E. Plockinger (ed.), *Lebendige Altertumswissenschaft: Festgabe zur Vollendung des 70. Lebensjahres von Herman Vetters* (Vienna, 1985), 348–53.

explained by his employment of two contradictory sources: a pro-Phokas family history and an account antagonistic to the emperor. It has been suggested that this pro-Phokas family history may also underpin certain episodes within his coverage of the reign of John Tzimiskes (969–76) and the early years of Basil's reign, particularly on those occasions when the Phokas family are at the centre of the narrative. Arguments for and against the incidence of pro-Phokas material in Skylitzes' testimony for Basil's reign will be explored at greater length in Chapter 5.[62] Meanwhile, another possible source has been identified for the reign of John Tzimiskes. It has been suggested that a war diary may have provided Skylitzes with material for his extensive descriptions of this emperor's campaign against the Rus in Bulgaria in 971. Skylitzes' testimony for this passage of warfare will be analysed in Chapters 4 and 5 of this volume.[63]

---

[62] The idea that pro- and anti-Phokas material was used by both Leo the Deacon and Skylitzes was first developed by M. Siuziumov, 'Ob istochnikakh Leva Diakona i Skilitsii', *Vizantiiskoe Obozrenie 2* (1916), 106–66, and taken up by Každan, *ODB*, iii, 1217. See also Hunger, *Hochsprachliche profane Literatur*, i. 368, 390; C. Roueché, 'Byzantine Writers and Readers: Story Telling in the Eleventh Century', in R. Beaton (ed.), *The Greek Novel* (London and Sydney, 1988), 127; R. Morris, 'The Two Faces of Nikephoros Phokas', *BMGS* 12 (1988), *passim*; eadem, 'Succession and Usurpation: Politics and Rhetoric in the late Tenth Century', in P. Magdalino (ed.), *New Constantines: the Rhythms of Imperial Renewal in Byzantium* (Aldershot, 1994), 206; Flusin and Cheynet, *Jean Skylitzès*, pp. xiii–xiv; see also below 5.2.3.

[63] The possibility that Skylitzes drew on a war diary (*Kriegesbuch*) for his coverage of the reign of John Tzimiskes, was first raised by Moravcsik, *Byzantinoturcica*, 398–9; see more recently Flusin and Cheynet, *Jean Skylitzès*, pp. xiii–xiv; S. McGrath, 'The Battles of Dorostolon (971): Rhetoric and Reality', in T. S. Miller and J. Nesbitt (eds.), *Peace and War in Byzantium: Essays in Honor of George T. Dennis* (Washington DC 1995), 152–64; see also below 4.2.2 and 5.2.3.

As for Basil's reign, none of Skylitzes' underlying source materials survive, although piecemeal evidence has suggested to some modern historians that a lost history composed by Theodore of Sebasteia may have been one of the texts which underpinned Skylitzes' account. Like Theodore Daphnopates, Theodore of Sebasteia is named in the preface of the *Synopsis Historion* as one of Skylitzes' sources.[64] However, the evidence supporting any link between this Theodore and Skylitzes is also very weak. The only textual support from within the main narrative body of the *Synopsis Historion* to link Skylitzes to Theodore of Sebasteia comes from a notice interpolated in manuscripts [A] and [E]. Here it is stated, 'the one from Sebasteia says that Basil II was crowned as emperor on the eleventh day of the month of January.'[65] Independent evidence that Theodore of Sebasteia composed a history of Basil's reign comes from the *Peri Metatheseon*, a twelfth-century treatise concerned with the translation of incumbent bishops to other dioceses. One version of this text claims that Bishop Agapios of Seleukeia Pieria, 'was moved to the patriarchate of Antioch during the reign of Basil Porphyrogenitus during the revolt of Skleros, as Theodore of Sebasteia wrote, he who composed the *chronikon biblion* of lord Basil Porphyrogenitos'.[66] Yet while

---

[64] Skylitzes, *Synopsis*, 4.

[65] Ibid. 313.

[66] *Traité*: 'Le Traité des transferts', ed. J. Darrouzès, *REB* 42 (1984), 181. This entry contains erroneous information. Agapios was in fact bishop of Aleppo when he was translated to Antioch (Yahya, *PO* 23, pp. 375–6). See below 6.3.3. The *Peri Metatheseon* contains another corrupt entry that refers to Agapios. This entry states that he was translated to Jerusalem rather than to Antioch (*Traité*, 181).

these two allusions suggest that Theodore of Sebasteia composed a history about Basil II, they are too insubstantial to
establish the nature of this text and its exact relationship
to Skylitzes' own production.[67]

One recent attempt to provide a link between Skylitzes'
text and Theodore of Sebasteia was that made by Nikolaos
Panagiotakes just before his death in 1997. Panagiotakes
argued that two miracle stories of Saint Eugenios of Trebizond compiled in the fourteenth century by John Lazaropoulos, but set during the revolt of Bardas Phokas (987–9)
and Basil II's campaigns against the Iberians (Georgians) in
1021–2, contain material extracted from the lost eleventh-
century history of Theodore of Sebasteia.[68] He noted that
the miracle stories were prefaced with narrative passages
of political history, some of which resembled passages in
Skylitzes and the twelfth-century world chronicle of
John Zonaras, but others of which had no parallel with the

---

[67] In a brief aside during his study of the origins and activities of the
Kometopouloi in Bulgaria Werner Seibt suggests an alternative relationship
between Theodore of Sebasteia and Skylitzes' text. He argues that Michael of
Devol, who was responsible for producing the interpolations relating to
western Macedonia in manuscript [U] *c.* 1118, used material from Theodore
of Sebasteia to expand Skylitzes' testimony. He does not indicate whether he
thinks that Skylitzes also used Theodore's history as a source for his original
synopsis (Seibt, 'Untersuchungen zur Vor- und Frühgeschichte der "bulgarischen" Kometopulen', 96, n. 22). The likelihood that both Skylitzes and his
later interpolators used Theodore is put forward by M. Gyóni, 'Skylitzes et les
Vlaques', *Revue d'Histoire Comparée*, 25 (1947), 169. A link between Theodore and Skylitzes is also noted by Flusin and Cheynet, *Jean Skylitzès*, p. xiv.
Certainly Schlumberger, *L'Épopée byzantine*, i. 586–7, assumed that Theodore
was one of Skylitzes' sources. Yet none of these modern historians explains
why they identify Theodore as a source for Skylitzes.

[68] Panagiotakes, 'Fragments', 321–57.

testimonies of these historians. Thus, during the revolt of Phokas, the Eugenios Miracles mirror Skylitzes' and Zonaras' account of the deployment of rebel troops on the Asian side of the Bosphoros, but go on to include additional material about the emperor's plans to resupply the capital by sea from Trebizond, and the rebels' decision to raid the Pontus coast using an Iberian army.[69] In the case of Basil's Iberian offensive of 1021–2, the Miracles allude to the emperor's decision to winter in Trebizond during a break in his campaign, information absent from the accounts of Skylitzes and Zonaras.[70] The principal conclusion that Panagiotakes drew from his comparison of these various narratives was that Lazaropoulos, Skylitzes, and Zonaras all drew on the same underlying lost historical account for at least part of their coverage of the reign of Basil II. Yet, in identifying Theodore of Sebasteia as the author of this lost history, Panagiotakes provided no other supporting evidence apart

[69] Panagiotakes, 'Fragments', 327, claims that this attack on the Pontus is not attested elsewhere. However, while this is true for the Greek evidence, eastern texts are more forthcoming. Yahya ibn Sa'id mentions the alliance between the Phokas family and the Iberians in the east during the period 988/9. According to Yahya, the Iberians defeated an imperial army led by Gregory Taronites that was marching from Trebizond to the Euphrates frontier (Yahya, *PO* 23, p. 424).

[70] Panagiotakes, 'Fragments', 330. Once again, although Panagiotakes is correct to say that no Greek source mentions Basil's residence in Trebizond, his presence in the city is recorded by a variety of eastern narratives: Yahya, *PO* 47, p. 463; Matthew of Edessa, *Armenia and the Crusades*, 46; the Georgian Royal Annals, 283. The Armenian historian, Aristakes of Lastivert, does not refer to Trebizond by name, but says that Basil wintered in Chaldia, the theme of which Trebizond was the capital (Aristakes, *Récit des malheurs*, 15). The situation on this sector of the eastern frontier is discussed further in 6.3.1.

from the fragile allusions to Theodore in Skylitzes' preface and the *Peri Metatheseon* discussed above.[71]

So flimsy is the evidence linking the lost history of Theodore of Sebasteia to the account of Basil's reign contained in the *Synopsis Historion*, that it is unlikely that any greater understanding of Skylitzes' sources for Basil's reign will come from further investigation into the putative relationship between these two texts. In Chapters 4 and 5 the question of Skylitzes' source materials for the reign of Basil II will be explored further, most notably his use of encomia produced in honour of the senior generals Bardas Skleros and Eustathios Daphnomeles.[72] However, at this stage it is simply important to note the lack of sustained research into the source materials and working practices behind Skylitzes' testimony as a whole, and his narrative of Basil's reign in particular.

Indeed, the only substantial analysis of Skylitzes' working methods and treatment of source materials is that conducted by Jonathan Shepard more than twenty-five years ago into the 1028–57 section of the *Synopsis Historion*. This research was carried out as part of a series of rigorous examinations of Byzantine diplomatic relations with neighbouring powers during the mid-eleventh century, during which Shepard compared Skylitzes' testimony, often the only account of the relevant events in Greek, with narratives composed in other languages. Partly through these

---

[71] For further discussion of Theodore of Sebasteia as a historian operating during Basil's reign see Shepard, 'Sources for the Conversion of Rus', 81–5; Shepard does not try to link Theodore and Skylitzes.
[72] See below 4.2.2, 5.2.3–4, and 5.3.

intertextual comparisons, and partly by looking at the internal structures of the *Synopsis* itself, he then identified several key diagnostic elements that can help us understand how Skylitzes' text was composed. Shepard's research is of fundamental interest to the historian of Basil's reign since it illustrates how Skylitzes' *Synopsis Historion* can be approached when none of the text's underlying sources survive. Since Shepard's analysis has to be collated from several different articles, and since so many of the diagnostics he isolated are germane to the next three chapters, the main points of his analysis are summarized here. In addition some of the implications of his research for understanding Skylitzes' treatment of Basil's reign are also explored in detail.[73]

Some of Shepard's most important observations concern the overall structure of the *Synopsis Historion*. In the course of his examination, for example, Shepard noticed the ubiquity of short generalized summaries of events within Skylitzes' *Synopsis*, passages of text where the organizing principle is usually theme rather than chronology.[74] One example identified by Shepard is the analysis of Byzantine relations with Caucasia which Skylitzes inserted into his text immediately before his account of Leo Tornikios' revolt in

---

[73] The Shepard articles in question are: 'John Mauropous, Leo Tornices and an Alleged Russian Army: The Chronology of the Pecheneg Crisis of 1048–9', *JÖB* 24 (1975), 61–79; 'Byzantium's Last Sicilian Expedition: Skylitzes' Testimony', *Rivista di studi bizantini e neoellenici* 14–16 (1977–9), 145–59; 'Isaac Comnenus' Coronation Day', 22–30; 'Scylitzes on Armenia in the 1040s and the Role of Catacalon Cecaumenus', *REArm* (1975–6), 296–311; 'Byzantinorussica', *REB* 33 (1975), 211–25; 'A Suspected Source', 171–81.

[74] Skylitzes' fondness for thematic principles of organization and interpretation has also been noted by Flusin and Cheynet, *Jean Skylitzès*, pp. xvii–xix.

1047. This passage covers the empire's dealings with its neighbours on the north-eastern frontier from the end of the reign of Basil II to the reign of Constantine IX (1042–55).[75] As Shepard noted, the insertion of such material, much of it highly compressed, can have a seriously distorting effect on the continuity of the underlying narrative; different events become easily elided; chronologies are telescoped. One place where Shepard observed these phenomena at play is in that section of Skylitzes' text which acts as a preface to the Byzantine annexation of the Armenian princedom of Ani in the early 1040s. Shepard pointed out that in this passage Skylitzes implies that Prince Gagic of Ani departed for Constantinople at the same time as his Armenian territories were absorbed. In fact other evidence conclusively suggests that he left more than two years later.[76]

The kinds of confusions that Shepard has observed arising from summary passages in Skylitzes' mid-eleventh-century coverage also appear to characterize Skylitzes' account of Basil's reign. In chapter 20, for example, when Skylitzes discusses Byzantine relations with the eastern frontier during Basil's hegemony, he elides the emperor's campaigns of 995 and 999 against northern Syria, and his two separate expeditions against Iberia in 1000 and 1021/2, into a single offensive.[77] Chapter 21, which deals cursorily with legislation against the Powerful and the arrest of Eustathios Maleinos, has similar potential for chronological confusion. The chapter contains no dates; and although one may assume

---

[75] Shepard, 'John Mauropous', 73–4.
[76] Shepard, 'Scylitzes on Armenia', 292–5.
[77] Skylitzes, *Synopsis*, 339–40.

that the legislation in question is the novel of 996, it is impossible to know when Maleinos was arrested. Skylitzes claims that he was taken captive by Basil as the emperor marched through Cappadocia on his return from the eastern frontier. However, since Basil returned from eastern campaigns in 995 and 1000–1, one is unable to identify from Skylitzes' telescoped testimony which of these occasions witnessed the arrest of Maleinos.[78] Similar dating problems arise with chapter 39, the compressed summary chapter that deals with Byzantine–Rus naval action in the Black Sea and the surrender to Byzantium of Vaspurakan in Armenia. At the beginning of this chapter the year 6524 (1016) is mentioned. But this date can only safely be applied to the first of the events listed: the Byzantine–Rus mission to the north coast of the Black Sea. It cannot be assumed to be the occasion when Vaspurakan was annexed.[79]

Undoubtedly, the most confusing of such summary passages as far as Basil's reign is concerned are to be found in Skylitzes' Balkan material. Just before Skylitzes begins his account of Basil II's defeat at the hands of the Bulgars in 986, he inserts a summary that deals with the rise of the Kometopoulos family, one of whose members, Samuel, later became tsar of the Bulgarians (chapter 11). This passage also explores the relationship between the Kometopouloi and the former Bulgarian royal dynasty represented by Boris and Romanos, the sons of Peter, the Bulgarian emperor, who

---

[78] Skylitzes, *Synopsis*, 340.
[79] Ibid. 354–5; see below 6.3.4 and 8.4 for more discussion about the surrender of Vaspurakan. For further discussion of telescoped material see also below 4.1.

himself died *c*.969. It concludes by summarizing Bulgar attacks on the Byzantines during the early years of Basil's reign and highlighting the conquest of Larissa in the Thessalian plain by Samuel.[80] It is a passage which resembles earlier references to the Bulgarian royal dynasty that Skylitzes makes within his testimony of the reigns of Nikephoros Phokas and John Tzimiskes: all three sections of text are generalized, compressed, and devoid of hard chronological or toponymical data.[81]

Nor is the description of the rise of the Kometopouloi the only time that Skylitzes' Balkan material takes the form of telescoped thematic summaries which are free of dates. After Skylitzes' account of Nikephoros Ouranos' 997 victory over Samuel in the passes of the Pindos mountains at the River Spercheios (described in chapter 23), he includes a series of short chapters about Basil's conflict with the Bulgarians. But these chapters do not seem to be arranged according to chronological principles; instead they are thematically organized. Chapter 24, the chapter immediately following the Spercheios narrative, deals with events at the Adriatic town of Dyrrachion. It begins with a description of the city while it was under Bulgarian control. The Bulgarian commander was Ashot Taronites, an erstwhile Byzantine general captured by Samuel who defected to his captors and married

---

[80] Ibid. 328–30.

[81] Ibid. 255; 277; 288 ff. Despite its intractable nature, such material has nonetheless inspired considerable speculation about the origins of the Kometopouloi and their conflict with Byzantium. Adontz, 'Samuel l'Arménien', 347–407; Seibt, 'Untersuchungen zur Vor- und Frühgeschichte der "bulgarischen" Kometopulen', 65–98.

the Bulgarian tsar's daughter.[82] This narrative passage explains how Ashot and his wife eventually changed sides once again, going over to the Byzantines and leaving Dyrrachion by sea. Next, a reference is made to the city returning to Byzantine control when a local family of notables, the Chryselioi, decided to back Basil in return for titular and financial rewards. The narrative indicates that Eustathios Daphnomeles arrived in the city as the emperor's representative.[83] Usually these events are dated to *c.*1005 on the grounds that the eastern historian, Yahya ibn Sa'id, claims that Basil won a complete victory over the Bulgars after a four-year campaign beginning in 1001. Indeed, it has recently been argued that after the return of Dyrrachion to Byzantine control in 1005, Basil II and Samuel reached a peace agreement which lasted for nine years.[84] Yet, there is nothing within this passage to indicate that the uncertain state of Dyrrachion was resolved in 1005, nor indeed that a treaty was finalized in the same year. Instead the reference to Daphnomeles as commander in the city seems to refer most plausibly to a rather later passage of events, namely the administrative arrangements which were made at the very end of Basil's conflict with the Bulgarians in 1018. In a passage of his narrative located much later in his account of Basil's reign (chapter 42), Skylitzes indicates that Daphnomeles was given control over Dyrrachion after the general

---

[82] For more on Ashot's marriage arrangements and the confusions surrounding his alliance with Samuel see below 4.1.

[83] Skylitzes, *Synopsis*, 342–3; Stephenson, *Legend of Basil the Bulgar-Slayer*, 17–18.

[84] Stephenson, *Byzantium's Balkan Frontier*, 66–71.

surrender of the Bulgarians in 1018 as a reward for defeating the Bulgarian rebel commander Ibatzes.[85] In these circumstances it would appear that the best interpretation of the earlier Dyrrachion chapter (chapter 24) referring to Ashot, the Chryselioi, and Daphnomeles, is that it should be seen as a thematic unit with an internal chronology that stretches across the entire reign. Chapter 24 is certainly not a passage that forms part of a long, precise, continuous, and coherent master chronology of Balkan history during Basil's reign.

Thematic rather than chronological organization also seems to explain some of Skylitzes' other short Balkan chapters. Chapters 27 and 28, for example, are passages that deal with the turbulent relations between the emperor and a variety of Bulgarian commanders in the mountainous region to the west of the plains of Thessalonika and Thessaly, a western Macedonian buffer zone between Byzantium and Bulgaria. Skylitzes' narrative records the surrender of Dobromeros at Berroia, Nikolitzas at Servia, and Draxanos, the *katarchon* of an unnamed castle, possibly Bodina; in return these commanders received Byzantine titles.[86] Just as with the Dyrrachion chapter these short chapters are positioned in Skylitzes' overall narrative shortly after the 997 Ouranos victory at the River Spercheios; they are also located after chapter 26 in which Skylitzes refers to a Byzantine raid against eastern Bulgaria in 1000. Chapter 27 outlining Dobromeros' handing over of Berroia then begins with the rather vague temporal phrase: 'once again in the

---

[85] Skylitzes, *Synopsis*, 365.
[86] Ibid. 344–5.

next year'. As a result it is usually assumed that the surrender of the key western Macedonian border fortresses occurred in 1001. Often the capture of these forts has been treated by modern historians as a permanent conquest, one which contributed to Basil's gaining of the initiative in his wars with Bulgaria.[87] Yet, subsequent references in Skylitzes' narrative indicate that none of the sites in question remained under permanent Byzantine command until the final conquest of 1018.[88] The question which then arises is why did Skylitzes choose to include references to these forts' capitulation to Basil at such an early point in his narrative if they all too quickly returned to Bulgarian control? The most likely solution to this question is that these chapters are not primarily concerned with fitting the history of these key fortified sites into an exact chronology of Basil's Balkan wars, but instead with a common theme: that of untrustworthy surrender by enemy commanders and the rewards of infidelity to the Byzantine empire. For what unites these chapters is less the date of their capture, and more the moralizing message that Bulgarian commanders who went over to Basil and then defected back to Samuel suffered horrible punishments. Nikolitzas, having been taken to Constantinople and honoured as a *patrikios*, soon escaped, rejoined Samuel, and launched a new assault on Servia. At some later, unspecified, date he was recaptured by the

---

[87] Stephenson, *Byzantium's Balkan Frontier*, 66–7 sees these frontier sites in Byzantine hands by 1004; see also his discussion in *Legend of Basil the Bulgar-slayer*, 34–5.

[88] Skylitzes, *Synopsis*, 356 (Berroia); 364 (Servia); 352–6 (Bodina); this point was also noted by Adontz, 'Samuel l'Arménien', 379.

Byzantines and cast into prison. Meanwhile, Draxanos married the daughter of a Byzantine notable in Thessalonika but tried to rejoin Samuel on three occasions. Finally he was arrested and impaled. It is striking that in some senses these very brief thematic chapters reflect a concern visible in the advice book of Kekaumenos, written shortly before the *Synopsis Historion*, that local enemy commanders who accept Byzantine salaries and titles are never to be trusted.[89]

Further proof that thematic rather than chronological principles guide the organization of Skylitzes' Balkan material in his account of Basil's reign come from another short chapter which follows the Ouranos Spercheios victory narrative. Rather than dealing with Bulgarian perfidy, this chapter is concerned with the disloyalty of a variety of leading Byzantine political figures who either chose to defect to Samuel's Bulgaria or were suspected of conspiracy with opposition forces. Skylitzes lists these figures in chapter 25: Paul Bobos (*magistros*) one of the leading men of Thessalonika (ἀνὴρ τῶν ἐν Θεσσαλονίκῃ τὰ πρῶτα); Malakeinos (*protospatharios*), a man outstanding in thought and speech, who is probably to be identified with John Malakenos, the *strategos* of Hellas, whose disgrace is mentioned in the life of St Nikon of Sparta; and some *illoustrioi* from Adrianople, who held the position of *strategoi*, one called Batatzes and another called Basil Glabas.[90] The fate of the

---

[89] Kekaumenos, *Consilia et Narrationes*, 278–284; see also below 4.2.2 for further discussion of the didactic qualities of Skylitzes' text.

[90] Skylitzes, *Synopsis*, 343; *St. Nikon*, ch. 43. Basil Glabas is not attested elsewhere in the literary record; however, eight seals belonging to individuals of this name, some of whom held high military office, have been found at

Adrianopolitans is unknown; however, Skylitzes tells us that Paul Bobos was resettled in the western Anatolian theme of the Thrakesion while Malakeinos was transferred to Constantinople itself (a reference confirmed by the Life of St Nikon). If Skylitzes' text was organized chronologically, all these defections, or suspected defections, must have occurred after 997, since this list of perfidious behaviour on the part of Byzantine luminaries is to be found two chapters later than that describing the Battle of the River Spercheios. Yet, there is tantalizing documentary evidence from the archives of the monasteries on Mount Athos which suggests that at least one of these indicted figures was accused of treachery long *before* the victory of Ouranos in 997. A judicial judgement dated to November 6505 (996) issued by Nicholas the *krites* of Thessalonika, Strymon, and Drougoubiteia refers to property which had once belonged to Paul of Thessalonika but had then passed into the hands of the emperor.[91] It is possible that the Paul in question here is Paul Bobos, and the property at issue the estates that were confiscated from him by the imperial fisc. Moreover, it is clear from the text of the Athonite judgement that these estates had been the subject of dispute between several parties for some time since they had been sequestered

Preslav: three belonging to a *protospatharios* and *hypatos*; four to an *archestrategos* and *protovestes*, and one to a *vestarches*. There is little consensus over whether these seals belong to the same individual, and over the connection between the holder(s) of the seals and the Glabas mentioned in Skylitzes' testimony (Doimi de Frankopan, 'Workings of the Byzantine Provincial Administration', 83).

[91] *Actes d'Iviron I. Des origines au milieu du XIe siècle*, eds. J. Lefort *et al.* Archives de l'Athos XIV, (Paris, 1985), no. 10.

from Paul, something which could date Paul Bobos' treachery to well before 996. If this is true, then here is convincing evidence that Skylitzes' chapter 25, which deals with Bobos, Malakeinos, and the turn-coats from Adrianople, is organized according to the thematic principle of treachery rather than according to chronology. Just because these instances of perfidy are listed after Ouranos' victory at Spercheios does not mean that any, or all of them, actually happened after 997.

The principal conclusion to be drawn from examples such as the treachery of Bobos is that any information contained in summary passages in Skylitzes' *Synopsis Historion* can never be dated with confidence. However, the inescapable fact is that to understand Basil's reign, particularly events in the Balkans, the modern historian often has to rely on Skylitzes' telescoped and thematic material. Later in this volume, most notably in Chapters 7 and 8, the ways in which Skylitzes' summarizing material shapes and distorts our overall understanding of Basil's reign will be discussed further. In those chapters it will be argued that while the ubiquity of Skylitzes' summaries certainly make constructing a coherent and detailed narrative of events all but impossible, understanding his compositional methods can, paradoxically, help us to sketch out a plausible account of the different chronological periods of the reign in different geographical regions, including Bulgaria. But for the rest of this current chapter attention will turn away from analysis of these short summary chapters to some other dimensions of Skylitzes' compositional methods which have been analysed by Jonathan Shepard and which are important in understanding how to read Skylitzes' testimony of Basil's reign.

In his analysis of Skylitzes' mid-eleventh-century material Shepard noted that in contrast to the historian's fondness for compressed, telescoped, and thematic passages, Skylitzes also adorns the *Synopsis* with long detailed stories which describe single episodes. Shepard included within this category of composition the Byzantine defence of Messina in Sicily in the early 1040s, the 1048 campaign against the Turks, the 1048–9 battles against the Pechenegs, and Isaac Komnenos' coup of 1057.[92] Similar examples are also visible in Skylitzes' treatment of earlier periods. Nearly one third of Skylitzes' coverage of John Tzimiskes' reign (969–76) is concerned with the siege of Dristra (Dorostolon) on the Lower Danube in 971.[93] There are also several comparable episodes from Basil's reign, although none is as long as the Dristra narrative. Such episodes include the cunning defence of Nikaia by Manuel Erotikos during the first Skleros revolt;[94] Basil's defeat at the hands of the Bulgars in 986;[95] Skleros' escape from Baghdad towards the end of the same year;[96] Nikephoros Ouranos' victory over Samuel at the River Spercheios in 997;[97] the defeat of the Bulgarians at Kleidion in 1014;[98] the surrender of the Bulgarian royal family and the principal Bulgarian commanders in 1018;[99]

---

[92] Shepard, 'Byzantium's Last Sicilian Expedition', 155–8; idem, 'Scylitzes on Armenia', 270–79; idem, 'A Suspected Source', 172–6.
[93] Skylitzes, *Synopsis*, 298–309.
[94] Ibid. 323.
[95] Ibid. 330–1; an episode also discussed below in 3.3.2 and 4.2.2.
[96] Ibid. 332–4; an episode also discussed below in 5.2.4.
[97] Ibid. 341–2; an episode also discussed below in 3.3.2 and 4.1.
[98] Ibid. 348–9; an episode also discussed below in 3.3.2 and 4.1.
[99] Ibid. 357–61; an episode also discussed below in 4.2.1.

and Eustathios Daphnomeles' capture of the senior Bulgarian general Ibatzes.[100]

Just as important as his work in tracing the structures of Skylitzes' text is Shepard's research into the different genres of source material that the author used in compiling the *Synopsis Historion*. On the one hand Shepard has argued that some of the most vivid passages of narrative action were excerpted from contemporary panegyrics produced by the supporters of senior commanders within the Byzantine army. As far as Skylitzes' mid-eleventh-century material was concerned, one of these panegyrical accounts was an apologetic pamphlet produced by associates of the general George Maniakes in 1043 at the time of Maniakes' revolt against Constantine IX Monomachos. More important than Maniakes' apologia, however, for Skylitzes' mid-eleventh-century narrative was the encomiastic biography of the general Katakalon Kekaumenos. According to Shepard, this forms the core of Skylitzes' coverage of the period between 1042 and 1057. Several of the distinguishing features of the encomia used by Skylitzes are discussed in greater length in Chapter 5 of this volume, where it is argued that an apologetic text produced by the general Bardas Skleros underpins Skylitzes' early coverage of the reign of Basil II; another panegyric produced by a senior general during Basil's reign, Eustathios Daphnomeles, and utilized by Skylitzes is also discussed in Chapters 4 and 5.[101]

---

[100] Ibid. 361–3; Flusin and Cheynet, *Jean Skylitzès*, pp. xx–xxi; an episode also discussed below in 4.2.2.

[101] See below 4.2.2, 5.2.3–4, and 5.3.

In addition to panegyrical accounts, Shepard suggests that Skylitzes also used other sources. The proliferation of *annus mundi* and indiction dates in the material between 1029 to 1043 suggested to Shepard that Skylitzes had access to a set of annals that consisted of short entries about politics, diplomacy, and natural disasters. Shepard argued that these annals might also have been the source for some of the brief notices found at the end of Skylitzes' coverage of Basil II's reign, such as the description of the eunuch Orestes' expedition to Sicily in 1025.[102] If this is so, then it is possible that Skylitzes' dated references to the expedition to the north coast of the Black Sea (January, 6524), Basil II's Constantinopolitan triumph in celebration of his victory over the Bulgarians (6527), his final battle against the

---

[102] Shepard, 'Byzantium's Last Sicilian Expedition', 145. For Orestes' expedition see Skylitzes, *Synopsis*, 368. The existence of civic or court annals in medieval Byzantium is a much-debated matter. It is clear that in the 6th c. John Malalas used a series of civic annals from Antioch and Constantinople in his synoptic history. Such annals seem to have been used in the 7th-c. *Chronicon Paschale* and even by the Great Chronographer in the 8th c. (E. Jeffreys, 'Malalas' Sources', in E. Jeffreys *et al.* (eds.), *Studies in John Malalas* (Sydney, 1990), 208–13; B. Croke, 'City Chronicles of Late Antiquity' in *Christian Chronicles and Byzantine History, Fifth-Sixth Centuries'* (Aldershot, 1992), no. IV, 193). However, after the 8th c. there is little evidence to support the writing of either civic or monastic annals within Byzantium (C. Mango, 'The Tradition of Byzantine Chronography', *HUS* 12 (1988), 360–72). It is possible that accurately dated material entered the historical record through official bulletins contained in the imperial archives rather than through annals. Nonetheless, extant lists of imperial accessions, marriages, deaths, and even important military campaigns, compiled in the 11th and 12th c. suggest that authors such as Skylitzes could have had recourse to some primary materials rich in dates with which to supplement the narratives supplied by their main historical sources (*Kleinchroniken: Die byzantinischen Kleinchroniken*, ed. P. Schreiner, CFHB 12, 3 vols. (Vienna, 1975–9); Shepard, 'Isaac Comnenus' Coronation Day', 25–6).

Iberians (September, 7th indiction, 6531), and the notice of the emperor's death (December, 9th indiction, 6534), may come from these annals too.[103]

Shepard's principal conclusion about Skylitzes' recourse to different genres of source materials, including annals that contained many dates and laudations of senior generals that contained few, was that when Skylitzes tried to use both types of text the chronology of the narrative that resulted was often seriously disturbed. Shepard pointed to Skylitzes' coverage of Sicilian matters in the 1030s in which the historian attempts to integrate an undated section of the Maniakes' encomium into an annalistic entry. As a result Shepard implies that Maniakes was appointed to lead an expedition to Sicily in 1034–5. In fact, Maniakes only took up this position in 1037–8.[104] In view of such confusions in the *Synopsis*, Shepard concluded that where Skylitzes relies on a single source his chronological and factual details are likely to be at their most trustworthy; but if the text has been synthesized from a mixture of materials inaccuracies will occur.[105] And indeed in a Basil-related context, one can

---

[103] Skylitzes, *Synopsis*, 354, 365, 367–9.

[104] Shepard, 'Byzantium's Last Sicilian Expedition', 146–7.

[105] The only other historian who appears to have considered Skylitzes' 11th-c. source materials at all is Laiou, who detects an ecclesiastical voice within the *Synopsis Historion*'s testimony for the reigns of Romanos III and Michael IV. She attributes this voice to an underlying source written by Demetrios of Kyzikos, who was active as a religious propagandist slightly earlier in the 11th c. for Emperor Constantine VIII (1025–28). In the preface to the *Synopsis* (see below 3.1) Skylitzes includes Demetrios within his list of those hyperbolic historians whose testimony he intended to simplify and clarify in his synopsis. However, Laiou produces no evidence to link Demetrios explicitly to the main narrative of Skylitzes' text (Laiou, 'Imperial Marriages', 167–72; Skylitzes, *Synopsis*, 4).

suggest that just such an elision of materials may lie behind the narrative which deals with the surrender of the western Macedonian forts of Servia, Berroia, and Bodina to Basil *c*.1001 discussed a little earlier. On this particular occasion it is possible that Skylitzes has taken an annalistic text containing several dates for Byzantine expeditions against the Bulgarians between 1000 and 1002; onto this he has then tried to graft a series of moralizing narratives about the perfidious behaviour and subsequent punishment of those Bulgarian generals who surrendered these forts. These stories, however, refer to events long after 1001 itself.[106]

Although Shepard's analysis was conducted more than twenty-five years ago, his detailed examination of the internal structures of Skylitzes' *Synopsis* closely resembles methods advocated more recently for the reading of Byzantine historiography. One of the pioneers in this area of study was Jakob Ljubarskij, who followed modern theories of narrativity in unpicking the texts of several Byzantine historians.[107] Although Ljubarskij did not in the course of his life's work discuss Skylitzes in this light, it is clear that his structural approach, like that of Shepard, offers interesting ways of understanding the architecture of complex historical narratives. Like Shepard, Ljubarskij's method is particularly valuable in those instances where it is impossible to compare

---

[106] Skylitzes, *Synopsis*, 344–45; see above p. 105.

[107] J. N. Ljubarskij, 'Man in Byzantine Historiography from John Malalas to Michael Psellos', *DOP* 46 (1992), 177–86; idem, 'New Trends in the Study of Byzantine Historiography', *DOP* 47 (1993), 131–8; idem, 'Concerning the Literary Technique of Theophanes Confessor'; idem, 'Quellenforschung and/ or Literary Criticism. Narrative Structures in Byzantine Historical Writings', *Symbolae Osloenses* 73 (1998), 5–78 (esp. 5–21).

a historical text with its underlying source materials. Because it is concerned with structure it is an approach that may also provide additional clues about how to identify and deal with those occasions where the extant text becomes prone to chronological or thematic confusion.

One of Ljubarskij's more important claims is that historical narratives are often structured around a series of different episodes. The largest of such textual units he terms mega-episodes; within these subsist smaller narratives.[108] When applied to Skylitzes' testimony Ljubarskij's approach yields the following results. The first half of Skylitzes' coverage appears to break down into three mega-episodes: the first Skleros revolt (chapters 1 to 10); Basil's early engagements with the Bulgarians (chapters 11 and 12); the revolts of Phokas and the return of Skleros (chapters 14 to 19).[109] These three large units of text are united by the common theme: revolt against imperial power. For while Skleros and Phokas are identified by Skylitzes as rebels, so too are the emperor's Bulgarian adversaries: 'When the Bulgars rebelled at the same time as Emperor John died, four brothers were chosen to lead them.'[110] Meanwhile, the second half of Skylitzes' coverage is primarily concerned with a single mega-episode, Basil's conflict in the Balkans. Furthermore, scrutiny of Skylitzes' text makes it clear that within these mega-episodes smaller narratives also exist. Examples from

---

[108] Ljubarskij develops this theory particularly in relation to the structure of Anna Komnene's *Alexiad* and John Kinnamos' *Deeds of John and Manuel Komnenos*: Ljubarskij, 'Quellenforschung and/or Literary Criticism', 16–21.

[109] Skylitzes, *Synopsis*, 314–28, 328–31, 332–9.

[110] Ibid. 328.

Skylitzes' coverage of Basil's reign include Erotikos' defence of Nikaia, Skleros' flight from Baghdad, and the detailed descriptions of battles in the Balkans: indeed, precisely those extended passages of text that we have already identified as single-episode narratives. It is clear that these more minor narratives are then mortared together within the greater mega-episodes by the ubiquitous telescoped, thematic, summary passages that we have also already discussed. Sometimes these telescoped summary passages serve as links within the greater narrative whole; sometimes they act as textual dustbins into which stray odds and ends can be cast.

But while application of Ljubarskij's constellation of greater and lesser episodes may offer us a way of unpicking the overall structure of Skylitzes' treatment of Basil's reign, it also alerts us to the fact that Skylitzes' method of composition is likely to have resulted in yet more chronological distortion and confusion. Take, for example, the structure of the initial mega-episode of the reign, the first Skleros revolt, which Skylitzes divides very neatly into two sections: the Skleros revolt before the appointment of Bardas Phokas as the chief imperial commander, the *domestikos of the scholai* (chapters 1–7); and the story of the revolt once Phokas was appointed (chapters 8–10).[111] In the first half of the narrative Skleros is portrayed fighting a series of pusillanimous commanders, especially eunuchs closely associated with the imperial court, such as Peter the *Stratopedarches*, the former servant, or *doulos*, of Emperor Nikephoros Phokas, and Leo the imperial *protovestiarios*

---

[111] For more on the chronology of this revolt see below 5.1 and 8.2.

who was vested by the imperial court with plenipotentiary powers. In contrast, in the second half of the narrative Skleros finds himself up against a quite different adversary, Bardas Phokas: 'a warlike man who knew how to bear himself nobly and with a sense for strategy, and not, as before, against a castrated manikin accustomed to the bedchamber'.[112] Yet the effect of this division in the Skleros revolt narrative is further chronological confusion. Because Skylitzes chooses to focus the second section of the narrative exclusively on the struggle between Skleros and Phokas, other events that do not involve Phokas but which were nonetheless perpetrated while he was in charge of the imperial armies, are repositioned to earlier sections of the text. Thus, according to the contemporary historian Leo the Deacon, the city of Attaleia went over to the Skleros commander Michael Kourtikios, *after* Skleros had defeated Phokas in battle near Amorion in western Asia Minor. In Skylitzes' testimony, in contrast, this defection is placed *before* the appointment of Phokas.[113] In a similar way, Leo claims that warfare at sea continued *after* Phokas' defeat near Amorion; according to Skylitzes, Skleros had lost control of the sea *before* Phokas took control of the imperial army.[114]

While the structure of Skylitzes' treatment of the first Skleros revolt leads to the reordering of events and chronological confusion, elsewhere the imposition by the author of a narrative structure can result in the marginalizing of

---

[112] Skylitzes, *Synopsis*, 324.
[113] Ibid. 317–18; Leo the Deacon, *Historiae Libri Decem*, 170.
[114] Skylitzes, *Synopsis*, 322–3; Leo the Deacon, *Historiae Libri Decem*, 170.

important stories. Thus, because the first half of Skylitzes' treatment of Basil's reign is devoted to the theme of military revolt by army generals, it leaves no room for a detailed description of the deposition of the emperor's great-uncle and closest adviser, Basil the *Parakoimomenos*, in 985. Indeed, in order to be able to fit this story into his account at all, Skylitzes has to break away from his main narrative at a rather later point, during his treatment of the Phokas revolt (987–9), to explain in an aside that the *Parakoimomenos* had already been dismissed by Basil.[115]

John Skylitzes is a Byzantine historian relatively little studied by modern historians. Yet he is the author of one of the most frequently cited medieval Byzantine histories. While his text begins in 811, it takes on a special significance during the reign of Basil II and the first few decades of the eleventh century, when it becomes the only extant detailed narrative of Byzantine political history in Greek. This chapter has summarized the limited secondary scholarship dedicated to Skylitzes, outlining the work of modern scholars on the manuscript traditions of the *Synopsis Historion*, the author's biography, the text's sources and its internal narrative structures. It has also considered how this research can help us understand Skylitzes' presentation and interpretation of Basil's reign, particularly the vexed Balkan coverage. Above all it has demonstrated how theme rather than chronology

---

[115] Skylitzes, *Synopsis*, 335; for Michael Psellos' twisting of the order of events involving Basil the *Parakoimomenos* to fit an overarching narrative structure see above 1.2.1 and below 8.3.

is the dominant organizing principle within the *Synopsis Historion*. This necessarily means that Skylitzes' text can only be used as a chronological guide to reigns such as Basil's with the greatest degree of caution.

3

Basil II and the Testimony of John Skylitzes: Textual Analysis

The last chapter concluded with a detailed discussion of the structural framework of Skylitzes' *Synopsis Historion*. It examined how the architecture of Skylitzes' text can affect the presentation and interpretation of the history of the later tenth and eleventh centuries. It highlighted the serious factual distortions, including mistakes and lacunae in chronology, which can result from the thematic arrangement Skylitzes imposes on his text. What this chapter suggested was that in the study of those periods of Byzantine history for which the *Synopsis* is the only extant narrative source in Greek, such as the reign of Basil, analysis and understanding of structure is indispensable. However, while a sensitivity to structure is important for fathoming Skylitzes' treatment and interpretation of history, the modern historian also needs to be aware of the impact that other aspects of authorship may have had on Skylitzes' composition: aspects such as Skylitzes' own purpose in writing, his literary interests, his audience, and his own position within political society. To assess the impact of these dimensions we need to look at both the text itself and the contexts in which it was produced in a variety of other ways.

This chapter begins to examine such questions about authorship by looking in greater detail at the text itself. It begins with a brief analysis of the preface, the section of a synoptic text in which the voice of the compiler is likely to be at its most audible. It then examines how the authorial intentions outlined in the preface are realized in the main body of the text. Since Skylitzes' project involves the distillation of texts produced by other historians, the best way of examining how he meets the ambitions of his preface is to compare the main narrative of the *Synopsis* with one of its sources. As none of Skylitzes' underlying materials from Basil's reign survive, an earlier section of the *Synopsis Historion* for which a known source is still extant is analysed. Skylitzes' coverage of the reign of Romanos Lekapenos (920–44) is set against the narrative of his principal source, the sixth book of the Continuation of Theophanes (*Theophanes Continuatus*).[1] The results of this investigation are then used to shed light onto Skylitzes' treatment of the reign of Basil, in particular his coverage of the emperor's Balkan wars.

3.1 THE PREFACE TO THE *SYNOPSIS HISTORION*

The authorial voice that emerges in the preface of Skylitzes' *Synopsis Historion* is concerned with two issues: first, why a

[1] In its scope and detail this comparative study is, as far as I am aware, innovative. The need to test out the correspondences between Skylitzes' preface and the rest of his text has been signalled by I. Grigoriadis, 'A Study

synoptic, or shortened, history of recent times is necessary, and second, how that synoptic history should be written.[2]

In the very first sentence of his preface Skylitzes presents his preferred model for the writing of synoptic history: the *epitome* of history compiled by George the *Synkellos* and Theophanes at the beginning of the ninth century. Having identified his historiographical ideal, Skylitzes then goes on to explain why more recent historians have fallen short in their attempts to continue the work of the *Synkellos* and Theophanes. Some, such as Michael Psellos (described here by Skylitzes as the *hypertimos* Psellos) and the *didaskalos* Sikeliotes, have failed to deal with history in sufficient detail:

> But having undertaken the task in a desultory way, they both lack accuracy, for they disregard very many of the more important events, and they are of no use to their successors, since they have merely made an enumeration of the emperors and indicated who took imperial office after whom, and nothing more.[3]

of the *Prooimion* of Zonaras' Chronicle in Relation to other 12th-Century Historical *Prooimia*', *BZ* 91 (1998), 333. The only comparative analysis of Skylitzes' text was that by A. P. Kazdan which set *Skylitzes Continuatus* against its principal source, the *Historia* of Michael Attaleiates (A. P. Kazdan, 'The Social Views of Michael Attaleiates', in A. P. Kazdan and S. Franklin (eds.), *Studies on Byzantine Literature of the Eleventh and Twelfth Centuries* (Paris, 1984), 23–86). However, this investigation was predominantly concerned with the text of Attaleiates. There was little direct concentration on either the content, vocabulary, level of language, or style of the 'Continuation' produced by Skylitzes, nor on the wider literary, intellectual, or political contexts in which the author was writing.

[2] The preface to the *Synopsis Historion* is to be found in Skylitzes, *Synopsis*, 3–4. A full translation is included in Appendix B of this volume. For further discussion of Skylitzes' preface see Flusin and Cheynet, *Jean Skylitzès*, pp. viii–xii; Grigoriadis, 'The *Prooimion* of Zonaras' Chronicle', 331–3.

[3] ἀλλὰ παρέργως ἁψάμενοι τοῦ ἔργου τῆς τε ἀκριβείας ἀποπεπτώκασι, τὰ πλεῖστα τῶν καιριωτέρων παρέντες, καὶ ἀνόνητοι τοῖς μετ' αὐτοὺς γεγόν-

In other cases historians are criticized for bias and short sightedness:

each [historian] had his own agenda, the one proclaiming praise of the emperor, the other a *psogos* of the patriarch, another the encomium of a friend.... They wrote histories at length of the things which happened during their times and shortly before: one sympathetically, another with hostility, another in search of approval, another as he had been ordered. Each composing their

ασιν, ἀπαρίθμησιν μόνην ποιησάμενοι τῶν βασιλέων καὶ διδάξαντες,τίς μετὰ τίνα τῶν σκήπτρων γέγονεν ἐγκρατής, καὶ πλεῖον οὐδέν (Skylitzes, *Synopsis*, 3). It is usually argued that the historical writings of Michael Psellos to which Skylitzes applies this criticism are not Psellos' long appraisal of fourteen emperors known as the *Chronographia*, but instead the much shorter *Historia Syntomos*. This second text is a list of Roman and Byzantine emperors extending from Romulus to Basil II. Attached to each emperor's entry is a very brief account of the principal events of his reign. Modern scholarly opinion is, however, divided on the issue of whether Psellos was responsible for the *Historia Syntomos*. Snipes, Ljubarskij, and Flusin and Cheynet believe that he was, and that it is to this text that Skylitzes refers in his preface. On the other hand Aerts, the editor of the modern critical edition, believes that the text was written by another 11th-c. author, possibly John Italos (K. Snipes, 'A Newly Discovered History of the Roman Emperors by Michael Psellos', *JÖB* 32.2 (1982), 55; J. N. Ljubarskij, 'Some Notes on the Newly Discovered Historical Work by Psellos', in J. S. Langdon and S. W. Reinert (eds.), *To Hellenikon: Studies in Honor of Speros Vryonis Jr.*, 2 vols. (New Rochelle and New York, 1993), i. 213–28; Flusin and Cheynet, *Jean Skylitzès*, pp. ix–xi; Pseudo-Psellos, *Historia Syntomos*, pp. i–xxv). Turning from Psellos to Sikeliotes, it should be noted that there is no extant Byzantine historical work by a *didaskalos* of this name. It is possible that Skylitzes is referring to lost historical writings by John Sikeliotes, a rhetorician active at the end of the 10th c. Sikeliotes once made a speech (which is no longer extant) in the presence of Basil II at the Pikridion monastery near Constantinople (Hunger, *Hochsprachliche profane Literatur*, i. 45–6; ii. 476–7; *ODB*, ii. 1068). Alternatively Sikeliotes may refer not to a family name, but to a sobriquet 'Master of the Sicilian School'. This reading is preferred by Flusin and Cheynet, who identify Sikeliotes with the 9th-c. historian, Theognostes, whose testimony for the reign of Michael II can be found in both Skylitzes' narrative and that of *Theophanes Continuatus* (Flusin and Cheynet, *Jean Skylitzès*, p. ix).

own history, and differing from one another in their narrations, they have filled the listeners with dizziness and confusion.[4]

Some of these offenders are listed. They include those whose texts are still extant today, such as Joseph Genesios, as well as other historians whose compositions are now lost, such as Theodore of Sebasteia and Theodore Daphnopates.[5]

Skylitzes then explains how he intends to fulfil his ambition of continuing Theophanes. His principal intention is to produce a synoptic account of history which gives 'a very shortened account of the events in different times', following the death of Nikephoros I, the ninth-century emperor. His source materials he identifies as the histories of the writers that he has just criticized for encomium and *psogos*. As for his working methods, Skylitzes reports that having read these histories, he then removed 'that which was written in a state of emotion or in the search of approval', 'disregarded differences and inconsistencies', 'shaved off whatever we have found which is too close to legend', and ignored rhetoric. In his own opinion his final product is 'a nourishment which is soft and finely ground in language'. This literary fare he believes will be to the taste of his audience whom he divides into four categories: 'those who love history'; those 'who prefer that which is very easy to that which is more

---

[4] οἰκείαν ἔκαστος ὑπόθεσιν προστησάμενοι, ὁ μὲν ἔπαινον φέρε εἰπεῖν βασιλέως, ὁ δὲ ψόγον πατριάρχου, ἄτερος δὲ φίλου ἐγκώμιον... ἀποτάδην γὰρ τὰ κατὰ τοὺς αὐτῶν χρόνους συνενεχθέντα, καὶ μικρὸν ἄνωθεν, ἱστορικῶς συγγραψάμενοι, καὶ ὁ μὲν συμπαθῶς, ὁ δ'ἀντιπαθῶς, ὁ δὲ καὶ κατὰ χάριν, ἄλλος δὲ καὶ ὡς προσετέτακτο, τὴν ἑαυτοῦ συνθεὶς ἱστορίαν καὶ πρὸς ἀλλήλους ἐν τῇ τῶν αὐτῶν ἀφηγήσει διαφερόμενοι ἰλίγγου καὶ ταραχῆς τοὺς ἀκροατὰς ἐμπεπλήκασιν (Skylitzes, *Synopsis*, 4).

[5] For these historians and their relationship to Skylitzes' text see above 2.4.

wearisome'; those 'who are acquainted with histories'; and finally, those 'who are not yet acquainted with histories'.

3.2 THE REIGN OF ROMANOS LEKAPENOS: A HISTORIOGRAPHICAL ANALYSIS

Throughout his preface Skylitzes' self-portrait is of the active architect of his narrative in full control of his underlying texts, rather than the passive copyist chained to his sources. However, when attention is turned to the main body of the narrative itself, the energetic statement of purpose conveyed by the preface at first appears to suffer an ignoble collapse. Initial impressions of Skylitzes' treatment of *Theophanes Continuatus'* account of the reign of Romanos Lekapenos suggest that our compiler is rarely more than a simple copyist and summarizer.[6] In terms of content, Skylitzes

---

[6] Coverage of the reign of Romanos Lekapenos is to be found in Skylitzes, *Synopsis*, 213–32; and *Theophanes Continuatus*, ed. I. Bekker, CSHB (Bonn, 1838), 398–435. Several small textual points confirm that Skylitzes' main source is the 'Continuation' of Theophanes rather than one of the many versions of the Logothete such as *George the Monk Continuatus*. First, Skylitzes includes a compressed version of a eulogy of the Kourkouas family and a notice about marital relations between the Lekapenoi and the Argyroi which are only found in *Theophanes Continuatus* (Skylitzes, *Synopsis*, 229–30; *Theophanes Con.*, 426–9; Skylitzes, *Synopsis*, 213; *Theophanes Con.*, 399). Second, Skylitzes mentions that Peter, the emperor of Bulgaria, suffered a revolt by his brother Michael: this too is discussed only by the 'Continuation' of Theophanes (Skylitzes, *Synopsis*, 226; *Theophanes Con.*, 420). Finally, in the case of the second marriage of Constantine, third son of Romanos Lekapenos, the wedding is recorded in all three texts, but Skylitzes follows *Theophanes Continuatus* in identifying the first name of the bride, Theophano,

follows the narrative structure of his root source very faithfully, only once deviating to insert a story about the deposition of Tryphon, the patriarch.[7] In terms of language he
often retains many of the phrases from the original account
verbatim. A clear example of close verbal parallels occurs
in his account of a Bulgarian victory near the palace of
Pegai at the beginning of Romanos' reign. The appropriate
passage from Skylitzes' account is cited here, with those
phrases taken directly from *Theophanes Continuatus* underlined:

φεύγει μὲν ὁ ῥαίκτωρ Ἰωάννης, σφάττεται δὲ ὑπὲρ αὐτοῦ ἀγωνι-
ζόμενος Φωτεινὸς πατρίκιος ὁ τοῦ Πλατύποδος υἱὸς καὶ ἄλλοι οὐκ
ὀλίγοι. μόλις οὖν ὁ ῥαίκτωρ διασωθεὶς εἰσῆλθεν εἰς τὸν δρόμωνα.
τοῦτο καὶ Ἀλέξιος ὁ δρουγγάριος ποιῆσαι βουληθείς, καὶ μὴδυνη-
θεὶς ἀνελθεῖν, ἐν τῇ τοῦ δρόμωνος ὑποβάθρᾳ πεσὼν ἐν τῃ θαλά-
σσῃ σὺν τῳ αὐτοῦ πρωτομανδάτωρι ἀπεπνίγη.[8]

and her family name, Mamantos, whereas the Logothete fails to record the
bride's identity (Skylitzes, *Synopsis*, 229; *Theophanes Con.*, 423; *George the
Monk Continuatus*, 914). *Theophanes Continuatus* is also identified as the
principal source for Skylitzes' account by Flusin and Cheynet, *Jean Skylitzès*,
p. xiii.

[7] Skylitzes, *Synopsis*, 226–7; Flusin and Cheynet, *Jean Skylitzès*, p. xiii.
[8] Skylitzes, *Synopsis*, 215: *Theophanes Con.*, 401. My translation of Skylitzes' text: 'On the one hand the *rector* John fled, whereas Photeinos, the
patrikios, the son of Platypodos, who was fighting for him, was killed as were
several others. And so the rector, having barely escaped, boarded the *dromon*
(warship). And although Alexios, the admiral (*droungarios*) wanted to do the
same thing, he was not able to climb up on the deck of the *dromon*; he fell
into the sea and was drowned together with his *protomandator*.' Verbatim
copying can also be observed in *Skylitzes Continuatus'* coverage of the second
half of the 11th c. As Shepard has pointed out, Skylitzes often copies his
underlying text so closely that he retains the first person singular voice of the
root source (Shepard, 'Byzantinorussica', 217).

Furthermore, there is empirical evidence to suggest that in his role as a simple copyist Skylitzes was less than fully competent: several errors in his transmission of the original source can be identified. For example, when Skylitzes refers to the marriage agreements between the Lekapenoi and the Argyroi at the beginning of Romanos' reign, he misreads the information in *Theophanes Continuatus* and identifies Leo Argyros as the bridegroom of Agatha Lekapene. *Theophanes Continuatus*, however, makes it clear that it was Romanos, the son of Leo, who married the Lekapene.[9] Other mistakes in Skylitzes' coverage of Lekapenos' reign arise from the misreading of certain words. For example, although *Theophanes Continuatus* explains that rebels involved in the plot of Arsenios and Paul the *Manglabites* suffered a beating as part of their punishment, Skylitzes alleges that they were blinded. For the term τυφθέντες in Theophanes, Skylitzes appears to have miscopied τυφλωθέντες.[10] Another single word error involves an accident in the forum, which according to *Theophanes Continuatus* resulted in the deaths of six men, but according to Skylitzes involved sixty deaths.[11] In another instance Skylitzes seems to have read his source with undue haste, and thus attributed to two individuals the fate experienced by only one. In his report of Byzantine dealings with the emirate of Melitene, Skylitzes suggests that friendly Byzantine–Arab relations broke down in 934 when both Arab leaders Apochaps and Aposalath died. However,

---

[9] Skylitzes, *Synopsis*, 213; *Theophanes Con.*, 399; see also Polemis, 'Some Cases of Erroneous Identification', 77.

[10] Skylitzes, *Synopsis*, 213; *Theophanes Con.*, 399.

[11] Skylitzes, *Synopsis*, 226; *Theophanes Con.*, 420.

Theophanes Continuatus makes it clear that although Apochaps and Aposalath had been involved in the original peace deal with the Byzantines, it was only Apochaps who died before the arrangement disintegrated.[12] Skylitzes' most serious factual error concerns the misdating of the appointment of Romanos' son Theophylact as patriarch of Constantinople after the deposition of Tryphon. Skylitzes records that this appointment happened in February of the 2nd indiction; the original source records 2 February of the 6th indiction.[13]

Nonetheless, comparison of the *Synopsis* and *Theophanes Continuatus* demonstrates that it is too simplistic on the basis of individual errors to claim that Skylitzes was an incompetent scholar. At the simple level of copying, for example, Skylitzes can achieve a high level of accuracy. In the case of the Arab leaders from Melitene, the names of Apochaps and Aposalath are both transcribed correctly.[14] Skylitzes is also diligent in his copying of the names of the conspirators involved in the multitudinous plots at the beginning of Lekapenos' reign. His only slip occurs in the case of a certain *magistros* Stephen who was exiled to the island of Antigone: he omits *Theophanes Continuatus'* statement that this malcontent was from Kalomaria.[15] Equally Skylitzes usually transmits dates accurately. The error concerning the Patriarch Theophylact is the only glaring mistake in the nineteen dates included in the *Synopsis*.

---

[12] Skylitzes, *Synopsis*, 224; *Theophanes Con.*, 416.

[13] Skylitzes, *Synopsis*, 227; *Theophanes Con.*, 422.

[14] Shepard, 'Byzantinorussica', 212 n. 7, suggests that Skylitzes is usually accurate in his transmission of Russian names.

[15] Skylitzes, *Synopsis*, 213; *Theophanes Con.*, 398.

Furthermore, Skylitzes very rarely omits a date mentioned in *Theophanes Continuatus*. An exception to this general rule is his failure to register the date of the second sea battle involving the Rus in 941 (10 September).[16] More frequent than his complete failure to register a date are his omissions of the precise day when an event occurred. For example, although he records the month and indiction date when the Union of the Church was confirmed in the early part of Romanos' reign (July; eighth indiction), he omits the day (Sunday).[17]

Taken as a whole such plentiful evidence for Skylitzes' faithful copying of content and vocabulary lends weight to the contention put forward by Thurn, the editor of the critical edition of the *Synopsis Historion*, that Skylitzes is little more than a transcriber, who adheres so faithfully to his source material that it is impossible to attribute any idiosyncrasies of grammar, style, or vocabulary to him.[18] Furthermore, Skylitzes' closely observed transcriptions may at some level appear to be compatible with established literary practices in later eleventh- and twelfth-century Byzantium. For example, the mid-twelfth-century synoptic historian John Zonaras explicitly states in the preface to his own literary production that his narrative deliberately contains a conspicuous heterogeneity of language and tone

---

[16] Skylitzes, *Synopsis*, 229–30; *Theophanes Con.*, 425.

[17] Skylitzes, *Synopsis*, 213; *Theophanes Con.*, 398.

[18] Skylitzes, *Synopsis*, p. viii; this view was also subsequently commended by N. Oikonomides in a review article of Thurn's critical edition, *BZ* 69 (1976), 70.

because he wishes to retain the varying styles of his different sources.[19]

Nonetheless, although Skylitzes' account of the reign of Romanos Lekapenos follows the narrative structure, word order, and even vocabulary of his underlying text, it would be dangerous to assume that Skylitzes was merely a passive copyist and abbreviator whose testimony can be accepted as an accurate transmission of the materials he collates. Instead, further inspection of Skylitzes' treatment of *Theophanes Continuatus'* coverage of the reign of Romanos Lekapenos, reveals a number of subtle adaptations which when aggregated demonstrate that the compiler of the *Synopsis* exercised an active authorial role. Skylitzes' interventions are compatible with the intentions he outlines in his preface on some occasions. On others his manipulations appear to deviate from his own statement of purpose. More importantly for the historian of medieval Byzantium, Skylitzes' active authorship can impose serious distortions on the contents and interpretations of the underlying materials he transmits.[20]

---

[19] Zonaras (John), *Annales*, ii. 8–9; Hunger, *Hochsprachliche profane Literatur*, i. 417.

[20] Useful comparisons can be drawn with the 9th-c. synoptic historian Theophanes the Confessor. Although Theophanes usually follows the word order and phraseology of the texts which underpin his narrative very faithfully, he can make interventions of a very subtle order, sometimes involving no more than the insertion of single word, the omission of a phrase, or the repositioning of a date. While some of these alterations are accidental, others are deliberate, undertaken with the purpose of altering the sense of the text (Mango and Scott, *The Chronicle of Theophanes*, pp. xcii–xcv). That Skylitzes is a copyist who nonetheless has his own style and tone is an observation also made by Flusin and Cheynet, *Jean Skylitzès*, pp. xiv–xvi, xxi.

At the most basic of levels Skylitzes takes measures to ensure that his history is a synopsis rather than a simple copy. Thus, he sometimes elides two main verbal clauses from the underlying text into a single clause containing a main verb and a participle construction; the latter may take the form of a genitive absolute.[21] His enthusiasm for abbreviation is most visible whenever he tries to combine so many phrases and sentences from the underlying source into a single unit that the meaning of his narrative becomes elusive. For example, on several occasions he combines several main verbs from the underlying text into a more elaborate single-verb sentence, with the result that a large slice of prose is expressed in a case other than the nominative. Thus, when Skylitzes decides to make the emperor the subject of a long sentence about the dismissal in 944 of John Kourkouas, the *domestikos* of the *scholai*, the subsequent description of the career and exploits of the general has to be rendered with several accusative participles; to add to the confusion Kourkouas is also to be found earlier in the sentence in the genitive case.[22] A parallel example of the

---

[21] For example, Skylitzes uses two genitive absolutes to describe the defeat of the Arabs and the flight of Leo of Tripoli at the hands of the admiral (*droungarios*) John Radenos in the early 920s: ὁ Ῥαδηνὸς κατονομα-ζόμενος αἰφνίδιον ἐπιφανεὶς ῥᾳδίως ἐτρέψατο, τῶν Ἀγαρηνῶν σχεδὸν πάντ-ων ἀνῃρημένων, τοῦ δὲ Τριπολίτου μόνου φυγῇ τὴν σωτηρίαν πορισαμένου (genitive absolutes underlined; Skylitzes, *Synopsis*, 218); whereas *Theophanes Continuatus* uses two main verbs (bold) to describe the actions of the Arabs and Leo: ὁ Ῥαδινὸς κατονομαζόμενος αἰφνιδίως **ἐπέθετο** αὐτῷ· καὶ . . . θεοῦ συνεργίᾳ οἱ ὑπ' αὐτὸν **τρέπονται** Ἀγαρηνοί, μόλις δὲ μόνος ὁ Τρι-πολίτης φυγῇ **διασώζεται** (Theophanes Con., 405).

[22] Skylitzes, *Synopsis*, 230: φθόνου δὲ κινηθέντος κατὰ τοῦ δομεστίκου τῶν σχολῶν Ἰωάννου τοῦ Κουρκούα παρὰ τῶν ἄλλων βασιλέων (ἐβούλετο γὰρ Ῥωμανὸς ὁ Βασιλεὺς Εὐφροσύνην τὴν τοῦ δομεστίκου θυγατέρα νύμφην ἀγα-

inclusion of long accusative clauses occurs in Skylitzes' account of the campaigns of Nikephoros Phokas (959–63), the future emperor, who served as a general during the reign of Romanos II. Once again, because Emperor Romanos occupies the nominative position, Nikephoros Phokas and his many military exploits against the Arabs have to be expressed in a very long accusative phrase.[23]

Although Skylitzes' use of such complicated participle constructions fulfils his ambition to abbreviate his underlying texts, it is less clear how the obfuscation produced by such syntax enables the author to meet one of his other compositional injunctions, namely to write an account in easily digestible and finely ground prose. Indeed, his frequent inclusion of other sophisticated grammatical structures suggests that rather than simplifying his underlying text, Skylitzes was intent on elevating it.[24] For example,

γέσθαι τῷ οἰκείῳ ἐκγόνῳ Ῥωμανῷ ⟨τῷ υἱῷ⟩ τοῦ ἐσχάτου παιδὸς αὐτοῦ Κω-
νσταντίνου⟩ ἠναγκάσθη τῆς ἀρχῆς αὐτὸν παραλῦσαι, ἐπὶ δυσὶ καὶ εἴκοσι χρ-
όνοις καὶ μησὶν ἑπτὰ ἀδιαδόχως τὴν τοῦ δομεστίκου ἀρχὴν ἰθύναντα, καὶ
πᾶσαν, ὡς εἰπεῖν, τὴν Συρίαν καταδραμόντα καὶ ταπεινώσαντα; the first two
phrases in bold highlight Kourkouas in the genitive case; the last phrase
underlined moves into the accusative case.

[23] Skylitzes, *Synopsis*, 249: τούτῳ τῷ ἔτει Νικηφόρον μάγιστρον τὸν
Φωκᾶν, δομέστικον ἤδη προβεβλημένον τῶν σχολῶν τῆς ἀνατολῆς παρὰ Κωνσταντίνου τοῦ βασιλέως, καὶ πολλὰ τρόπαια στήσαντα κατὰ τῶν ἑῴων Σαρακηνῶν, καὶ τόν τε τῆς Ταρσοῦ ἀμηρᾶν Καραμώνην καὶ Χαμβδᾶν τόν τοῦ
Χάλεπ καὶ τὸν Τριπόλεως Ἰζὴθ ὁλοσχερῶς ταπεινώσαντα, πέμπει κατὰ τῶν
ἐν Κρήτῃ Σαρακηνῶν, πλῆθος ἐπιλέκτων στρατιωτῶν ἐπιδοὺς αὐτῷ καὶ στ-
όλον κατηρτισμένον καλῶς; Nikephoros and the phrase associated with him
in the accusative case are underlined.

[24] A conspicuous distinction between the promise to write in simple prose
and the complexity of the final prose product has also been observed in the
historical writings of Niketas Choniates (Grigoriadis, 'The *Prooimion* of
Zonaras' Chronicle', 338–9).

when Skylitzes describes the military achievements of the general John Kourkouas, he advises the reader who wishes for more information to consult the biographical history written by the historian Manuel. Skylitzes expresses this command by using a third person singular imperative ζητησάτω (let him seek). In contrast, his source *Theophanes Continuatus* uses a simple third person plural verb to instruct 'those readers who wish to learn more' of Kourkouas' exploits that they will find the information they are seeking in the books of Manuel: εὑρήσουσιν (they will find).[25]

On other occasions, rather than retaining a simple main verb, participle, or infinitive, Skylitzes prefers to create a phrase involving a noun. Thus κατασκοπῆσαι becomes ἐπὶ κατασκοπὴν while ἐκστρατευσάντων becomes εἰσβολὴν ποιησαμένων.[26] In other instances Skylitzes elevates the register by interpreting a section of the underlying text with a high-style cliché. For example, both in his rewriting of *Theophanes Continuatus*, and elsewhere in his text, he sometimes replaces the simple identification of Hagia Sophia or the *Megale Ekklesia* with a more involved circumlocution: τῷ θείῳ τεμένει τῆς τοῦ θεοῦ σοφίας (in the divine precinct of the Holy Wisdom).[27] When he describes the coronations of members of the Lekapenoi family Skylitzes replaces *Theophanes Continuatus'* simple στέφεται (he was crowned) with the altogether more elaborate phrase ταινιωθεὶς τῷ βασιλικῷ διαδήματι (having been bound

---

[25] Skylitzes, *Synopsis*, 230; *Theophanes Con.*, 427–8.

[26] Skylitzes, *Synopsis*, 214, 216; *Theophanes Con.*, 400, 402.

[27] Skylitzes, *Synopsis*, 214; *Theophanes Con.*, 399; see also Skylitzes, *Synopsis*, 270 for a similar example from the reign of Nikephoros Phokas.

with the imperial diadem).[28] This too is a phrase that occurs
in other parts of the *Synopsis Historion*: the coronations of
Nikephoros Phokas and John Tzimiskes are described in
very similar terms.[29] Nonetheless, such elevations or elabor-
ations are not always consistent: at other times Skylitzes
simplifies the language of his underlying source.[30] For example, he sometimes employs two main verbs where *Theophanes Continuatus* uses a genitive absolute. On at least one
occasion he replaces an optative with a simple main verb.[31]

Skylitzes displays greater consistency in meeting some of
the *other* intentions he outlines in the preface, in particular
his desire to erase those hyperbolic elements which were 'too
close to legend', as well as those instances of excessive encomium. For example, he excises completely the more elaborate antiquarian and ethnographic excurses of his core
source. During his account of the maritime invasion of the
Rus, *Theophanes Continuatus* digresses to explain the ethnic
background of the Rus in 941 ('and they are called *Dromitai*,
who originate from the race of the Franks'), the purpose of
the Pharos lighthouse, and the classical background behind
the renaming of the Black Sea from the unfortunate (*Kakox-
einos*) to the fortunate (*Euxeinos*), a transformation which

---

[28] Skylitzes, *Synopsis*, 213; *Theophanes Con.*, 398.

[29] Skylitzes, *Synopsis*, 259, 286.

[30] In a review article of Thurn's critical edition of *Ioannis Skylitzae Synopsis Historiarum,* Cyril Mango reflects on the inconsistencies of Skylitzes'
Attic prose (*JHS* 95 (1975), 304–5).

[31] During the story of the revolt of Bardas Boilas, the *strategos* of Chaldia,
Theophanes Continuatus informs the reader that the emperor forgave the
poorer rebels and allowed them to go wherever they wanted: ὅπη βούλοιντο,
whereas Skylitzes renders this phrase as ὅπῃ βούλονται (*Theophanes Con.*,
404; Skylitzes, *Synopsis*, 217).

was wrought by Heracles' defeat of a band of local pirates.[32] All of these grace notes are excluded by Skylitzes. Also omitted from Skylitzes' compilation is the moralizing aside. After the victory of Symeon of Bulgaria's forces at Pegai in the early 920s, *Theophanes Continuatus* concludes a description of events with the reflection: 'such is the terrible [consequence] of lack of planning and inexperience when it is in alliance with foolhardiness.' This is a sentiment ignored by Skylitzes: he concludes his account of this military disaster with the burning of the Pegai palace.[33]

Nonetheless, such sanitizing interventions on the part of Skylitzes remain relatively rare, possibly because such high-style ornaments occur only occasionally in the text of Theophanes Continuatus itself. Much more conspicuous are Skylitzes' attempts to remove the excesses of encomium from the underlying text. At one level this operation merely involves stripping key personalities of superlative descriptions. For example, Skylitzes always removes the praise routinely applied in *Theophanes Continuatus* to Theophanes, the *Protovestiarios* (later *Parakoimomenos*) of the Emperor Romanos.[34] In a similar fashion he removes references to the military bravery of the emir of Melitene.[35] Severe pruning is applied to the encomium of John Kourkouas. For instance, while *Theophanes Continuatus* alleges that Kourkouas, 'became unrivalled in matters of war, and established many

---

[32] *Theophanes Con.*, 423–4; Skylitzes, *Synopsis*, 229.

[33] *Theophanes Con*, 402; Skylitzes, *Synopsis*, 215.

[34] *Theophanes Con.*, 423; Skylitzes, *Synopsis*, 228–9; Flusin and Cheynet, *Jean Skylitzès*, p. xv.

[35] Skylitzes, *Synopsis*, 224; *Theophanes Con.*, 416.

great trophies, and extended the Roman boundaries and sacked very many Agarene cities', and makes reference to his 'outstanding virtue', Skylitzes rather more drily comments that he 'overran and humbled, so it is said, the whole of Syria'.[36]

However, it is to the Lekapenoi themselves that Skylitzes applies the most systematic textual amputations and even rewritings. A relatively small-scale pruning is to be seen in Skylitzes' removal of a favourable reference to the horse-loving Patriarch Theophylact, youngest son of the Emperor Romanos.[37] At a more general level the inclination of *Theophanes Continuatus* to interpret the first half of the tenth century in the light of the family history, or perhaps the family tragedy, of the Lekapenoi is diminished. Thus, while Skylitzes follows *Theophanes Continuatus* in recording the coronations of the sons of the Emperor Romanos at the beginning of the reign, and also notes all the Lekapenoi marriages, he omits all mention of the family distress when Maria Lekapene departed for Bulgaria in 927 as the bride of Tsar Peter, or of their grief over the death of the eldest son Christopher in 931.[38]

Most dramatic is Skylitzes' reshaping of the personality of Romanos Lekapenos. This recasting is achieved partly by the omission or dilution of the more panegyrical features, and

---

[36] Skylitzes, *Synopsis*, 230, *Theophanes Con.*, 426–9.
[37] *Theophanes Con.*, 422; Skylitzes, *Synopsis*, 228.
[38] Reference to John of Bulgaria: *Theophanes Con.*, 419, Skylitzes, *Synopsis*, 225; reference to Mary Lekapene's departure to Bulgaria: *Theophanes Con.*, 415, Skylitzes, *Synopsis*, 224; reference to Christopher's death: *Theophanes Con.*, 420, Skylitzes, *Synopsis*, 226.

partly by some very selective rewriting. Conspicuous among the dilutions is Skylitzes' dramatic abbreviation of *Theophanes Continuatus*' descriptions of Romanos' charitable deeds. Thus, the forty-line eulogy of Romanos' good works during the winter of 927 in *Theophanes Continuatus* is reduced to six in Skylitzes' version.[39] Later in his text Skylitzes not only compresses another twenty-five line passage of encomium, which describes Romanos' generosity to various monastic and charitable institutions, to less than ten lines, but he also makes the additional suggestion that Romanos' motives were primarily conditioned by the need to atone for the sins of his past life, and that the main object of his interest was always the development of his own monastic foundation in Constantinople, the Myrelaion.[40]

However, it is in the section dealing with Romanos' meeting with the Bulgarian leader Symeon in 924 that Skylitzes' reconditioning of the encomium of the emperor is at its most conspicuous. First, Skylitzes omits those elements in *Theophanes Continuatus*' account which contribute to an aura of sanctity. Although he mentions that Romanos entered the church of Blachernai before he met Symeon in order to pray and to put on the protective *omophorion* of the Virgin, he excises all references to Romanos weeping and imploring the Mother of God for her assistance.[41] Later in the account of the meeting of the two leaders Skylitzes excludes all allusions to the bravery of Romanos.[42] At this

---

[39] *Theophanes Con.*, 415–17; Skylitzes, *Synopsis*, 225.
[40] *Theophanes Con.*, 429–30; Skylitzes, *Synopsis*, 231.
[41] Skylitzes, *Synopsis*, 219; *Theophanes Con.*, 406–7.
[42] Skylitzes, *Synopsis*, 220; *Theophanes Con.*, 407–8.

point he substantially curtails a passage of direct speech in which Romanos exhorts Symeon to stall his wanton slaughter.[43] But it is in his concluding editorial comments about Romanos' encounter with Symeon that Skylitzes' deviation from *Theophanes Continuatus* is at its most obvious. For where the original text maintains that Symeon went back to his camp praising 'the intelligence and humility and... appearance of bodily strength and... dauntless spirit [of the emperor]', Skylitzes alleges that the Bulgarian leader returned to his associates and commented on the 'moderation of the emperor and his lavishness and generosity in matters of money'.[44] One explanation for Skylitzes' reshaping of Lekapenos' role could be that the compiler had access to anti-Lekapenos material, which he used to counter the rhetorical hyperbole of *Theophanes Continuatus*. However, given the extremely tight congruence between the narrative structures of the *Synopsis Historion* and the account of *Theophanes Continuatus*, it seems superfluous to suggest that Skylitzes draws on an alternative primary source. Instead his treatment of the Lekapenoi family is almost certainly the result of his own willingness to comment upon, reorder, and reshape his core source using his own powers of interpretation.

Nonetheless, it should be noted that Skylitzes does not completely jettison the laudatory excesses of his underlying sources. The encomium of the bridegroom of Agatha Lekapene, a member of the Argyros family, is reduced in length

---

[43] Skylitzes, *Synopsis*, 220; *Theophanes Con.*, 408.
[44] *Theophanes Con.*, 409; Skylitzes, *Synopsis*, 221.

in Skylitzes' version, but the essence of the praise of the protagonist's physical and intellectual merits is retained.[45] Equally, although Skylitzes brutally curtails the list of the military activities of John Kourkouas, his brother Theophilos and his son Romanos, he retains all the information relating to the intra-familial links between the three Kourkouas commanders. Moreover, he even updates the text so that whereas Theophanes imparts the information that Theophilos was the grandfather of John Tzimiskes, 'who became *domestikos* of the *scholai* under Emperor Nikephoros', Skylitzes tells us that he was the grandfather of John Tzimiskes, 'who was emperor after these things'.[46] Furthermore, even if he dismisses or dilutes the more obvious passages of panegyric, Skylitzes cannot entirely escape the viewpoint of the original subject of the encomium. Thus, although he reshapes *Theophanes Continuatus*' praise of Romanos Lekapenos and John Kourkouas, Skylitzes still has to accept the underlying source's identification of these two actors as the most important protagonists in the history of this period.

While omission and abbreviation comprise one dimension of Skylitzes' willingness to intervene in his underlying text, his active authorial role can also be detected within his *additions* to the coverage of *Theophanes Continuatus*. These

---

[45] *Theophanes Continuatus* says that the Argyros bridegroom was: ἄνδρα ὄντα ὑπερώμιον, καὶ κάλλει σώματος καὶ ἰδέᾳ καὶ συνέσει καὶ μάλιστα τῇ ἐλεημοσύνῃ καὶ ἐπιδόσει καὶ τῇ ἀγαθότητι καὶ ἁπλότητι κοσμούμενον (*Theophanes Con.*, 399); this eulogy is shortened in Skylitzes to ἄνδρα γενναῖον, καὶ κάλλει σώματος καὶ ἰδέᾳ ὑπερφέροντα, συνέσει τε καὶ φρονήσει κοσμούμενον (Skylitzes, *Synopsis*, 213).

[46] Skylitzes, *Synopsis*, 230; *Theophanes Con.*, 428.

additions usually take the form of brief link phrases designed to bring thematic or chronological order to the underlying material. At their most simple, such phrases can simply be used to sharpen the focus of the root text. During his abbreviated account of the Rus attack of 941, Skylitzes decides to retain the vivid depiction of the impalings and crucifixions inflicted by the Rus on the local inhabitants of the shores of Asia opposite Constantinople. However, in order to wrench his concise narrative back to the eventual and inevitable defeat of the Rus, he adds the phrase ἀλλὰ ταῦτα μὲν πρότερον (but these things happened before) to refer to the depredations he has just listed; another link phrase is then required to indicate the resumption of the main story: ὡς ἄνωθεν ἐρρέθη (as was said above).[47]

Other link phrases have the additional purpose of trying to make sense of the structure of the source Skylitzes is processing. For example, at the end of the passage describing the marriage of Tsar Peter of Bulgaria to Maria Lekapene Skylitzes inserts the simple phrase: 'and matters in the City came to an end in this way'.[48] This phrase is intended as a pointer to the next episode in the text, namely Byzantine relations with Melitene, which certainly were *not* matters pertaining to the City (of Constantinople), but instead took the reader out to the empire's eastern frontier. Another one-line explanatory interpolation occurs in Skylitzes' account

---

[47] Skylitzes, *Synopsis*, 229; *Theophanes Con.*, 425. For a discussion of link phrases in synoptic history as signs of active editing see Jeffreys, *Studies in John Malalas*, 21. On Skylitzes' fondness for such devices see Shepard 'Byzantium's Last Sicilian Expedition', 147–8.

[48] Skylitzes, *Synopsis*, 224.

of the conspiracy of Bardas Boilas, the *strategos* of Chaldia. When *Theophanes Continuatus* reports on this revolt he offers no explanation as to why this episode is included in his text, but simply begins with the allegation of a plot. Skylitzes, in contrast, wishes to make explicit the fact that this revolt is mentioned at this point in the narrative because it represents yet another rebellion of the sort that peppered the early years of Romanos' reign. Therefore, at the beginning of the episode he adds the explanatory phrase: 'another revolt happened against the emperor in Chaldia.'[49]

At a rather more interpretative level, Skylitzes makes additions to the text of *Theophanes Continuatus* which offer explanations for particular courses of action or individual motives. Distinction can be drawn between those additions that are made with no apparent reference to the underlying source, and those which try to make sense of *Theophanes Continuatus*. In a passage relating to Bulgarian attacks on the palace of Theodora and the Byzantine military riposte led by Saktikios, the commander of the army unit known as the *Exkoubitores*, both categories of additional explanation can be identified. At the beginning of this passage Skylitzes explains that the reason why the palace of Theodora was burned was because nothing was in the way. This explanation has no apparent background justification in the text of *Theophanes Continuatus*. In contrast, Saktikios' early success against the Bulgar camp is explained by the absence of most of the Bulgars, who were away raiding the surrounding countryside for supplies. While

---

[49] Skylitzes, *Synopsis*, 217; *Theophanes Con.*, 404.

Theophanes Continuatus does not actually say that this was the case, Skylitzes' hypothesis is at least partially supported by the allegation of the underlying source that once the Bulgars heard of the assault of Saktikios they all returned to the camp.[50] One might suggest that Skylitzes' treatment of Symeon's post-conference report in 924 on the qualities of Romanos is an explanatory addition in the same vein. For having alleged that Symeon was enormously impressed with the personal qualities of the emperor, *Theophanes Continuatus* goes on to highlight the largesse which Romanos displayed on Symeon's departure: 'and so having embraced one another they parted, with the emperor having bestowed magnificent presents on Symeon.' In these circumstances Skylitzes' decision to make Symeon stress the largesse rather than the virtue of Romanos seems perfectly justified.

Yet, the reader of Skylitzes should note that even the simplest tightening of the structure of the text to comply with thematic rigour may easily eliminate the deeper nuances of the core source. For example, we have already seen that in his treatment of the revolts which plagued the early years of Lekapenos' reign, Skylitzes not only retains and accurately records the names of most of the conspirators listed by *Theophanes Continuatus*, but also alerts the reader's attention to the thematic integrity of these early passages by interpolating explanatory phrases. Yet, he also chooses to control the overwhelmingly large dramatis personae of his core source by selectively omitting certain minor personalities. For example, when Symeon of Bulgaria died in 927

---

[50] Skylitzes, *Synopsis*, 216; *Theophanes Con.*, 402–3.

Theophanes Continuatus notes that he left four sons (Peter, Michael, John, and Benjamin). Shortly after Symeon's death Peter, the young ruler of the Bulgarians, and his uncle George Sousouboule, who appears to have acted as a regent figure, approached Romanos Lekapenos for a peace treaty and marriage agreement, a request that met with success. Skylitzes reports a similar chain of events. However, he omits the names of Peter's two youngest brothers and that of George Sousouboule from his narrative, thereby depriving the reader of any sense of the complexity of dynastic politics within Bulgaria in the post-Symeon era.[51] Skylitzes' preference for omitting minor personalities in his treatment of *Theophanes Continuatus* has a similar effect elsewhere in his text, on this occasion destroying fragile clues about the workings of Byzantine high court politics. In his account of the conspiracy of Arsenios and Paul the *Manglabites* towards the beginning of Romanos' reign Skylitzes retains the names of the plotters but excises a minor character called Leo, the *anthropos* of Arsenios, who acted as an informer to the imperial authorities.[52] Not only does this omission mean that the reader of the *Synopsis Historion* is furnished with less information about the chiaroscuro of rumour, coup and counter-coup in the embryonic period of a key reign, it also deprives the narrative of vital information about the role of the elusive John the Rector and *Mystikos*. *Theophanes Continuatus* tells his reader that it was John who had originally recommended Leo to the emperor and secured his

---

[51] *Theophanes Con.*, 411–12; Skylitzes, *Synopsis*, 222–3.
[52] The term *anthropos* is ambiguous, but probably means client or retainer, rather than merely a servant.

appointment in imperial service. In this scant information provided by *Theophanes Continuatus*, John the Rector emerges as a key political broker at court. Unfortunately Skylitzes' omission of a minor character such as Leo means that much less can be deduced about major figures such as John.[53]

One of the reasons why Skylitzes omits minor characters like Leo is because his prime concern is to focus the text more narrowly on the more prominent personnel of the narrative. This desire may also determine Skylitzes' enthusiasm for attributing additional personal details such as names, titles, and offices to the most important figures within the history, even where they are missing in the core source. Just as Polemis noted that Skylitzes was willing to insert patronymic details into his narrative with no support from his underlying texts in the course of his ninth- and early tenth-century coverage, evidence of a similar nature appears in his treatment of the reign of Romanos Lekapenos.[54] Alexander Každan noticed that Skylitzes is the first historian to record the family name Lekapenos in connection with Romanos I and his family. In *Theophanes Continuatus* he is simply called Romanos; in other tenth-century literature, including the *De Administrando Imperio*, he is

---

[53] Skylitzes, *Synopsis*, 213; *Theophanes Con.*, 399. John the Rector fought against Symeon of Bulgaria early in Lekapenos' reign (see above), conducted a diplomatic mission to Bulgaria in 929, and plotted to restore Stephen Lekapenos to the throne after Constantine VII Porphyrogenitus deposed the Lekapenoi in 944–5 (Guilland, *Recherches*, ii. 214). The degree to which Skylitzes omits key details from a narrative while still striving to maintain the flavour of an underlying story has also been observed in 9th-c. sections of his text (Flusin and Cheynet, *Jean Skylitzès*, pp. xx–xxi).

[54] Polemis' observations are discussed above in 2.4.

identified as Romanos the Elder.[55] Further examples of Skylitzes' fondness for embellishing the personal details of the
main characters in his narrative include awarding individuals titles, which cannot be corroborated from the root text
of *Theophanes Continuatus*, nor indeed from other tenth-
century sources such as the Logothete. Thus, the Arsenios
mentioned above is, for no apparent reason, given the title
of *patrikios* by Skylitzes. The same title is awarded to Bardas
Boilas, the rebellious general (*strategos*) of Chaldia. During
Byzantine military actions against Melitene, Melias, the
leader of the Armenian troops, is given the additional label
magistros.[56] The most likely explanation for Skylitzes' tendency to award titles out of thin air is that he may have tried
to grant officials the rank he believed they deserved on the
basis of comparative evidence from elsewhere in the underlying text. Thus, Bardas Boilas is probably given the title
patrikios because other *strategoi* during the reign of Romanos were described as having this title by *Theophanes
Continuatus*: for example, Bardas Phokas is described by
Theophanes during the invasion of the Rus in 941 as a
former *strategos* with the title of *patrikios*.[57]

Although Skylitzes' decision to award Boilas the title of
patrikios appears to reflect his sensitive understanding of the
administrative history of the empire in the early to mid-
tenth century, elsewhere his presentation of the administrative structure of empire imposes serious distortions. Thus,

---

[55] A. Každan, 'The Formation of Byzantine Family Names in the Ninth
and Tenth Centuries', *Byz Slav* 58 (1997), 90.

[56] Skylitzes, *Synopsis*, 213, 217, 224; *Theophanes Con.*, 399, 404, 416.

[57] *Theophanes Con.*, 424.

where *Theophanes Continuatus* refers to a certain Michael, son of Myroleo, as a *topoteretes*, a senior officer within the professional and centralized *tagmatic* army forces of the early tenth century, Skylitzes uses the rather generalized term *tagmatarchon*.[58] A similar example occurs during his treatment of the invasion of the Rus in 941. *Theophanes Continuatus* explains that the Rus threat to Constantinople was eventually averted by the arrival of the *domestikos* of the *scholai*, John Kourkouas, with the army of the east. However, while Skylitzes retains *Theophanes Continuatus'* allusion to Kourkouas and his office as it is in the original text, he merely notes that the Byzantine general was accompanied by some *tagmata*.[59] Any sense is immediately lost that Kourkouas was in charge of that section of the professional, centralized army which usually operated on the eastern frontier and that its return to Constantinople was dramatic evidence of the crisis induced by the Rus attack. One suspects that Skylitzes' generalized phraseology may either reflect his own ignorance of military and administrative structures in the early tenth century, or may be an attempt to make the intricacies of the organization of the army during an earlier period of history accessible to his later eleventh-century audience. The idea that Skylitzes attempted to explain earlier periods of history by homogenizing and generalizing his administrative terminology would of course be germane to his wider project to provide a digestible account of history for a contemporary audience

---

[58] *Theophanes Con.*, 400; Skylitzes, *Synopsis*, 214.
[59] *Theophanes Con.*, 424; Skylitzes, *Synopsis*, 229.

at the end of the eleventh century. Yet, it should be stressed that Skylitzes is not consistent in his attempts to render the offices of earlier periods comprehensible to himself or to his audience. For example, on another occasion he simply copies without emendation the office of *tourmarches*, a position which was held by a senior commander within the provincial thematic armies in the tenth century but which had fallen into disuse by the later eleventh century.[60]

One area in which Skylitzes' many reshapings of the text of *Theophanes Continuatus* can be seen working in the round is in his treatment of military material. Examination of this material also demonstrates why Skylitzes' processes of homogenization and generalization can make the *Synopsis Historion* so difficult for subsequent historians to use. At the most basic level the military material, in particular the narrative surrounding long-term campaigns and more complicated battle sequences, is routinely the victim of brutal compression or simple omission, with the result that the reader is deprived of tactical details and a sense of overall strategy. For example, Skylitzes so dramatically abbreviates *Theophanes Continuatus*' account of Byzantine action against the eastern emirate of Melitene in the later 920s and early 930s, that he provides no indication of the annual campaigns that were waged by imperial armies against the Arabs, nor of the events of the final siege which eventually forced the city to capitulate in 934. Whereas *Theophanes Continuatus* describes the Byzantines burning the

---

[60] Skylitzes, *Synopsis*, 228; *Theophanes Con.*, 421; N. Oikonomides, *Les Listes de préséance byzantines des IXe et Xe siècles* (Paris, 1972), 341; idem, 'L'Évolution de l'organisation administrative', 148.

countryside of the emirate, their use of siege equipment, and
the general John Kourkouas' impatience at his initial failure
to take the city, Skylitzes summarizes the twists and turns of
the drama in a single bland phrase: 'having confined those
inside by siege he [Kourkouas] compelled them to look for
agreements.'[61]

A comparable example is Skylitzes' treatment of the aftermath of the invasion of the Rus in 941. In *Theophanes
Continuatus*' account the Rus who survived the first naval
battle are shown crossing over to Bithynia on the Asian side
of the Bosphoros. The Byzantine general Bardas Phokas is
then deputed to shadow the Rus as they forage in this area.
After forays with Phokas' advance party, and later the main
army led by John Kourkouas, the Rus decide to sail home,
driven out of the empire by a lack of supplies and the onset
of winter. Skylitzes' version of this passage of events is not
only shorter than that of *Theophanes Continuatus*, but takes
place in a geographical and temporal vacuum. In the *Synopsis Historion* no mention is made of the location of Bithynia. There is no reference to the orders given to Bardas
Phokas, so that when he meets the Rus he appears to do so
for no good strategic reason except coincidence. Skylitzes
does not include the reflection that the Rus had to take to
their ships again because of the time of year; instead their
decision has no context except a lack of supplies. However,
it is interesting to note that the passage of action that Skylitzes does retain in greater detail is the catalogue of colourful outrages the Rus inflicted on those Byzantines they

---

[61] Skylitzes, *Synopsis*, 224; *Theophanes Con.*, 415–16.

encountered. Here, it might be suggested that the entertainment of a later-eleventh century audience is more important to Skylitzes than a sense of strategy.[62]

Skylitzes' lack of tactical, topographical, and geographical awareness is visible elsewhere in his coverage of the reign of Romanos. For example, *Theophanes Continuatus* explains that the Byzantines were defeated by the Bulgarians at Pegai in the early 920s because the troops of Symeon suddenly appeared from above and were able to charge down upon their adversaries from a height. The key word in *Theophanes Continuatus'* text is ἄνωθεν (from above). However, this tactical advantage is completely ignored by Skylitzes who simply says that the Bulgarians suddenly appeared and attacked the Byzantines. The sense of height advantage enjoyed by the Bulgars at the beginning of their manoeuvre is entirely omitted by Skylitzes because he replaces the crucial term ἄνωθεν with the much less specific ἐκεῖθεν (from there).[63]

Equally frustrating for the modern historian who wishes to extract reliable military material from the *Synopsis Historion* is Skylitzes' tendency to compress the underlying narrative by applying homogenizing clichés. These have the effect of suppressing the uniqueness of the events in question, erasing specific detail, and transforming each military engagement into a string of impenetrable stereotypes. Thus, in Skylitzes' text the joining of two sides in battle is frequently represented by the phrase

[62] Skylitzes, *Synopsis*, 229; *Theophanes Con.*, 424–5. For further discussion of the entertainment qualities to Skylitzes' text see below 4.1.

[63] Skylitzes, *Synopsis*, 215; *Theophanes Con.*, 401.

συμπλοκῆς γενομένης.[64] One of the protagonists, particularly in a hand to hand engagement, is always likely to be mortally wounded, (πληγὴν) καιρίαν δὲ τυπείς.[65] A protagonist will conduct a siege with or without care, ἐπιμελῶς/ἀμελῶς ἐπολιόρκει.[66] The recipient/s of a siege always resist with spirit, εὐψύχως τὴν πολιορκίαν ἐδέξατο,[67] until the protagonist presses them too hard, στενοχωρήσας.[68] When they surrender it is usually because they are in need (τῃ ἐνδείᾳ) of essential supplies.[69] Camps are always established, στρατόπεδον πήξας.[70] Those encamped will often scour the surrounding countryside for booty or spoils, ἐπὶ διαρπαγὴν σκύλων.[71] The term ἐνέδρα is preferred when denoting an ambush.[72] Triumph in battle is often achieved easily, ῥᾳδίως.[73] Attacks are launched with unstoppable strength, ῥύμῃ ἀνυποστάτῳ.[74] Those who chose to rebel often take refuge at a well-fortified castle, φρούριον ἐρυμνὸν.[75]

This enumeration of clichés forces us to ask whether Skylitzes' military shorthand could be used to construct a model military engagement that was not based on any genuine evidence at all. Here, the picture is mixed. On the one hand, a comparison of Skylitzes' text with the narrative

---

[64] Skylitzes, *Synopsis*, 216.   [65] Ibid. 214.   [66] Ibid. 218.
[67] Ibid. 218.   [68] Ibid. 224.   [69] Ibid. 218.
[70] Ibid. 219.   [71] Ibid. 216.   [72] Ibid. 214.
[73] Ibid.
[74] Ibid. Skylitzes is not alone among Byzantine historians in his tendency to generalize accounts of warfare (J. Haldon, *Warfare, State and Society in the Byzantine World 565–1204* (London, 1999), 190–1); indeed the use of standardized phrases and vocabulary to describe military action is a widely recognized phenomenon in historiography of all periods (J. Keegan, *The Face of Battle* (London, 1976, repr. Pimlico Press, 1996), 36–54).
[75] Skylitzes, *Synopsis*, 226.

of *Theophanes Continuatus* for the reign of Romanos, suggests that there is usually a concrete event underpinning most of his homogenizing interpretations. Yet, it is also equally true that Skylitzes embroiders his underlying source with additional comments composed entirely of clichéd phrases. When Adrianople comes under Bulgarian attack in the early 920s, Skylitzes expatiates on both the military bravery and stupidity of the commander of the Byzantine garrison, the *patrikios* Leo Moroleo, by using his own repertoire of bland generalization. With no support from the underlying text he alleges that the Byzantine commander very courageously warded off Bulgarian assaults from the city's walls, but then opened the gates, attacked with irresistible strength, and was easily defeated. It should be noted that this passage contains two of the commonplace generalizations we identified in the paragraph above: ἀναπεταννὺς ἐπετίθετο σὺν ῥύμῃ ἀνυποστάτῳ καὶ ῥᾳδίως ἐτρέπετο.[76]

One final example from the historiography of the reign of Romanos Lekapenos will show how Skylitzes' substitution of a standardized cliché in the service of narrative compression leaves the reader entirely uninformed about the underlying details represented by that standardized phrase. In his encomium of the Kourkouas family *Theophanes Continuatus* devotes considerable praise to the achievements of John's brother Theophilos. Although *Theophanes Continuatus'* text is bestrewn with rhetorical hyperbole, including a comparison between Theophilos and King Solomon, it also conveys the key information that Theophilos was the *strategos* of

[76] Skylitzes, *Synopsis*, 218; *Theophanes Con.*, 404–5.

Chaldia and Mesopotamia, and that during his tenure of the former position he was involved in the capture of Theodosioupolis (modern-day Erzerum) on the north-eastern frontier.[77] Thus, although *Theophanes Continuatus* overdoses his text with rhetoric, he identifies Theophilos' geographical sphere of military operations with some accuracy. In contrast, although Skylitzes removes the hyperbolic allusion to Solomon, he also completely excises all the substantive detail of the general's career by articulating Theophilos' achievements in a standardized and anodyne cliché. He sums up Theophilos' achievements as *strategos* in Mesopotamia with the phrase: ταπεινώσας καὶ τελέως ἀφανίσας τοὺς ἐκ τῆς Ἄγαρ ('having humbled and finally destroyed the sons of Hagar')[78]

3.3 APPLICATIONS: SKYLITZES' TESTIMONY FOR THE REIGN OF BASIL II

3.3.1 General observations

This chapter offers a new approach to making sense of those parts of the *Synopsis Historion* where Skylitzes' underlying source materials fail to survive. The method developed thus far has been to examine *another* section of the *Synopsis* where the underlying text *does* survive in order to uncover the most characteristic features of Skylitzes' treatment of

---

[77] *Theophanes Con.*, 428; see below 6.3.1 for the fall of Theodosioupolis to Byzantine armies in 949.

[78] Skylitzes, *Synopsis*, 230.

source materials. The next stage in the process is to apply these conclusions to periods where Skylitzes' underlying sources do *not* survive, such as Basil's reign. And it is with this stage that the rest of this chapter is concerned. What follows surveys Skylitzes' testimony of Basil's reign in the light of the detailed textual analysis already conducted, highlighting some of the principal problems and implications of his editorial and authorial techniques. Some of the insights explored here are followed up further in subsequent chapters.

Let us begin with Skylitzes the copyist who follows a single root source closely, deviating only rarely from the underlying narrative structure, while sometimes retaining vocabulary and phraseology verbatim. While one cannot be certain that because Skylitzes used very few sources in his earlier tenth-century coverage he was just as parsimonious in his later tenth- and eleventh-century testimony, it remains a plausible working hypothesis that Skylitzes customarily worked from only a very small number of narratives throughout the compilation of his *Synopsis*, probably in the case of Basil's reign calling on only two or three texts. In Chapter 5, it will be argued that Skylitzes' principal source for his treatment of the first half of Basil's reign seems to have been a pro-Skleros encomium; that is to say, Skylitzes either used a Skleros encomium directly or he drew on an intermediate text which had already incorporated a panegyric of this sort. In Chapter 4 it will also be suggested that Skylitzes drew on another laudatory martial account in his testimony of Basil's Balkan wars; in this case a description of the military exploits of the general Eustathios

Daphnomeles.[79] However, I believe that it is difficult to move beyond this simple identification of encomiastic material which exists at a relatively indeterminate level in Skylitzes' text to making or supporting more definite and concrete claims about the precise sources that the author used in constructing his narrative of Basil's reign. For instance, I have seen nothing in Skylitzes' analysis of Basil's hegemony that points firmly in the direction of his use of a history by Theodore of Sebasteia, as is sometimes alleged.[80]

A further important implication of Skylitzes' close and generally accurate copying of his root texts is that when mistakes and vagueness over dates, figures, and places occur in the *Synopsis Historion*, responsibility may not always lie with Skylitzes himself but with those authors he excerpts. Thus, the figure of 15,000 Bulgarian troops blinded by Basil II in 1014 after the Battle of Kleidion is a statistic that some modern historians have treated sceptically, not least because the rest of Skylitzes' account of this campaign does not suggest that the Bulgarians suffered final defeat during this year. In fact, in the same section of his narrative which deals with the Byzantine victory at Kleidion, Skylitzes also mentions a Bulgarian victory over the Byzantine general Theophylact Botaneiates. Moreover, after Kleidion, Basil was forced to return to Byzantium rather than press on into Bulgarian-held territory. The fact that the war continued for another four years after Kleidion clearly indicates that Basil's Balkan adversaries retained considerable fighting

---

[79] See below 4.2.2.
[80] Theodore's connection to Skylitzes is discussed above in 2.4.

capacity.[81] In these circumstances historians are probably correct to question the scale of this figure of casualties at Kleidion.[82] However, the important point to note here is that any exaggeration could easily have been the responsibility of a historian writing long before Skylitzes rather than of Skylitzes himself. Such large figures of Bulgarian casualties were certainly already in circulation by the end of the third quarter of the eleventh century. Kekaumenos writing in the 1070s reported that Basil blinded around 14,000 Bulgarians.[83]

If we move on from Skylitzes the copyist to Skylitzes the active author, then we can detect with some confidence interesting instances of compression, omission, expansion, explanation, and homogenization within the historian's coverage of Basil's reign. As we noted earlier in the chapter, one of the most tell-tale signs of compression within Skylitzes' narrative are those occasions when his syntax becomes particularly strained. Such instances occur frequently within his

[81] Skylitzes, *Synopsis*, 348–51.

[82] Adontz, 'Samuel l'Arménien', 373–4; Whittow, *Making of Orthodox Byzantium*, 387–8.

[83] Kekaumenos, *Consilia et Narrationes*, 152; see also the discussion in Stephenson, *Byzantium's Balkan Frontier*, 71–2. One way in which such large, and probably exaggerated, figures entered the historiography of Byzantium may have been through the intermediate agency of speeches and/or letters. These literary productions, which Byzantine historians probably used as raw source material, often contained hyperbolic claims. For example, in a letter to the Bulgarian tsar Symeon written *c*.924–5 on behalf of Emperor Romanos Lekapenos, Theodore Daphnopates refers to an exceptionally large number of Bulgarians, 'up to 20,000', seeking asylum in the Byzantine empire from Symeon's wars (Theodore Daphnopates, *Correspondance*, eds. J. Darrouzès and G. Westerink (Paris, 1978), 58–9; for the close connections between Daphnopates and 10th-c. historical writings see also above 2.4).

coverage of Basil's reign, especially during passages of indirect speech. Thus, the very first chapter of his treatment of the reign concludes with a compressed sentence which summarizes the reactions of the *Parakoimomenos* Basil Lekapenos and the general Bardas Skleros to Skleros's appointment as *doux* of Mesopotamia, an office which Skylitzes tells us Skleros regarded as demotion.

This vexed Skleros very much so that he was not able to keep his grief to himself magnanimously, but he protested out loud and uttered reproaches that if in return for his bravery and trophies he received such rewards, being demoted he would become a not inconsiderable trial to the *Parakoimomenos*, who was saying that he [Skleros] [should be] pleased with the things that had been given [to him] and [should] not intrigue further if he did not intend retiring [to be] guardian of his private household, rather than being an army commander.[84]

Similar strains in syntax emerge during other passages of indirect speech such as Basil II's message conveyed to the Buyids of Baghdad by his envoy Nikephoros Ouranos in the early 980s and Skleros' negotiations with the Buyids which prefaced his release from captivity in Baghdad.[85]

As we saw in the analysis of the preface to the *Synopsis Historion*, one of Skylitzes' most vociferous authorial

---

[84] Τοῦτο τὸν Σκληρὸν σφόδρα ἐλύπησεν, ὡς μηδὲ παρ'ἑαυτῷ δυνηθῆαι συγκαλύψαι τὴν ἀνίαν μεγαλοψύχως,   ἀλλ'ἐπεγκαλέσαι καὶ προσονειδίσαι, εἰ ἀντὶ τῶν ὑπ'αὐτοῦ γενομένων ἀνδραγαθημάτων τε καὶ τροπαίων τοιαύτας ἀντιλαμβάνει τὰς ἀμοιβάς, ἐπὶ τὸ χεῖρον   προκόπτων, κἄν ὀλίγον ἤ οὐδὲν τῷ   παρακοιμωμένῳ   ἐμέλησεν, ἀγαπᾶν εἰπόντι τοῖς δεδομένοις, καὶ μὴ   ἐπέκεινα πολυπραγμονεῖν,   εἰ μή που μέλλει ἀντὶ ἄρχοντος οἰκουρὸς ἔσεσθαι τῆς ἰδίας οἰκίας (Skylitzes, *Synopsis*, 315).

[85] Skylitzes, *Synopsis*, 327–8, 333–4.

ambitions is the omission of encomium and other ornate and superfluous textual ornaments. In his treatment of *Theophanes Continuatus'* testimony of the reign of Romanos Lekapenos we saw him putting his prescriptions into action, removing ethnographical excursuses and asides which refer to legend. Skylitzes also appears to have taken equally draconian action in his treatment of Basil's reign. He includes very few decorative textual flourishes, bar the occasional pun, metaphor, or maxim, located primarily within his account of the Skleros and Phokas rebellions. For example, Skylitzes explains Bardas Skleros' need for finances at the start of his first revolt with what appears to be a standard rhetorical maxim: 'since he [Skleros] understood that the one who throws the dice needs much money, without which what is desired will come to nought, just as the rhetor says.'[86] He also refers to Stephen of Nikomedia, an envoy sent to the Skleros rebels by the imperial court, in terms that make a pun on the harshness inherent in the family name of Skleros. Stephen is described as a man acclaimed in wisdom and virtue, competent to 'soften with persuasion a harsh purpose of mind'.[87] Yet, as we noted in his treatment of the reign of Lekapenos, while Skylitzes may strip his text of high-flown excesses such as over-exuberant encomium, he nonetheless is still forced to articulate the viewpoint of the main protagonist of his underlying source. In the case of Lekapenos' reign, that main protagonist was the emperor. In this case, the voice that Skylitzes echoes is that of Bardas

---

[86] Skylitzes, *Synopsis*, 316.

[87] Ibid. 317: ἀνὴρ ἐλλόγιμος καὶ ἐπὶ σοφίᾳ καὶ ἀρετῇ διαβόητος καὶ πειθοῖ μαλάξαι ἱκανὸς γνώμην σκληρὰν καὶ ἀτίθασσον.

Skleros, an act of ventriloquism we shall explore further in Chapter 5.

Another conspicuous authorial intervention visible in Skylitzes' treatment of Romanos' reign, the addition of small link phrases that bring thematic unity to the overall narrative, is also ubiquitous throughout the author's coverage of Basil.[88] Such phrases include the very common form 'as we have said' which is inserted in the text as a convenient cross-referencing device. This phrase is particularly used as an *aide memoire* to remind the reader of earlier appearances within the narrative of some of the main actors in Basil's reign. When Skylitzes describes a battle fought in the Taurus mountains between the general Michael Bourtzes and imperial forces during the first Skleros revolt, he introduces Bourtzes by saying: 'Skleros...sent Michael Bourtzes, who had already defected to him, *as we have said*'.[89] Equally common are vague temporal phrases such as 'at that time', 'before these things happened', 'in the same year'. As we discussed in the previous chapter the structure of Skylitzes' text often takes the form of a concatenation of long narrative passages (so-called 'mega episodes') and short thematic chapters.[90] In these circumstances the appearance of general temporal phrases in Skylitzes' coverage of Basil's reign should not necessarily be read as a sign that the events he describes happened in an exact chronological order. Instead, such vague time-related phrases are probably better seen as

---

[88] See above 3.2.
[89] Skylitzes, *Synopsis*, 319–20.
[90] See above 2.4.

deliberate insertions designed to provide superficial links between a series of disparate thematic chapters. Apart from vague temporal terms Skylitzes also inserts other bland linking phrases that enable him to knit together the discrete sections of his narrative. When Skylitzes finishes his report on the first Skleros revolt (the first mega-episode of his narrative of Basil's reign) and moves on to Basil's early campaigns against the Bulgars (the next mega-episode),[91] he notes that Basil decided to move against Samuel 'when he had shaken off his concerns about Skleros'.[92] The Greek word for concern in this instance is *phrontis*. It is striking that a very similar phrase occurs somewhat later in the narrative when Skylitzes concludes his account of the Phokas rebellion and the second Skleros revolt (the third mega-episode of his account) and moves on to deal with Byzantium's relations with the outside world, above all with the Bulgarians (the final mega-episode of his Basil narrative). He achieves this transition between the major sections of his narrative in chapter 20, a characteristic telescoped summary passage which deals with warfare and diplomacy. Here Skylitzes asserts that: 'when he [Basil] had been released from the civil wars and concerns, the emperor considered how he would handle the situation with Samuel.' Once again he uses the term *phrontis* to render the idea of concern.[93]

It is likely that Skylitzes also resorts to inserting more substantial material into his narrative to bring a greater

[91] See above 2.4 for the importance of Lujbarskij's narratological analysis of Byzantine historiography.
[92] Skylitzes, *Synopsis*, 330.
[93] Ibid. 339.

sense of order. In his treatment of the reign of Romanos Lekapenos, Skylitzes often elaborates on the motives and explanations of events without justification from his underlying source. There are certain instances where such intervention without proof also occurs in his coverage of Basil's reign. In chapter 20, that short thematic chapter dealing with the empire's relations with its overseas neighbours which is located after the end of the coverage of the Phokas and Skleros rebellions, Skylitzes claims that an Arab attack on Antioch, at that point under the control of a *doux* called Damian, occurred because Basil was occupied with the domestic insurrection. Yet, at this point Skylitzes is in a nonsensical position. The Phokas and Skleros revolts ended in 989/90; whereas we know from a variety of eastern materials, including the testimonies of Yahya ibn Sa'id and Stephen of Taron, that the attacks on Antioch, to which Skylitzes refers, occurred much later, in the period 995–8.[94] This entirely erroneous linking of two events which happened nearly a decade apart seems to be the result of Skylitzes' efforts to impose a cause-and-effect coherence upon his text. In this case, of course, Skylitzes' false join can be detected because there are eastern texts against which his narrative can be checked. In those parts of his text, particularly within his Balkan coverage, where far fewer independent checks exist, it is much more difficult to assess the veracity of Skylitzes' explanations for events. The most the modern historian can do is be alert to the possibility that the incidence of motives and reasons within Skylitzes' text may often be his

---

[94] See below 6.3.3 for the chronology of Byzantine Antioch in Basil's reign.

own interpretation of events rather than an accurate transmission of material within his underlying source.

One of the other diagnostic elements to Skylitzes' treatment of the reign of Romanos Lekapenos is his tendency to omit minor individuals from the narrative, a method that often diminishes the nuance and complexity of the political history described by the original narrative. Obviously without Skylitzes' sources for Basil's reign it is impossible to appraise the extent or impact of this editorial trait. Nonetheless, while those actors that Skylitzes omits from his original sources will never be detected, it is on the other hand clear that he still *retains* a large number of personalities within his narrative. Indeed the strong prosopographical interest in leading aristocratic families he exhibits in his treatment of Lekapenos' reign persists once he moves into the later tenth and early eleventh centuries. This is a subject that will be explored in much greater detail in the next chapter. However, for the moment it is worth simply drawing attention to the problems inherent in Skylitzes' prosopographical approach. We need, above all, to remember the frequency with which Skylitzes was happy in his treatment of *Theophanes Continuatus* to draw genealogical connections between individuals and to bestow offices and titles on the basis of little supporting evidence from his underlying sources. This attitude to evidence, somewhat cavalier in modern terms, must warn us against using Skylitzes too slavishly or simplistically in the reconstruction of the careers of the most politically significant individuals and families during Basil's reign. Care must also be taken with another authorial intervention: Skylitzes' tendency to replace precise administrative terms with homogenized generalizations. This clearly makes his a treacherous text for any historian attempting to explore changes and continuities within the history of the medieval Byzantine bureaucracy, a point that we will return to repeatedly in Chapters 6 and 7.

The final problem associated with Skylitzes' authorial intervention is his idiosyncratic treatment of military matters: his extreme enthusiasm for cinematic moments of dramatic action; his equally conspicuous lack of interest in the geographical and strategic backdrop to long campaigns; his use of homogenizing terms in the service of embroidery or compression. These observations are of particular relevance to the reign of Basil since so much of Skylitzes' coverage of the later tenth and eleventh centuries is dedicated to military action. In Chapter 5 the ways in which Skylitzes uses his military lexicon in his description of the Skleros and Phokas revolts will be explored further. Here it will be argued that a homogenizing repertoire is used to amplify the heroism of particular individuals, in particular the general Bardas Phokas.[95] However, in the final section of this current chapter I wish to discuss briefly how Skylitzes' idiosyncratic approach to military matters affects his treatment of Basil's wars in the Balkans.

3.3.2   Skylitzes and Basil II's Balkan wars

Skylitzes' treatment of Basil's wars in Bulgaria can be divided into two main categories of narrative: isolated references to

[95] See below 5.2.3.

raids and sieges, and more detailed discussions of single battles. Both types of narrative, however, display all the hallmarks of Skylitzes' approach to military material. Let us look first at raids and sieges, both of which tend to be described within Skylitzes' highly characteristic summary chapters. The very fact that episodes of this nature appear in such abbreviated chapters means that they are necessarily short and devoid of geographical or strategic context, and expressed almost entirely through Skylitzes' standardized military vocabulary. In the highly telescoped chapter about the rise of the Kometopouloi (chapter 11) that forms the preface to the more detailed narrative of Basil's disastrous Bulgarian campaign of 986, Samuel's military exploits are described with typical economy: 'being without fear, [Samuel] overran the entire West, not only Thrace and Macedonia and the environs of Thessalonika, but also Thessaly, Hellas, and the Peloponnese. And he besieged many fortified sites, of which the main one was Larissa.'[96]

It is noteworthy that a summary of raids orchestrated by Samuel of almost identical content is located shortly before Skylitzes' account of the Bulgarians' defeat at the hands of Nikephoros Ouranos at the River Spercheios in 997. Ouranos learned that, '[Samuel] ... was invading Thessaly and Boetia and Attica and even into the Peloponnese via the

---

[96] ἀδείας τυχὼν κατέδραμε πᾶσαν τὴν ἑσπέραν, οὐ μόνον θράκην καὶ Μακεδονίαν καὶ τὰ τῇ Θεσσαλονίκῃ πρόσχωρα, ἀλλὰ καὶ θετταλίαν καὶ Ἑλλάδα καὶ Πελοπόννησον. καὶ πολλὰ φρούρια παρεστήσατο, ὧν ἦν τὸ κορυφαῖον ἡ Λάρισσα (Skylitzes, *Synopsis*, 330).

isthmus of Corinth, and was laying waste to everything and taking booty.'[97]

Equally vague and repetitive are many accounts of those sieges and invasions conducted by Byzantine forces. Take, for example, a brief, undated six-line chapter dedicated to one of Basil's sieges in Bulgaria (chapter 31). This chapter is located shortly before the account of the destruction of the Holy Sepulchre by the Fatimids of Egypt in 1009, although given Skylitzes' thematic approach to history, it may of course refer to another period entirely: 'Having crossed from there [where?], the emperor went to Pernikos, whose guard was Krakras, an excellent man in matters of warfare. After spending a reasonable amount of time there and losing rather a considerable number of men in the siege, Basil went back to Philippoupolis, since he knew that the defence works were too good for a siege, and that Krakras was not being softened up by flatteries or other promises and embassies.'[98]

Yet, in contrast to the brutal economy applied to the strategy, geography, and economy of so many of the raids and sieges enumerated by Skylitzes, rather more substantial attention is directed towards the heroic exploits of individual protagonists. A good example is the story of the demise

---

[97] Θετταλίαν τε καὶ Βοιωτίαν καὶ Ἀττικὴνεἰσβαλόντα τε καὶ ἐν Πελοποννήσῳ διὰ τοῦ ἐν Κορίνθῳ ἰσθμοῦ, καὶ πάντα ταῦτα   δῃοῦντα καὶ ληϊζόμενον (Skylitzes, *Synopsis*, 341).

[98] Ἐκεῖθεν ὁ βασιλεὺς διαβὰς ἔρχεται πρὸς Πέρνικον, οὗ φύλαξ ἦν ὁ Κρακρᾶς, ἀνὴρ ἄριστος τὰ πολεμικά. ἐν ᾧ χρόνον οὐκ ὀλίγον διατρίψας καὶ λαὸν οὐκ ὀλίγον ἐν τῇ πολιορκίᾳ ἀποβαλών, ὡς ἔγνω κρεῖττον ὑπάρχον πολιορκίας τὸ ἔρυμα, καὶ οὐδ᾽ ὁ Κρακρᾶς θωπείαις ἢ ἄλλαις ὑποσχέσεσιν ἐμαλάσσετο καὶ ἐπαγγελίαις, μετέβη πρὸς Φιλιππούπολιν (Skylitzes, *Synopsis*, 347).

of the Taronites family, a narrative that forms a preface to the account of the arrival of Basil's senior general and close associate Nikephoros Ouranos in the Balkans and his overwhelming victory at the Battle of the River Spercheios (chapter 23). This prefatory narrative about the Taronites is concerned with an engagement in which a party of raiding Bulgarians ambushed Ashot Taronites and killed his father Gregory, the *doux* of Thessalonika. Here it is striking that while Skylitzes uses his generalized and bland military terminology to provide an account devoid of strategic context, he employs an equally homogenized martial vocabulary to praise the heroic qualities of the senior Byzantine commander:

Samuel had set out on campaign against Thessalonika, setting aside one group (of troops) into traps and ambushes, while sending out a few other forces on a raid as far as Thessalonika itself. When the *doux* Gregory learned of this attack, he sent his own son Asotios to observe and inspect the force and to bring him back intelligence, while he himself followed behind. He [Asotios] left, engaged with the advance party and was victorious; but he was then intercepted unawares in the middle of the ambushes. When Gregory learned this, he went to help his son as quickly as possible, eager to rescue him from being captured. But he was also surrounded by Bulgarians and was killed having struggled nobly and heroically.[99]

---

[99] Τοῦ δὲ Σαμουὴλ ἐκστρατεύσαντος κατὰ θεσσαλονίκης καὶ τὸ μὲν ἄλλο πλῆθος εἰς λόχους καὶ ἐνέδρας διαμερίσαντος, ὀλίγους δέ τινας εἰς ἐκδρομὴν ἄχρι θεσσαλονίκης αὐτῆς πεπομφότος, ἐπιγνοὺς τὴν ἔφοδον ὁ δοὺξ Γρηγόρι-ος τὸν μὲν οἰκεῖον υἱὸν Ἀσώτιον ἔπεμψεν ἰδεῖν καὶ κατασκοπῆσαι τὸ πλῆθος καὶ αὐτῷ γνῶσιν δοῦναι, αὐτὸς δὲ ὄπισθεν εἴπετο. ὁ δὲ ἐξελθὼν καὶ τοῖς προ-

Whereas summary passages of this nature are customarily denuded of context, rather more geographical and strategic detail is retained in those somewhat longer single-episode narratives that are sprinkled throughout Skylitzes' treatment of the reign. We are provided with several geographical indicators about Basil's invasion routes into Bulgaria in 986 in chapter 12: that he journeyed via the Rhodope Mountains beside the River Euros, negotiating the mountain passes, before camping at a place called Stoponion to prepare for the siege of Triaditza (also known as Sardica or Sofia). The route that Ouranos followed in 997 to meet Samuel on the banks of the River Spercheios is also clearly articulated. Attention is also paid to the heavy rainfall on the night before the battle, a deluge which persuaded Samuel that he could camp safely on the other side of the river without taking precautions against a Byzantine attack.[100] A similarly detailed description is provided of the topography of the Battle of Kleidion in 1014; reference is made to Samuel's blockade of the passes of Kiaba Longos and Kleidion, and to the location of Mount Balasitzes, the mountain around which the Byzantine commander Nikephoros Xiphias led a party of troops in order to attack Samuel's defences from the back.[101]

δρόμοις συμπλακεὶς καὶ τρεψάμενος ἔλαθεν εἰς μέσους τοὺς λόχους περιληφθείς. τοῦτο ὡς ὁ Γρηγόριος ἔμαθεν, ἐβοήθει διὰ ταχέων τὸν παῖδα τῆς αἰχμαλωσίας γλιχόμενος ἐκλυτρώσασθαι. ἀλλὰ καὶ αὐτὸς κυκλωθεὶς ὑπὸ τῶν Βουλγάρων καὶ γενναίως καὶ ἡροϊκῶς ἀγωνισάμενος ἔπεσεν (Skylitzes, *Synopsis*, 341).

[100] Skylitzes, *Synopsis*, 330–1.
[101] Ibid. 348–50.

Nonetheless, even though Skylitzes retains a little more topographical and strategic context in these rather longer episodes, it is striking that the descriptions of actual armed engagements in these narratives are still expressed almost entirely with Skylitzes' armoury of stock military phrases. When Byzantine forces began to withdraw from the siege of Sardica in 986, Samuel, 'supposing that the disorderly withdrawal was flight, since it seemed so, attacked in great numbers with a war cry and a shout and confused the Romans and compelled them to fly; and he seized the camp and gained control of all their equipment and of the imperial tent itself and of the imperial regalia. The emperor having scarcely got through the passes arrived safe at Philippoupolis.'[102]

The fighting surrounding Ouranos' victory at the River Spercheios in 997 is described in equally bland terms: 'After gathering his army during the night [Ouranos] crossed the river and attacked those around Samuel while they were sleeping without having taken precautions. And they killed the greater number, and when no one had dared to resist, Samuel himself and his son Romanos were struck with heavy blows. . . .'[103]

---

[102] ὁ δὲ Σαμουὴλ τὴν ἀσύντακτον ἀναχώρησιν φυγήν, ὡς εἰκός, εἶναι ὑποτοπάσας, ἐπιπεσὼν ἀθρόως μετ' ἀλαλαγμοῦ καὶ βοῆς τούς τε Ῥωμαίους κατέπληξε καὶ φυγεῖν ἠνάγκασε, καὶ τὸ στρατόπεδον κατέσχε, καὶ τῆς ἀποσκευῆς ἁπάσας ἐγένετο κύριος καὶ αὐτῆς τῆς βασιλικῆς σκηνῆς καὶ τῶν βασιλικῶν παρασήμων. μόλις δέ ὁ βασιλεὺς τὰ στενὰ διελθὼν εἰς Φιλιππούπολιν διασῴζεται (Skylitzes, *Synopsis*, 331).

[103] ἀγείρας νυκτὸς τὸν στρατὸν περαιοῦται τὸν ποταμὸν καὶ τοῖς περὶ τὸν Σαμουὴλ ἀμερίμνως καθεύδουσιν ἐπιτίθεται. καὶ σφάζονται μὲν ἀριθμοῦ κρείττους, μηδενὸς πρὸς ἀλκὴν ἀπιδεῖν τολμήσαντος, ἐπλήγη δὲ καὶ αὐτὸς ὁ Σαμουὴλ καὶ ὁ τούτου υἱὸς Ῥωμανὸς βαθείαις πληγαῖς (Skylitzes, *Synopsis*, 342).

Even the great Battle of Kleidion is reduced to a chain of
Skylitzes' martial and heroic commonplaces from the moment when Xiphias arrived to attack the Bulgarian rear:
'Suddenly from above with a war cry and a din, he [Xiphias]
appeared at the back of the Bulgarians. They having been
thrown into disarray by the surprise turned to flight. And
the emperor having broken through the blockade pursued
them. And so many fell, and many more were captured and
Samuel was scarcely able to escape the danger while his own
son met the attackers with energy bravely....'[104]

While these rather anodyne battle narratives confirm
what we observed in his treatment of military matters in
the reign of Romanos Lekapenos, that Skylitzes has little real
interest in the precise detail of martial engagement, nonetheless they also display another authorial preference visible
in Skylites' coverage of Lekapenos' reign: the retention of the
most entertaining, shocking, or edifying stories. In his account of the Battle of the River Spercheios Skylitzes dwells
on the fact that Samuel and his son Romanos were only able
to escape capture by lying as if dead among the corpses after
the battle was over.[105] Meanwhile, the blinding of the 15,000
Bulgarian troops and the heart attack that this outrage
provoked in Samuel is the most shocking and memorable
element of the Kleidion narrative.[106]

---

[104] ἄνωθεν ἐξαίφνης μετ'ἀλαλαγμοῦ καὶ δούπου κατὰ νώτου γίνεται τῶν
Βουλγάρων. οἱ δὲ τῷ ἀπροσδοκήτῳ καταπλαγέντες τρέπονται πρὸς φυγήν.
καὶ ὁ βασιλεὺς μονωθὲν διαρρήξας τὸ τεῖχος ἐδίωκεν. ἔπεσον οὖν πολλοί,
καὶ πολλῷ πλείους ἑάλωσαν, μόλις τοῦ Σαμουὴλ διαφυγεῖν δυνηθέντος τὸν
κίνδυνον συνεργίᾳ τοῦ ἰδίου υἱοῦ γενναίως τοὺς ἐπιόντας ὑποδεξαμένου
(Skylitzes, *Synopsis*, 349).

[105] Skylitzes, *Synopsis*, 342.   [106] Ibid. 349.

It is also possible that other, rather briefer, narratives retain a place within Skylitzes' Balkan material because of their entertaining curiosity value. Shortly before Basil's 986 Bulgarian invasion, Skylitzes refers to the death of Boris, the eldest son of the previous tsar, Peter, shot by a border guard from his own side as he fled from captivity in Constantinople back to Bulgaria. The reason for this friendly-fire accident was that Boris was dressed like a Byzantine. This incident is undated and forms part of the complex mélange of materials located in a telescoped chapter (chapter 11) that introduces the theme of Bulgaria into Skylitzes' account of Basil's reign, and acts as the introduction to the first principal narrative of the Balkan coverage, Basil's invasion and siege of Sardica (Triaditza) in 986.[107] This telescoped introductory chapter also deals with the dynastic history of the Bulgarian tsars and the rise of the Kometopouloi. The key importance of the death-of-Boris incident as far as the broader narrative is concerned is that it signals the death of the legitimate tsar of the Bulgarians. The exact details of the friendly-fire episode, particularly in such a highly compressed piece of prose, are to some extent superfluous. The best explanation for their preservation by Skylitzes is that they were unusual and memorable.

A similar explanation may lie behind the retention of a minor personality within Skylitzes' account of the negotiations between Basil and various Bulgarian princes after the death of Samuel in 1014. On three occasions reference is made to a Bulgarian envoy: a certain Roman (i.e. a

---

[107] Ibid. 328–9.

Byzantine) with a severed hand. On the first occasion the envoy appears promising the submission to Basil of Samuel's son Gabriel Romanos; at his second appearance he is accompanied by a representative of Samuel's nephew, John Vladislav, who informs the emperor that Gabriel has been killed by John Vladislav; on the third occasion the envoy appears promising that John Vladislav will subjugate himself to the emperor.[108] I would suggest that the repeated manifestations of the crippled envoy are retained by Skylitzes because they enhance the palpable sense of gloom, suspicion, and deception that characterized relations between Basil and the leaders of the Bulgars in the post-Samuel era. Certainly these references form the prelude to the growth of even greater hostility and distrust between Byzantines and Bulgarians within Skylitzes' narrative. For Skylitzes claims that Basil, 'knew that John had written the letters with trickery and subtle intelligence and was contriving the opposite of what he promised'. Given Skylitzes' penchant for invented motives, this allegation could, of course, be fictional. Less fictional was the severity of Basil's martial reply to the news about the accession of John Vladislav. He invaded Bulgaria, plundered the region around Pelagonia in western Macedonia, and blinded all his Bulgarian prisoners.[109]

---

[108] Skylitzes, *Synopsis*, 352–3.   [109] Ibid. 353.

4

Basil II and the Testimony of John Skylitzes: Contexts

The previous chapter explored the methods John Skylitzes employed in writing his history. It highlighted the extent to which Skylitzes intervened in his text to reshape his presentation of the past; it also considered how these interventions affect our reading of the reign of Basil II. This chapter continues the analysis of Skylitzes' presentation of the Byzantine past by widening the discussion to consider the broader literary, social, and political contexts within which the author was working. Discussion will focus on how the author who emerges from the close textual analysis of the last chapter can be related to the eleventh-century Constantinopolitan civil servant whose biography was discussed in Chapter 2.[1] This chapter will demonstrate how the relationship between Skylitzes' text and his career explains several key characteristics of the author's treatment of Basil II, above all his conspicuous interest in the Byzantine aristocracy and his fascination with the Balkans.

[1] See above 2.3.

4.1 LITERARY AND SOCIAL CONTEXTS

By tradition the system of literary classification proposed by Krumbacher in the latter part of the nineteenth century has dominated how scholars have approached Byzantine historical writers. In accordance with Krumbacher's scheme long, derivative historical compilations such as that written by Skylitzes have tended to be positioned within the genre of low-to middlebrow chronicle rather than highbrow history. Differences between these two genres of historical writing have often been sharply and systematically drawn. High-style histories are said to be typified by eyewitness testimony, classical allusions, ethnographical and geographical excurses, and an elevated level of language that consciously imitates the Attic style of the writers of the Second Sophistic of the second century AD. In contrast a different array of characteristics are attributed to chronicles: a great variety of written sources, more extensive chronological coverage, a simplified level of Greek, an absence of classicizing tags, and a concentration on sensational events including natural disasters and portents. As far as authors and audiences are concerned, the literary characteristics of these two genres imply that high-style histories were read and produced by a highly educated coterie of mandarin civil servants, who worked in the higher echelons of the imperial administration in Constantinople, while the authors and audiences of chronicles were located far from the literary milieu of the imperial court, often in monasteries.[2]

---

[2] Krumbacher, *Geschichte der byzantinischen Literatur*, 226–30, 319–23.

While this schematic and genre-driven approach to Byzantine historical writing continues to attract considerable support,[3] it is important to note that there have been dissenting voices. More than thirty-five years ago Hans-Georg Beck pointed out that very few chronicles were produced either by or for monks. Instead chroniclers, or more accurately synoptic historians, were active in secular and metropolitan milieus, working in the imperial court in Constantinople within the higher echelons of state administration, precisely the same professional world inhabited by many high-style historians.[4] With this observation Beck undermined the principle that lowbrow chronicles and high-style histories were composed in mutually exclusive literary environments, and therefore that audiences and authors of such literature should be sharply distinguished. Meanwhile, other critics of the Krumbacher model have observed that precise distinctions between the content and style of chronicle and history writing can rarely be drawn in practice. Alexander Každan, a consistent and vociferous critic of over-schematic approaches to Byzantine culture,

---

[3] Hunger, *Hochsprachliche profane Literatur*, i. 243–78; R. Browning, 'Byzantine Literature', *DMA*, ii. 511–17; C. A. Mango, *Empire of the New Rome* (London, 1980), 8–9, and also chs. 10 and 13. For Cyril Mango the differences between chronicle and high-style history are part of a more general distinction between the thought world of the 'average' Byzantine and that of a small clique of intellectuals who 'exerted no appreciable influence on the thinking of the public at large'. A recent formulation of the traditional distinction between chronicle and history is that made by A. Karpozelos, *Βυζαντινοὶ ἱστορικαὶ καὶ χρονογράφοι* (Athens, 1997).

[4] H.-G. Beck, 'Zur byzantinischen "Mönchskronik"', in *Speculum Historiale: Geschichte im Spiegel von Geschichtsschreibung und Geschichtsdeutung (Festschrift K. Adler)* (Freiburg and Munich, 1965), 188–97.

frequently argued that Byzantine literature was typified more by fluidity and innovation than by conservatism, inertia, and the paralysis of immutable genre.[5] Within historiography itself he noted parallels in material, presentation, and interpretation between higher and lower style productions. Každan pointed out that eleventh- and twelfth-century high-style historians such as Michael Attaleiates and Niketas Choniates were as fond of including notices about omens and natural phenomena in their texts as contemporary synoptic historians. In contrast, the narratives of many synoptic historians contain elements more usually associated with high-style productions.[6]

Initial examination of Skylitzes' biography and text suggests that here too the model proposed by Krumbacher is deficient. Rather than belonging to a literary and social world that was in every way distinct from that of high-style historians, Skylitzes composed his *Synopsis* in the same social and cultural milieu as high-style productions.

[5] A. P. Každan, 'Der Mensch in der byzantinischen Literaturgeschichte', *JÖB 29* (1979), 1–21; idem, 'Approaches to the History of Byzantine Civilisation from Krause to Beck and Mango', in A. P. Každan and S. Franklin (eds.), *Studies on Byzantine Literature of the Eleventh and Twelfth Centuries* (1984), 11–22.

[6] Každan, 'Der Mensch', 5. In rather earlier Byzantine historical writings close parallels have been detected between the conceptual worlds of 6th-c. classicizing historians such as Prokopios of Kaisareia and Agathias and their contemporary, the synoptic historian John Malalas of Antioch (R. Scott, 'Malalas and his Contemporaries', in E. Jeffreys *et al.* (eds.), *Studies in John Malalas* (Sydney, 1990), 67–85; A. Cameron, *Procopius and the Sixth Century* (London and New York, 1996), 24–32). For further criticism of adopting an overly schematic approach to Byzantine historiography, see the review article by E. Jeffreys of Karpozelos, Βυζαντινοὶ ἱστορικαὶ καὶ χρονογράφοι in *BZ 92* (1999), 132–3.

As we saw in Chapter 2 of this volume John Skylitzes was *eparch* of Constantinople in the later eleventh century; he also held the senior judicial position of *megas droungarios* of the *Bigla*.[7] The same observation could be made of other synoptic historians writing in the century after Skylitzes. John Zonaras served Emperor Alexios Komnenos (1081–1118) in the same position of *megas droungarios* of the *Bigla* and also as *protoasekretis*.[8] Although Zonaras dedicated himself to writing history once his career was at an end and he had retreated into a monastery, other synoptic historians completed their compositions while still active in Constantinople and in the employ of the emperor. Constantine Manasses, who served Emperor Manuel Komnenos (1143–80) as a diplomat, was commissioned to compile a synoptic history in verse by the emperor's sister-in-law Eirene before she died in 1153, and long before he left court to take up his position as metropolitan bishop of Naupaktos.[9] There is no reason to suppose that he did not work on his synopsis, either composing it or gathering materials, while he was active in government service.

Furthermore, recent research into the literary world of the later eleventh and twelfth centuries has made it clear that whenever authors were at work in a shared physical and professional environment considerable overlap between literary genres occurred. The evidence is strongest from the mid-twelfth century where several writers, who can be identified with service within the imperial court or with

---

[7] See above 2.3.
[8] Hunger, *Hochsprachliche profane Literatur*, i. 416.
[9] Ibid. 419.

members of the imperial family, participated in a ground-swell of contemporary literary activity, which was characterized by considerable innovation and cross-fertilization of language levels and genres.[10] Many demonstrated a willingness to experiment with different registers of language, introducing elements of vernacular grammar and vocabulary into high-level productions. Many, including several historians, also moved between genres. Michael Glykas, a secretary at the court of Manuel Komnenos, was a poet, the writer of theological treatises, and a synoptic historian. Constantine Manasses composed panegyric, *ekphrasis*, a verse romance *Aristandros and Kallithea*, and a verse account of his diplomatic mission to Palestine in 1160, as well as his verse synoptic history.[11]

Although there has been somewhat less scholarly interest in literary production in the later eleventh and early twelfth centuries, it is worth noting that here too innovation and cross-fertilization has been identified, particularly in works associated with the imperial court, the higher ranks of the civil service, and Constantinople. Scholars have noted the emergence in this period of a new interest in the telling of

[10] See e.g. R. Browning, 'Byzantine Scholarship', *PP*, 28 (1964), 13–17; A. P. Každan and A. Wharton-Epstein (eds.), *Change in Byzantine Culture in the Eleventh and Twelfth Centuries* (Berkeley, 1985), 83–6. Apart from historians, other writers who moved between genres and switched registers included Theodore and Manganeios Prodromos, the anonymous author of *Spaneas*, and the authors of the 12th-c. novels (R. Beaton, *The Medieval Greek Romance*, 2nd edn. (London, 1996), 9–15, 91–100).

[11] The literary achievement and career of Glykas are summarized in: Hunger, *Hochsprachliche profane Literatur*, i. 422–6; for Manasses see idem, 419–21; *ODB*, ii, 1280; and Jeffreys, 'The Attitudes of Byzantine Chroniclers', 202–15.

vivid stories. Although writers in locations outside Constantinople, such as Kekaumenos, who probably wrote in the 1070s, made use of entertaining narratives in their literary productions, this new interest was most conspicuous among those authors who moved in the highest social and political circles in the capital. A fondness for elaborate anecdotes, particularly those describing military endeavour, has been noted among high-style historians, such as Nikephoros Bryennios, and synoptic historians, such as Skylitzes.[12] It has even been argued that this greater interest in martial narrative was inspired during the latter years of the eleventh century by the arrival in Constantinople of provincial aristocrats fleeing the contemporary Turkish invasions of Asia Minor. Roderick Beaton has suggested that the epic/romance *Digenes Akrites* was composed in Constantinople in this period, as emigrés from central Anatolia sought to make a permanent written record of much older oral poems describing the daring-do of life on the ninth- and tenth-century Arab–Byzantine frontier.[13] Although other scholars, most notably Elizabeth Jeffreys and Paul Magdalino, believe that the Digenes epic was written down in Constantinople during the mid- rather than the early twelfth century, the

---

[12] Mullett, *Theophylact of Ochrid*, 69–78; Roueché, 'Byzantine Writers and Readers', 123–32; J. D. Howard-Johnston, 'Anna Komnene and the *Alexiad*', in M. Mullett and D. Smythe (eds.), *Alexios I Komnenos* (Belfast, 1996), 260–302. It should, however, be noted that this enthusiasm for military anecdotes was not an entirely new phenomenon. There are stories about heroic exploits in texts that predate the later 11th c., such as *Theophanes Continuatus* and the history of Leo the Deacon.

[13] R. Beaton, 'Cappadocians at Court: Digenes and Timarion', in M. Mullett and D. Smythe (eds.), *Alexios I Komnenos* (Belfast, 1996), 329–38.

importance of the arrival of aristocratic refugees from central Anatolia for developments within Byzantine literature throughout the Komnenian period has been widely accepted.[14]

Nonetheless, there is a potential objection to the view that synoptic and high-style histories must necessarily be seen as part of the same cultural phenomenon simply because they were produced by historians working within the same physical and temporal environment. This objection relates to the fact that contemporary Byzantine writers themselves indicate a quite explicit generic difference between these two literary productions. As early as the ninth century, George the Monk, in the preface to his synoptic history, criticized the writers of secular history for their ostentation, loquacity, incomprehensibility, and overweening desire for applause.[15] The prefaces to eleventh- and twelfth-century synoptic histories contain echoes of George's criticism. Despite his considerable classical erudition and his use of the Roman historian Dio Cassius as a source for his coverage of the Roman Republic, the mid-twelfth-century synoptic historian John Zonaras chastised historians who indulged in detailed descriptions of military matters, lengthy and irrelevant digressions, and improbable dialogues. Here Zonaras appears not only to have been criticizing ancient historians,

---

[14] Digenes Akrites: *Digenis Akritis: The Grottaferrata and Escorial Versions*, ed. E. Jeffreys (Cambridge, 1998), pp. xvii, lvi–lvii; P. Magdalino, '*Digenes Akrites* and Byzantine Literature: the Twelfth-Century Background to the Grottaferrata Version', in R. Beaton and D. Ricks (eds.), *Digenes Akrites: New Approaches to Byzantine Heroic Poetry* (London, 1993), 1–14.

[15] George the Monk: *Georgius Monachus Chronicon*, ed. C. de Boor (and P. Wirth), 2 vols. (Stuttgart, 1904, repr. 1978), i. 1–2.

but also the classicizing historians of more recent generations such as Anna Komnene and Nikephoros Bryennios. In contrast, Zonaras indicates that his own work belongs outside this tradition when he says that it is his ambition to produce a synopsis which will present a short but clear view of important past events.[16] Even Constantine Manasses mirrors the sentiments of contemporary twelfth-century synoptic historians when he promises his patroness Eirene, 'a clear and comprehensible treatise ... giving plain teaching in history', which will remedy the contradictory accounts of the writers of histories and chronographies.[17] However, it is Skylitzes himself who seems to provide the clearest distinction between synopsis and high-style history. As we saw in the previous chapter, Skylitzes uses the preface to his own *Synopsis Historion* to draw an explicit contrast between his short and readable continuation of George the *Synkellos* and Theophanes and the long *psogos-* and encomium-riddled appraisals of recent generations of historians.[18]

Nonetheless, while it is true that eleventh- and twelfth-century synoptic historians stress their differences from those writing in a higher style, it could be argued that they protest too much. In many cases they exaggerate the

[16] Zonaras, *Annales*, 4–6. For a close reading of Zonaras' preface see Grigoriadis, 'The Prooimion of Zonaras' Chronicle', 340–4. Hunger, *Hochsprachliche profane Literatur*, i. 417, sees Zonaras specifically criticizing Anna Komnene and Nikephoros Bryennios. For Zonaras' good knowledge of classical sources see M. di Maio, 'Smoke in the Wind: Zonaras' use of Philostorgius, Zosimos, John of Antioch and John of Rhodes in his Narrative of the Neo-Flavian Emperors', *B* 48 (1988), 230–55.

[17] Manasses, *Breviarum Chronicum*, 5.

[18] Skylitzes, *Synopsis*, 3–4; see above 3.1.

differences in form and content between their writings and those of their highbrow contemporaries, while failing to highlight the conspicuous similarities between the two genres. Indeed, as Iordanis Grigoriadis has pointed out, striking similarities abound in the ways in which historians of all hues in the eleventh and twelfth centuries view their productions. From the *Chronographia* of Michael Psellos onwards, historians denounce the use of excessive rhetoric, express their fear of indulging in excessive praise or slander, claim to be looking for a middle way of relating their narrative, declare themselves unworthy of their allotted task, and laud the need for a plain and clear account, while at the same time indulging in elaborate word play, rare vocabulary, and rhetorical excess.[19] John Zonaras, for example, couches his reasons for writing in the same terms as the high-style historian Michael Psellos. Both explain that it is only the encouragement of friends that has persuaded them to take up their pens.[20] Meanwhile, Zonaras' negative portrayal of Alexios Komnenos is a blatant *psogos* for which he, rather than his source, appears responsible.[21] Moreover, while sharing characteristics with those very high-style historians whom they claim to despise, many synoptic writers of the eleventh and twelfth century actually deviate greatly from the synoptic models they claim to admire and follow. They often ignore the annalistic chronological structure of their synoptic predecessors such as Theophanes, employ

---

[19] Grigoriadis, 'The Prooimion of Zonaras' Chronicle', 327–44.

[20] Zonaras, *Annales*, 4; Psellos, *Cronografia*, i. 266–9; Grigoriadis, 'The Prooimion of Zonaras' Chronicle', 332, 340.

[21] Zonaras, *Epitomae*, 726–68.

more elevated language, and take a less providential view of history.[22]

Yet, it is likely that what seems to us like generic inconsistency and confusion within late eleventh- and twelfth-century historiography may not have been regarded in the same light by contemporaries. It is not that different genres did not exist in Byzantium; as Margaret Mullett has pointed out, genre is of fundamental importance to all forms of written culture in the sense that it is one of many ways in which writers can communicate their intentions and interests to their readers. The more important point, however, is that genre does not stand still but instead constantly mutates and adapts to meet changes in social and literary circumstance.[23] In the case of the writing of history in Byzantium in the later eleventh and twelfth centuries, the composition of synoptic history appears to have become a genre of court literature expressed in a middling to high-style register of Greek with its own particular rhetoric. If court officials in this period wanted to write histories with a longer compass than their own lifetime, they adopted the chronicle form at a superficial level. In order to indicate the synoptic nature of the production to potential audiences, it was important that the preface to the composition should contain a statement that the author intended to produce a

---

[22] Even Krumbacher accepted that Zonaras was skilled in his appreciation and use of Attic Greek (*Geschichte der byzantinischen Literatur*, i. 370–4). Mango and Scott (*Chronicle of Theophanes*, p. lii) reflect on the failure of the synoptic successors of Theophanes to adopt his strictly annalistic structure. Flusin and Cheynet, *Jean Skylitzès*, p. viii, note the degree to which Skylitzes abandons the annalistic structure of his stated models.

[23] M. Mullett, 'The Madness of Genre', *DOP* 46 (1992), 233–43.

short, unbiased, and easily understandable account. But
thereafter, considerable innovation and overlap with the
methods and materials of higher style histories were
possible.[24]

And, indeed, it is in the sense of drawing a real and valid
distinction between two historical genres, which, nevertheless, enjoyed a mutual and symbiotic relationship, that Skylitzes' own preface is best read. Although Skylitzes criticizes
the high-style historians of the past two centuries, such as
Joseph Genesios, Theodore Daphnopates, and Theodore of
Sebasteia, on the grounds of their use of *psogos*, encomium,
and limited chronological coverage, he makes it clear that
his own synopsis will be crafted from precisely this genre of
history writing.[25] Furthermore, in his identification of his
target audience, Skylitzes suggests that his literary production should be regarded not as an antidote to high-style
historical literature, but rather as a guide. Having stated
his ambition to produce a synoptic account in digestible
prose, he continues: 'so that those who approach the books
of the said historians... may carry and visit this book
as a travelling companion and... [so that] others who
have not yet happened upon these histories may have this
epitome as a guide.'[26] In Skylitzes' eyes synopsis and high-
style histories were complementary rather than mutually

---

[24] See also C. Holmes, 'The Rhetorical Structures of John Skylitzes' *Synopsis Historion*', in E. Jeffreys (ed.), *Rhetoric in Byzantium* (Aldershot, 2003),
187–99.

[25] Skylitzes, *Synopsis*, 3–4; Flusin and Cheynet, *Jean Skylitzès*, p. vii; see
also above 3.1.

[26] Skylitzes, *Synopsis*, 4; for a full translation see Appendix B.

exclusive productions.[27] And, in fact, this principle that a strong symbiotic bond existed between synoptic history and high-style historical writings is not, of course, limited to historiography, but finds parallels in other forms of Byzantine literary culture. In his analyses of the different levels of style within Byzantine literature, I. Ševčenko has indicated the frequency with which a wide variety of high-style texts were reshaped into handbook paraphrases that were expressed in a middling level of Greek, precisely so that subsequent readers and writers could absorb the contents of verbose texts without being forced to read the originals.[28]

Yet, while there is plentiful evidence to prove that eleventh- and twelfth-century authors of synoptic histories were educated civil servants who used high-style histories in their production of historical handbooks, can we be certain that their audiences were also located within the same elite and professional environment? Since recent research has begun to present a more optimistic picture of levels of literacy and access to literature *outside* the higher echelons of the Byzantine civil service, it would perhaps be premature to limit the reception of Skylitzes' *Synopsis Historion* purely to those most senior ranks of the imperial administration and court familiar with the writing of high-style histories.[29]

---

[27] The need to look at chronicle and history as distinct genres that function in constantly changing symbiotic relationships has also been signalled by Ljubarskij, 'New Trends in Byzantine Historiography', 133–4.

[28] I. Ševčenko, 'Levels of Style in Byzantine Prose', *JÖB* 31.1 (1981), 309–10; idem, 'Some Additional Remarks to the Report on Levels of Style', *JÖB* 32.1–2 (1982), 228–9.

[29] It has usually been assumed that the high cost of book production meant that few individuals outside elite government circles had regular access

Certainly the incidence of nine Skylitzes manuscripts dating from the twelfth to fourteenth centuries indicates that his text had a long-term audience that far exceeded the narrow world of the later eleventh-century Komnenian elite.[30] The fact that the Madrid manuscript was copied in Norman southern Italy during the twelfth century indicates that the appeal of the *Synopsis Historion* extended beyond the political borders of the empire itself.[31] Nonetheless, although there is a *longue durée* story of the *Synopsis Historion* of Skylitzes as an organic text that snaked its way through many generations of later Byzantine libraries, readers, and interpolators, circumstantial and textual evidence suggests that the author's principal and original audience was to be found among those groups which composed the empire's ruling class in the later eleventh century. That is to say, Skylitzes' original readers were on the one hand senior court officials resident in Constantinople; on the other

to books in medieval Byzantium (C. Mango and I. Ševčenko (eds.), *Byzantine Books and Bookmen*, (Washington DC, 1975). However, Margaret Mullet has argued for a more optimistic view of literacy levels and the dissemination of literature outside the court elite (M. Mullett, 'Aristocracy and Patronage in the Literary Circles of Comnenian Constantinople', in M. Angold (ed.), *Byzantine Aristocracy* (Oxford, 1984), 173–201, and eadem, 'Writing in Early Medieval Byzantium', in R. McKitterick (ed.), *The Uses of Literacy in Early Medieval Europe* (Cambridge, 1990), 156–84).

[30] In 1201 the library of the monastery of St John on Patmos owned a copy of Skylitzes' history: C. Diehl, 'Le Trésor et la bibliothèque de Patmos au commencement du 13e siècle', *BZ* 1 (1892), 500, 522; C. Astruc, 'L'Inventaire dressé en septembre 1200 du trésor et de la bibliothèque de Patmos, édition diplomatique', *TM* 8 (1981), 28–9; Snipes, 'The "Chronographia" of Michael Psellos', 57.

[31] On the Madrid Skylitzes see also above 2.2.1.

they were members of senior families which were either associated with the imperial dynasty or in rivalry with it.

The circumstantial evidence which points to an audience among the social and political elite relates to the fact that Skylitzes' text is often preserved in manuscripts that transmit other, late eleventh-century, high-style literary works whose authors and audiences were principally court-based. Thus, one of the earliest manuscripts of the *Synopsis Historion* of Skylitzes, manuscript [C] [*Paris BN Coislin 136*] which is usually dated to the twelfth century, contains a variety of high-style materials including the *Historia* of the later eleventh-century lawyer and courtier Michael Attaleiates, and the speeches of Manuel Straboromanos, the *megas hetaireiarches* (head of the imperial bodyguard), during the final decade of the reign of Alexios I. Manuscript [E] also conveys Attaleiates' history.[32]

Confirmation of Skylitzes' predominantly elite original audience is also provided by his own text, not least by many of those idiosyncratic elements in his coverage of the reigns of Romanos Lekapenos and Basil II that have been identified in the previous chapter of this volume. In the first place Skylitzes' use of a middling to high language register, his complex syntax, and his occasional classicizing tags, appear compatible with an audience of well-educated civil servants.[33] Analogous parallels between language use and audience have been suggested in the case of the

---

[32] Skylitzes, *Synopsis*, p. xxi; P. Gautier, 'Le Dossier d'un haut fonctionnaire d'Alexis Ier Comnène, Manuel Straboromanos', *REB* 23 (1965), 168–204.

[33] See above 3.2 for discussion of Skylitzes' syntax and language register.

sixth-century synoptic historian John Malalas. It has been
argued by Elizabeth Jeffreys *et al.* that since Malalas was
probably a minor official in the offices of the *Comes Orien-*
talis in Antioch, his prose style may reflect the level of Greek
used in the daily administrative work of local civil servants
in Syria during the reign of Emperor Justinian. Moreover,
these civil servants may have constituted Malalas' principal
audience.[34] Although Malalas writes in a distinctly more
rudimentary register than Skylitzes, the general point that
there may be important connections between the language
levels of synoptic texts and the professional character of the
audience remains valid.

However, the best evidence that Skylitzes was writing, at
least in the first instance, in accordance with the competences and concerns of a narrow, high-ranking audience is
his consistent and conspicuous interest in the political elite
of the empire. In Chapter 3, Skylitzes' fondness for swash-
buckling military anecdotes and his willingness to embroi-
der heroic incidents was noted in his coverage of the reigns
of Romanos Lekapenos and Basil II. This enthusiasm seems
compatible with the almost obsessive interest in martial
valour that Alexander Každan has identified among the
senior aristocratic families of Byzantium in the later eleventh century.[35] More convincing evidence that Skylitzes was

---

[34] Jeffreys *et al.*, *Studies in John Malalas*, 6–11.
[35] See, e.g. Každan, 'Der Mensch', 18 ff.; idem, 'Aristocracy and the Imperial Ideal', in M. Angold (ed.), *Byzantine Aristocracy* (Oxford, 1984), 43–58;
Každan and Wharton Epstein, *Change in Byzantine Culture in the Eleventh*
and Twelfth Centuries, 104–17; Každan, 'The Social Views of Michael Attaleiates', 23–86.

writing for a late eleventh-century elite audience is the emphasis that he places upon recording the names, titles, and pedigrees of the principal protagonists of his narrative. This emphasis accords with another important social phenomenon identified by several scholars, among them Alexander Každan and Paul Magdalino: the growth during the eleventh century of a regard for family (*genos*) and lineage among the empire's ruling elite, an elite which most modern historians loosely term the Byzantine aristocracy.[36]

One of the ways in which Skylitzes' text accords with this later eleventh-century preoccupation with dynastic principles is the frequency with which the author pauses to embellish and explain the family and nicknames of key individuals within his narrative.[37] As we noted in the previous

---

[36] A. P. Každan and S. Ronchey, *L'aristocrazia bizantina del principo del XI alla fine del XII secolo* (Palermo, 1997); reviewed P. Magdalino, *BZ* 92 (1999), 530–2. See also Každan, 'Social Views of Michael Attaleiates', 28–9; idem, 'Aristocracy and the Imperial Ideal', 45; P. Magdalino, 'Byzantine Snobbery', in M. Angold (ed.), *Byzantine Aristocracy* (Oxford, 1984), 64; idem, 'Honour among the Romaioi: The Framework of Social Values in the World of Digenes Akrites and Kekaumenos', *BMGS* 13 (1989), 183–4, 193–6. The term aristocracy is widely used by Byzantinists when analysing the 9th- to 12th-c. period, but is often deployed with considerable looseness. Most scholars have been more concerned with the minutiae of prosopography, that is to say with identifying individuals and families who seem to belong to the category of aristocracy, rather than defining the category itself. The scope and nature of the Byzantine aristocracy has been best analysed by J.-C. Cheynet, in his *Pouvoir et contestations*, 191–318, and 'L'Aristocratie byzantine (VIIIe–XIIIe s.)', *Journal de Savants* (2000), 281–322.

[37] The conspicuous interest that Skylitzes shows in the aristocracy of the 9th- to 11th-c. Byzantine Empire is a phenomenon also observed by Dr Stamatina McGrath in her doctoral thesis, 'A Study of the Social Structure of Byzantine Aristocracy as seen through Ioannes Skylitzes' Synopsis Historiarum'. I became aware of this thesis towards the end of the period when I was writing up my own doctoral research on Skylitzes. At that time I was unable

chapter, Skylitzes applies the family name Lekapenos to Emperor Romanos I without support from his underlying source *Theophanes Continuatus*. As Alexander Každan pointed out, Skylitzes is in fact the earliest historian to refer to the Lekapenoi by their family name.[38] Similar interest in family names is displayed in Skylitzes' coverage of the reign of Basil. He refers explicitly in such terms to the general who encouraged Bardas Skleros to cross the Anti Taurus at the beginning of his revolt: 'a general Sachakios [Isaac] by name, Brachamios was his second name'.[39] Skylitzes also highlights the nickname of the *domestikos* of the *scholai* of the West at the time of Basil II's disastrous foray into Bulgaria in 986: 'Stephan. . . . whom they used to call Kontostephanos on account of the shortness of his height'.[40] A similar explanation for a nickname is linked to his identification of Nikolitzas, a Bulgarian general who displayed ambiguous loyalty to the emperor during the wars of Basil II: 'Nicholas, the guardian of Servia, whom those who give nicknames call Nikolitzas because of the shortness of his height'.[41]

to consult Dr McGrath's work because of a serious delay in the distribution of authorized facsimiles by UMI Dissertation Services. Since I finished my doctoral research in 1999 I have been able to consult Dr McGrath's dissertation in its UMI facsimile version, and have been interested to see the congruence between our respective readings of the text. The editors of the recent translation of Skylitzes' text have also noted the conspicuous interest of both the author and his readership in the great families of the Byzantine empire (Flusin and Cheynet, *Jean Skylitzès*, pp. xviii–xix).

[38] See above p. 144.

[39] Skylitzes, *Synopsis*, 318; see also McGrath, 'Social Structures of the Byzantine Aristocracy', 116.

[40] Skylitzes, *Synopsis*, 331; see also McGrath, 'Social Structures of the Byzantine Aristocracy', 35.

[41] Skylitzes, *Synopsis*, 344; also, see above p. 105

Skylitzes does not merely emphasize the family names or nicknames of some of his principal narrative actors; on other occasions he also emphasizes their pedigree, pointing out that they come from established families.[42] During the siege of Nikaia by Bardas Skleros at the beginning of Basil II's reign, Manuel Erotikos, the defender of the city, is described as: 'a well-born man and famous in virtue and bravery' (ἐκ γένους τε ἄνδρα καὶ ἐπ' ἀρετῇ διαβόητον καὶ ἀνδρείᾳ).[43] When Patriarch Sisinnios died he was replaced by Sergios, who Skylitzes tells us could trace his family back to Photios, the ninth-century patriarch of Constantinople: καὶ τὸ γένος ἀναφέρων πρὸς Φώτιον τὸν πατριάρχην.[44] A similar emphasis on pedigree is also visible in Skylitzes' treatment of Romanos Lekapenos' reign. As we noted in the last chapter, while Skylitzes often ignores the most blatant encomia of the leading protagonists of his narrative, he nonetheless scrupulously retains details of their lineages and marriage alliances. Particular attention in this regard is paid to the Lekapenos, Argyros, and Kourkouas families.[45] Nor is his interest in

---

[42] His interest in aristocratic pedigrees may also explain the conspicuous interest in marriage arrangements visible both in the *Synopsis Historion* and the materials Skylitzes wrote as a lawyer (Laiou, 'Imperial Marriages and their Critics', 165–76; see also above 2.3).

[43] Skylitzes, *Synopsis*, 323; see also McGrath, 'Social Structures of the Byzantine Aristocracy', 135–7.

[44] Skylitzes, *Synopsis*, 341; establishing dates for the tenure of the patriarchal office is notoriously difficult for Basil's reign. Darrouzès' reworking of the dates of the incumbencies of the first three patriarchs of the reign suggests that Sisinnios himself took up office in 996; according to Skylitzes, Sergios became patriarch of Constantinople three years later, thus in 999 (J. Darrouzès, 'Sur la chronologie du patriarche Antoine III Stoudite', *REB* 46 (1988), 55–60).

[45] See above 3.2.

such clans solely confined to the reign of Romanos Lekapenos. In the case of the Argyros family his attention persists
into the later tenth and early eleventh centuries. In his coverage of the reign of Constantine Porphyrogenitus (945–59) he
traces the career of Marianos Argyros, one of the emperor's
closest associates and *komes* of the imperial stable. Here again,
he dwells on the Argyros family history, telling his reader that
Marianos was the son of Leo Argyros.[46] A little later in the
Synopsis Historion, during his account of the reign of Basil II,
Skylitzes mentions twice another Argyros, this time Basil: first
as the *strategos* of Samos who was sent to fight the Italian rebel
Meles *c.*1010–11; second as the first Byzantine commander of
Vaspurakan.[47] Also recorded is the marriage of the sister of
Romanos Argyros to the Doge of Venice. She is explicitly
described as 'the sister of Argyros who was emperor after
these things'.[48]

---

[46] Skylitzes, *Synopsis*, 323, 327.

[47] Skylitzes, *Synopsis*, 348, 355; Basil Argyros' exact status during the
Italian expedition is unclear. He cannot have been *katepano* of Italy, since
independent historiographical and documentary evidence from southern
Italy indicates that this position was held between 1010 and 1016 by Basil
Mesardonites (*Lupus Protospatharius*, ed. G. H. Pertz, *MGH ss* 5 (Hanover,
1844), 57; V. von Falkenhausen, *Untersuchungen Herrschaft*, 86; also see
below 7.2). It is always possible that Basil Argyros actually had little to do
with the containment of Meles' revolt and that he is identified with the
southern Italian sphere simply because Skylitzes conflates these two Basils:
Basil Argyros, the *strategos* of Samos, and Basil Mesardonites, *katepano* of
Italy. This suspicion of conflation is enhanced by the fact that the account of
Argyros' Italian actions is located in one of Skylitzes' characteristically terse,
telescoped passages, ch. 34 of the *Synopsis Historion*. For further discussion of
such passages see also above 2.4. For Argyros in Vaspurakan see also below
6.3.4.

[48] Skylitzes, *Synopsis*, 343.

Indeed, Skylitzes' fascination with the personnel of the social and political elite of the empire is visible elsewhere in his coverage of the reign of Basil II. His narrative of the revolts of Bardas Skleros and Bardas Phokas is replete with the names of members of powerful aristocratic families: Michael Bourtzes, Anthes Alyates, Pegasios, Constantine Gauras, the Hagiozacharites brothers, Isaac Brachamios, Andronikos Doukas, Bardas Moungos, Christopher Epeiktes, and Leo Aichmalotos.[49] He is also careful to record the identities of many senior army commanders within both the Bulgarian and the imperial armies during his testimony of Basil's campaigns in the Balkans. It is particularly striking that Skylitzes accords a similar status to the Bulgarian commanders as he also attributes to representatives of leading aristocratic families within the Byzantine Empire of the same period. Just as he refers to the principal protagonists of the Phokas and Skleros revolts as *dynastai* and *megistanes*, he uses exactly the same collective nouns for the leading figures within the Bulgarian polity during the Balkan wars of Basil's reign.[50] The degree to which he views representatives of senior Balkan families in the same light as the leading

---

[49] Ibid. 314–39.

[50] Skylitzes describes the adherents of Phokas in 987 as the *megistanes* of the Romans: οἱ δὲ τῶν Ῥωμαίων μεγιστᾶνες (Skylitzes, *Synopsis*, 332). During his analysis of the motives of Bardas Skleros during the same period he refers to the Phokas party as *dynastai*: τῶν δυναστῶν (Skylitzes, *Synopsis*, 335). Several of the Bulgarian commanders who surrendered in 1018 to Basil II are described as the *megistanes* of the Bulgars: μεγιστᾶνες τῶν Βουλγάρων (Skylitzes, *Synopsis*, 359). The Bulgarian commander Ibatzes is termed a *dynastes* by his Byzantine adversary Eustathios Daphnomeles *c*.1018 (Skylitzes, *Synopsis*, 362; see also below 4.2.2 for further discussion of the episode involving Ibatzes in Skylitzes' text).

families of the Byzantine Empire becomes clear in his account of what happened to the widow of Sermon, the *archon* of Serbia, shortly after the Bulgarian surrender of 1018. In return for handing over Sermon's fortress of Sirmion to the Byzantines, she was transported to Constantinople and 'married to a man from the *megistanes* of the capital city'.[51] Away from the Balkans, Skylitzes demonstrates an equally conspicuous concern to record the names and family connections of those figures who entered Byzantine service from regions in the east, particularly from Armenia and Iberia. When Basil II annexed the Iberian princedom of Tao in 1000, Skylitzes informs the reader that Pakourianos, Phebdatos, and Pherses were raised to the rank of *patrikios* and entered the service of the emperor. They are specifically described as being 'foremost according to their family (*genos*) in Iberia'. During his account of Basil's Balkan campaign of 1016 Skylitzes returns to the family of Phebdatos. In his story of Bulgarian attempts to forge an alliance with the Pechenegs, he refers to Tzotzikios, the *strategos* of Dristra, as 'the son of the *patrikios* Theudatos (Phebdatos), the Iberian'.[52] Meanwhile he also picks up the name of Pherses later in his account of Basil's reign, this time in the context of the revolt of Nikephoros Xiphias and Nikephoros Phokas in 1022. He notes that Pherses alone of the rebels was executed because he killed four imperial *kouratores* and an imperial eunuch.[53]

[51] Skylitzes, *Synopsis*, 366.
[52] Ibid. 339, 356.
[53] Ibid. 367; see also the account of Pherses' role in this rebellion in Armenian and Georgian historical writings: Aristakes, *Récit des malheurs*,

So great, indeed, is Skylitzes' emphasis on senior families in his coverage of Basil's reign that the narrative is almost entirely presented through the prism of aristocratic names, with the result that the emperor himself is often nothing more than a fleeting presence. In the next chapter we shall see how Skylitzes' use of a pro-Skleros source means that the perspective of an aristocratic rebel dominates his account of the revolts of Bardas Skleros and Bardas Phokas. However, even once he moves beyond the civil war period and away from the pro-Skleros source into the middle and final decades of the reign, Skylitzes does not shift his focus towards the emperor, but continues to articulate his narrative through the actions of personalities from elite families. Examination of his post-989 Balkan testimony makes this point particularly forcefully. We know from references in a variety of eastern sources that Basil II himself campaigned in the Balkans during the 990s. Both Yahya ibn Sa'id and

21; Georgian Royal Annals, 283. Sigillographical evidence suggests that Pherses may have been the *strategos* of Cappadocia at the time of the Xiphias–Phokas revolt (J. Nesbitt and N. Oikonomides, *Catalogue of Byzantine Seals at Dumbarton Oaks and in the Fogg Museum of Art*, 4 vols. (Washington DC, 1991–2001), iv. 43.13: Pherses Tzotzikios, *anthypatos*, *patrikios*, and *strategos*); see below 8.8 for analysis of the revolt itself. The family of Pherses had an egregious military pedigree. In 979 Pherses' father, Tzotzikios, served in the Iberian army which joined forces with the imperial armies led by Bardas Phokas to defeat Bardas Skleros (Stephen of Taron, *Armenische Geschichte*, 142; this alliance is also discussed below at 5.1 and 8.2). Pherses himself led the Iberian contingent of a joint Ibero-Armenian army, which defeated the emir of Azerbaijan in 998 (Stephen of Taron, *Armenische Geschichte*, 205–6). Both Pherses and his father held the hereditary office prince of princes (*eristav eristavi*), second only in position to the dynastic ruler in western Caucasian polities; see also McGrath, 'Social Structures of the Byzantine Aristocracy', 40, for a brief discussion of this family.

Stephen of Taron mention that Basil led an army into Bulgaria in 991.[54] During the following years while Basil was busy fighting in Bulgaria, his principal commanders on the eastern frontier, including Michael Bourtzes, were involved in a war of attrition with the Fatimids of Egypt.[55] At this time at least one, and possibly two, embassies were sent to the emperor from the eastern client state of Aleppo. These embassies are explicitly stated to have met the emperor while he was on campaign in the Balkans.[56] Moreover, after Michael Bourtzes, *doux* of Antioch, was defeated by the Fatimids in 994, Basil is said to have abandoned, temporarily at least, his campaigns in Bulgaria and to have marched eastwards at speed. He arrived at Antioch unexpectedly in the spring of 995 and immediately launched a series of counter raids against Fatimid-held territory.[57] However, while the eastern sources indicate that Basil was personally active on campaign in the Balkans during the 990s, Skylitzes' account barely mentions Basil's presence. Instead his account focuses on the activities of the Taronites family and Nikephoros Ouranos.

Skylitzes' coverage of the Byzantine exploits in the Balkans in the 990s begins with the appointment of Gregory Taronites as *doux* at Thessaloniki; then he reports on the Bulgarian ambush that led to Gregory's death and Ashot's imprisonment.[58] His account of the Taronitai is extremely

---

[54] Yahya, *PO* 23, pp. 430–1; Stephen of Taron, *Armenische Geschichte*, 198.
[55] For Bourtzes' engagement with the Fatimids see below 6.3.3.
[56] al-Rudrawari, *Eclipse*, vi. 229, 232.
[57] Yahya, *PO* 23, p. 442.
[58] Skylitzes, *Synopsis*, 341; this episode is also discussed above in 3.3.2.

similar to a story conveyed by the Armenian historian Stephen of Taron; indeed the congruence between Stephen and Skylitzes stories at this point suggests that their evidence may come from a common historiographical tradition.[59] Given Stephen's patent interest in all things Armenian, it could be suggested that Stephen chose to dwell on the role of the Taronitai in his account of Basil's Balkan campaigns because this family had recently migrated to Byzantine service, giving up their control over the Armenian princedom of Taron.[60] Yet, it is striking that despite his pro-Armenian focus, Stephen is more willing than Skylitzes to locate the fate of the Taronitai within a context of active campaigning by Basil II. Stephen begins his account of these events by saying that Basil invaded the land of the Bulgarians in 991 'to take revenge on them'—revenge, one assumes, for the heavy defeat of 986. Stephen then describes Basil besieging Berroia. In contrast, Skylitzes introduces his Balkan material by merely remarking that after the end of the revolts of Phokas and Skleros, Basil decided to deal with Samuel. He went to Thessalonika, gave thanks to Saint Demetrios for his

---

[59] Stephen of Taron, *Armenische Geschichte*, 198. Stephen adds some extra details, describing how one Sahak of Handzith, who had often fought bravely against the Bulgarians in the past, was also captured during this ambush; he then went over to his opponents' side. The congruence between Skylitzes' and Stephen's testimonies has also been noted by Dr Timothy Greenwood of the Oriental Institute in Oxford. Dr Greenwood is preparing a new translation into English of Stephen of Taron's *Universal History*.

[60] For Stephen's preoccupation with an Armenian perspective, see above 1.2.2; for more on the history of the Taronites family see N. Adontz, 'Les Taronites en Arménie et à Byzance', *B* 9 (1934), 715–38; *B* 10 (1935), 540–551; *B* 11 (1936), 21–30; idem, 'Observations sur la généalogie des Taronites', in his *Études arméno-byzantines* (Lisbon, 1965), 339–45.

deliverance from civil war, and appointed Gregory *doux* with responsibility for fighting the Bulgarians.[61] There is no sign in this account that Basil ever participated actively in a Balkan campaign.

As we noted in the previous chapter, Skylitzes' description of the fate of the Taronitai forms a prelude to his principal Balkan narrative of the 990s: Nikephoros Ouranos' triumph at the Battle of the River Spercheios.[62] This triumph is entirely attributed to the ingenuity and acuity of Ouranos; no role is assigned to the emperor at all beyond the fact that he appointed Ouranos. Moreover, once his story of the Ouranos victory is complete, Skylitzes appends a coda that returns to the theme of the Taronitai. This final passage constitutes a report about a marriage that Samuel sanctioned between one of his daughters (called Miroslava according to a later interpolation by Michael of Devol in manuscript [U]) and his prisoner of war, Ashot Taronites. The accuracy of this story has sometimes been doubted by historians because it bears uncomfortable parallels to a similar tale reported in the narrative of the Priest of Diokleia about the marriage of a daughter of Samuel to Vladimir, the ruler of the Adriatic princedom of Diokleia.[63] Yet, whether the story is to be believed or not, the salient fact as far as Skylitzes' narrative is concerned, is that Skylitzes chose to dedicate a substantial part of his Balkan material for the 990s to an account, however fabulous, of a dynastic

---

[61] Skylitzes, *Synopsis*, 341.
[62] This episode is also discussed above in 3.3.2.
[63] Skylitzes, *Synopsis*, 342–3; Adontz, 'Samuel l'Arménien', 395–406.

marriage involving the Bulgarian royal family rather than concentrating on Basil II's own martial activities.

In his coverage of Byzantine warfare in the Balkans after the Byzantine victory at the Battle of Spercheios a slight shift is visible in Skylitzes' treatment of the emperor's role. Gradually, and in the most general of terms, he begins to refer more frequently to imperial participation in campaigns. For example, he explains how Basil set out from Thessalonika and forced the surrender of various frontier commanders such as Dobromeros, Nikolitzas, and Draxanos.[64] He also describes an imperially led campaign to Vidin on the middle Danube and an imperial victory over Samuel close to Skopje.[65] In the highly standardized phraseology so typical of Skylitzes' treatment of military narrative, our author suggests that in the period before 1014 and the Battle of Kleidion, Basil led his armies on annual campaigns into Bulgaria: 'for the emperor did not leave off invading Bulgaria every year.'[66] Yet, even in these passages Basil remains a shadowy figure; praise is reserved for his commanders. In his only reference to the fate of eastern Bulgaria during the whole of his testimony for Basil's reign, Skylitzes notes that: 'in the year 6508, in the thirteenth indiction, the emperor having sent out a heavy force against the Bulgarian castles on the other side of the Haimos, that was led by the *patrikios*

[64] Skylitzes, *Synopsis*, 344–5; see above 2.4 for the difficulty in dating these surrenders.

[65] Skylitzes, *Synopsis*, 346–7.

[66] Skylitzes, *Synopsis*, 348; see below 7.1 for further discussion of how this phrase relates to the vexed question of the length and intensity of Basil's campaigning in Bulgaria in the first two decades of the 11th c.

Theodorokan and Nikephoros Xiphias, *protospatharios*, took Great and Little Preslav and Pliska and the Roman force retired unharmed and with trophies.'[67] This notice, once again, is articulated entirely in the bland phraseology of Skylitzes' military lexicon so ubiquitous within his coverage of the Balkans in Basil's reign. Yet, it is striking that one of the effects of the use of such anodyne prose is that the names and titles of Theodorokan and Xiphias stand out with even greater clarity.

The most notable example of glory being attributed to an aristocrat rather than to the emperor occurs during Skylitzes' description of the Battle of Kleidion in the mountains north of Thessalonika in 1014, acclaimed as a crushing victory over the Bulgarians. Here Skylitzes attributes the success of imperial armies not to Basil himself, but to the inspiration of Nikephoros Xiphias. When the Byzantine armies could not break through the blockade that the Bulgarians had established in the pass of Kleidion, it was Xiphias who recommended that a party of men should be led through the mountains to attack the enemy from the rear. Xiphias himself then conducted this operation.[68] Nor does the aristocratic focus to Skylitzes' Balkan coverage end with the Battle of Kleidion. As we shall see shortly Skylitzes' coverage of Basil's annexation of Bulgaria in 1018 is dominated by the catalogue of the names of Bulgarian notables that surrendered to the emperor. Appended to this roll call is another pair of narratives that expatiate on the bravery and

---

[67] Skylitzes, *Synopsis*, 343–4.
[68] Skylitzes, *Synopsis*, 348–9; this episode is also discussed above in 3.3.2.

cunning of those senior Byzantine commanders who mopped up residual Bulgarian resistance after 1018. One of these narratives is the account of the death of Sermon, *archon* of Serbia, killed in an ambush by the Byzantine general Constantine Diogenes. The second, much longer, account is that of Eustathios Daphnomeles' capture of Ibatzes, a heroic narrative that will be discussed in greater depth later in this chapter.

The extent to which Skylitzes displays an overwhelming interest in the social and political elite of the empire becomes particularly obvious once his text is compared with that of the mid-twelfth-century history of John Zonaras. Despite using Skylitzes' *Synopsis Historion* as one of its principal sources, Zonaras' account of Basil's reign is almost barren of the names of members of aristocratic families. At key moments in his narrative of this period Zonaras mentions the collective activities of groups of aristocrats in a general sense, but with the exception of the principal actors, such as Bardas Skleros or Bardas Phokas, individual members of the elite are almost never identified. During his coverage of the first revolt of Skleros, Zonaras omits all Skylitzes' references to the rebel commanders Michael Bourtzes, Anthes Alyates, Pegasios, Constantine Gauras, the Hagiozacharites brothers, Isaac Brachamios, Andronikos Doukas, Bardas Moungos, Christopher Epeiktes, and Leo Aichmalotos.[69] He also omits the names of those Iberians who went over to Byzantine service in 1000.[70] In his Balkan

---

[69] Zonaras, *Epitomae*, 539–46; Skylitzes, *Synopsis*, 314–28.
[70] Zonaras, *Epitomae*, 557.

material he retains a few references to those individuals so prominent in Skylitzes' account: for example, Dobromeros, the commander at Berroia, and Nikolitzas at Servia. However, elsewhere he is ruthless in excising those whom Skylitzes privileges. He removes all references to the activities of the Taronites family. He omits most references to the career of Nikephoros Ouranos. He retains mention of the raids on Pliska and Preslav in 1000, but cuts out the names of Xiphias and Theodorakan. Xiphias is also removed from the account of the battle at Kleidion. There is no trace of the Daphnomeles' narrative.[71] By such methods Zonaras distances himself from interest in the exploits of the empire's aristocracy and refocuses the narrative around the person of the emperor himself.

While Zonaras' reshaping of Skylitzes' account highlights the degree to which the *Synopsis Historion* is infused with an interest in the empire's multifarious elite, Skylitzes' own preface indicates that this concentration on the aristocracy at the expense of the emperor may have been self-conscious and deliberate. Let us remember that in his preface he criticizes contemporary historians, among them Michael Psellos, for a view of history limited to a strictly imperial horizon: 'They both lack accuracy, for they disregard many of the more important events, and they are of no use to their successors since they have merely made an enumeration of the emperors and indicated who took imperial office after whom and nothing more.'[72] Here, Skylitzes seems to be

---

[71] Zonaras, *Epitomae*, 558–66.

[72] Skylitzes, *Synopsis*, 3; see also above 3.1. R. Scott, 'The Classical Tradition in Byzantine Historiography', in M. Mullett and R. Scott (eds.), *Byzan-*

implying that the deeds of the emperor were not the more important events of the past, and that he himself in the course of his compilation was about to depart from this traditional interpretation of history.

This is not to suggest that Skylitzes ignores entirely the person of the emperor as a unit around whom the rest of his text is organized. His narrative is to some extent structured around individual imperial reigns. Indeed, he usually demarcates his appraisal of each reign with dated references: at the beginning of the reign, he customarily includes an accession date; and at the end, he notes the date of the incumbent emperor's death and the length of his (or more rarely, her) reign.[73] Yet, within the narrative itself, the focus falls as much on individual members of the political and military elite as on emperors. While emperors merely provide the superficial building blocks of the *Synopsis Historion*, what really holds Skylitzes' narrative together is a complex web of fine threads, each relating to a single individual or family, many of which run across the textual divisions imposed by imperial reigns. In this chapter we have traced several such fragile narrative threads: an interest in the

---

tium and the Classical Tradition (Birmingham, 1981), 69–70, argues that in medieval Byzantium the reign of the emperor became the standard unit for the writing and interpretation of history.

[73] For Skylitzes' treatment of the beginning and end of Basil's reign see Skylitzes, *Synopsis*, 314, 368–9. Flusin and Cheynet, *Jean Skylitzès*, pp. xvi–xx, are more convinced by the idea that emperors are the central organizing principle of Skylitzes' text. Indeed, they argue that by the end of the 11th c., this was the usual method of arranging historiographical material. However, they too acknowledge that storylines within the narrative of the *Synopsis* often spill over the text's regnal divisions.

Argyros family that can be traced in the reign of Romanos Lekapenos, Constantine Porphyrogenitus, and Basil II; a concentration on the Iberian dynasties of Pherses and Phebdatos that runs through the second half of Skylitzes' Basil testimony. Similar narrative threads will be identified in this and later chapters of this book; of particular importance will be those skeins of narrative that connect Skylitzes' treatment of Basil's reign with his mid- and later eleventh-century material.[74] However, at this stage in the argument we need to move beyond simple recognition of the fact that Skylitzes focuses intensely on the personnel, lineage, familial interconnections, and deeds of the social and political elite of the empire and its immediate geographical neighbours; instead we need to probe more deeply into why he chooses to interpret the history of Byzantium between ninth and eleventh centuries as the history of the empire's aristocracy.

4.2. POLITICAL CONTEXTS

4.2.1 Aristocratic competition

One explanation for why Skylitzes' *Synopsis Historion* emerges as the history of the families, heroism, deeds, and even revolts of the aristocracy is that it was composed in the second half of the eleventh century at a time of immense political tension within the Byzantine political elite.

[74] See in particular 5.3.

Whether Skylitzes was writing the *Synopsis Historion* in the 1070s as Seibt suggests, or in the early 1090s as I think more likely, this was a period generally characterized by endemic competition for imperial power among the more important families of the Byzantine empire.[75] Competition began after the death of the last Macedonian empress Theodora in 1056. Rivalry intensified between 1071 and 1081 as the empire was torn apart by civil war between different dynasties: the Doukas, Komnenos, Diogenes, Botaneiates, and Bryennios families. The past in such circumstances was an important legitimizing tool. Within his generally encomiastic treatment of Emperors Constantine X (1059–67) and Michael VII Doukas (1071–8) in the *Chronographia*, Michael Psellos includes several references to the genealogy of the imperial family.[76] Michael Attaleiates' elaborate genealogy of Emperor Nicephoros III Botaneiates (1078–81) contained in his *Historia*, which traces the emperor's descent from the tenth-century Phokades and the first-century Fabii, demonstrates clearly how the writers of history looked to both the immediate and the remote past to bolster dynastic prestige.[77] Although Skylitzes' interest in the deeds and family trees of the empire's aristocracy cannot be directly compared with the genealogical enterprises of Attaleiates and Psellos, since the *Synopsis Historion* is a survey which ranges far

[75] For the dating of Skylitzes' text see above 2.3; on the more general point about aristocratic rivalry see Cheynet, *Pouvoir et contestations*, 345–69; Angold, *Byzantine Empire*, 71–80, 115–48.

[76] Psellos, *Cronografia*, ii. 282–5, 296–9.

[77] Attaleiates (Michael): *Historia*, ed. I. Bekker, CSHB (Bonn, 1853), 216–27; Každan, 'Social Views of Michael Attaleiates', 28–9; idem, 'Aristocracy and the Imperial Ideal', 45.

wider than the achievements and pedigrees of a single family, it is possible that his text was composed within the very specific political context of aristocratic rivalry at the end of the eleventh century.[78]

One can start unravelling this political context by starting from the observation that Skylitzes' *Synopsis Historion* often resembles a 'Who Was Who' of the 'Who Is Who' of the last quarter of the eleventh century.[79] That is to say, Skylitzes' text frequently displays a conspicuous interest in those figures from the Byzantine past whose ancestors enjoyed political significance in the later eleventh century. Let us take one striking example. In Skylitzes' narrative of the civil wars at the beginning of Basil's reign, he pays particular attention to one Anthes Alyates, a henchman whom Bardas Skleros sent to rescue his son Romanos from the imperial palace in Constantinople before launching his first revolt in the east. In describing Anthes to the reader, Skylitzes characteristically draws attention to his family name: 'and so straightaway he sent a certain Anthes by first name, Alyates by second name'. He then goes on to describe Alyates, using his idiosycratic generalized vocabulary of military heroism, as one of Skleros' most effective servants: τὰ μάλιστα ὄντα αὐτῷ τῶν

[78] Skylitzes' great interest in plots and intrigue has also been noted by Flusin and Cheynet, *Jean Skylitzès*, p. xvii.

[79] Analogous to the case of Skylitzes may be the 13th-c. synoptic history written by George Akropolites, the *megas logothetes* of Michael VIII Palaiologos (1258–82). Ruth Macrides argues that this history resembles a 'Who's Who' of the Empire of Nikaia. Like Skylitzes Akropolites demonstrates concern that the full names and titles of all officials and aristocrats should be accurately recorded: R. Macrides, 'The Historian in the History', in C. Constantinides *et al.* (eds.), *Φιλέλλην, Studies in Honour of Robert Browning* (Venice, 1996), 221–2.

δραστικωτάτων ὑπηρετῶν.[80] Later in the narrative Skylitzes picks up Alyates again. He records, in his characteristically bland heroic military prose, that Alyates died during an engagement with the imperial commander Eustathios Maleinos in the Anti Taurus mountains close to the Koukoulithos pass a few months later: 'Aluates, not holding back, gripped by passion, spurred on his horse with ineffable strength and charged the enemy; having achieved nothing worth speaking of, he fell mortally wounded.'[81] Yet, while Skylitzes depicts Alyates as a hero of the first Skleros revolt, at the same time his narrative betrays signs that Alyates was actually quite a minor figure. He is described merely as one of Skleros' servants, a *hyperetes*, a designation that seems to indicate that he was part of the general's personal retinue. He does not bear any imperial title or office. Given that Skylitzes usually retains such information with scrupulous care, we may be certain that the fact that Alyates is not attributed with senior titles or offices means that he did not possess them. Why then, if Alyates was so minor, does Skylitzes retain notice of him in the narrative of the Skleros revolt? As we saw in his treatment of the reign of the reign of Romanos Lekapenos, Skylitzes is often enthusiastic to excise minor figures as distractions to the overall thematic integrity of his narrative.[82] Why does Alyates survive?

One plausible explanation is that it was the political significance of the Alyates family in the later eleventh century

---

[80] Skylitzes, *Synopsis*, 315–16.

[81] The relatively lowly position of Alyates has also been noted by McGrath, 'Social Structures of the Byzantine Aristocracy', 25.

[82] See above 3.2.

rather than the importance of Anthes during the later tenth century which demanded that Skylitzes retain his name within his narrative of Basil's reign, and indeed enhance his reputation with lashings of heroic prose. In this context it is worth noting that by the second half of the eleventh century the Alyates family had become one of the senior dynasties of the Byzantine aristocracy. One of Anthes' descendants, a certain Leo Alyates, was a *strategos* during the reign of Romanos IV Diogenes, responsible for the strengthening of the fortifications at Cherson.[83] Meanwhile, a rather more famous contemporary relative, Theodore Alyates was a leading supporter of Romanos IV during the civil wars that overtook the Byzantine empire in 1071 after the battle of Manzikert. He was taken prisoner in battle and blinded by the forces of Michael VII Doukas. His career in the political ferment of the third quarter of the eleventh century is described by Michael Attaleiates. Significantly, he is a character in whom Skylitzes himself took an interest. When Skylitzes came to use Attaleiates' *Historia* to write the Continuation to his *Synopsis Historion*, he retained the story of Theodore Alyates. In this account Skylitzes notes that Theodore held the high-ranking title of *proedros*, was well-born, famous, and remarkable for his stature and appearance, in other words a classic Byzantine aristocrat of the later eleventh century: Θεόδωρον οὖν πρόεδρον τὸν Ἀλυάτην, ἄνδρα γενναῖον καὶ ἐπιφανῆ, μεγέθει τε καὶ θέᾳ θαυμασιώτατον.[84]

---

[83] I. Karagiannopoulos and G. Weiss, *Quellenkunde zur Geschichte von Byzanz (324–1453)*, 2 vols. (Weisbaden, 1982), ii, no. 375.

[84] Attaleiates, *Historia*, 170–1; *Skylitzes Continuatus*, 153; For Skylitzes' use of Attaleiates' *Historia* in his own 'Continuation' see above p.83 n.41. See

A selection principle shaped by contemporary (that is to say, later eleventh-century) prestige rather than the realities of power in the more remote past may also explain the nature of Skylitzes' treatment of other individuals and families in his later tenth- and early eleventh-century coverage. Let us take an individual called Anemas, who consistently crops up in Skylitzes' accounts of the reigns of Nikephoros Phocas and John Tzimiskes, the mid-tenth-century emperors. In Skylitzes' appraisal Anemas is mentioned as the son of the emir of Crete, who was taken prisoner by the Byzantines during the capture of the island by Nikephoros Phokas in 961. Later he receives two citations for bravery during the campaign led by John Tzimiskes against the Rus at Dristra on the Lower Danube in 971. He is first depicted fighting heroically as a member of the imperial bodyguard. In his second appearance he is killed after a valiant but abortive assault on the Rus prince Svyatoslav.[85] Yet, it is clear from other evidence relating to the name Anemas that Skylitzes' interest in this tenth-century individual may have been determined by the prestige of the family in the early Komnenian period, rather than by his importance to the tenth-century Byzantine polity. Just how important this family was during the later eleventh century is made clear by a variety of Byzantine authors. Anna Komnene includes an

also McGrath, 'Social Structures of the Byzantine Aristocracy', 96 n. 33; McGrath points out that another Alyates appears in the *Alexiad* of Anna Komnene; he was killed in a skirmish with the Normans *c*.1108.

[85] Skylitzes, *Synopsis*, 249, 304, 308; Leo the Deacon confirms that Anemas was a member of the imperial bodyguard and the son of the former Cretan ruler (Leo the Deacon, *Historiae Libri Decem*, 149); see also discussion by McGrath, 'Social Structures of the Byzantine Aristocracy', 44, 101.

account of the rebellion of the four Anemai brothers in the
Alexiad, her narrative of the reign of Alexios Komnenos
(1081–1118).[86] She indicates that the Anemai were leading
figures in the army.[87] The prominence of the Anemai in early
Komnenian political society is confirmed in the letters of
Theophylact, the contemporary archbishop of Ochrid. One
of his correspondents in the period 1093–5 was Nicholas
Anemas, who held a senior military position in Macedonia,
possibly as *doux* of Skopje.[88]

On several other occasions Skylitzes' decision to record
the arrival within the Byzantine elite of certain outsiders
during the later tenth and early eleventh centuries may also
have been determined by the political significance of aristocratic families with the same name at the end of the eleventh
century. Thus, the inclusion of the name Pakourianos
among the list of Iberians who entered the service of Basil
II in 1000, may stem from his perceived association with the
later eleventh-century general Gregory Pakourianos. The
role of this latter-day Pakourianos as a powerbroker within

[86] Anna Komnene: *Anne Comnène, Alexiade*, ed. B. Leib, 3 vols. (Paris,
1967), iii. 69–74. Although undated in the *Alexiad*, the revolt is usually
assumed to have occurred before 1102 (Cheynet, *Pouvoir et contestations*,
100–01; B. Skoulatos, *Les Personnages byzantins de l'Alexiade* (Louvain, 1980)
172, 200–02).

[87] Michael Anemas led a detachment of Byzantine troops against the
Cumans in 1094 (Skoulatos, *Les Personnages byzantins*, 200).

[88] Theophylact of Ochrid: letters 32, 34, 41. Gautier suggests that Anemas
held the position of *doux* of Skopje. He argues that Anemas returned to
Constantinople in 1094/5 (Theophylact of Ochrid: *Théophylacte d'Achrida
Lettres*, ed. Gautier, 39–40). Mullett goes no further than seeing Anemas as a
young friend of the bishop who was an official in Bulgaria (Mullett, *Theophylact of Ochrid*, 147, 183, 275–6). It is not clear whether Nicholas himself
was one of the four brothers who rebelled.

the Byzantine polity at the time of the Komnenian coup against Nikephoros III Botaneiates in 1081 is described in detail in the *Alexiad*. Created *megas domestikos* by Alexios as a reward for his loyalty, he was the founder of the Georgian monastery at Bačkovo in Bulgaria.[89] Although he himself appears to have died without children in 1086, one of his younger relatives, also called Gregory, was the son-in-law of Nikephoros Komnenos, the brother of Emperor Alexios. In the mid-1090s Theophylact of Ochrid noted that despite his youth this junior Pakourianos enjoyed free access to (*parrhesia*) and counsel with Emperor Alexios.[90] Another Pakourianos, Thathoul, probably one of the Armenian relatives that Gregory mentions in his will, was also an important political personality during the reign of Alexios, although he was located rather further afield. Around the year 1100 he held the very senior title of *protonobelissimos*, and as *archon* of the *archontes* governed the distant eastern town of Marash (Germankeia) on behalf of the emperor.[91] A comparable example concerns Skylitzes' record of the handover of Vaspurakan by the Armenian prince Senacherim in the final decade of Basil II's reign.[92] Once again

[89] Skylitzes, *Synopsis*, 339–40; Anna Komnene, *Alexiade*, i. 73–4; *Typikon*: P. Gautier, 'Le Typikon du sébaste Grégoire Pakourianos', *REB* 42 (1984), 5–145; P. Lemerle, *Cinq études sur le XIe siècle byzantin* (Paris, 1970), 114–91; Skoulatos, *Les Personnages byzantins*, 112–15.

[90] Theophylact of Ochrid: letter 68. Gregory was appointed to command in Macedonia during the mid-1090s possibly as governor of Ochrid (Mullett, *Theophylact of Ochrid*, 94, 130, 146, 186, 215, 276).

[91] *Zacos Collection of Byzantine Lead Seals* 2 (1999), nos. 128–9.

[92] Skylitzes, *Synopsis*, 354–5; sigillographical evidence suggests that Senacherim's wife was granted the extremely high-ranking title of *zoste*, while his son David received the rank of *magistros* (see also below p. 213 n. 101 for the

a member of a family with the same name was closely associated with the Komnenos regime at the end of the eleventh century. In May 1089 Theodore Senacherim, described as a close associate (*oikeios*) of Emperor Alexios, was sent to oversee the restoration of the Xenophon monastery on Mount Athos to its original founder.[93]

Of course both these late eleventh-century personalities may have had very little to do with their late tenth- and early eleventh-century namesakes. Indeed, in the *typikon* of his monastery at Bačkovo, Gregory suggests that his family had still been located in Iberia until very recent times. He identifies his father as Pakourianos, the '*archon* of the *archontes* of the very noble race of the Iberians'. After his father's early death he himself wandered through Armenia, Iberia, and Syria before seeking employment within the Byzantine Empire.[94] His Caucasian background was also noted by Anna Komnene.[95] However, the probity of genealogical connec-

same title being granted to Maria of Bulgaria) (J.-C. Cheynet, 'La Patricienne à ceinture: une femme de qualité', in P. Henriet and A.-M. Legras (eds.), *Au Cloître et dans le monde: Femmes, hommes et sociétés (ixe–xve siècle). Mélanges en l'honneur de Paulette L'Hermit-Leclerq* (Paris, 2000), 182, 186); for Senacherim see also below 6.3.4.

[93] *Actes de Xénophon*, Archives de l'Athos XV, ed. D. Papachryssanthou (Paris, 1986), 71. This later 11th-c. Senacherim may also be the senior fiscal official of whom Theophylact of Ochrid complained *c.*1094/5 (Theophylact of Ochrid, letter 77; Mullett, *Theophylact of Ochrid*, 130). The seal from another member of this family, Abu Sahl Senacherim, survives: he held the title *kouropalates* (*Zacos Collection of Byzantine Lead Seals* 2 (1999), no. 121). It has been suggested that this seal belonged to the Abu Sahl who was another of the sons of Senacherim that migrated to Byzantium in Basil's reign (J.-C. Cheynet, 'La Patricienne à ceinture', 182).

[94] *Typikon* (Pakourianos), 21, 92.

[95] Anna terms Pakourianos an 'Armenian' (Anna Komnene, *Alexiade*, i. 74). Pakourianos identifies himself rather more broadly. According to his

tions did not have to be Skylitzes' principal concern. The more important point is that these names from the tenth and early eleventh centuries fitted the political landscape of the later eleventh-century world very neatly.

The most conspicuous group of outsiders to attract Skylitzes' interest in the reign of Basil II was the Bulgarian royal family, which was removed from imperial office in 1018 and absorbed within the Byzantine aristocracy. As we noted in Chapter 2, the second half of Skylitzes' testimony for the reign of Basil II concentrates almost exclusively on relations with the First Bulgarian Empire. Within this narrative most attention is paid to the last four years of the war and the final Bulgarian capitulation.[96] One of the principal themes of the narrative of this period is the history of the Bulgarian royal family itself. On the one hand Skylitzes notes, albeit with some chronological confusion, the death of Samuel Kometopoulos—an event he attributes to the shock of Samuel's dramatic loss at the Battle of Kleidion in 1014.[97] He also

typikon he founded his monastery explicitly for the Iberians who had served with him in the Byzantine army and who only spoke Georgian (*Typikon*, 21). However, he added his signature to the *typikon* in Armenian script (ibid. 130), while at the same time mentioning that he had Armenian relatives (ibid. 129); cf. N. G. Garsoïan, 'Armenian Integration into the Byzantine Empire', in H. Ahrweiler and A. E. Laiou (eds.), *Studies on the Internal Diaspora of the Byzantine Empire* (Washington DC, 1998), 89–91.

[96] See above 2.1.

[97] Skylitzes, *Synopsis*, 349, 351. In ch. 35 of Skylitzes' text, the battle of Kleidion is dated to 29 July. Skylitzes alleges that after the battle Basil blinded 15,000 Bulgarian prisoners-of-war, leaving one in every hundred with a single eye to lead the others home. On seeing his men returning in such a state, Samuel suffered a seizure and within two days was dead. His death is undated by Skylitzes, but Michael of Devol inserted the date of 6 Oct., suggesting that Samuel's death happened over two months after the original

records the brief reign of Samuel's son Gabriel Radomir. This was cut short when the new Bulgarian ruler was assassinated by his cousin John Vladislav.[98] The father of John had been Aaron, who we already know from an earlier passage in Skylitzes' account had been murdered by his brother Samuel when he was suspected of favouring the Byzantines.[99] Vladislav himself was killed in 1018 in battle outside the city of Dyrrachion, the event that precipitated the final surrender of the Bulgarians.[100] More intriguing, however, than Skylitzes' awareness of the dynastic history of the Bulgarian empire, is his keen and extensive interest in those members of the royal family that submitted to Basil in 1018. He carefully records that when Maria, the widow of John Vladislav, was brought before Basil II at Ochrid, she was accompanied by three of her own sons and six daughters, as well as by two daughters and five sons of the previous tsar, Gabriel Radomir, and an illegitimate son of the tsar Samuel, Gabriel's father. Skylitzes goes on to record the surrender shortly afterwards of three more sons of John Vladislav.[101]

battle had taken place. This date of death, however, does not accord with a date given a little later in the same chapter by Skylitzes himself, where he alleges that Samuel's son, Gabriel Romanos, began his reign as early as 15 Sept. Further uncertainty occurs in the next chapter (36), when Skylitzes relays a post-Kleidion story, which claims that the death of Samuel only became known to the Byzantines on 24 Oct. The best explanation of this chronological confusion is that Skylitzes may have tried, unsuccessfully, to synthesize two separate accounts, each of which gave different information about Samuel's death. For further analysis of the difficulties presented by Skylitzes when he attempts to unite contradictory texts see above 2.4.

[98] Skylitzes, *Synopsis*, 353.

[99] Ibid. 329.

[100] Ibid. 357.

[101] Ibid. 359–60. All of the medieval manuscripts record that one of the six sons was Prousianos. Manuscript [U] adds the names Alousianos, Aaron,

Moving beyond Basil's reign, Skylitzes continues to chart the progress of the principal members of the family, stressing above all their participation in conspiracies and their marital connections with the Byzantine aristocracy as a whole. Two episodes of aristocratic unrest involving Prousianos, one of John Vladislav's sons, during the reigns of Constantine VIII and Romanos III are described by Skylitzes. In the first of these accounts the reader is told that that the sister of Prousianos was married to Romanos Kourkouas who was blinded by Constantine VIII on suspicion of conspiracy.[102] During the reign of Michael IV, Skylitzes records the participation of Alousianos, the brother of Prousianos, in the Balkan revolt of Peter Deljan. He begins his description with the reflection that Alousianos was the second son of Aaron (that is, John Vladislav), and that he was married to a wife with an estate in the Anatolian theme of the Charsianon.[103]

It is likely that Skylitzes displays such long-term interest in the family history of the house of John Vladislav because by the end of the eleventh century all the principal families of the empire, including the Komnenoi, had genealogical connections to the former Bulgarian ruling dynasty. During the revolt of Isaac Komnenos in 1057 Skylitzes cites the *magistros* Aaron, one of the sons of John Vladislav, as one of the commanders who remained loyal to Emperor Michael

---

Traianos, Radomir; manuscript [E] adds the name Klimen. Cheynet, 'La Patricienne à ceinture', 181, notes that Maria was given the extremely high-ranking title of *zoste* (see also above, n. 92).

[102] Skylitzes, *Synopsis*, 372, 376, 384.
[103] Ibid. 413–15.

VI. Nonetheless, he also mentions that Aaron's sister was married to Isaac.[104] This sister was called Catherine. She became empress when her husband Isaac overthrew Michael VI and became emperor. Two years later Isaac was forced to abdicate. According to Michael Psellos, Catherine held Psellos himself responsible for her husband's demise. However, Psellos seems to have had grudging admiration for Catherine, who he noted was descended from a very noble family.[105] Anna Komnene confirms the continuing significance of Bulgarian aristocratic ancestry to status within Byzantine political society at the end of the eleventh and beginning of the twelfth century. One obscure revolt against Alexios, she notes, was led by 'a man who traced his ancestry back to the famous Aarones on one side'.[106]

Before leaving the Byzantine descendants of the last royal family of the first Bulgarian empire, it is worth noting that the idea that a late eleventh-century aristocratic context lies behind Skylitzes' treatment of the Balkans, above all his narrative of the Bulgarian wars of Basil II, is not completely new. A similar hypothesis was volunteered in a little-known article more than twenty years ago by I. Đurić. He drew attention to two verse eulogies to a certain Aaron *doux* and *proedros* which were composed by Theophylact of Ochrid after the archbishop had met the general on campaign in the

---

[104]　Skylitzes, *Synopsis*, 493.

[105]　Psellos, *Cronografia*, ii. 278–83.

[106]　Anna Komnene, *Alexiade*, iii. 88–91. Cheynet, *Pouvoir et contestations*, 102. In 1107 this Aaron accompanied Emperor Alexios on his campaign in the western Balkans against Bohemond (Skoulatos, *Les Personnages byzantins*, 3–4).

Balkans. These encomia are fulsome, praising Aaron for the imperial qualities of philanthropy and hospitality.[107] Durić links this Aaron to a certain Aaron Radomir whose seals survive in some numbers.[108] As Durić suggests, it is likely that this Aaron Radomir is also the same general as that Rodomir who Anne Komnene tells us fought against and was imprisoned by the Turks, an episode that enabled him to learn Turkish. He later campaigned with Alexios Komnenos against the Pechenegs and was present at the great Byzantine victory at Levounion in 1092.[109] In 1097 he was among those Byzantine commanders who negotiated the surrender of Nikaia from the Turks during the course of the First Crusade.[110] While Durić's suggestion that this Aaron is the same individual as that member of the family who rebelled against Alexios seems unlikely, not least because Anna quite specifically says that Aaron the insurgent was illegitimate, his article nonetheless draws attention to the exalted careers and pre-eminent reputations that members of the former Bulgarian royal family continued to enjoy during the early Komnenian period. Moreover, Durić also suspects that the disproportionately large amount of

[107] I. Durić, 'Theophylacte d'Achrida sous la tente d'Aaron', *ZRVI* 27 (1988), 89–91.

[108] These seals usually invert the name to Radomir Aaron. Seals survive that give him the titles of *vestes* and *magistros* and office of *strategos* (N. Oikonomides, *SBS* 3 (Washington DC, 1993), 184; V. Laurent, *Les Sceaux byzantins du Médailler Vatican* (Vatican, 1962), no. 148); according to seals issued later he held the more senior positions of *proedros* and *doux* (J.-C. Cheynet, 'Du Prénom au patronyme: les étrangers à Byzance', in N. Oikonomides (ed.), *SBS* 1 (Washington DC, 1987), 58–60).

[109] Anna Komnene, *Alexiade*, ii. 138; iii. 15.

[110] *Zacos Collection of Byzantine Lead Seals* 3 (1999), no. 278.

coverage accorded to the family of John Vladislav by Skylitzes and his rather more cursory treatment of the dynasty
of Samuel, may be explained by the fact that the Aarones
were a much more famous later eleventh-century Byzantine
dynasty than the descendants of Samuel's family.[111]

4.2.2 Imperial authority

Skylitzes' treatment of families such as the Aarones, the last
Bulgarian royal dynasty, makes it evident that our author
did not simply conceive of the *Synopsis Historion* as a
genealogical address book of the past. Instead, his wider
interpretation of the history of the Byzantine empire, 'the
more important events of the past' as he terms it, was
centred on dynastic competition and revolt, particularly
among those families who were famous at the end of the
eleventh century. The regularity with which aristocratic
insurrection punctuated the senior levels of elite political
society in Byzantium during the decades following the death
of the last Macedonian empress, Theodora, in 1056, does
not make such an interpretation surprising. Nonetheless,
the idea that Skylitzes produced a compendium of revolt
for an audience composed predominantly of aristocrats, at
first sight sits uneasily with his position as a highly placed
and trusted official within the administration and inner
court circle of Emperor Alexios I Komnenos. However, a
political context developed within Paul Magdalino's analysis

---

[111] Durić, 'Theophylacte d'Achrida', 91.

of Komnenian government suggests one way in which Skylitzes' professional career as a top-ranking Komnenian official could be compatible with this author's interpretation of the past as a story of aristocratic rivalry.

Magdalino has suggested that the regime of Emperor Alexios Komnenos was characterized by its inclusive policies towards other leading aristocratic families. One manifestation of this greater inclusiveness was frequent intermarriage between the great dynasties of the empire, such as the Komnenoi, the Doukai, the Kontostephanoi, and the Bryennioi. In the early years of Alexios' reign Magdalino believes that this strategy of intermarriage was not simply a form of imperial reward for loyal supporters, but a conciliatory policy explicitly designed to placate recent opponents.[112] While one cannot know whether Skylitzes' history was sponsored or commissioned by the emperor, it is possible that the articulation of history presented in the *Synopsis Historion* by one of the emperor's most loyal servants may be related to this official policy of division-healing within the aristocracy. The emphasis which it places on the predecessors of contemporary aristocratic families, their valiant deeds, their long-standing associations with high politics, and their frequent intermarriages, certainly suggests that the *Synopsis Historion* of Skylitzes contains echoes of the Komnenian propaganda which accompanied the processes of dynastic integration.

[112] Magdalino, *Manuel Komnenos*, 187, 202–6; Cheynet, *Pouvoir et contestations*, 359–60, 369–75.

The idea that a context of greater political inclusiveness underpins Skylitzes' production could certainly help to explain the appearance and elaboration of other kinds of materials within the *Synopsis Historion*. For example, at several key junctures in his later tenth- and eleventh-century testimony Skylitzes describes the interventions of the military saints, Theodore *Stratelates*, George, and especially Demetrios. He records that after the fall of Preslav in Bulgaria in 971 to Emperor John Tzimiskes, the Rus were defeated in open battle on the feast day of Saint George. During Tzmiskes' final victory over the Rus at Dristra in 971, Saint Theodore was said to have appeared on a white horse offering assistance to the imperial armies. Skylitzes also mentions Tzimiskes' subsequent support for the cult of Theodore at Euchaneia in Paphlagonia.[113] An aside inserted into the text shortly after Basil II's victory over Bardas Phokas at Abydos records the emperor's pilgrimage to the tomb of Saint Demetrios at Thessalonika.[114] Later in the text during Skylitzes' coverage of the revolt of the Bulgarians led

[113] Skylitzes, *Synopsis*, 300, 308–9. The emperor rebuilt the church containing the tomb of Saint Theodore at Euchaneia and renamed the town Theodoroupolis. N. Oikonomides, 'Le Dédoublement de Saint Théodore et les villes d'Euchaïta et d'Euchaina', *AB* 104 (1986), 327–35, argues that Euchaina/Euchaneia, the cult centre of Saint Theodore the General, *Stratelates*, was probably a hilltop site near the city of Euchaita, the location of the tomb of Saint Theodore the Recruit, *Tiron*. The tombs of both St Theodores were popular pilgrimage sites during the 11th c. (E. Malamut, *Sur la route des saints byzantins* (Paris, 1993), 42).

[114] Skylitzes, *Synopsis*, 339. It was probably during this pilgrimage to Thessalonika, which preceded his 991 campaign against the Bulgarians, that Basil met St Photios, the monk who became his spiritual guide and accompanied him on campaigns thereafter. During his lifetime Basil made pilgrimages to the tombs of the warrior martyrs St George, St Theodore *Tiron* and

by Peter Deljan *c.*1040, Saint Demetrios is also attributed with the relief of the siege of the city of Thessalonika.[115] It is possible that these stories were purposefully included, or retained, in Skylitzes' text because by the mid- to later eleventh century, military saints were a powerful propaganda tool for the rallying of aristocratic solidarity. The popularity of military saints among soldiers and aristocrats is nowhere more visible than on the lead seals of many members of the Byzantine political elite, especially those who held senior military positions, and no one was more fond of these saints than the Komnenoi.[116] The seals issued by Alexios Komnenos himself before he became emperor depict Demetrios. The seals of his brothers Isaac and Adrian feature Saints Theodore and George respectively.[117] The Komnenian emperors also used depictions of military saints on some of their issues of coinage. Alexios' own choice fell on Saint Demetrios.[118]

St Theodore *Stratelates* (Crostini, 'The Emperor Basil II's Cultural Life', 78; Schlumberger, *L'Épopée byzantine*, i. 646; ii. 46–7; see also discussion of this text above in 1.3).

[115] Skylitzes, *Synopsis*, 413. Kekaumenos, who conveys a shorter narrative of the same siege, does not mention the intervention of St Demetrios (Kekaumenos, *Consilia et Narrationes*, 160–2).

[116] For further discussion of the relationship between aristocratic political competition and the iconography of seals see J.-C. Cheynet, 'Par Saint Georges, Par Saint Michel', *TM* 14 (2002), 115–34.

[117] See e.g. G. Zacos and A. Veglery, *Byzantine Lead Seals*, 3 vols. (Basel, 1972), i, nos. 2701–2 (Isaac brother of Alexios); nos. 2704–07 (Alexios before he became emperor); no. 2708 (Adrian).

[118] Mullett, *Theophylact of Ochrid*, 51 and n. 213. The St Demetrios issue was struck at Thessalonika. Although the recent study of military saints by Walter deals with depictions on a variety of media, it does not deal extensively with sigillographical representations: C. Walter, *The Warrior Saints in*

But of greater significance to the argument that Skylitzes' *Synopsis Historion* is predicated on the desirability of cohesion within the early Komnenian polity, is the fact that most of the miraculous interventions cited by Skylitzes occur in Balkan contexts. At the end of the eleventh century the principal theatre of Byzantine warfare was located in the Balkans. In the first two decades of Alexios' reign Byzantine armies were engaged with Normans in the west of the region and nomads in the north. Anna Komnene's accounts of Alexios' Balkan expeditions in this period make it clear that many leading aristocrats occupied positions of high command within the Byzantine campaign armies. Yet, research by Jean-Claude Cheynet has argued the Balkan policy of the early years of Alexios' reign may have been unpopular with many members of the Byzantine elite. Cheynet notes that most incidents of aristocratic discontent against the Komnenian regime occurred shortly after imperial victories

Byzantine Art and Tradition (Aldershot, 2001). It is interesting to note Walter's point that the earliest depictions of warrior saints tend to date from the reigns of late 10th-c. emperors, including most famously of all, the roundels containing busts of the military saints which surround Basil II in the frontispiece to that emperor's psalter. However, it was only in the 11th c. that the cults of these saints as soldiers began to gather pace. This was the case, according to Walter, at least as far as the two Theodores (*Tiron* and *Stratelates*) and George were concerned. He doubts whether the cult of Demetrios had developed a military dimension before the 13th c., although by the 11th c. troops stationed in Thessalonika already anointed themselves with myrrh from the saint's tomb before going into battle. However, sigillographical and numismatic materials from the 11th c., as well as contemporary carved images in ivory and precious stones, suggest that Demetrios was already seen as a soldier saint by the end of the 11th c. (Walter, *Warrior Saints*, 48–65, 78–90, 126–33, 274–83; Cheynet, 'Grandeur et décadence', 132; Evans and Wixom, *Glory of Byzantium*, 134–6).

in the Balkans; whereas, once Alexios turned his attention to Asia Minor in the second half of his reign such dissent evaporated.[119] If Skylitzes was at work on the *Synopsis Historion* in the first half of Alexios' reign, perhaps during the 1090s, then he was writing at a time when imperial attention was still predominantly focused on the Balkans. In these circumstances, it seems reasonable to argue that one of Skylitzes' motivations in writing may have been to allay contemporary aristocratic suspicion of the geographical trajectory of Alexios' campaigns. Such a motivation would explain two conspicuous preoccupations within Skylitzes' text: first, the overwhelming interest which his narrative takes in the Balkans; and second, the author's frequent demonstration that it was the bravery of earlier aristocratic generations that had regained the Balkans for the empire in the reigns of John Tzimiskes and Basil II.

Both of these preoccupations are visible throughout the whole of Skylitzes' text. As we have already seen, the second half of Skylitzes' treatment of the reign of Basil is almost entirely devoted to the Bulgarian wars. During the course of that narrative he lionizes senior army generals such as Nikephoros Xiphias.[120] He also dedicates more than two-thirds of his coverage of the reign of John Tzimiskes (969–76) to the Balkan sphere, the context in which the heroics of Anemas are recorded. Other aristocratic names who receive Skylitzes' attention during his Balkan coverage in the later tenth and early eleventh centuries include Gregory and

---

[119] Cheynet, *Pouvoir et contestations*, 362, 368.
[120] See discussion of episodes involving Xiphias above at 3.2.2 and 4.1.

Ashot Taronites, Theophylact and Michael Botaneiates, Constantine Diogenes, and David Areianites.[121] These were exactly the families who enjoyed immense political authority at the end of the eleventh century and whose loyalty Alexios needed to consolidate. For example, the Taronitai were a high-profile family related to the Komnenoi by marriage, and as we have seen to the Bulgarian royal family of Samuel.[122] The Diogenes family had already provided one emperor of recent times, Romanos IV (1068–71); by the 1090s his son Nikephoros was perceived to be the most dangerous of Alexios' rivals. Despite serving with the imperial campaigns of the 1080s against Normans and Pechenegs, and being appointed governor of Crete, Nikephoros was eventually blinded in 1094 on charges of conspiracy.[123] Meanwhile, the scion of another leading family, Nikephoros III Botaneiates, had occupied the imperial throne before Alexios became emperor. Even families featured in Skylitzes' tenth- and early eleventh-century Balkan coverage with less prestigious later eleventh-century credentials remained influential in the period when Alexios came to power. Towards the end of the eleventh century, for example, a certain

---

[121] Skylitzes, *Synopsis*, 339–42 (Taronites); 350 (Botaneiates); 352, 355–6, 365 (Diogenes); 345, 354–5, 358 (Areianites).

[122] John Taronites was the brother-in-law of Alexios Komnenos (Cheynet, *Pouvoir et contestations*, 277); for their relationship to the Bulgarian royal family see above 4.1.

[123] Nikephoros participated in military actions against the Normans in 1081 and Pechenegs 1087 (Anna Komnene, *Alexiade*, i. 155; ii. 90, 96, 100); Anna also outlines his subsequent conspiracy (ibid. ii. 169–84); see also for the careers of Diogenes family members during Alexios' reign, Cheynet, 'Grandeur et décadence', 133–5.

Leo Areianites held the senior rank of *protoproedros* and was *katepano* of the theme of the Optimatoi.[124]

Further support for the idea that late eleventh-century demands of greater political inclusiveness conditioned Skylitzes' view of the Balkans emerges if we examine closely the ways in which our author interprets and recasts several episodes within his Bulgarian coverage from the later tenth and early eleventh centuries. Let us begin with his treatment of John Tzimiskes' siege of Dristra against the Rus in 971. During a detailed study of the Greek sources which report on this battle, Stamatina McGrath has observed that both Leo the Deacon and Skylitzes composed their accounts of this campaign using the same basic source material. She argues that Leo's account was much more faithful to original detail, whereas Skylitzes was vaguer and more generalized. For example, where Leo reports that Svyatoslav, the leader of the Rus, was hit between the neck and the shoulder by the Byzantine hero Anemas, Skylitzes merely reflects that he was hit on the head. Equally where Leo alleges that one of the Byzantine generals, John Kourkouas, was killed while he was drunk, divinely punished for pilfering some Bulgarian holy vessels, Skylitzes maintains more prosaically that he was killed while heroically defending a siege machine.[125] It seems likely that Skylitzes is calling upon his ubiquitous

---

[124] Nesbitt and Oikonomides, *Byzantine Seals at Dumbarton Oaks*, iii. no. 71.27.

[125] McGrath, 'The Battles of Dorostolon', 152–62; Skylitzes, *Synopsis*, 304, 308; Leo the Deacon, *Historiae Libri Decem*, 148 (Kourkouas), 153 (death of Anemas). For the possibility that Leo the Deacon and John Skylitzes used the same source, probably a war diary (*Kriegsbuch*), see above 2.4.

generalizing and homogenizing military vocabulary to describe both of these martial encounters.[126] Yet, the fact that Skylitzes went to the trouble of altering the narrative involving John Kourkouas requires more explanation than simple standardization of vocabulary. The clue to this emendation may be lurking in the career of one of Kourkouas' late eleventh-century descendants. In 1092, close to the time when Alexios finally defeated the nomad Pechenegs at the Battle of Mount Levounion, a certain Gregory Kourkouas was *doux* of Philippoupolis, a crucial position in the defence system of the Balkans.[127] With such an important Balkan city in the hands of Kourkouas, Skylitzes had a powerful motive for obscuring the fact that during that glorious campaign which had first taken Byzantine frontiers back up to the Danube in 971, one of Gregory's forebears had been drunk at his post.

In rather different ways Skylitzes' treatment of Basil II's disastrous expedition to Bulgaria in 986 drives home a similar message to his potential readers: that success in the Balkans is dependent on aristocratic co-operation and enthusiasm; without such consensus catastrophe ensues. As we noted in previous chapters, the Byzantine invasion and

---

[126] For more discussion of this standardized vocabulary see above 3.2 and 3.3.2.

[127] Kourkouas' position as *doux* of Philippoupolis is known from sigillographical and epigraphical evidence. It is a dated inscription at Plovdiv (Philippoupolis) which indicates that he held the position of *doux* in 1091–2 (I. Jordanov, 'Medieval Plovdiv According to the Sphragistic Data', in N. Oikonomides (ed.), SBS 4 (Washington DC, 1995), 119–21). The prominence of the Kourkouai at the end of the 11th c. may also explain why their pedigree is retained in Skylitzes' coverage of the reign of Romanos Lekapenos; for the retention of pedigrees see above 3.2.

attempted siege of Sardica in 986, and the emperor's subsequent defeat by Samuel, is one of the longer narratives within Skylitzes' coverage of Basil II's reign, yet a narrative that is also characterized by the ubiquitous use of Skylitzes' anodyne military lexicon, which glosses over the precise strategic and martial details of the campaign.[128] Yet, what is striking is that over this rather pallid strategic background, Skylitzes paints a very strong picture of why in his view Basil's invasion failed: a picture of acute aristocratic rivalry and distrust. At the very beginning of his narrative he mentions that Leo Melissenos, *magistros*, was left to keep watch over the army's rearguard, enabling Basil himself to enter Bulgaria and besiege the city of Sardica; meanwhile, Samuel and his Bulgarian forces looked on from their mountain fastnesses, afraid to encounter the emperor in open battle. But once the siege was underway Stephen (or Kontostephanos), the *domestikos* of the west, out of jealousy warned the emperor that he should return to Constantinople because Melissenos was about to seize power. Frightened by this rumour Basil ordered the army to break camp; as his troops withdrew they were savagely attacked by Samuel; the Bulgarians seized everything including the imperial tent. When the remnants of the army reached Philoppoupolis, where Melissenos was stationed, the rumour of the emperor's imminent deposition proved to be false. Basil reacted angrily; he and Kontostephanos argued at length; eventually the emperor seized Kontostephanos by the beard and threw him to the ground. As is often the case with his

---

[128] Skylitzes, *Synopsis*, 330–1; see also above 2.4 and 3.3.2.

longer narratives, Skylitzes concludes his account with a particularly colourful, entertaining image.[129]

Yet, if Skylitzes' account is compared with more contemporary extant narratives of the same campaign, then suspicions arise that he has used some of his characteristic narrative techniques—bland military narrative, stress on aristocratic names, and a strong final punchline—to obfuscate the military failings of the Byzantine army of the tenth century, and recast the story according to the political exigencies of the later eleventh. Leo the Deacon, an eye-witness who travelled with Basil to Bulgaria in 986, does not mention an altercation between Melissenos and Kontostephanos at all; instead in a detailed description of the siege of Sardica and the subsequent disorderly Byzantine withdrawal, he consistently indicates that the campaign failed because of incompetence and complacency on the part of Basil's generals, and a critical lack of supplies which distracted the large army from their principal military tasks. Rather than simply being intercepted by the Bulgarians as they returned home, as Skylitzes suggests, the Byzantine army was subject to constant raids much earlier in the campaign, notably during the siege of Sardica when small parties were attacked as they tried to gather food and fodder.[130]

While the validity of Skylitzes' account cannot be challenged simply because Leo offers an alternative set of causes to the defeat of 986, nonetheless, there is independent evidence to support Leo's rather than Skylitzes' conclusions.

---

[129] For more on Skylitzes' desire to entertain see above 3.3.2.
[130] Leo the Deacon, *Historiae Libri Decem*, 171–3.

This comes from the *Taktikon Vári,* that military manual customarily dated to the later tenth or early eleventh century, which deals primarily with Byzantine warfare in the Balkans. It dwells on those dimensions of warfare it considers critical to military success in a Balkan context: the need to establish a strong and well-organized camp; the need to maintain a regular line of supplies from the empire itself—the army cannot expect to live off the land in Bulgaria, a region that the author of the treatise considers impoverished; the need to protect oneself against attack in the passes. So close are the parallels between these recommendations and the basic military errors that Leo identified in his account of the 986 expedition, that it has been suggested that the *Taktikon Vári* was composed in response to the disaster of that year, and that it was subsequently used as a blueprint for Basil's later campaigns in Bulgaria.[131]

The very terse account of the 986 campaign related by the contemporary Armenian historian, Stephen of Taron, also seems to confirm that the Byzantines were defeated in 986 because of inexperience and incompetence, especially in dealing with warfare in the mountain passes, rather than because of a dispute between Melissenos and Kontostephanos. Stephen indicates that the imperial army was completely destroyed by Bulgarian ambushes. Of course, it is important to remember that Stephen may exaggerate the extent of the Byzantine defeat for his own pro-Armenian polemical purposes: according to Stephen, Basil only

---

[131] 'Campaign Organisation and Tactics', 246–326. For the suggestion that this treatise was written in response to the 986 defeat see ibid. 242.

escaped back into imperial territory because he was saved by the Armenian infantry.[132] Nonetheless, while the accounts of contemporary historians such as Leo and Stephen could be shaped by subtexts and agendas as idiosyncratic and polemical as those of later historians such as Skylitzes, comparison of the different appraisals of the 986 campaign appears to indicate that incompetence and inexperience were fundamental to Byzantine defeat. This is a context that Skylitzes chooses to ignore. Instead using anaemic martial prose, he creates a featureless military backdrop onto which he pins his more important later eleventh-century message: that military disaster in the Balkans springs directly from aristocratic dissent.

A third, and final, example from the end of Basil II's Bulgarian campaigns illustrates conclusively Skylitzes' efforts to draw together the twin themes of conquest in the Balkans and the bravery of earlier generations of aristocrats. This example concerns the capture of the renegade Bulgarian general Ibatzes by the Byzantine commander Eustathios Daphnomeles. It represents the longest single narrative in Skylitzes' Balkan coverage of Basil II's reign, extending to nearly three sides of printed text, and occurs halfway through Skylitzes' general description of the Bulgarian surrender to the Byzantines in 1018.[133] It tells the story of the senior Bulgarian commander Ibatzes, who fled to a remote and moutainous fortified palace site with the hope of ruling Bulgaria for himself. He was obdurate against all forms of

---

[132] Stephen of Taron, *Armenische Geschichte*, 186–7.
[133] Skylitzes, *Synopsis*, 360–4.

imperial flattery and bribery. As a result Basil was forced to suspend his triumphant progress around Bulgaria and his receipt of the subjugation of local princes and commanders; instead he confined himself to Devol for fifty-five days while he waited for Ibatzes to concede. At this point Eustathios Daphnomeles, the new Byzantine governor (termed, with typical vagueness, *archon* by Skylitzes) took it upon himself to remedy the impasse. He inveigled his way into the crowds that celebrated the Feast of the Dormition of the Virgin at Ibatzes' palace. Once inside the palace he announced himself to Ibatzes, who was amazed at the daring of the Byzantine commander, but who assumed that Daphnomeles intended to join him in his resistance to Basil. Soon the two generals withdrew into a heavily wooded glade within the palace gardens for further negotations. At this point Eustathios wrestled Ibatzes to the ground, pinioned him with his knee, called on his two associates to stuff Ibatzes' mouth with cloth, blinded him, and then cast him back into the hall of the palace. The Byzantine assailants then ran to an upper room of the palace while anguished crowds gathered below seizing staves, bows, spears, torches, and whatever came to hand that would serve as a weapon. At this point Daphnomeles delivered an impassioned speech that persuaded the crowds to submit to the emperor and hand over Ibatzes.

Skylitzes' justification for inserting this story into his main account of the Bulgarian surrender to Basil is that the narrative, 'contains something sweet and wondrous' (ἔχει γὰρ ἡδύ τι καὶ θαυμαστὸν ἡ διήγησις).[134] But what

---

[134] Ibid. 360.

exactly does Skylitzes mean here? Certainly the Ibatzes story is much more detailed and vivid than is customary for the *Synopsis Historion.* It has an unusually strong sense of place and time. It also includes a long speech; again a rarity, for as we noted in Chapter 3 of this volume, Skylitzes usually chooses to compress extended addresses.[135] One obvious reason for Skylitzes' retention, or insertion, of the Ibatzes' story into his wider narrative is that it was highly entertaining. It has a high quotient of strategic cunning and gratuitous violence, qualities that we have already indicated appealed to later eleventh-century aristocratic audiences.[136] Yet, both the position of the Ibatzes–Daphnomeles episode within the general account of the Bulgarian surrender, and the contents of the episode itself, suggest that this sweet and wondrous narrative served purposes other than mere entertainment, or inconsequential and light-hearted digression. Instead, examined closely, this episode proves to be Skylitzes' most patent articulation of the principle that Basil II's Balkan conquests were achieved through the bravery and initiative of an aristocracy willing to sacrifice its own selfish interests to the greater good of the empire.

As with so many other episodes in the coverage of Basil's reign, Skylitzes accords only a very slight and indirect role in this narrative to the emperor himself. Skylitzes makes it clear that the emperor desired the capitulation of Ibatzes, but the

---

[135] See above 3.2.

[136] See above 4.1; Charlotte Roueché has identified the Daphnomeles–Ibatzes narrative in the *Synopsis Historion* as one of the first examples of a new interest in fictional narrative in later 11th-c. Byzantine literature (Roueché, 'Byzantine Writers and Readers', 128).

means by which these wishes are conveyed to Daphnomeles are unstated. Instead the power of the episode lies in the fact that Daphnomeles decides to fulfil this general imperial desire through his own bravery and initiative. Also noteworthy is the fact that the narrative colour in this episode occurs at the beginning of Skylitzes' tale, from the time when Daphnomeles enters the palace of Ibatzes to the moment when the distraught crowds become aware of the blinding of their leader. So powerful and immediate is the action in this passage that it is probably copied verbatim from Skylitzes' underlying source, an authorial strategy which we know Skylitzes sometimes adopts.[137] However, once Ibatzes' assailants escape upstairs, the nature of the narrative changes radically. As so often with Skylitzes' Balkan coverage, it is at this point that we take leave of original detail and re-enter the universe of military platitudes and homogenous heroic prose. These are diagnostics that should immediately alert the reader to the possibility that the second section of the Ibatzes–Daphnomeles episode has either been reglossed or manufactured from scratch by Skylitzes himself, a recasting that will allow the author's own message to come across all the more clearly.

Initial signs of the intrusion of Skylitzes the interventionist author occur when Eustathios encourages his small band of comrades to be brave, not to yield, or betray themselves and fall into the hands of those who would seek their destruction, but instead either accept salvation from their

---

[137] For this strategy see above 3.2.

adversaries or a pitiable and painful death.[138] Such generalized exhortations to bravery before armed encounter litter
the pages of Skylitzes' tenth- and eleventh-century testimony.[139] However, more intriguing is the speech that
Eustathios delivers to the crowd of Bulgarians. For it is
here that the full range of Skylitzes' most important aristocratic and Balkan interests can be found clustered in a single
passage. In this address Eustathios stresses the amity and
common political society that could and should exist between the Bulgarian and Roman (Byzantine) aristocracy:
'I reserve no hatred for your dynast.' It is striking that Skylitzes, through Eustathios, applies the same generic aristocratic label (*dynastes*) to Ibatzes as he uses for members of
the Byzantine political elite.[140] Eustathios also notes the
potential common ground between Bulgarians and Romans,
not just those Romans who come from Thrace and Macedonia, but also those who come from far away in Asia
Minor. If Cheynet and Magdalino are correct in suggesting
that many members of the late eleventh-century Byzantine
aristocracy were more interested in fighting the Turks in
Asia Minor than protecting the empire in the Balkans,
then here is a powerful message from an eastern aristocrat
that in more successful times the energies of all were directed

---

[138] Skylitzes, *Synopsis*, 362.

[139] See e.g. Skylitzes' account of how Bardas Phokas motivated himself
before meeting Basil II in battle at Abydos in 989 (Skylitzes, *Synopsis*, 337; see
also below 5.2.3). Skylitzes attributes similar sentiments to Bardas in his
account of the rebellion of 971 against Emperor John Tzimiskes (Skylitzes,
Synopsis, 293–4).

[140] See above p. 191.

towards the west.[141] And yet Eustathios, and Skylitzes, make it clear that such reckless, and apparently hopeless, acts of bravery are dictated by a higher cause: service to the emperor: 'The more prudent of you will realize that I have not undertaken such a deed heedlessly or in vain, but that some compulsion impelled me. For I would not have thrown myself so madly into manifest danger and despise my own life, if there was not another reason forcing me to approach the deed. You should know that this action is the order of the emperor, whom I in obedience serve as a tool.'[142]

Nonetheless, while service to the emperor may be the underlying rationale of such desperate heroism, this is not risk without recompense. Instead, Skylitzes uses the pithy punchline that concludes so many of his narratives to drive across the real message of this particular story: that service to the emperor in the Balkans brings reward. For after Ibatzes was handed over and commended to prison, Daphnomeles was appointed *strategos* of Dyrrachion and granted all his Bulgarian adversary's movable wealth.[143]

The degree to which personal reward was the traditional final outcome of service to the emperor in the Balkans is mirrored in another narrative from Skylitzes' Balkan coverage of Basil's reign. This is the story of the annexation of Sirmion by Constantine Diogenes, an episode that replicates the Ibatzes–Daphnomeles narrative in theme but which is expressed rather more briefly. Like Ibatzes, Sermon the

---

[141] Magdalino, *Manuel Komnenos*, 187, 202–6; Cheynet, *Pouvoir et contestations*, 359–77.

[142] Skylitzes, *Synopsis*, 362.

[143] Skylitzes, *Synopsis*, 363.

archon of Serbia, with his principle fortress at Sirmion, refused to surrender to the emperor; like Daphnomeles, Constantine Diogenes took it upon himself to resolve the situation. As in the Ibatzes–Daphnomeles episode, Sermon was tricked into a meeting which rapidly turned into an ambush. On this occasion, however, the Balkan commander was killed rather than blinded. As we have already seen, Sermon's wife was dispatched to Constantinople to be married.[144] The more striking parallel between the Ibatzes and Sermon episodes, however, is the punchline: the reward that the triumphant Byzantine commander received from his victory. Here Skylitzes states laconically, 'And Diogenes was appointed to rule in the newly acquired lands.' In fact, as Paul Stephenson has pointed out, direct Byzantine control of the region of Serbia and the fortress of Sirmion appears to have been relatively short-lived; Diogenes was soon withdrawn from this frontier area, and control was ceded back to local commanders, or župans.[145] However, the longevity of the precise rewards that service to the emperor in the Balkans brought individual aristocratic families was unlikely to have been the principal issue for Skylitzes. Instead, in general terms he was simply concerned to demonstrate that rewards from service in the Balkans were forthcoming in the past and could be so again in the future. More importantly, by dwelling on official positions and material recompense he was able to demonstrate how the

---

[144] See above p. 192; see also Cheynet, 'Grandeur et décadence', 123.

[145] Stephenson, *Byzantium's Balkan Frontier*, 66, 124; idem, 'The Balkan Frontier in the Year 1000', in P. Magdalino (ed.), *Byzantium in the Year 1000* (Leiden, 2002), 122–3, 125–6; idem, *Legend of Basil the Bulgar-slayer*, 45–6.

rise to prominence of many of the great families of the later eleventh century, such as the Diogenes, was originally based on their contribution to Basil II's wars in Bulgaria.

Of course in linking the prestige of leading aristocratic dynasties of the late eleventh century to the martial successes of Basil's reigns, Skylitzes was not alone. Other historians of the same period were making precisely the same point, although in ways rather more partial to single families. Nikephoros Bryennios begins his account of the deeds of Alexios Komnenos by relating how John and Isaac Komnenos, the father and uncle of Alexios, were entrusted as young boys into Basil's II tutelage by their father and were trained as soldiers within the imperial army.[146] Meanwhile according to Michael Attaleiates, Nikephoros the grandfather of Nikephoros Botaneiates III (1078–81) was single-handedly responsible for bringing Basil's Bulgarian campaigns to a successful conclusion. Attaleiates also alleges that Michael Botaneiates, Nikephoros III's father, who fought with imperial armies in Bulgaria and later in Iberia, was regarded as the emperor's son.[147] Such references make it clear that by the later eleventh century the wars of Basil II were routinely manipulated by rival families in the service of dynastic prestige and promotion. These preoccupations suggest that Skylitzes was wise to stress the aristocratic component of previous emperors' Balkan campaigns, above all those of Basil II. Even if most late eleventh-century aristocrats were more concerned with contemporary Asia Minor, the

---

[146] Bryennios (Nikephoros): *Nicephori Bryennii Historiarum Libri Quattuor*, ed. and trans. P. Gautier, CFHB 9 (Brussels, 1975), 75.
[147] Attaleiates, *Historia*, 229–36.

Balkans received a privileged position within their own dynastic propaganda. If Skylitzes was serious in promoting a joint imperial–aristocratic alliance in the Balkans in the final decades of the eleventh century, his decision to highlight the bravery and achievements of the ancestors of the contemporary Byzantine aristocracy gave him the greatest chance of a receptive audience.

For Skylitzes writing at the end of the eleventh century the history of the reign of Basil II fell into two neat sections. The first comprised a period of aristocratic conflict in which the empire suffered. The ambitions and rivalries of Bardas Skleros and Bardas Phokas framed Basil II's disastrous foray into Bulgaria, an invasion that was itself doomed by aristocratic competition. The second half of the reign was typified by the ingenuity, energy, and co-operation of the aristocracy, both Byzantine and Bulgarian. While the empire remained politically fragmented during the later eleventh century, Skylitzes' reading of history made sense in contemporary eyes. But by the mid-twelfth century Skylitzes' analysis was obsolete. As the Komnenoi secured their imperial dynasty, there was no need to interpret the past in terms of rival aristocratic families, whose co-operation led to imperial success, and whose dissent boded disaster. When the later Komnenoi looked to exploit the legacy of Basil's reign, they did so in radically different ways. For Manuel Komnenos, Basil's reign was not a tissue of elite rivalries, heroism, and machinations. Instead it was a period of self-confident imperial splendour. According to an anonymous poem written in the reign of Manuel Komnenos, the emperor built a new refectory at the monastery of Mokios, a foundation once restored by Basil II himself. This refectory was decorated with portraits of the three Komnenian emperors, Alexios, John, and Manuel, as well as Basil II.[148] Meanwhile, Skylitzes' text survived within the substrata of later historians' works. His narrative provided the fundamental structure for mid-twelfth-century synoptic historians such as Zonaras and Glykas. But, as we saw in the case of Zonaras' use of the *Synopsis Historion,* Skylitzes' rather dated concerns about a fragmented and competitive aristocracy could by this point be cast aside.

This chapter has explored the later eleventh-century literary, social, and political contexts within which John Skylitzes composed the *Synopsis Historion.* It has argued that the text itself was compiled by an author who worked within the upper echelons of the imperial administration during the first two decades of Komnenian rule. It was deliberately written for an aristocratic audience based primarily in the Constantinopolitan court. This hypothesis is supported not only by the fact that Skylitzes held a senior position within the imperial government of Alexios Komnenos, but also by textual evidence from within the *Synopsis Historion* itself. Skylitzes' devotion to the deeds and pedigrees of the leading aristocratic families of the Byzantine empire has been discussed in depth and located in a very distinct political context: the internal and external insecurity of the Byzantine Empire during the later eleventh century. Hostility between rival aristocratic families encouraged Skylitzes to interpret

---

[148] C. A. Mango, *The Art of the Byzantine Empire* (Toronto, 1986), 226; Stephenson, *Legend of Basil the Bulgar-slayer,* 87–94.

the Byzantine past in terms of dynastic connections and competition. His interest in the Balkans seems to have been shaped by a desire that all the major aristocratic families should work together to protect the empire from external attack.

These later eleventh-century literary, social, and political contexts clearly shaped Skylitzes' presentation of the reign of Basil II, sometimes in distorting ways. Skylitzes' prosopography of Basil's reign is often conditioned by his interest in the 'Who's Who' of the Komnenian period. This has the potential to confuse our understanding of the relative importance of individuals and families within political society during the reign of Basil: Skylitzes may mention minor characters, such as the Skleros rebels and a variety of imperial outsiders, more because of the political significance of their eleventh-century descendants than because of their own political importance. It is also clear that Skylitzes' enthusiasm for interpreting the Byzantine past through the achievements of the great aristocratic families can obscure the role and authority of the emperor, and offer a false impression of the balance of power between imperial authority and leading members of the political elite. While such a balance of power in favour of the aristocracy was the context within which the later eleventh-century politics of Skylitzes' own lifetime were played out, the political situation in the reign of Basil II was quite different. As the rest of this book will demonstrate, the reign of Basil was a period when imperial authority was far from moribund either at home or abroad. The challenge for Basil was not how to rebuild imperial authority through negotiating and rewarding a fragmented and recalcitrant aristocracy; this was the challenge that the Komnenian emperors faced. Instead, Basil's task was completely different: how to gain and retain control of the core institutions of imperial governance.

5

The Revolts of Skleros and Phokas: Historiography and the Skleros Manifesto

5.1 HISTORICAL OUTLINE

The last two chapters have explored the main Greek narrative of Basil's reign, the *Synopsis Historion* of John Skylitzes. Both discussions have been predicated on the premiss that Skylitzes' treatment of the reign of Basil II is best approached through an understanding of how his text as a whole was put together at the end of the eleventh century. One of the key reasons for adopting this broader historiographical focus is the lack of other historical accounts covering the period 976–1025 against which Skylitzes' coverage of Basil's reign can be compared directly. However, there is one period of Basil's reign where the problem of scarcity of evidence is less acute, and where a relatively substantial section of Skylitzes' account can be set against several other detailed historical narratives. This period comprises the first thirteen years of the reign (976–89), when Emperor Basil and Constantine VIII, Basil's brother and co-emperor, were challenged for imperial power by the generals Bardas

Skleros and Bardas Phokas. In addition to accounting for approximately half of Skylitzes' coverage of Basil's reign, these revolts represent the dominant narrative in the analyses of the reign presented by Leo the Deacon and Michael Psellos.[1] Meanwhile allusions to the revolts also occur in Greek hagiographical materials: in the *Miracles of St Eugenios* of Trebizond and the *Vita* of St Nikon Metanoiete of Sparta.[2] More striking, however, is the extent to which the revolts also command considerable attention from contemporary historians and hagiographers working on the eastern periphery of the Byzantine world in languages other than Greek. These writers include Stephen of Taron and Grigor Narekac'i (both writing in Armenian), Yahya ibn Sa'id (in Arabic), and the author of the Georgian *Life of John and Euthymios*.[3] Even historians writing in Arabic in locations far away from Byzantium, whose interest in the domestic history of the empire was rather more occasional, such as Ibn Miskawayh and Abu Shudja al-Rudhrawari, pay close attention to internal Byzantine affairs during this period.[4]

Beyond the principal historical accounts, our understanding of the revolts is enhanced by an array of epigraphical evidence, manuscript colophons, and archive documents

[1] Skylitzes, *Synopsis*, 314–39; Leo the Deacon, *Historiae Libri Decem*, 169–75; Psellos, *Cronografia*, i. 8–43.

[2] *Miracles of Saint Eugenios*, 343–52; *St Nikon*, ch. 39.

[3] Stephen of Taron, *Armenische Geschichte*, 140–3, 187–9; J.-P. Mahé, 'Basile II et Byzance vus par Grigor Narekac'i', *TM* 11 (1991), 555–72; *Life of John and Euthymios*, 67–142; Georgian Royal Annals, 373–4; Yahya, *PO* 23, pp. 372–89, 398–402, 418–27.

[4] Ibn Miskawayh, *Eclipse*, v. 424–5, 436–9; al-Rudhrawari, *Eclipse*, vi. 6–7, 23–35, 115–19.

from several different language traditions. A series of documents (or rather, as we shall see below, quasi-documents)
from Iraq, which were written in Arabic, still survive and
relate to the period between 980 and 987, when Bardas
Skleros was held captive by the Buyid emir of Baghdad.
These documents include letters, treaties, and eye-witness
narrative accounts: an edited version of the original diplomatic report of the envoy Ibn Shahram who was sent to
Constantinople from Baghdad in 981/2;[5] a propaganda letter of Adud al-Daula, the Buyid emir, issued when the
embassy of Ibn Shahram returned, which is contained in
the letter collection of a contemporary, al-Shirazi;[6] an eyewitness account of the release of the Skleroi from Baghdad;[7]
the treaty formulated at the time of the Skleros release
between the Byzantine rebels and their former Buyid captors; and a letter to Bardas Skleros from the Buyid general
Chutur written in March 990 once the rebels had returned
to Byzantium.[8] Several contemporary manuscript colophons, and an inscription at Zarzma near Akhaltzikhe in
southern Georgia, add supplementary prosopographical details to what is known about Iberian and Armenian partici-

---

[5] al-Rudhrawari, *Eclipse*, vi. 23–34; for extensive discussion of this report
see A. Beihammer, 'Der harte Sturz des Bardas Skleros. Eine Fallstudie zu
zwischenstaatliche Kommunikation und Konfliktführung in der byzantinisch-arabischen Diplomatie des 10. Jahrhunderts', in R. Bösel and H. Fillitz
(eds.), *Römische Historische Mitteilungen* 45 (Vienna, 2003), 21–57.
[6] Adud al-Daula: J. C. Bürgel, *Die Hofkorrespondenz Adud ad-Daulas*
(Wiesbaden, 1965), 155–6.
[7] al-Rudhrawari, *Eclipse*, vi. 116–17.
[8] M. Canard, 'Deux documents arabes sur Bardas Sklèros', *Studi bizantini e
neoellenici*, 5 (1939), 55–69.

pation in the revolts on both the imperial and rebel sides.[9] From the west of the empire in Cyprus another inscription also alludes to the revolt period.[10]

This plethora of sources has two important implications: first, that information and interpretation presented in one account can be cross-checked against other accounts; and second, that a more detailed narrative of this period can be constructed than for any other phase of the reign. And indeed, it is on this 976–89 period that most historians of Basil's reign have tended to concentrate, with the result that a reasonably coherent narrative picture of events has been distilled.[11] According to this narrative, Emperor John Tzimiskes died in January 976 leaving Basil II and his brother Constantine, sons of a former emperor, Romanos II, in full control of the empire. However, shortly after their accession to full adult rule, Basil and Constantine were threatened by a serious revolt led by Bardas Skleros, the *doux* of Mesopotamia, the general in charge of the army based east of the Anti Taurus mountains. In the spring or early summer of 976, Skleros declared himself emperor. His initial revolt lasted for three years and was punctuated by several pitched battles between imperial and rebel forces. Victory for the emperors was only achieved after Bardas Phokas, the nephew of another former emperor, Nikephoros II Phokas, was recalled

[9] N. Adontz, 'Tornik le moine', *B* 13 (1938), 143–64; Forsyth, 'The Chronicle of Yahya ibn Sa'id', 386.

[10] T. C. Papacostas, 'A Tenth-Century Inscription from Syngrasis, Cyprus', *BMGS* 26 (2002), 42–64.

[11] The most detailed and well-rounded account of the revolts is to be found in Forsyth, 'The Chronicle of Yahya ibn Sai'd', 370–462. See also Adontz, 'Tornik', 143–64; Seibt, *Die Skleroi*, 29–58. For place names see Map 1.

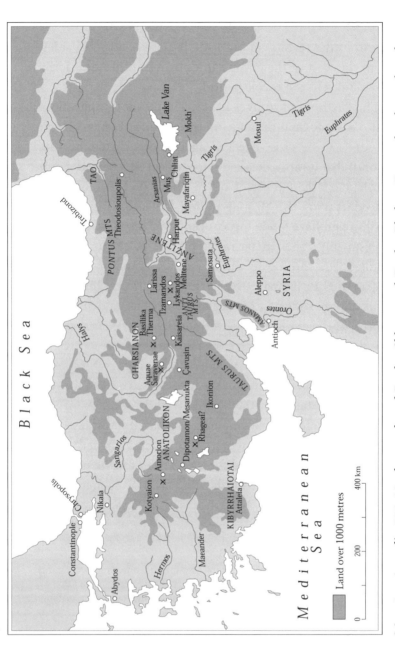

MAP 1. Anatolia 976–89: the revolts of Bardas Skleros and Bardas Phokas. Drawn by the author from: M. Whittow, *The Making of Orthodox Byzantium, 600–1025* (London, 1996).

from internal exile to lead a Byzantine army reinforced with troops sent from David the prince of the Iberian (Georgian) state of Tao. Skleros was finally defeated by Phokas and this Georgian army in March 979.

But the suppression of the rebels did not preface a period of peace and stability. Skleros and his immediate retinue of about three hundred men took refuge with, or were imprisoned by, the ruler of Iraq, Emir Adud al-Daula, and remained a potential threat off-stage in Baghdad. Skleros' residence in Arab territory was the subject of intense diplomatic exchange between the Byzantine court and the Buyids during the early 980s. The Buyid envoy Ibn Shahram makes it clear that Basil himself was willing to contemplate ceding the empire's client state of Aleppo in northern Syria to the Buyids if Adud surrendered Skleros. But this was a policy opposed both by military chiefs such as Bardas Phokas, and the emperor's great-uncle and chief adviser at court, Basil the *Parakoimomenos*.[12] Internal political tensions reached a denouement in 985. First it was rumoured that Basil the *Parakoimomenos* was about to incite a palace coup against his great-nephew. In response the armies of the east suspended their operations in northern Syria, apparently in preparation to intervene in support of the *Parakoimomenos*. But their expectations were premature. Rather than removing the emperor, the *Parakoimomenos* was himself dislodged from power. Then the emperor went on to reorganize the military high command on the eastern frontier to the dissatisfaction of a series of leading generals including Bardas

---

[12] al-Rudhrawari, *Eclipse*, vi. 31–3; Beihammer, 'Der harte Sturz', 37–44.

Phokas. Their dissatisfaction grew even greater when Basil attempted to wrest the foreign policy initiative for himself by attacking Bulgaria the following year.[13]

When Basil's foray to Sardica (also known as Triaditza or Sofia) ended in disastrous retreat, a second period of civil war ensued. Skleros was released by Baghdad in the winter of 986–7. He soon relaunched his rebellion in the east of the empire in the area around Melitene. Phokas announced his own imperial candidature and seduced Skleros into a military alliance. He then reneged on the terms of the alliance and imprisoned Skleros in the Anti Taurus. For two years Phokas' forces threatened Constantinople from the Asian side of the Bosphoros. It was only in late 988 or early 989 that Phokas' forces led by Kalokyros Delphinas were defeated at Chrysopolis.[14] Shortly afterwards reinforcements arrived to support Basil from the Rus, part of a deal in which Basil's sister was dispatched as a bride for Vladimir, the prince of Kiev, while Vladimir in turn converted to Orthodox Christianity. In April 989 these Rus troops helped Basil to defeat and kill Phokas at the Battle of Abydos. Yet even after the defeat of Phokas, the spectre of rebellion endured. Bardas' younger son Leo held out at Antioch until November 989. Meanwhile, Skleros was released from prison by Phokas' widow and launched his third insurrection. This revolt however was of short duration and the Skleroi capitulated at some point before 6 March 991, the date when Bardas himself died.[15]

[13] For this chronology see also below 6.3.3.
[14] For the problems associated with dating the Battle of Chrysopolis see Forsyth, 'The Chronicle of Yahya ibn Sa'id', 439–40.
[15] Yahya, *PO* 23, pp. 430–1.

This, then, is the outline narrative that has been reconstructed by a series of scholars of the early years of Basil's reign. In this chapter I do not intend to re-examine the medieval sources which refer to the Skleros and Phokas revolts in order to refine this narrative. Instead what I want to do is compare these different medieval testimonies to understand the Greek historiographical tradition of Basil's reign more clearly, above all the *Synopsis Historion* of John Skylitzes. The chapter looks principally at which dimensions of the revolts attracted medieval historians' attention and why that was so. It suggests that in the construction of their accounts of the first thirteen years of Basil's reign both Skylitzes and Michael Psellos used a now-lost Greek panegyrical manifesto dedicated to Bardas Skleros. The chapter argues that this source was chosen by both historians in accordance with eleventh-century literary, social, and political concerns, rather than because it was an accurate reflection of later tenth-century political realities, a line of reasoning which accords with the argument developed in earlier chapters of this book.

5.2   HISTORIOGRAPHICAL DISCUSSION

5.2.1   General historiographical interest

It is not difficult to see why so many medieval historians from so many different traditions of history writing working in so many different languages were so intrigued by the revolts of Bardas Skleros and Bardas Phokas. However they are to be interpreted, it is clear that these rebellions marked a conspicuous hiatus in the tenth-century expansionist enterprise of Byzantium. With the outbreak of rebellion key resources were diverted away from the offensive on the frontiers and channelled into a debilitating struggle for mastery over Anatolia and Constantinople. During the first Skleros revolt rival armies fought in the passes of the Taurus and Anti Taurus and on the Anatolian plateau; Nikaia and Abydos were besieged; naval engagements were joined off the western Asia Minor littoral and in the Sea of Marmara. Localized fighting occurred in Antioch.[16] During the Phokas revolt military action was less widespread, but once again Abydos came under siege.[17] Civil war also enfolded Arab, Armenian, and Iberian buffer states into alliances with imperial and rebel armies, and offered encouragement to hostile powers beyond the empire, such as the Fatimids of Egypt and the Buyids of Iraq.[18]

This was a reversal in fortune which was immediately apparent to contemporaries. According to Stephen of Taron, the empire was torn apart during the first Skleros revolt: town was pitted against town; village against village.[19] News of the first Skleros revolt reached the village of Syngrasis near Salamis in Cyprus, where an inscription refers to a shipwreck which occurred when the empire was 'in a state of disorder, being troubled by Bardas Skleros'.[20] In Iraq the court historian Ibn Miskawayh greeted the sight of the

[16] Forsyth, 'The Chronicle of Yahya ibn Sa'id', 370–93.
[17] Ibid. 433–43.
[18] For the implications of the revolt for relations with Byzantium's eastern neighbours see below 6.2, 6.3.2–3, 8.2, and 8.4.
[19] Stephen of Taron, *Armenische Geschichte*, 141.
[20] Papacostas, 'Tenth-Century Inscription', 51.

respective ambassadors of Basil and Skleros fawning at the feet of Adud al-Daula in the aftermath of the first Skleros revolt with the reflection that, 'nothing like this had ever happened before; it was one of the glories of Adud.'[21] Ibn Miskawayh's reflections are undoubtedly somewhat exaggerated. As one of Adud's most loyal civil servants, he was eager to promote the standing of his political master. But to a certain extent his surprise at the suddenness of the demise of Byzantine prestige was justified.[22] The strategic balance had, after all, so recently been otherwise. Less than a decade earlier, in 972, Emperor John Tzimiskes had led an invasion of the Upper Tigris which triggered riots in Baghdad when the citizens became convinced that the Byzantines were intending to invade Iraq.[23]

According to other contemporary or near-contemporary historians, the collapse in the Byzantine position was even more profound: not only had the offensive against the neighbours ceased, but the neighbours had begun to fight back on all fronts. Yahya ibn Sa'id reports that the prolonged period of Byzantine civil war allowed the armies of the Bulgarian state, based in western Macedonia and led by the Kometopoulos family, to raid deep into mainland Greece and the Peloponnese.[24] Stephen of Taron points out that

[21] Ibn Miskawayh, *Eclipse*, v. 436.
[22] For Ibn Miskawayh as a servant of Adud see Forsyth, 'The Chronicle of Yahya ibn Sai'd', 44 ff.
[23] Ibn Miskawayh, *Eclipse*, v. 326–9; Yahya, *PO* 23, pp. 353–8; M. Canard, 'La Date des expéditions mésopotamiennes de Jean Tzimiscès', *Mélanges Henri Grégoire, Ann. de l'Inst. de Phil. et d'Hist. Or. et Slav.* 10 (1950), 99–108. This invasion is also discussed below at 6.2, 6.3.2, and 8.1.
[24] Yahya, *PO* 23, p. 430; Skylitzes, *Synopsis*, 329–30, 339. For the rise of the Kometopouloi see Seibt, 'Untersuchungen', 65–98; see also below 7.1 and 8.5.

Bad ibn Dustuk, a Kurdish emir who controlled Chliat on Lake Van, took advantage of the general mayhem in Caucasia to sack the town of Muş.[25] But perhaps it is Leo the Deacon who conveys most dramatically the incomprehensible scale and suddenness of the reversal in Byzantine fortunes during the early years of Basil's reign. As a member of the palace clergy and a writer of speeches at the court of Basil II, Leo represents a contemporary, Constantinopolitan perception of the disasters of the post-976 period. His summary of the Skleros and Phokas revolts, the 986 failure in Bulgaria, and the humiliating intervention of the Rus, stand in elegiac contrast to his more detailed accounts of the martial achievements of Basil's imperial predecessors.[26] His sombre reflections are mirrored by some of the poems written by John Geometres and John of Melitene in the last quarter of the tenth century which lament the evil consequences of civil war, the shame of the arrival of Rus troops in Constantinople, and the opportunities which internal weakness afforded to the Byzantine Empire's Bulgarian adversaries.[27]

---

[25] Stephen of Taron, *Armenische Geschichte*, 141; on Bad see also below 6.2 and 6.3.1–2.

[26] Leo the Deacon, *Historiae Libri Decem*, 169–78. Leo's pessimism has recently also been interpreted as part of a more widespread late 10th-c. concern about the approach of the millennium: Magdalino, 'The Year 1000 in Byzantium', 233–70, esp. 242; see also a rather briefer discussion by Mango, *Empire of the New Rome*, 211.

[27] See e.g. the poems, εἰς τὴν ἀπόστασιν; εἰς τὰς τῶν Ἰβήρων ἁρπαγάς; εἰς τοὺς Βουλγάρους; εἰς τὸν Κομιτόπουλον (Geometres (John): *Anecdota Graeca, E Codd. Manuscriptis Bibliothecae Regiae Parisiensis*, ed. J. A. Cramer, 4 vols. (Oxford, 1839–41), iv. 271–3, 282–3; Skylitzes, *Synopsis*, 282–3). See also Schlumberger, *L'Épopée byzantine*, i. 641–6, 725; ii. 34, 43–4; Poppe, 'The Political Background to the Baptism of the Rus', 214–17; Ševčenko, 'Poems on the Deaths of Leo VI and Constantine VII', 189. The general gloominess of

Of course, the fundamental importance of these revolts to the political history of Basil's reign is not the only reason why these revolts are so fully reported in the extant sources. In some cases medieval interest in the revolts reflects the accident of textual survival. Very little would be known, for example, about Iberian involvement in the first Skleros revolt were it not for an extant saint's life in Georgian about two late tenth-century Athonite monks, John and Euthymios. Forced to rely on Skylitzes' coverage of this period, we would merely know that after Skleros' victories in 978, the Byzantine general Bardas Phokas sought armed assistance from the Iberian *kouropalates*, David prince of Tao. On the other hand, the *Life of John and Euthymios* presents a much fuller picture of the diplomatic contacts established between the Byzantine court and David. It details the activities of Tornik, a Georgian monk from Mount Athos and a general formerly in the employ of

Geometres' poetry is noted by Lauxtermann, 'John Geometres', 368–9; idem, 'Byzantine Poetry', 202, 207; idem, *Byzantine Poetry*, 234–5. Lauxtermann suggests that John Geometres' sombre tone may also reflect disappointment in the failure of his own career. Lauxtermann has identified Geometres, a former soldier, as part of a network of officials close to the emperor's uncle, Basil the *Parakoimomenos*, who were highly critical of the emperor's policies towards the empire's neighbours. Lauxtermann hypothesizes that Geometres may have been dismissed from public office in 985 at the same time as his patron, the *Parakoimomenos* (Lauxtermann, 'John Geometres—Poet and Scholar', 370–1; idem, 'Byzantine Poetry', 202, 213; idem, *Byzantine Poetry*, 36–7, 40–1, 158–9). For further examination of the demise of Basil the *Parakoimomenos* see below 8.3. It should be noted that one poem of this period usually attributed to Geometres, a eulogistic epitaph of Emperor Nikephoros Phokas which indirectly criticizes Basil II for calling in the Rus in 988, has recently been attributed by Lauxtermann to John the Metropolitan of Melitene (Lauxtermann, 'Byzantine Poetry', 207–8; idem, *Byzantine Poetry*, 234–6, 305–16).

David, who travelled from Constantinople to western Caucasia on an imperial mission to enlist the support of the prince of Tao. It also refers to the rewards offered to the Georgian monastery of the Iviron on Mount Athos after Skleros' defeat.[28]

Interest in the Skleros and Phokas revolts can also be explained by other factors. Many of the Arabic documents which bear first-hand witness to relations between Skleros, Constantinople, and Baghdad in this period were preserved primarily because they provided useful templates for diplomatic practice throughout the Arab medieval world. Thus, the treaty containing the terms of the release of the Skleroi from Baghdad in 987 is to be found in the later diplomatic manual of the Mamluk secretary al-Kalkashandi.[29] The re-

---

[28] Life of John and Euthymios, 89–92; Adontz, 'Tornik', 143–64; P. M. Tarchnishvili, 'Le Soulèvement de Bardas Sklèros', *BK* 17–18 (1964), 95–7. Imperial patronage for the Iberians on Athos in the aftermath of the Skleros revolt can be corroborated by various Georgian manuscript colophons and by documents from the archives of the Iviron monastery itself: *Actes d'Iviron: Des origines au milieu du XIe siècle*, eds. J. Lefort, N. Oikonomides, and D. Papachrysanthou, Archives de l'Athos XIV (Paris, 1985), 7–31, 117 ff. Equally, the after-life of this Athonite saint's life also demonstrates how one single narrative can penetrate many different sources. Thus, the Iberian intervention mentioned in some versions of the Georgian Royal Annals, a heterogeneous collection of 11th- to 14th-c. historical and historiographical materials, proves to be nothing more than a paraphrase of the historical background contained in the Life of John and Euthymios which was interpolated into the Annals during the 18th c. (Georgian Royal Annals, 373–4).

[29] Canard, 'Deux documents arabes', 65–8. A similar text to Kalkashandi is the *Kitab al Daha'ir wa-l-tuhaf*, another later medieval Egyptian text with roots in the later 11th c. (Hamidullah, 'Nouveaux documents', 281–98). This text is a list of embassies and diplomatic gift exchanges. It includes the most detailed account of the famous 917 Byzantine embassy to Baghdad, the list of Emperor Romanos Lekapenos' gifts to the Ikhshidid leader of Egypt, as well as notes on Basil II's relations with the Fatimids of Egypt and the rulers of Sicily.

port of the Buyid envoy, Ibn Shahram, who journeyed to Constantinople in 981–2, survives because it was included in the later eleventh-century annalistic account of the historian al-Rudhrawari.[30] It has recently been argued that it was edited and then inserted into al-Rudhrawari's text for didactic reasons. That is to say, what we now have is not the full text as Ibn Shahram presented it to Adud al-Daula, but a redaction which focused on issues of central importance for diplomats of the future: concerns such as how to behave as an envoy in Byzantium, and how to identify and manipulate the weak points of one's diplomatic adversaries to win concessions.[31] As well as being preserved in histories for utilitarian purposes, documents concerned with the revolt may have survived, either in their entirety or in edited forms, for other literary reasons as well. For instance, Ibn Shahram's report and a detailed eyewitness account of the ceremonial surrounding the release of the Skleroi five years later may have been preserved because they were thought to conform to a general Arab literary enthusiasm for the distant, the foreign, and the exotic.[32] Certainly, in the case of

---

[30] al-Rudhrawari, *Eclipse*, vi. 23–34.

[31] Beihammer, 'Der harte Sturz', 28–9, 46–50.

[32] Ibid. 223–4, 116–17. This enthusiasm had its roots in a genre of Arabic literature known as *adab*. Taking material from a variety of other literary genres, including poetry, oratory, and grammar, *adab* was primarily concerned with rendering its reader more courteous, urbane, and erudite. As Arab contact with non-Arab peoples grew, so *adab* came to be informed by the written traditions of Iran, India, and the Greek-speaking world. As a result it encouraged widespread interest in the cultures which fostered these exotic literary forms (*EI*, i. 175–6; A. Miquel, *La Géographie humaine du monde musulman jusqu'au milieu du 11e siècle*, 3 vols. (Paris, 1967), ii. 152–89). Marius Canard frequently suggested that many allusions to Byzantium in

al-Rudhrawari's report on the release of the Skleroi, there is striking evidence of a fascination with the exotic as it applied to Byzantium, above all the explicit reference to the fact that the Skleroi spoke Greek during the ceremonial which preceded their departure from Baghdad.[33]

---

medieval Arab literature were conditioned by the traditions of *adab*: M. Canard, 'Quelques "à côté" de l'histoire des relations entre Byzance et les Arabes', *Studi medievali in onore di G. Levi della Vida*, 2 vols. (Rome, 1956), i. 98–119; expanded in idem, 'Les Relations politiques et sociales entre Byzance et les Arabes', *DOP* 18 (1964), 35–56.

[33] 'As Ward [i.e. Bardas (Skleros)] approached, he bowed his head slightly and kissed the prince's hand. A chair with a cushion was placed for him and he sat down thereon. Samsam al-daulah proceeded to make civil inquiries, and he [Ward] invoked a blessing on the prince and *thanked him in Greek, the conversation being conducted through an interpreter*' (al-Rudhrawari, *Eclipse*, vi. 116–17). Nor was the interest that al-Rudrawari displays in the exoticism of Byzantium without precedent in Arab historiography. Political defectors from Byzantium to Islamic territories always attracted attention. The flight of Andronikos Doukas *domestikos of the scholai* to Baghdad in 907 is documented by historians writing in Arabic from as early as al-Tabari in first decades of the 10th c. to Ibn Haldun in the late 14th. That *adab* played some role in the retention of such material within Arabic literature is best illustrated by the mid- 10th-c. writings of Masudi. More than a simple geographer or a historian, Masudi was an intellectual with a broad range of cultural interests, a master *adib*, fascinated by exotica from distant lands. Included among his stories about Byzantium is the flight of Andronikos Doukas. Most telling in an *adab* context, however, is the shape that Masudi's narrative takes; rather than dwelling on the political situation within Byzantium that led up to Andronikos' decision to flee, Masudi focuses on the fact that the Byzantine general was forced by the caliph to convert to Islam once he arrived in Baghdad (A. A. Vasiliev, *Byzance et les Arabes*, 3 vols. (Brussels, 1935–68), ii/1. 181–92; ii/2. 19–21 (Tabari), 58 (Arib), 259 (Ibn Haldun), 398 (Masudi); see also S. Tougher, *The Reign of Leo VI (886–912): Politics and People* (Leiden, 1997), 208–18; M. Canard, 'Deux episodes des relations diplomatiques arabo-byzantines au Xe siècle', *Bulletin des Études Orientales de l'Institut Français de Damas* (1949–50), 54–62).

5.2.2   Pro-Skleros interest in Skylitzes' Synopsis Historian

There are many reasons, then, why medieval writers were fascinated by the Skleros and Phokas revolt period. But if we go beyond a general interest in the rebellions as a whole, and focus more closely on the ways in which these revolts are reported in the medieval historiographical record, then rather more interesting observations arise. For example, if one looks closely Skylitzes' account of this period in the *Synopsis Historion*, then it is striking that the author devotes far more attention to the insurrection of Bardas Skleros than that of Bardas Phokas. This is a surprising trend, which sits uneasily with evidence from more contemporary Greek and non-Greek sources and with circumstantial evidence contained in Skylitzes' *own* account, testimonies which suggest that it was Phokas rather than Skleros who presented the greater threat to the emperor.

There are three principal diagnostic elements in Skylitzes' treatment of these revolts which suggest that Skleros was of greater interest to our author than Phokas:

1. It is the Skleros rebellion of 976–9 which is narrated at much greater length and in greater detail than the Phokas revolt of 987–9. For example, Skylitzes' account of the itineraries of Skleros' campaigns in Asia Minor between 976 and 979 is full of detailed information. In contrast, he has virtually no hard evidence on how Phokas crossed Anatolia from his campaign headquarters in central Anatolia to the Asian shores of the Bosphoros when he rebelled in the summer of 987. Even Skylitzes' description

of the Phokas blockade of Constantinople is exceptionally thin.[34]

This discrepancy in the length and detail of coverage can best be illustrated by comparing a section of Skylitzes' account of Skleros' first march across Asia Minor in 976/7 with his analysis of the early stages of the 987 Phokas revolt. It is important to note that even in a very small section of Skylitzes' coverage of the Skleros rebellion, the reader is presented with a high concentration of very specific information about personnel, place-names, and titles (highlighted in bold font in the text produced below), as well as a reasonably coherent picture of a key battle. On the other hand, Skylitzes' account of the outbreak of the Phokas revolt *as it involved Phokas* amounts to no more than two very short passages (also produced below). Not only are these passages short, they convey exceptionally little detail about the few bald facts they present.

Itinerary of the first march of Skleros across Asia Minor

As he advanced on **Kaisareia** Skleros dispatched advance parties and spies in order to scout about and to find out where the enemy might be, and to prepare the road for him. And **Anthes Alyates**

---

[34] The most detailed account of the key battles fought in the extreme west of Asia Minor between 987 and 989 is to be found outside the Greek tradition in the history of Stephen of Taron (Stephen of Taron, *Armenische Geschichte*, 188–9); Yahya ibn Sa'id's account contains the crucial information that the final battle of Abydos was fought on 13 April 989 (Yahya, *PO* 23, pp. 419–31). However, Yahya's more detailed coverage of the revolt is usually concerned with events on the eastern frontier, especially in Antioch and Trebizond (see below 6.3.3).

had been selected as the leader of those who were sent. When these men came up against and chanced upon a part of the imperial army which had as its leader **Eustathios Maleinos, magistros,** in a pass (they call the place **Koukoulithos**), they tested out the enemy and made attacks.... And after **three days** he (Skleros) reached **Lapara.** This place was part of **Cappadocia,** which is now called **Lykandos,** so named because of its wealth and abundance. Once the **stratopedarches** had learned this, he employed a night march for fear of Skleros passing by, and camped opposite the enemy. And up to this point they [both] hesitated, and shirked open battle and attempted to steal victory. Bardas outwitted his opponents, having prepared many meals, as if about to get his own army to eat; thus he deceived the enemy. For on the assumption that he was not about to initiate the battle during that day, they themselves turned to feasting. Skleros, when he knew this (for he had the forces prepared for battle), suddenly sounded the warcry with the trumpet and attacked the enemy as they were eating. But they... defended themselves stoutly for a while. Then Bardas, after making outflanking manoeuvres and causing the enemy to fear that they were being encircled, sent out the **tribute troops** against the rear, and turned the enemy to flight and inflicted much bloodshed, with the **doux of Antioch, Bourtzes,** withdrawing first.... And he [Skleros] seized the whole camp with its baggage and from there he acquired boundless wealth. From there, he came once again to the place called **Tzamandos.** The city of **Tzamandos** lay on a precipitous rock, well populated and dripping with wealth. Having taken this city from the willing inhabitants he collected much wealth. This victory disturbed many of the adherents of the emperor and compelled them to desert to Skleros. For **Bourtzes** was the first to desert, and the *patrikios* **Andronikos Lydos,** the *doux,* with his sons. And the **Attaleians** imprisoned the admiral of the emperor and went over with the whole fleet to

Michael Kourtikios, sent by Skleros to be *strategos* of the **Kibyr-rhaiotai**.[35]

The early stages of the Phokas revolt

But the greatest men of the Romans were very angry with the emperor... they gathered together in **Charsianon** in the house of **Maleinos**, on the 15th August, of the 15th indiction, and proclaimed **Bardas Phokas** emperor, having crowned him [literally: set the diadem around him] and the rest of the recognizable regalia of empire....

[Bardas] himself delegated part of the army to the *patrikios* **Kalokyros Delphinas** and sent it to **Chrysopolis** on the other shore from the capital. Leading the rest of the forces with him, he went to **Abydos**, in the hope that with the straits under his control, he would win over the citizens who were oppressed by need.[36]

A similar unevenness in the narrative coverage afforded to Skleros and Phokas is visible in Skyltizes' account of the final battle between the two generals at the tail end of the first Skleros revolt. This battle was, of course, won by Phokas at the head of the joint imperial and Iberian army. However, it is striking that we learn much more about this battle as it concerned Skleros than Phokas.[37] For instance, in the account of the duel between the two generals that forms the centrepiece to Skylitzes' narrative of the battle, Skleros' individual manoeuvres are recorded with some precision.

[35] Skylitzes, *Synopsis*, 318–20. See Map 1 for all geographical references in this passage.
[36] Skylitzes, *Synopsis*, 332, 336.
[37] Ibid. 326–7.

He cut off the right ear of Phokas' horse and severed the animal's bridle with a blow from his sword. In contrast Phokas' contribution to the dual is described in rather more general terms drawn from the Skylitzes' military lexicon: 'having beaten him [Skleros] on the head with his mace, he [Phokas] threw him down over the neck of his horse with the weight of the blow.'[38] Despite his apparent victory in the hand-to-hand fighting, Phokas then mysteriously disappeared up a hill, leaving the reader to concentrate on Skleros. We are told that Skleros went to wash himself clean of the blood of warfare, assuming that Phokas' disappearance signalled his defeat. At this point the general's horse, whose name is given—Aegyptios—escaped his handlers and ran through the rebel army lines causing mayhem. Skleros' troops assumed their general had fallen, and in their panic to escape they began to jump into the Halys river. At this point Phokas reappeared and won the day.[39]

2. The second diagnostic feature which suggests that Skylitzes was more interested in Skleros than in Phokas is that most of his narrative dealing with the Phokas rebellion of 987–9 is concerned with the *story and viewpoint of Skleros*, rather than the deeds of the principal rebel Phokas. For example, in contrast to the extreme brevity of his description of Phokas' preparations for war, Skylitzes devotes a much longer section of text to a tortuous excursus exploring

---

[38] ὁ δὲ Φωκᾶς τῇ κορύνῃ πατάξας αὐτὸν κατὰ τῆς κεφαλῆς τοῦτον μὲν ἐπὶ τοῦ τραχήλου τοῦ ἵππου ῥιπτεῖ τῷ βάρει τῆς πληγῆς κατενεχθέντα (Skylitzes, *Synopsis*, 326).

[39] For further discussion of the date and accuracy of reporting about this battle see below 8.2.

Skleros' conundrum about which side he should support in the forthcoming conflict. The following passage illustrates how long and detailed is Skylitzes' treatment of Skleros' internal musings:

He [Skleros] was uncertain and changeable in his thoughts. For, on the one hand, he judged that he was too weak to continue and hold fast to the revolt on his own. But he thought it ignoble and unmanly to move over to Phokas or to the emperor. And so having discussed at length with his supporters, in the end he calculated that for him to be hailed as emperor on his own was reckless and unprofitable, because it was impossible, and yet he hated the idea of going over to one of the dynasts and rejecting the other, because of the uncertainty of the future. And so he decided that as far as was possible, he would win over both powers, in order that in any unfortunate eventuality he should have the help and support of at least one of them. And so he himself sent letters to Phokas asking for a joint plan of action and for a partition of the empire, if they were able to conquer the emperor. But with *very clever judgement and calculation,* he secretly sent his son Romanos to the emperor, as though he [the son] were a deserter, so that if Phokas prevailed, he himself [Skleros] would be the saviour of his son, and if the emperor proved the stronger, he himself [Skleros] would be saved from danger, as the beneficiary of the intercession of that man [Romanos]. And Romanos, having assumed the appearance of flight, went to the emperor.[40]

3. The third diagnostic element in Skylitzes' testimony which seems to emphasize the actions and views of Skleros rather than Phokas is the frequency with which attention is drawn to the cunning and acumen of Skleros. Two ex-

---

[40] Skylitzes, *Synopsis,* 334–5.

amples occur in passages already cited above. In his analysis of Skleros' first march across Asia Minor, Skylitzes describes how Skleros cleverly used deception to gain an advantage at the battle of Lapara. In the passage which expatiates on Skleros' vacillations in 987, the general's decision to send his son Romanos to the emperor is explicitly interpreted by Skylitzes as a sign of shrewdness.

None of the foregoing argument about the ubiquity of Skleros in Skylitzes' account and the fleeting presence of Phokas is intended to suggest that Skleros and his allies were never dangerous. Indeed, all the evidence, both within and also outside Skylitzes' account, points to the fact that during his first revolt Skleros clearly presented a major threat to the security of Basil and his regime. In his capacity as a military commander on the eastern frontier Skleros was able to call upon considerable fiscal, physical, and manpower resources. When he launched his first insurrection against Basil he established his campaign headquarters at Charpete (also known as Harput in Armenian, and Hisn Ziyad in Arabic), a strong point in the Anzitene, the region east of the Anti Taurus which he controlled in his capacity as *doux* of Mesopotamia.[41] Next, he sequestered the fiscal

---

[41] Ibid. 315–16; Yahya, *PO* 23, pp. 372–3; J. D. Howard-Johnston, 'Crown Lands and the Defence of Imperial Authority in the Tenth and Eleventh Centuries', *Byz Forsch*, 21 (1995), 93; idem, 'Byzantine Anzitene', in S. Mitchell (ed.), *Armies and Frontiers in Anatolia* (Oxford, 1983), 248–50; A. Bivar, 'Bardes Skleros, the Buwayids and the Marwanids at Hisn Ziyad in the Light of an Unnoticed Arab Inscription', in S. Freeman and H. Kennedy (eds.), *Defence of the Roman and Byzantine Frontiers* (Oxford, 1986), 9–21; T. Sinclair, *Eastern Turkey: An Architectural and Archaeological Survey*, 4 vols. (London, 1987–90), iii. 13–35. See Map 1.

revenues of nearby Melitene. Finally, he secured additional troops from outside the empire by contracting military alliances with the regional powers which neighboured Byzantine Mesopotomia. The Armenian prince of Mokh, a region south of Lake Van, fought alongside Skleros' forces; the Hamdanid emir of Mosul, Abu Taghlib, provided light cavalry troops in return for a marriage agreement.[42] These local allies were both rich and powerful. The traveller and geographer Ibn Hawkal makes several references to the immense rental revenue of the family of Abu Taghlib, the Hamdanids of Mosul. Hints of large Hamdanid estates also emerge from a gazette of contemporary Baghdad gossip collated by al-Tanukhi. Ibn Miskawayh describes the immense cash reserves he saw accumulated in Hamdanid mountain fortresses when he made an inventory of Abu Taghlib's possessions for Adud al-Daula in 979. In the course of his negotiations with the Byzantines in the early 980s, Ibn Shahram, the Buyid envoy, stressed how valuable had been the support of Abu Taghlib to Skleros' insurrection: 'You are well aware that when Abu Taghlib . . . assisted Ward [Bardas Skleros] he foiled the Byzantine sovereigns.' [43] Equally, the

---

[42] For Skleros' Armenian support see: Stephen of Taron, *Armenische Geschichte*, 140–1; Skylitzes, *Synopsis*, 320–1. Skylitzes also mentions that the Armenians of the Byzantine army were the first to hail Skleros as emperor (Skylitzes, *Synopsis*, 315–16). For relations with Abu Taghlib see Skylitzes, 315–16; Yahya, *PO* 23, pp. 398 ff.; and Ibn Miskawayh, *Eclipse*, v. 424–6. Seibt, *Die Skleroi*, 38, and Forsyth, 'The Chronicle of Yahya', 377.

[43] Ibn Hawkal: *La Configuration de la terre,* trans. J. H. Kramers and G. Wiet, 2 vols. (Beirut and Paris, 1964), p. 205; al-Tanukhi: *Table Talk of a Mesopotamian Judge,* trans. D. Margoliouth (London, 1922), 195–201; Ibn Miskawayh, *Eclipse*, v. 312, 415, 421–5, 431–4; al-Rudhrawari, *Eclipse*, vi. 26–7; Beihammer, 'Der harte Sturz', 47. Ibn Miskawayh and Yahya make indirect

extent of Skleros' military success, at least during his first revolt, should not be understated. Apart from defeating several imperial field armies, he was recognized as emperor in Antioch, controlled part of the thematic navy, and besieged the key point of Abydos by land and by sea, thus threatening the supply of grain into Constantinople.[44]

Nevertheless, all the evidence indicates that as Skleros' first revolt progressed, fundamental weaknesses within his power structure emerged. It soon became obvious that Skleros' real hope of success had rested in a swift knockout punch; the longer the campaigns went on, the more his challenge to imperial authority waned. Critical to Skleros' ultimate lack of success was his inability to threaten Constantinople permanently. Whenever he approached the capital, a new imperial field army always emerged to drive him back. For example, having defeated imperial forces at the Battle of Lapara in the eastern theme of the Lykandos at the beginning of his revolt, Skleros and his army marched west and camped at Dipomaton on the western reaches of the Anatolian plateau, near the Lake of the Forty Martyrs, modern Akşehir Gölü. In response to the arrival of Skleros in the west, an imperial army under the command of Peter the Stratope-

references to the legendary wealth of Abu Taghlib in their reports about the expulsion of the Hamdanids from Mosul by Adud al-Daula in 978/9. They allege that Adud was afraid that Abu Taghlib would use rumours about his immense fortune to persuade the Fatimids of Egypt to help him regain control of northern Syria and the Djazira from the Buyids (Ibn Miskawayh, *Eclipse*, v. 434; Yahya, PO 23, p. 402).

[44] Skylitzes, *Synopsis*, 315–27; Yahya, *PO* 23, pp. 372–89, 398–402; J. T. Teall, 'The Grain Supply of the Byzantine Empire', *DOP* 13 (1959), 104, 119, on the importance of Abydos, located on the Straits of the Dardanelles, in the passage of basic foodstuffs into Constantinople from the 8th to the 10th c.

darch and Leo the *protovestiarios* set out from Kotyaion, marched past the rebel camp at night, and so drew Skleros' forces south and east towards Ikonion and away from Constantinople. Although Skleros defeated his enemies in the subsequent pitched battle at Rhageai, his victory was achieved at the price of turning eastwards.[45] Less than a year later Skleros was once again forced back onto the plateau, when imperial armies crossed the Bosphoros under the command of Bardas Phokas and began marching towards Kaisareia. Once again Skleros was victorious in the field battles which ensued; but once again these victories were achieved at the price of moving eastwards. For while Skleros defeated Phokas at the Battle of Pankaleia near Amorion in the theme of the Anatolikon in June 978, he was unable to prevent Phokas from regrouping imperial forces, and continuing his march away from Constantinople. When Skleros won a second engagement later in 978, it was far to the east at Basilika Therma in the theme of the Charsianon, and despite his military success, Skleros was forced to spend the winter in this area of Anatolia. Thus, even though Skleros had remained undefeated during 978, his threat to the capital had been thoroughly dissipated by Phokas' march east. Moreover, during the winter of 978, Skleros' position worsened considerably. By March 979 the imperial forces led by Phokas had been reinforced by the Iberian army dispatched

---

[45] Skylitzes, *Synopsis*, 319–32; Skleros' itineraries across Asia Minor during his first revolt can be traced in several of the volumes produced by the *Tabula Imperii Byzantini* project: F. Hild and M. Restle, *TIB, Kappadokien* (Vienna, 1981), 93–4; K. Belke and M. Restle, *TIB, Galatien und Lykaonien* (Vienna, 1984), 71; K. Belke and N. Mersich, *TIB, Phrygien und Pisidien* (Vienna, 1990), 96–7. For place-names see Map 1.

by David of Tao. On 24 March 979 this joint Ibero-Byzantine army defeated Skleros at Sarvenisni (Aquae Saravenae) in the theme of Charsianon. Skleros and his immediate retinue fled across the Diyar Bakr to Mayafariqin, where they were taken into custody by the Buyid forces of Adud al-Daula.[46]

Meanwhile, even though his first revolt had lasted more than two years, Skleros' power-base always remained prey to the uncertain loyalty of many of his supporters. His rebellion was, from the very beginning, afflicted by defections. Before Skleros had even crossed the Anti Taurus at the start of his revolt, he was forced to have his chief of staff (the *hetaireiarches*) murdered to prevent him from swapping sides. As early as 977 the Hagiozacharites brothers defected to the *protovestiarios* Leo; when they were captured by Skleros at the Battle of Rhageai they were blinded as a punishment for their disloyalty. An even more significant defector was the *basilikos* Obeïdallah, Skleros' lieutenant at Antioch.[47] This gradual withering of domestic support was paralleled by the ongoing disintegration of his diplomatic alliance in the east. Severe stresses began to appear as soon as Abu Taghlib was attacked by the Buyid armies of Adud al-Daula, and was forced to flee from Mosul in 978. At first Abu Taghlib took refuge at Hisn Ziyad, Skleros' main command centre in the east, and requested military aid from his Greek ally. Skleros responded by telling Abu Taghlib that more Hamdanid troops were needed to secure a victory against Bardas Phokas

---

[46] Skylitzes, *Synopsis*, 323–5; Yahya, *PO* 23, pp. 375, 399; Stephen of Taron, *Armenische Geschichte*, 142–3; Hild and Restle, *Kappadokien*, 94, 143–4, 156–7.

[47] Skylitzes, *Synopsis*, 318, 322; Yahya, *PO* 23, 376–7. See below 6.4 for the career of Obeïdallah.

before he could come east to fight the Buyids. Although Abu Taghlib dispatched some fresh troops, he himself left Hisn Ziyad and fled back to the Djazira, and thence to Syria the moment he heard that Skleros had been defeated by Phokas and the Iberians of Tao in March 979.[48]

In contrast, fragility of support and limited resources do not seem to have been typical of the 987–9 Phokas revolt. While information about the events of the Phokas rebellion is much less readily available, rebel forces appear to have presented a much more consistent danger to imperial authority in Constantinople than was the case during the Skleros insurrection. The very fact that the key battles between rebel and imperial armies were fought at Chryso-polis and Abydos, in the extreme west of Asia Minor, close to Constantinople itself, suggests that it was impossible for Basil and his ministers to muster the forces from within the empire necessary to drive Phokas back onto the Anatolian plateau. Second, the fact that David of Tao supported Pho-kas meant that the emperor was unable to call upon allied forces from Iberia to bolster the imperial army as had

[48] Yahya, *PO* 23, pp. 397–402; Ibn Miskawayh, *Eclipse*, v. 420–43. The chronology of Abu Taghlib's wanderings on the Djazira frontier is confused, since the accounts of Yahya and Ibn Miskawayh which deal with his expulsion from Mosul and his flight into exile do not coincide exactly (Forsyth, 'The Chronicle of Yahya', 315–16). However, it is clear that Abu Taghlib's fortunes were on the wane from the moment that Adud al-Daula took control of Baghdad at the end of May 978. Buyid troops loyal to Adud were besieging Mosul by the end of June 978 (Ibn Miskawayh, *Eclipse*, v. 420–1); Beihammer, 'Der hart Sturz', 47–8, has also suggested that the Arabic texts overplay Abu Taghlib's significance in the events of Skleros' revolt; in the case of Ibn Shahram this exaggeration of his role was part of the Buyid envoy's diplo-matic strategy for forcing concessions from Basil's court.

been the case in 978–9 when dealing with Skleros. Instead Basil was forced to look northwards to the prince of Kiev for supplementary troops, a deal that involved an unprecedented marriage of a porphyrogenita princess to a ruler of the Rus, and a strategy which clearly provoked considerable disquiet among the citizens of Constantinople.[49]

The fate that this group experienced after they were defeated by Basil also strongly indicates that the Phokas axis was seen as the greater threat to the emperor's authority. After Phokas himself was killed at Abydos in April 989, his head was conveyed around the empire as a warning to other rebels. A few months before, following the defeat at Chrysopolis, Kalokyros Delphinas, one of Phokas' generals had been impaled (or crucified); one of Phokas' other officers, Atzupotheodore, may also have been impaled.[50] In contrast, when the Skleroi finally surrendered in 989, they were allowed to retain their offices, estates and titles.[51] Later in the reign they

---

[49] See above 5.2.1.

[50] Leo the Deacon, *Historiae Libri Decem*, 174–5 (crucified); Skylitzes, *Synopsis*, 336 (impaled). Stephen of Taron agrees with Leo that Delphinas was crucified (Stephen of Taron, *Armenische Geschichte*, 188). Basil appears to have ensured that the fate of Delphinas should endure as a terrifying exemplar. A column in Delphinas' memory was erected at the place where he was executed. Symeon the New Theologian discovered this column when he was exiled to Chalcedon from Constantinople early in the 11th c. (St Symeon the New Theologian, 132; McGuckin, 'Symeon the New Theologian', 30). The reference to Atzupotheodore comes from an interpolation in manuscript [U] of Skylitzes' *Synopsis Historion* and may therefore represent an addition by Michael of Devol (see above 2.2.1).

[51] Skylitzes, *Synopsis*, 338; Psellos, *Cronografia*, i. 36–41; al-Rudhrawari, *Eclipse*, vi. 119; Yahya, *PO* 23, pp. 426–7, 430–1. Yahya also refers to estates in northern Syria bestowed on Skleros and his brother Constantine in 989/90: these included Raban, a town populated by Armenians who had ejected their Islamic overlords and declared their loyalty to Basil II *c*.980 (Yahya, *PO* 23,

held top-ranking military posts. For example, Romanos Skleros, the son of Bardas, led a Byzantine army against Fatimid forces near Antioch in *c*.992.[52] A certain Bighas (also known as Pegasios) a servant of Skleros, is identified by Yahya ibn Sa'id as a Byzantine army commander in the Antioch area during the Arab revolt of al-Acfar in 1004/5. He had previously served as Skleros' governor at Nikaia after that city fell to the rebel army in 977–8.[53]

Nor is it just circumstantial evidence which suggests that Bardas Phokas presented a greater threat to Basil than Bardas Skleros. Michael Psellos, writing in the middle of the eleventh century, also comes to this conclusion in his account of Basil's reign in his *Chronographia*. While, as we shall see shortly, Psellos, like Skylitzes, concentrates at much greater length on the events of the Skleros revolt, nonetheless, he states very clearly that it was Bardas Phokas who presented the greatest danger.[54]

5.2.3   Pro-Skleros or pro-Phokas source materials?

The idea that it is Skleros rather than Phokas that Skylitzes chose to focus upon has important implications for our

pp. 405–6; E. Honigmann, *Die Ostgrenze des byzantinischen Reiches von 363 bis 1071* (Brussels, 1935), 73.

[52] Stephen of Taron, *Armenische Geschichte*, 199; Cheynet, *Pouvoir et contestations*, 334–5; Seibt, *Die Skleroi*, 62–4. It is unclear whether Romanos was *doux* of Antioch at this time; see below 6.3.3.

[53] Yahya, *PO* 23, p. 466; Skylitzes, *Synopsis*, 323; Cheynet, *Pouvoir et contestations*, 334–5.

[54] Psellos, *Cronografia*, i. 18–21; for more on Psellos' *Chronographia* see above 1.2.1.

understanding of the source materials that this author used in constructing his history of Basil's reign. As we saw in Chapter 2, it is widely assumed that a lost Phokas family chronicle was utilized by several later Greek historians, including John Skylitzes, in the course of their coverage of the second half of the tenth century.[55] However, the minimalist treatment of Phokas and the extensive coverage of Skleros in Skylitzes' appraisal of the revolt period of 976–89, must cast some doubt on how extensively pro-Phokas material was used in the *Synopsis Historion*, at least as far as coverage of the reign of Basil is concerned. Instead, the evidence seems to point in a contrary direction, suggesting that Skylitzes may have been more interested in source materials that focused on the activities and ambitions of Bardas Skleros.

One of the reasons, of course, for the supposition that a pro-Phokas source underpins much Greek historiography is that members of the Phokas family, above all Bardas Phokas, are customarily cast in a heroic light within such texts. Skylitzes himself includes accounts of several battle scenes in which Bardas Phokas is portrayed as a fighter of heroic and gigantic proportions. One example occurs during the first Skleros revolt. Here Skylitzes portrays Phokas in the thick of an engagement with an advance party of Skleros supporters. In the heat of the engagement Phokas kills one of Skleros' adjutants, Constantine Gauras, with his mace: 'This man [Phokas] on seeing him and recognizing who he was, went forth to meet him and struck him on the head

---

[55] See above 2.4.

with his mace, and he [Gauras] immediately fell down lifeless from his horse with the unstoppable force of the blow.'[56]

Yet what is particularly striking about Phokas-related passages such as these is that their content is usually very brief, vague, and repetitive. In the course of the final, and decisive, battle at the end of the first Skleros revolt in 979, Skylitzes describes a duel fought between Phokas and Skleros in very similar terms to that between Phokas and Gauras: 'Then Phokas, having seen his own army giving ground little by little and on the point of flight, and judging that a renowned death was better than an ignoble and reproached life, broke through the enemy phalanxes and attacked Skleros with all his might.... And Phokas, having beaten him on the head with his mace, threw him down over the neck of his horse with the weight of the blow.' [57]

Likewise, when Skylitzes describes Phokas' final battle against Basil II at Abydos in 989, he explains both the

---

[56] ὃν οὗτος ἰδὼν καὶ ὅστις εἴη κατανοήσας, ἠρέμα τὸν ἵππον παρενεγκὼν καὶ ὑπαντιάσας παίει κορύνῃ κατὰ τῆς κόρυθος. καὶ ὁ μὲν λειποθυμήσας τῇ ἀνυποστάτῳ φορᾷ τῆς πληγῆς πίπτει παραυτίκα τοῦ ἵππου (Skylitzes, *Synopsis*, 325).

[57] ἐνταῦθα τὸν ἑαυτοῦ λαὸν θεασάμενος ὁ Φωκᾶς κατὰ μικρὸν ἐνδιδόντα καὶ πρὸς φυγὴν βλέποντα, βέλτιον εἶναι κρίνας τὸν εὐκλεῆ θάνατον τῆς ἀγεννοῦς καὶ ἐπονειδίστου ζωῆς, τὰς τῶν ἐναντίων συγκόψας φάλαγγας πρὸς αὐτὸν μετὰ σφοδρότητος ἵεται τὸν Σκληρόν... καὶ ὁ μὲν Σκληρὸς τοῦ ἵππου τοῦ Φωκᾶ τὸ δεξιὸν οὖς σὺν τῷ χαλινῷ παίσας ἀποκόπτει τῷ ξίφει. ὁ δὲ Φωκᾶς τῇ κορύνῃ πατάξας αὐτὸν κατὰ τῆς κεφαλῆς τοῦτον μὲν ἐπὶ τοῦ τραχήλου τοῦ ἵππου ῥιπτεῖ τῷ βάρει τῆς πληγῆς κατενεχθέντα (Skylitzes, *Synopsis*, 326). Note at the beginning of this passage the general exhortation to bravery before armed encounter; a similar exhortation appears in Skylitzes' narration of the daring deeds of Eustathios Daphnomeles in Bulgaria (see above 4.2.2).

general's motivation for fighting, and his actual military action, in terms which are identical to his account of Phokas' earlier engagement with Skleros in 979: '*having nobly selected an honourable death rather than an ignoble life*, when Phokas saw the emperor from a distance... he reasoned with himself that if he were to triumph over this man [i.e. Basil] he would easily vanquish the rest; *having spurred on his horse, he charged violently against him, and slicing the enemy phalanxes in two, to everyone he appeared unstoppable.*'[58]

Indeed, rather than emanating from a family chronicle, it seems likely that scenes such as these were constructed from phrases out of Skylitzes' bland, generalizing, and homogenizing military lexicon, which was discussed in earlier chapters.[59] For example, it is not surprising to note that two of these excerpts depict either Phokas or his military initiatives through the use of one of Skylitzes' favourite adjectives: ἀνυπόστατος (unstoppable). Others describe Phokas spurring on his horse as a prelude to deadly action, μυωπίσας: another favoured motif from Skylitzes' catalogue of military manoeuvres described with one of his most characteristic martial terms. A more convincing alternative to complete fabrication, however, is the likelihood that Skylitzes drew on a narrative account which at some level contained pro-Phokas material, but that he then chose to compress that

---

[58] ὁ Φωκᾶς τοῦ ζῆν ἀγεννῶς τὸ γενναίως ἀποθανεῖν εὐγενῶς προκρίνας, τὸν βασιλέα θεασάμενος πόρρωθεν... καὶ πρὸς ἑαυτὸν λογισάμενος, ὡς, εἰ τούτου ἐπιτυχὴς γένηται, ῥᾷον ἂν καὶ τοὺς λοιποὺς καταγωνιεῖται, τὸν ἵππον μυωπίσας ῥαγδαίως ἵκετο κατ' αὐτοῦ, τὰς ἐναντίας φάλαγγας διακόπτων καὶ ἀνυπόστατος τοῖς πᾶσι φαινόμενος (Skylitzes, *Synopsis*, 337).

[59] See esp. 3.2 and 3.3.2.

material brutally by using his homogenizing and heroic language. The result was that all signs of the original Phokas narrative immediately disappeared. Whichever of these hypotheses is correct, it nonetheless remains the case that there is little sign of the widespread adherence to pro-Phokas material in Skylitzes' account. In contrast, the overwhelming interest in the activities and attitudes of his rival, Bardas Skleros, points to the probability that Skylitzes made extensive use of a pro-Skleros source either directly or through an intermediary.[60]

The first occasion in the *Synopsis Historion* when the reader becomes convinced that Skylitzes used a pro-Skleros source in his composition, or at the very least an intermediate history that drew on pro-Skleros material, occurs in the years before Basil came to the throne during the reign of John Tzimiskes (969–76). The general narrative context to the entry of pro-Skleros material into Skylitzes' text is the Byzantine attempt in 970–1 to defeat the Rus; those armies who had been invited into the Balkans by Emperor Nikephoros Phokas (963–9) to fight Byzantium's Bulgarian neighbours, but who had then refused to return to Kiev when their task was complete.[61] The exact episode where the pro-Skleros source itself becomes visible is the defence of Arkadioupolis in Thrace by Bardas Skleros in 971.[62] All those characteristics observed during Skylitzes' coverage of

[60] The only historian who has ever raised this possibility is Roueché, 'Byzantine Writers and Readers', 127.

[61] See below 8.5 for the historical background to Byzantine–Bulgarian–Rus relations in this period.

[62] Skylitzes, *Synopsis*, 287–91; see also a translation of this episode in McGeer, *Sowing the Dragon's Teeth*, 294–8.

Skleros' role in the reign of Basil II are visible here too. First of all the episode is dealt with at length: thirty per cent of Skylitzes' coverage of the reign of Tzimiskes is dedicated to this single encounter. While this account, like every other martial episode in Skylitzes' *Synopsis Historion*, has been reglossed with the author's characteristic military phraseology, nonetheless, it also contains a large degree of first-hand detail. The names and titles of Skleros' commanders are mentioned: Skleros, *stratelates* and *magistros*, his brother Constantine, *patrikios*, and his principal lieutenant John Alakasseus, *patrikios*. Accurate information is also supplied about the complex formation of the enemy army, which is correctly described as an alliance of northern peoples rather than a purely Rus force. Bulgars and Rus fought together; another part of the army was made up of Turks (Magyars) who 'lived in Pannonia to the west', while the final section comprised Patzinaks (Pechenegs).[63] While the size of this enemy army is exaggerated for dramatic effect (it is said to number 12,000), the precision of the number of Byzantine casualties appears to be a more plausible detail: 'twenty-five Byzantines fell in the battle but nearly every last one of them was wounded.'[64] Equally first-hand appear to be some cameo touches from a duel that Bardas' brother Constantine fought with a Rus cavalryman; after cutting off the head of his adversary's horse, he then grabbed the Rus soldier by the beard, before severing his head too.[65]

Another tell-tale sign that Skylitzes' account of the battle at Arkadioupolis draws on pro-Skleros material is the fact

---

[63] Skylitzes, *Synopsis*, 289.   [64] Ibid. 291.   [65] Ibid. 290–1.

that we learn about what happened, and why it happened, from Bardas' own viewpoint. It is Bardas who perceives that his numbers were vastly inferior to those of the enemy; it is Bardas who decides to defeat them with stratagems; it is Bardas who waits inside Arkadioupolis as though afraid, a pretence that the Rus and their allies take to reflect genuine Byzantine terror; it is Bardas who 'thinks long and hard about how he might attack the enemy'; it is Bardas who gives John Alakasseus his precise orders on how to entrap the barbarian army, suggesting that his lieutenant charges the enemy and then feigns a retreat, a withdrawal that will entice the enemy into a Byzantine ambush; it is Bardas, who despite winning an initial martial encounter with the barbarians, has the experience to act on fresh reconnaissance information that the rest of the enemy army awaits him in battle array; it is Bardas and his brother Constantine who win important duels with Rus commanders during the final passage of fighting. The fact that the feigning of fear, and the setting and springing of the Alakasseus ambush, are explicitly interpreted as clever stratagems concocted by Bardas himself offers further proof that the information in this account emanates from a source close to the Skleroi. As we saw earlier in this chapter, Skleros is habitually associated with clever ploys in Skylitzes' acount of Basil II's reign.

Paradoxically it is another Greek text, the contemporary history of Leo the Deacon, which lends further support for the idea that Skylitzes' report on the defence of Arkadiou-polis emanates from a text that is sympathetic to Skleros. For while Leo certainly admires the general, asserting that he was well born (*gennaios*) and active (*rhektes*), the Skleros that he portrays in conflict with the Rus is a man of sudden energy, rapidly conceived plans, and above all, good fortune.[66] Rather than reporting on a Skleros who ponders at length and with deviousness on his next move behind the walls of Arkadioupolis, Leo depicts the general impatient in the field of battle. He directs Alakasseus to reconnoitre among the Rus and to return swiftly so that battle may be joined forthwith. Speed is of the essence. Once Alakasseus returns, Skleros positions two ambuscades on either side of his army and leads his own forces into enemy lines. After much hectic fighting, the signal is given for the Byzantine ambush forces to attack the Rus in the rear, causing panic and flight.[67] Moreover while comparison between the two texts points to radical differences in the substance of the battle and the temperament of the Byzantine general, it also suggests that the Skleros narrative, as it is conveyed by Skylitzes, contains a substantial degree of exaggeration. For while the Byzantines are certainly outnumbered, Leo suggests that the enemy army is only a quarter of the size of that reported by Skylitzes, 3,000 rather than 12,000. Meanwhile, although Leo attributes to Bardas Skleros a certain amount of personal valour during the course of the fighting, he also reports that the Byzantine general was very nearly killed by a Rus warrior; it was only the dramatic intervention of Bardas' athletic brother Constantine that saved his skin. Furthermore, while Skylitzes offers the entirely plausible figure of

[66] Elsewhere in his narrative of the reign of John Tzimiskes, Leo expresses admiration for Skleros, describing him as 'extraordinarily vigorous and effective' (Leo the Deacon, *Historiae Libri Decem,* 116).

[67] Leo the Deacon, *Historiae Libri Decem,* 108–11.

twenty-five fatalities on the Byzantine side, Leo reports a figure more than twice as big, namely fifty-five.[68] While textual comparison between Greek sources points to the penetration of pro-Skleros material in John Skylitzes' text, it is evidence from non-Greek texts that best indicates the extent to which this pro-Skleros narrative shapes Skylitzes' coverage of Basil's reign. These texts are the various narratives and documentary records from Buyid Iraq that concern themselves with Skleros' imprisonment and release from Baghdad. Just as Leo's portrait of Skleros' battles with the Rus suggests that the account in Skylitzes' *Synopsis Historion* is somewhat exaggerated in its regard for Skleros' ingenuity and acumen, so the Buyid texts demonstrate that the heroism and cunning which Bardas is said by Skylitzes to have displayed while in exile, are simply the confections of a pro-Skleros party. According to a detailed, lively, and heroic account conveyed by Skylitzes, the Skleroi were released from Baghdad, because the Buyid authorities in Iraq had become so hard pressed by their own enemies that they needed to draft the stern and sturdy Romans into the ranks of their own pusillanimous troops. But at first Skleros 'was crafty and with dissimulation asked how men who had been imprisoned for such a long time would be able to handle weapons'.[69] Eventually he accepted his commission, but refused to receive additional supplies or troops from his former captors. Instead, the hardy Byzantine prisoners were let out of gaol, given a bath, and sent into battle, where they routed the opposition. Rather than returning to Baghdad,

---

[68] Leo the Deacon, *Historiae Libri Decem*, 111.
[69] Skylitzes, *Synopsis*, 333.

the Romans then spurred on their steeds, and completed a heroic charge out of Iraq and into the empire.[70]

An alternative story emerges from the Buyid evidence. Both the eyewitness accounts of the release of the Skleroi in the history of al-Rudhrawari, and the treaty in the diplomatic handbook of al-Kalkashandi which details the terms of their departure from Baghdad, indicate that the former rebels were set free under the strictest of conditions, and provided by the Buyids with the necessary troops and supplies to enable them to reach the empire.[71] Skleros promised, in the event of his becoming emperor, to set free all Muslim prisoners of war, to protect the property and families of Muslims, to prohibit any Byzantine army from marching on the eastern frontier, and to hand over seven border fortresses to the control of the authorities in Baghdad.[72] Furthermore, it is also clear from the subsequent correspondence dated to 990 between the Buyid general Chutur

---

[70] Ibid. 332–4; Michael Psellos also reports this story albeit more briefly (Psellos, *Cronografia*, i. 20–3).

[71] al-Rudhrawari, *Eclipse*, vi. 116–17; Canard, 'Deux documents', 59–62, 65–8. Yahya also reports that the Skleroi returned to Byzantium under the escort of Buyid troops (Yahya, *PO* 23, pp. 419–20).

[72] Canard, 'Deux documents', 59–62, locates these seven fortresses in the extreme north of the Diyar Bakr in the area of the Upper Tigris. Canard argues that they had fallen into Byzantine hands during Tzimiskes' campaigns on the Mesopotamian frontier in 972 (see above 5.1 and below 6.2 and 6.3.2). They were at the centre of negotiations between the Buyids and Byzantines at the time of Ibn Shahram's embassy in 981–2; see also Forsyth, 'The Chronicle of Yahya ibn Sa'id', 402–9, 426; C. Holmes, 'Byzantium's Eastern Frontier in the Tenth and Eleventh Centuries', in D. Abulafia and N. Berend (eds.), *Medieval Frontiers: Concepts and Practices* (Aldershot, 2002), 100–1.

and Skleros, that Baghdad was prepared to bankroll Skleros' enterprises once the rebel was back in Byzantium.[73]

5.2.4   The Skleros manifesto: dates and motives

The identification of pro-Skleros material within John Sky-litzes' narrative demands answers to two important questions: when, and why, would such a panegyrical source have been written? The strongest likelihood must be that this pro-Skleros material represents an encomium which was composed at some point after Skleros returned to Byzantium in 987 and before his death in March 991.[74] However, within this general time-frame, two rather more specific contexts can be suggested. The first is that the text was written as part of the propaganda war which *preceded* Skleros' surrender to Basil II in 989. The second is that it was composed *after* Skleros laid down his arms and met the emperor at a conference of reconciliation in late 989 or early 990.

There is persuasive evidence for the first interpretation. Like all rebels, Skleros had always sought to manipulate public relations. During his first revolt he let it be known that his spiritual guide, a certain monk, had foreseen Bardas' elevation to the imperial purple in a dream.[75] Both Bardas Skleros and Bardas Phokas are said to have taken great comfort in the popular contemporary prophecy that the

---

[73] Canard, 'Deux documents', 63–4, 68–9.

[74] The date is provided by Yahya, *PO* 23, pp. 430–1.

[75] Skylitzes, *Synopsis*, 316–17; Jean-Claude Cheynet points out the need for rebels against imperial authority in the 10th to 12th c. to disseminate effective propaganda (Cheynet, *Pouvoir et contestations*, 161–2).

name of the future emperor would begin with the letter *beta*, failing to recognize that their adversary, the emperor Basil, had a name with the same initial letter.[76] However, by the final stages of his revolt in 989, Skleros had rather different propaganda needs. Instead of being engaged in a quest for the imperial purple, he was involved in a game of diplomatic bluff to ensure his own survival. Indeed, since his return to the empire in Baghdad in 987 Skleros had been struggling to keep afloat. Despite being escorted back to the empire by Bedouin and Kurdish horsemen, and seizing the revenues from his erstwhile base at Melitene, he had been unable to build the *auld alliances* which had underpinned his first revolt a decade earlier. The Bedouin and Kurdish troops had soon left his service, and in his vulnerability he had joined Phokas.[77] At this point his son Romanos defected to Basil II. As we have seen Skleros claims, in the account refracted by Skylitzes, that this defection was part of an elaborate family plan, an insurance policy in case the Phokas alliance misfired.[78] However, this explanation is not corroborated by the more contemporary account of Yahya ibn Sa'id. Instead, he claims that Romanos left his father because he mistrusted Phokas, a fear that was realized when Bardas was taken captive by his namesake Bardas Phokas.[79] Moreover, Bardas Skleros' position continued to be perilous after his release from captivity by the Phokas family in March or

---

[76] Skylitzes, *Synopsis*, 338, interpolation in manuscripts [U] and [E].

[77] Yahya, *PO* 23, pp. 421–3; Stephen of Taron, *Armenische Geschichte*, 187–8; Skylitzes, *Synopsis*, 334–6.

[78] For this claim see above 5.2.2.

[79] Yahya, *PO* 23, p. 422.

April 989. References within his correspondence with the Buyid general Chutur indicates that as late as June 989, more than three months after his release from imprisonment by the Phokades in the Anti Taurus mountains, Skleros was still to be found in the plain of Larissa in eastern Cappadocia.[80] There is no evidence that he ever advanced any further west. Instead, he seems to have set up a laager in eastern Anatolia from which he negotiated his surrender to the emperor.

Central to Skleros' strategy was a need to persuade the emperor that despite his lack of resources he remained a potent foe. Delaying in Larissa, safely distant from the hinterland of the capital, was one element to this strategy. Allowing the emperor to believe that preparations were underway for a resumption of revolt was another strand.[81] Yet another could have been the production of a narrative which contained examples of the heroism of the Skleroi, above all extensive coverage of their fabulously exotic military exploits in the distant regions of Buyid Iraq. Certainly there is independent evidence to suggest that Basil feared Skleros' qualities as a general, especially his ability to raise light cavalry troops from neighbouring eastern powers. Although Skleros' return to Byzantium in 987 proved to be a false dawn, Yahya ibn Sa'id reports that the emperor was terrified of the arrival of the erstwhile usurper and his nomad escort. So great, indeed, was his concern that he

---

[80] Canard, 'Deux documents', 63, 68–9.

[81] It is interesting that in referring to the renewal of Skleros' revolt in 989, Skylitzes uses a verb meaning 'to get into training for war': ὁ Σκληρὸς πάλιν ἀνελάμβανεν ἑαυτὸν καὶ τὴν προτέραν ἐσωμάσκει ἀποστασίαν (Skylitzes, *Synopsis*, 338).

reappointed Bardas Phokas to the position of *domestikos* of the *scholai*, commander-in-chief of the army, only to see Phokas himself organize a much more potent rebellion.[82] Furthermore, Skleros' continuing correspondence with the Buyid authorities, after his release from captivity by the Phokades in 989, might have suggested that this long-term dissident still had the contacts necessary to build a future eastern alliance.

Yet, although it is possible that the pro-Skleros encomium was composed before the rebel and emperor came to terms, I suspect that it is more likely to have been written after the Skleros surrender. My suspicions are based not so much on evidence that comes directly from Skylitzes' narrative, but more on the account of Basil's reign in Michael Psellos' *Chronographia*. As we have seen above, Michael Psellos was happy to make the general point that it was Bardas Phokas who was the principal threat to Basil's security in the first thirteen years of his reign.[83] Nonetheless, this allegation does not appear to have prevented Psellos from also making extensive use of the pro-Skleros historiographical tradition in his own narrative treatment of the reign. Signs of that pro-Skleros material are scattered throughout his testimony. Psellos, like Skylitzes, picks up on the general theme of Skleros' cunning and strategic awareness. He favourably compares Skleros' abilities as a commander with those of Phokas.[84]

[82] Yahya, *PO* 23, 421–3.

[83] Psellos, *Cronografia*, i. 18–21; see also above p. 268.

[84] 'This man Skleros, although apparently not to be compared with Phokas in physical prowess, was a greater exponent of military strategy and management. It was also said that he was more resourceful.' (Psellos, *Cronografia*, i. 34–5; trans. Sewter, *Michael Psellus*, 41).

He expatiates on Skleros' resourcefulness during his revolts in great detail, describing the skill with which Skleros deprived both Constantinople and the imperial field armies of essential supplies.[85] He also includes the daring-do version of Skleros' escape from Baghdad found in Skylitzes' testimony.[86] Yet another place where Psellos seems to have drawn on a pro-Skleros narrative is in his account of the conference between Basil and Bardas, which took place after the general had capitulated to the imperial authorities. And it is this description which, above all, supports the notion that the whole pro-Skleros encomium was composed *after* agreement was reached between the two parties.

Early on in his description of the eventual meeting between Basil and Skleros, Psellos contrasts the experience and dignity of the rebel favourably with the juvenile irascibility of the emperor. He vividly describes Skleros approaching the emperor, still wearing the red shoes symbolic of imperial rule. According to Psellos, Basil 'saw all this from a distance and shut his eyes in annoyance, refusing to see him at all until he first clothed himself like an ordinary citizen'.[87] More significantly, however, this is the occasion at which Skleros' ingenuity is presented by Psellos as the quality which allows him to transcend the ignominy of defeat. Despite failing to take the throne himself, the battle-hardened general is still able to call upon his idiosyncratic cunning, and thus give the

---

[85] Psellos, *Cronografia*, i. 34–7. Psellos tells his reader that Skleros diverted naval convoys, blocked roads, and siphoned off merchandise for his own troops.

[86] Psellos, *Cronografia*, i. 20–3.

[87] Ibid. 38–41.

emperor some crafty advice on how to prevent future disorder:

After this the emperor questioned him, as a man accustomed to command, about power, and how his rule could be protected, free from dissension? Skleros proposed advice which was not typical of a general, but more like a *cunning* plot: destroy the governors who are overproud; let no generals have too many resources; exhaust them with unjust exactions, so that they are kept busy with their own affairs; admit no woman to the palace; be accessible to no-one; share with few your most intimate plans.[88]

But why should such encomiastic material have been necessary *after* Skleros' surrender? One of the reasons may have been that Skleros needed to justify his political career to the Byzantine political elite at large, to members of his own family, and even to himself. Amid the complexities and confusions presented by the Skleros narrative in the Greek record, it is easy to forget the enormous cost of Bardas' revolt to his immediate supporters. By refusing to surrender to Basil at the end of his first revolt in 979 with the rest of the rebel party, Skleros had led his immediate family and entourage into a ten-year political cul-de-sac. This impasse had involved at least six years' of imprisonment in Baghdad, two years' confinement by Phokas, and more important still, many years without the benefits that service within the upper echelons of the Byzantine military could bring.

Another reason for the production of a Skleros panegyric in the post-989 conference period may have been that

---

[88] Ibid. (trans. adapted, Sewter, *Michael Psellus*, 43). This story is also briefly alluded to by Kekaumenos, although Skleros is not actually named in his account (Kekaumenos, *Consilia et Narrationes*, 284).

imperial authorities still needed to be persuaded that the Skleroi were worth rehabilitating. In this context it is important to stress the completely supine position of the Skleroi after they capitulated. Far from meeting the emperor on equal terms in 989, Skleros appeared before Basil as a broken man. Both Psellos and Skylitzes record what they allege is a well-known story, that Basil greeted the appearance of Skleros in the imperial tent with disdain.[89] According to this account, which appears to have its origins outside the tradition of the Skleros source, Basil sneered, 'the one whom I have feared and trembled before comes led by the hand.' In a particularly obscure phrase Skylitzes hints that the reason for Skleros' decrepitude was the fact he had been blinded during the course of his journey to meet Basil: 'for having been struck during the journey by a lack of sight, he threw away sighted knowledge, and was led blind before the emperor.'[90] In such unpropitious circumstances it was imperative for the future of the Skleros family that the imperial authorities should be reminded of their military daring and expertise. More important, it was vital that these qualities were recognized as indispensable to the future well-being of the Byzantine state.

The need to convince the imperial authorities that the Skleroi were worth rehabilitating may explain why the pro-Skleros source, as it is refracted through the accounts of Skylitzes and Psellos, often reads as a narrative version of many of the tactics enumerated in the military manuals

---

[89] Skylitzes, *Synopsis*, 338–9; Psellos, *Cronografia*, i. 38.
[90] Skylitzes, *Synopsis*, 338–9.

of the tenth century. In his study of Byzantine warfare in the tenth century Eric McGeer has noted how Skylitzes' account of Skleros' action at Arkadioupolis represents a perfect real-time enactment of the tactics recommended by the *Praecepta Militum*, that manual written from the field notes of Nikephoros Phokas, the great military emperor. In Skylitzes' rendition of this battle Skleros offers a copybook example of how to deal with an enemy of superior numbers; of how to use skirmishing cavalry men to harrass foes; of how to collect and act upon intelligence; and of how to engage in the hand-to-hand cavalry fighting required of those heavily armoured *kataphraktoi* that formed the nucleus of the Byzantine field armies of the tenth century.[91] Copybook adherence to the dictates of contemporary military *taktika* is visible elsewhere in the eleventh-century Greek historical record of Skleros' military action. Michael Psellos praises the excellent order maintained by Skleros' cavalry during their flight from Iraq when they were under pressure from superior numbers of troops.[92] He also describes the personal touch that Skleros deployed in order to inspire loyalty among his troops during his later revolts against the emperor: he bound them into one coherent body, reconciled their differences, ate at the same table, drank from the same cup, and addressed them by their own name.[93] As a result he suffered no desertions from his cause. Such claims tally closely with the recommendations of contemporary military manuals that generals should seek to build army units

---

[91] McGeer, *Sowing the Dragon's Teeth*, 298.
[92] Psellos, *Cronografia*, i. 20–3; Haldon, *Warfare, State and Society*, 224.
[93] Psellos, *Cronografia*, i. 36–7.

around pre-existing bonds of friends, neighbours, and family, and that officers should be quartered with the troops under their command.[94]

In fact, as we have already observed, many of Skleros' claims were either extremely far-fetched, or more simply blatant lies. Despite Skleros' protestation that he was able to inspire loyalty among his troops, his revolts were always plagued by desertions; instead of fighting his way out of Iraq using a classic *kataphraktoi* charge, Arabic evidence indicates that he returned to Byzantium as a Buyid client. How is the presence of such complete fabrication within the Skleros source to be explained unless as a piece of desperate propaganda? Such radical reworkings of the events of the immediate past suggest that Bardas was not interested in reshaping his career in subtle ways, offering his readers a favourable angle on events; his was not a gentle exercise in retrospective self-justification from the armchair of retirement for decisions that had gone wrong. Instead his purpose was much more immediate. Skleros needed to prove that he and his connection were superlative troops, indispensable to the well-being of the empire; the only way of doing this was by insisting that as a commander he always played it by the book. In this case the book, or books, were contemporary military manuals. Moreover, there are substantial grounds for thinking that despite the enormity of the falsehoods that Skleros' apologia contains, lies or exaggerations of which contemporaries must surely have been aware, his cavalier

---

[94] *Praecepta Militum*: McGeer, *Sowing the Dragon's Teeth*, 13, 39, 59; *Ouranos Taktika (b)*, 89, 117.

approach to his own past was a gamble worth taking. For while Skleros himself was in a desperate situation, so was Basil II. In the emperor's case desperation came from the external context: war with the empire's neighbours.

In the later 980s and early 990s, the empire of Basil II was threatened on at least two fronts, by the Bulgarians in the west, and by the Fatimids of Egypt in the east. Meanwhile, control over the far north-east of the empire had been ceded since 979 to the Iberian (Georgian) princes and nobles of Tao in return for their assistance in defeating the first rebellion of Bardas Skleros.[95] In such dire international circumstances experienced generals were needed. However, with the death of Bardas Phokas and Kalokyros Delphinas at Abydos in 989, and the deposition of the remaining Phokades from army command after the revolt was over, the emperor faced an acute shortage of generals. So acute indeed was this shortfall that even in the immediate aftermath of victory at Abydos, Basil was unable to dismiss all his former Phokas adversaries. Leo Melissenos, who had been in command of rebel troops during the siege of Abydos in 988, was spared the humiliation of being paraded through Constantinople. By 994 he was once again involved in warfare on the eastern frontier, leading a party of reinforcements from Constantinople to assist in the war effort against the Fatimids.[96] Other commanders whose loyalty must have been open to doubt, such as Michael Bourtzes, who had once

---

[95] Forsyth, 'The Chronicle of Yahya ibn Sa'id', 388–93; for this surrender of territory to the Iberians see above 5.2 and below 6.2, 6.3.4, and 8.4.

[96] Forsyth, 'The Chronicle of Yahya ibn Sa'id', 134; Skylitzes, *Synopsis*, 338; Leo the Deacon, *Historiae Libri Decem*, 171–3; Yahya, *PO* 23, p. 440.

supported Bardas Skleros, continued to occupy high-ranking military offices after 990.[97] More to the point, while Basil II found himself hamstrung by a lack of suitable generals, his desperation offered the Skleroi an obvious route to rehabilitation. One member of the Skleros family had, of course, already taken advantage of this situation. When Bardas' son, Romanos Skleros, defected to Basil in 987 he received a warm welcome, precisely because the emperor was bereft of experienced commanders and knew that Romanos was 'a skilful man, effective and very resourceful in military matters'.[98] Where Romanos had led, by 989 his father believed that he could follow.

The appearance of other members of the Skleros axis at the head of Byzantine armies during the subsequent decades of Basil's reign proved Bardas Skleros correct. Military expertise in times of political and military crisis was a safe route back to political fortune. Yet Bardas Skleros and his brother Constantine did not themselves live to see this revival.[99] Having been resettled in Thrace by the emperor, where it is possible that they were kept under house arrest, both died before the end of March 991, in circumstances that at least one later medieval Arab historian found suspicious.[100] Given the brevity of the time that intervened between the surrender and death of Skleros, it is likely that the

---

[97] See examples from the Antioch region in 6.3.3.

[98] Skylitzes, *Synopsis*, 335; for more on Romanos' alliance with Basil see above 5.2.2.

[99] See above 5.2.2 and below 6.3.3 for the post-989 careers of Bardas' son Romanos and the rest of the Skleros entourage.

[100] al-Rudhrawari notes that some reports alleged that Bardas Skleros died of poison (al-Rudhrawari, *Eclipse*, vi. 119).

encomium preserved in the accounts of Skylitzes and Psellos was written at some point in 990.

5.3   THE SKLEROS MANIFESTO AND THE WRITING OF HISTORY

Having identified traces of a pro-Skleros source behind the eleventh-century Greek historical record of the first thirteen years of Basil's reign, the most pressing question must be: why did historians such as Skylitzes and Psellos choose to articulate their appraisals around this historiographical tradition? One reason for their choice could, of course, have been the accident of survival: when they came to write their respective accounts in the mid- to late eleventh century, this was all they had available. But this is not the only possibility; and, indeed, there is evidence to suggest that paucity of source materials was not the factor that dictated their choice of narrative. For example, Skylitzes himself says that an alternative account about the activities of the Skleroi in Baghdad existed: that they fought for the Buyids, were well treated, and that as Adud al-Daula lay dying he ordered his son to grant the Romans their freedom.[101] In addition, an alternative Byzantine narrative also seems to have entered the Arabic tradition, represented by the annalistic historian, al-Rudhrawari. Inserted into his text just before mention of the Ibn Shahram embassy of 981/2, is

---

[101] Skylitzes, *Synopsis*, 334.

a summary account of domestic Byzantine history from the death of Basil and Constantine's father, Romanos II, in 963, to the arrival of Skleros in Baghdad.[102] This account seems to have been taken from a Greek original since it displays an accurate rendering of Byzantine names and titles, which is unusual in most Arab historiography.[103] More striking, however, is the fact that this narrative does not portray Skleros the astute military hero, but rather Skleros, the leader of a motley band, on the point of being abandoned in 979 by most of his supporters:

Before the arrest of Ward his chief followers assembled in his presence, and told him that they saw no likelihood of their negotiations with Adud ending in the latter's furnishing effective aid. They said ... our right course is to return to Byzantine territory peacefully if we can, or if we must fight then doing our utmost with the prospect of winning, or else leaving this world with honour unimpaired. He replied that this proposal was worthless, that he had a high opinion of Adud ... when he resisted their proposals ... many of them abandoned him.[104]

However, while the contemporary source that made its way into the Iraqi historical tradition may have been a more

[102] al-Rudhrawari, *Eclipse*, vi. 4–7.

[103] For typical instances of inaccuracy in such matters see M. Canard, 'Les Sources arabes de l'histoire byzantine', 296–7, n. 7; idem, 'Quelques noms de personnages byzantins dans une pièce du poète Abu Firas', *B* 11 (1936), 452, n. 5; Miquel, *La Géographie humaine*, ii. 387–91, comments on the habitual inaccuracy displayed by Arab geographers in describing Byzantium.

[104] al-Rudhrawari, *Eclipse*, vi. 7–8. Wesem Farag also notes that while Skylitzes claims that Skleros went voluntarily to Adud in Baghdad, all the eastern narratives, both Arabic and Armenian, claim that Skleros and the remnants of his party were taken captive by the Buyid emir (Farag, 'Byzantium and its Muslim Neighbours', 81 n. 57).

accurate account of events at the end of the tenth century, it is possible that Psellos and Skylitzes selected their underlying source materials with criteria *other* than precision and truthfulness in mind. In the previous two chapters it has been suggested that Skylitzes' *Synopsis Historion* was compiled in accordance with many of the requirements and expectations of history-writing of the latter stages of the eleventh-century. In concluding this chapter I would like to suggest that the ubiquity of pro-Skleros material in Skylitzes' and Psellos' accounts, both of which were written in the second half of the eleventh century, is to be explained by the political and literary demands of the period in which these historians themselves were writing, rather than because this material accurately represented the political history of the reign of Basil II or because it was the only source that these historians had to hand. Psellos and Skylitzes, in other words, made an active choice to include this material.

At the most basic level we should note the extent to which the pro-Skleros source meets the general requirements of history-writing in the second half of the eleventh century. In earlier chapters in this book we have already observed a widespread enthusiasm among both authors and audiences in the later eleventh century for lively narratives which contained large doses of vivid military heroism.[105] The long and detailed military accounts within the Skleros source, in particular the narratives describing the general's rout of the Rus at Arkadioupolis in 970, and his heroic flight from Iraq in 987 certainly meet this fascination. Moreover,

---

[105] See esp. 4.1 and 4.2.2.

the ubiquity of praise for Skleros' ingenuity and cunning within this source may also have satisfied a contemporary fascination with military acumen and clever strategies. Alexander Každan certainly believed that these were topics that preoccupied the writers and readers of late eleventh- and twelfth-century historical literature.[106]

If we look more specifically at Skylitzes, then it is clear that here too a pro-Skleros source would fit with his later eleventh-century working methods and use of source materials. As we saw in Chapter 2, Jonathan Shepard has argued that eulogistic narratives of senior generals were among Skylitzes' preferred core sources in the writing of history. While looking at Skylitzes' coverage of the mid-eleventh century, Shepard concluded that two of the author's most important sources were a laudatory account of the general Katakalon Kekaumenos and an apologetic text produced to justify the revolt of George Maniakes (1043).[107] If Skylitzes was prepared to use encomia produced by senior generals as the main vehicle for his articulation of the history of the empire in the mid-eleventh century, then there is no reason why he should not have used similar source materials in his account of Basil's reign. Indeed, as we saw in Chapter 4, Skylitzes seems to have used a root text of this nature in building up his narrative of the heroic exploits of the general Eustathios Daphnomeles in the Balkans.[108] In this context, it

---

[106] Každan, 'Aristocracy and the Imperial Ideal', *passim*; 'Social Views of Michael Attaleiates', 63–73; Každan and Wharton-Epstein, *Change in Byzantine Culture*, 99–118, and esp. 104, 112.

[107] See above 2.4.

[108] See above 4.2.2.

is also worth pointing out that the ways in which the pane-gyrics of Kekaumenos and Maniakes shape Skylitzes' eleventh-century testimony closely resemble the impact of the Skleros narrative on the author's coverage of Basil's reign. Narrative passages connected to the exploits of Kekaumenos and Maniakes tend to be long and detailed. The careers of these generals are minutely explained. Their tactical cleverness and strategic awareness are frequently stressed. It is their viewpoint which is most overwhelmingly audible. All these are diagnostic traits which we have traced in those parts of Skylitzes' coverage of the reigns of John Tzimiskes and Basil II taken from the Skleros source.

Moreover, Skylitzes' use of pro-Skleros material in his historical writings also reflects one of his other later eleventh-century interests, namely, prosopography and the author's desire to express the Byzantine past through the deeds and achievements of the ancestors of the aristocracy of the early Komnenian period.[109] In this context, it is worth noting that the Skleroi were not only an important family during the reign of Basil II, but were also still a very important dynasty at the end of the eleventh century, during the early decades of the reign of Alexios Komnenos. For instance, at the Synod of Blachernai in 1094–5, one Andronikos Skleros held the extremely senior title of *protonobelissimos*. Another member of the family who participated at the same synod, Michael, possessed the senior rank of *kouropalates*.[110] A further sign of the political prominence of the

---

[109] See Ch. 4 above, *passim*.
[110] Magdalino, *Manuel I Komnenos*, 501–2; Seibt, *Die Skleroi*, 97–101.

family in the early Komnenian period is the participation of an unnamed member of the family in the Anemas revolt, an insurrection which has been dated to the period 1100–1.[111] Moreover, it is clear that the family were too politically important to be irreparably damaged by their association with this conspiracy. Instead, their star continued to rise. By 1104, Andronikos, who was a *protonobelissimos* in 1094, held the title of *sebastos*. Seibt, the principal modern prosopographer of the Skleros family, has suggested that this elevation in status may even reflect the fact that Andronikos had recently married into the imperial family.[112] While this hypothesis has yet to be substantiated by other evidence, Andronikos' senior title clearly indicates his importance within the highest echelons of Byzantine political society in the first decade of the twelfth century.

The idea that Skylitzes selected pro-Skleros source material in his analysis of Basil's reign because of the political importance of this family in his own lifetime, gains support from the appearance of similar material in the account of Basil's reign in Michael Psellos' *Chronographia*. Although the exact date of the composition of Psellos' *Chronographia* remains unclear, it is likely that Psellos was at work on the principal section of his historical writings (those dealing with the period leading up to the fall of Isaac Komnenos in 1059) several decades before Skylitzes wrote the *Synopsis Historion*.[113] Just as the Skleroi enjoyed political prominence

---

[111] Anna Komnene, *Alexiade*, iii. 70; see above 4.2.1 for further discussion of the Anemas revolt.

[112] Seibt, *Die Skleroi*, 98.

[113] Psellos seems to have completed the first section of the *Chronographia*, which ends with the abdication of Isaac, before 1063 (Kaldellis, *Argument of*

at the end of the eleventh century, when Skylitzes was writing, so they occupied the highest echelons of Byzantine elite society when Psellos was active. Among the leading Skleroi of the mid-eleventh century were Basil Skleros, *strategos* of the theme of the Anatolikon in the late 1020s and early 1030s; Romanos Skleros, *doux* of Antioch on two separate occasions during the 1050s, and a leading protagonist in the 1057 coup which unseated Michael VI; and two female members of the family.[114] The first of these women was the wife of Constantine Monomachos, who died before her husband became emperor in 1042. The second, called Maria, was Constantine's long-standing mistress both before and after his accession to the imperial purple.[115]

The prominence of the family at this time was certainly recognized by Psellos himself. In the early stages of his

---

Psellus' Chronographia, 11). The date of composition of the second section of his text, that dealing with the reigns of the Doukas and Diogenes families, is less certain. Psellos' account, which at this stage is far less coherently organized and argued than the pre-1059 coverage, contains material from the reign of Michael VII (1071–8), and yet Psellos shows no sign of knowledge of Michael's fall. According to this logic, Psellos would have finished his work in the mid-1070s; Kaldellis, *Argument of Psellus' Chronographia*, 11, follows the traditional dating set by R. Anastasi, *Studia sulla Chronographia di Michele Psellos* (Catania, 1969). However, since Psellos may not have died until the 1090s, there is a very slight possibility that he was writing the final section of his work in the reign of Alexios Komnenos. The notion that Psellos continued to write in the Komnenian period has been propounded principally by Každan, 'Social Views of Michael Attaleiates', 53–5; idem, 'An Attempt at Hagio-Autobiography: The Pseudo-Life of "Saint" Psellos', *B* 53 (1983), 546–56; *ODB*, iii. 1754–5; see also, P. Gautier, 'Monodie inédite de Michel Psellos sur le basileus Andronic Doucas', *REB* 24 (1966), 153–64.

[114] Seibt, *Die Skleroi*, 65–8, 76–85; Romanos Skleros' career is discussed further in 6.3.3.

[115] Seibt, *Die Skleroi*, 70–6.

account of the reign of Constantine Monomachos (1042–55) he refers at length to the emperor's Skleraine mistress.[116] However, it is his much briefer reference to another Skleraine, the member of the family who had been Monomachos' wife, which is the more interesting for our purposes. According to Psellos, this woman was 'descended from the very famous Skleros family'.[117] In this brief phrase the reader gains an elusive hint of the extent to which the political identity of mid-eleventh-century members of the Skleros family was articulated through the fame and renown of their ancestors. This conclusion is substantiated by the contents of a letter written by Michael Psellos to Romanos Skleros, former *doux* of Antioch, in the mid-1050s. In this letter Psellos notes: 'I neither saw your grandfather nor lay eyes on your father. But reputation has it that they were noble (*gennaioi*) men and the paragons of good birth (*eugeneia*).'[118] While Seibt's prosopographical research suggests that Bardas Skleros, the rebel of Basil's reign, was too old to have been either the father or grandfather of the *doux*

---

[116] Psellos, *Cronografia*, i. 296–309.

[117] ἣν ἐκ τοῦ τῶν Σκληρῶν ἐπιφανεστάτου γένους ἠγάγετο (Psellos, *Cronografia*, i. 296).

[118] ἀλλ'ἐγώ σοι οὔτε τὸν πάππον εἶδον οὔτε τὸν πατέρα τεθέαμαι· ἡ φήμη δὲ τούτους γενναίους ἄνδρας καὶ εὐγενείας ἔχει ἀγάλματα (Psellos (Michael), *Scriptora Minora: Michaelis Pselli Scripta Minora*, ed. E. Kurtz and F. Drexl, 2 vols. (Milan, 1937–41), ii. 102). Romanos Skleros was not the only member of this family with whom Psellos corresponded. At a rather later date, in the early 1070s, Psellos wrote to Nicholas Skleros, at that time a *proedros* and *krites* of the theme of the Aegean Sea (Psellos, *Scriptora Minora*, ii, letters 37, 44, 56 and 63; Seibt, *Die Skleroi*, 94–5). By 1084 Nicholas had been appointed to the senior judicial position of *megas droungarios* of the *Bigla*. He may even have been Skylitzes' predecessor in this post (see above 2.3 for Skylitzes' biography).

Romanos,[119] the comments of Michael Psellos offer strong circumstantial evidence that stories glorifying the earliest members of the Skleros dynasty were ubiquitous in mid-eleventh-century Byzantium. Given the continuing import-ance of the Skleroi within Byzantine political society at the time Psellos was writing, it may not be entirely surprising that he chose to use one such Skleros narrative, that of Bardas, the founder of the Skleros family, as one of his sources for his appraisal of the reign of Basil II.

Although connections between Michael Psellos and the pro-Skleros panegyric are somewhat more provisional than those between Skylitzes and this encomiastic material, none-theless, both eleventh-century historians appear to have used a historiographical tradition that favoured Bardas Skleros extensively in their accounts of Basil's reign. This contention is another stage in the argument outlined in earlier chapters in this book: that the first step towards uncovering the history of Basil's reign lies in understanding the eleventh-century Greek historiography that reports on that history; furthermore, to understand that historiography one needs to know more of the social, literary, and political contexts within which it was written. However, locating this later historical literature in its appropriate contexts is not enough. What has yet to be discussed is what these discov-eries mean for our reading of political realities during Basil's reign itself. In other words, how should we now interpret Basil's reign in the knowledge that the later Greek

[119] Romanos' father was probably the brother of the Basil Skleros, the *strategos* of the Anatolikon mentioned above. His grandfather was Romanos, the son of Bardas Skleros (Seibt, *Die Skleroi*, 64–5, 76).

historiography plays up the political significance of Bardas Skleros and underplays that of Bardas Phokas? This is a question which will be explored further in the next chapter, particularly in the discussion of the nature of military command on the tenth- and early eleventh-century eastern frontier. It will also shape the very final chapter of this volume, when a new analytical interpretation of Basil's reign will be offered.

6

Administration and Imperial Authority on the Eastern Frontier

6.1   METHODS AND SOURCES

The first five chapters of this book have focused on that source material which is central to any coherent understanding of the reign of Basil II, namely the medieval historiographical record. Particular attention has been paid to the principal account of the reign written in Greek, the testimony offered by John Skylitzes in his *Synopsis Historion*. It has been argued that the content and interpretation of Skylitzes' text, which was written more than fifty years after the death of Basil, were shaped by the literary, social, and political conditions of the later eleventh century. The same argument has been applied somewhat more briefly to Michael Psellos' account of the reign. These chapters have suggested that the mid- to later eleventh-century concerns of Skylitzes and Psellos constitute an important and sometimes distorting lens between the modern reader and Basil. Nonetheless, these chapters have also shown that once the historian is aware of this intermediate lens, he or she can still utilize these later Greek texts to reconstruct and interpret the important political, diplomatic, and military processes and structures of Basil's hegemony. In these early chapters I have shown how such reconstruction and interpretation can be applied to individual episodes during the reign, particularly during the Skleros and Phokas revolts and the emperor's wars in the Balkans. In the final chapter I will offer an interpretation of the whole reign based on such rereadings of the medieval Greek historical record.

However, before we move on to this final reconstruction, I would like to examine two other critical concentrations in the evidence for Basil's reign. The first of these comprises contemporary narratives written in languages other than Greek. The other is the plethora of lead seals belonging to imperial officials from the later tenth and early eleventh century. In the next two chapters I want to use these narratives and contemporary lead seals to construct a picture of governance in Basil's Byzantium which reflects later tenth- and early eleventh-century political and administrative realities rather than the concerns of later eleventh-century historians such as Skylitzes and Psellos. The analysis will focus on the empire's frontiers, those regions where the survival of a relatively strong narrative record offers a chronological context to changes in governance reflected in the sigillographical material. By combining the narrative and sigillographical evidence I hope to show how Byzantine governance worked on the ground in real time.

This chapter will focus on the eastern frontier; the next will look at the Balkans and southern Italy. Both will build upon evidence for frontier governance provided by a list of imperial offices drawn up in the final decades of the tenth century, which is known as the *Escorial Taktikon*. This list of official precedence documents some of the most important changes in military governance on Byzantium's frontiers following territorial conquests by imperial armies in the east and west between the reigns of Romanos Lekapenos (920–44) and John Tzimiskes (969–76).[1] The most significant of those changes in frontier governance, according to Oikonomides, the modern editor of the *Taktikon*, was the division of the conquered territories into a series of small new themes placed under the authority of overarching regional units called duchies or katepanates. Each of these regional authorities was commanded by a senior officer from the Byzantine field army who was known either as *doux* or *katepano*. This senior officer, located at a key frontier fortress, was in charge of a large garrison of troops drawn from the empire's central field army; he also exercised gubernatorial powers over the localities under his command including responsibility for civil affairs. By the time Basil came to the throne in 976, there were three regional katepanates in the east, centred on Antioch in the south, Mesopotamia in the south-east and Chaldia in the north-east respectively. To these would be added during Basil's reign the katepanate of Iberia created after the absorption of the

---

[1] Oikonomides offered a *terminus post quem* of 971 to the *Taktikon* on the grounds that it includes mention of those small Balkan themes that were conquered by John Tzimiskes in 971. The fact that the *Taktikon* fails to mention those minor themes in northern Syria, such as Laodikeia and Balanias, which were absorbed into the empire during Tzimiskes' final military campaign in the east offers according to Oikonomides a *terminus ante quem* of 975 (Oikonomides, *Listes*, 258–61).

Georgian principality of Tao, and the katepanate of Vaspurakan, which came into being after the annexation of the
eponymous Armenian princedom south of Lake Van. In
the west the *Escorial Taktikon* lists *doukes* for Thessalonika
and Adrianople in the Balkans and a *katepano* of Italy. Later
in Basil's reign the office of *katepano* of Bulgaria came into
being.[2]

Nonetheless, while the *Escorial Taktikon* can be utilized as
a rough guide to administrative structures and processes, it
should be noted that its use to the modern administrative
historian is in many ways limited, above all because it is not
a detailed manual of frontier governance, but instead a
seating plan drawn up by imperial officials who organized
banquets within the Great Palace in Constantinople. As such
it amounts to an occasional and approximate outline of the
hierarchy of the principal office holders within the Byzantium, which could easily include offices that had fallen into
temporary abeyance or complete desuetude.[3] Instead, in
order to find out more about the contemporary operation
and transformation of frontier governance we need to turn
to local narratives and seals. It is these which allow us to

---

[2] N. Oikonomides, 'L'Organisation de la frontière orientale de Byzance
aux Xe–XIe siècles et le taktikon de l'Escorial', *Acts of the 14th International
Congress* 1971, 3 vols. (Bucharest, 1974), i. 285–302, 285–302; idem, *Listes*,
344–6, 354–63; idem, 'L'Évolution', 148; H. J. Kühn, *Die byzantinische Armee
im 10. und 11. Jahrhundert: Studien zur Organisation der Tagmata* (Vienna,
1991), 158–69; W. Treadgold, *Byzantium and its Army 284–1081* (Stanford,
Calif., 1995), 114–15; Howard-Johnston, 'Crown Lands', 86–91; Haldon,
Warfare, State and Society, 84–9.

[3] The same point has been made in respect of lists of precedence from the
9th c., such as the *Kleterologion* of Philotheos (F. Winkelmann, *Byzantinischen
Rang- und Ämterstruktur im 8. und 9. Jahrhundert* (Berlin, 1985), 28).

observe the quotidian operation of local power and to see that the organization of Byzantine frontiers in this period was a piecemeal, ad hoc process, constantly reshaped by changing political, diplomatic, and military circumstances. In addition, such evidence reveals that senior Byzantine military officials sent out from Constantinople to govern the frontiers were only one part of a highly flexible form of governance that sought to adapt to the heterogeneous nature of the local populations in the border regions. Such conclusions feed into a wider point: that once we see Byzantine administration at work in chronological and geographical context, many of the stereotypes about Basil's draconian governance, most of them based on a loose reading of Michael Psellos' analysis of Basil as a man of steel, prove to be misplaced.[4]

6.2   THE EASTERN FRONTIER: A BACKGROUND

In the second and third quarters of the tenth century Byzantine armies had taken advantage of the demise of the Abbasid caliphate, and extended the empire's territorial boundaries over the Taurus and Anti Taurus mountains into Cilicia, northern Syria, and northern Mesopotamia, thus territorially redefining a Byzantine east that for the previous three centuries had been limited to the Anatolian plateau. Yet, when Basil himself came to the throne in 976,

---

[4] See above 1.2.1 and below 8.3 for Psellos' characterization of Basil.

few of these annexations had been consolidated. Melitene, conquered in 934, the oldest of the great territorial gains of the tenth century, had been under Byzantine suzerainty for less than half a century. Most permanent conquests were even more recent. Cilicia, absorbed in 964–5, had been under Byzantine rule for little more than a decade. Antioch in northern Syria had only surrendered to the Byzantines in 969. Other sites in northern Syria, such as Barzouyah and Saoune, ceded to the Byzantines during Emperor John Tzimiskes' last eastern campaign in 975, had been under imperial rule for less than a year when Basil assumed the imperial purple.[5] From the very beginning of his reign, therefore, Basil was faced with the challenge of governing a series of eastern regions that had only very recently been subordinated to imperial control. Among the problems he faced was how to deal with extremely heterodox local populations, few of whom spoke Greek as their first language or practised Orthodox Christianity. Far more numerous than Greek settlers in the Byzantine east were local Armenian and Syrian populations as well as small Muslim communities which chose to live under Byzantine hegemony when their co-religionist leaders were removed from power.[6] Finding

[5] See Map 2 for all geographical references in this chapter; for a summary of these eastern conquests see Vasiliev, *Byzance et les Arabes*, ii/1. 261–307, 341–65; Honigmann, *Die Ostgrenze*, 72–102; Whittow, *Making of Orthodox Byzantium*, 317–34.
[6] For further discussion of the very mixed ethnic and religious complexion of the Byzantine east in the 10th and 11th c. see G. Dagron, 'Minorités ethniques et religieuses dans l'Orient byzantin à la fin du Xe et au XIe siècles: L'Immigration syrienne', *TM* 6 (1976), 177–216; Garsoïan, 'Armenian Integration', 53–124; C. Holmes, ' "How the East was Won" in the Reign of Basil II', in A. Eastmond (ed.), *Eastern Approaches to Byznatium* (Aldershot, 2001), 41–56.

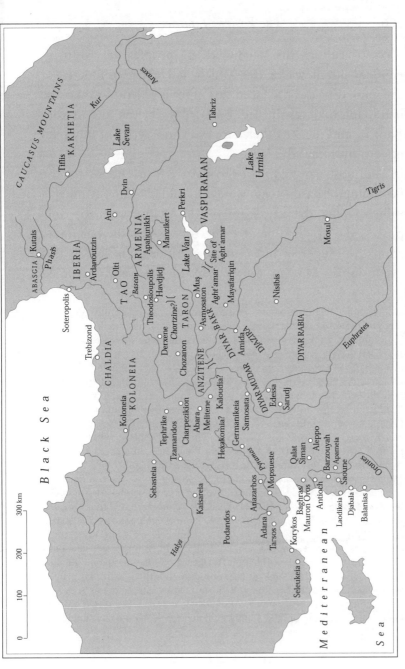

MAP 2. The eastern frontier: Byzantium and its eastern neighbours c.950–1050. Drawn by the author from: N. Oikonomides, *Les Listes de préséance byzantines des IXe et Xe siècles* (Paris, 1972); M. Whittow, *The Making of Orthodox Byzantium, 600–1025* (London, 1996).

ways of ruling this patchwork of peoples was difficult enough, but it was a task which had to be conducted at the same time as Basil faced two other problems: on the one hand, internal revolts led by Bardas Skleros and Bardas Phokas, and on the other, threats from a series of powerful eastern overseas adversaries.

The most dangerous of those eastern neighbours at the beginning of Basil's reign were undoubtedly the Fatimids, a militant Shia dynasty from north Africa, who not only possessed a powerful land army composed of Berber forces from the Maghreb, but also a large fleet.[7] In 969/70 this expansionist Muslim power had invaded and occupied

---

[7] For a detailed discussion of imperial relations with Fatimid Egypt and Aleppo, Byzantium's client state in northern Syria, in Basil's reign, see: Schlumberger, *L'Épopée byzantine*, i, ch. 9; ii, chs. 2, 3, 7; H. Kennedy, *The Prophet and the Age of the Caliphates* (London, 1986), 282–4, 318–38; Whittow, *Making of Orthodox Byzantium,* 367–9, 379–82; Forsyth, 'The Chronicle of Yahya ibn Sa'id', 416–23, 478–557; Farag, 'Byzantium and its Muslim Neighbours', chs. 4–5; idem, 'The Aleppo Question: A Byzantine–Fatimid Conflict of Interest in Northern Syria in the Later Tenth Century', *BMGS* 14 (1990), 44–60; R. J. Bikhazi, 'The Hamdanid Dynasty of Mesopotamia and North Syria 254–404/868–1014', Ph.D. Thesis (Michigan, 1981), 973–80. Fatimid activities in Syria, which brought the dynasty into contact with the Byzantines from 969 onwards, are also covered in depth by T. Bianquis, *Damas sous la domination fatimide (359–468/969–1076): Essai d'interprétation de chroniques arabes médiévales,* 2 vols. (Damascus, 1986–9), ii. 37–456; see also M. Brett, *The Rise of the Fatimids: The World of the Mediterranean and the Middle East in the Fourth Century of the Hijra, Tenth Century C.E.* (Leiden, 2001), 308–16, 331, 346–58, 417–23; see also below 8.4. Relatively little attention is paid to Fatimid–Byzantine relations in an important new publication on the Fatimid world: P. E. Walker, *Exploring an Islamic Empire: Fatimid History and its Sources* (London, 2002), although in two articles Walker has explored early contacts between the two sides in Syria: 'A Byzantine Victory over the Fatimids at Alexandretta (971)', *B* 42 (1972), 431–40; idem, 'The "Crusade" of John Tzimisces in the Light of New Arabic Evidence', *B* 47 (1977), 301–27.

Egypt. By the autumn of 970, Fatimid armies had seized Palestine and Syria, and their sights were set on Byzantine northern Syria. During the winter of 970–1 they besieged Antioch for five months. Although this siege was swiftly disbanded once a Byzantine relief force arrived, Fatimid armies constituted a perennial threat to Byzantine security in northern Syria during the first half of Basil's reign, with competition between the two powers focused on two strategic targets: first, the coastal ports of northern Syria and Lebanon, such as Laodikeia, Balanias, Tripoli, Tyre, and Beirut; and second, Aleppo, the Hamdanid emirate in northern Syria which had become a Byzantine, tribute-paying, client state in the year 969–70. During the 980s, warfare between Byzantium and the Fatimids was somewhat sporadic; this changed, however, in the 990s, when the Fatimids under the caliph al-Aziz went onto a more sustained offensive, repeatedly besieging Aleppo and defeating Byzantine armies in battle on three occasions, in 992, 994, and 998. On two occasions, in 995 and 999, Basil himself was forced to campaign in the east to retrench the Byzantine strategic position. It was only during the caliphate of al-Aziz's son, al-Hakim, that the Fatimid threat was assuaged. In 1001 the two sides reached a truce, which lasted without serious rupture until 1016, when the Fatimids briefly occupied Aleppo.[8] Although competition was renewed at this point, rivalry between the two powers remained highly localized up to the end of Basil's reign.

---

[8] For further narrative details see below 8.4.

Further east, in the Djazira, on the frontier that stretched along the Upper Euphrates and Upper Tigris rivers in Mesopotamia and northern Iraq, there were several local Muslim opponents to Byzantine territorial power at the beginning of Basil's reign.[9] In 973, less than three years before Basil came to power, the Hamdanid emirate of Mosul had defeated a Byzantine field army near Amida, south of the Anti Taurus, taking Melias, the *domestikos* of the *scholai*, captive in the course of the battle. Although the Hamdanids were expelled from Mosul and the Diyar Bakr cities of Mayafariqin and Amida in 978–9, they were replaced by a more potent military threat: forces loyal to Adud al-Daula. Adud was a member of the Shia Buyid clan that controlled most of the Iranian plateau. He himself was the emir of Fars in southern Iran. After ousting his cousin, Izz al-Daula, from power in Baghdad in the spring of 978, he also controlled Iraq. For the next five years, until he died in 983, Adud threatened to unify a vast territorial landmass, which stretched from Persia in the east to the Diyar Bakr in the west. More important, although Adud's hegemony was brief, it occurred at the very beginning of Basil's reign, when the emperor himself was threatened by the first revolt of Bardas Skleros. Indeed, Adud was enthusiastic to exploit his imperial neighbour's insecurity for his own territorial gain. As we saw in

---

[9] Relations between Byzantium and Buyid Iraq are outlined in: Canard, 'La Date des expéditions mésopotamiennes de Jean Tzimiscès', 99–108; idem, 'Deux documents', 55–69; Whittow, *Making of Orthodox Byzantium*, 365–7; Kennedy, *Prophet and the Age of the Caliphates*, 225–36. Forsyth, 'The Chronicle of Yahya ibn Sa'id', 393–416, 478–557; Farag, 'Byzantium and its Muslim Neighbours', chs. 2–3.

Chapter 5, Skleros was offered sanctuary by Adud in Baghdad after his defeat by imperial armies in 979. Adud's hope was that he could use Skleros as a pawn either to recover a series of mountain fortresses in the Diyar Bakr from the Byzantines, or to realize an even greater territorial ambition, control over Aleppo in northern Syria.

Even after Adud died, Buyid Baghdad continued to use Skleros as a political pawn, and when the general returned to Byzantium in 987, it was with the sponsorship of Buyid gold.[10] Nonetheless, by the time that Skleros left Baghdad and re-entered the empire, Buyid power on the Byzantine frontier was disintegrating in the face of pressure from Arab and Kurdish nomad tribes. The last Buyid governor left Mosul in 996, and henceforth this city was under the control of the Bedouin Uqalids. Meanwhile, the Diyar Bakr was absorbed within a Kurdish emirate founded by Bad ibn Dustuk. This emirate, ruled by the Marwanid dynasty, not only encompassed regions south of the Anti Taurus, but also a variety of urban sites on the northern shores of Lake Van in southern Armenia.[11] The military potency of this new Kurdish power was visible during the revolt of Bardas Phokas, when Bad took advantage of the mayhem inside Byzantium to raid the plain of Muş in Taron, an Armenian princedom annexed by the Byzantine empire as recently as 966/7.[12] It

---

[10] For Skleros' relationship with the Buyids see above 5.2.3.

[11] For more on the Marwanids see T. Ripper, *Die Marwaniden von Diyar Bakr: Eine kurdische Dynastie im islamischen Mittelalter* (Würzburg, 2000), 109–41; Farag, 'Byzantium and its Muslim Neighbours', 145–7.

[12] Stephen of Taron, *Armenische Geschichte*, 141; Ripper, *Die Marwaniden*, 109–15.

was only in 992/3, after Bad's death and a series of Byzantine punitive raids around Lake Van, that Basil was able to negotiate a lasting peace with the Kurdish emirate.[13]

North of the Djazira frontier lived a variety of eastern Christian neighbours, princes whose prosperity and political confidence were in the ascendant.[14] Their economic prosperity stemmed from the taxes they extracted from the international trade routes that ran through their domains.[15] They then invested these revenues in extensive building programmes: constructing churches, monasteries, and even cities.[16] Greater political confidence came with increasing

---

[13] al-Rudhrawari, *Eclipse*, vi. 262; Stephen of Taron, *Armenische Geschichte*, 200–3; Ripper, *Die Marwaniden*, 135–40.

[14] For relations between Byzantium and the Caucasian princedoms in Basil's reign see: Forsyth, 'The Chronicle of Yahya ibn Sa'id', 464–78, 557–81; C. Toumanoff, 'Armenia and Georgia', in J. Hussey (ed.), *The Cambridge Medieval History*, iv. *The Byzantine Empire: Byzantium and its Neighbours* (Cambridge, 1967), 615–20; Toumanoff, 'The Bagratids of Iberia from the Eighth to the Eleventh Centuries', *Le Muséon* 74 (1961), 37–42; V. Minorsky, 'New Light on the Shadaddids of Ganja (951–1075)', *Studies in Caucasian History* (London, 1953), 14–20; A. Ter Ghevondyan, *The Arab Emirates in Bagratid Armenia* (Lisbon, 1976), 101–21.

[15] H. A. Manandian, *The Trade and Cities of Armenia in Relation to Ancient World Trade*, trans. N. G. Garsoïan, (Lisbon, 1965), 136–72; see also below 8.4.

[16] C. Toumanoff, 'Armenia and Georgia', 615–16. In the first half of the 10th c. the Artsruni princes of Vaspurakan constructed several palace complexes of which the most famous was that at Aght'amar, situated on an island in Lake Van. The palace church is still extant (Thomas Artsruni, *History*, 355–61; A. Manoukian (ed.), *Documents of Armenian Architecture/Documenti di Architettura Armena*, 19 vols. (Milan, 1974), vol. viii); L. Jones, 'The Visual Expression of Power and Piety in Medieval Armenia: The Palace and Palace Church at Aghtamar', in A. Eastmond (ed.), *Eastern Approaches to Byzantium* (Aldershot, 2001), 221–41. Later in the 10th c. the Bagratids of Širak sponsored the construction of a new walled city at Ani in northern Armenia (Stephen of Taron, *Armenische Geschichte*, 138, 192, 213; Manoukian, *Documents of Armenian Architecture*, vol. xii). Within Georgian-speaking Caucasia

military success against the Muslim emirates of Lake Van and even, on occasion, against the emirs of Ganja and Azerbaijan. Foremost of these princes in 976 was David of Tao. His authority among his princely peers in Caucasia, whether Armenian- or Georgian-speaking, Chalcedonian or Monophysite, was such that he frequently acted as an arbiter in regional disputes, and as the co-ordinator of military action against Islamic foes.[17] As we have seen in the last chapter, David's role as a key political player on the eastern frontier became particularly apparent to the Byzantines when in 978–9 he supplied Basil II with the large cavalry force which enabled imperial armies to crush the first Skleros revolt. Among David's rewards was the stewardship for his lifetime of key imperial territories on the north-eastern reaches of the frontier.[18] David's regional power was somewhat reduced when, having participated in the Phokas revolt on the side of the rebels, he was forced to make Basil II the legatee of his princedom of Tao.[19] This agreement destroyed a previous arrangement by which David had made his adopted son Bagrat III of Abasgia his heir.[20] Yet, David remained a powerful force within

enthusiastic sponsors of churches and monasteries included David of Tao (d. 1000) and Bagrat III of Abasgia (d. 1014) (W. Z. Djobadze, *Early Medieval Georgian Monasteries in Historic Tao, Klarjet'i and Šavšeti* (Stuttgart, 1992); Evans and Wixom, *Glory of Byzantium*, 336–49).

[17] Stephen of Taron, *Armenische Geschichte*, 138, 192; Georgian Royal Annals, 272–7. David was the only Georgian-speaking member of the Ibero-Armenian Bagratid family to mint his own coins (Toumanoff, 'Bagratids of Iberia from the Eighth to the Eleventh Centuries', 40).

[18] See below 6.3.1.

[19] Yahya, *PO* 23, pp. 424, 429, 460.

[20] Georgian Royal Annals, 273–5.

Caucasian politics until his death in 1000.[21] And indeed, although Basil marched eastwards to secure his inheritance in 1000, for much of the second half of the emperor's reign Byzantine influence in this region was eclipsed by a newly emergent Georgian state which was ruled, until 1014, by Bagrat III, king of Abasgia and Iberia. Disputes between the two sides continued over the subject of Tao, and it was in this context that Basil campaigned in Iberia close to the end of his reign in 1021–2. This was a period also notable for the offer by the Armenian prince of Ani, John Smbat, to make Basil his heir, and the more dramatic step of his neighbour, Senacherim, the Artsruni prince of Vaspurakan, to surrender his hereditary lands in the region south and east of Lake Van to Byzantium.[22]

The key question, then, in this chapter is: how did the Byzantine administration of the east evolve during Basil's reign in the context of pressures from a heterodox local population and a plurality of Muslim and Christian neighbours? In order to answer this question, discussion will focus primarily on the history of the katepanates of the east; but in order to understand fully the administrative changes and continuities that occurred during the reign of Basil itself, analysis of each katepanate will be set in rather wider chronological contexts. Analysis of those katepanates existing at the beginning of Basil's reign (Chaldia, Mesopo-

---

[21] In the final decade of the 10th c. David not only seized Manzikert near Lake Van from its Muslim overlords, but also constructed an armed alliance among Christian princes in Caucasia which defeated Mamlan, the Rawwaddid emir of Azerbaijan in 998/9 (Stephen of Taron, *Armenische Geschichte*, 202–5).

[22] For these surrenders see also below 6.3.4 and 8.4.

tamia, and Antioch) will begin in the mid-tenth century
with those innovations introduced as a result of the military
conquests in the Anti Taurus Mountains achieved by
Romanos Lekapenos' senior general, John Kourkouas.[23]
Investigation of each katepanate, including Iberia and Vaspurakan, the new units founded during the early eleventh
century, will then be taken beyond the end of Basil's reign
into the mid-eleventh century. In addition to military administration, civil bureaucracy on the frontier will also be
discussed, once again within a wide chronological framework. What the chapter will demonstrate is that Basil realized that the key to good governance on the frontier was, on
the one hand, flexibility of command, and on the other,
diplomacy tempered by occasional force.

6.3   MILITARY ADMINISTRATION IN THE
EASTERN FRONTIER *c.*950–1050

6.3.1   The katepanate of Chaldia

The *doux* of Chaldia has customarily been seen as the official
responsible for the far north-east section of the frontier, a
region including the Black Sea coast and Pontus Mountains
east of Trebizond, the former emirate of Theodosioupolis
centred on the Basean plain, and the former Armenian
princedom of Taron.[24] A lack of primary written materials

[23] Howard-Johnston, 'Crown Lands', 86–7.
[24] Oikonomides, *Listes*, 263, 354; Forsyth, 'The Chronicle of Yahya ibn
Sa'id', 371; see also Map 2.

makes it difficult to know when a commander officially designated as the *doux* of Chaldia first appeared. Sigillographical and literary evidence suggests that such an office certainly did not exist in the first half of the tenth century, when the region known as Chaldia was still a theme governed like the rest of Anatolia by a *strategos*.[25] Instead, it is only with the more ambitious eastern military enterprises which characterized the middle of the tenth century, that the first signs of commanders in Chaldia with broader authority than that of a mere *strategos* begin to emerge. Such signs appear for the first time during the conquest of Theodosioupolis in 949, when the victorious Byzantine military commander, Theophilos Kourkouas, the brother of John Kourkouas, and the grandfather of Emperor John Tzimiskes, is described as *monostrategos* of Chaldia, a position which may imply greater seniority than that of a mere thematic *strategos*.[26] Stronger signs of the concentration of regional military power in the hands of a single individual occur

[25] Many of the seals of these 10th-c. *strategoi* are listed in A. Bryer and D. Winfield, *The Byzantine Monuments and Topography of the Pontus*, 2 vols. (Washington DC, 1985), i. 316; see also G. Schlumberger, *Sigillographie de l'empire byzantin* (Paris, 1884), 290, nos. 2–3; Nesbitt and Oikonomides, *Byzantine Seals at Dumbarton Oaks*, iv. 32.37–32.41. One *strategos* of Chaldia who appears in the literary sources was Bardas Boilas. He rebelled against Romanos Lekapenos (920–44) in the third decade of the 10th c. (*Theophanes Con.*, 404).

[26] Theophilos is described as *monostrategos* of Chaldia by the 10th-c. historian Theophanes Continuatus. The *De Administrando Imperio*, compiled c.952, names him as *strategos* of Theodosioupolis. However, this appellation may indicate that he was commander in Chaldia with his main base at Theodosioupolis (*Theophanes Con.*, 428; *De Administrando Imperio*, ed. G. Moravcsik and trans. R. J. H. Jenkins, (Washington DC, 1967) 212 (hereafter *DAI*)).

during the reign of Nikephoros Phokas (963–9). According to both the contemporary tenth-century historian Leo the Deacon and to John Skylitzes, the emperor's nephew Bardas held the position of *doux* of the border region of Chaldia and of Koloneia. The latter location was a theme established in the mid-ninth century on the eastern fringes of the Anatolian plateau.[27]

It is important to note that this is the first mention of the position of *doux* in a frontier context in the Byzantine historical record. Yet, it would be premature to assume that this appointment necessarily represents a radical and permanent reorganization of the administration of the whole of the eastern frontier. Instead, it can be persuasively argued that the appointment of Bardas Phokas was driven by short-term military pressures both within and outside the empire. On the one hand the greater focus of regional military authority in the hands of Phokas reflected the demands of internal security. Bardas' uncle Nikephoros needed a strong and loyal hand in the furthest reaches of north-eastern Anatolia, a region where the authority of rival families such as the Lekapenoi and Kourkouai had

[27] Skylitzes, *Synopsis*, 284; Leo the Deacon, *Historiae Libri Decem*, 96; Oikonomides, *Listes*, 354; Kühn, *Die byzantinische Armee*, 184–5. Skylitzes also mentions on two other occasions that Bardas Phokas was a *doux*. The first reference is to be found in his coverage of Bardas Phokas' revolt against Emperor John Tzimiskes in 971. In a passage of direct speech Bardas recalls his former position as a *doux*, although without specifying the geographical location of his responsibilities (Skylitzes, *Synopsis*, 293–4). The second reference occurs during Skylitzes' account of the first Skleros revolt, when he notes that David *archon* of Tao and Bardas Phokas had become friends while the latter was *doux* in Chaldia (Skylitzes, *Synopsis*, 326).

traditionally been strong.[28] Equally Bardas' appointment reflects a growth in the intensity of Byzantine diplomatic and military relations with neighbouring regions in western Caucasia during the reign of Nikephoros. In 966–7 Bagrat and Gregory, the princes of the neighbouring Armenian princedom of Taron, handed over their territories to Nikephoros Phokas in return for the title of *patrikios* and estates within the Byzantine empire.[29] In 968/9 Byzantine raiding armies passed through Taron on their way to raid the Arab emirates of Lake Van.[30]

When Nikephoros Phokas was murdered by John Tzimiskes in 969, his nephew Bardas was removed from his position as *doux*. A lack of written evidence means that it is impossible to know exactly what happened next in Chaldia. However, using the evidence provided by tenth- and eleventh-century lead seals, it is clear that administrative power was far from permanently settled when Bardas was dismissed. Instead, frontier authority in Chaldia was consistently characterized throughout the tenth and eleventh centuries by a high degree of flexibility. One sign of the ad hoc nature of this authority is the frequency with which commanders could exercise responsibility for more than one region. This principle of overlap had, of course, been visible in the career of Bardas Phokas himself, in his control of both Chaldia and Koloneia. A similar phenomenon can be detected on the eleventh-century seal of a certain Nicho-

[28] Cheynet, *Pouvoir et contestations*, 216, 321–4.
[29] Skylitzes, *Synopsis*, 279.
[30] Yahya, *PO* 18, p. 825; Canard, 'La Date des expéditions mésopotamiennes de Jean Tzimisces', 100.

las *patrikios*, who was *katepano* of both Chaldia and Mesopotamia. This seal indicates that on occasion the supreme
regional military commander of the northernmost section
of the frontier could also exercise authority over Mesopotamia, the border region lying further south among the plains
and mountains of the Anti Taurus and the Upper Euphrates
and Upper Tigris rivers.[31] Moreover, the seals of several non-
military officials in the later tenth and eleventh centuries
indicate the extent to which administrative authority based
principally in Chaldia could be linked with neighbouring
districts. For example, several *protonotarioi* and *kritai* exercised authority over Chaldia and Derxene, regions lying to
the west of Theodosioupolis.[32] Other *kritai* exercised jurisdiction over the theme of Koloneia as well as Chaldia, thus
mirroring the geographical scope of Bardas Phokas' authority as *doux*.[33] Meanwhile, in a case not directly involving
Chaldia, but still pertinent to the administrative history of
the northernmost sector of the frontier, a certain Leo, *protospatharios*, was *strategos* of both the small themes of

---

[31] Nesbitt and Oikonomides, *Byzantine Seals at Dumbarton Oaks*, iv. 55.10;
see below 6.3.2 for the possibility that Skleros may have held joint command
over Chaldia and Mesopotamia.

[32] *Protonotarios*: Nesbitt and Oikonomides, *Byzantine Seals at Dumbarton
Oaks*, iv. 61.2; *kritai*: Nesbitt and Oikonomides, *Byzantine Seals at Dumbarton
Oaks*, iv. 61.3–61.6; J.-C. Cheynet, *Sceaux de la collection de Zacos (Bibliothèque Nationale de France) se rapportant aux provinces orientales de l'Empire
byzantin* (Paris, 2001), nos. 27–8, 37; see also the seal of a *chartoularios*
of Chaldia and Derxene: Nesbitt and Oikonomides, *Byzantine Seals at Dumbarton Oaks*, iv. 61.2; likewise the seal of an *artoklines* and *anagrapheus* of
Chaldia and Derxene: Cheynet, *Sceaux de la collection de Zacos (BN)*, no. 29.

[33] *Krites* of Chaldia and Koloneia: Nesbitt and Oikonomides, *Byzantine
Seals at Dumbarton Oaks*, iv. 48.2.

Derxene and Taron in the last years of the reign of John Tzimiskes.[34]

Evidence for the development of the office of *doux* in Chaldia during the reign of Basil II is extremely meagre. It is impossible to know which of those officials whose seals are discussed above held office during Basil's reign itself. Meanwhile, the only literary evidence for the history of the Chaldia region during the reign comes from the *Miracles of Saint Eugenios*. This hagiographical text notes that during the revolt of Nikephoros Xiphias and Nikephoros Phokas in 1022, a certain Basil was *doux* of Chaldia and Trebizond.[35] While this example demonstrates that officials bearing the responsibilities of *doux* continued to be appointed to Chaldia in the first quarter of the eleventh century, it does not indicate whether this was a position that was permanently occupied. Indeed, the officials who are more frequently found in the eleventh-century sigillographical record of this region are *strategoi* of Chaldia.[36] There are several possible explanations for this unbalanced ratio of *doukes: strategoi* seals. The mismatch could reflect a demotion in

[34] Matthew of Edessa, *Armenia and the Crusades*, 27–8.

[35] Panagiotakes, 'Fragments', 356. This Basil was probably the *gawar* (governor) of Chaldia referred to by Aristakes of Lastivert, who was instructed to sell as slaves the prisoners-of-war taken during Basil's campaign against George of Iberia and Abasgia in the autumn of 1021 (Aristakes of Lastivert, *Récit des malheurs*, 12). Another late 10th- or early 11th-c. *doux* of Chaldia seems to have been the *protospatharios* Niketas (K. M. Konstantopoulos, Βυζαντιακὰ μολυβδόβουλλα τοῦ ἐν Ἀθήναις Ἐθνικοῦ Νομισματικοῦ Μουσείου (Athens, 1917) (hereafter *Molybdoboulla*), no.158a).

[36] J.-C. Cheynet, C. Morrisson, and W. Seibt, *Sceaux byzantins de la collection Henri Seyrig* (Paris, 1991), no. 174; Nesbitt and Oikonomides, *Byzantine Seals at Dumbarton Oaks*, iv. 32.43; see also Bryer and Winfield, *Monuments of the Pontus*, i. 316.

Chaldia's status from an area controlled by a *doux* back to a theme under the authority of a *strategos*. This demise could have occurred when the katepanate of Iberia was created, making a duchy of Chaldia irrelevant.[37] An alternative reason for the incidence of eleventh-century *strategoi* could be that the original theme of Chaldia continued to exist alongside the regional duchy of the same name throughout the later tenth and eleventh centuries. With command over a much smaller area than the entire duchy, the *strategos* of Chaldia would have been subordinate to the regional *doux* or *katepano*.[38] However, the explanation that accords most closely with the context provided by the historical narrative evidence, is that while the office *strategos* of Chaldia may have continued to be filled regularly, the much more senior position of *doux* was only rarely occupied. This was because for much of the later tenth and early eleventh centuries, the responsibility for the military security of this section of the frontier was ceded to one of the empire's neighbours, rather than being exercised directly by a senior Byzantine military commander.

The first imperial neighbour potentate to gain control of the northern reaches of the imperial frontier during Basil's reign was the Christian prince, David of Tao. In return for dispatching troops to help suppress the first Skleros revolt, David was granted control over several key towns annexed by Byzantium earlier in the tenth century, including

[37] On the Iberian katepanate see below 6.3.4.

[38] This is a hypothesis first volunteered H. Ahrweiler, 'Recherches sur l'administration de l'empire byzantin aux IXè–XIè siècles', *BCH* 84 (1960), 48.

Theodosioupolis.[39] In those areas previously held directly by the Byzantines, one of David's local lieutenants was a leading local Iberian noble called Bagrat, who also held the Byzantine titles of *patrikios* and *magistros*.[40] Contemporary Armenian historians suggest that Bagrat was the brother of Tornik, the famous military commander who had led the Iberian contingent in the imperial army that defeated Skleros, and whose family were local landowners in Taron and Derxene, regions to the south-west of Theodosioupolis.[41] Although David and his lieutenants sided with the rebels during the Phokas revolt (first defeating an imperial force led by Gregory Taronites, and later suffering a defeat at the hand of an imperial army led east by one Zan Patrik),[42] David continued to serve as the empire's lieutenant in this northerly section of the frontier after 990.[43] This arrange-

[39] Stephen of Taron lists those regions ceded to David (Stephen of Taron, *Armenische Geschichte,* 141–2); see also Yahya, *PO,* 23, pp. 424, 429; Skylitzes, *Synopsis,* 326; *Life of John and Euthymios,* 89–91; Panagiotakes, 'Fragments', 348. Some of the regions granted to David, such as Theodosioupolis (referred to as Karin, its Armenian name, by Stephen of Taron) and the plain of Basean were within the north-eastern frontier regions of the empire (see Map 2). Others, such as Harkh and Apahunikh, north of Lake Van, were not under the direct political control of the empire in 979. In the case of these territories Byzantium seems merely to have acknowledged David's right to launch military attacks against the Muslim emirates of the Lake Van region; for more on these emirates see *DAI,* ch. 44; Adontz, 'Tornik', 150–1. Other areas named by Stephen of Taron within the grant made to David have yet to be identified accurately. For further analysis see Forsyth, 'The Chronicle of Yahya ibn Sa'id', 464–78; Forsyth summarizes not only the primary evidence but also the extensive and contradictory secondary literature concerned with the 979 grant.

[40] Yahya, *PO,* 23, pp. 424, 429; Panagiotakes, 'Fragments', 348.

[41] Stephen of Taron, *Armenische Geschichte,* 190; Adontz, 'Tornik', 143–64.

[42] Probably John the *patrikios*.

[43] Stephen of Taron, *Armenische Geschichte,* 190.

ment only broke down with the death of David in 1000 and Basil's campaign to claim those regions he had ceded in 979 as well as those areas of Tao to which he had become heir after the Phokas revolt.

Yet, despite Basil's campaign and a follow-up expedition organized by Nikephoros Ouranos, the Byzantine commander at Antioch, the Byzantines did little to consolidate their position in this north-east part of the frontier permanently. Instead in the period between 1000 and the 1021, supreme military tutelage over the northern and central sections of Byzantium's eastern frontier appears to have been devolved to another neighbouring power, the Marwanid emirs whose power-base stretched from the Lake Van region into the Diyar Bakr south of the Anti Taurus. In 1000 Basil II granted Muhhamid al-Daula, the nephew of Bad ibn Dustuk, the title of *magistros* and the office of *doux* of the East, a bestowal of honours on a Muslim that historians have struggled to explain. Yet this appointment makes sense if Muhhamid is seen as a replacement for David of Tao, who became at one and the same time a client of the empire and its representative in the east. Certainly, we know that the Marwanids campaigned on behalf of the empire. In 1009–10 they provided troops for an expedition to Aleppo to reinstall another Byzantine client family as emirs.[44]

Indeed, the historical record suggests that it was only in 1018, the year when Basil finally annexed Bulgaria, that the imposition of central military control from Constantinople in the northern stretch of the Byzantine eastern frontier was

[44] Yahya, *PO* 47, pp. 392–3.

contemplated once again. It was in this year that the fortifications of Theodosioupolis were repaired.[45] Three years
later Basil launched his only sustained expedition against the
empire's neighbours to the north-east when he attacked
George, who had succeeded Bagrat III as king of Abasgia
and Iberia in 1014. As far as Basil was concerned George was
guilty of intruding on his territory in Tao. Basi's first incursion into Iberia took place in the autumn of 1021, an
inconclusive expedition which eventually saw imperial
armies withdraw westwards for the winter to Trebizond in
Chaldia. Basil relaunched his attack the following spring,
and despite the distractions caused by a contemporaneous
revolt by Nikephoros Phokas and Nikephoros Xiphias, the
emperor eventually won a crushing victory over his Georgian foes. The striking point here, though, is that the only
mention of a *doux* of Chaldia during the reign of Basil II
comes in this particular and highly bellicose context, suggesting that this appointment was one of many special
arrangements for war against the Iberians rather than a
permanent gubernatorial position on the frontier with responsibility for a demarked territorial region.

6.3.2   The katepanate of Mesopotamia

The central sector of the eastern frontier has customarily
been seen by historians as the responsibility of the *doux* of
Mesopotamia. The region comprises those isolated plains

---

[45] Aristakes of Lastivert, *Récit des malheurs*, 11.

and passes in the Anti Taurus mountains annexed by the general John Kourkouas in the middle of the tenth century. The list of minor *strategoi* in the *Escorial Taktikon* indicate that while the fertile plains of Melitene and the Anzitene lay at the heart of this sector of the frontier, Byzantine authority could extend as far south as Germanikeia (Marash) on the Ceyhan (Pyramos) river and Samosata on the Euphrates.[46]

This is an extensive territorial region, yet despite its size, there is little evidence that this sector of the frontier was governed by a supra-thematic military commander such as a *doux* or a *katepano* before the reign of Basil II began. Instead, during the reign of Basil's predecessor John Tzimiskes, the only reference to a military commander of Mesopotamia concerns the *strategos* of Mesopotamia. When the Fatimids attacked northern Syria during the winter of 970–1, an anonymous *strategos* of Mesopotamia was sent to deal with the incursion.[47] This *strategos* was almost certainly the military governor of the theme of Mesopotamia which was established in the Anti Taurus region north of Melitene during the first decade of the tenth century. The theme itself covered a considerably smaller geographical area than the central sector of the frontier as a whole.[48] Moreover, sigillographical evidence also suggests that *strategoi* of the theme of Mesopotamia continued to be appointed throughout the second half of the tenth century.[49] The persistence of the

[46] See Map 2.
[47] Skylitzes, *Synopsis*, 287; Farag, 'The Aleppo Question', 47; Walker, 'A Byzantine Victory over the Fatimids', 431–40.
[48] *DAI* 239.
[49] Schlumberger, *Sigillographie*, 288; Nesbitt and Oikonomides, *Byzantine Seals at Dumbarton Oaks*, iv. 55.11–13.

office of *strategos* of Mesopotamia does not mean in itself, of course, that a *doux/katepano* could not have existed at the same time. As was the case with Chaldia, it is possible that a *doux* and *strategos* could have exercised office simultaneously, with the latter being subordinate to the former.

Yet in the case of Mesopotamia there is no evidence that a supra-thematic senior regional commander, such as a *doux* or *katepano*, was appointed to the central sector of the frontier as early as the reigns of either Nikephoros Phokas or John Tzimiskes. Instead, it is only at the beginning of the reign of Basil II that the first signs of an overarching military authority in this region begin to emerge. On this occasion the evidence comes from the *Synopsis Historion* of John Skylitzes, and his report that Bardas Skleros was appointed *doux* of Mesopotamia shortly after Basil came to the throne. Yet, any understanding of the nature of Skleros' appointment is, unfortunately, prejudiced by Skylitzes' characteristic working methods, and his use and abuse of underlying texts. In this case Skylitzes' use of a pro-Skleros source in his account of the reign of Basil II means that it is Skleros' justification of his revolt, rather than the wider strategic context on the eastern frontier, which underpins the analysis of this appointment in the *Synopsis Historion*.[50] According to Skylitzes, Basil Lekapenos, the *Parakoimomenos*, was so distrustful of Skleros' political ambitions, that he released the general from his position of *stratelates* (supreme commander of the field army), and installed him instead as *doux* of the *tagmata* in

---

[50] Skylitzes, *Synopsis*, 314–15; see Ch. 5 of this volume for discussion of the pro-Skleros source in Skylitzes' narrative.

Mesopotamia. In Skleros' place he appointed Peter the eunuch as *stratopedarches* of all the *tagmata* of the east. Meanwhile, Skleros was so vexed by this series of events, 'that he was not able to conceal to himself his grief magnanimously, but protested out loud'.[51]

Yet, it would be a mistake to use Skylitzes' interpretation of Skleros' appointment as evidence that a duchy/katepanate of Mesopotamia was already well established in 976, or indeed that it had come to represent a regional backwater.[52] Instead, this was a frontier that had seen recent and bloody warfare. In 972 Emperor John Tzimiskes had led an expedition from the Anzitene in Byzantine Mesopotamia into the Djazira to raid the cities of Edessa and Nisibis. So convinced were the inhabitants of Baghdad that Tzimiskes' real target was Iraq that they rioted in the streets.[53] In response to this

---

[51] Skleros was originally appointed *stratelates* of the east by John Tzimiskes in 970 in order to deal with the Rus invasion of Thrace (Skylitzes, *Synopsis*, 288; see also above 5.2.3). The rest of Skleros' career during the reign of Tzimiskes is obscure. He was still in charge of the eastern army at the battle for Dristra in 971 (Skylitzes, *Synopsis*, 300). However, by 972–3 the general in charge of the eastern army was Melias (Canard, 'La Date des expéditions mésopotamiennes de Jean Tzimisces', 102). It is possible that Skleros had been deprived of control over the eastern army by Tzimiskes as the result of an unsuccessful conspiracy. According to a brief allusion in Skylitzes' testimony, Skleros had been accused of plotting against Tzimiskes at an unspecified point in the reign (Skylitzes, *Synopsis*, 314). However, the fact that Skleros once again held the office of *stratelates* of the east by the end of Tzimiskes' reign suggests that he was rehabilitated before Tzimiskes' death. He may have been rehabilitated after Melias was taken prisoner by the Hamdanids of Mosul in 973 (Seibt, *Die Skleroi*, 35).

[52] Most modern historians have followed Skylitzes in interpreting Skleros' appointment as *doux* in 976 as a demotion to the margins of the military and political hierarchy: Seibt, *Die Skleroi*, 36; Forsyth, 'The Chronicle of Yahya ibn Sa'id', 375.

[53] For Tzimiskes' attack see also above 5.2.1.

Byzantine attack the Hamdanids of Mosul launched a counter strike through the Bitlis pass north of the Diyar Bakr,
laying waste to the Byzantine territory of Taron.[54] Another
Byzantine offensive followed swiftly, as the *domestikos* of the
scholai Melias set out from the Anzitene in the summer of
973 and arrived at the gates of Amida in the Djazira. It was at
this battle that Melias was taken captive by the Hamdanids.[55]

With such a recent legacy of bloody military encounters,
it is clear that this frontier in 976 was a highly sensitive
region to which only the most competent and trusted commander, with highly effective and professional troops, would
have been dispatched. Indeed, Skleros' appointment makes
more sense when it is interpreted in this light rather than in
terms of a demotion. It is noteworthy that the only other
historian to report on Skleros' arrival on this stretch of the
eastern frontier, Yahya ibn Sa'id, does not consider his
appointment a demotion. Instead, he merely notes that
Bardas Skleros was appointed the governor of Bathn Hanzit
and Khalidiyat.[56] Moreover, Skleros was not simply given

---

[54] See Map 2.

[55] Ibn Miskawayh, *Eclipse*, v. 326–8; Yahya, *PO* 23, pp. 353–8; Canard, 'La
Date des expéditions mésopotamiennes de Jean Tzimiscès', 99–108.

[56] Yahya, *PO* 23, p. 372. The term for governor used by Yahya is the Arabic
wali. Controversy still persists about the exact geographical regions that
Yahya believed to be under Skleros' command. It is generally agreed that
Bathn Hanzit denotes Mesopotamia. This is the Arab name for the region
known in Greek as the Anzitene, the plain in the Anti Taurus at the centre of
Byzantine Mesopotamia. Identification of al-Khalidiyat, however, has proved
more difficult. Seibt (*Die Skleroi*, 36) has argued that it should be identified
with Kaloudia, one of the small frontier themes on the west bank of the
Euphrates downstream from Melitene. It is equally possible that al-Khalidiyat
denotes Chaldia. As noted above in 6.3.1, there is sigillographical evidence to
support the idea that command over both the northern and central sections
of the frontier could be vested in a single individual.

command over the light cavalry and infantry forces of the small themes (*Armeniaka themata*). Instead, as even Skylitzes notes, he was placed in charge of *tagmata*, or field army troops. The most likely context for his appointment as *doux* of Mesopotamia was that he was expected to continue the struggle against the Hamdanids of Mosul, which had been set in motion by the campaigns of Melias and John Tzimiskes. However, instead of fighting the Muslim enemy, Skleros took advantage of his control over the field army troops and rebelled against the emperor. Forced to justify his decision to turn the Byzantine field army under his command on Constantinople rather than on the Djazira, he manufactured the excuse that he was disappointed with his treatment by the imperial authorities. It is this excuse which then enters the historical record via Skylitzes' account.

Although the military administrative history of Mesopotamia at the beginning of Basil's reign has to be analysed through the distorting lens of Skylitzes' testimony, certain conclusions can still be drawn about the development of regional authority in the central sector of the Byzantine frontier in the later tenth century. First, the position of *doux* appears to have been novel at the time Skleros was appointed. It was not a well-established office within a highly developed system of frontier administration put in place by Basil's predecessors John Tzimiskes or Nikephoros Phokas.[57] Second, the position was connected to command

---

[57] This viewpoint contrasts with Kühn, *Die byzantinische Armee*, 182–3, who believes that Nikephoros Phokas was responsible for instituting the katepanate of Mesopotamia. However, Kühn's argument is based on supposition. Having attributed the creation of the katepanates of Chaldia and

over troops from the centralized army in pursuit of military victory over neighbouring adversaries. At this point the office of *doux* was not a sedentary administrative position with authority over a strictly defined geographical area.

It is difficult to know how the military administration of the central sector of the frontier evolved after Bardas Skleros revolted in 976, since the only information available comes from seals. The sigillographical record indicates that *doukes/ katepanes* of Mesopotamia continued to be appointed during the eleventh century, yet it is impossible from the material record to know whether this position was permanently occupied during the later tenth and early eleventh centuries, or whether it was an occasional appointment shaped by wider political and diplomatic circumstances. While the material record is of little help in determining the chronology of the duchy and the responsibilities of senior commanders on the frontier, the general strategic position of the empire vis à vis its neighbours in this period may have meant that *doukes/katepanes* rarely needed to be appointed between the exile of Bardas Skleros to Baghdad in 979/80 and the annexation of Vaspurakan in the final decade of Basil's reign. The collapse of the Hamdanids of Mosul in 978–9 and the disintegration of Buyid power in Baghdad after the death of Adud al-Daula in 983 diminished the Muslim threat to the central sector of the Byzantine eastern

Antioch to Nikephoros Phokas, he argues that Mesopotamia must have been given this status at the same time, since any other decision would have left a hole in the organization of the frontier. However, Kühn's argument demands that the katepanates of Chaldia and Antioch were fully developed by Nikephoros Phokas, an assertion which, as I demonstrate in this chapter, is unsustainable.

frontier.[58] In these circumstances there was little need to maintain a large contingent of troops from the centralized Byzantine army under the command of a senior *doux*. Although Bad ibn Dustuk, the Marwanid emir, attacked Byzantine positions during the Phokas revolt operating from his base in the Diyar Bakr, south of the Anti Taurus, after his death his successors came to terms with the empire. When Muhhamid al-Daula was appointed *magistros* and *doux* of the east any need to appoint a Byzantine *doux* from Constantinople evaporated completely.

This situation only changed in the final decade of the reign when Basil annexed Vaspurakan, the Armenian principality which lay to the east of Byzantine Mesopotamia. It is this sudden territorial expansion that may provide a context for those *doukes/katepanes* who appear in the sigillographical record in the early to mid-eleventh century. At least one seal of a *katepano* of Mesopotamia has been dated to the 1020s or 1030s, the period of the consolidation of Byzantine power in Vaspurakan.[59] From this period on, seals of *katepanes* of Mesopotamia become more frequent again.[60] Nonetheless, it should be stressed that even in the eleventh century a large degree of flexibility was still associated with ducal command

---

[58] On the collapse of Buyid power see below 8.4.

[59] Seibt, *Die byzantinischen Bleisiegel in Österreich*, 260 (Constantine Parsakoutenos).

[60] D. Theodoridis, 'Theognostos Melissenos, Katepano von Mesopotamia', *BZ* 78 (1985), 363–4; Nesbitt and Oikonomides, *Byzantine Seals at Dumbarton Oaks*, iv. 55.8 (Leo *anthypatos, patrikios*); ibid. 55.9 (Michael *vestarches*). The sigillographical evidence from the 11th c. seems to contradict Kühn's view that the katepanate of Mesopotamia withered after the annexation of Vaspurakan (Kühn, *Die byzantinische Armee*, 183).

over this geographical area. This flexibility is at its most visible in the frequency with which such officials continued to be assigned responsibility for more than one region. Thus, just as Bardas Phokas held command in Chaldia and Koloneia in the tenth century, so the *patrikios* Nicholas exercised power as *katepano* of both Chaldia and Mesopotamia during the eleventh. Nor was Nicholas alone: in the 1040s or early 1050s Gregory Pahlawuni simultaneously exercised power as *katepano* of Mesopotamia, Taron, and Vaspurakan.[61] The fundamental principle that one commander could hold an array of regional commands seems to have remained constant between the mid-tenth and mid-eleventh centuries.

6.3.3   The katepanate of Antioch

The best evidence for the development of a supra-thematic, regional, military authority on the eastern frontier during the later tenth and early eleventh centuries comes from Antioch, where the sigillographical record is supported by epigraphical evidence and a variety of literary texts. Foremost among the literary evidence is the history of Yahya ibn Sa'id, who arrived in northern Syria in 1014–15, and was an

---

[61] For an analysis of the positions held by Pahlawuni on the eastern frontier see K. N. Yuzbashian, 'L'Administration byzantine en Arménie aux Xe et XIe siècles', *REArm* 10 (1973–4), 147; see also Nesbitt and Oikonomides, *Byzantine Seals at Dumbarton Oaks*, iv. 76.2 for Gregory's seal when he was *doux* of Vaspurakan and Taron. Yuzbashian expressed doubts about whether a single individual could have held all three commands at once. However, the evidence produced here demonstrates that several eastern frontier commands (whether military or non-military), could be held simultaneously across several regions by the same individual.

eyewitness of Byzantine rule in the final decade of Basil's reign.[62] Taken together these sources all emphasize the ad hoc, piecemeal, and flexible nature of the development of Byzantine military administration on the southernmost section of the eastern frontier. As the forthcoming discussion will indicate, malleability of military command was at its most visible in the early decades of Byzantine rule, when this region faced a series of challenges to imperial authority both from within and outside the empire. In contrast, by the final decades of Basil II's reign, greater political and military stability within the empire and on the frontier meant that administrative practice could stabilize. The responsibilities of the *doux/katepano* of Antioch become clearer and more firmly established. However, even at this point the katepanate of Antioch was not a rigid institution, but instead retained the flexibility to be able to respond to political and military pressures when the need arose.

It is frequently alleged that Antioch was put under the command of a *doux* or *katepano* by Emperor Nikephoros Phokas when it was conquered by Byzantine armies in October 969.[63] Yet, evidence from within the literary and sigillographical records does not support such an early dating. As long ago as 1962, Laurent pointed out that neither of the commanders who led the victorious armies in 969,

[62] Yahya, *PO* 18, p. 708; Forsyth, 'The Chronicle of Yahya ibn Sa'id al Antaki', 1. Excellent use is made of both the literary and material evidence in the reconstruction of the contours of the military, civil, and ecclesiastical administrative history of the katepanate of Antioch in the 10th and 11th c. by K.-P. Todt, 'Region in Griechisch-Orthodoxes Patriarchat von Antiocheia in mittelbyzantinischer Zeit (969–1084)', *BZ* 94 (2001), 239–67.

[63] Oikonomides, *Listes*, 354; Kühn, *Die byzantinische Armee*, 170–1.

namely Peter the *stratopedarches* and Michael Bourtzes, became *doux* of the city when it fell.[64] Instead, Peter left Antioch at the head of the imperial field army and proceded to besiege Aleppo.[65] Nor did he return to Antioch after the siege of Aleppo. Instead, he next appears in the historical record as leader of the *tagmata* of Thrace and Macedonia during John Tzimiskes' campaign against the Rus at Dristra in Bulgaria in 971.[66] Meanwhile in 969, Bourtzes travelled back to Constantinople, where he incurred imperial displeasure over his actions during the conquest of Antioch.[67] He joined the co-conspirators of John Tzimiskes, and participated in the assassination of Nikephoros Phokas in De-

[64] V. Laurent, 'La Chronologie des gouverneurs d'Antioche sous la seconde domination byzantine', *Mélanges de l'Université St-Joseph de Beyrouth* 38 (Beirut, 1962), 227.

[65] Skylitzes, *Synopsis*, 271–2; Yahya, *PO* 18, pp. 816–17, 823–4.

[66] Skylitzes, *Synopsis*, 300; Laurent, 'Gouverneurs d'Antioche', 227.

[67] The reason why Bourtzes incurred imperial displeasure is uncertain. According to Skylitzes, Bourtzes exceeded the orders he had been given during the course of the siege. Originally appointed *strategos* of Mauron Oros, a small theme based in the Amanos Mountains close to Antioch, he was commanded merely to raid the countryside surrounding the city. However, in search of personal glory Bourtzes took the unilateral decision to occupy one of the upper towers of the circuit walls of Antioch. When his position became desperate, he was forced to send for emergency help from the imperial field army under the leadership of Peter the *stratopedarches*. When the field army arrived, Antioch itself fell. However, as a result of his earlier disobedience Bourtzes was dismissed from his position as *strategos* of Mauron Oros (Skylitzes, *Synopsis*, 271–3). Yahya ibn Sa'id conveys a slightly different story. Although Bourtzes was rewarded for his role in the fall of Antioch, his recompense was much smaller than expected. This was because Nikephoros Phokas was angry with him for allowing Antioch to be burned (Yahya, *PO* 18, p. 825). Leo the Deacon confirms that Bourtzes led an advance party into Antioch and set the city on fire (Leo the Deacon, *Historiae Libri Decem*, 81–2).

cember 969.[68] An inscription on a late tenth-century reliquary suggests that rather than Bourtzes or Peter, the first commander of Antioch was the *anthypatos* and *patrikios* Eustathios Maleinos. Yet, this epigraphical evidence makes it clear that Maleinos did not hold the position of *doux*. Instead he was *strategos* of Antioch and the theme of Lykandos which had been established in the early tenth century in the broken countryside between the eastern plateau and the Anti Taurus mountains.[69]

The appointment of Maleinos to command in Antioch is paradigmatic of how short-term political considerations often underpinned appointments in the immediate aftermath of eastern conquests. In the first place, close family ties between the Maleinos and Phokas families made Eustathios a commander whom the emperor Nikephoros Phokas could trust.[70] Members of both families had frequently fought side by side during Byzantium's battles with the Hamdanids of

[68] Leo the Deacon, *Historiae Libri Decem*, 85; Yahya, *PO* 18, p. 829; Skylitzes, *Synopsis*, 279.

[69] W. B. R. Saunders, 'The Aachen Reliquary of Eustathius Maleinus 969–970', *DOP* 36 (1982), 211–19; see also Todt, 'Patriarchat von Antiocheia', 241. The foundation of the theme of Lykandos in the early 10th c. by an Armenian commander called Melias has been widely discussed: *DAI* 238–40; G. Dédéyan, 'Les Arméniens en Cappadoce aux Xe et XIe siècles', in C. D. Fonseca (ed.), *Le aree omogenee della civiltà rupestre nell'ambito dell'impero bizantino: la Cappadocia* (Lecce, 1981), 76–80; C. Dédéyan, 'Mleh le grand, stratège de Lykandos', *REArm* 15 (1981), 73–102; Oikonomides, 'L'Organisation de la frontière orientale', 286–7, and in the same congress proceedings, H. Ahrweiler, 'La Frontière et les frontières de Byzance en Orient', i. 219–23.

[70] Eusthathios Maleinos and Nikephoros Phokas were cousins. Nikephoros' mother was Eustathios' aunt (Cheynet, *Pouvoir et contestations*, 268). Blood ties between the two families were strengthened by spiritual links. Eustathios' uncle was Michael Maleinos, the *hegoumenos* of a monastery on Mount Olympos in Bithynia, who was also a spiritual adviser to Emperor Nikephoros. Indeed, on the night Nikephoros was killed by

Aleppo and Mosul in the mid-tenth century. In 960, the emir of Aleppo, Sayf al-Daula, was ambushed by a Byzantine army led by Leo Phokas, Nikephoros' brother, and Constantine Maleinos, Eustathios' father.[71] Eustathios' uncle Leo, meanwhile, had been killed in 953/4, in an engagement near Germanikeia during which Nikephoros' brother Constantine was taken captive.[72] Furthermore, the fact that Maleinos was the member of a family with a distinguished track record in eastern warfare gave him an invaluable degree of natural authority within the Byzantine field army. Finally, Maleinos' position as *strategos* of Lykandos indicates that he did not simply have to rely on his family's pedigree to exert his authority, but was also able to call upon his own standing as military commander and administrator. Taken together it was Maleinos' status as a relative and political ally of the Phokas family, and as the governor of a well-established eastern Anatolian theme, which determined his appointment at Antioch.[73] As such Maleinos' position at Antioch demonstrates the extent to which military experience, high standing within the army, and political loyalty to the emperor, underpinned the military organization of the frontier. Furthermore, Maleinos' command over both Lykandos and Antioch once again illustrates the frequency

Tzimiskes and his henchmen, the emperor was lying on a rough covering he had been given by Michael (Skylitzes, *Synopsis*, 280).

[71] *Theophanes Con.*, 479; M. Kaplan, 'Les Grands Propriétaires de Cappadoce', in *Le aree omogenee della civiltà rupestre nell'ambito dell'impero bizantino: la Cappdocia*, ed. C. D. Fonseca (Lecce, 1981), 145.

[72] Yahya, *PO* 18, p. 771; Canard, 'Quelques noms de personnages byzantins', 456.

[73] Hild and Restle, *Kappadokien*, 224–6.

with which command over several regions in the Byzantine east could be vested in a single individual.

Powerful analogies exist for Maleinos' position in the immediate aftermath of the conquest of Antioch. Sigillographical evidence suggests that the first commander of Anazarbos and Mamistra (Mopsuestia), the Cilician cities conquered by Nikephoros Phokas in 964, was a certain George Melias *protospatharios,* the *strategos* of the eastern Anatolian theme of Tzamandos.[74] Just as at Antioch, therefore, the new conquests of Mamistra and Anazarbos were put under the command of an officer who already exercised military command on the easternmost reaches of the plateau, in this case Tzamandos. Moreover, George Melias also exercised considerable authority within the Byzantine army. Like Maleinos, he could call upon a considerable family pedigree of service in the eastern

---

[74] Schlumberger, *Sigillographie,* 671. Seibt, *Bleisiegel,* 261, and P. Stephenson, 'A Development in Nomenclature on the Seals of the Byzantine Provincial Aristocracy in the Late Tenth Century', *REB* 52 (1994), 195 n. 43, have both cast doubt on the transcription of this seal, arguing that since Tzamandos lay outside Cilicia, this must be a misreading. Instead, they have argued that the owner was the *strategos* of Anazarbos, Mamistra, and Adana, that his name was Melissenos, and that the seal, on epigraphical grounds, should be dated to the 11th c. However, there are stronger arguments for supporting a 10th- rather than an 11th-c. dating. First, the title of *protospatharios* would appear to be too lowly for a commander of three themes in the middle of the 11th-c. Moreover, as the Maleinos reliquary indicates, it was not unusual for military commanders in the chaotic conditions of the 10th-c. frontier to exercise command both in the eastern plateau and in newly annexed regions. Tzamandos, like Lykandos, was a region developed by the early 10th-c. commander Melias; it was originally a *tourma,* a subdivision of a full theme (*DAI* 240). By the early 10th c. the town at the centre of the theme was the site of a Chalcedonian bishopric, and by 954 a Syrian metropolitan had taken up residence there (Hild and Restle, *Kappadokien,* 91–2, 116–18, 300–1; Cheynet, Morrisson, and Seibt, *Sceaux byzantins de la collection Henri Seyrig,* no. 276; Dagron, 'Minorités ethniques et religieuses', 192).

plateau region. It was his eponymous ancestor, Melias, who had been responsible for establishing Byzantine control over the eastern Anatolian regions of Lykandos and Tzamandos early in the tenth century.[75] Sigillographical evidence indicates that the family continued to exercise military command in the eastern plateau throughout the tenth and eleventh centuries.[76] Moreover, if George, the owner of the seal, can be identified with the Melias who rose to the position of *domestikos* of the *scholai* of the east by 973, then his authority, just like that of Maleinos, was built on his own military skills as well as the reputation of his ancestors.[77]

---

[75] *DAI* 238–40.

[76] Apart from George Melias, there also exists a seal of Theodore Melias, *kandidatos*, who was *taxiarches* (infantry commander) in the theme of the Lykandos (Konstantopoulos, *Molybdoboulla*, no. 224a; Dédéyan, 'Mleh le grand', 101–2) The Zacos collection contains an 11th-c. seal of a *strategos* called Melias (Zacos, *Byzantine Lead Seals II*, no. 572). In 1991 a seal dated to the first half of the 11th c. appeared at auction that belonged to a Basil Melias, *strategos* (Oikonomides, *SBS* 3, 189). In neither the second nor the third seal is the geographical region under the command of these *strategoi* indicated.

[77] It is possible that at an earlier point in his career Melias may have been the *strategos* of the small theme of Chortzine, which lay north-west of the plain of Muş in Taron (Zacos, *Byzantine Lead Seals II*, no. 227; Oikonomides, *Listes*, 359). Melias may have come to Tzimiskes' attention in the context of the Cilician campaigns of Nikephoros Phokas. As *domestikos* of the *scholai* in the mid-960s, Tzimiskes was a leading protagonist of warfare in Cilicia (Skylitzes, *Synopsis*, 267–8; Yahya, *PO* 18, p. 793). Certainly fresco decoration of the Great Pigeon House church in Cappadocia indicates that the two men had already developed close connections during the reign of Nikephoros Phokas. This church depicts Nikephoros Phokas and the empress Theophano in the north apse. On the north wall of the church, the forty martyrs of Sebasteia are represented as a line of infantry soldiers. At the head of the line ride John Tzimiskes and Melias on horseback (L. Rodley, 'The Pigeon House Church at Çavuşin', *JÖB* 33 (1983), 301–39; N. Thierry, *Haut Moyen-âge en Cappadoce: Les Églises de Çavuşin*, 2 vols. (Paris, 1994), i. 56).

However, while the appointment of officials such as Melias and Maleinos was driven by short-term domestic and external political needs, such imperatives could also make their tenure of command on the frontier very brief. Thus, within a year of the death of his political ally Nikephoros Phokas in December 969, Eustathios Maleinos found himself transferred from Antioch to the position of *strategos* at Tarsos in Cilicia.[78] His place at Antioch appears to have been taken by Nicholas the eunuch. Nicholas was sent east at the head of an imperial field army by the new emperor, John Tzimiskes, during the winter of 970–1 to deal with an attack from Fatimid Egypt.[79] However, it is unlikely that Nicholas was in Antioch for long, since as soon as the Fatimid threat was contained, the imperial field army was recalled to the west to deal with the invasion of the Rus in Bulgaria. Thereafter, although the picture of the organization of military administration in Antioch is exceptionally unclear, no commander appears to have exercised control in the city for longer than a few months. During the reign of Tzimiskes, the only mention of a senior military official at Antioch after the departure of Nicholas the eunuch, concerns Michael

[78] Saunders, 'Reliquary of Aachen', 215–16. As governor of Tarsos during the reign of Tzimiskes, Maleinos was responsible for arresting those inhabitants of Antioch who had murdered Christopher the Melkite Patriarch of Antioch in 966 (M. Canard, 'Une vie du patriarch melkite d'Antioche, Christophore', review of H. Zayyat, 'Vie du patriarche melkite d'Antioche, Christophore (967) par le protospathaire Ibrahim b. Yuhanna, document inedit du Xe siècle', *B* 18 (1953), 565). Maleinos still occupied this post at the beginning of Basil's reign (Yahya, *PO* 23, p. 373).

[79] Yahya, *PO* 23, p. 350; Skylitzes, *Synopsis*, 287; Saunders, 'Aachen Reliquary', 211–12; Walker, 'Byzantine Victory over the Fatimids', 431–40; Laurent, 'Gouverneurs d'Antioche', 227–8.

Bourtzes. According to Yahya, when a severe earthquake caused considerable damage to the circuit walls of Antioch, Bourtzes was dispatched to the city by Tzimiskes in order to oversee the necessary repairs.[80] Unfortunately his position of command within the Byzantine hierarchy at this time is not specified. Yet, he does not seem to have been given a permanent office or called *doux*. Instead, when the refortification was completed, Bourtzes returned to active service within the mobile Byzantine field army. According to Skylitzes, when John Tzimiskes died Bourtzes commanded the *tagma* of the *stratelatai* within the army led by Bardas Skleros.[81]

Indeed, the very first mention of the office of *doux* in an Antiochene context only occurs after the death of John Tzimiskes in 976 at the very start of Basil's reign. Once again this first citation occurs in the testimony of Skylitzes, who reports that at the same time as Skleros was named *doux* of Mesopotamia, Bourtzes was appointed *doux* of Antioch-on-the-Orontes.[82] Unfortunately, the exact nature of Bourtzes' responsibilities as *doux* at Antioch is obscured by the fact that Skylitzes interprets his deployment on the eastern frontier within the wider context of Skleros' appointment as *doux* of Mesopotamia. Thus, Skylitzes claims that Bourtzes was sent to Antioch so that he would not conspire with Skleros against the emperors in Constantinople. Reading Skylitzes' interpretation of events, it is tempting to see Bourtzes' appointment as part of a broader

---

[80] Yahya, *PO* 23, p. 351.   [81] Skylitzes, *Synopsis*, 315.
[82] Ibid.

imperial decision in 976 to marginalize the leading figures of the Byzantine field army. Yet such a view would be misconceived. Indeed, just as it has been demonstrated that military and diplomatic relations with neighbouring Muslim powers to the east, rather than imperial fears of revolt, underpinned Skleros' deployment on the central sector of eastern frontier, a similar model can be outlined for Bourtzes' appointment. That is to say, just as Skleros was appointed *doux* so that he could lead Byzantine field army detachments on campaigns against the Hamdanids of Mosul, so Bourtzes was given command at Antioch so that he could keep up the offensive against the principal Muslim adversary on *his* sector of the frontier, namely the Fatimids.

That such strategic thinking underpinned Bourtzes' appointment is supported by the testimony of Yahya ibn Sa'id. He notes that at the beginning of Basil's reign, Bourtzes led an invasion of Muslim territory. During an exploratory expedition in the spring of 976 the Byzantines raided the coastal town of Tripoli, returning to Antioch with lots of booty. Plans were soon afoot for a second expedition.[83] Clearly, this military action was part of a wider strategy to apply pressure to Fatimid positions on the coast of northern Syria and the Lebanon. As such it represented a continuation of the tactics of the latter stages of the last eastern campaign of John Tzimiskes. This campaign had taken place in the summer of 975, less than a year before Bourtzes' appointment as *doux* in Antioch. The most colourful element of Tzimiskes' incursion into Muslim territory had been

[83] Yahya, *PO* 23, p. 372.

his march into central Syria, and his appearance outside the walls of Damascus.[84] Yet, in many ways the more strategically significant component of the 975 campaign was its conclusion. Having devastated the interior of Syria, Tzimiskes returned northwards along the littoral of the Levant, raiding or rendering tributary port towns such as Sidon, Beirut, Djubayl, Tripoli, Djabala, and Balanias. The ambition of this campaign must surely have been to deprive the powerful Fatimid fleet of as many strategic points on the coast as possible.[85] When he was appointed *doux* of Antioch in the spring of 976, Bourtzes was expected to continue this strategy.

However, while Michael Bourtzes' appointment as *doux* of Antioch in 976 makes more sense if it is set against the background context of military and diplomatic relations with the Fatimids, rather than political machinations among palace officials in Constantinople, it should be stressed that Bourtzes' frontier role seems to have been limited to his command over a military force. There is little sign that he was appointed as a permanent governor with responsibility for civilian as well as military matters on the frontier. Instead, in Yahya's brief narrative coverage of fron-

[84] Yahya, PO 23, pp. 368–9. M. Canard, 'Les Sources arabes de l'histoire byzantine', 293–5, transmits the testimony of Ibn al-Kalanisi.

[85] The outlines of this coastal campaign are reported in Yahya, *PO* 23, p. 369. The most detailed account, however, comes from Tzimiskes' own letter to Ashot III, Armenian king of Ani, which is transmitted in the 12th-c. Armenian history of Matthew of Edessa (Matthew of Edessa, *Armenia and the Crusades*, 31–2). The campaign itself is analysed in detail by Walker, 'The "Crusade" of John Tzimisces', 301–27; Bianquis, *Damas sous la domination fatimide*, 93–6.

tier warfare around Antioch in the spring of 976, the city itself appears as little more than a convenient garrison base for troops leading the offensive against the Fatimids. Bourtzes himself was simply the commander in charge of that garrison.

When the Skleros revolt broke out in the spring of 976, Bourtzes was instructed to leave Antioch, join forces with Eustathios Maleinos, the *strategos* of Tarsos, and prevent rebel armies from progressing westwards across the Anti Taurus.[86] From this point onwards the military administrative history of Antioch becomes very obscure. For a short while after Bourtzes left the city, command was held by Bourtzes' son. However, as soon as Bourtzes himself decided to defect from the emperor and join the Skleros party, he instructed his son to leave Antioch and entrust the city into the hands of the *basilikos* Kouleïb.[87] During the remaining years of the Skleros revolt, the most significant figures in the governance of the city of Antioch were first Kouleïb, and later Oubeïdallah, two Christian Arab administrators, both of whom held the office of *basilikos*. The significance of this office and the responsibilities undertaken by Kouleïb and Oubeïdallah will be discussed in the later section of this chapter that deals with civilian administration.[88] However, for now it is worth noting that it is only in September 985, six years after the end of the first Skleros revolt, that the historical record once again makes mention of the office of *doux*.

---

[86] Yahya, *PO* 23, p. 372.   [87] Yahya, *PO* 23, p. 373.
[88] See below 6.4.

In 985 the holder of the office of *doux* was the general, Leo Melissenos.[89] Yet, there is little about his appointment to suggest that the office he held had become a permanent gubernatorial position. Instead, nearly ten years into Basil's reign, the office was still an ad hoc appointment shaped by short-term political and military exigencies. According to Yahya ibn Sa'id, Melissenos' original appointment was made in the context of a particular, and clearly defined, military goal: the siege of the coastal town of Balanias, which had recently been occupied by the Fatimids. However, a conjunction of more pressing political and military conditions both within and outside the empire ensured that Melissenos' tenure of the position of *doux* was brief. For after he had captured and fortified Balanias, he was swiftly recalled to Constantinople. In part Melissenos' recall was motivated by the distrust he had inspired in the emperor while he had been on active service in the east. He had briefly called a halt to the siege of Balanias when he thought that Basil was about to be deposed by Basil Lekapenos the *Parakoimomenos*. He had only resumed military operations after the emperor commanded him to continue with the siege or face having to pay the soldiers' wages out of his own pocket. However, another reason for the recall of Melissenos was that Basil II needed this general's expertise during his forthcoming campaign against Bulgaria, planned for the summer of 986.[90]

The flexible and ad hoc nature of command on the eastern frontier is further demonstrated by the history of

[89] Yahya, *PO* 23, pp. 416–17.
[90] Ibid., p. 417; Skylitzes, *Synopsis*, 330; Laurent, 'Gouverneurs d'Antioche', 232. It is possible that during the Bulgarian expedition Melissenos

the Antiochene region in the year which separated Leo's departure from Antioch and the outbreak of the revolt led by Bardas Phokas in August 987. In some senses Leo was replaced at Antioch by Bardas Phokas. According to Yahya, at the same time as Leo was recalled to Constantinople in 986, Bardas was relieved of his position of *domestikos* of the *scholai* of the east, supreme commander of the field army. Instead he was appointed *doux* of the east and governor of Antioch and the provinces of the east.[91] Yet Yahya's description of Phokas' appointment suggests that unlike Leo Melissenos' limited responsibilities as *doux*, Bardas' new duties were extremely broad, and not purely confined to military matters or to command over the immediate environs of Antioch. So vast, indeed, is the geographical scope implied in this title, that Phokas' role may have been that of an imperial plenipotentiary on the frontier.

---

fulfilled the position of *domestikos* of the *scholai* of the west. This argument has been advanced by Jordanov from the evidence of two seals belonging to Leo Melissenos *domestikos* that were found during excavations at Preslav in eastern Bulgaria. On one seal Leo is attributed with the title *magistros*; on the other *patrikios* (I. Jordanov, 'Molybdobulles de domestiques des scholes du dernier quart du Xe siècle trouvés dans la stratégie de Preslav', in N. Oikonomides (ed.), *SBS* 2 (Washington DC, 1990), 208–9). However, it should be noted that Skylitzes maintains that Stephen Kontostephanos was the *domestikos* of the west during the 986 Bulgarian campaign. Skylitzes relates that Melissenos was given responsibility for guarding the city of Philippoupolis during the expedition (Skylitzes, *Synopsis*, 331). As yet there is insufficient evidence to resolve who led the field army of the west and the exact nature of Melissenos' command. The contribution of Melissenos and Kontostephanos to the 986-expedition is also discussed above in 4.2.2 and below in 8.5.

[91] Yahya, *PO* 23, p. 417. Laurent sees Bardas' position as simply *doux* of Antioch (Laurent, 'Gouverneurs d'Antioche', 233).

Such an interpretation would be compatible with the broader military position of the empire at the time. With a summer campaign against Bulgaria planned, a large part of the professional field army stationed on the eastern frontier was required to return to Constantinople to fight in the west, including generals such as Leo Melissenos. In these circumstances there was little sense in leaving Bardas Phokas in the position of *domestikos* of the *scholai* when there were few *scholai* to lead. Instead, Phokas was given wide-ranging powers to supervise the eastern frontier while Basil himself was on campaign in Bulgaria. Yet, even Phokas' appointment proved to be an ad hoc provision that had to be hastily rearranged when new external and internal political and military pressures arose.[92] These pressures were the ignominious failure of Basil's 986 invasion of Bulgaria, and the appearance of a new threat in the east: the arrival in February 987 of Bardas Skleros, who had recently been released by the Buyid authorities in Baghdad. With the need for a greater armed presence in the east, Phokas was restored to the position of *domestikos* at the head of the mobile field army. However, once the imperial field army returned eastwards to deal with Skleros, Phokas himself rebelled.[93]

---

[92] This is not to say that Phokas was necessarily happy with this division of military command. One of the reasons adduced by Skylitzes for Phokas' revolt in 987 was that he had been left behind from the Bulgarian offensive (Skylitzes, *Synopsis*, 332). Nonetheless, given Skylitzes' fondness for ascribing motives to characters within his narratives without any independent corroboration, one should perhaps be wary of taking this claim too literally; for further general discussion of this characteristic of Skylitzes' composition, see above 3.2).

[93] Skylitzes, *Synopsis*, 330–4; Leo the Deacon, *Historiae Libri Decem*, 171–5; Yahya, *PO* 23, pp. 418–21; Stephen of Taron, *Armenische Geschichte*, 186–90.

Ambiguity about the nature of command at Antioch persisted throughout the Phokas revolt itself and during the last decade of the tenth century. For example, according to Yahya, Leo Phokas, the son of Bardas, took his father's place at Antioch in 987 when the rebellion first broke.[94] However, Leo's exact position is unclear. It is impossible to know whether Leo was his father's replacement as *domestikos* of the *scholai*, or as *doux*. Unfortunately there are only two narrative passages concerned with Leo's role in the rebellion. It is, therefore, difficult to interpret the nature of his command from the historical written record. In the first, Yahya shows Leo tricking Agapios, Patriarch of Antioch, whom the Phokades suspected of treachery, into leaving the city.[95] The second episode occurs in Yahya's account of the very end of the Phokas rebellion after Bardas' death at Abydos in April 989. According to Yahya, Leo continued the Phokas insurrection in Antioch until November 989. Then he surrendered to the citizens of Antioch and was handed over to Basil's new lieutenant in the city, Michael Bourtzes. At the time of Leo's surrender he was supported by a small armed force, which included Armenians and Muslims. Together they had mounted last-gasp resistance from a tower in the city walls.[96] Nonetheless, such a meagre shard of evidence from the final, embattled stages of the revolt does not enable us to reconstruct the nature of Leo's power earlier in the rebellion.

---

[94] Yahya, *PO* 23, p. 425; Laurent, 'Gouverneurs d'Antioche', 233.
[95] Yahya, *PO* 23, p. 425.
[96] Ibid., pp. 427–8.

Equally confusing is the nature of military command in Antioch between the end of the Phokas revolt in 989 and the early 990s. It is clear that by 992 Michael Bourtzes had taken control. When Byzantine armies were defeated by Fatimid forces in 992, and later in 994, it was Michael who was at their head.[97] Yet, the situation during the three years before 992 is less clear. Usually it is argued that Bourtzes was appointed *doux* of Antioch when he arrived in the city in 989 to arrest Leo Phokas.[98] However, a reference in Stephen of Taron's account to an engagement in 991 in the Antioch region between a Fatimid army and a small force led by Romanos Skleros, the son of the former rebel Bardas, persuaded Werner Seibt to argue that Skleros was *doux* in the city between 989 and 991. Seibt believed that Bourtzes only took over as *doux* in 992.[99] However, modern historians may be creating a false problem here. In the context of the intensified warfare between Fatimid and Byzantine armies which characterized northern Syria in the last decade of the tenth century, it is possible that responsibilities for the defence of the southern sector of the frontier were shared among a number of senior military officers, all with experience of warfare in the Byzantine east. Indeed, the narrative of Yahya illustrates this principle of multiple command in action. When the Byzantines were defeated in 994 by the Fatimids in the Ruj valley north of Apameia, their army was led by Bourtzes, but also contained fresh troops recently sent from Constantinople under the command of Leo Melisse-

[97] Yahya, *PO* 23, 438–40.
[98] Laurent, 'Gouverneurs d'Antioche', 233–4.
[99] Stephen of Taron, *Armenische Geschichte*, 199; Seibt, *Die Skleroi*, 63–4.

nos, himself a former *doux* of Antioch.[100] It is possible that an analogous position pertained in the early 990s, with Romanos Skleros being sent to the eastern frontier with responsibility for a similar mobile relief force. Thus, *c.*991–2 Romanos may have held an office such as *domestikos* of the *scholai* at the head of *tagmata* dispatched from Constantinople, while Bourtzes was, at the same time, *doux* of Antioch.[101]

Clearer than the nature of the command exercised by Bourtzes in the early 990s is the fact that his conduct in office did much to dissatisfy the emperor Basil. Not only did Bourtzes lose two major field army engagements with the Fatimids (in 992 and 994), forcing Basil II himself to campaign in northern Syria in 995, he was also accused of exacerbating the conflict by imprisoning a Fatimid envoy.[102] By 995 Basil had tired of Bourtzes, and replaced him with Damian Dalassenos.[103] However, Damian's duties are also difficult to interpret. Little can be resolved from the historical record, since a variety of labels are used to describe his position. He is called *Doux* of the East by Yahya, in a phrase that echoes the plenipotentiary position held by Bardas Phokas in 986–7.[104] On the other hand when two

---

[100] Yahya, *PO* 23, p. 440.

[101] This is the solution also offered by J.-C. Cheynet and J.-F.Vannier, *Études prosopographiques* (Paris, 1986), 21–2.

[102] Yahya, *PO* 23, p. 438.

[103] Ibid., pp. 443–4; Laurent, 'Gouverneurs d'Antioche', 234.

[104] Yahya, *PO* 23, p. 444; Cheynet and Vannier, *Études prosopographiques*, 77; Cheynet, 'Basil II and Asia Minor', 88, is inclined to see Dalassenos as a plenipotentiary for Basil.

later Arab historians, whose common source was the eleventh-century Iraqi historian Hilal al Sabi, comment on the death of Dalassenos in battle against the Fatimids in 998, they merely call him *doux*.[105] In contrast, the Armenian historian Stephen of Taron refers to Damian by his title, *magistros*, rather than by his office.[106] Meanwhile, with characteristic vagueness Skylitzes notes, in the midst of a telescoped and confusing summary passage about Byzantine relations with the east (chapter 20 of the *Synopsis Historion*), that Damian ruled in Antioch.[107] Although no sigillographical evidence has ever been directly linked to Damian Dalassenos, it is possible that he was the owner of a seal in the Dumbarton Oaks collection belonging to a Damian *doux*.[108] Yet, even this seal does not add much to any understanding of the nature of Damian's command at Antioch. More information is forthcoming from the description of Damian's actual responsibilities in Yahya ibn Sa'id's narrative. This indicates that Damian's position was still primarily that of an active military commander. For two years after his appointment he led raids down the north Syrian coast to

---

[105] al-Rudhrawari, *Eclipse*, vi. 239–40 (writing in the later 11th c.); Ibn al-Kalanisi (writing in the mid-12th c.) in Canard, 'Les Sources arabes de l'histoire byzantine', 299–300; Forsyth, 'The Chronicle of Yahya ibn Sa'id al Antaki', 101–39.

[106] Stephen of Taron, *Armenische Geschichte*, 201–2.

[107] ὅς ἦρχεν Ἀντιοχείας (Skylitzes, *Synopsis*, 340); see above 2.1 and 2.4 for Skylitzes' tendency to telescope narratives, especially those dealing with eastern affairs; see above 3.2 and 3.3.1 for the difficulties involved in using Skylitzes' testimony to discuss administrative history.

[108] Unpublished seal from Dumbarton Oaks: 58.106.4100. This seal is not discussed by Cheynet and Vannier, *Études prosopographiques*, 76–8, in their analysis of Damian's career.

Tripoli. In the third year his attacks were focused further inland, as he tried to capture the town of Apameia on the east bank of the Orontes, then in Fatimid hands. However, when the Fatimid governor of Damascus arrived to relieve Apameia in July 998, Damian was killed in battle.[109]

Damian's replacement was Nikephoros Ouranos, who took up command late in 999.[110] For the four years prior to his arrival in Antioch he had been *domestikos* of the *scholai* on active service in the Balkans, where he had gained universal renown as the result of an unexpected, but convincing, victory over a Bulgarian army at the River Spercheios near Thermopylae in 997.[111] It is clear that despite the peace that was agreed between Byzantine and Fatimid authorities in 1000–1, military affairs continued to dominate Ouranos' attention once he arrived on the eastern frontier. Shortly after his appointment to command in Antioch he accompanied Basil II on his campaign to annex Tao in the spring of 1000.[112] During the following year he returned to Tao to repel the incursion led by Gurgen of Iberia.[113] Several years later in 1006/7 Ouranos marched from Antioch to Sarudj in the Diyar Mudar, where he won a victory over an Arab dervish insurrectionist called al-Acfar and his Bedouin allies the Banu Noumeir and the Banu Kilab.[114] Several

---

[109] The most detailed account of this battle is that preserved in the history of Ibn al-Kalanisi (Canard, 'Les Sources arabes de l'histoire byzantine', 297–300).

[110] Skylitzes, *Synopsis*, 345; Yahya, *PO* 23, pp. 400, 460, 466–7; Laurent, 'Gouverneurs d'Antioche', 235–6.

[111] For further discussion of this battle see below 8.5.

[112] Yahya, *PO* 23, p. 460.

[113] Stephen of Taron, *Armenische Geschichte*, 212; see also above 6.3.1.

[114] Yahya, *PO* 23, pp. 466–7.

letters sent by the contemporary *krites* of Tarsos, Philetos Synadenos, to Ouranos while he was stationed in Antioch, praise him for his military valour and may refer to this campaign.[115]

However, it is clear from both literary and sigillographical materials that Ouranos' responsibilities were broad in their definition and extended over a vast geographical area. According to the seals he issued while stationed in Antioch he was: Nikephoros Ouranos, *Magistros* and Ruler (*Ho Kraton*) of the East.[116] The amorphous and universal nature of Ouranos' power is reflected in the fact that most contemporary literary sources, including Yahya ibn Sa'id, Stephen of Taron, and Philetos Synadenos, simply refer to Nikephoros by his title of *magistros*.[117] Indeed, when addressing Ouranos, Synadenos was apt to reflect on the august nature of Ouranos' position with the superlative invocation, *peribleptos magistros*.[118] The seniority, ambiguity, and idiosyn-

[115] Synadenos (Philetos): letters 8–13; McGeer, 'Tradition and Reality', 131; Todt, 'Patriarchat von Antiocheia', 242, 248. Al-Acfar had been an irritant in the borderland areas between Antioch and Aleppo for some two years before Ouranos' action. He was eventually incarcerated by Byzantium's principal regional ally, Emir Loulou of Aleppo (Yahya, *PO* 23, p. 467).

[116] Νικηφόρῳ μαγίστρῳ τῷ κρατοῦντι τῆς ᾿Ανατολῆς τῷ Οὐρανῷ (Nesbitt and Oikonomides, *Byzantine Seals at Dumbarton*, iii.99.11; also published in McGeer, 'Tradition and Reality', 139–40; see also Cheynet, 'Basil II and Asia Minor', 88).

[117] Yahya refers to Ouranos as *magistros* in the context of his expedition against al-Acfar (Yahya, *PO* 23, p. 367). However, in his testimony for the period 1000–1 he calls Ouranos *doux* (ibid., p. 460). Stephen of Taron refers to Ouranos in 1000 by his title, *magistros*, and by the responsibility he had fulfilled in imperial service during the early 980s, *epi tou kanikleiou* (keeper of the imperial inkstand) (Stephen of Taron, *Armenische Geschichte*, 212); see below 6.4 for more on the correspondence between Synadenos and Ouranos.

[118] Synadenos (Philetos), letters 8–13, especially letter 11.

cratic nature of the office fulfilled by Ouranos on the eastern frontier suggests that Nikephoros may have been invested with plenipotentiary powers which extended far beyond control over Antioch and the field army which was garrisoned there. It is likely that after he had resolved a peace with the Fatimids in 1000–1, Basil was able to concentrate his full resources on warfare with Bulgaria.[119] Therefore, just as he had appointed Phokas as his plenipotentiary in the east during the Bulgarian campaign of 986, he now used Ouranos in this broad-based eastern office while he himself campaigned in the Balkans. The difference, however, between Phokas and Ouranos was that the latter was unquestionably loyal to the emperor, whereas the former had betrayed him. Yet, it is likely that Ouranos was appointed as much for his ability to maintain the recently agreed peace with the Fatimids as for his ability to prosecute war. Certainly Ouranos was an experienced diplomat as well as soldier. Before beginning his military career in the Balkans in the later 990s, Ouranos had worked both in central civil administration and in eastern diplomacy, undertaking two missions to Baghdad to negotiate with the Buyids about the exiled rebel general Bardas Skleros.[120]

---

[119] The connection in timing between campaigns in the east and west is discussed further below in 8.4–5.

[120] See below 6.4 for Ouranos' earlier career in imperial service. For more on the tactical manual that he wrote, some of the contents of which reflect his experience at Antioch, see *Ouranos Taktika (a)*: de Foucault, 'Douze chapitres', 281–310; *Ouranos Taktika (b)*: McGeer, *Sowing the Dragon's Teeth*, 88–162; A. Dain, *La 'Tactique' de Nicéphore Ouranos* (Paris, 1937); McGeer, 'Tradition and Reality', 129–40.

The history of command on the eastern frontier in the region of Antioch is much less full for the second half of Basil's reign than the first. This is mainly because Yahya ibn Sa'id's coverage of the events in northern Syria is very thin between the years 1000 and 1016.[121] The most that can be said of this largely unrecorded sixteen-year period is that Ouranos held power between at least 1000 and 1007, the year when he campaigned against al-Acfar. By 1011 one Michael *koitonites* was *doux* of Antioch, indicating that Ouranos had lost power in Antioch by the end of the first decade of the eleventh century.[122] However, the very fact that Ouranos was in command at Antioch for more than seven years signals an important change in administrative practice on the frontier. Whereas during the first thirty years of Byzantine rule in Antioch, external and internal political pressures had entailed a series of ad hoc military commands and a very rapid turnover in office holders, now, in the predominantly peaceful conditions which followed the 1000–1 accord with the Fatimids, short-term expediency was able to give way to a greater degree of permanent command.

---

[121] In most of his coverage for these years Yahya is concerned with Egyptian history (*PO* 23, pp. 462–520). In particular he concentrates on the eccentric behaviour of the contemporary Fatimid caliph, al-Hakim, who was responsible for persecuting and expelling some members of the Egyptian Christian and Jewish communities, including Yahya himself. Most infamous of his attacks on the Christian communities under his authority was his destruction of the Church of the Holy Sepulchre in Jerusalem in 1009 (Yahya, *PO* 23, p. 492; Forsyth, 'The Chronicle of Yahya ibn Sa'id al Antaki', ch. 5; M. Canard, 'La Destruction de l'Église de la Resurrection par le Calife Hakim et l'histoire de la descente du feu sacré', *B* 35 (1965), 16–43).

[122] Yahya, *PO* 23, p. 501; Laurent, 'Gouverneurs d'Antioche', 236.

By the final decade of Basil's reign, there are further signs of the consolidation of military administration on the frontier, most notably in the regularity with which the contemporary literary and sigillographical records refer to the senior commanders at Antioch as either *doux* or *katepano*. For example, in 1016 Yahya ibn Sa'id mentions an anonymous *katepano* of Antioch. In 1024 he cites Constantine Dalassenos as the *katepano*.[123] The seal of Niketas of Mistheia, who took command in Antioch between 1030 and 1032, indicates that he was *patrikios, rector,* and *katepano*.[124] Another individual identified by sigillographical evidence as a *doux* is Theophylact Dalassenos (1032 to 1034).[125] Sigillographical evidence has added the *protospatharios* Pankratios (whose term in office has been dated to the reign of Basil himself), the *anthypatos* and *patrikios* Leo, Constantine Bourtzes *magistros,* and Michael Kontostephanos *magistros* to the list of early to mid-eleventh-century

---

[123] Yahya, *PO* 47, pp. 401, 477; Laurent, 'Gouverneurs d'Antioche', 237, 239.

[124] N. Oikonomides, *A Collection of Dated Byzantine Lead Seals* (Washington DC, 1986), no. 80. Both Yahya and another Arab historian, Kemal al-Din, report that Niketas was the *katepano* of Antioch (Laurent, 'Gouverneurs d'Antioche', 239). It should be noted, however, that Skylitzes retains a characteristic vagueness when he reports on Niketas' frontier command. On one occasion he merely states that Niketas was the leader (*hegemon*) of Antioch: ἀπαίρων δὲ τῆς Συρίας δομέστικον μὲν τῶν σχολῶν ἀποδείκνυσι Συμεὼν τὸν τοῦ πενθεροῦ αὐτοῦ Κωνσταντίνου θεράποντα, ἡγεμόνα δὲ Ἀντιοχείας Νικήταν τὸν ἐκ Μισθείας (Skylitzes, *Synopsis*, 382); on another, the ruler (*archon*) of Antioch: κατόπιν δὲ ἦλθε καὶ ὁ Πινζαράχ, προπεμπόμενος καὶ δυροφορούμενος παρὰ τοῦ χρηματίσαντος ἄρχοντος Ἀντιοχείας Νικήτα τοῦ ἐκ Μισθείας (Skylitzes, *Synopsis*, 383).

[125] Cheynet, Morrisson, and Seibt, *Sceaux byzantins: Henri Seyrig,* no. 156: *anthypatos, patrikios* and *doux* of Antioch; Cheynet and Vannier, *Études prosopographiques,* 84.

doukes/katepanes.[126] Further sigillographical evidence that
the office only became more stable towards the end of Basil's
reign is provided by the fact that the Seyrig collection, with
its impressive array of tenth- and eleventh-century seals
from the eastern frontier, contains seven seals of the *doux/
katepano* of Antioch: none predates Theophylact Dalassenos
(1032–4).[127]

Yet, while the increased stability in the office of *katepano*
in this period points to a degree of consolidation of military
administration in northern Syria, it would be a mistake to
overemphasize the martial character of the frontier in the
latter decades of Basil's reign. Yahya gives little indication
that after Ouranos, *katepanes* of Antioch led many long-
distance military campaigns. When Basil II chose to support
the Hamdanid prince Abu al-Hayja in his attempt to regain
control of Aleppo from the ruling emir, Mansour ibn Loulou, in 1009, he preferred to leave the fighting to armies
provided by local nomad powers, including the Marwanids
and another regional Byzantine ally from among the Bedouin, the Mirdasids.[128] Even when conditions in northern

---

[126] Pankratios (Zacos, *Byzantine Lead Seals II*, no. 664; see also Cheynet,
'Grandeur et décadence', 128); Leo (Schlumberger, *Sigillographie*, 309); for
both office-holders see also Cheynet, Morrisson, and Seibt, *Sceaux byzantins:
Henri Seyrig*, 114. Constantine Bourtzes (J.-C. Cheynet, 'Sceaux byzantins
des musées d'Antioche et de Tarse', *TM* 12 (1994), no. 48; Laurent, 'Gouverneurs d'Antioche', 237); Michael Kontostephanos (*The George Zacos Collection of Byzantine Lead Seals, 1* (Auction 127, Spinks catalogue, 7 October
1998), no. 43).

[127] Cheynet, Morrisson, and Seibt, *Sceaux byzantins: Henri Seyrig*, nos.
156–62.

[128] Yayha, *PO* 47, pp. 392–3; for discussion of the Mirdasids see, Kennedy,
Prophet and the Age of the Caliphates, 302–6; Forsyth, 'The Chronicle of Yahya
ibn Sa'id', 537–57.

Syria deteriorated after the Fatimids reoccupied Aleppo in 1016 at the expense of Mansour, Basil's reaction was muted. The emperor simply ordered the walls of the citadel at Antioch to be strengthened and imposed a trade embargo.[129] When the deposed emir, Mansour, took refuge at Antioch, he was granted a salary and a local estate which he fortified. However, this castle appears to have been little more than a listening post, a position where Mansour could monitor conditions within his former emirate. At no point does he seem to have been given a large detachment of troops. Indeed, the 700 soldiers that he brought with him from Aleppo were detached from his service and put onto the pay roll of the garrison at Antioch.[130] The demilitarized nature of the frontier in this period is also illustrated by the fate of the monastery of Qalat Siman, which had been strengthened by Nikephoros Phokas during the Byzantine assault on Antioch in 968. In 1017 when it was raided by a Fatimid army, it was no longer manned or strongly protected.[131] Finally even when one of the Byzantine's regional allies, the Mirdasids, seized Aleppo from the Fatimids, Basil remained unenthusiastic about offering military support to his Arab clients. In 1024 the Mirdasids were attacked by the Fatimids. The *katepano* of Antioch at this time, Constantine Dalassenos, sent 300 infantrymen to assist in the defence of

---

[129] This embargo is discussed in greater detail below at 8.4.

[130] Yahya, *PO* 47, pp. 399–403.

[131] For its original fortification see W. B. R. Saunders, 'Qalat Siman: a Frontier Fort of the Tenth and Eleventh Centuries', in S. Freeman and H. Kennedy (eds.), *Defence of the Roman and Byzantine Frontiers* (Oxford, 1986), 291–305; for the Fatimid attack see Yahya, *PO* 47, p. 405; see also Todt, 'Patriarchat von Antiocheia', 246.

the city. However, these troops were withdrawn when the emperor disapproved of Dalassenos' action. The message was clear: Basil would allow his *katepano* to act as a diplomat; he would pay the garrison at Antioch; but he would not allow the *katepano* to prosecute war without his permission.[132]

That such demilitarized conditions continued to be the quotidian frontier experience in the Antioch region after the death of Basil is also suggested by testimonies other than that of Yahya ibn Sa'id. In 1048–9, Ibn Butlan, a Christian Arab doctor who travelled through northern Syria from Baghdad, visited Antioch and commented in his travelogue of that journey on the garrison of 4,000 men stationed there. However, aside from this reference, Ibn Butlan had nothing more to say about the military complexion of this area. Instead, his account dwelt on the region's agricultural and commercial well-being and its heterodox population. In a detailed description of Laodikeia, a port town which had been at the forefront of raiding activity against the Fatimids in the final quarter of the tenth century, Ibn Butlan makes no mention of the city's fortifications nor of a military garrison. Instead, his interest is drawn to the city's harbour, its ancient monuments, a former temple which had served the town both as a mosque and more recently as a church, its other surviving mosques, its market places and market inspectors, and its merchants. The principal responsibility of the town's governor in this period of peace appears to have

[132] Yahya, *PO* 47, p. 477; Laurent, 'Gouverneurs d'Antioche', 237, 239.

been the regulation of the town's prostitutes.[133] Ibn Butlan also implies that the rural districts of northern Syria were demilitarized zones of local prosperity. During his visit to the village of Imm he enumerates a host of intriguing features, including churches, a mosque, prostitutes, pigs, fish in local rivers, and mills. He comments at length on the prosperity of the local countryside.[134] Notably absent from his report is any mention of a garrison, despite the fact that Imm had been an important fortified site controlled by the *doux* Michael Bourtzes within the theme of Artah (listed in the *Escorial Taktikon*) during Byzantium's wars with the Fatimids in the early 990s.[135] Nor is it likely that this tendency to demobilize fortifications when there was no obvious threat was limited to the Antiochene sector of the frontier. A similar tendency has been observed at Melitene, where the city walls were not rebuilt after the fall of the city to the Byzantines in 934.[136] Mothballing of fortifications also seems to have occurred on the empire's north-eastern frontier. During the Byzantine attack on Theodosioupolis in the late 930s and 940s, a position called Hafdjidj was fortified and garrisoned as a forward attack

---

[133] Ibn Butlan: *The Medico-Philosophical Controversy between Ibn Butlan of Baghdad and Ibn Ridwan of Cairo*, ed. and trans. J. Schlacht and M. Meyerhof (Cairo, 1937), 57.

[134] Ibid. 54.

[135] Ibid. 54–5. See also Yahya, *PO*, 23 (1932), p. 438; Oikonomides, *Les Listes*, 268–9; Bar Hebraeus: *Chronography*, 218.

[136] F. Tinnefeld, 'Die Stadt Melitene in ihrer späteren byzantinischen Epoche (934–1101)', *Acts of the 14th International Congress 1971*, 3 vols. (Bucharest, 1974), ii. 436–8.

base.[137] But after Theodosioupolis fell in 949 Hafdjidj appears to have lost its martial dimension. Although the *Escorial Taktikon* lists a *strategos* of Chauzizion, the Greek name for Hafdjidj, it is likely that this office had already been suppressed. When Basil II passed through this area in 1000 the fortress of Hafdjidj had to be reoccupied, indicating that under normal circumstances it was not garrisoned.[138]

Nonetheless, administrative phenomena typical of peacetime conditions, such as stability in the office of *katepano* and demobbed fortifications, may have been limited as far as Antioch was concerned to the first half of the eleventh century. In the second half of the century, internal and external political and military pressures wrought changes. In Antioch at least there are strong signs from the career of Romanos Skleros, the great-grandson of the rebel Bardas, that by the middle of the eleventh century the office of *doux/katepano* once again had to become more flexible in response to changing strategic conditions. In 1054 Romanos held the position of *doux* of Antioch. However, when he was reappointed to command in Antioch in the latter part of the decade he held the joint position of *stratopedarches* of the east (head of the mobile field army in the east) and *doux* of Antioch. Two contexts can be suggested for the widening of

---

[137] *DAI* 206–14; Vasiliev, *Byzance et les Arabes*, ii(1) 284; ii(2) 122. The fortress has yet to be located by modern historians although it is assumed to lie north of the Bingöl Dağı, near the source of the Araxes River (J. D. Howard-Johnston, 'Procopius, Roman Defences North of the Taurus and the New Fortress of Citharizon', in D. H. French and C. S. Lightfoot (eds.), *The Eastern Frontier of the Roman Empire* (Oxford, 1989), 79–80, 195).

[138] Oikonomidès, *Les Listes*, 266–7; Stephen of Taron, *Armenische Geschichte*, 210; Aristakes of Lastivert, *Récit des malheurs*, 4.

his responsibilities: first, that Skleros was appointed to this enhanced military position as a reward for supporting Isaac Komnenos' revolt against Michael VI in 1057; and second, that as Turkish invasions became more frequent and dangerous, reaching as far as Melitene in 1057, and Sebasteia in 1059/60, more flexibility was required of the Byzantine military presence across the whole eastern frontier.[139]

Another component of greater flexibility may have been the dusting-off and reuse of long-abandoned fortifications. In the Antioch area the fortresses of the small theme of Artah, including Imm, were regarrisoned in the reign of Romanos IV (1068–71).[140] Meanwhile, there are signs in the sigillographical and historiographical records that the small theme located in the Amanos Mountains, Mauron Oros, was remanned. Created as a theme, fortified and garrisoned by Michael Bourtzes during Nikephoros Phokas' campaign to conquer Antioch in the later 960s, Mauron Oros appears to have been abandoned shortly after the city fell to Byzantine armies in 969. It does not appear as a theme in the *Escorial Taktikon* which was composed soon after the conquest of northern Syria. However, at the end of the eleventh century traces of the theme reappear: the Seyrig collection contains the seal of a *strategos* of Mauron Oros; the theme is also mentioned in the Treaty of Devol drawn up

[139] Laurent, *Sceaux byzantins du Médailler Vatican*, no. 94; Cheynet, Morrisson, and Seibt, *Sceaux byzantins: Henri Seyrig*. nos. 158, 159; Cheynet, *Sceaux de la collection Zacos (BN)*, no 5; Seibt, *Die Skleroi*, 79–83; Laurent, 'Gouverneurs d'Antioche', 242; C. Cahen, *Pre-Ottoman Turkey: A General Survey of the Material and Spiritual Culture and History*, (trans. J. Jones Williams) (London, 1968), 69–71.

[140] Bar Hebraeus, *Chronography*, 218.

between Bohemond of Antioch and Alexios I in 1108.[141] Similar phenomena are witnessed elsewhere in the Byzantine east in the chaotic conditions of the later eleventh century. For example, in Melitene the city walls were rebuilt during the reign of Constantine X Doukas (1059–67) when the indigenous notables of the city lobbied for their repair to prevent raids by Turkish nomads and local Armenian brigands.[142]

6.3.4   The katepanates of Iberia and Vaspurakan

The only significant territorial expansion achieved by the Byzantine Empire during the reign of Basil II in the east was in western Caucasia. In the north of this region this extension comprised the annexation of the princedom of Tao in 1000, and the territorial gains added in 1022 following Basil's campaigns against George of Abasgia. In the south, it amounted to the absorption of the territories of the Artsruni principality of Vaspurakan south and east of Lake Van. Broadly speaking it was from these new territories that the katepanates of Iberia and Vaspurakan were created.

[141] Skylitzes, *Synopsis*, 271–2; Cheynet, Morrisson, and Seibt, *Sceaux byzantins: Henri Seyrig:* no. 183; Honigman, *Ostgrenze*, 127; Anna Komnene, *Alexiade*, iii. 133–6. Those sites enumerated in the Treaty of Devol have been used by Todt, 'Patriarchat von Antiocheia', 245–9, to trace the territorial extent of the original katepanate (or ducate, as he terms it) of Antioch. It is important to remember, however, that not all of these sites were occupied simultaneously or continuously.
[142] Tinnefeld, 'Die Stadt Melitene', 436–8.

Unfortunately, however, fundamental problems of geography and chronology hamper any attempt to reconstruct the origins and development of these katepanates. In the north debate centres on two issues: first, the extent of the lands ceded to Basil by David of Tao in 1000 and those added in 1022; and second, whether a katepanate existed as early as 1000, or was only first established in the early 1020s after Basil's final campaign against the Abasgians and Iberians.[143] In the south, the most intractable problem is ascertaining the date of the surrender of Vaspurakan.[144] Furthermore, a lack of reports about these katepanates in the historical record means that even after annexation itself, the early years of Byzantine rule are often opaque. It is only with the absorption of the northern Armenian principality of Ani in the early 1040s that the primary sources, above all the historical accounts of Skylitzes and Aristakes of Lastivert, begin to dedicate more sustained coverage to the Caucasian katepanates. Thus, a fuller picture of frontier command only begins to emerge in the historical record fifteen years after the death of Basil II.[145]

Despite these problems, a certain amount of scholarship has been devoted to the early history of the Caucasian katepanates, with useful contributions coming from Yuzbashian, Janssens, Seibt, and Arutjunova-Findanjan.[146]

---

[143] For further discussion of these campaigns see below 8.4.

[144] Ibid.

[145] An analysis of political and military relations on the north-east frontier during the 1040s has been expertly pieced together by Shepard, 'Scylitzes on Armenia in the 1040s', 296–311.

[146] Yuzbashian, 'L'Administration byzantine en Arménie', 139–83; F. Janssens, 'Le Lac de Van et la stratégie byzantine', *B* 42 (1972), 388–404; W. Seibt,

However, many issues remain unexplored, most notably how these katepanates should be interpreted in the wider history of the organization of the Byzantine eastern frontier in the tenth and eleventh centuries.[147] While a broad-based history of the Caucasian katepanates is not given here, I include some brief remarks about the early history of the organization of the Byzantine eastern frontier in Caucasia, because they reflect many of the developments in frontier command already observed in the cases of Chaldia, Mesopotamia, and Antioch. Above all, they demonstrate the overriding principle that the military administration of the Byzantine east was always organized on a highly flexible footing, particularly in the immediate aftermath of annexation.

Of the two katepanates the origins of Iberia are the most obscure. Not only is it difficult to ascertain whether Byzantine rule extended into Tao permanently in 1000 or only after 1022, it is also impossible to identify any commander in Iberia before the appointment of Niketas of Pisidia in 1025/6.[148] In contrast, the early history of imperial rule in

'Die Eingliederung von Vaspurakan in das byzantinische Reich (etwa Anfang 1019 bzw. Anfang 1022)', *HA* 92 (1978), 49–66; V. A. Arutjunova-Fidanjan, 'Sur le problème des provinces byzantines orientales', *REArm* 14 (1980), 157–69; eadem, 'The Social Administrative Structures in the East of the Byzantine Empire', *JÖB* 32.3 (1982), 21–34; eadem, 'Some Aspects of Military Administrative Districts in Armenia during the Eleventh Century', *REArm* 20 (1986–7), 309–20; eadem, 'The New Socio-Administrative Structure in the East of Byzantium', *Byz Forsch* 19 (1993), 79–86.

[147] A rare, but brief, attempt to interpret the katepanates of Iberia and Vaspurakan within the wider military command structure of the frontier is undertaken by Kühn, *Die byzantinische Armee*, 186–93.

[148] Skylitzes, *Synopsis*, 370: Niketas' office is identified as that of *doux* of Iberia (Kühn, *Die byzantinische Armee*, 188). It was probably Niketas who was the anonymous *katepano* who returned Bagrat, the son of George of Abasgia,

Vaspurakan is less opaque. Although the exact date of the surrender of the southern Lake Van principality is difficult to establish, it is at least possible to identify the first two commanders in this region from the testimony of John Skylitzes, although it should be noted that with characteristic vagueness Skylitzes fails to mention either the date of their appointment or their exact office: 'Basil Argyros, *patrikios*, having been sent out to rule this land, and having failed in all respects was released from office. And Nikephoros Komnenos, *protospatharios*, was sent as his replacement, who through using a mixture of force and persuasion on his arrival there, made the land subject to the emperor.'[149]

to his homeland in 1025 (Georgian Royal Annals, 284). Bagrat had been taken hostage as part of the peace agreement reached between Basil II and George after the emperor's campaigns on the north-eastern frontier in 1021–2. It is possible that this Niketas was also the owner of a seal in the Zacos collection belonging to a Niketas, *patrikios* and *katepano* of Iberia (Zacos, *Byzantine Lead Seals II*, no. 1026). For Yuzbashian, however, Romanos Dalassenos was the first *doux* of Iberia, appointed in 1023 in the aftermath of Basil's Georgian campaigns (Yuzbashian, 'L'Administration byzantine en Arménie', 156, 183). Yet, his identification of Dalassenos as the first *doux* rests on the naming of Romanos as such by an inscription on the Iberian gate at Theodosioupolis/Erzerum which is now lost. The inscription itself was dated to 991–2, a date which historians have traditionally rejected because of their belief, largely based upon evidence of silence, that the katepanate was founded by Basil in 1023. With the disappearance of the inscription, it is impossible to know when Romanos exercised authority over Iberia. On the basis of sigillographical evidence Cheynet and Vannier, *Études prosopographiques*, 83–4, believe that Romanos' brother Theophylact may have been one of the earliest *katepanes* of Iberia, perhaps in 1021. Once again the chronology of this appointment cannot be solidly substantiated, although it is clear from seals which belonged to Theophylact that he served in this position at some point in his career; equally he also held the office of *katepano* of Vaspurakan (Cheynet, *Sceaux de la collection de Zacos (BN)*, no. 50).

[149] ἧς ἄρχειν ἀποσταλεὶς Βασίλειος πατρίκιος ὁ Ἀργυρὸς καὶ τοῖς ὅλοις πταίσας παραλύεται τῆς ἀρχῆς. καὶ διάδοχος αὐτοῦ πέμπεται Νικηφόρος πρ-

Despite his lack of specificity about the office exercised by Komnenos and Argyros, Skylitzes provides some useful clues about the nature of frontier command in this region of the Byzantine east, particularly when his testimony is aggregated with evidence from other historians. In the first instance, Skylitzes' observation about Komnenos' use of force to exert Byzantine rule as well as more peaceful methods demonstrates that military action was at the centre of a commander's responsibilities. This impression is confirmed by the Armenian historian Aristakes of Lastivert, who comments on the brigades of Cappadocian troops under Komnenos' command.[150] As the commander of a full-time garrison prepared to fight to impose Byzantine authority, Komnenos' role in Vaspurakan closely resembled that of commanders on the Antiochene frontier during the first half of Basil's reign, such as Michael Bourtzes and Damian Dalassenos.

ωτοσπαθάριος ὁ Κομνηνός, ὅς κατὰ χώραν γενόμενος καὶ τὰ μὲν πειθοῖ, τὰ δὲ βίᾳ χρώμενος ὑπήκοον τῷ βασιλεῖ τὴν χώραν ἐποίησεν (Skylitzes, *Synopsis*, 355).

[150] Aristakes, *Récit des malheurs*, 26–7; these Cappadocians were almost certainly soldiers recruited in central Asia Minor who were sent to the frontiers to serve with the *tagmata* of the empire's main field army. For the 11th-c. practice of raising of troops from the Anatolian themes to serve in *tagmata* see Kühn, *Die byzantinische Armee*, 251–7; J.-C. Cheynet, 'Du Stratège de thème au duc: Chronologie de l'évolution au cours du XI siècle', *TM* 9 (1985), 181–94. This is a practice usually dated to the mid-11th c. However, its incidence during Basil's reign may point to rather earlier origins. *Tagmata* troops from Anatolia were also to be found elsewhere on the empire's frontiers during Basil's reign. In the mid-990s John Chaldos served in Thessalonika as *doux* at the head of a garrison of troops recruited from the Asia Minor themes of the Armeniakon and Boukellarion (*Actes d'Iviron*, no. 8; for Chaldos and his troops, see discussion also below in 7.1 and 8.5).

Furthermore, Aristakes' evidence demonstrates the importance which military experience and authority within the army itself assumed in the deployment of commanders to the frontier. Just as these attributes were fundamental to the command exercised by Eustathios Maleinos and George Melias in Antioch and Cilicia during the reign of Nikephoros Phokas, so they underpinned the appointment of the eleventh-century *katepanes* of Vaspurakan. According to Aristakes, Komnenos was a brave and bellicose man. He had made himself famous by his 'courageous actions and boldness ... and had become renowned through all the east'.[151] Meanwhile, Basil Argyros was also a military figure with considerable experience in the field. At the beginning of the second decade of the eleventh century he was *strategos* of the maritime theme of Samos. While exercising this office he may also have been dispatched to deal with the revolt of Meles in southern Italy.[152] The frequency with which experienced veterans of the Balkan wars of Basil's reign, both Byzantine and Bulgarian, later held command in the Caucasian katepanates, indicates the degree to which military competence remained an essential quality for commanders on this stretch of the eastern frontier. For example, in 1034, Nicholas Chryselios served as *katepano* of Vaspurakan.[153] He was the member of a family of local notables who had surrendered Dyrrachion to Byzantine control during Basil's reign and had been rewarded with titles within the

---

[151] Aristakes, *Récit des malheurs*, 26–7.
[152] See above p. 190 n. 47.
[153] Skylitzes, *Synopsis*, 388; Felix, *Byzanz und die islamische Welt*, 123.

Byzantine hierarchy.[154] The military pedigree of the Chryselioi is demonstrated by the fact that an eleventh-century
member of the family became *domestikos* of the Optimatoi.[155] Although Nicholas was removed as *katepano* of Vaspurakan in 1035, his replacement was another Balkan war
veteran. This was Niketas Pegonites, who had led the Byzantine army in the battle outside Dyrrachion in 1018 at
which John Vladislav, the last Bulgarian tsar, had been
killed.[156] Other mid-eleventh-century *doukes/katepanes* of
Iberia and Vaspurakan included at least two of John Vladislav's sons, Aaron and Alousianos.[157]

However, while military pedigree was a prerequisite for
command in the Caucasian katepanates, it is clear that
martial experience alone did not guarantee a long career in
one location. Indeed, one of the most striking features of the
early history of the katepanate of Vaspurakan outlined above

[154] Skylitzes, *Synopsis*, 342–3; for further discussion of the surrender of
Dyrrachion see above 2.4 and below 8.5.

[155] Theodore Chryselios, *protospatharios*: Nesbitt and Oikonomides, *Byzantine Seals at Dumbarton Oaks*, iii. 71.12.

[156] Skylitzes, *Synopsis*, 357, 388; Grégoire, 'Du Nouveau sur l'histoire
bulgaro-byzantine', 289–91. The office held by Niketas in 1018 appears to
have been *strategos* of Dyrrachion.

[157] For Aaron as *katepano* of Vaspurakan see Skylitzes, *Synopsis*, 448–52;
Zacos, *Byzantine Lead Seals II*, no. 352; as *magistros* and *doux* of Ani and
Iberia, see Nesbitt and Oikonomides, *Byzantine Seals at Dumbarton Oaks*, iv.
75.1; Kühn, *Die byzantinische Armee*, 189–94. Alousianos was described by
Skylitzes as a *strategos* in Theodosioupolis in 1040 (Skylitzes, *Synopsis*, 413).
His location in the town of Theodosioupolis in the far north-east of Anatolia
indicates that he almost certainly held the position of *katepano* or *doux* of
Iberia. Theodosioupolis appears to have been the centre of the katepanate of
Iberia before the annexation of Ani in 1042. See above 4.2.1 for further
analysis of the role of the sons of John Vladislav within 11th-c. Byzantine
political society and administration.

is the rapid turnover in senior commanders, a characteristic already observed in other sections of the frontier during the first half of the reign of Basil. Yet, as the careers of Argyros, Komnenos, and Chryselios illustrate, a variety of factors propelled this high turnover. Basil Argyros was removed from office during the reign of Basil himself on the grounds of incompetence. Here we can detect clear echoes of the replacement of Michael Bourtzes at Antioch in 995. Incompetence was also the reason why Chryselios was dismissed in 1035. He was blamed for allowing the Lake Van city of Perkri, which had only recently come under Byzantine control, to fall once again into the hands of local Muslims.[158] Yet, the reason for the short duration of Komnenos' command at Vaspurakan was rather different. Nikephoros Komnenos was removed from office not by Basil, but instead by Constantine VIII, either in 1026 or early in 1027. The reason for Komnenos' dismissal was that he was accused of wishing to rule the East, and of allying with George, the king of Iberia and Abasgia, in an attempt to further his plans.[159] Thus, just as dismissals and appointments at Antioch and Mesopotamia during the second half of the tenth century had often been shaped by political tensions between generals on the frontier and the emperor in Constantinople, so in the short turbulent reign of Constantine VIII, distrust between centre and periphery also contributed to a high turnover in staff on the borderlands.

---

[158] Skylitzes, *Synopsis*, 388. Aristakes claims that Perkri was lost because the troops left to guard the city became drunk (Aristakes, *Récit des malheurs*, 36).

[159] Aristakes, *Récit des malheurs*, 26–7; Skylitzes, *Synopsis*, 371–2.

6.4   CIVIL ADMINISTRATION ON THE EASTERN FRONTIER: *c.*950–1050

Administration in all regions of the Byzantine Empire was not simply about the principles and logistics underpinning military defence and attack. Instead, imperial authority was also articulated in the localities through the provision of justice and the exploitation of resources. However, the question of the civil administration of the eastern frontier during the tenth and eleventh centuries has attracted much less interest among modern scholars than the structures of military organization on the periphery. Comment has usually been limited to reflections on the apparent lack of a civil bureaucracy in the easternmost regions of the empire, or to generalized assumptions that functionaries from the former regimes were absorbed within the superstructure of the Byzantine state.[160] Such a lack of interest is curious. For the second half of Basil's reign, and the reigns of many of his eleventh-century successors, peaceful conditions prevailed on the eastern frontier, particularly in regions bordering Muslim neighbouring powers. In these circumstances it might be expected that military matters assumed a relatively low administrative significance in comparison with other dimensions of local government, particularly the collection of taxation and the administration of justice.

---

[160] See e.g., Cheynet, Morrisson, and Seibt, *Sceaux byzantins: Henri Seyrig*, no. 120.

In the final section of this chapter I wish to look briefly at civil administration in the Byzantine east, in particular in those areas which had been wrested from Muslim control during the second and third quarters of the tenth century. On the basis of both literary and sigillographical evidence I will argue that governance in the east differed markedly from that in other areas of the empire where Byzantine administrative practices were more solidly entrenched. Instead of introducing alien administrative practices and practitioners into these newly conquered regions, imperial authorities were willing to acknowledge the logic that in regions where languages and customs were so different, substantial benefits in terms of security and fiscal revenue were most likely to occur with minimal administrative change. The administrative practices followed by imperial authorities in this period had the effect of establishing a quasi-tribute relationship between the heterodox populations of the periphery and Constantinople. Moreover, although this relationship was subject to tighter control by the imperial capital during the second half of Basil's reign, a principle of administrative devolution still pertained during this period and, indeed, during the decades which followed the emperor's death.

One sign that civil administration in the eastern frontier regions, especially in those areas that belonged to the former Muslim emirates, differed radically from contemporary bureaucratic structures in the heartland of the empire, is the paucity of extant lead seals which belonged to officials with judicial and fiscal responsibilities. For example, while there is much evidence, including a plethora of lead seals, to suggest that judges were a burgeoning administrative phenomenon in the themes of western and central Asia Minor in the later tenth and eleventh centuries, seals of judges (*kritai* or *praitores*) in the eastern borderlands are much less prolix. They are also much less conspicuous than those of their military counterparts, the *doukes/katepanes*.[161] Moreover, even when they do appear within the sigillographical record, it is clear that the authority of a single judge was very thinly spread over a vast geographical distance. Most of the surviving seals of judges belonged to officials whose authority coincided with one of the great katepanates such as Mesopotamia, Iberia, or Antioch or even with the former emirate of Melitene.[162] On occasion their authority could range even further, extending into neighbouring districts as well. Single judges could preside over joint themes in the interim area between the eastern plateau and the Anti Taurus such as Lykandos and Sebasteia, or Lykandos and

[161] For instance the Seyrig collection, which contains a large number of eastern seals, includes examples of seven *doukes/katepanes* of Antioch and only one of a *praitor* of the region (Cheynet, Morrisson, and Seibt, *Sceaux byzantins: Henri Seyrig*, nos. 156–62 and 163). There are no seals of Antiochene *kritai* in the collection. In contrast, for the ubiquity of judges in the administration of the core themes (provinces) of Byzantium in the later 10th and 11th c., see Ahrweiler, 'Recherches sur l'administration de l'empire byzantin', 46, 51–2, 68–9, 74; Oikonomides, 'L'Évolution de l'organisation administrative de l'empire byzantin', 148–9; C. Holmes, 'Basil II and the Government of Empire (976–1025)', D.Phil. Thesis (Oxford, 1999), 248–56.

[162] Melitene: Zacos, *Byzantine Lead Seals II*, no. 952; Mesopotamia: Nesbitt and Oikonomides, *Byzantine Seals at Dumbarton Oaks*, iv. 55.7; Konstantopoulos, *Molybdoboulla*, no. 155g; Antioch: Cheynet, Morrisson, and Seibt, *Sceaux byzantins: Henri Seyrig*, no. 163; Iberia: Zacos, *Byzantine Lead Seals II*, no. 387; Konstantopoulos, *Molybdoboulla*, no. 177a.

Melitene.[163] Equally the small border themes, sometimes known as *Armeniaka themata,* do not appear to have had their own judges. Instead, these areas were grouped together under the jurisdiction of a single judge.[164] Finally, the lack of seals of judges is mirrored by a more general paucity in eastern regions of seals belonging to other sorts of civilian officials which are so frequently found in themes in the Byzantine heartland. Very few seals have been found among the former emirates which pertain to officials concerned with fiscal lands (*epi ton oikeiakon*), or even with customs' receipts (*kommerkiarios*).[165]

---

[163] Zacos, *Byzantine Lead Seals II,* no. 803; Nesbitt and Oikonomides, *Byzantine Seals at Dumbarton Oaks,* iv. 53.5; Cheynet, *Sceaux de la collection de Zacos (BN),* no. 42. Ahrweiler has also observed the granting of two frontier regions to a single judge. She cites examples of the twinning of Melitene and Mesopotamia, Lykandos and Melitene, and Iberia and Mesopotamia; she also observes the more general phenomenon of a lack of judges in the east (Ahrweiler, 'Recherches sur l'administration de l'empire byzantin', 84–5).

[164] Schlumberger, *Sigillographie,* 296; Zacos, *Byzantine Lead Seals II,* no. 503; Nesbitt and Oikonomides, *Byzantine Seals at Dumbarton Oaks,* iv. 56.3–12; Cheynet, *Sceaux de la collection de Zacos (BN),* nos. 17–20.

[165] The seal of Autoreianos, *protonotarios* of the *oikeiakon,* was found at Adana in Cilicia (J.-C. Cheynet and C. Morrisson, 'Lieux de trouvaille et circulation des sceaux', in N. Oikonomides (ed.), *SBS* 2 (Washington DC, 1990), 124). Only three seals of *kommerkiarioi* in the east have been found, and all refer to Antioch: see Cheynet, 'Basil II and Asia Minor', 81–2, n. 40, for further references. For an analysis of the much greater increase in the activities of the office of the *epi ton oikeiakon* elsewhere in the empire during the later 10th and 11th c., see Oikonomides, 'L'Évolution de l'organisation administrative', 136–7; idem, 'Terres du fisc et revenu de la terre aux Xe et XIe siècles', in V. Kravari, J. Lefort, C. Morrisson (eds.), *Hommes et richesses,* 2 vols. (1989–91, Paris), ii. 321–2; Kaplan, *Les Hommes,* 321; J.-C.Cheynet, 'Épiskeptitai et autres gestionnaires de biens publics (d'après les sceaux de l'IFEB)', in W. Seibt (ed.), *SBS* 7 (Washington DC, 2002), 87–117. Evidence for the widespread incidence of *kommerkiarioi* in the long-established Anatolian and Balkan themes of the empire during the 10th and 11th c. can be found in all the

However, the general absence in the former emirates of lead seals belonging to officials usually associated with civilian administration in the Byzantine provinces, should not be taken as evidence of a lack of civilian administration in these eastern regions. Instead, when other sigillographical and literary materials are examined, it becomes clear that the civilian administration of the east was simply configured in different ways from that in longer established themes. Whereas areas like the west and centre of Asia Minor were becoming increasingly characterized in the tenth and eleventh centuries by the penetration of large numbers of civilian officials dispatched from the empire's capital city, the Constantinopolitan presence in the east was on a much smaller scale. This was because bureaucracy on the eastern frontier was more indirectly managed. Local administration, above all the collection of taxes, largely remained in indigenous hands and was articulated according to indigenous practices. These indigenous functionaries were then responsible to a thin tier of senior Byzantine officials appointed by the emperor in Constantinople. As a result, the centrally appointed official was more like a guarantor of tribute than the collector of fiscal dues or the manager of imperial assets.[166]

major collections of Byzantine seals. The author of the military manual 'Skirmishing', which was produced either during or shortly after the reign of Nikephoros Phokas (963–9), confirms that increasing numbers of civil officials sent from Constantinople were penetrating the inner themes of the empire during the 10th c. He alludes disparagingly to the appearance in Anatolia of 'tribute-levying mannikins who contribute absolutely nothing to the common good [but] . . . store up many talents of gold' ('Skirmishing', 109–11; trans. (adapted): Dennis, *Three Military Treatises*, 217).

[166] These were conclusions that I reached in the course of my doctoral research completed in 1999, and were ideas I presented in an article written in

The starting point for this hypothesis of a tribute-based form of local governance is a very particular phenomenon in the sigillographical record which has often been observed by historians, but only recently investigated in much greater detail by James Howard-Johnston. This phenomenon concerns the marked incidence of seals of one particular variety of civil official in many locations along the entire length of the eastern frontier, namely *kouratores* or *episkeptitai*.[167] Now, elsewhere in the empire these officials are usually identified with the direct management of crown estates,

2001: Holmes, ' "How the East was Won" ', 41–56. Around the same time Todt went to press quite independently with some very similar ideas, particularly concerning the katepanate of Antioch, in his 'Patriarchat von Antiocheia', also published in 2001. In what follows here I include references to Todt's work where it enhances or refines my own analysis.

[167] Oikonomides, 'L'Évolution de l'organisation administrative', 138; Kaplan, *Les Hommes*, 316–17; Howard-Johnston, 'Crown Lands', 75–100 especially 88 ff.; Cheynet, 'Épiskeptitai', 88–91, 98–116; Howard-Johnston's list of these officials from the eastern borderlands includes: *kouratores* from Melitene, Chaldia, Derxene, Rachais/Rachab, Hafdjidj (Chauzion), Artze, Taron, Manzikert and Inner Iberia, Tarsos, Antioch, Artach, Mesopotamia; *episkeptitai* from Seleukeia, Mesopotamia, Arabissos, Podandos, Abara, Rodandos, and Tephrike (Howard-Johnston, 'Crown Lands', 89–91, nn. 41–57). To this list should be added: John, *spatharokandidatos* and *kourator* of Antioch (Cheynet, 'Sceaux byzantins des musées d'Antioche et de Tarse', no. 47); Euthymios Karabitziotes, *exaktor, krites* of Hippodrome, Seleukeia and *kourator* and *anagrapheus* of Tarsos (Oikonomides, *SBS* 3, 192); John Hexamilites *krites* of Seleukeia and *kourator* of Tarsos (J. Nesbitt and M. Braunlin, 'Selections from a Private Collection of Byzantine Bullae', *B* 68 (1998), no. 13); Himerios Solomon, *megas kourator* of Antioch, Katotikos, *pronoetes* of the *megas kourator* of Antioch, and Epiphanios Katakalos, *episkeptites* of Rodandos (Cheynet, *Sceaux de la collection de Zacos (BN)*, nos. 8, 9, 43). The degree to which *kouratores* were an established part of the Byzantine administrative landscape in the Byzantine east by the end of Basil's reign is indicated by the fact that during the revolt of Nikephoros Phokas and Nikephoros Xiphias in 1022 four imperial *kouratores* were killed in these regions (Skylitzes, *Synopsis*, 367).

and indeed, historians seeking to explain the incidence of such seals in this more eastern context, including Howard-Johnston himself, have hitherto worked within this administrative paradigm. As a result, it has been widely assumed that these seals demonstrate that large areas of the eastern emirates, in particular those lands deserted by Muslims fleeing Byzantine conquest, were turned into imperial estates and directly managed for the crown in Constantinople.[168] Yet, there are reasons to doubt this interpretation. First, given the marked paucity of civilian officials in all other spheres of local government on the eastern frontier, it seems odd that the imperial authorities had the manpower to place such emphasis on a single and relatively specialized area of administration. Second, when the seals of these officials are set in the context of the historical texts which record the annexation of former Muslim emirates, it makes much more sense to see their owners as the guarantors of tribute rather than the managers of estates.

The strongest support for the idea that *kouratores* and analogous officials were the collectors of tribute comes from the only historical account to mention an eastern *kouratoria*. This is the description of the turning of Melitene into a *kouratoria* when the city was annexed by the Byzantines in 934. According to *Theophanes Continuatus*: 'They [the Byzantine army] reduced Melitene to such shortage, that they suddenly captured it, and razed it to the ground, and not only Melitene but also its neighbouring cities and districts which were highly productive and very fertile and <could>

---

[168] Kaplan, *Les Hommes*, 316; Howard-Johnston, 'Crown Lands', 91–2.

yield many other revenues. Having then turned Melitene into a *kouratoria*, the emperor had many thousands of [pounds?] of gold and silver raised annually in revenues from there.'[169] Here, the crucial term indicating that many of the *kouratoriai* of the Byzantine east were compatible with a tribute paradigm of local government, is the verb used for the raising revenues: δασμοφορεῖσθαι. The principal meaning of δασμός in Greek is that of tribute.[170]

Although no other literary source comments explicitly on the imperial *kouratoriai* in the Byzantine east, there is other unambiguous literary evidence that the payment of tribute was how the imperial authorities most readily conceived of the reward they could expect from the conquest of Muslim regions. This expectation is most clearly stated in the case of the Byzantine military manoeuvres which preceded the fall of Antioch in 969. In the autumn of 968 the hinterland of the city was softened up by a large raid. As the main imperial field army withdrew to Cappadocia in Anatolia for the winter, key forward-attack bases in the mountains and roads that surrounded the city of Antioch were fortified. From these bases Byzantine commanders were encouraged to raid the countryside around Antioch itself each day, thus persuading the inhabitants within the city to surrender. One

---

[169] εἰς τοσαύτην στένωσιν τὴν Μελιτινὴν περιέστησαν ὥστε αὐτὴν συντομώτατον ἐκπορθῆσαι καὶ ἕως ἐδάφους καταστρέψαι, οὐ μόνον δὲ ταύτην ἀλλὰ καὶ τὰς ὁμόρους αὐτῇ πόλεις καὶ χώρας πολυφόρους τε καὶ πιοτάτας οὔσας καὶ οἵας πολλὰς παρέχειν προσόδους. ταύτην οὖν τὴν Μελιτινὴν εἰς κουρατωρίαν ἀποκαταστήσας ὁ βασιλεὺς πολλὰς χιλιάδας χουσίου καὶ ἀργυρίου ἐκεῖθεν δασμοφορεῖσθαι ἐτησίως πεποίηκεν (*Theophanes Con.*, 416–17; Tinnefeld, 'Die Stadt Melitene', 436).

[170] H. G. Liddell and R. Scott (H. S. Jones and R. McKenzie), *A Greek-English Lexicon*, 2nd edn. (Oxford, 1968), 370.

such base was that at Baghras in the Amanos mountains, where Michael Bourtzes was left as *strategos* of the newly created theme of Mauron Oros. His instructions were to 'prevent the inhabitants of Antioch from coming out and collecting the supplies necessary for living', during the winter.[171] In a tribute-related context, Leo the Deacon's account of the strategic reasoning behind this attritional strategy is particularly striking. In a passage of direct speech, which Leo attributes to the emperor himself, Nikephoros Phokas is to be found arguing that the object of his military policy was to compel Antioch to become *tributary* (*hypospondos*) to the Byzantines.[172]

A tribute relationship between centre and locality in the civil administration of the eastern frontier also helps to explain the important but rather ambiguous position of officials described in the historical record as *basilikoi*. Whenever *basilikoi* are discussed by modern historians they are

---

[171] Yahya, *PO* 18, p. 816; Leo the Deacon, *Historiae Libri Decem*, 73–4. Skylitzes gives the name of the theme, Mauron Oros, although he wrongly locates it in the Taurus rather than the Amanos range, a mistake which some modern historians of Byzantium have copied (Skylitzes, *Synopsis*, 271–2; Ahrweiler, 'Recherches sur l'administration de l'empire byzantin', 46). Skylitzes suggests that the castle controlled by Bourtzes was built from scratch in 968. However, the Arab geographer, Ibn Hawkal, indicates that the site was already fortified before the period of Byzantine rule (Ibn Hawqal, *Configuration*, 182); Mauron Oros is also discussed above in 6.3.3.

[172] ὥστε καθ'ἑκάστην ἐπεξελάσεσι καὶ καταδρομαῖς, καὶ ἐπιτιτηδείων διαρπαγαῖς τὴν Ἀντιόχου ταπεινώσωσι, καὶ εἰς ἀμηχανίαν δεινὴν κατακλείσαντες καὶ ἄκουσαν ἀναγκάσωσι Ῥωμαίοις γενέσθαι ὑπόσπονδον ('so that with daily attacks and raids, they [the Byzantine troops] should lay Antioch low by depriving it of essential supplies; and having reduced the city to a state of desperate helplessness, they should compel it against its will to become tributary to the Romans') (Leo the Deacon, *Historiae Libri Decem*, 73–4; my trans.).

usually attributed with a general role in fiscal and judicial administration. Sometimes they are seen as analogous to *kouratores*. Yet their role is rarely discussed in detail, and it is widely assumed that they were lower-ranking functionaries subordinate to more senior officials such as the provincial *krites*.[173] However, the position of *basilikoi* on the eastern frontier in the aftermath of the tenth-century Byzantine conquests was of much greater significance than this modest definition implies. Instead, as the careers of two very famous *basilikoi* from the later tenth-century frontier demonstrate, these were the figures on whom the emperor in Constantinople, and even usurpers such as Bardas Skleros, had to depend in order to mobilize the resources of the great former emirates.

One of these *basilikoi* was Kouleïb,[174] whose career is predominantly known from the historical testimony of Yahya ibn Sa'id. He was a Christian Arab and servant of the Hamdanid regime at Aleppo, who surrendered the fortresses of Barzouyah and Saoune in northern Syria to John Tzimiskes in 975, during that emperor's last great eastern campaign. In return Tzimiskes gave him the senior title of *patrikios* and the office of *basilikos* of Antioch. During the Skleros revolt Kouleïb surrendered Antioch to the rebels,

---

[173] Ahrweiler, 'Recherches sur l'administration de l'empire byzantin' 73–4; J.-C. Cheynet, 'L'Apport arabe à l'aristocratie byzantine des Xe–XIe siècles', *Byz Slav* 61 (1995), 141–2; idem, 'Basil II and Asia Minor', 81–2, also discusses Kouleïb in this light.

[174] According to the spelling of Arabic names in *EI* (the system to which I have tried to adhere in a simplified fashion in this volume), the name Kouleïb should be rendered as Kulayb. However, since Kouleïb is the form used by the editors of Yahya ibn Sa'id's text, I have retained it.

and was appointed *basilikos* in Melitene instead. When Skleros fled to Baghdad in the aftermath of the failure of his revolt, Kouleïb did not go with him. Instead, he retained his position at Melitene. When Skleros returned to the empire from Baghdad in 987, nearly a decade later, Kouleïb still exercised authority in Melitene.[175]

However, it is when other evidence is aggregated with Yahya's testimony, that Kouleïb's role as a lynch-pin of eastern politics and diplomacy becomes particularly manifest. When the Buyid envoy Ibn Shahram travelled westwards from Baghdad to Constantinople in 981, as part of the long-running negotations between the empire and Adud al-Daula concerning the captivity in Iraq of Bardas Skleros, he met Bardas Phokas, the *domestikos* of the *scholai*, in the theme of the Charsianon in eastern Anatolia. Among the members of Phokas' party was Kouleïb. In his account of his meeting with Phokas, Ibn Shahram indicates that Kouleïb was the key intermediary between the imperial military high command in the east and Aleppo, the Hamdanid emirate in northern Syria which was a Byzantine client state. It was Kouleïb, for example, who was able to ensure the annual delivery of the tribute of Aleppo. As a result of these intermediary skills, he alone of Skleros supporters had received a pardon when the first Skleros revolt had collapsed in 979. Moreover, he had been allowed to keep the estates he had been granted by John Tzimiskes in 975.[176] Further signs that

---

[175] Yahya, *PO* 23, pp. 369, 373, 420; Laurent, 'Gouverneurs d'Antioche', 231.

[176] al-Rudhrawari, *Eclipse*, vi. 23–4; see Ch. 5 above for the first Skleros revolt.

Kouleïb was a high-profile figure in the frontier world who was well rewarded by authorities at the centre, can be detected in an early eleventh-century Syriac monastic chronicle from Melitene, which Michael the Syrian inserted into his history in the twelfth century. According to this contemporary chronicle, Kouleïb, who was also known by his Greek name and title Eutychios the *patrikios*, sponsored the monastery of Bar Gagai near Melitene in 987/8.[177] It is even possible that Kouleïb and his family were so important to relations between the centre, the periphery, and the emirates beyond the empire's eastern border, that they survived the turmoil of the second phase of Skleros' insurrection (987–9) and continued in the service of the Byzantine state after 989. The Zacos Collection contains a seal belonging to Bardas, the son of Kouleïb.[178]

Another *basilikos* of critical political importance at the start of Basil's reign was Obeïdallah, another Arab Christian.[179] In 976 he was *basilikos* of Melitene. By surrendering

[177] Michael the Syrian, *Chronique*, 125–6; the date 987/8 is that provided by Michael the Syrian's account. However, according to the much later testimony of the 13th-c. historian Bar Hebraeus (who used Michael the Syrian as one of his sources), Kouleïb supported Bar Gagai a decade earlier in 977/8. Given that Michael is the more contemporary source, his is probably the account to be accepted. Bar Gagai rapidly became a great centre of Syriac learning. A manuscript from the monastery dated to 994 is to be found at the monastery of Saint Mark in Jerusalem. Another manuscript, now found at Mosul, was copied at Bar Gagai in 1013 (Dagron, 'Minorités ethniques', 192, 197).

[178] Zacos, *Byzantine Lead Seals II*, no. 371; Cheynet, 'Du Prénom au patronyme', 60–2; Guilland, *Recherches*, 288.

[179] According to the spelling of Arabic names in *EI* the name Obeïdallah should be rendered as Ubayd Allah. However, since Obeïdallah is the form used by the editors of Yahya ibn Sa'id's text, I have retained it.

the city to the rebel forces of Bardas Skleros, he enabled Skleros to sequester the fiscal revenues of the former emirate, and openly declare revolt against the emperor. Still in the service of Skleros, Oubeïdallah became Kouleïb's successor as *basilikos* of Antioch.[180] Basil II was only able to regain Antioch for the imperial side in 977/8 by promising Oubeïdallah the position of 'governor' for life.[181] Yahya ibn Sa'id's account of Oubeïdallah's actions during the civil war at Antioch make it clear that the *basilikos* exercised not only civilian responsibilities, but even some degree of military power. For example, once he had defected to the emperor, Oubeïdallah defended Antioch against armed attack by two senior Skleros lieutenants: Sachakios Brachamios and Ibn Baghil. Furthermore, he suppressed a revolt by local Armenians. Although Yahya ibn Sa'id claims that the citizens of the city were his chief source of political support, Oubeïdallah's ability to beat off attack by leading Skleros commanders such as Brachamios indicates he must also have had some authority over an armed garrison.[182]

Yet, while Kouleïb and Oubeïdallahs' authority as *basilikoi* may have been heightened by the exigencies of civil war, the very broad nature of their jurisdiction is echoed in the responsibilities of other *basilikoi* who exercised power in the former emirates, but who are only known through the sigillographical record. At least three such seals are extant: Chosnis, *basilikos* of Tarsos; John, *krites* of the central Con-

---

[180] Yahya, *PO* 23, p. 373.
[181] Ibid., pp. 375–7; the term used by Yahya to denote governor is the Arabic *wilaya*; Laurent, 'Gouverneurs d'Antioche', 231–2.
[182] Yahya, *PO* 23, p. 378.

stantinopolitan court of the Hippodrome, *basilikos* of Melitene and the *Armeniaka themata*; and Solomon, *basilikos* of
Melitene, and *megas chartoularios* of the main Constantinopolitan tax-collecting bureau of the *Genikon*.[183] The wide
range of responsibilities exercised by the last two examples,
John and Solomon, demonstrate the judicial and fiscal authority of *basilikoi*, competences which as we have seen were
practised by Oubeïdallah and Kouleïb. However, it is worth
noting the Constantinopolitan affiliations of the other judicial and fiscal offices held by these eleventh-century *basilikoi*,
a connection that was absent from the careers of *basilikoi*
active in the tenth century such as Kouleïb or Oubeïdallah.
This development suggests that greater political stability
within the empire itself, and peaceful relations with the
eastern neighbours during the eleventh century, meant
that the key intermediary functionaries on the eastern frontier could increasingly be drawn from Constantinople, rather than from former Hamdanid servants or other local
notables.[184]

A brief examination of the ecclesiastical and secular history of northern Syria and Cilicia indicates that the greater
use of Constantinopolitan officials in the exercise of intermediate power on the eastern frontier almost certainly
began in the last decade of the tenth century, during the

---

[183] Zacos, *Byzantine Lead Seals II*, no. 108 (Chosnis); Nesbitt and Oikonomides, *Byzantine Seals at Dumbarton Oaks*, iv. 56.2 (John), 68.1 (Solomon).

[184] A conclusion also reached by Todt, 'Patriarchat von Antiocheia', 249–
50, on the basis of wide-ranging investigation into the sigillographical record
of Antioch and Tarsos.

reign of Basil II himself. Central to an understanding of this change is the career of Agapios, the later tenth-century patriarch of Antioch, another key figure on the frontier whose authority originally sprang from his ability to mediate between imperial authority in Constantinople and the local populations of the Byzantine east. Agapios' rise to power began during the first Skleros revolt with the death of the incumbent patriarch of Antioch, Theodore, in May 976. Motivated by opportunism Agapios, the bishop of Aleppo, travelled to Constantinople to persuade the emperor to appoint him as Theodore's replacement. In return he promised to persuade Oubeïdallah, the rebel *basilikos* of Antioch, to declare for the emperor.[185] Despite Agapios' relatively junior status as bishop of Aleppo, Basil and his advisors were so desperate to regain political control of Antioch that they agreed to this plan.[186] Agapios returned to Antioch, entering the city secretly. He came to terms with Oubeïdallah, and was installed as patriarch in January 978.[187] During the next decade he used the authority he had been granted by Constantinople to secure his own position in the locality. At the heart of Agapios' policy was the promotion of the Antiochene Melkite church at the expense of the local Syrian Monophysite Church. According to later Syrian historians, Agapios burnt the books of Syrian

---

[185] Yahya, *PO* 23, pp. 375–6; the careers of Theodore and Agapios are discussed by Todt, 'Patriarchat von Antiocheia, 258–9.

[186] Eli, the Chalcedonian patriarch of Alexandria, consistently refused to recognize Agapios as patriarch of Antioch on the grounds that he was far too junior to have been granted such a lofty position (Yahya, *PO* 23, pp. 378–89).

[187] Yahya, *PO* 23, p. 377.

churches, forced local notables to have their children rebaptized as Chalcedonians, and then deployed these converts as local clergy in rural northern Syria.[188]

However, Agapios' power as a mediator between locality and centre, living on the periphery of the Byzantine Empire, was short-lived. Twelve years later in the aftermath of the Phokas revolt, Basil II decided to extricate himself from dependence on local figures such as Agapios. Accused of colluding with the Phokas family, Agapios was summoned to Constantinople and secluded in a suburban monastery.[189] As the emperor's authority strengthened during the 990s, he began to extend his authority even more energetically into the localities. In 996 Agapios was officially deposed. His replacement was a Constantinopolitan, John the *chartophylax* of the Hagia Sophia.[190] Soon John was joined in the east by other Constantinopolitan officials, including his friends and correspondents, Philetos Synadenos, *krites* of Tarsos, and most famous of all, the supreme military commander in the east, Nikephoros Ouranos.[191]

As we saw earlier in this chapter, Ouranos arrived in Antioch in 1000–1 as, 'the one who rules the east', with plenipotentiary powers over the whole eastern frontier. At the most basic of levels this was a military position. Yet, in other respects, Ouranos' appointment as plenipotentiary represented an imperial desire to use a Constantinopolitan

---

[188] Michael the Syrian, *Chronique*, 131–2.

[189] Yahya, *PO* 23, p. 428.

[190] Ibid., pp. 445–6; Todt, 'Patriarchat von Antiocheia', 259.

[191] For letters exchanged between John, Nikephoros and Philetos, see Darrouzès, *Épistoliers byzantins, passim.*

official to fulfil the intermediary position previous occupied by local functionaries such as the *basilikoi* Kouleïb and Oubeïdallah. Certainly Ouranos was ideally suited to such a wide-ranging role. In addition to his impressive military pedigree, Ouranos was also able to call upon extensive experience in administrative and diplomatic affairs, competences that had been fundamental to the authority of Kouleïb and Oubeïdallah. Ouranos' early professional life had been spent in Constantinople within the imperial palace and the upper echelons of central administration. By 982 he was keeper of the imperial inkstand, a position which required him to become competent in the handling of sophisticated documents including imperial chrysobulls.[192] His knowledge of the administrative practices and court politics of Constantinople was so well regarded that at some point during the mid- to later 980s, while he was still keeper of the imperial inkstand, he was appointed *epitropos,* or lay guardian, of the Athonite monastery of the Lavra.[193] In the exercise of this responsibility Ouranos must have gained valuable experience in acting as an intermediary between

[192] Several of Nikephoros' own letters seem to date from the period when he was still keeper of the imperial inkstand (Ouranos: letters 3–6; V. Laurent, *Le Corpus des sceaux de l'empire byzantin,* ii. *L'Administration centrale* (Paris, 1981), 102). In his letter to Anastasios, the metropolitan of Laodikeia, he displays his familiarity with the handling of imperial chrysobulls (Ouranos: letter 3). He asks the metropolitan to submit all the chrysobulls of the see for his perusal. It is possible that a seal of Nikephoros, *anthypatos, patrikios* and *epi tou kanikleiou,* may have belonged to Ouranos (Zacos, *Byzantine Lead Seals II,* no. 861).

[193] Ouranos' appointment must post-date 984 and pre-date 999 (*Actes de Lavra,* 19–20, 45–6, 52, and no. 31; McGeer, 'Tradition and Reality', 130–1; see also below p. 477).

the interests of a locality and central government. Moreover, his early career also brought him into contact with the machinations of high politics and diplomacy with Byzantium's eastern neighbours. During the early 980s, he was involved in the intense diplomatic negotiations with the Buyids that surrounded the exile of Bardas Skleros in Baghdad. He became a close acquaintance of the Buyid envoy Ibn Shahram during the latter's mission to Constantinople over the winter of 981/2. When Ibn Shahram returned to Baghdad, Ouranos travelled with him as the Byzantine ambassador to the court of Adud al-Daula. On this occasion he may have been vested with plentipotentiary powers.[194] Shortly after his arrival in the Buyid capital, Adud al-Daula died, and Ouranos found himself, like Skleros, confined to prison.[195] He was eventually released early in 987, the date when Skleros himself returned to the empire.[196] However, even these relatively barren years may not have been wasted. As a result of his friendship with Ibn Shahram and his captivity in Iraq, it is possible that he even learnt some rudimentary Arabic. All these skills would have stood him in good stead for his plenipotentiary role on the frontier in the first decade of the eleventh century.

Moreover, there is clear evidence from both contemporary seals and letters that Ouranos may not have been the only official from the capital drafted into a frontier role that

[194] As Farag has pointed out, Ibn Shahram requested that Ouranos be sent to Baghdad with full negotiating powers (Farag, 'Byzantium and its Muslim Neighbours', 94–5).

[195] al-Rudhrawari, *Eclipse*, vi. 25–34; Skylitzes, *Synopsis*, 327; Yahya, *PO* 23, pp. 400–2.

[196] Yahya, *PO* 23, p. 420.

demanded a full portfolio of competences. After Ouranos was posted to Antioch, he summoned Philetos Synadenos to Tarsos.[197] Although *krites* of Tarsos is the office attributed to Synadenos in the later eleventh-/early twelfth-century manuscript in which copies of his letters appear, the responsibilities he undertook when he arrived in the east may have extended more widely than those of a judge.[198] If, for example, Synadenos held the same offices indicated on the seals of many other senior officials at Tarsos in the tenth and eleventh centuries, then it is likely that his real responsibilities were as *krites* of Seleukeia and *kourator* of Tarsos.[199] Moreover, it is possible that he was the owner of a seal belonging to Philaretos, *Krites* of the East, *Exaktor,* and *Illoustrios.*[200] Much like the office of *krites,* the office of *exaktor* was concerned with

---

[197] 'Ouranios [the heavenly one] made me come' (Synadenos: letter 11). The exact date of Philetos' arrival in Tarsos is uncertain. But he must have been in the east by 1007 since he wrote to Ouranos congratulating him on his victory over al-Acfar in this year.

[198] Synadenos' letters appear in manuscript 706 from the monastery of Saint John on Patmos (Darrouzès, *Épistoliers byzantins*, 9–12); for further discussion of the career and responsibilities of Philetos Synadenos, see Todt, 'Patriarchat von Antiocheia', 249–50.

[199] Eustathios Romaios, *krites* of Seleukeia and *megas kourator* of Tarsos (Konstantopoulos, *Molybdoboulla,* no. 147a); Nicholas Serblias, *krites* and *megas kourator* of Tarsos and Seleukeia (Cheynet, *Sceaux de la collection de Zacos (BN),* no. 44) see above, p. 373 n. 167 for Euthymios Karabitziotes *exaktor, krites* of the Hippodrome and Seleukeia, and *kourator* and *anagrapheus* of Tarsos and John Hexamilities, *krites* of Seleukeia, and *kourator* of Tarsos.

[200] Nesbitt and Oikonomides, *Byzantine Seals at Dumbarton Oaks,* iii. 86.34. The editors believe that the owner of the seal was merely the *krites* of the theme of the Anatolikon on the grounds that the responsibilities of a single judge could not have extended over an area as great as the East. However, as this chapter has demonstrated, individuals in both military and civilian offices in the easternmost regions of the Byzantine empire customarily exercised authority over very large regions indeed.

both the provision of justice and the exercise of fiscal responsibility. As both a *krites* and *exaktor*, the owner of this seal clearly exercised a host of judicial and financial competences over a wide geographical area, a formula typical of administration on the eastern frontier. Furthermore, while it is dangerous to read substantive meanings into the elusive literary artefacts which passed between senior officials such as Synadenos and Ouranos, it is possible that an elliptical allusion to the incompatibility of learning and the bearing of arms contained in one of Synadenos' letters to Nikephoros, may reflect the wide range of duties, including military service, that officials on the frontier were expected to undertake in imperial service. If this is so, Philetos implies Ouranos was better equipped than himself:

On the one hand I have lost the capacity to be wise and to be called wise, and on the other, I am completely inexperienced in the bearing of arms, the rattling of a spear, the drawing and firing of an arrow, and the brandishing of a spear against the enemy, and as much as is required to make war against the foe—for I am not hardhearted or very daring, but someone undaring and feeble—I have failed at both: for I am now neither wise nor daring in the face of the enemy. And so tell me who I am, wise *Strategos*. As for me, what I had I have thrown away, what I had not, I am unable to take hold of, and that which I am, as you see, I have lost.[201]

It is clear from Philetos' self-pitying statement that officials appointed to act as intermediaries on the frontier experienced a profound sense of frustration and bewilderment at the panoply of commitments which greeted them on their

---

[201] Synadenos: letter 8.

arrival from Constantinople. Yet, paradoxically, their trauma is also very strong evidence of the relatively limited nature of the administrative changes set in train by Basil II during the second half of his reign. For while it is true that officials such as Ouranos and Synadenos represented a new Constantinopolitan presence in the locality, nonetheless by acting as intermediate plenipotentiaries they continued to exercise the same role once fulfilled by local notables such as Kouleïb and Oubeïdallah. While the appointment of such Constantinopolitan figures indicates that the role of inter-mediary was subject to greater control from the centre after 1000, there is little sign that their presence represented a profound shift in the governance of the locality at an every-day level. There is no evidence, for example, to suggest that during the second half of the reign of Basil there was any change in the basic tribute relationship between locality and centre. Instead, during the eleventh century, eastern regions continue to be characterized by the lack of seals of civilian officials found elsewhere in the empire.

This trend within the sigillographical data militates against the possibility that new fiscal and judicial adminis-trative structures and practices were imposed on the frontier region, or that large numbers of officials from the capital began to arrive in the east to take up junior positions within provincial bureaucracy. Instead, it seems more likely that underneath a thin tier of centrally appointed officials such as Ouranos and Synadenos, the quotidian management of the frontier remained in the hands of indigenous officials. More investigation into the sigillographical record is needed, par-ticularly into surviving bilingual seals (Greek/Armenian,

Greek/Syriac, Greek/Arabic, Greek/Georgian), if this conclusion is to be substantiated. However, as Todt has recently
pointed out, shortly after Basil's reign ended, in 1034, the
inhabitants of Antioch rebelled against the *katepano* of Antioch and one of his tax officials: that official, according to
Skylitzes, was called Salibas, an individual whom Todt suggests was probably an Arab-speaking Melkite Christian from
Antioch.[202]

Any understanding of the administration of the Byzantine
eastern frontier during the reign of Basil II must, through
paucity of evidence, particularly outside Antioch, remain
hazy and incomplete. However, this chapter has pointed to
some very general and provisional principles of frontier
governance.

As far as the military administration of the frontier is
concerned, case studies of the region's *doukes* and *katepanes*
suggest that military command before, during, and after
Basil's reign was always very flexible. Apart from in Chaldia,
no military officer on the frontier can be identified as a *doux*
or a *katepano* before the death of John Tzimiskes in 975. The
earliest identification of such officials outside Chaldia occurs in the first year of Basil's reign in the shape of Michael
Bourtzes and Bardas Skleros, *doux* of Antioch and Mesopotamia respectively. However, as *doukes*, commanders like
Skleros and Bourtzes were military leaders of mobile units
of field army troops conducting warfare against the empire's

---

[202] Todt, 'Patriarchat von Antiocheia', 255; see also Skylitzes, *Synopsis*,
395–6.

eastern adversaries, rather than governors of clearly defined geographical regions. The military context to many appointments meant that commands were customarily arranged on an ad hoc basis, with senior officers often exercising authority over more than one geographical area. On occasion the senior commander in the east could be invested with plenipotentiary powers. This was most likely to happen when the military energies of the empire were concentrated on warfare in the Balkans. In the first half of the reign, the interplay of internal and external political pressures dictated a swift turnover in staff. Very little is known about the organization of any of the katepanates in the middle decades of the reign. In the northern and central sections of the frontier, the Byzantine military presence may have been light, with the exigencies of military security left in the hands of neighbouring potentates. Before 1000 the empire's chief custodian in this region was David of Tao; after 1000 the Marwanids. Further south peace with the Fatimids in 1000–1 brought more stability to the organization of the eastern frontier, particularly in the office of *doux/katepano* of Antioch. The origins of the katepanates of Iberia and Vaspurakan are very unclear. Nonetheless, some of the features of their early histories display striking parallels with developments elsewhere on the eastern frontier in earlier periods.

In the case of civil governance, Byzantium's relationship with its eastern territories was consistently typified by a tribute relationship between centre and locality. At the beginning of Basil's reign the vital intermediary representatives of the centre were often local notables or employees of

Muslim regimes recently replaced by Byzantine authority. However, by 1000 senior intermediaries were more usually nominees dispatched by Constantinople. Yet, the indirect, tribute-paying relationship over which they presided remained essentially unaltered from arrangements first established in the tenth century. Successive tenth- and eleventh-century emperors, including Basil II himself, acknowledged the logic that in order to govern the eastern localities cost-effectively, it was essential to utilize local officials.[203]

[203] A conclusion which accords closely with the thesis of indirect frontier governance recently propounded by J.-C. Cheynet, 'Les Limites du pouvoir à Byzance: Une forme de tolerance?' in *Toleration and Repression in the Middle Ages. In Memory of Lenos Mavromatis* (Athens, 2002), 17–28.

7

Administration and Imperial Authority on Byzantium's Western Frontiers

The last chapter of this book looked in some detail at the administration of Byzantium's eastern frontier before, during, and after the reign of Basil II. Case studies of the region's katepanates (also known as doukates) suggested that the military administration of the frontier was always highly flexible and responsive to internal and external political pressures. In the case of civil governance the relationship between Constantinople and the eastern frontier was structured around the payment of tribute. In both military and civil administration these broad conclusions remain true for the whole of the reign, although after 1000 frontier governance appears to have become increasingly stable and subject to greater control by the emperor in Constantinople. Yet, while that control became greater, it continued to be predicated on indirect methods of rule in which local official and neighbouring potentates often had an important part to play.

In this chapter I want to ask whether the eastern experience is any way similar to that on two other frontier areas during Basil's reign. Above all, I want to establish whether all Byzantine borderlands in this period were characterized by similar principles of flexible civil and military governance, or whether the individual strategic, economic, and demographic environments provoked very different administrative responses in each borderland. In examining these questions, I will compare the eastern frontier with, on the one hand, the northern and western Balkans, areas where the Byzantines encountered an aggressive Bulgarian state; and on the other hand, with southern Italy, where the empire came face to face with local Lombard princes as well as encountering more distant neighbours, such as the Ottonians emperors of Germany and northern Italy, and the Muslim rulers of the Maghreb. Both frontier areas, while not as rich in historiographical materials as the eastern borderlands, are still reasonably well represented in the extant medieval historical narratives; both also have strong sigillographical records. In looking at these regions I will be relying heavily on the research of other scholars, particularly those detailed analyses of local Byzantine governance developed by Paul Stephenson (for the Balkans), and Vera von Falkenhausen and Jean-Marie Martin (for Italy). My ambition is principally comparative: to see how my own conclusions about Byzantine governance on the eastern frontier compare with models of frontier administration uncovered elsewhere. However, in the course of this comparison I will also try to demonstrate how the very peculiar historiography of Basil's reign supports, refines, and challenges established pictures of frontier governance. In particular, I want to demonstrate how Skylitzes' methods and preoccupations as a historian (outlined in earlier chapters of this book) shape our apprehension of the governance of the Balkans and Italy.

7.1 THE BALKANS

At the outset of this discussion it is important to stress the degree to which any understanding of the Balkan frontier is conditioned by the nature of the surviving evidence. In an impressive number of recent publications, which synthesize and discuss both primary sources as well as scattered and relatively ill-known secondary literature about the Balkan region in the tenth to twelfth centuries, Paul Stephenson has conclusively demonstrated that the historian of Byzantium's Balkan frontier can call upon a wealth of material evidence, including seals, coins, and archaeological remains, to reconstruct the political, administrative, and military history of this area.[1] Nonetheless, while the evidence Stephenson uses

---

[1] See for the 10th- and 11th-c. period Stephenson, *Byzantium's Balkan Frontier*, chs. 2–4 which builds on his Ph.D. thesis 'The Byzantine Frontier in the Balkans in the Eleventh and Twelfth Centuries' (Cambridge, 1995). For further and more detailed exposition see Stephenson's 'Byzantine Policy towards Paristrion in the Mid-Eleventh Century: Another Interpretation', *BMGS* 23 (1999), 43–66; idem, 'The Byzantine Frontier at the Lower Danube in the Late Tenth and Eleventh Century', in D. Power and N. Standen (eds.), *Frontiers in Question: Eurasian Borderlands, 700–1700* (Basingstoke and London, 1999), 80–104; idem, 'The Byzantine Frontier in Macedonia', *Dialogos* 7 (2000), 23–40. Stephenson examines the evidence base for Basil's reign closely in his 'The Balkan Frontier in the Year 1000', 109–33, and most recently in *Legend of Basil the Bulgar-Slayer*, chs. 2–3.

is extremely exciting and likely to provide a host of new questions as well as answers to the mysteries of Balkan history in the tenth and eleventh centuries, it is important to be aware before setting out of some of the problems involved in interpreting the material record.

Most of these problems arise, paradoxically, not from the material record itself, but from difficulties associated with the extant narrative texts: that is to say from John Skylitzes' confused history of Byzantine relations with the Balkans; the much later *History of the Priest of Diokleia*; and a handful of anecdotes about relations between various Byzantine and Bulgarian commanders in Basil's wars which crop up in Kekaumenos' *Consilia et Narrationes*.[2] One particularly important problem is the fragmented nature of these texts, a characteristic which makes it extremely difficult to establish a reliable chronology against which the material evidence, much of which is itself undated, can be interpreted. None of the surviving narratives provide the kind of sustained narrative backbone that the detailed account of Yahya ibn Sa'id offers for the Antiochene sector of the eastern frontier. As we have seen in the previous chapter, it is this solid chronology, emanating from a reliable medieval narrative, which facilitates a more rounded interpretation of other varieties of evidence, many of which are often difficult to date, such as seals and inscriptions.[3] In contrast, the Balkan narratives only offer a series of occasional snapshots during the complex wars between Basil and his Bulgarian adversaries.

---

[2] See above 1.2.2 for a brief analysis of these narrative texts.
[3] See esp. above 6.3.3.

Another important point is the relatively narrow geographical focus of many of the narrative texts which report on the Balkans: they reveal more, for example, about the frontier in western Macedonia than about Byzantium's relations with eastern Bulgaria and the Middle Danube regions. Of course, all is not lost, for while the Balkan historiographical base is less secure than that from the eastern half of the empire, the historian of the Balkan frontier does have recourse to other sources of written evidence. Particularly important in this regard is a small reservoir of documents from the Athonite monasteries which often refer to the activities of local imperial officials. Although the focus of these archives on the region around Thessalonika means that once again more can be said about Macedonia than about the rest of the Byzantine Balkans, nonetheless, when used in combination with the extant sigillographical record and anecdotal narratives, these documents offer some glimpses of how borderland governance worked on the ground.

Bearing in mind the difficulties with the source materials outlined above, I have attempted in this chapter a sketch of Byzantium's administration on its Balkan frontier during the later tenth and early eleventh centuries. We will begin, as in the previous chapter, with the *Escorial Taktikon*, that list of imperial precedence compiled in the early 970s, which within its presentation of the empire's official hierarchy registers the most important of Byzantium's frontier commands. As we have seen, in the east of the empire it records *doukes* for the border regions of Chaldia, Mesopotamia, and Antioch; turning to the Balkans it mentions *doukes* for Thessalonika and Adrianople, those towns commanding

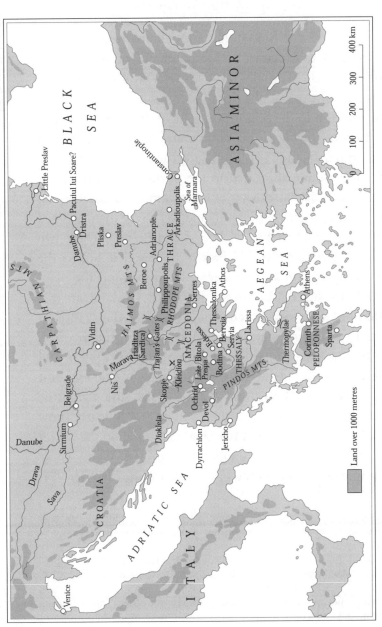

MAP 3.   The Balkans c.971–1025. Drawn by the author from: D. Obolensky, *The Byzantine Commonwealth: Eastern Europe, 500–1453* (London, 1971); M. Whittow, *The Making of Orthodox Byzantium, 600–1025* (London, 1996); P. Stephenson, *Byzantium's Balkan Frontier* (Cambridge, 2000).

BLACK SEA

Little Preslav
Păcuiul lui Soare?
Danube
Dristra
Pliska
Preslav

CARPATHIAN MTS

Vidin

HAIMOS MTS

Beroe
Adrianople
THRACE
Arkadioupolis
Constantinople
Sea of Marmara

Morava
Niš
Serdica (Sardica)
Trajan's Gates
Skopje
×Kleidion
Ohrid
Devol
Prespa
Lake Bitola
Bodina
Essa
Berroia
Servia
THESSALY
Larissa

Philippoupolis
RHODOPE MTS
MACEDONIA
Serres
Athos
Thessalonika

ASIA MINOR

AEGEAN SEA

PINDOS MTS

Thermopylae

Corinth
PELOPONNESE
Sparta
Athens

Belgrade
Sirmium
Danube
Drava
Sava
CROATIA

Diokleia
Dyrrachion
Jericho
ADRIATIC SEA
ITALY
Venice

Land over 1000 metres

0   100   200   300   400 km

the hinterlands of Macedonia and Thrace respectively; it also records a *katepano* of Mesopotamia of the West, a position which is usually taken to refer to a command in the region of the Danube delta.[4]

In addition to the senior positions of *doux* and *katepano*, the *Escorial Taktikon* also enumerates several *strategoi* of small border themes.[5] These include the themes of Strymon and Drougoubiteia, located to the north of the important eastern Macedonian towns of Thessalonika and Serres respectively. Further to the south and west were themes based around the fortified sites of Edessa and Berroia. These two fortresses guarded the complex of routes that linked the plain of Thessalonika in eastern Macedonia and the plain of Thessaly in central Greece with that lakeland area of western Macedonia, which would become the centre of Samuel's Bulgarian state. Meanwhile, the *Escorial Taktikon* also lists several *strategoi* with commands in central and eastern Bulgaria, including the officials who enjoyed joint command over Thrace and Ioannoupolis (the Byzantine name for Preslav), Beroe, a theme in central Bulgaria (now Stara Zagora), and at least two themes located on the Lower Danube, Dristra and Mesopotamia of the West. These themes seem to have come into existence shortly after 971,

---

[4] Oikonomides, *Listes*, 262–9; idem, 'Recherches sur l'histoire du Bas-Danube au Xe–XIIe siècles: Mésopotamie d'Occident,' *RESEE* 3 (1965), 57–79; see Map 3 for place names.

[5] For all these small themes, see Oikonomides, *Listes*, 264–7, 355–63; see also Ahrweiler, 'Recherches sur l'administration de l'empire byzantin', 47–8, for other evidence apart from the *Escorial Taktikon* which supports the model of small themes appearing on the Balkan as well as the eastern frontier during the later 10th and 11th c.

the year when John Tzimiskes (969–76), Basil's imperial predecessor, had invaded eastern Bulgaria and taken Preslav, the capital city of the Bulgarians, which had been built by the great ninth- and early tenth-century tsars of Bulgaria, Boris and Symeon. In taking Preslav Tzimiskes captured the last tsar of the Bulgarians, another Boris, who was later paraded in victory through the streets of Constantinople along with his imperial regalia. Tzimiskes then moved northwards to the Lower Danube to expel a rogue Rus army which had originally been invited by the Byzantines to attack the Bulgarians but which had reneged on the original settlement and now seemed eager to settle permanently in the western Black Sea region. The result of this campaign was that Tzimiskes destroyed the Bulgarian empire based around Preslav.[6] Finally to complete this list of small themes in the Balkans recorded by the *Escorial Taktikon*, one should head much further west and add Jericho, which was located south of Byzantium's key listening point on the Adriatic, Dyrrachion, which had itself been a theme since the mid-ninth century.

Nonetheless, just as was the case in the east, behind the apparently straightforward information in the *Escorial Taktikon* existed a much more complex frontier world. This becomes apparent when alternative sources of written and material evidence are considered. Using a cache of seals discovered at Preslav, Paul Stephenson has suggested that the early administration of those regions of eastern Bulgaria

---

[6] For the narrative of Tzimiskes' conquest see in the first instance Stephenson, *Byzantium's Balkan Frontier*, 47–55.

conquered by John Tzimiskes in 971 was extremely fluid. During Tzimiskes' reign official commands held by individuals such as Leo Sarakenopoulos constantly mutated. Sometimes Ioannoupolis and the more long-established Byzantine administrative zone of Thrace were held as a joint command, with a separate *strategos* located at Dristra (renamed Theodoroupolis by Tzimiskes); on other occasions the same individual exercised authority over both Ioannoupolis and Dristra, or over Thrace and Dristra. This period of initial conquest was also marked by a rapid turnover in officials. Both these phenomena, of joint command and rapid turnover, have striking parallels with initial periods of rule on newly conquered frontiers in the east. However, what Stephenson also shows is that while there was considerable flexibility in the delegation of command, there was considerable solidity in the physical demarcation and protection of the Byzantines' new territories. Coin finds from a variety of sites on the Lower Danube indicate that a series of positions were fortified to protect the Mysian plain between the river and the Haimos Mountains from Rus attack. The most impressive of these sites was the naval base on the island of Pacuiul lui Soare.[7]

As he moves from the reign of Tzimiskes to that of Basil, Stephenson makes a determined effort to tease a plausible

---

[7] Stephenson, *Byzantium's Balkan Frontier*, 55–8; although see the comments by P. Doimi de Frankopan about the difficulty of being sure of the dates when Leo Sarakenopoulos held office (Doimi de Frankopan, 'Workings of the Byzantine Provincial Administration', 88–9). For more on the cache of seals see I. Jordanov, *Pechatite ot strategiiata v Preslav, 971–1088* (Sofia, 1993). For parallels between the east and the Balkans in the matter of high office turnover see above 6.3.

chronology of administrative developments out of the material evidence from eastern Bulgaria, that is to say, from coins, seals, and archaeological remains.[8] However, the difficulties he encounters indicate just how hard it is to track from material evidence alone the timetable of the consolidation of Byzantine power in the region under Tzimiskes, the collapse of Byzantine authority in eastern Bulgaria in the early years of Basil's reign, and the rise of the new Bulgarian empire of Samuel Kometopoulos in western Macedonia. At the root of the problem is the confused narrative of Skylitzes' *Synopsis Historion*, which as we shall see in the next chapter provides very little help with reconstructing Balkan chronology between 971 and 990. For example, Skylitzes deals very briefly and in a confused fashion with the rise of Kometoupoulos power in two characteristically telescoped passages: one located during his coverage of the regency of the empress Theophano which preceded the reign of Nikephoros Phokas and one during Basil's reign itself.[9] Indeed, even when they are aggregated together, the most that the narrative accounts of Skylitzes, Kekaumenos, Yahya, and Stephen of Taron can tell us about the respective positions of the Byzantines and Bulgarians during the first fifteen years of Basil's reign is that by 986 Samuel was threatening Byzantine authority throughout the Balkans, and that few

---

[8] Stephenson, *Byzantium's Balkan Frontier*, 59 ff; idem, *Legend of Basil the Bulgar-Slayer*, 12 ff.

[9] Skylitzes, *Synopsis*, 255–6, 328–30; see also below 8.5 for the rise of the Kometopouloi; for Skylitzes' tendency to telescope narratives see above 2.4; for further discussion of this particular passage of Skylitzes' text see above pp. 102–3.

areas north of the Haimos Mountains remained for long under direct Byzantine control. Such is the picture that underpins the various reports on Basil's ill-fated Balkan expedition of 986, a campaign which attempted to besiege and conquer Triaditza (also known as Sardica, modern-day Sofia), but which was destroyed by Bulgarian ambushes.[10] The fact that this expedition was directed against Triaditza indicates that by this point the Byzantines had lost control of central Bulgaria. The situation further east is more obscure, although Byzantine raids against eastern Bulgarian towns such as Preslav and Pliska around the year 1000 point to a collapse of Byzantine authority in this region as well during the early decades of Basil's reign.[11] Indeed, an index of the weakness in the imperial position across the whole Balkan peninsula in the first half of the reign is the fall to Samuel in 986 of Larissa, the city which dominated the large and agriculturally important plain of Thessaly in central Greece.[12]

A more rounded picture of governance on Byzantium's Balkan frontier only begins to emerge in the 990s, the point at which Skylitzes begins to take a rather more consistent, if confused, interest in the region, and as a result provides a

[10] Skylitzes, *Synopsis*, 330–1; see also above 3.3.2, 4.2.2, and below 8.5 for further discussion of these events.

[11] Skylitzes, *Synopsis*, 343–4; see also above 2.4 for further discussion of this period. Skylitzes' evidence militates against a recent reading of the history of eastern Bulgaria in the first two decades of Basil's reign, which argues for continuity in Byzantine governance rather than rupture (Doimi de Frankopan, 'Workings of the Byzantine Provincial Administration', 86–9).

[12] Skylitzes, *Synopsis*, 330, 349–50; Kekaumenos, *Consilia et Narrationes*, 250–2; P. Lemerle, *Prolégomènes à une édition critique et commentée des 'Conseils et Récits' de Kékauménos* (Brussels, 1960), 43–5, 58.

sketchy narrative context for other sources of evidence. It is only, therefore, at this point, when narrative and material evidence begin to coincide, that a detailed comparison between the frontier experience of the Balkans with the situation in the eastern borderlands during Basil's reign really becomes possible.

Let us begin an analysis of the administration of the Balkan frontier in the post-990 period with the most senior position listed in the *Escorial Taktikon*, that of *doux*. Just as was the case in the east, this position emerges in the Balkans as a flexible command, liable to mutate according to circumstances within and outside the empire. The first time that a Balkan *doux* can be identified in the narrative record occurs when Skylitzes relates the story of the death of the *doux* of Thessalonika, Gregory Taronites, an event which is not dated precisely by the historian but appears to have occurred in the early 990s.[13] Besides his reference to Taronites, Skylitzes makes other references to commanders at Thessalonika, sometimes calling them *doux*, sometimes *strategos*, and sometimes merely recalling that they ruled (using various forms of the verb *archein*). This vague reference to regional rule is typical of Skylitzes' treatment of administrative terminology; as we saw in the previous chapter, Skylitzes also uses various forms of *archein* in his discussion of frontier commands in the east.[14] However, while Skylitzes offers little precision in his treatment of senior command in the

---

[13] See above 3.3.2, 4.1, and below 8.5 for further discussion of this episode.

[14] Apart from his reference to Taronites as *doux*, Skylitzes only mentions the term '*doux* of Thessalonika' on one other occasion during his coverage of Basil's reign, when referring to Nikephoros Kabasilas in 1024 (Skylitzes,

Balkans, important confirmation that a *doux* of Thessaloniki existed by the middle of the 990s is to be found in the contemporary documentary record. According to an Athonite charter confirming a fiscal exemption to the monastery of the Iviron, John Chaldos was *doux* in around 995.[15] While evidence for Adrianople is much thinner than for Thessalonika, sigillographical and epigraphical sources indicate that a *doux* was at some time appointed here too in Basil's reign. A seal of one Theodorokan, *patrikios* and *doux* of Adrianople, has been discovered at Preslav.[16] Moreover, in 1007, a copy of the Gospels in Armenian was commissioned in Adrianople by one John, the *proximos* of the *doux* Theodorokan.[17]

Synopsis, 368). His more usual term is *archein* which he uses in reference to Taronites himself and to another presiding officer at Thessalonika, Nikephoros Botaneiates (ibid. 339, 350). He also refers to Constantine Diogenes as the *strategos* at Thessalonika after Botaneiates (ibid. 352). For Skylitzes' use of homogenized terminology see above 3.2, 3.3.2; and for its use in an eastern frontier context see above 6.3.3–4.

[15] *Actes d'Iviron*, no. 8. Although the year in which this document was issued is not indicated clearly in the text itself, 995 seems the most likely. Certainly it had to be issued before John Chaldos, the *doux* of Thessalonika, had been taken prisoner by the Bulgarians *c*.996. For Chaldos' capture see Skylitzes, *Synopsis*, 347. Later in his account Skylitzes mentions that Chaldos was released at the time of the general Bulgarian surrender in 1018 after twenty-two years of captivity: Skylitzes, *Synopsis*, 357. The Iviron document also suggests that Chaldos was *doux* in around 995, for although it contains no annualized date, it claims to have been issued in the ninth indiction which tallies with the year 995. For more information about the family of Chaldos, see Cheynet, 'Basil II and Asia Minor', 84, 93.

[16] I. Jordanov, 'Les Sceaux de deux chefs militaire byzantins trouvés à Préslav: Le Magistros Leo Mélissenos et le patrice Théodorokan', *Byzantinobulgarica* (1986), 187–9.

[17] Evans and Wixom, *Glory of Byzantium*, 357–8, no. 239; Nersessian, *Treasures from the Ark*, 182–3.

Just as the primary role of *doukes* and *katepanes* on the eastern frontier was as the commander of detachments of troops from the centralized professional army, the *doukes* of the Balkan frontier exercised similar responsibilities. Chaldos was the leader of *tagmata* (crack cavalry regiments in the empire's centralized field army) manned by soldiers recruited in the central Anatolian themes.[18] Meanwhile, Theodorokan was a hardened professional soldier who probably began his career in the east. Before his appointment to Adrianople he was *strategos* of the small eastern frontier theme of Artze; he was also *archegetes* of the east, the leader of the infantry within an imperial field army; his first position in the Balkans may have been as *strategos* of Philippoupolis.[19] Further evidence that detachments of central army troops were located in the Balkan frontier region comes from another Athonite document that refers to a *topoteretes*, one of the most senior officials within a *tagma*. This *topoteretes*, Paspalas, was

[18] The Athonite document which refers to Chaldos names him as *doux* of Thessalonika, the Boukellarioi, and Armeniakoi (*Actes d'Iviron*, no. 8). This seems to suggest that he was the commander of troops raised in Asia Minor (Boukellarion and Armeniakon) who then served in the Balkans.

[19] Dumbarton Oaks Unpublished F2093 (Artze); Konstantopoulos, *Molybdoboulla*, no. 594 (*archegetes* of the east); Skylitzes, *Synopsis*, 343, 345 (Philippoupolis); for a partial reconstruction of his career see Cheynet, Seibt, and Morrisson, *Sceaux byzantins: Henri Seyrig*, 150. It is possible that Theodorokan was one of those Iberians from Tao who entered Byzantine service in 990 when Basil II annexed the lands of David of Tao; on these Iberians see further discussion in 4.1 and 8.4. Skylitzes seems confused about Theodorokan's career. He believed that his last appointment was as *strategos* of Philippoupolis and seems to know nothing of his service at Adrianople (Skylitzes, *Synopsis*, 345). An explanation for Skylitzes' muddle is offered later in this chapter. For more on the office of *archegetes*, see Oikonomides, *Listes*, 335.

responsible for dealing with the aftermath of a Saracen raid on the island of Gymnopelagisia in 992, an attack which led to the capture by Arab pirates of a Serbian embassy on its way to visit the emperor.[20]

Yet, while *doukes* can be identified in Balkan contexts in the 990s, it is important to stress that in this period their military duties were primarily defensive, designed to protect the plains of eastern Macedonia and Thrace against attack by the armies of Samuel of Bulgaria. The defensive quality of ducal responsibilities emerges in Skylitzes' narrative concerning Gregory Taronites at Thessalonika. Gregory was appointed shortly after the end of the Phokas revolt with the explicit purpose to 'prevent and drive back the raids of Samuel'.[21] That this was Taronites' main responsibility is verified by Skylitzes' account of Gregory's death, when the historian explains that Taronites died in the context of an attack on the region around Thessalonika by Samuel's Bulgarians. Hearing of the imminence of a Bulgarian raid, Gregory sent Ashot his son to collect intelligence, while he followed from behind. In the initial skirmishes, Gregory was successful, but he perished when he fell into a Bulgarian

---

[20] *Actes de Lavra*, no. 8. For further analysis of *topoteretai* see Oikonomides, *Listes*, 110–11, 118–19, 329; for the 992 Serb mission see Ostrogorsky, 'Une ambassade serbe', 187–94; see also below 8.5.

[21] Skylitzes, *Synopsis*, 339. It is unlikely that Taronites was appointed to command in the Balkans before the end of the Phokas revolt. During that rebellion he had led an expedition to the eastern frontier on behalf of the emperor to try to raise an eastern alliance that would attack Phokas from the rear. This expedition was defeated by Iberian contingents organized by David of Tao (Yahya, *PO* 23, pp. 424–5; *Miracles of Saint Eugenios*, 348–50).

ambush.[22] This is not to say, of course, that there was no offensive military activity on Byzantium's Balkan frontier during the 980s or 990s. However, where offensives occurred they appear to have involved the imperial field army led by Basil II himself rather than expeditions led by his subordinate *doukes* at Thessalonika. These imperially led campaigns include a rather obscure four-year series of offensives beginning in 991 to which Yahya and Stephen of Taron allude in general terms.[23] While the precise details of these campaigns are unknown, a variety of eastern sources confirm that Basil was on active service in the Balkans in the autumn of 994. At least one, and possibly two, embassies from Aleppo met the emperor when he was on active campaign in the Balkans.[24] It was from the Balkans that Basil led his field army eastwards to relieve northern Syria from Fatimid attack in early 995.[25]

It was this threat of external attack, both by Bulgarians and also Arab pirates, which seems to have conditioned another striking aspect of Byzantine administration on the Balkan frontier in the early decades of Basil's reign: the survival of many elements of provincial government which had been developed in earlier centuries to protect imperial themes both in Anatolia and Byzantine Europe from

---

[22] Skylitzes, *Synopsis*, 341; see above 3.3.2 and 4.1 for further discussion of this narrative passage. Another *doux* of Thessalonika, John Chaldos, also seems to have been the victim of a Bulgarian ambush shortly after the death of Taronites (see above, p. 404 n. 15).

[23] Yahya, *PO* 23, p. 431; Stephen of Taron, *Armenische Geschichte*, 198.

[24] al-Rudhrawari, *Eclipse*, vi. 29, 232.

[25] Yahya, *PO* 23, p. 442.

external attack.[26] The survival of such long-established modes of provincial governance is visible in that Athonite charter confirming a fiscal exemption to the monastery of the Iviron issued by the *doux* John Chaldos in 995.[27] It lists those local imperial officials who are forbidden from imposing taxes and dues on the property and tenant farmers (*paroikoi*) of the Iviron monastery; these include officials more usually associated with local governance in the ninth and early tenth centuries: *tourmachai, merarchai, kometes* of the tent, *droungarokometes*, and thematic *domestikoi*.[28] Other Athonite documents from the period 996–1008 bear witness to the survival of many of these officials into the second half of Basil II's reign.[29] The fact that Chaldos does not mention any *strategoi* among those officials from whom the monks are to be immune suggests that by the 990s the position of *strategos* of Thessalonika may have ceased to be

[26] For the development and mainly defensive operation of this traditional thematic administration see Oikonomides, *Listes*, 341–4; Whittow, *Making of Orthodox Byzantium*, 113–26, 165–81; Haldon, *Warfare, State and Society*, 112–15.

[27] *Actes d'Iviron*, no. 8; see also discussion of this charter earlier in this chapter.

[28] These officials are listed by Philotheos in the late 9th c. (in the list of precedence known as the *Kleterologion*) as the most senior members of the military hierarchy of a Byzantine theme (Oikonomides, *Listes*, 108–11, 341–4). Another Athonite charter shows the same officials at work in the region of Thessalonika in the mid-10th c.: *Actes du Prôtaton*, Archives de l'Athos VII, ed. D. Papachryssanthou (Paris, 1975), no. 6. This charter from 943 lists *komes* of the tent, *chartoularios* of the theme, *protomandator, domestikos* of *vestaritai*).

[29] *Actes d'Iviron*, no. 10 (dated to 996, mentions a *tourmarches*); no. 13 (dated to 1007: former *droungarios*); no. 15 (dated to 1008: former and current *droungarioi*); *Actes de Lavra*, no. 14 (dated to 1008: *tourmaches* and *droungarios*); no. 18 (before 1016: former *droungarios*).

filled. Instead, the *strategos* had been replaced by a *doux*. In these circumstances, officials such as Taronites and Chaldos can in some ways be considered primarily as the heads of provincial military governments whose principal *raison d'être* was defence rather than attack. In order to fulfil their responsibilities they received the additional support of garrisons from the central army. This position contrasts with the east, where officials such as Michael Bourtzes, Leo Melissenos, and Damian Dalassenos enjoyed a much more active role as *doukes* during the first decades of Basil's reign, participating in offensive operations, primarily against the Fatimids.

Some signs of change are discernible towards the end of 990s. At some point after the death of Gregory Taronites, Nikephoros Ouranos arrived in Thessalonika vested with broader powers than his predecessors. According to Skylitzes, he was *doux* of the whole west.[30] A manuscript from the Vatopedi monastery on Mount Athos states that he was *domestikos* of the *scholai*; Yahya ibn Sa'id refers to him merely as *domestikos*.[31] Certainly he seems to have been equipped with a rather larger army than his predecessors. In 997 he marched south from Thessanolika with a force that inflicted a large defeat on the army of Samuel at the

---

[30] Skylitzes, *Synopsis*, 341–2, 364.

[31] McGeer, 'Tradition and Reality', 130–1 n. 13; Yahya, *PO* 23, pp. 446–7. Several seals belonging to a Nikephoros, *magistros*, *domestikos* of the west have been attributed to Ouranos. According to Jordanov, two such seals exist: one from Preslav in eastern Bulgaria, the other from Dristra on the Lower Danube: Jordanov, 'Molybdobulles de domestiques des scholes', 210–11; see also Zacos, *Byzantine Lead Seals II*, no. 863. McGeer, 'Tradition and Reality', 130–1, is less certain that these seals can be attributed to Ouranos since neither refers to Nikephoros by his family name.

River Spercheios, a victory that delighted and indeed greatly surprised his friends and contemporaries such as Leo, Metropolitan of Synada.[32] Of course it is difficult to know from such meagre evidence whether Ouranos combined responsibility for the defence of Thessalonika with a role in charge of the mobile field army, or whether an alternative *doux* of Thessalonika also existed at the same time as Ouranos was active in the Balkans, an official who perhaps protected the *domestikos*' rearguard while he was on campaign. Whatever the answer, the fact that Ouranos went on to fulfil a plenipotentiary role at Antioch in 1000–1 suggests that his earlier appointment in the Balkans may have been of a similar nature.[33]

The exact reason why Basil II appointed a plenipotentiary at Thessalonika with access to a substantial army in the later 990s is as yet obscure; however, it is possible that instability elsewhere in the empire in the second half of the 990s demanded that the emperor spend more time in Constantinople and less in the Balkans. As we have already seen, the mid-990s saw an increase in tension between Fatimids and Byzantines, culminating in the defeats of Michael Bourtzes (in 994) and Damian Dalassenos (in 998), military set-backs that required Basil himself to abandon fighting in Bulgaria

---

[32] Skylitzes, *Synopsis*, 341–2. Leo of Synada wrote to Nikephoros congratulating him on his success against the Bulgarians while he himself was serving as the imperial envoy to the Ottonians in the later 990s (Leo of Synada, letter 13); see also Stephenson, *Legend of Basil the Bulgar-Slayer*, 17. For more discussion of representations of, and reactions to, the battle, see above 3.3.2, 4.1, and below 8.5.

[33] For Ouranos' eastern responsibilities see above 6.3.3 and 6.4.

and lead lightning raids against northern Syria.[34] On the other hand, there are signs in the hostile poetry that critics of the regime, such as John Geometres, continued to produce in the 990s that the emperor enjoyed little popularity in Constantinople itself during this period.[35] In such circumstances, long absences from Constantinople were unwise. It is possible that a combination of internal and external pressures led the emperor to delegate some responsibility for military affairs in the Balkans to a trusted second-in-command; as with the east, arrangements on the Balkan frontier were responsive to developments elsewhere in the empire.

According to Skylitzes, when Ouranos left for Antioch his successor at Thessalonika was David Areianites.[36] Unfortunately we are told nothing of Areianites' activities, which means that little more can be said of either his role or that of Ouranos. The paucity of dated information in Skylitzes' testimony for the Balkans in the period 1000–14 makes it difficult to discern the role of the frontier commanders such as *doukes* in the post-Spercheios period, just as it makes it impossible to speculate on other frontier arrangements. The lack of securely dated evidence for this period, for example,

[34] These raids are discussed above in 6.2, 6.3.3, and below in 8.4.

[35] Lauxtermann, 'John Geometres', 372, believes that some of Geometres' verses bewailing Bulgarian victories can be dated as late as 997–8. In these verses Geometres is aghast at Samuel's temerity in crowning himself emperor of the Bulgarians. The fact that Leo the Deacon's rather negative portrait of the early years of Basil's reign was produced *c.*995 is further testimony to the generally gloomy atmosphere which seems to have prevailed in Constantinople throughout the 990s and which is discussed above in 1.2 and 1.3.

[36] Skylitzes, *Synopsis*, 345.

makes it difficult to know whether Samuel and Basil came to a peace agreement in 1005, an agreement whose existence has recently been hypothesized, but against which I will argue in the final chapter of this book.[37]

Yet, even when Skylitzes' testimony becomes more detailed in the period 1014–18, his evidence about administrative arrangements on the western frontier must be handled carefully. So great is Skylitzes' interest in those martial exploits achieved in the Balkans by the ancestors of famous families from the end of the eleventh century, that he runs the danger of losing sight of the contemporary hierarchy of office-holders and their responsibilities in the Balkans during Basil's reign itself.[38] Nonetheless, there are signs within Skylitzes' testimony that just as in the period before 1000, the *doux* of Thessalonika's principal responsibility continued to be primarily defensive: protecting the Byzantine coastal plains from Bulgarian attack, and providing a solid base from which field armies, especially those led by the emperor himself, could operate without fear of attack from the rear. Such operational principles can be detected during the Byzantine campaign of 1014. While the main Byzantine field army under the command of Basil II was engaged with attacking the pass at Kleidion, a Bulgarian counter-offensive was sent to raid Thessalonika under the command of David Nestoritzes. It was the responsibility of the then *doux*, Nikephoros Botaneiates, to meet and defeat this Bulgarian riposte. Having successfully warded off the Bulgarian raid,

---

[37] See below 8.5.
[38] Skylitzes' late 11th-c. focus is discussed above in 4.1 and 4.2.2.

Botaneiates was then charged with securing the road between western Macedonia and Thessalonika so that Basil's army could withdraw safely for the winter. Unfortunately at this point Botaneiates fell into an ambush and was killed.[39] Although there is less evidence about frontier command further east in Thrace than in Thessalonika, there are signs that commanders such as the *doux* of Adrianople and the *strategos* of Philippoupolis were also expected to offer back-up support for imperial campaigns. In an undated reference Skylitzes informs his reader that Theodorokan was left by the emperor to guard Philippoupolis while he attacked Triaditza (Sofia). If the location of this reference in the text is to be trusted, then this expedition seems to have occurred shortly after Ouranos' victory at Spercheios and before 1000.[40] Needless to say, given Skylitzes' preference for arranging his text according to thematic principles rather than chronology, this conclusion must remain provisional. What Skylitzes makes rather clearer, however, is that while Thracian commanders were expected to protect and support imperial expeditions from the rear, they may also have enjoyed a more positive campaigning role themselves. We know from a dated reference in Skylitzes' testimony that Theodorokan led raids against eastern Bulgaria around 1000, at a time when he was probably still *strategos* of Philippoupolis.[41] It is sometimes alleged that Skylitzes' testimony for this attack proves that eastern Bulgaria was fully

---

[39] Skylitzes, *Synopsis*, 348–51; for further discussion of the Battle of Kleidion see also above 3.3.2, 4.1, and below 8.5.

[40] Skylitzes, *Synopsis*, 343.

[41] Ibid. 343–4.

conquered in this year. Yet, it is likely that the ambition of this expedition was simply that of a raid, part of an ongoing struggle between the empires of Samuel and Basil on several different sectors of the Balkan frontier. Skylitzes himself construes the campaign of 1000 as a morale-boosting assault with limited objectives rather than an attempt at permanent occupation: 'In the year 6508 the emperor, having sent out a heavy force against the Bulgarian castles (*kastra*) on the other side of the Haimos, which was led by the *patrikios* Theodorokan and the *protospatharios* Nikephoros Xiphias, took Great and Little Preslav and Pliska *and the Roman army withdrew unharmed and with trophies*.'[42]

Indeed, a Bulgarian attack launched against Adrianople in 1002 during the Feast of the Dormition of the Virgin, while Basil II was far away campaigning against Vidin on the Middle Danube, suggests that the struggle for eastern Bulgaria continued into the early years of the eleventh century. The attack on Adrianople may also indicate that its commander (perhaps Theodorokan) was away campaigning with the emperor.[43] The most that can be said is that the struggle for eastern Bulgaria, as well as for the Lower and

---

[42] Given that Skylitzes' evidence cannot be used to prove conclusively that eastern Bulgaria was completely reconquered at this point, any reconstruction of the contours of the Byzantine administration that followed this reconquest must remain somewhat provisional; Stephenson offers an outline of the post-1000 administrative developments in this region using sigillographical evidence. He assumes complete reconquest of the area, and reoccupation of those Lower Danube forts originally constructed by John Tzimiskes (Stephenson, *Byzantium's Balkan Frontier*, 63–4; idem, *Legend of Basil the Bulgar-Slayer*, 18–19). I am less certain about whether such a clear-cut chronology can be drawn from the available evidence.

[43] Skylitzes, *Synopsis*, 346.

Middle Danube regions, is highly obscure for much of Basil's reign. Indeed, the first positive sign in the textual record that Byzantine armies had reoccupied eastern Bulgaria and taken the Byzantine frontier back up to the Danube comes as late as 1016. Skylitzes mentions that at this time Tzotzikios, son of Phebdatos, one of the Georgians who entered imperial service in 1000, was the *strategos* at Dristra.[44]

Nonetheless, while it is unlikely that commanders in Thrace led a sudden expansion of Byzantine authority into eastern Bulgaria and up to the Danube c.1000, the careers of officials such as Theodorokan are interesting in another respect. Even allowing for chronological inaccuracy in Skylitzes testimony, it is clear that frontier commanders in the Balkans enjoyed relatively stable careers after 1000, a phenomenon that we have already witnessed in the east in the same period. Theodorokan served at Philippoupolis and at Adrianople for at least seven years (from 1000 to 1007).[45] Meanwhile, Nikephoros Xiphias began his service as early as 1000 as part of Theodorokan's army that raided the Preslavs

[44] Ibid. 356. For discussion of the Georgians entering Byzantine service at this point see above 4.1. Although Stephenson would see positions on the Lower Danube being reoccupied by the Byzantines rather earlier than this, he too comments on the relatively small amount of material evidence for a Byzantine presence in this region during the reign of Basil, particularly a paucity of numismatic finds. His explanation for this phenomenon is that the Lower Danube was no longer a high defensive priority for Byzantium, partly because the peace treaty with the Rus which Basil agreed in 988 meant that Rus attack across the Black Sea and up the Danube River was no longer such a threat, and partly because the Rus themselves were preoccupied with fighting the Pechenegs (Stephenson, *Legend of Basil the Bulgar-Slayer*, 20; see also S. Franklin and J. Shepard, *Emergence of Rus* (Cambridge, 1996), 169–80).

[45] For more on Theodorokan's career see above p. 405.

and Pliska.[46] An undated reference in Skylitzes' testimony indicates that Xiphias later became *strategos* of Philippoupolis in Thrace. Skylitzes claims that he replaced Theodorokan when the latter became too old to hold office. However, this ageist explanation may be an intervention on the part of Skylitzes, who shows no sign of realizing that Theodorokan moved on to the ducal office at Adrianople.[47] More significant, however, as far as the career of Xiphias is concerned, is that he was still *strategos* of Philippoupolis when he appeared at the battle of Kleidion in 1014.[48] Of course it is impossible to know whether Skylitzes identifies Xiphias and Philippoupolis so frequently because he is reporting accurately from his underlying sources, or because he is choosing to make his account more interesting and convincing by adding prosopographical details which may in fact be completely erroneous. Yet there is external evidence verifying that at the very least Xiphias had a long service record in the Balkans during Basil's reign, even if he was moved from office to office within that general region. In 1022 Nikephoros Xiphias encouraged Nikephoros Phokas, son of Bardas Phokas, to rebel against the emperor. In his report on this rebellion, Yahya ibn Sa'id explains that when the insurrection was over the emperor punished Xiphias only lightly in recognition of his past services: 'He made Xiphias a monk and gave him a monastery outside Constantinople. The

[46] Skylitzes, *Synopsis*, 343.
[47] Ibid. 345; for Skylitzes' fondness for tying up loose prosopographical ends without independent corroboration see above 3.2.
[48] Skylitzes, *Synopsis*, 348–9.

emperor kept in mind Xiphias' previous services ... during his campaigns against the Bulgarians.'[49]

Despite the extremely fragmentary nature of the evidence about the military organization of the Balkan frontier in Macedonia and Thrace in the decades preceding the 1018 annexation of Bulgaria, a plausible working hypothesis is that the main responsibilities of the *doukes* of Thessalonika and Adrianople, and other commanders on the frontier such as the *strategos* of Philippouplis, were twofold: to protect the Byzantine position against external attack; and to support the major campaigns of the main Byzantine field army led by Basil II. While the role of the *doux* always retained a strongly defensive complexion, it is likely that as the reign progressed the *doux* increasingly became an important part of the emperor's offensive against the Bulgarians, particularly after the 1001 peace agreement between the Fatimids and Basil II enabled the emperor to divert the military energies of the empire towards the Balkans. Nonetheless, all arrangements were always open to modification as the position of Ouranos in the second half of the 990s suggests, an appointment that was laced with the kind of flexibility visible on the contemporary eastern frontier.

Indeed, the discussion of the eastern frontier in the last chapter drew attention to the extent to which military officials such as Ouranos were not only expected to undertake active fighting but also to exercise other skills, especially diplomacy with neighbouring potentates. From Skylitzes' account of Byzantine relations with the Balkans in the

---

[49] Yahya, *PO* 47, p. 469. Eng. trans. Feras Hamza.

period leading up to the annexation of Bulgaria in 1018 we see little sign of the *doukes* of Thessalonika or Adrianople flexing their diplomatic muscles. However, this is not to say that frontier commanders in the Balkans in the first four decades of Basil's reign did not negotiate with local powers, or that diplomacy was absent from relations between Balkan powers and Byzantines. Indeed, quite the contrary. In 1002, during an imperial campaign on the Middle Danube at Vidin, a local Magyar chieftain, Ajtony, was baptized. It has been argued that he may have accepted baptism in return for favourable trading arrangements along the Danube with the Byzantine Empire.[50] In 1016 Skylitzes reports on the diplomatic intelligence dispatched to the emperor by Tzotzikios, the *strategos* of Dristra, Byzantium's key listening post on the Lower Danube frontier. Tzotzikios warned that the Bulgarians were on the point of an alliance with the Pechenegs, the nomad confederation located north of the river.[51] Another frontier commander whose responsibilities included a portfolio of diplomatic skills such as negotiation and intelligence gathering was the *strategos* of Dyrrachion, the Byzantine listening post located on the Black Sea, where information about the Adriatic context was customarily filtered.

Even during the campaigns that led up to the annexation of Bulgaria in 1018, diplomacy as well as sheer brute force was used. Of course, Skylitzes' interest in the martial enterprises

---

[50] Stephenson, *Byzantium's Balkan Frontier*, 65; idem, *Legend of Basil the Bulgar-Slayer*, 21.

[51] Skylitzes, *Synopsis*, 356; see also above 3.2.2 for further discussion of Skylitzes' detailed narrative about negotiations between Basil and John Vladislav, in which a crippled envoy plays a crucial role.

of the ancestors of his favoured eleventh-century families means that he concentrates with greatest attention on the military dimension of the conflict. He enumerates the series of raids that were launched against Bulgarian positions in western Macedonia by leading Byzantine commanders: David Areianites, Constantine Diogenes, Eustathios Daphnomeles, Nikephoros Xiphias, Niketas Pegonites, Nikephoros Botaneiates and the eunuch Orestes. Yet, even Skylitzes accepts that there was a strong diplomatic context to the annexation of Bulgaria. He alludes indirectly to the complex of negotiations that formed the diplomatic backdrop to the period 1014–18: to embassies that passed between Basil, John Vladislav, the Bulgarian tsar, senior Bulgarian commanders such as Krakras, and other regional powers, such as Vladimir, the ruler of the princedom of Diokleia.[52] In the narrative of the Priest of Diokleia, the diplomatic context to the annexation of Bulgaria is articulated with much greater clarity: here Basil is openly accused of persuading John Vladislav to murder Gabriel Radomir, the son of Samuel who ruled as Bulgarian tsar briefly after his father's death in 1014.[53] Meanwhile, Yahya ibn Sa'id claims that Basil was actually invited to take control of Bulgaria by local commanders after the death of John Vladislav, Gabriel's successor, in 1018.[54] Moreover, as Paul Stephenson has shown, the testimonies of Skylitzes, Kekaumenos, and the Priest of Diokleia contain a multiplicity

[52] Skylitzes, *Synopsis*, 348–56; Stephenson, *Legend of Basil the Bulgar-Slayer*, 27–30.

[53] Priest of Diokleia, 336–7; Ferluga, 'Die Chronik des Presters von Diokleia', 444.

[54] Yahya, *PO* 47, p. 407.

of short stories which illustrate the extent to which a combination of force and diplomacy had typified frontier relations and governance in the Balkans for many decades, long before Basil II's final assault on the Bulgarians in the period after 1014.[55] These stories usually concern the cajoling strategies deployed to persuade the commanders of small frontier fortifications from both sides, Bulgarian and Byzantine, to surrender or defect. Such strategies included the granting of titles, salaries, and offices within the Byzantine administrative hierarchy. In Chapter 2 of this book, attention has been drawn to the short narratives written by Skylitzes involving the surrender to Basil of the Bulgarian commanders of those mountain fastnesses which guarded the routes between Thessalonika and western Macedonia: locations such as Berroia, Servia, and Bodina.[56]

But if a mixture of force and diplomacy typified the Byzantine frontier experience in the Balkans during the four decades of Basil's reign, what was the situation after the annexation of Bulgaria in 1018? Superficial scrutiny of Skylitzes' account leaves the reader with the overwhelming impression that the annexation was consolidated largely through military means. Skylitzes mentions the seizure of

[55] Stephenson, 'The Balkan Frontier in the Year 1000', 130; idem, *Legend of Basil the Bulgar-Slayer*, 3–5; Stephenson explores this theme further in the post-Basil history of the Balkans (see esp. his *Byzantium's Balkan Frontier*, ch. 4).

[56] Skylitzes, *Synopsis*, 344–5. Whereas Stephenson has tended to see the surrenders enumerated by Skylitzes as permanent handovers achieved in c.1000–5, I would argue that they were temporary arrangements (Stephenson, 'The Balkan Frontier in the Year 1000', 130; see discussion above 2.4 and below 8.5).

Bulgarian fortifications and the building of new castles, including the erection of twin forts named after Basil and his brother Constantine at Lake Prespa.[57] He dwells on the heroic post-conquest exploits of various Byzantine commanders against local Bulgarian commanders and princes, most notably Eustathios Daphnomeles against Ibatzes and Constantine Diogenes against Sermon of Sirmion.[58] Yet, once again it is important to recall that Skylitzes' account was composed according to the cultural and political interests of the later eleventh century, rather than with an intense interest in recording the practicalities of Byzantine–Bulgarian relations in the reign of Basil II. Thus, while Skylitzes stresses the martial nature of the post-annexation experience, other evidence, including incidental material in his own account of the reign, suggests that Byzantine administration in the newly conquered regions was characterized by a considerable degree of flexibility and the involvement of local Bulgarians in both military and civil administration.

First, it is important to note that the imperial field army was withdrawn from the Balkans shortly after 1018. Once Basil had completed his imperial progress through the Bulgarian lands he had conquered, he moved south to celebrate a triumphal entry into Athens. He then returned to Constantinople, for another imperial triumph. In the capital he put in place arrangements for a new imperial expedition, this time against Iberia in the east.[59] Various historical

---

[57] Skylitzes, *Synopsis*, 359–60.

[58] For further discussion of the Daphnomeles and Diogenes narratives see above 4.2.2.

[59] Skylitzes, *Synopsis*, 364–6.

narratives hint that within the imperial armies that campaigned in Caucasia there were complements of Bulgarian
troops, whom the Byzantines may have been steadily
recruiting since the death of Samuel's son Gabriel.[60] Meanwhile, other troops from the main field army which had
been located until so recently in Bulgaria served in forces
sent to Italy to fight under the command of the *katepano* of
Italy, Basil Boiannes.[61] Those troops left in Bulgaria were
placed under the command of David Areianites at Skopje. If
Skylitzes is correct in calling Areianites *strategos autokrator*,
then it seems possible that he may have exercised the kind of
plenipotentiary role held in earlier decades by Ouranos both
in the Balkans and in the east.[62] If this is so, then once again
we have very strong evidence to suggest that when Basil was
on campaign elsewhere in the empire he preferred to leave

[60] Skylitzes suggests that *c.*1015 a series of Bulgarian commanders, including Dometianos Kaukanos, Gabriel Kaukanos, and Elitzes, the *archon* of
Moglena, surrendered to Basil and were sent to Vaspurakan (Skylitzes,
Synopsis, 352; see also below 8.5). In the course of his discussion of Basil's
conquest of Bulgaria, Aristakes of Lastivert mentions the depredations that
Bulgarian troops would later inflict on the east (Aristakes of Lastivert, *Récit
des malheurs*, 7). The Georgian tradition speaks of Basil's army of 1021–2
being composed of innumerable foreigners (Georgian Royal Annals, 282).
Certainly many former Bulgarian commanders served Basil's imperial successors in Caucasia; see above 6.3.4.

[61] The army that travelled to join Boiannes in Italy in 1024 to open up an
offensive against Muslim Sicily included Bulgarians, Vlachs, and Macedonians as well as Turks and Russians according to local Italian sources (Annals
of Bari, 53; see below 8.6).

[62] Skylitzes, *Synopsis*, 358; an interpolation by Michael of Devol, c.1118,
in manuscript [U] of the *Synopsis Historion* calls Areianites *katepano* of
Bulgaria. In referring to a David who ruled in Bulgaria the *Miracles of
Eugenios* appear to allude to Areianites (*Miracles of Eugenios*, 356); see also
Stephenson, *Byzantium's Balkan Frontier*, 74.

other frontiers under the overarching authority of a trusted second-in-command.

Nonetheless, after Areianites' appointment, the history of supreme command in the newly conquered areas of Bulgaria becomes rather obscure. Yahya ibn Sa'id claims that Basil turned Bulgaria into a katepanate.[63] Sigillographical evidence appears to support Yahya in this claim. However, the seals of the earliest *katepanes* and *doukes* of Bulgaria make it clear that the military responsibilities enjoyed by senior military commanders extended far beyond the newly conquered regions around Skopje and Ochrid, the centres of Samuel's empire. Some of these commanders exercised joint command over Thessalonika and Bulgaria;[64] one, a certain Constantine, whose seal is in the Lvov collection in Ukraine, was *doux* of Bulgaria, Thessalonika, and Serbia. It is likely that this particular seal belonged to Constantine Diogenes, whom the historiographical record records as holding senior military command in Thessalonika, Bulgaria, and Sirmion (Serbia) during the reigns of Basil II, Constantine VIII, and

---

[63] Yahya, *PO* 47, p. 407.

[64] See e.g. an anonymous *katepano* of Thessalonika and Bulgaria, who held the title of *protospatharios* (L. Maksimovic and M. Popovic 'Les Sceaux byzantins de la région danubienne en Serbie', in N. Okonomides (ed.), *SBS* 3 (Washington DC, 1993), no. 15); or Christopher, *katepano* of Thessalonika and Bulgaria (Zacos, *Byzantine Lead Seals II*, no. 969). If, as Stephenson suggests, the owner of this seal is to be identified with the Christopher who was *protospatharios* and *katepano* of Longobardia in 1028, then it is likely that he was also the patron of the Church of Panaghia ton Chalkeon in Thessalonika (Stephenson, 'The Balkan Frontier in the Year 1000', 125; idem, *Legend of Basil the Bulgar-Slayer*, 44–5; C. A. Mango, *Byzantine Architecture* (London, 1986), 113–15; J.-M. Spieser, 'Inventaires en vue d'un recueil des inscriptions historiques à Byzance. I. Les inscriptions de Thessalonique', *TM* 5 (1973), 163–4).

the early years of Romanos III. While the exact identity, geographical responsibility, and indeed chronological order of succession of some of these early *katepanes* or *doukes* are all difficult matters to resolve, it is clear that senior military officials in the Balkans could hold command over extremely large geographical areas. The size of the region under their authority and the flexibility of their function are reminiscent of the ad hoc plenipotentiary authority often enjoyed by *katepanes* and *doukes* on the eastern frontier.[65]

If the experience of the newly conquered areas of the Balkans was at all similar to administrative practice on Byzantium's eastern frontier at locations such as Antioch, then those senior Byzantine military commanders appointed directly from Constantinople to exercise overarching

---

[65] The plenipotentiary point is also made by Stephenson, 'The Balkan Frontier in the Year 1000', 125–6, and in his *Legend of Basil the Bulgar-Slayer*, 39–40. I am less sure, however, whether one can be as certain as Stephenson about the exact chronology of the office-holding undertaken by Areianites, Diogenes, and the *katepano* Christopher in the Balkan region, largely because the timetable relies too substantially on the order in which Skylitzes attributes titles and official positions to these individuals. As we have seen in earlier chapters of this book, Skylitzes' cavalier and anachronistic application of administrative terminology to the principal characters within his narrative makes using his testimony to construct the careers of particular individuals a perilous activity (see above 3.2 for a series of cases from his coverage of the reign of Romanos Lekapenos). I would apply the same caveat to the certainty with which Jean-Claude Cheynet identifies Constantine Diogenes and places him within the chronology of Byzantine regional commanders in the Balkans post-1014. Cheynet sees Diogenes succeeding Theophylact Botaneiates as *doux* of Thessalonika; he also identifies Constantine Diogenes with Diogenes Philomates, who according to sigillographical evidence was *katepano* of Thessalonika, and who we know from an inscription was responsible for building a fortress at Megale Gephyra in Thessaly in 1015 (Cheynet, 'Grandeur et décadence', 123–7).

authority in Bulgaria were almost certainly supported by a detachment of full-time professional troops from the imperial field army. This garrison was probably located at Skopje, the initial base of Areianites' authority. The discovery of copper coins datable to Basil's reign and the restoration of ramparts at fortresses such as Sirmion and Belgrade, signs of more superficial repairs at Margum, and indications of entirely new building at Braničevo, all sites on the Middle Danube, suggest that garrisons were also installed elsewhere in the conquered regions.[66] As we saw in Chapter 4, Skylitzes provides an entertaining narrative of how Constantine Diogenes, the local Byzantine commander close to Sirmion consolidated Byzantine power in this region. Constantine killed Sermon, the Serb ruler of Sirmion, using an elaborate ruse, before dispatching Sermon's widow to Constantinople to be married off to a suitable Byzantine husband.[67]

However, it would be a mistake to overemphasize either the scale or longevity of the presence of the central Byzantine army in post-conquest Bulgaria. As Stephenson has noted, shortly after the death of Basil II Diogenes was recalled from the Sirmion region to defend the empire against Pecheneg attack.[68] The fortifications in this region of the Middle Danube appear to have passed back into indigenous hands around the same time. The Life of St Symeon of Mount Sinai indicates that by 1030 Belgrade was in the hands of a

[66] Stephenson, *Byzantium's Balkan Frontier*, 65–6; idem, 'The Balkan Frontier in the Year 1000', 121; idem, *Legend of Basil the Bulgar-Slayer*, 41–2.
[67] See above 4.2.2.
[68] Skylitzes, *Synopsis*, 373; Stephenson, 'The Balkan Frontier in the Year 1000', 125; idem, *Legend of Basil the Bulgar-Slayer*, 45–6.

local župan. One explanation for this retreat of Byzantine military might be that Basil II's imperial successors were less willing than the great emperor himself to countenance the expense of a strongly fortified frontier region, either in the Middle Danube, or further east in Paristrion, as the region encompassing the Lower Danube and Mysian plain came to be known in the eleventh century.[69] Yet, even during Basil's own reign it is clear that the empire's iron presence on the different sectors of the Balkan frontier was selective. First, as Stephenson himself has shown, Basil appears to have done little to fortify inland and upland areas such as the region west of the Velika Morava corridor between Nis and Skopje. Furthermore, sigillographical evidence datable to the early eleventh century suggests that Basil continued to use diplomacy rather than force to extend Byzantine authority, particularly in the western Balkans; certainly seals survive which show neighbouring potentates in Croatia and Dalmatia accepting Byzantine titles.[70] Finally Yahya ibn Sa'id, whose comments on the administrative arrangements in Bulgaria in the early eleventh century are the most contemporary witness to these events, indicates that Basil was circumspect in his use of fortifications and garrisons. Yahya indicates that Basil appointed commanders to the

[69] Stephenson, *Byzantium's Balkan Frontier*, 80–9, 122–30; idem, 'The Balkan Frontier in the Year 1000', 126.

[70] Stephenson, 'The Balkan Frontier in the Year 1000', 123–5; idem, *Legend of Basil the Bulgar-Slayer*, 42–4; although note that such diplomacy could be accompanied by the selective use of force. In 1024 the *katepano* of Italy, Basil Boiannes, raided Croatia, taking the wife and son of King Kresimir III back to Constantinople (von Falkenhausen, 'Byzantine Italy in the Reign of Basil II', 149).

most powerful fortresses; yet he also stresses that many other fortifications were dismantled. Among those dismantled fortifications may have been those at Ochrid. According to a reference in the Continuation to Skylitzes' *Synopsis Historion*, after Basil ransacked Samuel's palaces at Ochrid, the former capital of the Bulgarian empire was left unfortified.[71]

Indeed, rather than the widespread installation of large and ubiquitous garrisons in the newly conquered regions, what is striking about Basil's administration is his adherence to that most characteristic principle of tenth- and eleventh-century frontier governance: how to achieve maximum fiscal benefit with minimum dislocation on the ground.[72] It is this rationale that surely explains why Basil ordered those Byzantines and Armenians who had been captured by Samuel and settled on the land in Bulgaria, to remain as farmers in their new homes if that was their wish.[73] It is this rationale that explains why the emperor allowed the Bulgarians to be taxed in kind as had been the case under their previous rulers, a practice that was only changed, with disastrous consequences, after the emperor's death.[74] It is this rationale which explains why Basil was happy to

[71] Yahya, *PO* 47, p. 407; *Skylitzes Continuatus*, 164.
[72] See here too, Stephenson, *Legend of Basil the Bulgar-Slayer*, 37.
[73] Skylitzes, *Synopsis*, 363.
[74] Skylitzes does not refer to the preservation of the existing tax regime during his testimony for Basil's reign; instead he mentions it during his coverage of the revolt of Peter Deljan which broke out when Michael IV (1034–41) attempted to commute long-standing Bulgarian taxes in-kind to cash payments (Skylitzes, *Synopsis*, 411–12). Skylitzes provides further corroboration of Basil's decision to retain Samuel's fiscal arrangements in the 'Continuation' to the *Synopsis Historion* (*Skylitzes Continuatus*, 162–3); Stephenson, *Legend of Basil the Bulgar-Slayer*, 37.

guarantee to the Bulgarian church the protected fiscal status it had enjoyed during Samuel's reign.[75] Yet, Basil's decision to leave fiscal affairs undisturbed does not mean that he was impervious to the financial state of the newly conquered territories. Instead, Yahya tells us that he appointed *basilikoi* to manage the finances.[76] Whether such *basilikoi* were local notables or appointees from Constantinople has yet to be established. However, if a parallel between financial and episcopal governance can be drawn, there are strong grounds for thinking that the management of finances may have been devolved to locals. In the case of ecclesiastical governance, Basil II deprived the Bulgarian church of its status as an independent patriarchate, yet he granted the Metropolitan of Ohrid an autocephalous position and control over several neighbouring bishoprics at the expense of his ecclesiastical rivals at Larissa, Dyrrachion, Thessalonika, and Naupaktos. More to the point, the new head of the Bulgarian church, whose name was John, was both a local and indeed the former head of the Bulgarian church; he seems to have been none other than the erstwhile Bulgarian patriarch.[77]

---

[75] N. Oikonomides, 'Tax Exemptions for the Secular Clergy under Basil II', in J. Chrysostomides (ed.), Καθηγήτρια: *Essays presented to Joan Hussey for her Eightieth Birthday* (Camberley, 1988), 318–20.

[76] Yahya, *PO* 47, p. 407; see also Stephenson's comments to the same effect, *Legend of Basil the Bulgar-Slayer*, 36–7.

[77] For the charters outlining these episcopal arrangements see Gelzer, 'Ungedruckte und wenig bekannte Bistumsverzeichnisse', *BZ* 2, 42–6; Mullett, *Theophylact of Ochrid*, 64–6; Oikonomides, 'Tax Exemptions for the Secular Clergy', 317–18; Stephenson, *Byzantium's Balkan Frontier*, 75; idem, 'The Balkan Frontier in the Year 1000', 126; idem, *Legend of Basil the*

7.2   SOUTHERN ITALY

While a lack of sustained narratives stymie the reconstruction of a convincing chronology of governmental developments on Byzantium's Balkan frontier in Basil II's reign, the
history of the administration of southern Italy in the same
period is somewhat easier to piece together. Important
sources for an enterprise of this nature are historical and
hagiographical narratives from across southern Italy, including non-Byzantine areas controlled by Lombard princes. Of
particular significance, however, are two related local chronicle traditions from Byzantine-held territory in the region,
the Annals of Bari and *Lupus Protospatharius.* These texts
record the arrival and departure of senior administrative
officials from Constantinople, especially in the western
region of Longobardia (Apulia). Further accurately dated
information about local administration is provided by a
relatively rich series of archive sources.[78] When combined,
annalistic and documentary evidence give a convincing narrative backdrop against which to contextualize the rather
bald accounts of Byzantine action in southern Italy provided
by the principal historical accounts of Basil's reign, such
as Skylitzes' *Synopsis Historion.* They also provide an

Bulgar-Slayer, 46–7. An interpolation in Skylitzes' account by the bishop
Michael of Devol *c.*1118 indicates that a Constantinopolitan called Leo was
only appointed to the metropolitan position at Ochrid in the reign of
Michael IV (Skylitzes, *Synopsis,* 400; Mullett, *Theophylact of Ochrid,* 57–8).

[78] See e.g. the list of documents mentioning *katepanes* and *strategoi* from
this region drawn up by von Falkenhausen, *Untersuchungen,* 161–91.

important backdrop to the surviving sigillographical, epi-graphical, and archaeological evidence. One particularly important result of this relative wealth of sources is that local administration in southern Italy has been studied in some depth by modern scholars, most notably by Vera von Falkenhausen and Jean-Marie Martin.[79] As a result the southern Italian experience can add an important new di-mension to our perceptions of frontier administration from elsewhere in the empire.

Once again the *Escorial Taktikon* provides the starting point for a discussion about the nature of military com-mand on the frontier. Just as it mentions *doukes* in the east and the Balkans, so it records a *katepano* of Italia, thereby suggesting that by the reign of John Tzimiskes, when the *Escorial Taktikon* is usually believed to have been composed, Byzantine southern Italy had become the responsibility of a single commander who was appointed from the central army.[80] In some senses this picture is backed up by sources

---

[79] For administrative developments see von Falkenhausen, *Untersuchun-gen, passim*; eadem, 'Zur byzantinischen Verwaltung Luceras am Ende des 10. Jahrhunderts', *Quellen und Forschungen aus italienischen Archiven und Bibliotheken*, 53 (1973), 395–406; eadem, 'A Provincial Aristocracy: The Byzantine Provinces in Southern Italy' in M. Angold (ed.), *Byzantine Aris-tocracy* (Oxford, 1984), 211–35; eadem, 'Byzantine Italy in the Reign of Basil II', 119–49; J-M. Martin, 'Une frontière artificielle: La Capitanate italienne', *Acts of the 14th International Congress 1971*, 3 vols. (Bucharest, 1974), ii. 379–85; idem, *La Pouille du VIe au XIIe siècle* (Rome, 1993), 258–68, 693–714; idem, 'Les Problèmes de la frontière en Italie mériodionale (VIe–XIIe siècles): L'Approche historique', *Castrum*, 4 (1992), 267–8; J.-M. Martin and G. Noyé, 'Les Façades de l'Italie du sud', *Castrum*, 7 (1995), 492–6; for place-names, see Map 4.

[80] Oikonomides, *Listes*, 262–3; for discussion of the dating of the *Taktikon* see above 6.1.

MAP 4. Byzantine southern Italy *c*.950–1025. Drawn by the author from: J.-M. Martin and G. Noyé, *La Capitanata nella del storia Mezzogiorno medievale* (Bari, 1991); J.-M. Martin, *La Pouille du VIe au XII siècle* (Rome, 1993); G. Loud, *The Age of Robert Guiscard: Southern Italy and the Norman Conquest* (Harlow, 2000).

that can be accurately dated. An act of confirmation indicates that a *katepano* existed as early as 970.[81] Meanwhile, the narrative record may push the establishment of a *katepano* back earlier. The *Chronicle of Salerno* suggests that a single official from the central army was placed in supreme command in Byzantine Italy at the tail-end of the reign of Nikephoros Phokas (963–9). The *patrikios* Eugenios seems to have been appointed to lead a military and diplomatic offensive against Otto I, the Saxon ruler who had been crowned emperor in the West in 962 and who, by the end of the 960s, was attempting to extend Ottonian influence over the Lombard principalities of Capua-Benevento and Salerno, as well as over the Byzantine themes of Calabria and Longobardia.[82] If Eugenios was appointed as *katepano* of Italy towards the end of the reign of Nikephoros Phokas (963–9), then his position can perhaps be compared with the appearance of the emperor's nephew Bardas Phokas as *doux* of Chaldia on the northernmost sector of the empire's eastern frontier.[83]

However, just as the position of *doux* of Chaldia proved to be a flexible command which fluctuated in accordance with conditions elsewhere in the empire, similar observations have been made by von Falkenhausen of the situation in southern Italy.[84] While *katepanes* were originally appointed as commanders of offensives against external enemies, with the death of Nikephoros their responsibilities changed rap-

---

[81] von Falkenhausen, *Untersuchungen*, 45, 83.

[82] *Chronicon Salernitanum: A Critical Edition with Studies on Literary and Historical Sources and on Language*, ed. U. Westerbergh (Stockholm, 1956), 175–6. Eugenios was perhaps too energetic in his enforcement of Byzantine authority; on account of his cruelty he was recalled to Constantinople by Emperor Nikephoros.

[83] See above 6.3.1.

[84] von Falkenhausen, *Untersuchungen*, 45–7.

idly, particularly as conditions elsewhere in the empire meant that the southern Italian frontier became a backwater, a region accustomed more to soaking up pressure from outside foes rather than launching attacks on its enemies. The downgrading of the Italian frontier began in the reign of Nikephoros' imperial successor, John Tzimiskes (969–76), who soon came to terms with the Ottonians, marrying his relative Theophano to Otto I's son, Otto II.[85] Peace in the west meant that the emperor was able to liberate the troops necessary for his campaigns elsewhere in the empire, especially in the east. Meanwhile, conditions after Tzimiskes' death did not lend themselves to a fresh military interest in southern Italy. The outbreak of civil war at the beginning of Basil's reign, the rise of the Kometopouloi in Bulgaria, and the ongoing struggle with the Fatimids in the east, meant that there was little spare military capacity for action in Italy, even when the Byzantine position was threatened by external attack or internal revolt.[86] Indeed, Basil's attention only turned towards Italy in a military sense in the second half of his reign, particularly after his annexation of Bulgaria. At least two major expeditions were sent to deal with a local revolt led by Meles, a Lombard notable from Bari, during the second decade of the eleventh century. Then, in 1024–5 Basil himself planned an invasion of Sicily. An advance party led by the eunuch Orestes, a veteran of the Bulgarian campaign, had already left for the west when the emperor died.[87]

While southern Italy was rarely a priority for the imperial authorities in Constantinople, nonetheless, a reasonable

---

[85] A. Davids, *The Empress Theophano: Byzantium and the West at the Turn of the First Millennium* (Cambridge, 1995).

[86] von Falkenhausen, 'Byzantine Italy in the Reign of Basil II', 141–3.

[87] For the Sicilian expedition see below 8.6.

amount can be gauged about its administration, both military and civil, during Basil's reign. The first important observation concerns *katepanes*. While such officials were frequently to be found at the head of local bureaucracy, it is clear that they were dispensable in times of crisis elsewhere in the empire. For much of the 990s, that decade when Byzantine energies were at their most extended, involved in defending the Balkans against Bulgarian attack and the eastern frontier against Fatimid advance, there appears to have been no *katepano* in Italy at all. Instead, command over local civil and military administration appears to have been in the hands of a senior officer from the *tagma* of the *exkoubitores*, a regiment of central government troops based in Bari, the headquarters of Byzantine authority in southern Italy.[88] Of course the presence of the *exkoubitores* is, of itself, significant. It indicates that a small detachment of central army troops remained in the region throughout Basil's reign, an impression confirmed by the incidence of senior *tagmata* officials in contemporary documentary and sigillographical sources.[89] Whatever the pressures elsewhere in the empire, southern Italy was, then, never fully abandoned by Basil. Nonetheless, it is clear that it was only in the final two decades of Basil's reign that large numbers of troops were dispatched to southern Italy. If we can believe Skylitzes' rather confused testimony, *strategoi* from the naval

[88] A *praitorion*, or governor's HQ, had been built in Bari before 1011 (Martin, *La Pouille*, 705).

[89] This commander seems to have taken control during the interregnum between the *katepanes* John Amiropoulos (988–9) and Gregory Tarchaneiotes (998–1006) (von Falkenhausen, *Untersuchungen*, 117–18, 122; G. Loud, 'Byzantine Italy and the Normans', in J. D. Howard-Johnston (ed.), *Byzantium and the West* (Amsterdam, 1988), 218; Martin, *La Pouille*, 702). For the presence of field officers of the various *tagmata* see also von Falkenhausen, 'Byzantine Italy in the Reign of Basil II', 152; Martin, *La Pouille*, 700–3.

themes of Samos and Kephalonia were dispatched *c.*1011 with troops to help suppress the first rebellion of Meles. The *katepano* in charge of southern Italy in this period was Basil Mesardonites.[90] When Meles recommenced his rebellion in 1017, allying with a band of Norman mercenaries to defeat a Byzantine army led by the *katepano* Kontoleo Tornikios, a new Byzantine force was dispatched led by Basil Boiannes.[91]

It is striking that in periods of emergency in southern Italy itself, when large numbers of troops from the central army were employed, the position of *katepano* took on the supra-thematic military nature with which it had been invested in the later 960s. Thus, in 982 during the invasion of the German emperor, Otto II, a certain Romanos *patrikios* was vested with authority over Italy and Calabria.[92] In 1017 Boiannes was appointed *katepano* of the whole region of southern Italy, of Calabria as well as Langobardia. Indeed Boiannes may have enjoyed the kind of plenipotentiary position familiar from the careers of Nikephoros Ouranos and David Areianites.[93] As von Falkenhausen has pointed

---

[90] Skylitzes, *Synopsis*, 348. For confusion in Skylitzes' record of this expedition, particularly over the precise identity of the *strategos* of Samos, see above p. 190 n. 47.

[91] Skylitzes does not refer to Boiannes' exploits during his coverage of Basil's reign, but refers to them later in the *Synopsis Historion* in a characteristically telescoped passage about the history of Byzantine command in southern Italy which forms the preface to his account of the revolt of George Maniakes during the reign of Constantine IX Monomachos (Skylitzes, *Synopsis*, 426); see also von Falkenhausen, 'Byzantine Italy in the Reign of Basil II', 138. Boiannes' exploits are easier to trace in Italian and northern European historical writings than in Byzantine texts: *Lupus Protospatharius*, 57; Ralph Glaber, *Historiarum Libri Quinque*, 97–8; Ademar of Chabannes, *Chronicon*, 173–4; Leo Marsicanus, *Chronica Monasterii Casinensis*, 236–43, 261; William of Apulia, 102–4; Amatus of Monte Cassino, *Storia de'Normanni* 24–40; for further discussion of all these texts see above 1.2.2.

[92] von Falkenhausen, *Untersuchungen*, 49, 84.

[93] Ibid. 86–7. The late 11th-c. verse account of the deeds of Robert Guiscard by William of Apulia succinctly summarizes the all-encompassing

out, however, this aggregation of powers into the hands of a single military commander was quite rare during the later tenth and early eleventh centuries. Instead, she has argued that it was more usual for the *katepano* of Italia to fulfil the role which had been exercised by the *strategos* of Langobardia earlier in the tenth century. In other words that the *katepano* of Italy (or Longobardia—the terms appear to be used by contemporaries synonymously during this period) was simply a *new* term for an *old* office: that of *strategos* of Longobardia (a region which approximately equates to modern-day Apulia). The quotidian responsibilities of this *katepano* were twofold and limited: he organized the defence of the locality from external foes and watched over the civil administration of the province.[94] Parallel authority was exercised in Calabria by a separate *strategos*, an official whose survival into the eleventh century is visible in documentary and sigillographical materials.[95]

That Byzantine southern Italy retained a large element of its earlier thematic governance is visible in other forms of evidence. Documentary, sigillographical, and historiographical sources all demonstrate the survival of those officials within thematic administration familiar from the ninth and tenth centuries, including *tourmachai*, *kometes* of the tent, and *droungarioi*.[96] The reason for the retention of a bureau-

---

responsibilities of a *katepano*: 'Quod catapan Graeci, nos iuxta dicimus omne, Quisquis apud Danaos vice fungitur huius honoris, Dispositor populi parat omne quod expedit illi, Et iuxta quod cuique dari decet omne ministrat' (William of Apulia, 102–4).

[94] von Falkenhausen, *Untersuchungen*, 49–50, 104–5; see also Martin, *La Pouille*, 700–1.

[95] von Falkenhausen, *Untersuchungen*, 63–5, 99–104.

[96] Ibid. 108–15; Martin, *La Pouille*, 705.

cratic structure based on the traditional administrative imperative of defence is easily detected. Throughout the reign of Basil, the whole of Byzantine southern Italy was prey to sporadic raids by western powers and sustained attacks by Arabs operating from Sicily and North Africa. Otto II attacked Byzantine southern Italy in 982 before meeting disastrous defeat at Stilo (in Calabria) at the hands of the emir of Sicily. In 1021 Henry II, the German emperor, entered Byzantine territory, an expedition that the Byzantines did little to resist actively, despite the fact that Basil Boiannes had increased size of the garrison in Bari and established a double line of fortified urban settlements in the borderland region of northern Apulia. Meanwhile, the raiding activity of Muslim states from the south regularly devastated large areas of Byzantine-held territory, particularly in the first half of Basil's reign. These Muslim raids are recorded in brief entries in the annals from Byzantine southern Italy. Yet, despite the brevity of their description of such raids, the local histories make it clear that Muslim incursions became both more frequent and serious during the period 986 to 1009. In 986 Gerace in Calabria was occupied briefly and the walls of nearby Cosenza destroyed; in 988 and 1003 Bari was threatened; in 1009 Cosenza was reoccupied. A powerful sense of the catastrophe such raids wrought to local society is provided by a landowner from Conversano who refers to misery in the hinterland of Bari in 992.[97]

---

[97] Annals of Benevento, 176; Annals of Bari, 53–4; *Lupus Protospatharius*, 55–7. For the general narrative of these raids see Gay, *L'Italie méridionale et l'empire byzantin*, 333–424; Kreutz, *Before the Normans*, 119–23. See also von Falkenhausen, 'Byzantine Italy in the Reign of Basil II', 141–3, 148–51; she

The limited defensive nature of the responsibilities of the *katepanes* of Italy/Longobardia, and their more junior *strategos* colleagues in Calabria, during Basil's reign was shaped by two pressures: the relative neglect of the military administration of the frontier by the imperial authorities in Constantinople and the danger of external attack. The defensive quality of the role of the senior Byzantine military officials in southern Italy and the survival of the substructure of the thematic government over which they exercised authority has its most obvious parallels in the Balkans, particularly in Thessalonika, where as we have seen earlier in this chapter, administration was shaped, at least until 1018, by another powerful external threat, the Bulgarians. Yet, while the Italian sphere may have been neglected more than other borderlands, distinct parallels between the military administration of this frontier in the extreme west and elsewhere in the empire of Basil II can still be observed. Just as elsewhere, senior commanders in Italy were required to be skilled diplomats. During the worst Arab raids, those which occurred at the beginning of the eleventh century, Byzantine commanders on the ground in Italy had to co-operate with overseas allies to protect the strongholds of imperial authority in the region. At some point between 1002 and 1004 Bari, the headquarters of the *katepano* of Italy, was only rescued from Arab siege by a Venetian navy; in 1006 a Pisan maritime force supported the Byzantine

argues that Calabria was affected by Arab raids more severely than Apulia, and that in the first half of Basil's reign it experienced substantial depopulation. For more on Boiannes' fortifications see below p. 441.

position in Calabria.[98] This use of regional allies for the prosecution of defensive campaigns is a phenomenon observed on other frontiers, and a strategy that Basil II used frequently, particularly when his main field army was occupied elsewhere in the empire. The employment of nascent maritime Italian cities to defend Byzantium's periphery recalls the activities of David of Tao on the eastern frontier in the period before 1000, and alliances with the Marwanids and Mirdasids after this date.[99] An additional parallel between the Italian context and the military administration of other frontiers in Basil's reign is the fragility of senior command in the decades before 1000, and its greater robustness after this date. Just as was the case in the east and in the Balkans, the early decades of Basil's reign were characterized by a very rapid turnover in senior commanders. Many *katepanes* of Italy, such as Kalokyros Delphinas (982–3) and John Amiropoulos (988–9), lasted for little more than a year.[100] However, from *c*.1000 onwards, senior command in southern Italy was characterized by greater longevity and stability. Several *katepanes* held power in Italy for between six and ten years. Gregory Tarchaneiotes, who arrived in Italy in 998, was recalled in 1006; Basil Mesardonites ruled between 1010 and 1016; Basil Boiannes arrived to deal with

---

[98] For the Venetian intervention see: *Lupus Protospatharius*, 56 (dated to 1002); Annals of Bari, 53 (dated to 1003); John the Deacon, *Cronaca Veneziana*, 166–7 (rescue of Bari dated to 1004); Nicol, *Byzantium and Venice*, 44–6; also see Gay, *L'Italie méridionale et l'empire byzantin*, 368–70; von Falkenhausen, 'Byzantine Italy in the Reign of Basil II', 144; for these events also see below 8.6.

[99] See above 6.3.1–3.

[100] von Falkenhausen, *Untersuchungen*, 84.

Meles in 1017; he was only recalled from Italy a decade later at the beginning of the reign of Romanos III (1028–34).[101]

Parallels between southern Italy and peripheral zones elsewhere in Byzantium surface not just in military governance but also in civil administration. Both von Falkenhausen and Martin have observed the degree to which a highly centralized state based on Constantinople was willing in practice to work with considerable flexibility in absorbing local administrative practices, indigenous bureaucrats, and provincial power structures. Such practices meant that a peripheral region such as southern Italy was characterized by a bureaucracy that differed considerably from administration at the heart of the empire. Both von Falkenhausen and Martin argue that from the period when the Byzantines first began to expand their authority in southern Italy, in the later ninth century, they customarily accommodated the plurality of local faiths, languages, and laws. They recognized the practical differences between largely Greek-speaking areas such as Calabria and the region around Bari, where the Orthodox faith was also at its strongest, and the predominantly Latin-speaking Longobardia (Apulia), whose inhabitants tended to worship according to the Latin rite and follow Lombard law. Some regions were governed according to Greek law, others according to Lombard law. Where Lombard law prevailed, the chief legal officials were local *gastalds* or *iudices*. Signatures on contemporary documents indicate that these *gastalds* could be either Greek- or Latin-speaking. Moreover, many positions

---

[101] von Falkenhausen, *Untersuchungen*, 84–7.

within the hierarchy of thematic government were filled by indigenous notables. *Tourmachai*, who exercised both military and civil responsibilities, and were second in rank only to the *strategos* or *katepano*, were almost always local figures, as were bishops and archbishops.[102]

Moreover, while adoption of and adaptation to local practices appears to have been a constant throughout Byzantine-controlled southern Italy, it was in the frontier regions of the province that differences between local and metropolitan structures were at their most visible, as Jean-Marie Martin's analysis of the fortification of the remote and lightly populated northern borderlands of Apulia demonstrates. Certainly textual and archaeological evidence suggests that the initiative for fortifying this region, known as the Capitanata, in the last decade of Basil's reign came from the imperial authorities. Latin chroniclers explicitly refer to the role that the *katepano* Basil Boiannes played in founding new fortified settlements at sites such as Civitate, Dragonara, Florentino, Montecorvino, Tertiveri, and Troia.[103] The fact that many of these were new foundations may point to considerable investment on the part of the

[102] Ibid. 103, 109–11, 128–9; von Falkenhausen, 'Zur byzantinischen Verwaltung Luceras', 395–406; eadem, 'A Provincial Aristocracy', 217–18; eadem, 'Byzantine Italy in the Reign of Basil II', 139, 152–3, 155–6; Martin, *La Pouille*, 695–99, 705–10; see also Loud, 'Byzantine Italy and the Normans', 218; Kreutz, *Before the Normans*, 125–9.

[103] See, e.g. Leo Marsicanus: 'cum iam dudum Troiam in capite Apulie construxisset, Draconian quoque et Florentinum ac Civitatem, et reliqua municipia que vulgo Capitanata dicuntur edificavit, et ex circumpositio terries habitatores convocens deinceps habitari constituit' (Leo Marsicanus, *Chronica Monasterii Casinensis*, 261).

Constantinopolitan centre.[104] Yet, those who actually settled in the newly fortified region were Lombards. The *katepano* issued privileges in 1019 (and perhaps again in 1024) encouraging Lombards from outside Byzantine territory to move to the region; one of the main inducements to migrate was the confirmation of Lombard law in the new settlements.[105] The fact that far less evidence (whether material or documentary) for the presence of imperial authorities has been retrieved from the Capitanata than from most other regions of Byzantine southern Italy suggests that the internal governance of this frontier region was left almost entirely to local power-structures and processes. The only imperial officials, indeed, who appear in the historical record of the Capitanata were officers from the imperial army, particularly those bearing the responsibility of *komes*. They were probably in charge of small numbers of troops garrisoned in the newly fortified sites.[106]

Nonetheless, it is important to note that despite their remote location the fortified settlements of the Capitanata were far from impoverished. As I have suggested earlier in

[104] Some of the cash for this investment may have been raised by taxing areas of southern Italy occupied by the Byzantines since the later 9th c. There is evidence for the widespread imposition of the fortification-building tax (*kastroktisia*) in Oria, Trani, Bari, and Monopoli, in the late 10th and early 11th c., although it is also clear that exemptions from this due were granted to some favoured individuals (Martin, *La Pouille*, 713; Oikonomides, 'Tax Exemptions for the Secular Clergy', 321–2).

[105] Martin, 'Une frontière artificielle', 379–85; idem, *La Pouille*, 259–63; idem, 'Les Problèmes de la frontière', 263, 268; J.-M. Martin and G. Noyé, *La Capitanata nella del storia Mezzogiorno medievale* (Bari, 1991), 201–6; von Falkenhausen, *Untersuchungen*, 55–7; eadem, 'Provincial Aristocracy', 213–14.

[106] Martin, *La Pouille*, 699–700, 711–14.

this book, both on the eastern frontier and in the Balkans a powerful motive for the Byzantine preservation of local administrative practices and officials was the practical rationale of achieving maximum fiscal benefit at minimal administrative expense. This is a view also propounded by von Falkenhausen as far as the overall governance of Byzantine southern Italy is concerned.[107] That strong economic and fiscal motives underpinned frontier governance in Basil's Byzantium is also supported by Martin's analysis of Boiannes' policies in the Capitanata. For as Martin points out, one of the outstanding results of Boiannes' policy of fortification was to turn a region which had once been a wasteland into an area of strong economic development. Within two decades of the issue of privileges, local charters record a surge in economic activity: the excavation of irrigation canals, the erection of mills, and the presence of vines.[108]

This increase in the prosperity of a frontier region, driven by non-Greek speaking and non-Orthodox professing migrants who were deliberately encouraged to settle by the imperial authorities, has important parallels in Byzantium's eastern borderlands. Indeed, the most well-known

[107] von Falkenhausen, 'Provincial Aristocracy', 218.

[108] Martin, 'Une frontière artificielle', 382–3; idem, 'Les Problèmes de la frontière', 268; on increasing local prosperity in southern Italy in the latter stages of Basil's reign see also von Falkenhausen, 'Byzantine Italy in the Reign of Basil II', 151, 157–8. Similar arguments for 11th-c. prosperity in those regions of southern Italy which had previously been made desolate by raiding have been made by Guillou with respect to 11th-c. Calabria and the cultivation of mulberry trees, the feeding of silk worms, and silk production (A. Guillou, 'Production and Profits in Southern Italy (9th to 11th century)', *DOP* 38 (1974), 91–109.

comparative example is that of the emperor Nikephoros
Phokas (963–9) choosing to repopulate Melitene in the
960s with Syrian Monophysites from Muslim-controlled
territories.[109] These Syrians were part of a wider trading
network which included communities living along the Tigris
River in cities like Tikrit and Mosul. One of these families,
the Banu Abu Imran, were so wealthy that they were able to
lend Basil II enough money to support the entire Byzantine
field army when he stayed in Melitene during the winter of
1022 after campaigning against the Iberians and in Azerbaijan.[110] But the Syrians were not alone among non-Greek
speaking and non-Orthodox professing migrants to the
eastern reaches of the Byzantine Empire. During the supremacy of the Armenian *katholikos* Khachik (972–92),
enough Armenians had migrated to Tarsos and Antioch
for new Armenian sees to be established.[111] Meanwhile,
new Armenian churches were built across the easternmost
reaches of Anatolia[112] and Armenian monasteries were
recorded in the Amanos Mountains during Basil's reign.[113]
In the first half of the eleventh century substantial numbers
of Georgian Chalcedonian monks were also active in the

[109] Michael the Syrian, *Chronique*, 130–2; Dagron, 'Minorités ethniques',
186–204; Holmes, 'Basil II and the Government of Empire', 157.

[110] Michael the Syrian, *Chronique*, 145; Bar Hebraeus, *Chronography*, 178;
Dagron, 'Minorités ethniques', 193–4; see also below 8.4 and 8.8 for Basil's
campaign of 1021–3.

[111] Stephen of Taron, *Armenische Geschichte* 196; Garsoïan, 'Armenian
Integration into the Byzantine Empire', 56–7, 71.

[112] Michael the Syrian, *Chronique*, 132–4; Bar Hebraeus, *Chronography*,
179; M. Thierry, 'Données archéologiques sur les principautés arméniennes
de Cappadoce orientale au XI siècle', *REArm* 26 (1996–7), 119–72.

[113] Matthew of Edessa, *Armenia and the Crusades*, 47–8.

same region, most notably at the monastery of St Symeon Stylites the Younger on the Wondrous Mountain.[114]

Further analogies between the experience of the eastern frontier and that of southern Italy emerge if we consider the relationship between the representatives of Constantinopolitan power, local notables, and indigenous populations. In the case of the eastern frontier, it has been suggested that administration was characterized by a thin layer of senior, centrally appointed officials, who acted as the key intermediaries between Constantinople and local society. That this was also the case in Italy is suggested by the fact that while the most senior officials such as the *katepanes*, *strategoi*, and *kouratores* were appointed directly from Constantinople, almost all other officials, whether Greek- or Latin-speaking, were locals.[115] Moreover, whenever Constantinopolitan appointees do appear in the documentary record, it is clear that they were few in number, and that their responsibilities stretched thinly over vast distances,

[114] W. Z. Djobadze, *Materials for the Study of Georgian Monasteries in the Western Environs of Antioch-on-the-Orontes* (Louvain, 1976); idem, *Archaeological Investigations in the Region West of Antioch-on-the-Orontes* (Stuttgart, 1986). At St Baarlam's monastery on Mt Kasios, 65 kilometres south-west of Antioch, three anonymous copper *folles* of issues A1 and A2 have been discovered (Djobadze, *Archaeological Investigations*, 218–19.) These issues are usually dated to the period 969–76 (A1) and 976–1028 (A2): V. Ivanisevic 'Interpretations and Dating of the Folles of Basil II and Constantine VIII— the Class of A2', *ZRVI* 27 (1989), 37–39). Specifically on the Wondrous Mountain see Ibn Butlan, *Medico-Philosophical Controversy*, 56; Djobadze, *Archaeological Investigations*, 59, 204–11. Several 11th-c. seals issued by the monastery survive: Cheynet, Morrisson, and Seibt, *Sceaux byzantins: Henri Seyrig*, no. 288; V. Laurent, *Le Corpus des sceaux de l'empire byzantin*, v. *L'Église* (Paris, 1963–72), no. 1559.

[115] von Falkenhausen, 'Provincial Aristocracy', 211–12, 217–18; Martin, *La Pouille*, 703–7.

often beyond southern Italy itself. Among such senior officials dispatched from the centre of the empire with extensive duties in the eleventh-century localities was John Xeros, a *dioiketes* of the Peloponnese and *kourator* of the West and Longobardia.[116]

Another theme developed in Chapter 6 of this book was the idea that on the eastern frontier senior officials presided over a relationship between Constantinople and the locality that was predicated on tribute payments. In a more limited sense the same may have been true of Italy. While areas which had been under direct Byzantine control since the late ninth century were taxed according to the same regime as in the heartlands of the empire, albeit through the agency of officials indigenous to southern Italy, in those remote inland regions where the Byzantines had traditionally exerted much less influence, such as the Capitanata and the hinterland of Taranto, looser arrangements closer to tribute payments may have been current.[117]

An *apodeixis* (receipt) sent to one Kinnamos in 1016 by the *katepano* Basil Mesardonites seems to support this hypothesis. The *apodeixis* acknowledged the receipt of 36 *nomismata* in the form of a tax known as the *synetheia* sent from the *kastron* of Palagiano. This location was one of those small sites fortified in the early eleventh century in the

[116] von Falkenhausen, *Untersuchungen*, 131; Laurent, *Vatican*, no. 111. For more on this family's service in central government see Cheynet, *Pouvoir et contestations*, 201 (nn. 12, 13), 257, 375–6; Laurent, *Le Corpus des sceaux de l'empire byzantin,* ii. *L'Administration centrale* (Paris, 1981), no. 327.

[117] For the idea that long-occupied areas were taxed in line with arrangements in the heartlands of the empire, albeit through the agency of officials of local origin, see Martin, *La Pouille*, 710–13.

hinterland of Taranto as part of a system of deep defence against Arab attack.[118] Kinnamos himself was a local notable who held the office of *kalligraphos*, a position which may equate to that of local notary. For von Falkenhausen, the principal significance of this document is that senior commanders in the west of the empire continued to be paid their salary directly by the local populace in the eleventh century, a situation which was in direct contrast to the east of the empire where salaries were traditionally paid by the emperor in cash.[119] But just as important, it seems to me, is the extent to which this arrangement suggests that the relationship between remote local communities in southern Italy and the principal representative of Constantinopolitan authority took the form of one-off cash payments which were unmediated by any intermediate, lesser-ranking imperial official sent from the capital. If this is so, then the agreement between Kinnamos and Mesardonites can be construed as a tribute agreement. In addition it provides further proof that the number of senior Byzantine bureaucrats on the frontiers in the tenth and early eleventh centuries was often extremely restricted, and that day-to-day governance of such peripheral regions remained largely in the hands of indigenous power-structures, even during the final decade of Basil's reign when imperial authority across the empire was at its zenith.

---

[118] von Falkenhausen, *Untersuchungen*, 131; Martin, 'Les Problèmes de la frontière', 267; idem, *La Pouille*, 268–7.

[119] von Falkenhausen, *Untersuchungen*, 131.

8

The Reign of Basil II: A Reconstruction

8.1 BACKGROUND

When Basil II and his younger brother Constantine VIII became senior emperors in 976 they inherited an empire which had expanded considerably in territorial terms since the foundation of the Macedonian dynasty by their great-great-grandfather Basil I in 867. Forward momentum in the east had prospered as the Abbasid caliphate in Baghdad slowly disintegrated. During the later ninth and first half of the tenth centuries that expansion had been piecemeal, with the most conspicuous Byzantine territorial conquest coming in 934 at Melitene. It was only in the middle of the century that the drive eastwards had begun to accelerate significantly, as Byzantine armies broke through the Taurus and Anti Taurus ranges, conquering the cities of the Cilician Plain and forcing Antioch in northern Syria to submit in 969. Meanwhile in the west, military action had also been undertaken shortly before the reign of Basil began. After a Byzantine decision to persuade the Rus of Kiev to attack their Bulgarian neighbours had misfired badly in the late

960s, Emperor John Tzimiskes had been forced to campaign against both the Rus and the Bulgarians. Following imperial victories at Preslav and Dristra in 971 Byzantium had annexed much of eastern Bulgaria.[1]

Such was the military glory and territorial expansion which preceded Basil's reign. However, with this glory and expansion had also come substantial internal instability. When Romanos II had died in 963 leaving his sons Basil and Constantine as minors and his widow Theophano as their regent, the senior general Nikephoros Phokas had seized power in Constantinople with the aid of the boy emperors' great-uncle Basil Lekapenos, the *Parakoimomenos*, who was the chief eunuch in charge of the Great Palace.[2] Having married Theophano, Nikephoros had acted as guardian and senior emperor to Basil and Constantine. Indeed, all three emperors appeared on the coinage produced during Nikephoros' reign. But in 969 instability had returned, with the assassination of Nikephoros by another general, John (I) Tzimiskes. After being prohibited by Patriarch Polyeuktos from marrying Theophano, Tzimiskes had sent the empress into exile while keeping her sons in Constantinople. It was only in January 976, when Tzimiskes

---

[1] For an outline of the history of Byzantium in the later 9th and 10th c. see in the first instance, Whittow, *Making of Orthodox Byzantium*, chs. 8 and 9; J. Shepard, 'Byzantium in Equilbrium', and idem, 'Byzantium Expanding', in T. Reuter (ed.), *NCMH* iii (Cambridge, 1999), 553–66, 586–604.

[2] A short account of this coup is related in Skylitzes, *Synopsis*, 256–9. For a rather more detailed and contemporary history of this period, see Leo the Deacon, *Historiae Libri Decem, passim*; Ostrogorsky, *Byzantine State*, 283–98; Treadgold, *Byzantine State and Society*, 498–513.

himself died, that Basil and Constantine finally assumed full rule as adult emperors.[3]

8.2   THE YEARS OF REVOLT: 976–89

During the first thirteen years of his reign Basil faced external adversaries as well as severe threats from within Byzantium. In the west attacks came from Bulgaria; in the east from the Fatimids of Egypt, the Buyids of Iraq, and a variety of Kurdish and Bedouin tribes. However, the principal danger was domestic: from revolts led by the generals Bardas Skleros and Bardas Phokas. Plentiful coverage of these revolts by medieval historians means that a reasonably clear picture of what happened during the civil wars of 976 to 989 can be distilled.[4] Nonetheless, Skylitzes' use of a pro-Skleros source, which we identified in Chapter 5 of this book, introduces certain important distortions in the narrative of the early years of Basil's reign.

The first period of civil war was precipitated in the spring or early summer of 976, when Bardas Skleros, *doux* of Mesopotamia (the general in charge of the army based east of the Anti Taurus mountains) rebelled. From his base at Kharput (Hisn Ziyad) in the Anzitene plain, Skleros marched westwards. Once he had captured Melitene, he

---

[3] Establishing Basil's exact age is difficult. Psellos claims that he was 71 when he died; Skylitzes that he was 70. This would mean that Basil was born some time around 956 (Psellos, *Cronografia*, i. 54–5; Skylitzes, *Synopsis*, 369).

[4] See above Ch. 5; for place names see Map 1.

declared himself emperor. An imperial embassy led by Stephen, the metropolitan of Nikomedia, was unable to dissuade Skleros from this action.[5] The early phases of the war were dominated by a series of inconclusive skirmishes in the Anti Taurus between Skleros' armies and imperial forces led by Eustathios Maleinos and Michael Bourtzes, the *doux* of Antioch.[6] Skleros drew on a wide support base: Armenians in the army, local eastern Christian populations and dignitaries, and even neighbouring Arab Muslim princes, such as Abu Taghlib, Hamdanid prince of Mosul. Yet although it was wide, this alliance was also fragile. Before he even crossed the Anti Taurus, Skleros had to execute his *hetaireiarches*, the head of his immediate retinue, on suspicion that he was about to desert to Basil.[7] Once Skleros finally mustered the strength to cross the Anti Taurus he encountered an imperial army in open combat at Lapara on the eastern Anatolian plateau. The date of this battle is unknown: either late 976 or early 977. It was a Skleros victory.[8] Shortly afterwards Michael Bourtzes was captured and his deputy at Antioch surrendered to Skleros.[9] According to Skylitzes, Skleros then secured control of the important fleet of the theme of the Kibyrrhaiotai based at Attaleia through the agency of his admiral Michael Kourtikios, although Leo the Deacon, a more contemporary historian, suggests that this event did not occur until after Bardas

---

[5] Skylitzes, *Synopsis*, 314–17; Yahya, *PO* 23, pp. 373–4.
[6] Skylitzes, *Synopsis*, 318; Yahya, *PO* 23, p. 374.
[7] See above 5.2.2.
[8] Skylitzes, *Synopsis*, 319–20; also discussed above 5.2.2.
[9] Skylitzes, *Synopsis*, 319; Yahya, *PO* 23, p. 373.

Phokas became involved in the fighting in 978. It is Leo's testimony that should probably be trusted here. As we indicated in Chapter 2, this discrepancy in the dating between the two texts is likely to be the result of Skylitzes' subsequent reordering of the narrative of events.[10] What seems more certain is that after Skleros' victory at Lapara, another imperial embassy, this time led by Leo the *proto-vestiarios*, was sent to negotiate with Skleros; but this too proved unable to come to terms with the rebel.[11]

For the next two years the rebels held the initiative. Skleros achieved another victory over an imperial field army at Rhageai, an unknown location in Phrygia in western Asia Minor.[12] The city of Nikaia, guarded by Manuel Eroti-kos, who was an important forebear to Emperor Alexios Komnenos, also fell to the rebels.[13] Abydos was also success-fully besieged by Skleros' son Romanos, an action which threatened grain supplies to Constantinople.[14] So difficult was the imperial position that by the spring of 978 Basil the *Parakoimomenos* recalled Bardas Phokas, the nephew of Emperor Nikephoros II Phokas, from internal exile. He was appointed *domestikos* of the *scholai*, head of the imperial field army. He headed for Kaisareia in Cappadocia where he raised an army, which included those, like Michael Bourtzes,

---

[10] Skylitzes, *Synopsis*, 319; Leo the Deacon, *Historiae Libri Decem*, 170; see above 2.4 for discussion of the dating of this episode.

[11] Skylitzes, *Synopsis*, 320.

[12] Skylitzes, *Synopsis*, 321–2; Stephen of Taron, *Armenische Geschichte*, 140–1.

[13] Skylitzes, *Synopsis*, 322–3.

[14] Ibid. 324.

whose precise loyalties during the early years of the revolt had been uncertain.[15]

What happened next is a matter of controversy. According to Skylitzes at least three battles were fought between Phokas and Skleros in Anatolia; the first a victory for Skleros at Amorion in the west; the second another Skleros victory at Basilika Therma in the east; the third, a victory for Phokas on the plain of Pankaleia by the Halys River, achieved only after imperial forces had been reinforced by several thousand Iberian (Georgian) troops from the principality of Tao.[16] In contrast, Yahya alludes to only two battles: the first at Pankaleia on 19 June 978, which Skleros won; the second at an unknown location on 24 March 979, where Phokas was victorious.[17] As John Forsyth has shown, this confusion can to some extent be reconciled by using evidence from other contemporary, or near contemporary, sources: Leo the Deacon, the Georgian Life of John and Euthymios, and an inscription from the Georgian monastery of Zarzma which refers to the Iberian intervention from Tao. According to this resolution, the first battle was fought at Pankaleia close to Amorion on the western reaches of the Anatolian Plateau in June 978, while the second and final battle took place at Basilika Therma in the eastern Anatolian theme of the Charsianon in March 979. Forsyth's belief is that the third battle reported by Skylitzes, in which Skleros and Phokas fought a single-handed duel at the Halys River,

---

[15] Skylitzes, *Synopsis*, 324, Yahya, *PO* 23, p. 374.
[16] Skylitzes, *Synopsis*, 324–7.
[17] Yahya, *PO* 23, pp. 375, 399.

did not occur. For him, this engagement was nothing more than a literary figment on the part of Skylitzes.[18]

Having examined Skylitzes' working methods in detail in this book, I am inclined to agree with Forsyth that Skylitzes has almost certainly embellished his account of the Battle of the River Halys, probably by using his military lexicon to add spurious heroic detail to his description of the fighting. Indeed, in Chapter 5, we saw how frequently Skylitzes uses his own particular martial language to articulate how duels were fought, including this encounter between Phokas and Skleros.[19] One can perhaps go further and suggest that Skylitzes may have used the motif of a duel as a convenient way of manufacturing laconic descriptions of military encounters which were much messier and inconclusive in his underlying texts. Nonetheless, my examination of Skylitzes' use and abuse of his sources would not go so far as to support the idea that he simply made things up without support from an original authority. As we saw when analysing his treatment of *Theophanes Continuatus'* coverage of the reign of Romanos Lekapenos in Chapter 3, Skylitzes' additions to his underlying texts tend to take the form of the explanation of motives or insertion of prosopographical details, rather than the introduction of entirely new episodes.[20] In this sense then, I would suggest that the third battle cannot be purely the result of Skylitzes' invention, but instead has its roots in Skylitzes' underlying source: in other

---

[18] Forsyth, 'The Chronicle of Yahya ibn Sa'id', 384–93; see also above 5.2.1 and 6.2 for more on the Iberian intervention.

[19] See above 5.2.3.

[20] See above 3.2.

words, in the pro-Skleros text on which Skylitzes drew heavily to write this part of the *Synopsis*. That there is some solid, Skleros-related evidence in Skylitzes' description of the battle at the Halys River was demonstrated in Chapter 5. Here attention was drawn to the concrete incidental detail, such as the name of the rebel general's horse, which typifies Skylitzes' treatment of Bardas Skleros at this point; this, indeed, contrasts with his much thinner and more cliché-ridden coverage of Phokas.[21]

When all these strands are pulled together, two possibilities seem to be left. One is that the spurious third battle between Skleros and Phokas is at heart a fiction on the part of the author of the pro-Skleros source, designed to create a heroic false finale to Skleros' first war against Basil.[22] The other possibility is that Skylitzes himself found a genuine episode of military action somewhere in the midst of the pro-Skleros source which he then moved to the very end of his narrative of the first Skleros revolt for the purposes of entertaining or providing a military and/or political lesson to his reader.[23] Adjudicating between these possibilities is all but impossible. The most that can be said is that at some level this spoof final battle has a kernel of truth about it. Equally true, is that however this final battle came to reside in the *Synopsis Historion*, Skylitzes added lashings of heroic detail to his narrative. Finally it is clear that the decisive last

---

[21] See above 5.2.2.

[22] See above 5.2.4 for the propaganda aspects to the pro-Skleros source that Skylitzes used.

[23] See above 3.3.2 and 4.2.2 for motives of entertainment and didactic purposes in Skylitzes' composition.

battle of the first Skleros revolt was that reported by Yahya, which took place in the Charsianon in March 979.[24]

Between 976 ad 979 Skleros presented an important challenge to Basil's imperial rule. But it is important not to overstate the severity of that challenge. Skylitzes certainly interprets this three-year period as a relentless Skleros initiative against a pusillanimous imperial court. Yet, this depiction may owe much to his use of a pro-Skleros source. Other evidence suggests that Skleros was rather less dangerous. He was never able to threaten Constantinople permanently. Whenever he approached the city, imperial armies consistently drove him back onto the plateau.[25] He failed to take control of an important source of revenue at the height of his authority in the east, the caravan carrying tribute payments from Aleppo to Constantinople.[26] His power at sea was only partial. Important naval victories were won for the emperor by Bardas Parsakoutenos and Theodore Karantenos.[27] At a crucial point in his campaign

---

[24] Yahya, *PO* 23, p. 399.

[25] See above 5.2.2.

[26] Skylitzes, *Synopsis*, 320–1.

[27] Skylitzes reports that Theodore Karantenos, as *droungarios* of the imperial fleet based at Constantinople, defeated Michael Kourtikios, head of the Attaleia fleet, off Phokaia in the coastal waters of western Asia Minor (Skylitzes, *Synopsis*, 322). It is likely, however, that Skylitzes is conflating two naval engagements here. Leo the Deacon, a contemporary, relates that Bardas Parsakoutenos rather than Karantenos was the head of the central fleet. Indeed, this fleet used Greek fire to destroy a navy loyal to Skleros off Abydos (Leo the Deacon, *Historiae Libri Decem*, 170). There seem, therefore, to have been two serious Skleros defeats at sea: the first suffered off the western coast of Anatolia by Kourtikios at the hands of Karantenos, who seems likely to have been the *strategos* of another naval theme; the second fought much closer to Constantinople between the imperial navy led by Parsakoutenos and

Skleros lost his wealthy eastern Hamdanid allies, when Abu Taghlib, emir of Mosul, was defeated by the Buyids. In short, although Skleros was a good general, he simply did not have the resources to defeat Basil II.[28]

The defeat of the Skleros rebels did not, of course, bring an end to political uncertainty. Skleros and his personal following of about three hundred men were taken into custody by the Buyid ruler of Baghdad, Adud al-Daula, a move which led to fevered diplomatic exchanges between the Byzantine court and Iraq during the early 980s. Byzantine ambassadors to Baghdad included Basil's closest associate at court, Nikephoros Ouranos, the keeper of the imperial inkstand.[29] One of the Buyid envoys who travelled to Constantinople, Ibn Shahram, left an invaluable account of his own expedition to Constantinople *c.*981. In this testimony he indicates that Basil wanted to surrender the empire's client state of Aleppo in northern Syria in return for taking delivery of Skleros. This policy was anathema to many of Basil's advisers including leading generals such as Bardas Phokas and Leo Melissenos, and his own great-uncle, Basil the *Parakoimomenos,* the most important official at court.[30] These tensions came to a head in 985. First there were rumours that Basil Lekapenos was about to incite a

another Skleros maritime force whose commander is unknown. Werner Seibt has also pointed to the likelihood that Skylitzes conflates the two battles (Seibt, *Die Skleroi,* 42).

[28] See above 5.2.2.

[29] Skylitzes, *Synopsis,* 327; Yahya, *PO* 23, p. 400–1, 420; Stephen of Taron, *Armenische Geschichte,* 142–3; for more on Ouranos' career see above 6.3.3, 6.4, 7.1, and below 8.4, 8.5.

[30] al-Rudhrawari, *Eclipse,* vi. 23–34.

palace coup against his great-nephew. Next the armies of the east suspended their operations against the Fatimids in northern Syria. But their expectations of a change of regime proved premature. Rather than removing Basil, the *Para-koimomenos* found *himself* dislodged from power.[31] The emperor then reorganized military high command in the east, recalling Leo Melissenos, *doux* of Antioch, and replacing him with Bardas Phokas, who was transferred from the office of *domestikos* of the east.[32] Meanwhile, Basil took control of foreign policy by attacking Bulgaria in August 986.[33]

When this initiative collapsed in ignominious defeat against the Bulgarians, a second period of civil war ensued. First of all Bardas Skleros was released from Baghdad in the winter of 987. He re-entered imperial territory and immediately revived his rebellion in the area around Melitene. His operation was bankrolled by Baghdad; his troops were drawn from local Bedouin and Kurdish tribesmen.[34] By spring 987 Phokas was hastily reassigned to his erstwhile position of *domestikos* to deal with the Skleros threat.[35] However, his loyalty to the emperor soon evaporated. By August, or September at the very latest, Phokas had declared himself emperor.[36] He probably spent the summer

---

[31] Yahya, *PO* 23, pp. 415–17.

[32] For this chronology see also above 6.3.3.

[33] Yahya, *PO* 23, p. 418; Skylitzes, *Synopsis*, 330–1; Stephen of Taron, *Armenische Geschichte*, 186–7.

[34] Yahya, *PO* 23, pp. 419–20; Stephen of Taron, *Armenische Geschichte*, 187–8; al-Rudhrawari, *Eclipse*, vi. 115–18.

[35] See above 6.3.3.

[36] Forsyth, 'The Chronicle of Yahya ibn Sa'id', 429–32.

negotiating a military alliance with Skleros which included as one of its terms the eventual division of the empire between the two generals. The exact timing and nature of the Phokas–Skleros agreement are obscure, but it is possible that Phokas offered Skleros the role of *domestikos* of the *scholai* in the east while he himself became emperor.[37] One of the reasons why working out what happened during the Phokas–Skleros negotiations and their subsequent joint revolt is so difficult is because once again Skylitzes' testimony exaggerates Skleros' strengths. As we saw in Chapter 5, Skylitzes claims that Skleros was so clever that he allied himself with Phokas, while at the same time dispatching his son Romanos to work for Basil II just in case the emperor was victorious. Yahya, in contrast, maintains that Romanos distrusted Phokas and went over to the emperor of his own accord. Yahya's account is more plausible. Shortly after the two generals agreed terms Phokas imprisoned Skleros. The truth was that Skleros was in a much weaker position than Skylitzes indicates. He had been forced into alliance with Phokas because his Bedouin and Kurdish troops had deserted him.[38]

---

[37] This may be one way of reconciling the apparent discrepancy between Skylitzes' and Yahya's reports of the agreement. According to Yahya, Phokas was to rule in Constantinople while Skleros was to have power outside the capital; according to Skylitzes, Skleros was to exercise power in Antioch and on the eastern frontier while Phokas would be, 'ruler of the empire itself' (Yahya, *PO* 23, 420–1; Skylitzes, *Synopsis*, 336). This putative division of power between Skleros and Phokas is usually explained in territorial terms (see e.g. Forsyth, 'The Chronicle of Yahya ibn Sa'id', 429–30; Seibt, *Die Skleroi*, 52–3) but it may make more sense if it is seen in terms of office-holding instead.

[38] See above 5.2.2–4.

In contrast, while Skylitzes provides relatively little information about the Phokas rebels, they were clearly more dangerous opponents for Basil. Once rebellion broke out in the summer of 987 they consistently threatened Constantinople from the Asian side of the Bosphorus. It was impossible for Basil to drive Phokas back from the coast of Asia Minor as had been the case with Skleros a decade previously. Phokas commanded the loyalty of all the eastern armies and most senior commanders. Only the smaller western armies and a handful of generals stayed loyal to the emperor. Romanos Skleros helped Basil to defend crucial sites such as Abydos.[39] Gregory Taronites (another erstwhile Skleros supporter) tried unsuccessfully to rally local leaders along the eastern frontier only to find himself defeated by troops from Tao loyal to the Phokades.[40] The peril which Basil faced demanded a desperate solution. He sent his sister Anna as a bride to Vladimir, prince of Kiev, in return for around six thousand Rus mercenary troops. This was a spectacular, and ultimately successful, gamble. In late 988 or early 989, Rus troops helped Basil to destroy a rebel army led by Kalokyros Delphinas at Chrysopolis. On 13 April 989 the emperor took the field against Phokas in battle at Abydos carrying the Blachernai icon of the Virgin.[41] Basil's brother Constantine was also present, later claiming that his was the spear which slew the rebel.[42] Yet, as both

[39] See above 5.2.2.

[40] Yahya, *PO* 23, pp. 424–5; *Miracles of Saint Eugenios*, 348–50.

[41] Skylitzes, *Synopsis*, 336–7; Psellos, *Cronografia*, i. 22–9; Leo the Deacon, *Historiae Libri Decem*, 173–5; Yahya, *PO* 23, pp. 424–6; Stephen of Taron, *Armenische Geschichte*, 188–90.

[42] Psellos, *Cronografia*, i. 26–7.

Skylitzes and Psellos acknowledge, the exact fate of Phokas was unknown. Some contemporaries believed he fell in battle; others that he was poisoned. What is clear is that Basil decided to make brutal examples of the rebels. Delphinas had been impaled after his defeat. After Abydos, Phokas' head was sent on a grisly tour of the empire.[43] The terrifying warning was successful. By November 989 Leo Phokas ceded Antioch. Meanwhile at an uncertain date, but certainly before his death on 6 March 991, Bardas Skleros surrendered to the emperor.[44] The civil wars were over.

8.3 AFTER 989: LEGISLATION AND PROPAGANDA

While it is relatively straightforward to construct a narrative account of the civil wars of 976 to 989, particularly once the impact of the pro-Skleros source is taken into account, it is much more difficult to understand what was at stake politically. Often it is argued that these revolts were the culmination of a long, tenth-century conflict between the Macedonian emperors and Byzantium's great aristocratic families over the material resources of the empire. In fomenting revolt the Skleros and Phokas families displayed the potency of the greater families; in brutally defeating the rebels and later crushing their families Basil re-established

[43] Psellos, *Cronografia*, i. 26–9; Leo the Deacon, *Historiae Libri Decem*, 175; Yahya, *PO* 23, p. 426.

[44] Yahya, *PO* 23, pp. 426–7; Skylitzes, *Synopsis*, 338–9; Psellos, *Cronografia*, i. 36–41; see also above 5.2.4.

imperial power.[45] Two pieces of evidence appear to support this view. The first is a long series of novels issued by the Macedonians during the tenth century which tried to prevent the so-called 'Powerful' (*Dunatoi*) from accumulating estates at the expense of the 'Poor' and the imperial fisc. The last, and most draconian, novel in the corpus was issued in 996 by Basil II. As we saw in Chapter 1, this novel required that all properties acquired by the Powerful within free peasant *choria* since 927 should be restored to their former owners without compensation. It also abolished the prevailing practice that such properties were immune from investigation after the passage of forty years. Furthermore, it identified the Phokades as typical of the worst kind of Powerful offenders. The second strand in the evidence is Michael Psellos' literary sketch of the emperor which appears to suggest that after defeating Skleros and Phokas, Basil crushed the greater families of the empire and took sole control of imperial governance.

However, there are reasons for doubting that the civil wars were primarily about a struggle between an increasingly enfeebled emperor and an aristocracy whose power was vested in private reserves of landed property and manpower. In the first place it is unlikely that the balance of material resources was slipping in the tenth century inexorably away from the emperors towards the aristocracy. Contemporaries within and outside the empire consistently point to the Byzantine emperors' substantial income. The

---

[45] Ostrogorsky, *Byzantine State*, 303–8; see also above 1.1 for modern historiographical interpretations of Basil's reign.

author of the mid-tenth-century military manual *De velita-tione* (also known as *Skirmishing*), representing the conservative voice of the serving military officer in the Anatolian provinces, complained about the disturbances caused by civil officials sent from Constantinople, trouble-makers whom he identified as 'tribute levying manikins [who] contribute absolutely nothing to the common good...but store up many talents of gold'.[46] Writing from outside the empire at approximately the same time, the Arab geographer Ibn Hawkal observed a similar phenomenon. He noted that while part of the customs receipts at Trebizond on the Black Sea had once been pocketed by local officials, now all receipts were collected on behalf of the emperor.[47] Such imperial wealth had also, of course, been significantly augmented by the eastern conquests of Basil's imperial pre-decessors.[48]

Events during the civil wars themselves also indicate the degree to which the rebels were not sustained by their own private wealth and manpower but instead by their tenure of public office, especially their command over imperial armies.[49] Whenever Skleros and Phokas held high military office they were dangerous: as generals they were able to negotiate alliances with neighbouring states, hold imperial

---

[46] *Skirmishing*: G. Dagron and H. Mihăescu, *Le Traité sur la guérilla (De velitatione) de l'empereur Nicéphore Phokas* (Paris, 1986), 109–11; translation from Dennis, *Three Byzantine Military Treatises*, 217.

[47] Ibn Hawkal, i. 193.

[48] Howard-Johnston, 'Crown Lands ', 86–95; Cheynet, 'Basil II and Asia Minor', 76–8.

[49] This view of aristocratic resources and power is also held by J.-C. Cheynet; see e.g. his 'L'Aristocratie byzantine', 303–4.

fortresses, and sequester taxes. Without public office they lost these resources and their revolts immediately fizzled out. This is exactly what happened when Skleros returned from exile in 987. For, as we have seen, although Skleros was initially given some manpower and money by the authorities in Baghdad, on his return to Byzantium his allies soon fell away, leaving him with only his personal retinue. Within a very short time he was taken prisoner by Phokas.[50] One could perhaps argue that Skleros' threat was less potent in 987 because his estates had been confiscated by the imperial authorities while he was in exile.[51] However, if we turn away from the Skleros family and look instead at the Phokades, then we find the same phenomenon: that such families only presented a powerful threat when they held senior military positions. Bardas Phokas for example was deprived of the office of *doux* of Chaldia by Emperor John Tzimiskes in 971. At this stage as a private individual he attempted to launch a rebellion from his private estates in Asia Minor, but he attracted few adherents and his revolt ended swiftly.[52] In contrast, when he revolted against Basil II in 987, he held the office of *domestikos* of the *scholai*, controlled the entire field army of the east, and had access to the fiscal resources

---

[50] Yahya, *PO* 23, pp. 421–3; Stephen of Taron, *Armenische Geschichte*, 187–8; Skylitzes, *Synopsis*, 334–6; Canard, 'Deux documents', 63–4, 68–9.

[51] This confiscation of Skleros-related estates was confirmed by Ibn Shahram during the course of his encounter with the *basilikos* Kouleib in eastern Anatolia *c*.981; see further discussion above in 6.4.

[52] Skylitzes, *Synopsis*, 291–4; Leo the Deacon, *Historiae Libri Decem*, 112–26; Cheynet, *Pouvoir et contestations*, 24–5.

of the eastern half of the empire. His revolt lasted for nearly two years.[53]

Another reason for thinking that the revolts were not primarily about an irreconcilable hatred between the greater families and the emperor, is the fact that after insurrection was over many rebels were treated generously. The Skleros family had their lands returned and were restored to public office. Bardas Skleros even received the title of *kouropalates*. Even the Phokas nexus were not treated as severely as is sometimes alleged. Certainly, some rebels were executed or imprisoned: as we have seen, Bardas Phokas was killed on the battlefield and his head was paraded around the empire as a warning to others, while one of his commanders, Kalokyros Delphinas, was either impaled or crucified, a fate which may also have befallen another lieutenant, Atzupotheodore.[54] Yet not all Phokas rebels were punished so harshly. Eustathios Maleinos, another of the Phokades' closest allies, remained in control of his estates for several years after the Phokas revolt was defeated. It was only later that he was put under house arrest in Constantinople, and only after he died that his estates were confiscated by the fisc.[55] Meanwhile, rather than losing all his lands, Bardas Phokas' son, Nikephoros, was given a new estate once the revolt was over. Moreover, at the end of Basil's reign Nikephoros and his brother Bardas held the senior titles of *patrikioi*.[56] While

---

[53] Skylitzes, *Synopsis*, 332–8; Leo the Deacon, *Historiae Libri Decem*, 173–4; Yahya, *PO* 23, pp. 417–26; Stephen of Taron, *Armenische Geschichte*, 187–90; see also 6.3.1.

[54] See above 5.2.2.

[55] Skylitzes, *Synopsis*, 332, 340.

[56] Yahya, *PO* 23, p. 420; Skylitzes, *Synopsis*, 366, 372.

the Phokas family were probably deprived of public office for the rest of Basil's reign, several of their allies, including the general Leo Melissenos, were restored to command.[57] As research into the prosopography of Basil's reign indicates, the emperor continued throughout his reign to employ great families within his armies, particularly during his conflict with the Bulgarians.[58]

Rather, then, than turning on implacable opposition between emperor and aristocracy, the conflicts which characterized the early years of Basil's reign were more about foreign policy and control of the army. That the army was a critical structural element within the Byzantine state was a principle long recognized by contemporaries, including

---

[57] The Armenian historian Aristakes of Lastivert describes the frustration that the Phokades felt throughout Basil's reign because they were deprived of official responsibilities. Aristakes uses a powerful metaphor: that they ranted like caged lions (Aristakes of Lastivert, *Récit des malheurs*, 16–17). It is intriguing that the Greek historian John Skylitzes uses similar imagery in his description of Eusathios Maleinos' house arrest in Constantinople. He depicts Emperor Basil keeping Maleinos ensnared within privilege: 'Supplying him plentifully with everything he needed, Basil detained Eustathios as if he were nourishing a wild beast in a cage' (Skylitzes, *Synopsis*, 340). For the rehabilitation of Melissenos see discussion above 5.2.4, 6.3.3.

[58] Sifonas, 'Basile II et l'aristocratie byzantine', 118–33. Skleros' son Romanos fought the Fatimids in 992–3 and his lieutenant Pegasios served in northern Syria in the first decade of the 11th c. (see above 5.2.2). Michael Bourtzes, who defected to the Skleros party in 977–8, served as *doux* of Antioch in the first half of the 990s (see above 6.3.3). Members of the Taronites family, who had originally rebelled with Skleros, helped Basil suppress the Phokas revolt and served in the Balkans in the 990s (see discussions above in 3.2.2 and 7.1). Meanwhile, Zaphranik of Mokh, an Armenian prince who supported Skleros in his first revolt, became a *manglabites* (member of the imperial *hetaireia* or palace guard) during the 980s (Stephen of Taron, *Armenische Geschichte*, 141; Mahé, 'Basile II et Byzance vus par Grigor Narekac'i', 560, 565–7).

Basil's grandfather Constantine VII in the mid-tenth century: 'As the head is to the body, so is the army to the state; as their condition varies, so too must the whole undergo a similar change. He who does not subject these matters to great care errs with respect to his own safety especially if he must regard the commonwealth as his own realm of security.'[59] The coups of Nikephoros Phokas and John Tzimiskes had set the precedent for experienced generals to seize imperial power. When Basil came to the throne in 976 he was very young. Those with greater experience clearly wished to dominate his decisions, particularly about military affairs, and if necessary replace him. Conflict was the result. When he visited Constantinople in 981 Ibn Shahram reported that Basil himself believed that his argument with Bardas Phokas about imperial policy towards Aleppo could lead to his deposition. Skylitzes alleges that one of the reasons for the Phokas rebellion in 987 was that many leading generals had been denied a role in the Bulgarian expedition of 986.[60] But if control over the army and foreign policy rather than competition for private resources lay at the heart of political tensions during the early years of Basil's reign, it is clear that the emperor's defeat of Skleros and Phokas in 989 did little to alleviate the difficulty. For while power remained vested in the army, whoever commanded the army would continue to threaten the emperor. And indeed, as we have already seen, for several years after 989, military commanders, particularly those in the east, worried Basil persistently. The

[59] Svoronos, *Novelles*, 118; trans. E. McGeer, *The Land Legislation of the Macedonian Emperors* (Toronto, 2000), 71.

[60] al-Rudhrawari, *Eclipse*, vi. 28–35; Skylitzes, *Synopsis*, 332

foremost example was Michael Bourtzes, an experienced soldier whose loyalty to the emperor during the first Skleros revolt had wavered, and whose relationship with Basil remained tense during the 990s when he was *doux* of Antioch until he was dismissed from office in 995.[61] I would suggest that it was only after 1000-1, when Basil was able to reach a peace settlement with the Fatimids, that the problem caused by the eastern generals could be resolved (see below).

Yet, if the Phokas and Skleros revolts were primarily conflicts about control of the army, how should we interpret Michael Psellos' allegations and the provisions of the 996 novel? My reading is that neither of these texts is primarily about conflict between Basil and the great families. In the novel itself the emperor's hostility towards the Powerful families is of secondary significance. As Nicholas Svoronos, the modern editor of the text has shown, the novel survives in two versions, one which represents Basil's original decree, the other a later eleventh-century reworking; and it is only in this second version that the great families, such as the Phokades and Maleinoi, are identified as representatives of the Powerful who need to be reined in by imperial authority.[62] Such explicit, or indeed implicit identification of these

---

[61] See above 6.3.3 and below 8.4.

[62] According to Svoronos the first version of the novel was written in a learned style; the second version retains some passages of the learned original intact, while abbreviating others, and removing or paraphrasing technical administrative terms which by the mid- to later 11th c. had become obsolete. The second version also contains additional passages of text in the form of concrete examples of members of the Powerful whom imperial authority regarded as offenders. These concrete examples included the Phokades, Maleinoi, and Mouselai (Svoronos, *Novelles*, 190–2, 194–7; idem, 'Remarques sur la tradition du texte de la novelle de Basile II concernant les

great families is missing from the original text. Indeed, instead of being preoccupied with attacking the great families, the novel seems to have been issued with a rather different concern in mind: to impose Basil's authority over a court and administration, which had for so long been dominated by the influence and reputation of his great-uncle, Basil the *Parakoimomenos*. This Basil was the illegitimate son of Emperor Romanos Lekapenos (920–44). Unlike his half-brothers, he survived the deposition of the Lekapenoi by Constantine Porphyrogenitus in 945, and went on to serve a variety of emperors during the second half of the tenth century, including his great-nephew Basil II.[63] In the process he became the pivot of Byzantine political society, striking deals with court officials within Constantinople itself and with leading military commanders on the frontiers. It was, for example, the *Parakoimomenos'* influence within the Great Palace and his control over Constantinople that enabled Nikephoros Phokas to enter the city and be crowned emperor in 963.[64] Basil was not only a central figure at court, he was also a literary figure and military commander in his own right.[65] He remained

puissants', *Recueil des Travaux de l'Inst. d'Ét. byz,, Mélanges G. Ostrogorsky* II, 2 vols. (Belgrade, 1964), ii. 433).

[63] The *Parakoimomenos'* half-sister Helen, the daughter of Romanos Lekapenos, was the paternal grandmother of Basil II and Constantine VIII. John Geometres explicitly compared the *Parakoimomenos'* relationship with his great-nephews Basil and Constantine as one of father to son (Lauxtermann, *Byzantine Poetry*, 40).

[64] Skylitzes, *Synopsis*, 258.

[65] W. G. Brokkaar, 'Basil Lacapenos: Byzantium in the Tenth Century', *Studia Byzantina et Neohellenica Neerlandica*, 3 (Leiden, 1972), 199–234.

powerful in the early years of Basil II's reign, but increasingly his authority was rejected by his great-nephew, Emperor Basil. As Ibn Shahram, the Buyid envoy from Baghdad reported, by 981 the two were estranged over the future of Aleppo.[66] Basil II finally dismissed his great-uncle from office in 985. The *Parakoimomenos* died shortly afterwards.[67]

Yet the struggle between the two Basils for control over the central levers of power continued long after this date. This much can be ascertained from the original version of the novel of 996, which indicates that more than ten years after the *Parakoimomenos'* death Basil II was still trying to annul the grants and privileges issued by his great-uncle, still trying to unpick a complex web of political affiliations, and still trying to browbeat his officials into recognizing his own omniscient and omnipotent position at the heart of Byzantine government.[68] Nowhere is the desire to create this image of the all-seeing, all-powerful emperor clearer than at the most famous point in the 996 novel, at which Basil abolished the customary immunity from inquiry and confiscation granted to those who had illegally seized lands from the Poor when forty years had passed.[69] In rescinding this measure Basil granted the fisc unrestricted powers to

---

[66] al-Rudhrawari, *Eclipse*, vi. 23–35; see also above 5.1.

[67] For the death of the *Parakoimomenos* see Yahya, *PO* 23, pp. 416–17; Skylitzes, *Synopsis*, 335; Leo the Deacon, *Historiae Libri Decem*, 172; see also above 2.4, 6.3.3. For confusion in the medieval Greek tradition about how his death fits into the overall narrative of Basil's reign see above 1.2.1, 2.4 and below in this chapter.

[68] Svoronos, *Novelles*, 214. This repeated attack on the *Parakoimomenos*, long after his death, has also been noted by Farag, 'Byzantium and its Muslim Neighbours', 125.

[69] Svoronos, *Novelles*, 200, 212.

review the landed position of any member of the Powerful, a group explicitly identified as comprising the same senior imperial office- and title-holders as those listed in Emperor Romanos Lekapenos' novel of 934.[70] While it was, of course, impossible for imperial authorities in Constantinople to control precisely what its functionaries did in the locality, by including this open-ended provision Basil sent out a brutal message to his officials that the state *could*, if it chose, strike them down at any point. Nor did Basil merely warn of his intentions. He also provided a terrifying exemplar in a certain *protovestiarios* from his court, who as his career in imperial service progressed had accumulated lands within his native *chorion*, but whose estates were then confiscated by the emperor and returned to his original neighbours.[71]

Interpreted in this way, the novel of 996 becomes part of the changes that occurred when one member of the Macedonian-Lekapenos imperial family, Basil II, replaced another, Basil Lekapenos, as the fulcrum of imperial government. That Basil wished to place himself explicitly

---

[70] Ibid. 204–5. Romanos enumerated among the Powerful: *magistroi* and *patrikioi*, as well as those honoured with offices, magistracies, and imperial dignities (civil and military), thematic officials and ex-officials, metropolitans, archbishops, bishops, *hegoumenoi*, heads of pious foundations and those, 'who have in some way attained worldly or ecclesiastical eminence' (Svoronos, *Novelles*, 91; trans. McGeer, *Land Legislation*, 59). It is only in the second version of Basil's novel that this list of officials is reiterated in detail (and the office of *protokentarchos* is added); in the original version issued in 996 rather than naming every official, the emperor merely states that he is following his great-grandfather's general principle.

[71] It is only in the second, later, version of the novel that this *protovestiarios* is named as Philokales (Svoronos, *Novelles*, 202–3). In the first version of the novel he is left anonymous.

at the centre of the state in the minds of his subjects and officials may also explain some of the material artefacts of his reign. Imperial omnipotence is graphically represented in the frontispiece to the Psalter commissioned by Basil II which is now located in Venice. Here Basil appears in military dress, in the guise of an emperor of Late Antiquity, crowned by Christ, supported by his friends the military saints, and receiving the submission of a multitude of peoples. Recent research suggests that these peoples were as likely to be Basil's own subjects as his overseas adversaries.[72] Another index of Basil's all-seeing, all-knowing self-image is the epitaph to his tomb. The emperor describes his constant vigilance: 'for none saw my spear lie still from the time the emperor of heaven called me great emperor autokrator of the earth.... now campaigning manfully to the west.... now to the very borders of the east.'[73] This rhetoric was absorbed by contemporary historians. The obituary for Basil recorded by Yahya ibn Sa'id may have been taken from an official eulogy issued at the time of the emperor's death. Yahya describes Basil as an emperor who 'throughout his reign looked into every matter, great or small in his empire'.[74]

A rather similar picture surfaces in Michael Psellos' austere portrait of Basil. He describes Basil's omniscience and

---

[72] Cutler, 'The Psalter of Basil II'; Stephenson, *Legend of Basil the Bulgar-Slayer*, 51–6.

[73] Mercati, 'Sull' Epigrafio di Basilio II Bulgaroctonos', ii. 230; Stephenson, *Legend of Basil the Bulgar-Slayer*, 49–51; trans. Jonathan Shepard; see also Lauxtermann, *Byzantine Poetry*, 236–8; Walter, *Warrior Saints*, 90, 278.

[74] Yahya, *PO* 47, p. 483; trans. Feras Hamza.

conscientious scrutiny of every aspect of government; he reports Basil's constant watchfulness over the empire's frontiers; he stresses the emperor's fondness for modest attire and his disdain for luxury; he emphasizes Basil's successful expansion of the imperial treasury, an achievement also picked up by Yahya. More to the point he describes, in very similar terms to the novel of 996, the emperor's attempt to censor his great-uncle's legislation.[75] Indeed recent research suggests that Psellos' account of Basil's reign may best be seen as a diptych of the two Basils: emperor and *Parakoimomenos*. As Barbara Crostini has shown, in his account Psellos even reorders events so that the demise of the *Parakoimomenos* forms the centre-point of his narrative.[76] This structural change means that Psellos makes the demise of the *Parakoimomenos* the catalyst which changes Basil II from a dilettante into an autocrat. Intriguingly, this textual reordering also suggests that for Psellos the conflict between the two Basils was more important than the emperor's conflict with the powerful families. In Psellos' account Skleros and Phokas become two of many problems that Basil faced rather than the central problem. Psellos' focus on the *Parakoimomenos* has recently been interpreted in a variety of ways. Perhaps Psellos saw in the story of the rise and fall of the *Parakoimomenos* something of his own thwarted career in imperial service?[77] Perhaps as a proto-pagan, who was hostile towards established religion, Psellos dwells on the *Parakoimomenos* because he wants to savour

---

[75] Psellos, Cronografia, i. 8–55; Yahya, *PO* 47, p. 483.
[76] Crostini, 'The Emperor Basil II's Cultural Life', 55–80.
[77] Ibid. 64.

the moment when the emperor destroyed that most potent symbol of his great-uncle's power, his monastery?[78] Matters may, however, be more straightforward. I would argue that Psellos makes the conflict between the two Basils the central event of the reign because this was how contemporaries during the reign itself saw the matter. In stressing the extent to which the rise of Basil the emperor sprang from the demise of Basil the *Parakoimomenos*, Psellos merely echoes the novel of 996. Indeed, so closely does Psellos' interpretation of the reign mirror contemporary propaganda that one suspects that he may have constructed his account using materials from the emperor's own records. As an official at the imperial court in the second and third quarters of the eleventh century Psellos certainly had access to imperial archives.[79]

Basil II faced considerable domestic problems in the first half of his reign: civil wars fomented by his generals; a long struggle for control over the central government with his great-uncle. Psellos seems to suggest that the fundamental question of Basil's reign was: who was to guide the ship of state? The erosion of the imperial fisc and the growth of private estates were at most secondary issues. From as early as Ibn Shahram's embassy to Constantinople in 981, it is clear that Basil wanted to be in charge. His struggle to achieve this goal would take him many years. However,

---

[78] Kaldellis, *The Argument of Psellos' Chronographia*, 82–5.

[79] Marc Lauxtermann also subscribes to the view that Psellos had seen documentation produced during the reign of Basil, on the grounds that Psellos makes a point of noting the unembellished language that the emperor used in his dictated orders (Lauxtermann, 'Byzantine Poetry', 203–4).

after 1000, as we shall see below, reality began to align with the emperor's rhetoric.

8.4 EAST

The area where imperial policy changed most dramatically as a result of Basil's determination to captain the ship of state was Byzantium's eastern frontier. For much of the century before Basil came to power this region had been the focus of Byzantine military aggression, with imperial armies forcing their way over the Taurus and Anti Taurus mountains into the northern reaches of the Fertile Crescent. As we saw in Chapter 6, when Basil came to the throne Byzantium's new eastern territories were areas where administrative structures still remained very fluid and imperial authority had yet to be fully imposed. The empire also faced a series of potentially hostile Muslim neighbours in the east, of whom the most dangerous were the Fatimids of Egypt.

During the first half of Basil's reign, competition between Byzantium and the Fatimids focused on twin targets: the coastal ports of northern Syria and Lebanon, and the city of Aleppo, the Hamdanid emirate in northern Syria, a Byzantine client state since 969/70. Various generals were involved in conflict with the Fatimids between 976 and 988, including Michael Bourtzes, Leo Melissenos, and Bardas Phokas.[80]

---

[80] See above 6.2, 6.3.3. For a more detailed survey of Byzantine relations with the Fatimids and Hamdanids in the period 976–88 see Forsyth, 'Chronicle of Yahya ibn Sa'id', 416–23; Farag, 'Byzantium and its Muslim Neighbours', 182–8, 235–6.

A brief period of peace occurred in 988 when the Fatimids agreed to a Byzantine embassy, which requested a truce so that Basil's energies could be devoted to fighting the Phokas revolt.[81] When conflict broke out again with greater seriousness during the 990s, Fatimid armies repeatedly besieged Aleppo, and inflicted a series of defeats on Byzantine armies based at Antioch. In 994 the *doux* of Antioch, Michael Bourtzes, was defeated for a second time by the Fatimids. At this point Basil II left his campaign in Bulgaria with a detachment of the Byzantine field army, crossed Anatolia in a little over two weeks, and arrived unexpectedly in northern Syria in the early spring of 995. The Fatimid army fled and Michael Bourtzes was sacked as *doux*.[82] This was not the last occasion that Basil was forced to intervene personally in warfare on the frontier shared with the Fatimids. In 998 Byzantine forces based at Antioch under the command of the new *doux*, Damian Dalassenos, suffered another defeat. Basil responded by ravaging Fatimid-held territory in the Orontes valley before cutting westwards to the coast to besiege Tripoli. Although the siege was unsuccessful, Basil's swift military response to the defeat of Dalassenos persuaded the advisers surrounding the young Fatimid caliph, al-Hakim, to come to terms. The result was a peace which lasted without serious rupture from 1001 to 1016. It was

---

[81] Forsyth, 'Chronicle of Yahya ibn Sa'id', 434–35; Farag, 'Byzantium and its Muslim Neighbours', 235–6.

[82] See above 6.3.3. For further coverage of Fatimid–Byzantine warfare in the early 990s, see Forsyth, 'Chronicle of Yahya ibn Sa'id', 481–93.

unshaken even by al-Hakim's destruction of the Church of the Holy Sepulchre in Jerusalem in 1009.[83]

For at least the first seven years of this period of peace Basil's close associate Nikephoros Ouranos served as the emperor's second-in-command on the eastern frontier. Known as *Kraton* of the East, according to his seals at least, Nikephoros appears to have exercised plenipotentiary powers over the whole eastern frontier, in command of both civil and military administration.[84] Not much can be ascertained of his career in the east, although his military manual and letters give us some clues about Byzantine tactics in eastern warfare at the end of the tenth century.[85] Only occasional glimpses of Nikephoros' military activities and his fearsome reputation are visible in the eastern historical narratives and the letters of his friend the judge of Tarsos, Philetos Synadenos.[86] Yet, perhaps the sources' silence, especially that of Yahya, during this period is significant. We learn little of Nikephoros and the eastern frontier simply because very little happened. The most Nikephoros had to do was deal with localized revolts, like that of Gurgen of Iberia in 1001 and the dervish insurrectionary al-Acfar in

[83] See above 6.3.3; Forsyth, 'Yahya', 493–510, 532–45; Farag, 'Byzantium and its Muslim Neighbours', 255–72. For recent discussion of Byzantine–Fatimid relations in the context of the destruction of the Holy Sepulchre and its eventual reconstruction, see Biddle, *The Tomb of Christ*, 74–8. There is good evidence from the much later Mamluk historian, al-Makrizi, for a regular exchange of friendly embassies between Cairo and Byzantium, particularly in the period 1012–14 (Farag, 'Byzantium and its Muslim Neighbours', 272).

[84] See above 6.3.3, 6.4.

[85] McGeer, 'Tradition and Reality', 129–40.

[86] Darrouzès, *Épistoliers*, 256, 258–9.

the Diyar Mudar in 1006–7.[87] Peace with the Fatimids in 1001 allowed Basil to concentrate the empire's military energies in the west, safe in the knowledge that his frontier army in the east was under the tutelage of his most loyal associate. And although this situation deteriorated to some extent when Fatimid forces occupied Aleppo in 1016, Byzantine–Fatimid rivalry remained highly localized. There was no return to the full-scale hostilities that characterized the pre-1000 period.[88]

East of the frontier with the Fatimids, the Djazira borderlands were still an area of active hostility between Byzantium and local Muslim powers in 976. At the time when Basil came to the throne Bardas Skleros found himself appointed to military command in this area as *doux* of Mesopotamia. According to Skylitzes, Skleros regarded this appointment as a backwater posting. Yet, events preceding Skleros'

---

[87] Yahya, *PO* 23, pp. 466–7.

[88] In 1016 after the explusion of Mansur ibn Loulou, a Byzantine ally, from Aleppo by the Fatimid governor of Apameia, Basil II shut the border between Aleppo and Antioch to local trade. The only regional power to gain an exemption from this prohibition was a local Bedouin tribe called the Mirdasids (Yahya, *PO* 47, p. 401). However, longer distance trade with Egypt and Syria, much of which must have travelled by sea, may not have been affected. While it is usually asserted that an embargo was also imposed by Basil on long-distance trade between Byzantium and the Fatimids (Felix, *Byzanz und die islamische Welt*, 40; Forsyth, 'The Chronicle of Yahya ibn Sa'id', 545; Farag, 'The Aleppo Question', 59–60), it is not certain that the rather convoluted Arabic text supports such a reading. Moreover, circumstantial and literary evidence make a long-distance trade embargo unlikely. Documents from the Cairo Geniza refer to trading relationships between Fatimid Egypt and Byzantium during the 1020s (Farag, 'The Aleppo Question', 60). For deeper inquiry into Fatimid–Byzantine relations between 1016 and the end of Basil's reign, see Forsyth, 'Chronicle of Yahya ibn Sa'id', 545–54; Farag, 'Byzantium and its Muslim Neighbours', 274–80.

appointment suggest that Skylitzes was mistaken in this impression. Far from being a backwater this was a hot frontier where Byzantine armies during the reign of John Tzimiskes had been particularly active. One can speculate that the imperial authorities in Constantinople on the death of Tzimiskes wanted to scale back the offensive. But a reining-in of the offensive rather than the remoteness of his command is more likely to have been the real nub of Skleros' complaints and the catalyst to his revolt. Unfortunately the fact that Skylitzes used a pro-Skleros apology as his main narrative source for his coverage of the early part of Basil's reign obscures the domestic political wranglings within Byzantium which led up to Skleros' decision to rebel.[89] But while the exact cause of Skleros' revolt must remain obscure, it had an immediate impact on this sector of the frontier. The Byzantine offensive stopped. And when the Buyid emir, Adud al-Daula, expelled Abu Taghlib, Skleros' regional ally, from Mosul, Mayafariqin, and Amida in 978–9, the empire found itself faced by a potent foe. For the next five years, until he died in 983, Adud controlled a vast swathe of Iraq, western Iran, and northern Mesopotamia from his base in Baghdad. Moreover, he hoped to expand further by capitalizing on Byzantium's domestic strife. Having given the Skleros party sanctuary in a Baghdad prison in 979, Adud's negotiations with Basil turned on the premiss that he would return Skleros in exchange for either a series of mountain fortresses in the Diyar Bakr or control of Aleppo. Although the potency of the Buyid threat waned with

---

[89] See above Ch. 5 and 6.3.2.

Adud's death, Buyid Baghdad continued to sponsor Skleros when he returned to the empire in 987.[90] As we have seen, by the time Skleros returned to Byzantium, Buyid power was beginning to give way to Arab Bedouin and Kurdish tribes in the Djazira. Most powerful of these new forces was the emirate of the Marwanids, founded by Bad ibn Dustuk, which preyed upon both Armenian and Byzantine territory south and west of Lake Van during the Skleros revolt and afterwards. Peace only finally came to this stretch of the frontier in 1000 when Basil awarded Bad's nephew and successor, Ibn Marwan, the title of *magistros,* the office of *doux* of the east, and the promise that imperial troops would assist the Marwanids if they came under outside attack.[91]

In western Caucasia Byzantium's neighbours were pre-dominantly Christian princes, who rarely threatened the empire directly, but who were becoming both militarily and economically stronger in the later tenth century. For the first half of Basil's reign, the most important of these princes was David of Tao, whose regional prominence grew considerably as a result of his vital support for Basil's hegemony during the Skleros revolt. His reward for supply-ing Basil II with armed reinforcements with which to defeat Skleros in 979 was the lifetime stewardship of key imperial territories in Byzantium's north-east borderlands, including the city of Theodosioupolis and the plain of Basean. To some extent his good fortune changed at the end of the 980s, when his support for Bardas Phokas was punished by Basil II who made himself David's legatee in Tao.

[90] See above 6.2, 6.3.2.   [91] See above 6.2, 6.3.1–2.

Nonetheless, for the next ten years David remained de facto politically powerful in the north-east of Byzantium, almost certainly continuing to serve as the empire's principal client in this region.[92] Indeed, it was only when David died early in 1000 that Basil made any effort to impose Byzantine authority directly in this region by marching eastwards to collect his inheritance. Having dispersed token resistance to the Byzantine take-over from the local Georgian nobility, the emperor garrisoned the key fortresses of Tao. He also accepted obeisance from a variety of neighbouring Caucasian princes, Muslim as well as Christian, who were rewarded with imperial titles. Among them was Ibn Marwan. The following year, one of these princes, Gurgen of Iberia (K'art'li), unhappy that he had only received the title of *magistros*, invaded Tao. His attempts were thwarted by a Byzantine army led by Nikephoros Ouranos, the new *doux* of Antioch.[93] Yet, despite this Byzantine victory, little further effort was made to impose imperial authority. Instead while Basil was busy fighting the Bulgarians in the west, a powerful Georgian state began to emerge. In 1008 Bagrat III, ruler of Abasgia, and erstwhile adopted son of David of Tao, inherited Iberia (K'art'li) from his natural father Gurgen, thus uniting a region which extended from the eastern shore of the Black Sea to the foothills of the Caucasus mountains. Bagrat also conquered the princedom of Kakhetia, northeast of Tiflis, and acquired the city of Ardanoutzin, a trading

[92] See above 6.2, 6.3.1.

[93] Yahya, *PO* 23, p. 460; Georgian Royal Annals, 374; Stephen of Taron, *Armenische Geschichte*, 210–12; for further discussion see Forsyth, 'The Chronicle of Yahya ibn Sa'id', 464–78, 557–60.

station north of Tao, which enjoyed an immense customs
revenue, and which was also coveted by successive tenth-
century Byzantine emperors including Basil II.[94] When he
died in 1014 Bagrat left his son George a considerable legacy,
including a longstanding claim to those territories in Tao
which were in Byzantine hands. It was in relation to control
over Tao that relations with Christian Caucasia became
more important during the final decade of Basil's reign.
With the accession of George in 1014, a disagreement immediately broke out about David's patrimony. Having
warned George to stay out of David's former princedom,
Basil sent an imperial army to crush Iberian resistance in
1014. This army was decisively defeated. However, once the
annexation of Bulgaria was completed in 1018, preparations
for a larger-scale campaign were set in train, beginning with
the refortification of Theodosioupolis. Three years later
Basil marched east. Although his first incursion into Iberia
in the autumn of 1021 proved to be inconclusive, another

---

[94] For the general expansion of Bagrat's authority: Georgian Royal Annals,
275–81, 374; Toumanoff, 'Armenia and Georgia', 616–19; idem, 'The Bagratids of Iberia', no. 60; Rapp, 'Imagining History at the Crossroads', 569–79.
The appeal of Ardanoutzin was recognized by the Byzantines earlier in the
10th c. Constantine Porphyrogenitus (945–59) commented that: 'The commerce of the region of Trebizond, and of Iberia and of Abasgia and from the
whole country of Armenia and Syria comes to it, and it has an enormous
customs revenue from this commerce.' During the reign of his imperial
predecessor, Romanos Lekapenos (920–44), the empire had unsuccessfully
tried to occupy the city (*DAI*, 216–23). When Bagrat III occupied Ardanoutzin he expelled his cousins, Bagrat and Demetrios, members of a cadet branch
of the Iberian Bagratids. These cousins took refuge with Basil II in Constantinople. During the reign of Constantine VIII (1025–8) a Byzantine army
tried unsuccessfully to retake the city on their behalf (Georgian Royal Annals,
287, 375; Toumanoff, 'The Bagratids of Iberia', nos. 58 and 59).

offensive in the spring of 1022 resulted in a crushing victory. In return for peace, George handed over several fortresses and his son Bagrat as a hostage.[95]

Meanwhile, Basil's interest in Caucasia did not stop with Georgia but extended into Armenia. In the winter of 1021/2 John Smbat, prince of the Armenian principality of Ani, made Basil his heir. His territories eventually passed to the Byzantines in 1042, long after Basil had died.[96] At around the same time Senacherim, the Artsruni prince of Vaspurakan, took a rather similar decision. He surrendered his hereditary lands south of Lake Van to Byzantium in return for a miscellany of titles, offices, and estates within the empire, including if Skylitzes is to be believed, the position of *strategos* of the central Anatolian theme of Cappadocia. The date of this agreement is, however, obscure because Skylitzes alludes to the subject in one of his characteristic telescoped miscellaneous chapters in the *Synopsis Historion*. This chapter contains the date 1016. However, this date probably does not refer to the handover of Vaspurakan but to a completely different event which is also present in this summary chapter: Byzantium's military alliance with the Rus against northern Black Sea regions.[97] Yahya ibn Sa'id is equally vague, merely mentioning that Vaspurakan was handed over to Byzantium at around the same time as Basil's

[95] Georgian Royal Annals, 281–4, 374; Aristakes of Lastivert, *Récit des malheurs*, 11–21; Yahya, *PO* 47, 459–63, 467–9; Skylitzes, *Synopsis*, 366–7; Forsyth, 'The Chronicle of Yahya ibn Sa'id', 560–81.

[96] Aristakes of Lastivert, *Récit des malheurs*, 15–16; Matthew of Edessa, *Armenia and the Crusades*, 46–7; Forsyth, 'The Chronicle of Yahya ibn Sa'id', 579–81.

[97] Skylitzes, *Synopsis*, 354–5; this passage is also discussed above in 2.1.

campaign against Iberia.[98] Meanwhile, only the later
eleventh-century Armenian historian, Aristakes of Lastivert,
gives slightly more precise dating indications. He suggests
that Senacherim and his son David had already gone over to
Basil before the outbreak of the Phokas–Xiphias revolt in
1021–2. Indeed, according to both Aristakes and his fellow
Armenian historian, Matthew of Edessa, the house of Artsruni was responsible for helping to crush the revolt.[99]
Equally unclear is the strategic context to the surrender.
Although Matthew of Edessa writing in the early twelfth
century asserts that the decision was precipitated by Turco-
man raids, it is likely that pressure on the Artsruni came
from elsewhere: either the Marwanids of the Diyar Bakr, the
Shaddadids of Dvin, or the Rawwaddids of Azerbaijan.[100]
That the Rawwaddids may have been an important danger
is suggested by the action Basil took after he defeated
George of Abasgia in 1022. When he left Tao, he marched
to Vaspurakan, and then headed east to the Plain of Her
(modern-day Khoy in western Iran), west of Lake Urmia.
Although the emperor was forced to turn westwards when
the early autumn snows fell, Basil's target may have been the
emirate of Azerbaijan located to the east of Lake Urmia.[101]

[98] Yahya, *PO* 47, p. 463.

[99] Aristakes of Lastivert, *Récit des malheurs*, 19; Matthew of Edessa,
Armenia and the Crusades, 47. For further discussion see Seibt, 'Die Eingliederung von Vaspurakan', 49–66.

[100] For the Muslim powers near Lake Van see Minorsky, 'New light on the
Shadaddids of Ganja (951–1075)', 14–20; Ter Ghevondyan, *Arab Emirates*,
101–21.

[101] Aristakes of Lastivert, *Récit des malheurs*, 24–5; Matthew of Edessa,
Armenia and the Crusades, 47. Basil was forced to spend the winter in
Melitene, only returning to Constantinople in 1023 (Michael the Syrian,
Chronique, 145; Bar Hebraeus, *Chronography*, 178).

Nonetheless, it is also possible that we may be mistaken in trying to identify one single event or threat which precipitated the handover of Vaspurakan and Basil's subsequent campaign to the Plain of Her. Instead there are signs that the surrender of the Artsruni lands may have been the culmination of a long, symbiotic diplomatic courtship. As J.-P. Mahé has demonstrated, from very early in Basil's reign Armenians from Vaspurakan cultivated and celebrated links with the Byzantine world, while in turn Byzantium maintained and fostered diplomatic ties in the Lake Van region. Using evidence principally from a panegyrical poem written by the Armenian poet Grigor Narek'ci, Mahé has shown how Zapranik, a lesser princeling, from the tiny principality of Mokh, south-east of Lake Van, took part in the first Bardas Skleros revolt on the Skleros side. After the defeat of Skleros in 979, he was pardoned by Basil II and took up a position within the Byzantine army in the relatively minor position of *manglabites*. By 983 Zapranik and other family members managed to secure some imperial relics from Basil which were taken back to Mokh to be inserted in a new monastery church at Aparank. Present at the ceremony which accompanied the consecration of this new church complete with its new relics were the Artsruni princes of the more substantial principality of Vaspurakan. Here then is evidence that from a very early date in Basil's reign southern Armenians were already engaged in a positive diplomatic relationship with Byzantium. This was a relationship which was considerably strengthened in 1000 when the princes of Vaspurakan, Gurgen and Senacherim, met Basil on his campaign in the east and were granted titles, silks, and horses, in a transaction which resembled that forged at the same time between Basil and the Muslim Marwanids.[102]

Basil II's final expedition to the east lasted for nearly three years. Yet, this aggressive interest in the east at the very end of the emperor's life was relatively unusual in the context of the reign as a whole. Before the annexation of Bulgaria in 1018 Basil preferred to use diplomacy to conduct relations with his neighbours in the east, both Christian and Muslim. In this outlook Basil departed radically from his imperial predecessors, Nikephoros Phokas and John Tzimiskes. Basil rarely campaigned in the east. Even during his campaigns of 995 and 999–1000 his interest was focused on using force to compel his neighbours to accept treaties and alliances. After 1000 local potentates, most notably the Marwanids, but also the princes of Vaspurakan, under the distant supervision of the *doux* of Antioch, were used to police much of the Byzantine frontier. As we saw in Chapter 6, many forts were abandoned or even deliberately destroyed. Employment of local potentates and the dereliction of fortresses must have reduced the need for a large number of Byzantine garrisons. Meanwhile, eastern territories within the Byzantine Empire were governed and taxed through indigenous officials who reported to a small number of centrally appointed Constantinoplitan administrators.[103] Economic

---

[102] Mahé, 'Basile II et Byzance vus par Grigor Narekac'i', 555–72; Stephen of Taron, *Armenische Geschichte*, 211–12; for Zapranik as a rehabilitated member of the Skleros axis see above 8.3. See also below 8.8 for another context for the Artsrunik handover of power in Vaspurakan.

[103] See above 6.3.3, 6.4.

policies inaugurated by Nikephoros Phokas which encouraged eastern Orthodox communities, such as Monophysite Armenians and Syrians, to settle in Byzantine eastern territories were continued.[104] As tenth- and eleventh-century Arab geographers and visitors to the Byzantine east noticed, even Muslims were allowed to remain in the empire if they paid a head tax.[105]

8.5   BULGARIA

It is relatively easy to track Basil's policies and achievements in the east because so many historical texts report on this region. In contrast Basil's relations with Bulgaria are much harder to trace in the medieval historical record. Only John Skylitzes provides any detailed treatment of the region in his account of Basil's reign in the *Synopsis Historion*. Some of his coverage is typified by colourful narrative. More usual, however, are short chapters full of isolated references to raids and sieges. Such chapters are devoid of strategic context and expressed through bland military vocabulary. Information is brutally edited and often telescoped. Dates and topographical data are casualties. Chronology is often sacrificed to theme. It is particularly difficult to know what to make of the large geographical and chronological confusions and lacunae in the text. Do they mean that Basil was only

[104] See above 7.2.
[105] Ibn Hawqal, 186; Ibn Butlan, 54–7; see also Holmes, ' "How the East was Won" ', 43–4.

sporadically at war with the Bulgarians? Or do they meant that Basil II was constantly at war with Bulgaria but that this reality is obscured by Skylitzes' methods of composition and his particular historical interests?[106]

Working out why and when Basil and Bulgaria came to blows in the first place is a considerable problem. Not much is known about Byzantine–Bulgarian relations after 971 when, as we have seen in earlier chapters, John Tzimiskes won important victories over a joint Rus-Bulgarian army in eastern Bulgaria. At this point the Rus were expelled from Bulgaria and Boris, the Bulgarian tsar, was captured and paraded with his imperial regalia in Constantinople. But, from this point on the picture of Bulgaria becomes obscure, illuminated only by coins, seals, inscriptions, archaeology, and the *Escorial Taktikon*. From such evidence it appears that Preslav/Ioannoupolis in eastern Bulgaria became the centre of a Byzantine province, while Roman forts on the Danube were rebuilt to defend the Balkans from further Rus attack. Yet, establishing how these new administrative and military structures then developed is problematic because so little of the surviving evidence can be dated with pinpoint accuracy. Sigillographical and textual evidence can be used to reconstruct the careers of several individuals who held offices in the Balkans in the later tenth and early eleventh centuries. But it is more difficult to build a convincing narrative of Byzantine rule simply by synthesizing these careers with Skylitzes' confused chronology. As far as the late tenth century is concerned, the available evidence

---

[106] See discussions above in 2.4, 3.3.2, 4.2.2, 7.1.

cannot really indicate how far Byzantine administration penetrated into Bulgaria during the 970s, and how long it survived the death of Tzimiskes in 976.[107]

The main problem with working out what happened to Byzantine rule in Bulgaria after 971 stems from Skylitzes' method of composition. Rather than offering a chronological account, Skylitzes summarizes events between 971 and Basil's first invasion of Bulgaria in 986 in two separate summary chapters. The first chapter is chronologically displaced, occurring, rather disconcertingly, in his narrative about Nikephoros Phokas' rise to power during the regency of Theophano in 963. The second chapter forms a preface to his longer narrative treatment of Basil II's 986 invasion.[108] Both passages lack detail. In the first Skylitzes refers to Peter, emperor of the Bulgarians, who sent his two sons to the Byzantines as hostages. He goes on to mention the death of that emperor (Peter) and how the two sons were subsequently dispatched by the Byzantines to fight the rebels David, Aaron, Samuel, and Moses Kometopouloi, sons of the most powerful *komes* in Bulgaria. The second passage states that the Kometopouloi rebelled only when John Tzimiskes died. At this time Peter's sons, Boris and Romanos, escaped to Bulgaria from Constantinople. Boris died en route, shot by a friendly-fire arrow.[109] Romanos stayed in Bulgaria before returning to Constantinople at an unstated time in the future. Meanwhile, all the Kometopouloi died except for Samuel. Moses and David perished in battle;

---

[107] See above 7.1.
[108] Skylitzes, *Synopsis*, 255–56, 328–30.
[109] See above 3.3.2.

Aaron was killed by Samuel for favouring the Byzantines. Finally, Samuel overran Thrace, Macedonia, the suburbs of Thessalonika, Thessaly, Hellas, and the Peloponnese. He besieged and took many places, including Larissa, the main city in the fertile plain of Thessaly.

Some of confusions in these summary accounts can be unravelled using other evidence. Alternative narrative material in Skylitzes' own account of Tzimiskes' reign and in Leo the Deacon's history demonstrates that Peter's son Boris was not held hostage continuously in Constantinople between 963 and the 970s. Instead he was emperor of the Bulgarians between 969 and 971.[110] Unfortunately, however, very few reconstructions of this type are possible because other sources of evidence are either non-existent or extremely difficult to date. My own reading of the evidence is that if Skylitzes' testimony is analysed in the context of his own working methods, then it soon becomes clear that assembling a reliable chronology to the outbreak of Bulgarian–Byzantine hostility (and indeed to the rest of the conflict) is all but impossible. In these first two summary passages, Skylitzes is not even trying to provide an accurately dated appraisal of the rise of Bulgarian power. Instead, he is sketching a general background to form a backdrop for his account of Basil's expedition in 986.[111] It is not at all clear that the limited information in these summary chapters necessarily preceded August 986; some events may have happened later. Support for this idea comes from an

---

[110] Skylitzes, *Synopsis*, 288, 297, 310; Leo the Deacon, *Historiae Libri Decem*, 136, 158.
[111] Skylitzes, *Synopsis*, 330–1.

interpolation made into Skylitzes' text by Michael of Devol, the early twelfth-century Macedonian bishop who took an interest in Basil's conflict with the Bulgarians and annotated his text accordingly.[112] According to Michael, Aaron Kometopoulos was still alive when Basil invaded in 986. Indeed he was part of the Bulgarian army that fought with the Basil as the emperor withdrew through the Gates of Trajan.[113] In these circumstances the most we can say about the period *before* 986 is that there was a serious revival in Bulgarian political power, although it is impossible to know how extensive this was by 986 itself, and how far the Byzantine gains of 971 had been eroded. It is likely, although difficult to prove, that the Kometopouloi were able to consolidate their power in western Macedonia while the empire's resources were focused on fighting Skleros, the Fatimids, and the Buyids in the east.

Whatever the state of Bulgarian and Byzantine relations before 986, Basil's invasion in August of that year paradoxically tipped the balance towards Bulgaria. This invasion is a rare occasion in the course of Basil's relations with the Balkans where other narrative sources can be used to refine the picture presented by Skylitzes. According to Skylitzes, Basil's army invaded Bulgaria with the intention of besieging the city of Triaditza (also known as Sardica, modern-day Sofia). At first Samuel and his Bulgarian forces looked on from their mountain fastnesses, afraid to meet the emperor in open battle. But once the siege was under way, distrust

---

[112] For Michael see above 2.2.1.
[113] Skylitzes, *Synopsis*, 331.

spread among the senior officers of the Byzantine army. Stephen Kontostephanos, who held the office *domestikos* of the west, accused his rival Leo Melissenos of plotting against the emperor. Basil and his army withdrew in panic, only to be attacked by Samuel as they retreated. When rumours of a conspiracy proved to be false, Basil reacted angrily, and according to Skylitzes threw Kontostephanos by his beard to the ground.[114] Yet, as we have seen, Skylitzes' interpretation of events may be misleading. When his story is compared with the other accounts of the expedition rather different reasons emerge for Basil's defeat in 986. Leo the Deacon, an eyewitness, stresses Byzantine incompetence, complacency, and meagre supplies, an interpretation backed by other contemporary sources: Stephen of Taron and an important military manual, the *Taktikon Vári*. In Chapter 4, I suggested that the reason why Skylitzes presents events rather differently from the contemporary evidence is because he sought to subordinate the narrative of Basil's campaign to his later eleventh-century political purposes, above all, of persuading a recalcitrant aristocracy that it was important for the well-being of the empire to support Alexios Komnenos during *his* campaigns in the Balkans.[115] As far as Basil's reign is concerned, however, defeat in Bulgaria precipitated new rebellions by Skleros and Phokas.[116] Trapped in Constantinople Basil was unable to contemplate action in the Balkans between 987 and 989. Instead, it is likely that the Bulgarians continued to gain the upper hand.

[114] Skylitzes, *Synopsis*, 330–1.
[115] See above 4.2.2.
[116] See above 5.1, 8.2.

Documentary evidence from Mt Athos refers to Bulgarian raiding against the town of Hierissos near Thessalonika. The sombre poetry of John Geometres, a former soldier and critic of Emperor Basil, refers to a constant Bulgarian menace in this period.[117] It was only when the civil wars were over that the emperor could turn once again to Bulgaria.

Various eastern sources allude to a renewed Byzantine offensive in the Balkans led by Basil early in the 990s. Yahya and Stephen of Taron both mention an invasion in 991, while it is clear that a number of envoys from Aleppo travelled to meet the emperor when he was on active campaign in the Balkans[118] It was only the Fatimid victory over Michael Bourtzes in 994 that forced Basil to turn his attentions away from Bulgaria to the eastern frontier.[119] In addition to military campaigns the emperor also clearly attempted to counter the Bulgarians through diplomatic alliances. Documentary evidence from Athos refers to a Serbian embassy (possibly sent by the prince of Diokleia) in 992.[120] Meanwhile, it is possible that an alliance struck in 992 between the Byzantines and Venice by which the Venetians were granted trading privileges in Constantinople may have been formulated with the view to encouraging the Venetians to harry the Bulgarians in the Adriatic.[121]

---

[117] *Actes de Lavra*, no. 8; Geometres, iv. 271–3, 282–3; for more on Geometres, see above 1.3.

[118] Yahya, *PO* 23 (1932), pp. 430–1; Stephen of Taron, *Armenische Geschichte*, 198; al-Rudrawari, *Eclipse*, vi. 229, 232.

[119] See above 8.4.

[120] *Actes de Lavra*, no. 10; Ostrogorsky, 'Une ambassade serbe', 187–94; Stephenson, *Legend of Basil the Bulgar-Slayer*, 17.

[121] The chrysobull confirming this alliance only exists in a Latin translation of the Greek original: A. Pertusi, 'Venezia e Bisanzio nel secolo XI', i. 195–8.

Nonetheless, the peculiarities of Skylitzes' testimony make it difficult to trace this picture of active military and diplomatic campaigning on the part of Basil. Instead Skylitzes' late eleventh-century interest in the past deeds and pedigrees of the great aristocratic dynasties means that he tends to concentrate instead on the activities of the emperor's commanders. For example, in earlier chapters we have noted the wealth of his material on Gregory Taronites, the *doux* of Thessalonika: the commander's heroic death in an ambush, the capture of his son Ashot, and the subsequent marriage of that son into the Bulgarian royal family. That Skylitzes' aristocratic interests can give a misleading picture of the Balkans during Basil's own reign is made clear by the testimony of a contemporary, Stephen of Taron. Like Skylitzes Stephen mentions the Taronitai, yet unlike Skylitzes he sets their achievements in the context of active campaigning by Basil II.[122]

The extremely fragmentary nature of the historical record makes it difficult to assess the successes and failures of Basil's initiative. Yet it is likely that for much of the 990s the emperor's position remained parlous. Several Byzantine senior military officials were eliminated by Bulgarian attack: in addition to Ashot Taronites, John Chaldos, another *doux* of Thessalonika, was also taken captive.[123] Skylitzes claims

---

Venetian historians seem to allude to the treaty but in more general terms: John the Deacon, *Cronaca Veneziana*, 149, 193; Andrea Dandolo, *Chronicon Venetum*, 193; see also Nicol, *Byzantium and Venice*, 39–40.

[122] Skylitzes, *Synopsis*, 341–2; Stephen of Taron, *Armenische Geschichte*, 198; for further discussion of Skylitzes' treatment of the Taronitai' activities see above 3.3.2, 4.1, 7.1.

[123] See above p. 404 n. 15.

several local commanders and prominent townsmen in Byzantine-held territory conspired with Samuel, included *strategoi* from Adrianople, and possibly from the theme of Hellas (central Greece) as well. Only partial faith can be placed in Skylitzes' testimony here, since he relates these allegations in a summary chapter dedicated to the theme of defection, which may quite possibly include material from outside the 990s. However, evidence from Athos suggests that at least one individual Skylitzes accuses of collusion, Paul Bobos, an *archon* in Thessalonika, was found guilty during this decade.[124] Paradoxically, the strongest evidence for Byzantine weakness during the 990s comes from the empire's greatest triumph, the crushing victory that Basil's close associate Nikephoros Ouranos achieved over Samuel at the River Spercheios in 997. The unexpected glee, relief, and surprise that this victory caused among Byzantine contemporaries, such as Nikephoros' associate and correspondent, Leo of Synada, reflect just how dangerous Byzantines believed the Bulgarians to be.[125]

Ouranos' victory at Spercheios is one of those rare events to which Skylitzes dedicates a reasonably full description.[126] However, tracing what happened in the Balkans after Ouranos' triumph from Skylitzes' testimony is more difficult. He makes some superficial dated references to precise events. In 1000 a large Byzantine army was sent against targets in eastern Bulgaria including Preslav and Pliska. In 1001 Basil himself led an army against a series of mountain

---

[124] This passage of Skylitzes' testimony is discussed in greater detail in 2.4.
[125] Leo of Synada: letter 13.
[126] Skylitzes, *Synopsis*, 341–2.

forts west of Thessalonika. In 1002 Basil led a campaign against Vidin on the Middle Danube; on his return south he raided Skopje in the region of the Macedonian lakes, the heartland of Samuel's empire.[127] Such brief references are usually used to support the idea that by the early eleventh century Basil had restored Byzantine control over eastern Bulgaria, the central Danube, and the frontier west of Thessalonika. It has even been suggested that by 1005 Basil had succeeded in pinning Samuel back inside the Macedonian Lakes area. Control over the Adriatic had been re-established through the empire's ally the Doge of Venice, who by 1000 was calling himself *doux* of Dalmatia. Meanwhile the key Adriatic port of Dyrrachion came back into Byzantine hands when the ruling local family, the Chryselioi, surrendered the city. At this point, the emperor agreed a ten-year peace deal with Samuel on terms favourable to the Byzantines.[128]

Nonetheless, it seems to me that the contents of the *Synopsis Historion* and Skylitzes' own working methods may militate against this interpretation of events. First, as we have seen in the last chapter, there are several reasons for thinking that eastern Bulgaria was not fully conquered in 1000. Skylitzes himself construes the campaign of 1000 as a morale-boosting assault rather than a permanent occupation; while Basil II was campaigning against Vidin in 1002, the Bulgarians were able to strike back and raid Adrianople; only with Skylitzes' identification of a *strategos* at Dristra on

---

[127] Skylitzes, *Synopsis*, 343–6.
[128] Stephenson, *Byzantium's Balkan Frontier*, 66–71; idem, *Legend of Basil the Bulgar-slayer*, 18–25.

the Lower Danube *c.*1016 is there any positive evidence that Byzantine armies had reoccupied eastern Bulgaria.[129] Meanwhile, even the forts along the western Macedonian mountain frontier were probably not permanently conquered in the early years of the eleventh century. As we discussed in Chapter 2, stories of the surrenders of locations such as Berroia and Servia are to be found in two of Skylitzes' characteristic summary chapters, which in this instance are dedicated to the theme of disloyal defectors. As we have seen throughout this volume, none of the data in such summary chapters can be accurately dated. Furthermore, even Skylitzes indicates that few of these Macedonian fortresses were held securely by the Byzantines before 1014. For when he describes the situation in the Balkans *c.*1014, he demonstrates that many of the wesern Macedonian fortresses were back in Bulgarian hands.[130] The situation in the Adriatic is equally uncertain. In the first place it is unclear whether Venice's actions can be tied to the Bulgarian conflict. John the Deacon, an exact contemporary, interprets the Venetian action as a unilateral decision to rid the area of Croat pirates rather than part of an alliance against the Bulgarians.[131] Meanwhile, the status of Dyrrachion is hard to determine for the first two decades of the eleventh century. References to the city's return to Byzantine rule occur in an undated summary chapter in Skylitzes' narrative. As we have seen in Chapter 2, this chapter does not refer to a

---

[129] Skylitzes, *Synopsis,* 343–6, 356; see also above 7.1.

[130] See above 2.4; Skylitzes, *Synopsis,* 350–60.

[131] John the Deacon, *Cronaca Veneziana,* 155–60; Andrea Dandolo, *Chronicon Venetum,* 197.

single episode but instead to a series of events from across the whole reign which have Dyrrachion as a common theme. As a result the data that it contains cannot be used to support the contention that the city was surrendered by the Chryselios family to Eustathios Daphnomeles in 1005. Indeed Eustathios, I would argue, had little connection with Dyrrachion until the conquest of 1018, when he became the city's *strategos* as a reward for capturing the renegade Bulgarian general, Ibatzes.[132]

If it is impossible to be certain of the date of the return of Dyrrachion to Byzantine control then the arguments that Basil and Samuel agreed a peace treaty in 1005 look fragile. My own sense is that warfare continued between Basil and Samuel at a low level for most of the period between 1005 and 1014. Skylitzes himself alleges that Basil invaded Bulgaria every year, a statement that I would take to mean that the historian was summarizing an excess of material in his underlying sources which he found dull rather than fictionalizing events which did not occur.[133] It is, after all, striking just how many other writers from very different milieux refer to Basil's long wars with the Bulgarians: the author of the life of St Nikon, al-Rudhrawari, Elias of Nisibis, and Ademar of Chabannes.[134] It is possible, of course, that these annual invasions were merely seasonal raids. The

---

[132] Skylitzes, *Synopsis*, 342–3; for discussion of Daphnomeles' career see above 2.4, 4.2.2.

[133] Skylitzes, *Synopsis*, 348; for Skylitzes' willingness to abbreviate that which bores him see above 3.2.

[134] al-Rudhrawari, *Eclipse*, vi. 119; Elias of Nisibis, *Chronographie*, 142; Arbagi, 'The Celibacy of Basil II', 41–5.

all-year-round campaigns Psellos mentions in his character sketch of the emperor may only include Basil's eastern adventures of 999–1000 and 1021–3.[135] Yet, still there is a strong case for annual raids led by the emperor supported by low-level frontier warfare. As Paul Stephenson has shown, the testimonies of Skylitzes, Kekaumenos, and the Priest of Diokleia are replete with short stories about warfare and diplomacy among border warlords from the first half of the eleventh century, including Basil's reign.[136] As we have seen, it is in the context of annual campaigns led by the emperor that Skylitzes refers to the Battle of Kleidion, that contest in the passes near Stroumitza north of Thessalonika, during which a Bulgarian blockade was broken by an attack from the rear by Basil's general Nikephoros Xiphias. According to one narrative strand in Skylitzes' account, which is also picked by the advice book of Kekaumenos, this victory was so overwhelming that Basil blinded some fifteen thousand Bulgarian captives, an event which caused Samuel to die from a heart attack.[137] Yet, the contemporaneous defeat of Byzantine forces led by Theophylact Botaneiates, *doux* of Thessalonica, at the hands of the Bulgarian commander, David Nestoritzes, meant that Byzantine victory was far from complete. Theophylact's defeat persuaded Basil II to retreat after Kleidion; he only decided to winter in the Balkans when the death of Samuel was announced to him.

[135] Psellos, *Cronografia*, i. 46–7.
[136] Stephenson, *Byzantium's Balkan Frontier*, chs. 2 and 4, *passim*; see also above 7.1.
[137] Skylitzes, *Synopsis*, 348–50; Kekaumenos, *Consilia et Narrationes*, 152; an episode discussed above in 3.3.2, 4.1, 7.1.

Even then, it still took four years for Basil to turn victory into final surrender.[138]

In his relatively detailed account of the events which led up to Byzantine victory in 1018, Skylitzes stresses the punitive raids that were conducted by Basil's senior generals.[139] Yet, diplomacy was clearly equally important to Basil's success. Embassies passed between Basil and a variety of local potentates: Samuel's son Gabriel Romanos, Samuel's nephew John Vladislav (the son of Aaron), Vladimir the prince of Diokleia, and a host of other Bulgarian warlords. This diplomatic dimension is particularly stressed by the narrative of the Priest of Diokleia, who accuses Basil of persuading John Vladislav to murder Gabriel Radomir.[140] Whether or not Basil lay behind the murder of Gabriel in 1015, he continued to face a hostile Bulgarian state led by Gabriel's assassin John Vladislav. Basil responded with brutal force and hidden diplomacy. The emperor invaded Bulgaria, plundered the plains of western Macedonia, and once again blinded all his Bulgarian prisoners. John Vladislav's response was to entrench himself in the newly strengthened fortifications at Bitola.[141] Vladislav himself was eventually killed in 1018 in battle outside the city of Dyrrachion, the event which finally persuaded the Bulgarian

[138] Skylitzes, *Synopsis*, 350; Whittow, *Making of Orthodox Byzantium*, 387–8; Stephenson, *Legend of Basil the Bulgar-Slayer*, 24–31.

[139] Skylitzes, *Synopsis*, 350–65 for the period 1014–18; raids discussed above in 7.1.

[140] The Priest of Diokleia, 336; Stephenson, *Legend of Basil the Bulgar-Slayer*, 27; but see also Skylitzes, *Synopsis*, 350–65.

[141] For epigraphical evidence pointing to this fortification see discussion of inscriptions in 1.3.

royal family and senior army commanders to surrender to the emperor.[142] Yahya ibn Sa'id records that when the Bulgarian dignitaries surrendered to Basil they were sent to Constantinople and given Byzantine brides.[143] But it is Skylitzes who records the surrenders in greatest detail, almost certainly because at the time when he was writing many Byzantine aristocrats claimed descent from the Bulgarian royal family, particularly the branch represented by John Vladislav.[144] This surrender clearly involved much public spectacle, as did Basil's celebration of his victory: Basil first journeyed through Macedonia receiving submissions from the Bulgarian leaders and acclaim from his army. A stage was especially constructed for these displays. Then he went to Athens to give thanks at the Church of the Virgin (the Parthenon). Finally he returned to Constantinople, where he entered the city in triumph wearing a crown of victory (*toupha*) and displaying the human and material booty he had acquired from his Balkan conquests. Among the human captives paraded before the citizens of Byzantium's capital were Maria, the wife of John Vladislav, and many of the daughters of Samuel.[145]

As we have seen in earlier chapters, the administration of Bulgaria after Basil's conquest is difficult to reconstruct. Skylitzes presents a picture of military rule: old fortifications were seized; new castles were built; senior commanders,

---

[142] Skylitzes, *Synopsis*, 357; Grégoire, 'Du nouveau sur l'histoire bulgaro-byzantine,' 289–91.

[143] Yahya, *PO* 47, pp. 407–8.

[144] The significance of these surrenders for Skylitzes is discussed above in 4.2.1.

[145] Skylitzes, *Synopsis*, 364–5; the *toupha* worn by Basil is discussed further in Stephenson's *Legend of Basil the Bulgar-Slayer*, 56–62.

such as Eustathios Daphnomeles and Constantine Diogenes, heroically continued the conquest in more remote areas. However, other evidence suggests that just as on the eastern frontier, Basil preferred to govern with a relatively light hand. Apart from a permanent garrison at Skopje operating under the authority of a regional military commander with the powers of a plenipotentiary, Byzantium's military presence in the Balkans was soon modified. Garrisons briefly installed at renovated late Roman forts on the Middle Danube were soon withdrawn, if not by Basil himself then by his immediate successors. Many fortifications were dismantled during Basil's own reign. Meanwhile, just as in the east, Basil disdained fiscal and administrative dislocation. Former Byzantine prisoners of war settled in Bulgaria by Samuel were allowed to retain their holdings rather than rejoin the Byzantine army. The local population continued to be taxed in kind. It is likely that local notables were retained within positions of financial responsibility; a similar situation seems to have prevailed in senior clerical appointments.[146]

8.6   WEST

While an understanding of Byzantium's relations with Bulgaria in Basil II's reign is complicated by a confusing narrative record, the history of Byzantine activity in southern

---

[146] See above 7.1; see also above 4.2.2 for the role played by Daphnomeles and Diogenes.

Italy is somewhat easier to piece together from annals and archive documents. These sources suggest that the emperor's attention was rarely devoted to the Byzantium's western periphery, presumably as a result of the more pressing concerns of civil war during the first thirteen years of his reign and subsequent conflicts with Byzantium's neighbours. In some senses it appears to have only been in the final decade of his reign that Basil was able to dedicate substantial imperial resources to the empire's western periphery. Nonetheless, as the previous chapter made clear, while the western frontier was rarely a priority, the governance of southern Italy and the related matter of diplomatic relations with Byzantium's western neighbours may have been of greater interest to Basil than modern historians have sometimes allowed.[147]

Local annals and saints' lives offer vivid testimony to the fact that the first half of Basil's reign was characterized by regular raids on Byzantine southern Italy by the Muslims of Sicily and North Africa.[148] Such raids affected not only the Byzantine provinces but other areas of southern and central Italy too. It was ostensibly to deal with this Arab threat that the German emperor, Otto II, invaded Byzantine southern

---

[147] A lack of engagement with southern Italy by Basil is a powerful theme in the work of Gay, *L'Italie méridionale et l'empire byzantin*, 324–429; a more recent corrective comes from Kreutz, *Before the Normans*, 119–25, 150–1, who argues that while Byzantine commitment was always conditioned by circumstances elsewhere in the empire, imperial interest in southern Italy was never completely absent; indeed in the first decades of the 11th c., the Byzantine presence became more active not just in military endeavours but also in cultural projects.

[148] See above 7.2.

Italy in 982. The Byzantines appear neither to have supported nor opposed this invasion. When Otto was eventually defeated it was by the emir of Sicily at Stilo in Byzantine Calabria.[149] Subsequent Byzantine action involved containing Muslim attack rather than taking the offensive. Nonetheless, southern Italy was not entirely abandoned. Senior army commanders from Constantinople were dispatched throughout Basil's reign to act as governors. A garrison of troops from the main Byzantine field army was constantly deployed at Bari, the main Byzantine administrative centre.[150] Active diplomacy was also pursued. The protection of southern Italy was one context for relations between Byzantium and Venice. In 1003 Venice helped a Byzantine force to defend Bari from Arab siege.[151] This joint action may have been the practical result of a marriage deal that was struck early in the eleventh century between the son of Doge Peter Orsoleo and Maria Argyrina, the daughter of a prominent member of Basil's court in Constantinople.[152] But the Pisan help that was afforded to the Byzantines in a naval victory off Reggio in Calabria in 1006 indicates that Venice was not Byzantium's only Italian naval ally.[153] Indeed, references in Arabic histories to embassies arriving from Basil II

[149]   Gay, *L'Italie méridionale et l'empire byzantin,* 327–41; Kreutz, *Before the Normans,* 119–22.

[150]   See above 7.2.

[151]   Ibid.

[152]   John the Deacon, *Cronaca Veneziana,* 168–70; Andrea Dandolo, *Chronicon Venetum,* 193–4. The marriage unfortunately came to a swift end in 1008 when both Maria and her husband John died from the plague (Andrea Dandolo, *Chronicon Venetum,* 202–3); Nicol, *Byzantium and Venice,* 45–7; Ciggaar, *Western Travellers,* 265–6.

[153]   See also above 7.2.

at Cordoba suggest that the Byzantines may have looked beyond Italy to the Umayyad caliphs in Spain for naval support against their mutual maritime enemies, the Muslims of Sicily and North Africa.[154] Basil may also have attempted to use more direct diplomatic channels to mitigate the impact of Muslim attacks. The survival of a list of gifts sent from the emperor to the Kalbid emir of Sicily suggests that the emperor tried to bribe the local Arabs into ceasing hostilities.[155]

The surviving chronicles indicate that the worst of the Arab raids were over after the first decade of the eleventh century. Yet, after this the Byzantines faced a new problem: internal revolt, especially the insurrection led by Meles, a rich citizen from Bari. The first mention of this revolt comes in 1009 when Meles led a local conspiracy against the *katepano* John Kourkouas. This revolt was suppressed within a year by Kourkouas' successor, Basil Mesardonites, possibly with support from a fleet led by Basil Argyros, the *strategos* of Samos.[156] Six years later, however, revolt broke out again, after Meles had built an alliance of outside protagonists who included the Lombard rulers of Capua-Benevento, and a motley assortment of Norman mercenaries and pilgrims. Together they defeated a Byzantine army led by the *katepano* Kontoleo Tornikios. In December 1017 Byzantine reinforcements arrived led by a new *katepano*, Basil Boiannes. Meles was defeated and took refuge with the German emperor,

---

[154] Ibn al-Kardabus, 85; Wasserstein, *Rise and Fall of the Party Kings,* 135.
[155] Hamidullah, 'Nouveaux documents', 291–6.
[156] See above 7.2.

Henry II, north of the Alps.[157] A few years later, in 1025, Boiannes took part in a campaign against Sicily. He joined the eunuch commander Orestes, a veteran of the Bulgarian campaigns, who had sailed with an advance party of troops and landed in Messina. Basil II's death, however, meant that the main expeditionary force did not set off and the mission against Sicily failed.[158]

The arrival of Boiannes in southern Italy is usually seen as the beginning of a more offensive Byzantine policy. Boiannes was particularly active in consolidating Byzantine authority in the wastelands bordering the territories of neighbouring Lombard princes to the north. Fortified settlements and small forts were built in the Capitanata as part of a defence against attack by Lombard princes, Norman mercenaries, and German emperors; in the south, the hinterland of Taranto was fortified to withstand Arab attack. In both regions garrisons were installed.[159] Pandulf, the Lombard prince of Capua to the north of imperial-held territory became a Byzantine client and participated in joint Lombard–Byzantine military actions.[160] Yet, it is possible that rather than being a new initiative, Boiannes' actions were merely a stage in a gradual reimposition of Byzantine authority in southern Italy which had been under way for

---

[157] *Lupus Protospatharius*, 57; Ralph Glaber, *Historiarum Libri Quinque*, 97–8; Ademar of Chabannes, *Chronicon*, 173–4; William of Apulia, 98–104; Amatus of Monte Cassino, *Storia de'Normanni*, 24–40; Leo Marsicanus, *Chronica Monasterii Casinensis*, 236–43, 261; also see above 7.2.

[158] Annals of Bari, 53; Lupus Protospatharius, 57; Skylitzes, *Synopsis*, 368.

[159] See above 7.2.

[160] Gay, *L'Italie méridionale et l'empire byzantin*, 417–8; von Falkenhausen, 'Byzantine Italy in the Reign of Basil II', 147–50.

much of the second half of Basil's reign. There are several signs of a long-term strengthening of the Byzantine position. Several commanders sent from Constantinople after 995 served for very long periods, in contrast to the turbulent early years of Basil's reign when many senior officers in the region served for only a few months.[161] Nor was Boiannes the first *katepano* to flex his muscles among neighbouring Lombard princes. In 1011, after the first Meles revolt had been crushed, Basil Mesardonites had conducted a progress through Lombard territory.[162] Greater Constantinopolitan interest in southern Italy may also be visible in the region's architectural record. Art historians have detected metropolitan support for the building of a series of large basilical churches at Bari, Taranto, Bovino, and Vieste in the early eleventh century.[163]

Nonetheless, while Constantinople may have taken a greater interest in southern Italy as Basil's reign progressed, it is important not to overstate the case. In the first place it is

---

[161] See above 7.2.

[162] Leo Marsicanus, *Chronica Monasterii Casinensis*, 237 ff.; Gay, *L'Italie méridionale et l'empire byzantin*, 403; von Falkenhausen, 'Byzantine Southern Italy in the Reign of Basil II', 147. Such assertive action on the part of Byzantine commanders was not unknown earlier in the reign. After the defeat of Otto II at Stilo, the *katepano* Kalokyros Delphinas extended Byzantine authority into northern Apulia, recovering the inland site of Ascoli. A sign of the greater reach of Byzantine authority from this point on is the dating of documents in the Lucera region according to Byzantine imperial reigns (von Falkenhausen, 'Byzantine Italy in the Reign of Basil II' 143; eadem, 'Zur byzantinischen Verwaltung Luceras', 397–406).

[163] A. Wharton-Epstein, *The Art of Empire: Painting and Architecture of the Byzantine Periphery: A Comparative Study of Four Provinces* (Pennsylvania State University, 1988), 147–56; Kreutz, *Before the Normans*, 150–1; Martin, *La Pouille*, 264–5.

clear that when the region came under sustained attack, as in 1021–2 during an invasion by Henry II, the German emperor, there was very little that the Byzantine senior commanders could do except wait patiently in Bari until the enemy's alliances with local Lombard princes fell apart and concerns beyond the Alps diverted their energies northwards again.[164] Moreover, in southern Italy as on other Byzantine frontiers, imperial authority, in order to survive, had to adapt to local administrative practices, indigenous bureaucrats, and provincial power structures. Encouraging settlement was just as important as building fortifications. As we saw in Chapter 7, the case of the towns of the Capitanata and the hinterland of Taranto suggest that capitalizing on local talent also made sound fiscal sense for the imperial authorities in Constantinople.[165]

Further afield, Byzantine relations with other western states were almost exclusively characterized by diplomacy rather than military might. This was certainly true of relations between Basil and the German empire in the decades between Otto II's disastrous expedition of 982 and Henry II's invasion in 1021–2. As early as 991 Otto III, son of Otto II and the Greek princess Theophano, sent two embassies to Byzantium with requests for an imperial bride. The progress of these marriage negotiations in the later 990s is illuminated by the letters of Leo of Synada, the Byzantine envoy to the Ottonians. They not only indicate how intense diplomatic contacts could be at this time, but also highlight the

---

[164] Gay, *L'Italie méridionale et l'empire byzantin*, 419–24.
[165] See above 7.2.

complex web of rivalry and co-operation which typified Byzantine–Ottonian relations. Competition for control over and influence in Rome was particularly fierce. At one point during Leo's embassy (996–8) the Byzantines backed an alliance between the Crescenti, a local Roman family, and Otto's tutor Philagathos, a Greek monk from southern Italy. Together they deposed Otto III's candidate, Gregory V, and declared Philagathos pope.[166] Although Otto returned to Rome, reinstalled Gregory, and later appointed Gerbert of Aurillac as Pope Sylvester II, he found it difficult to impose full control over the city. After Otto died in 1002 relations between the Ottonians and Basil become harder to trace, although in 1021–2 Byzantine and German interests clearly clashed once again when Henry II invaded southern Italy.

The surviving source materials mean that we know more about Byzantine contacts with Germany than with any other western power during Basil's reign. Yet contacts may also have been established with other states north of the Alps. Nascent western aristocratic and royal families consistently tried to associate themselves with Byzantine imperial splendour and charisma. In 988 Hugh, the first Capetian king of France, seems to have requested a Byzantine bride from Basil II for his son.[167] By the 1020s and 1030s aristocratic pilgrims began to appear regularly at the Byzantine court in Constantinople on their way to Jerusalem. Meetings with the Byzantine emperor usually yielded gifts of fine fabrics and

---

[166] Leo of Synada: letters 1–13.
[167] Gerbert of Aurillac, *Letters*, letter 119; for discussion of this text see above 1.3.

even relics, charismatic items to be taken back to northern Europe and used in the adornment of family monasteries.[168]

8.7   NORTH

Basil II's reign is significant in many different respects. It marked the high-water point in the medieval history of Byzantium. It brought Bulgaria within the Byzantine political sphere. It resonates through the modern history of the Balkans as Greek, Bulgarian, and Macedonian nationalists have used and abused Basil's personality and achievements in the construction and destruction of national claims.[169] But it is in connection with the long-term history and identities of the Russians that Basil's reign, almost by accident, enters what one might term World History. For it was during Basil's reign in 988 that Vladimir prince of Kiev converted to Orthodox Christianity. Even if, as historians now believe, there were many Rus conversions in this period and many Rus principalities, the importance of 988 lay in the fact that the *Russian Primary Chronicle*, compiled in its current form in the early twelfth century, chose to record the conversion of Vladimir as the seminal moment in the creation of Kiev, that principality to which all others eventually became subordinate.[170] But while the *Russian Primary*

[168] Ralph Glaber, *Historiarum Libri Quinque*, 97–8; Ciggaar, *Western Travellers*, esp. chs. 1–2 and pp. 168–9.
[169] Stephenson, *Legend of Basil the Bulgar-Slayer*, 113–37.
[170] *Russian Primary Chronicle*, 90–135.

Chronicle dedicates extensive coverage to the events surrounding the conversion of Vladimir, it is striking that historians writing from within the Byzantine empire registered little interest in the acceptance of Christianity among the Rus. Skylitzes notes the context to the conversion of the Rus: the marriage of Basil's sister Anna to Vladimir and the arrival of Rus troops to fight Bardas Phokas. But he says nothing of the conversion itself.[171] Indeed it is only Arab historians who make it clear that Vladimir's acceptance of Christianity was part of a nexus of arrangements with the Byzantines involving a marriage and the dispatch of mercenaries.[172] Such a fragmented source-base means that the precise chronology and the detail of the component events of Vladimir's conversion remain highly contested. Particularly uncertain is the motivation behind the episode which saw a Rus attack on the Byzantine outpost of Cherson in the Crimea. Was this a friendly action on the part of Vladimir, who was determined to help his brother-in-law Basil against rebel Phokas supporters in Cherson? Or was it that Vladimir grew tired when Basil failed to dispatch Anna in accordance with the agreement struck between the two rulers?[173]

[171] Skylitzes, *Synopsis*, 336. Neither Leo the Deacon nor Michael Psellos mentions the conversion of the Rus. Leo the Deacon does not even refer to the participation of Russian troops within the imperial army during the Phokas revolt, while Psellos makes only a passing allusion to their presence (Leo the Deacon, *Historiae Libri Decem*, 173–4; Psellos, *Cronografia*, i. 22–3).

[172] Yahya, *PO* 23, pp. 423–60; al-Rudhrawari, *Eclipse*, vi. 119; see Shepard, 'Sources for the Conversion of Rus', 71–4.

[173] Poppe, 'The Political Background to the Baptism of the Rus', 196–244, favours the first reading. The second, and more traditional, reading is preferred by Obolensky, 'Cherson and the Conversion of the Rus', 244–56. These debates are summarized by Franklin and Shepard, *Emergence of Rus*,

The enormous scholarly effort applied to understanding Byzantine–Rus relations at the time of the conversion itself is in some senses a reflection of modern preoccupations with the birth of a nation.[174] It also reflects the fact that most of the medieval written evidence about Byzantine–Rus relations in Basil's reign clusters around these events. References outside the Slavonic record to other Rus activities in Basil's reign are extremely rare and somewhat inconsequential. Skylitzes records two apparently random episodes: a joint Byzantine–Rus attack on the northern Black Sea coast in 1016 involving Sphengos the brother of Vladimir; and the adventures of Chrysocheir, another relative of Vladimir, who came to Byzantium towards the end of Basil's reign as a mercenary. On his arrival in Constantinople Chrysocheir argued with imperial authorities, attacked Abydos, and was eventually defeated at sea off the island of Lemnos.[175] Other historians of Basil's reign mention the presence of Rus mercenaries in Byzantine armies campaigning on all of the empire's frontiers.[176]

159–62. Elsewhere, Shepard suggests we should follow the *Primary Chronicle*'s chronology of events, arguing that Vladimir attacked Byzantine Cherson in a pre-emptive strike designed to force Byzantium into a new relationship. For Shepard, the context to this raid was Vladimir's relative insecurity as a new ruler and his search for political legitimacy (Shepard, 'Sources for the Conversion of Rus', 93–6).

[174] See e.g. the whole issue of *HUS* 12–13 (1988–9).

[175] Skylitzes, *Synopsis*, 354, 367.

[176] Rus troops were employed in the army that travelled with Basil to attack Fatimid positions in northern Syria in 999; they burned a church at Hims where local inhabitants had sought sanctuary (Yahya, *PO* 23, p. 458). Armenian historians comment on the cruelty of Rus troops who marched against Tao in 1000 (Stephen of Taron, *Armenische Geschichte*, 210; Aristakes of Lastivert, *Récit des malheurs*, 4). Rus contingents were also part of the army

Yet, while references such as these are elusive, they suggest that Vladimir's acceptance of Christianity had the very practical impact of strengthening and extending long-standing strategic, religious, and commercial ties between the Byzantine and Rus. The *Russian Primary Chronicle*, Byzantine historians, administrative texts such as the *De Administrando* and *De Cerimoniis*, as well as archaeological evidence, all demonstrate that such connections had begun to develop long before Vladimir converted. Rus trade routes from Kiev to Constantinople down the Dniepr River had begun to open up from the early tenth century onwards.[177] Rus troops had participated in Byzantine expeditions to southern Italy in 935 and Crete in 949.[178] Vladimir's grandmother Olga had travelled to the Byzantine court in Constantinople to negotiate military and trading alliances, as well as converting to Orthodox Christianity during the reign of Constantine Porphyrogenitus.[179] Such ties were considerably strengthened by Vladimir's own conversion. At the most obvious level

that fought with Boiannes against Meles in southern Italy (Ademar of Chabannes, *Chronicon*, 173–4); more Rus troops were dispatched westwards at the end of Basil's reign to attack Sicily (*Annals of Bari*, 53); see also S. Blondal and B. S. Benedikz, *The Varangians of Byzantium* (Cambridge, 1978), 45–52.

[177] *DAI*, 56–63; Franklin and Shepard, *Emergence of Rus*, 91–111.

[178] *Constantini Porphyrogeniti Imperatoris De Cerimoniis Aulae Byzantinae Libri Duo*, ed. J. J. Reiske (Bonn, 1829–30), bk. 2, ch. 44 (Italy, 935); ch. 45 (Crete, 949).

[179] *Russian Primary Chronicle*, 45; Skylitzes, *Synopsis*, 329; *De Ceremoniis*, 597–8. The issue of when and where Olga was baptized is disputed (Kiev or Constantinople; 946 or 957); see e.g. D. Obolensky, 'Ol'ga's Conversion: The Evidence Reconsidered', *HUS* 12–13 (1988–9), 145–58; J. Featherstone, 'Olga's Visit to Constantinople', *HUS* 14 (1990), 293–312; idem, 'Olga's Visit to Constantinople in *De Cerimoniis*', *REB* (forthcoming); I am grateful to Dr Featherstone for allowing me to see an early draft of this article; A. Poppe, 'Once Again Concerning the Baptism of Olga, Archontissa of

Vladimir's conversion precipitated a growing traffic in religious personnel and objects. Priest, bishops, artists, architects, and precious objects were all transported to Kiev. Some were sent by Basil as gifts; others were bought or employed by Vladimir; some were more brutally sequestered, above all during the Rus sack of Cherson. But besides religious contact, pragmatic links also grew exponentially. In addition to the greater use of Rus mercenaries in Byzantine armies, trading connections seem to have blossomed. Archaeological evidence suggests that an island in the Dniepr estuary, once prohibited to Rus merchants, became an active trading station. Vast numbers of fragments of Byzantine imported amphorae, glass, and jewellery have been discovered here. It has been suggested that one reason why Vladimir inaugurated an ambitious building programme of earthworks and fortified settlements around Kiev was to protect Rus ships bound for Constantinople from nomad attack. Greeks who were skilled in baking bricks seem to have built the forts.[180]

Finally, while Basil may initially have been reluctant to send his sister Anna to Kiev and to support Rus conversion, there are signs that for the rest of his reign, he monitored and exploited political events north of the Black Sea for his own ends. The German historian Thietmar of Merseberg indicates that when Boleslav, king of Poland, entered Kiev on behalf of the Rus prince Svyatopluk in 1018, the king immediately sent envoys to inform Constantinople of what had happened.[181] It

Rus', *DOP* 46 (1992), 271–3. For a summary of the crucial debates, see Franklin and Shepard, *Emergence of Rus*, 133–8.

[180] Franklin and Shepard, *Emergence of Rus*, 162–80.
[181] Thietmar of Merseburg, 532.

has also been argued that Byzantium's joint expedition with Sphengos to the northern Black Sea coast in 1016 could be interpreted as a naval alliance struck between Basil and another princely competitor for supremacy among the Rus, perhaps Mstislav of Tmutokoran, who was powerful at this time in the Sea of Azov and eastern Black Sea regions. Khazaria in this case may refer to the Kasogian, peoples of the Kuban and northern Caucasus region who it is known from other sources were conquered by Mstislav.[182] In a characteristically muddled passage Skylitzes alleges that the Rus and Byzantines captured the local ruler George Tzoulas. It is unlikely that Tzoulas was the leader of the Kasogians; he may, however, have been a notable at the Byzantine outpost of Cherson. The Tzoulas family are known from seal evidence to have been prominent in the Byzantine Crimea.[183] While it is difficult to say why the expedition attacked Cherson, the important general point is that in the decades which separated Rus conversion from Basil's death, Byzantine and Rus relations blossomed and multiplied at many different levels.

8.8   THE END: THE REVOLT OF PHOKAS AND XIPHIAS

When Basil died in 1025 he left the Byzantine Empire with strong frontiers. He had imposed imperial authority on frontier territories and on the empire's neighbours with a

---

[182] Franklin and Shepard, *Emergence of Rus*, 200.
[183] I. V. Sokolova, 'Les Sceaux byzantins de Cherson', *SBS* 3, 104.

mixture of force and diplomacy. Basil had used warfare most extensively in Bulgaria. Elsewhere he had preferred, if possible, to use diplomacy. However, even where he deployed force to conquer territories, he was often happy to consolidate imperial rule through the use of indigenous civil administrators and local fiscal and ecclesiastical practices. With the exception of the revolt of Meles in southern Italy, there is little sign that Basil's style of governance faced serious opposition during the second half of this reign. Obituaries in eastern sources refer to the emperor's astute management of his empire and his sound political sense.[184] Yet, for all the favourable comment that Basil earned when he died, it is clear that at the very end of his reign his position of security came under unexpected challenge. Suddenly, and without warning, he faced armed opposition from within the empire which was more serious than any he had encountered since the death of Bardas Phokas in April 989. It is opposition which has often been overlooked by modern historians, almost certainly because Michael Psellos ignored the revolt during his own outline of Basil's reign.[185] This decision on the part of Psellos seems to have been taken on aesthetical grounds. To have intruded domestic opposition at the end of the reign would have been to disturb the perfect equilibrium of his imperial portrait.

---

[184] See above 1.1.

[185] One exception to the lack of interest in this revolt from modern historians is H. Grégoire and N. Adontz, 'Nicéphore au col roide', *B* 8 (1935), 203–12. The rebellion is also briefly mentioned by Cheynet, *Pouvoir et contestations*, 36–7, 333.

Psellos' depiction of the sybaritic dilettante turned by harsh circumstance into a military man of steel could not allow for failure in the emperor's waning years.[186] More difficult, however, than explaining why Psellos concealed the problems which emerged in the sunset of Basil's career is determining precisely what those problems were and why they occurred.

The most serious insurrection that Basil faced at the end of his reign occurred in central Anatolia during the course of his final campaign against the Georgians in Tao and Inner Iberia. The revolt was led by the generals Nikephoros Xiphias and Nikephoros Phokas, and broke out in Cappadocia in 1022, a mere four years after the emperor's annexation of Bulgaria. The many medieval narratives that cover these events (in contrast to the complete silence on the part of Psellos), whether written in Greek, Arabic, Georgian, or Armenian, all agree that this insurrection was extremely serious. Not only did the revolt involve large numbers of rebels within the empire, but the insurrectionists were widely believed to be in contact with forces outside the empire, including George prince of the Iberians, and possibly the Fatimid caliph, al-Hakim.[187] Some historians have interpreted these events as a return of the inexorable threat of the Powerful families; the financial and manpower resources of clans like the Phokades proved too strong for the emperor to hold at bay for ever. Indeed, a corollary of this

---

[186] For Psellos' delineation of the reign see above 1.2.1.

[187] Aristakes of Lastivert, *Récit des malheurs*, 17–22; Skylitzes, *Synopsis*, 366–7; Georgian Royal Annals, 283; Yahya, *PO* 47, pp. 463–7; Matthew of Edessa, *Armenia and the Crusades*, 46–7.

argument is that it was these domestic pressures from the Powerful who held lands in central Asia Minor that persuaded Basil to encourage the house of Artsruni to surrender their princedom of Vaspurakan in the final decade of his reign. According to this view, Basil then deliberately settled his new Armenian allies on crown estates in eastern central Asia where they could challenge the landed authority of families like the Phokades.[188]

While it is true that the family of Senacherim were granted lands and titles in central Asia in return for supporting the emperor during the Phokas–Xiphias revolt, I would, nonetheless, argue against this reading of domestic tensions in the Byzantine polity at the end of Basil's reign. In the first instance it is clear that the migration of the Artsruni into the Byzantine Empire during Basil's reign belongs to much deeper and broader contexts than a putative struggle between the emperor and the Powerful families of central Asia Minor. One context was diplomatic. As we have already seen, Basil spent much of his reign building up contacts with the Artsruni as part of his wider conduct of diplomatic and military relations with Byzantium's neighbours in Transcaucasia and the Diyar Bakr.[189] Other important contexts were economic and demographic conditions. From long before Basil's reign began Armenians of all stations had migrated westwards in search of opportunities within the Byzantine Empire. For some those opportunities were commercial; others, particularly men from the Armenian aristocracy,

---

[188] Howard-Johnston, 'Crown Lands', 97–8; Seibt, 'Die Eingliederung von Vaspurakan', 59–60.
[189] See above 8.4.

such as Melias in the early tenth century, and the Taronites family rather later on, searched for different openings, above all service in the Byzantine armed forces.[190] It is within these broad contexts that the surrender of the Artsruni should be primarily understood. That they received lands in central Asia Minor for helping Basil defeat the rebels of 1021–2 was merely a circumstantial reward rather than the prime motive of the Artsrunik migration.

But if the Phokas–Xiphias revolt was not about the balance of tenurial resources inside the Byzantine Empire, what was it about? I would argue, that as with the revolts of Bardas Skleros and Bardas Phokas which occurred at the very beginning of the reign, the causes of the Phokas–Xiphias revolt only really begin to emerge when the many historical accounts that report on it are compared closely. These make it clear that this revolt was not in fact about the resurgence of private magnate power; instead unrest was rooted in uncertainty about who was to succeed Basil II as emperor. In this context, it is important to remember that at the time of the revolt Basil was about 66 years old; his brother Constantine, 63; Basil's nieces were unmarried and in their forties. There was no male heir. In these circumstances the search for a new emperor had to begin. One important requisite was an imperial claim from the distant past. The contemporary historian, Yahya ibn Sa'id, indicates that Nikephoros Phokas was chosen as the front man for his revolt precisely because, 'many Byzantines had a liking for Phokas and ... their

---

[190] See above p. 336 (Melias); 3.3.2, 7.1, 8.3 (Taronites); for more discussion of commercial opportunities see above 7.2.

affection for his ancestors made him their choice.'[191] Among these ancestors of course was Emperor Nikephoros Phokas.[192] Other candidates for the imperial throne actively considered during the 1020s were the Argyros family because of their links with the incumbent dynasty. Three years after Basil's death Constantine VIII married his daugher Zoe to Romanos Argyros. As Yahya notes, 'The choice fell on Romanos on account of the closeness of kin between him and Constantine's ancestors: both their fathers were maternal cousins ... [descended] from two sisters, the daughters of Romanos the Old' (i.e. Romanos Lekapenos).[193]

However, the immediate catalyst for the revolt of Phokas and Xiphias, that is to say the emperor's age, is less important for understanding how Byzantine political society operated during the second half of Basil's reign, than the identity of the chief protagonist of rebellion, the character whom many of the medieval historians claim was the real force behind the rebellion. That figure was not Nikephoros Phokas but Nikephoros Xiphias, one of Basil II's most successful generals during the Bulgarian wars. After the annexation of Bulgaria, Xiphias had been transferred to the position of *strategos* of the central Anatolian theme of the Anatolikon.[194]

---

[191] Yahya, *PO* 47, p. 465; trans. Feras Hamza.

[192] For the ubiquity of texts celebrating the Phokas family throughout the 10th and 11th centuries see in the first instance A. Markopoulos, 'Byzantine History Writing at the End of the First Millennium', in P. Magdalino (ed.), *Byzantium in the Year 1000* (Leiden, 2002), 195–6.

[193] Yahya, *PO* 47, pp. 486–7; trans: Feras Hamza.

[194] Skylitzes, *Synopsis*, 366–7; Yahya, *PO* 47, pp. 463–9; Aristakes, *Récit des malheurs*, 17–19; Georgian Royal Annals, 283. For more on the career of Xiphias, see above 3.3.2, 4.1, 4.2.2.

At this point, Yahya tells us, Xiphias 'entertained ideas of taking over the empire and had corresponded with Phokas asking him to join in his plans'.[195] What the role of Xiphias in this revolt suggests is that rather than signalling the return of the Powerful families, the Xiphias–Phokas insurrection represented a bid for power by a senior general in the twilight years of Basil's reign. At issue in 1021–2 was that long-standing tension within the Byzantine tenth- and eleventh-century state: control over the army. Since the turn of the century Basil had been in control. But as the emperor approached his seventieth birthday, his control was subject to challenge. That Basil himself recognized this fact is indicated by his own response to the revolt. For while the revolt itself subsided quickly once an imperial armed contingent led by Theophylact Dalassenos had been mustered and Xiphias in panic had killed his rebellious ally, Basil had the head of Nikephoros Phokas brought from Cappadocia and paraded amid the imperial forces, so concerned was he that this insurrection might have eroded irreparably the loyalty and enthusiasm of the troops involved in the offensive against the Iberians.[196] Meanwhile, Xiphias was stripped of office and sent to a monastery, a relatively light punishment for which Yahya adduces two reasons. First that the emperor was compassionate about the depression from

---

[195] Yahya, *PO* 47, pp. 464–5.

[196] Yahya, *PO* 47, p. 465; Aristakes of Lastivert, *Récit des malheurs*, 20. Both Yahya and Aristakes note the number of rebel sympathizers inside the imperial camp. Aristakes considered Basil's display of Phokas' head an opportune propaganda coup after the revolt was over. Yahya alleges that Phokas' head was also sent to George of Iberia to dissuade him from making an alliance with the rebels.

which Xiphias suffered; second he recognized Xiphias' good service record in Bulgaria.[197]

There were other signs that the end of Basil's reign was characterized by worries about who was going to control the main instruments of state when the emperor died. According to Aristakes of Lastivert, so great was the uncertainty in Constantinople itself that the emperor went on parade through the city to reassure the citizens that he was still alive. It is clear that few of Basil's senior advisers wanted his brother Constantine to become senior emperor. They discouraged Basil from summoning Constantine to the imperial palace when he was on his deathbed and only reluctantly delivered the letters which Basil sent to his brother summoning him to Constantinople from his residence in Nikaia.[198]

The extent to which Constantine ever played an active role in imperial governance during Basil's reign is an uncertain matter. As we have seen, Constantine occasionally emerges from his brother's shadow. He was present, for example, at the Battle of Abydos, claiming, indeed, that his was the spear that killed Bardas Phokas.[199] However, Michael Psellos indicates that at some undated point after Abydos, Constantine was demoted to the status of decorative political non-entity: 'To Constantine he allotted a mere handful of guards, as though he grudged him protection of a more dignified or imposing nature... He gradually

---

[197] Yahya, *PO* 47, p. 469.

[198] Aristakes of Lastivert, *Récit des malheurs*, 25.

[199] Psellos, *Cronografia*, i. 26–7. Stephen of Taron, *Armenische Geschichte*, 189.

decreased his authority too. He left him to enjoy the beauties of the country, the delights of bathing and hunting, his special hobbies, while he himself went out to the frontiers.'[200]

Modern historians have sometimes questioned this picture, suggesting that Constantine may have exercised rather more authority than Psellos allows, perhaps governing in Constantinople and the imperial palace while Basil himself was absent campaigning on the frontiers.[201] This seems unlikely. Close scrutiny of the fragmentary evidence points instead to the probability that Constantine rarely fulfilled more than a ceremonial role, even *before* the death of Phokas in 989. He is, for example, completely absent from that detailed picture of court politics and intrigue in the account of Ibn Shahram, the Buyid envoy to Constantinople *c*.981. Ibn Shahram makes it clear that at this early point in the reign the most important actors at the Byzantine centre were Emperor Basil, Basil the *Parakoimomenos*, and the emperor's chief assistant and confidante, keeper of the imperial inkstand, Nikephoros Ouranos.[202] As we have seen, Ouranos went on to enjoy a spectacular career in diplomacy, warfare, and governance of the Byzantine provinces in both east and west from the mid-980s to the early 1000s.[203] If there was an alter ego whom Basil trusted to rule in regions where he

[200] Psellos, *Cronografia*, i. 32–5 (trans. Sewter, *Michael Psellus*, 40).

[201] S. Runciman, 'The Country and Suburban Palaces of the Emperors', in *Essays in Honor of Peter Charanis*, ed. A. E. Laiou-Thomadakis (Rutgers, NJ, 1980), 219.

[202] al-Rudhrawari, *Eclipse*, vi. 23–34.

[203] See above 6.3.3, 6.4, 7.1.

could not be present himself for much of his reign it was Nikephoros rather than his brother Constantine. Indeed, we know that Constantine was not left to govern Constantinople during at least one of Basil's great campaigns. During the emperor's eastern foray against the Fatimids in 995 Constantine travelled with Basil's army. He advised Basil to attack and occupy Byzantium's Hamdanid client city of Aleppo. So little was Constantine's authority, and so out-of-touch his advice with Basil's own preferred, indirect, style of governance, that the emperor disregarded his brother's views entirely.[204] It is also clear that Constantine was absent from the centre of power in Constantinople at the very end of Basil's reign. Instead the most important Constantinopolitan official was John, the *Protonotarios*.[205] It was individuals like John who were concerned lest power was about to be handed over to Constantine, someone they clearly regarded as a senile cipher.

Uncertainty about the future may explain another unusual characteristic of the end of Basil's reign. Rather than resting on his Bulgarian laurels, Basil continued after 1018 to campaign and plan new offensives, in Italy and in the east, right up to the time of his death. Endless fighting was probably the only way of keeping control over the levers of state power, in particular maintaining the emperor's grip over that most important lever, the army. Controlling the key institutions of the state may also have dictated the emperor's rather unusual choice of burial place. Rather

---

[204] Farag, 'The Aleppo Question', 53.
[205] Skylitzes, *Synopsis*, 369.

than being interred in the elaborate tomb that he had prepared for himself in the Mausoleum of Constantine at the Church of the Holy Apostles in the centre of Constantinople, Basil suddenly decided to be buried in the church of the monastery of St John the Evangelist, an establishment that he had refounded outside the walls of the city. This monastery was located at the Hebdomon, close to the imperial parade grounds. In death, as in life, Basil wanted to keep watch over his troops.[206]

8.9   BASIL'S LEGACY

When Basil II died the frontiers of the Byzantine Empire were at their most extensive since the reign of Herakleios, the emperor whom later Byzantines considered Basil's only equal.[207] Basil's reign has usually been regarded as the acme of medieval Byzantium. Yet, as we saw in the first chapter of this book, some very recent thought about the emperor has been rather less positive. For Michael Angold, at least, Basil's empire was doomed in the long term by the emperor's style of governance. His personal control of the institutions of the state, his efforts to curb the Powerful, and his heavy taxation, all stymied the commercial growth of the empire. His territorial conquests destroyed erstwhile buffer zones; guarding the new frontiers imposed a catastrophic financial

[206] Skylitzes, *Synopsis*, 369; Yahya, *PO* 47, pp. 481–3. Stephenson, *Legend of Basil the Bulgar-Slayer*, 49–51.
[207] Choniates, *Epistulae*, 285.

burden on the empire's resources. Angold's Basil is an over-weening autocrat who handed his successors an impossible legacy. According to this model, later eleventh-century do-mestic strife and defeat at the hands of external adversaries such as the Normans, Pechenegs, and Turks can all be traced back directly to Basil II's own policies.[208] While I have not constructed this book with the explicit aim of replying to this revisionist picture, in view of the interest that Basil's reign provokes among historians of eleventh-century Byzan-tium, I would like in these final pages briefly to explore the principal implications which the evidence and arguments presented in the last eight chapters have for appraising the legacy of Basil's reign.

In some senses, Angold's charge that Basil came to control all the institutions of the Byzantine state, thereby making himself the mainspring of the empire's governance, is jus-tified. Nowhere is this centralizing quality to Basil's reign more apparent than in the emperor's efforts to control the waging of war. Ibn Shahram's comments about the em-peror's desire to dictate policy towards the Buyids and Aleppo in the east, and Basil's own campaign against Bul-garia in 986, demonstrate the extent to which the emperor sought to take the martial and strategic initiative from very early on in his reign. By 1001, after making peace with the Fatimids, Basil was able to dictate with much greater ease when, where, and under whom the army fought. He himself was able to lead that army on campaign. In a similar way, the emperor's attacks on Basil the *Parakoimomenos* from the

---

[208] For references to Angold's critique see 1.1.

early 980s until the issuing of the 996 novel illustrate Basil's sustained effort to locate himself at the centre of the imperial court in Constantinople and civil administration. As far as Basil's legacy is concerned, there is some evidence to suggest that this desire to become the fulcrum of governance, both military and civil, stored up problems for the future. As we have seen in this chapter, Basil himself struggled to control the key institutions of Byzantium, especially the army, as he neared the end of his life.

Furthermore, while it is true that Basil correctly identified the army as the central tension in the relationship between the emperor and the rest of political society, it could be said that his methods merely exacerbated the problem. If Basil's military success bound martial prowess ever more tightly to imperial legitimacy, not only did this mean that Basil himself had to campaign until the very end of his reign, but also that later eleventh-century emperors were forced to emulate Basil's martial example. Certainly, it is true that shortly after Romanos III (1028–34) took power, he proceeded to invade northern Syria despite having little military experience. Signs that Romanos was trying to compete with Basil II's record emerge in his decision to assault Aleppo, a city that Basil had himself considered too dangerous to attack and hold. The campaign, undertaken in the heat of summer, and against the advice of many of Basil's own generals, was a fiasco.[209] Nonetheless, while it is true that the emperor sought to place himself at the centre of Byzantine governance, it is important as far as his legacy is concerned to make

[209] Yahya, *PO* 47, pp. 495–501.

sure that Basil's rhetoric of sole control does not seduce us into thinking that sole control was all there was to Basil. Put another way, we need to take full account of the complex interplay between the emperor's rhetoric of autocracy and the reality of his preference to devolve administration wherever possible.

That Basil wished to be seen by his contemporaries as omnipotent and omniscient is very clear from the propaganda that he disseminated: the illustrations in his Psalter, the provisions of the 996 novel, the sentiments in his own epitaph, and the traces of self-promotion that survive in Michael Psellos' character sketch. This was a rhetoric that gained in power as the reign progressed and continued to resonate deep into the eleventh century. Even if the Bulgarslayer legend dates from the late twelfth century, eleventh-century witnesses, such as Ademar of Chabannes and Aristakes of Lastivert, attest to the almost supernatural fear that Basil provoked before and after his death.[210] This fear was partly conjured by written and visual rhetoric, but it had also been consolidated by Basil's actions. While it is quite possible that eleventh-century Greek accounts of Basil's brutality are exaggerated, not least the numbers of Bulgarian prisoners blinded by him after the Battle of Kleidion, nonetheless it is clear that Basil often took fearsome reprisals at key political and military junctures. Impalings and crucifixions followed the defeat of Bardas Phokas.[211] Bedouin

[210] Ademar of Chabannes, *Chronicon*, 154; Aristakes of Lastivert, *Récit des malheurs*, 25; for the later 12th-c. context to the Bulgar-slayer sobriquet, see Stephenson, *Legend of Basil the Bulgar-Slayer*, ch. 6.

[211] See above 5.2.2, 8.2–3.

prisoners taken during Basil's campaign in northern Syria in 995 had their hands cut off.[212] Mass blindings of Georgian prisoners attended the first stage of Basil's 1021–2 campaign against Iberia.[213] Yet, while such actions shocked and un-nerved contemporaries, it is important not to forget the functional context of this brutality. Brutality was, above all, another form of rhetoric; a way of propagating and maintaining the image of omnipotence that the emperor cultivated elsewhere in other forms of propaganda. Cer-tainly, the rhetoric of omnipotence and fear had a terrible reality of its own. It dictated that many people from within the Byzantine Empire and from Bulgaria and Transcaucasia, most of whom were fellow Christians, died or were muti-lated at Basil's hands. Equally Basil's rhetoric, whether per-formed after battle in grotesque circumstances, or whether spoken, written, and illustrated, had another reality, in the sense that it shaped the behaviour of those whom Basil governed or sought to govern. Those who feared the em-peror obeyed his dictums. Yet, it is important to stress that rhetoric, whether enacted or inscribed, was not the only tool by which Basil governed.

As we have seen throughout the second half of this vol-ume, diplomacy and delegation were just as central to Basil's governance of his empire. He devolved immense power to regional plenipotentiaries, of whom Nikephoros Ouranos was only the most prominent. Some of his regional lieuten-ants were the rulers of the empire's immediate neighbours.

---

[212] Yahya, *PO* 23, p. 443.
[213] Yahya, *PO* 47, p. 461.

As the reign progressed, loyal senior army officers served for long stretches in key provincial commands. Finally, throughout Byzantine frontier regions, Basil built civil administration on the solid bedrock of local power-structures, following indeed long-standing advice in the *Taktika* of Leo VI, Basil's great-grandfather, about the worth of keeping taxes low and locals happy.[214] As far as Basil's legacy is concerned, this practical devolution of power has important implications. On the one hand, long-standing practices of delegation meant that successor emperors to Basil did *not* have to run *all* organs of governance by themselves. Basil left his successors with experienced personnel, and strong, flexible structures of governance. All those imperial successors had to do to govern successfully was to create, as Basil had done, the illusion that they were in charge. A second implication of Basil's extensive devolution of power concerns Angold's belief that Basil stripped away the empire's buffer zones and over-burdened taxpayers with an expensive military frontier. Yet if Basil's local power-structures, particularly on the frontiers, were as devolved as they seem, then some of these concerns evaporate. Alliances with rulers and peoples on the frontiers clearly alleviated the need to maintain large border garrisons. This must have kept costs down. The built environment may have been equally inexpensive. As we have seen in Chapters 6 and 7, far more fortifications in conquered areas were destroyed or neglected than refurbished; the only region where immense imperial efforts

---

[214] Leo VI, *Taktika*, *PG* 107, cols. 896–97, chs. 37–40. I would like to thank Dr Jonathan Shepard for this reference.

were deployed in frontier fortification was the Capitanata in southern Italy. Meanwhile, as we have seen, while old buffer zones certainly disappeared during Basil's reign, new ones were created: among the Bedouin, Kurds, and Armenians in the east, among the Rus in the north, among the Serbs and Croats in the Balkans, and among the Lombards in Italy.[215]

Other charges brought against Basil by Angold are more difficult to answer on the basis of the research presented in this volume. For example, without having dedicated more space to fiscal matters, it is difficult for me to assess the extent to which Basil stifled the empire's economy by imposing heavy taxes especially on the Powerful. Yet, here too I am tempted to believe that Angold's worries may be misplaced. Evidence presented in Chapters 6 and 7 concerning the growth of commercial and agricultural life in the eastern borderlands and southern Italy suggests that Basil and his senior lieutenants did little to curtail economic growth and much to encourage it in the frontier provinces at least. Indeed, there is more positive proof that on the empire's eastern frontier taxes were less punitive than among Basil's neighbours. According to Yahya, *c.*1012 Syrian Christians chose to leave areas of Palestine controlled by the Bedouin Jarrahid dynasty to settle in Antioch and Laodikeia in northern Syria, precisely because the fiscal burden was less onerous.[216] Moreover, the flexible taxation arrangements which prevailed across the empire's borderlands suggest a concern

---

[215] This point is also made by Cheynet, 'Basil II and Asia Minor', 104 ff.
[216] Yahya, *PO* 23, p. 505.

to keep taxes light. Certainly in the Balkans fiscal revolts only began to break out when Basil II's imperial successors revoked his decision to tax the Bulgarians in kind according to established practice under Samuel and tried instead to impose money dues.[217]

Whether Basil was as generous towards the heartlands of his empire as to the frontiers is not a question this volume has investigated. My silence on this subject is in many ways the reflection of a belief that the evidence which might allow one to reach firm conclusions about fiscal changes in these regions during Basil's reign simply does not exist. Certainly modern historians have pointed to the gradual penetration of imperial tax officials into the local governance of the core Byzantine themes during the tenth and eleventh centuries.[218] The evidence for this penetration comes partly from incidental comments in written sources, but above all from the ubiquity of lead seals belonging to such officials in the provinces of western and central Asia Minor as well as in Greece and the maritime themes of the Aegean.[219] Furthermore, it has been widely acknowledged that as more civil

---

[217] See above 7.1; see also Stephenson, *Legend of Basil the Bulgar-Slayer*, 47.

[218] Ahrweiler, 'Recherches sur l'administration de l'empire byzantin', 46, 51–2, 68–70; Oikonomides, 'L'Évolution de l'organisation administrative de l'empire byzantin', 136–7, 148; the modern historiography is also discussed above in 6.4.

[219] Even the swiftest perusal through the catalogues of major sigillographical collections indicates the greater incidence of seals of judges and other civilian officials in these provinces in the later 10th and 11th cs. than in earlier periods. See e.g. the first three volumes of *Catalogue of Byzantine Seals at Dumbarton Oaks and in the Fogg Museum of Art*, ed. by Nesbitt and Oikonomides. For more detailed exploration of this contention from a sigillographical perspective see my doctoral thesis, Holmes, 'Basil II and the Government of Empire', 248–71, esp. at 248–50.

(judicial and fiscal) officials rose to prominence in local governance, the military administration of the core themes in the tenth and eleventh centuries was reduced. Indeed, many military officials, where they survived, took on civil responsibilities, especially in tax collecting.[220] Since the sequence of these seals clearly stretches across the tenth and eleventh centuries, one can safely assume that Basil II did little to stem the fiscalizing of the inner provinces of the Byzantine Empire. However, there is no evidence whatsoever which can allow us to say that he accelerated the process. There is little sign of harsh taxation in the historiographical record, which in any event is all but silent as far as Anatolia is concerned after 989 and has virtually nothing to say about Greece and the Aegean for the duration of the reign.[221] This silence is in marked contrast to the vociferous treatment in the medieval historical record of tenth-century emperors, such as Nikephoros Phokas, whose taxation policies were considered to be oppressive.[222] Meanwhile, since

[220] For the case that the theme armies gradually withered in the later 10th and early 11th cs. see among others, Ahrweiler, 'Recherches sur l'administration de l'empire byzantin', 2, 23; Kühn, *Die byzantinische Armee, passim;* Fine, 'Basil II and the Decline of the Theme System', 44–7; M. Grigoriou-Ioannides, '*Themata* et *tagmata*: Un problème de l'institution de thèmes pendant les Xe et XIe siècles', *Byz Forsch*, 19 (1993), 35–41. Kekaumenos comments on the increasing number of fiscal duties (*demosiake douleia*) that provincial military officials were taking on in the 11th c. (Kekaumenos, *Consilia et Narrationes*, 154); for further discussion of this point, see Holmes, 'Basil II and the Government of Empire', 234–48.

[221] For the silences in the medieval historiographical record see above 1.2.

[222] See, e.g., Skylitzes' catalogue of complaints about the heavy taxation imposed by Nikephoros Phokas, a picture which is confirmed by Liudprand of Cremona (Skylitzes, *Synopsis*, 273–5; Liudprand of Cremona: *Relatio de Legatione Constantinopolitana*, ed. and trans. B. Scott (London, 1993), ch. 63).

virtually none of the seals which attest to the phenomenon of fiscalization in these regions during the tenth and eleventh centuries can be precisely dated to the reign of Basil, we cannot from sigillographical evidence alone say that more fiscally related offices were appointed per annum during Basil's reign than at other periods in the tenth or eleventh centuries. Nor can we point to a sudden speeding up or slowing down of such change during his reign.

One important reason for the usual assumption that Basil taxed his subjects very heavily is the immense wealth that he is said to have collected by the end of his reign. Michael Psellos refers to the emperor's vast underground treasury. Yahya also expounds on the emperor's fortune in his end-of-reign obituary.[223] Yet, careful reading of medieval evidence suggests that rather than coming from unduly heavy internal taxation, most of Basil's wealth accrued from other sources. Psellos, possibly using imperial records, indicates that Basil became rich in three different ways: partly by confiscating property from those who had rebelled against him; partly by limiting his expenses; but primarily from the spoils of war.[224] Other historians offer more detailed narrative evidence for how substantial wealth was accumulated from abroad. Skylitzes refers to the ransacking of Samuel's palaces in western Macedonian, above all at Ochrid where Basil found 'much money and crowns of pearls and gold-embroidered clothes and one hundred *kentenaria* of gold

---

[223] Psellos, *Cronografia*, i. 44–7; Yahya, *PO* 47, p. 483. 11th-c. Fatimid sources also comment on Basil's exceptional wealth (Hamidullah, 'Nouveaux documents', 298).

[224] Psellos, *Cronografia*, i. 44–7.

stamped materials'.[225] In the east Aristakes suggests that the sale of prisoners-of-war may have been a lucrative part of Basil's wars. The narrator notes that at the end of the first, rather inconclusive, stage of Basil's final campaign against the Iberians in 1021–2, large numbers of prisoners were taken. These were then sold at Trebizond where Basil and his army withdrew for the winter. It was only in the spring that Basil turned east again to defeat his enemy.[226] What this evidence suggests is that in the final decade of his reign Basil indulged in exceptionally lucrative campaigns. No doubt it was the revenue gained from one conquest which provided the investment for the next: thus as Bulgaria was overcome, so resources were diverted to Iberia; with Iberia conquered, Basil went on to plan to campaign against Sicily.

It is surely in this context of wealth begetting wealth that two brief references in Skylitzes' *Synopsis Historion* to the tax known as the *allelengyon* are best understood. The first time that Skylitzes mentions this imposition it is in a characteristically terse, undated, chapter which probably refers to the early years of the eleventh century. At this point Skylitzes claims that Basil decided that where there was a shortfall in taxation payments because the Poor were unable to meet their tax burden, the Powerful were obliged to make up the payment; this was a measure opposed by Patriarch Sergios. Skylitzes mentions the tax again immediately after his description of Basil's victory in Bulgaria, when once again the patriarch petitioned for the tax to be lifted.[227] Usually

---

[225] Skylitzes, *Synopsis*, 359.
[226] Aristakes of Lastivert, *Récit des malheurs*, 16.
[227] Skylitzes, *Synopsis*, 347, 365.

these two brief Skylitzes references are used to support the
case that Basil II imposed onerous fiscal burdens on his
wealthiest and most influential subjects as part of his dominant concern to oppress the Byzantine aristocracy.[228] However, this is to take the two allusions out of their narrative
context. If they are read in that context then the significance
of the *allelengyon* becomes rather different. It is important to
realize that both references to the *allelengyon* appear in
connection with warfare in Bulgaria: the first, when Basil
was still engaged in annual campaigns against Samuel; the
second, after his wars against the Bulgarians had finally
come to an end. It is particularly significant that Skylitzes
connects neither reference to the theme of an attack on the
Powerful. Instead the first reference suggests that the *allelengyon* was a tax which was first imposed to help the
Byzantine war effort in the early eleventh century. The
location of the second reference is even more intriguing.
For Skylitzes mentions Sergios' unhappiness with Basil's
maintenance of the tax immediately after his description
of Basil's victory parade through Constantinople, when the
emperor put on display the booty gained from his triumph
over the Bulgarians. What Skylitzes seems to be suggesting is
not that Sergios attacked the *allelengyon* because it was
oppressing the Powerful, but because it simply no longer
seemed necessary. Visual evidence of the triumph and
wealth of the empire had just been provided on the streets
of Constantinople; why were wartime taxes still necessary?
The answer, of course, was that Basil had not finished

---

[228] See above 1.1.

fighting. Instead, he was readying himself to take his armies east to Iberia, an intention of which only he, and possibly his inner circle, had knowledge. Yahya, a near contemporary, comments on the fact that imperial policy was a matter known only to the emperor in his description of the prelude to Basil's Iberian expedition in 1021: '[Basil] left Constantinople and went to Philomelion, his intentions known only to himself.' Yahya goes on to indicate that Basil's decision to attack Iberia was a surprise. Most contemporaries thought that he intended to attack northern Syria.[229]

The Basil who has emerged in this final chapter is an emperor who knew his own mind, was determined to formulate his own policies, wished to convince others that he was in sole control, but who in the matter of quotidian governance was happy to delegate extensively in both military and civil affairs. While the tying of military prowess to the imperial image created a formidable precedent for later emperors to follow, it was no more difficult a model than the imperial style that Basil himself inherited from those highly successful tenth-century emperor-generals, Nikephoros Phokas and John Tzimiskes. Indeed, the military triumphs against the Bulgarians and Iberians at the end of Basil's reign meant that his successors inherited rather more quiescent frontiers than he himself had known when he came to the throne in 976. Meanwhile, the coffers were full rather than empty as they had been some fifty years earlier.[230] Basil's immediate successors, therefore, were left with an eminently

---

[229] Yahya, *PO* 47, p. 461.
[230] Ibid., p. 483.

palatable legacy, as indeed the Byzantine Empire's relative peace, prosperity, and continued territorial expansion of the next twenty-five years indicate. While some emperors unsuited to the battlefield like Romanos III felt they needed to prove themselves a New Basil, the wily Constantine IX (1042–55) governed for more than a decade as an armchair emperor, successfully facing down challenges from the generals Leo Tornikios and George Maniakes.

But if Basil's legacy was so gilded and benign, why had his empire all but collapsed by 1081, the year that Alexios Komnenos came to the throne? The answer to this question surely lies with the strength of Byzantium's external enemies during the mid- to later eleventh century. The crucial difference between Basil II and the later eleventh-century successor emperors, particularly those who ruled after Constantine IX, was that few enjoyed a luxury of choice as to where they sought to channel the empire's energies and resources. Rather than selecting to campaign first against Bulgaria, and then in the Iberian borderlands, and then in Sicily, as Basil was able to do, they found themselves faced with assault on three frontiers, from the Normans in the west, the Pechenegs in the north, and the Turks in the east. That Byzantium was vulnerable when it came under attack on more than one frontier was a danger that Basil himself had acknowledged; hence his eagerness to come to terms with the Fatimids in the east so that he could engage with Samuel in Bulgaria. Moreover, as John Haldon and Paul Magdalino have argued recently, all three of these external adversaries were aggressive and highly decentralized politics. As such they challenged existing Byzantine military and diplomatic

structures in unprecedented ways. Byzantine frontier administration found it difficult to contain sustained raiding from
three directions. The centralized field army, which relied on
large numbers of heavy cavalry and infantry forces, proved
unwieldy in open battle against adversaries who often
used guerrilla tactics. Meanwhile, traditional Byzantine diplomatic methods designed for employment in the courts of
centralized states proved less persuasive when deployed
against powers each with a multiplicity of leaders.[231]

Yet, as Haldon points out, while the Turks, Normans, and
Pechenegs certainly challenged the structures of the Byzantine state, these structures had been developed during the
reigns of emperors between the mid-tenth and mid-eleventh
centuries against a rather different strategic background.
Between the 930s and the early 1040s Byzantium rarely
came under serious external threat, and usually only then
in periods of internal strife, such as the first thirteen years of
Basil II's reign. Sustained assaults on more than one front
were exceptionally rare. Indeed, for much of this period
Byzantium was on the military offensive. It was in these
contexts of confidence that Byzantine military and diplomatic structures had evolved. That in the middle of the
eleventh century new adversaries appeared and challenged
these structures cannot be blamed on those who developed
them much earlier for entirely different situations.

Indeed, if blame is to be apportioned anywhere for collapse in the eleventh century, Haldon has argued that it

---

[231] Haldon, 'Approaches to an Alternative Military History', 64–71;
P. Magdalino, 'The Medieval Empire (780–1204)', in C. A. Mango (ed.),
The Oxford History of Byzantium (Oxford, 2002), 182–92.

should be directed not towards those who governed Byzantium in the later tenth and early eleventh centuries, but instead at that political elite which dominated central government from the reign of Constantine Monomachos (1042–55) onwards. He suggests that a mixture of arrogance towards the new *barbaroi* threatening the empire, a reduction in military expenditure, demilitarization of certain key frontiers, and disintegration of army morale, weakened the Byzantine capacity for effective defence.[232] Recalling the much older analysis of Speros Vryonis, Haldon suggests that disagreements about the defence of the frontiers began to divide members of the empire's political elite into civil and military parties, leading ultimately to civil war.[233] One can, of course, question whether periods of domestic instability which followed the death of Basil's niece, the empress Theodora, in 1056 were precipitated solely by such policy debates or whether they also turned on competition to fill the imperial shoes of the Macedonian dynasty. What is more certain is that few Byzantines fully recognized the dangers of the triple threat which faced them, particularly during the decade that followed defeat against the Turks at the Battle of Manzikert, 1071. In the civil war that followed this military debacle, many competing Byzantine aristocratic families exacerbated the problem of external

---

[232] Haldon, 'Approaches to an Alternative Military History', 60–74; idem, 'The Organisation and Support of an Expeditionary Force: Manpower and Logistics in the Middle Byzantine Period', in K. Tsiknakes (ed.), *Byzantium at War (9th to 12th c.)* (Athens, 1997), 145–6.

[233] Haldon, 'Approaches to an Alternative Military History', 68–9; Vyronis, *Decline of Medieval Hellenism*, ch. 2.

pressure by inviting members of Byzantium's new enemies, the Turks, Normans, and nomads, to fight in their own small armies.[234] In this time of desperate struggle rival families also drew, as we have seen in earlier chapters of this book, on every possible resource, including the Byzantine past. It was in the context of a searching for imperial legitimacy that families like the Botaneiatai and Komnenoi increasingly began to turn to the reign of Basil II for evidence of their family's dynastic pedigree and martial heroism.[235]

When Alexios I came to the throne in 1081, the practice of associating dynastic prestige with Basil's reign was already well established. The challenge that the new Komnenian emperor faced was to unite a fragmented domestic aristocracy to withstand the empire's three foreign foes. It has been the contention of this volume that political unity in the face of external danger was the message that one close associate of the new Komnenian regime tried to broadcast in his synoptic history.

That Komnenian official was John Skylitzes; his history, the *Synopsis Historion*. Skylitzes' interests centred on aristocratic families and Balkan warfare. It was in the light of these twin obsessions that he articulated the reign of Basil II. His methods and interpretations cast a very thick veil over the history of the reign of Basil itself. The most important need for the modern historian of Basil's reign is to know that this veil exists. Beyond that simple knowledge, the fragmentary quality of the other evidence relevant to Basil's hegemony

---

[234] Cheynet, *Pouvoir et contestations*, 345–57; idem, 'Grandeur et décadence', 119, 135.
[235] See above 4.2.

means that for some periods and some places, even where we perceive the veil, we cannot lift it. Some aspects of the reign will be forever dark. But there are periods and places where we can both see the veil and have enough evidence to look beyond it. Those periods and places are: the revolts of the first thirteen years; the east; the Balkans; and Italy. And it is in these times and places that Basil emerges as a figure striving to occupy the centre stage.

Basil began his reign as a lonely figure. His courtiers told Ibn Shahram that the emperor thought that many around him were, 'indifferent as to whether it be I or someone else who is emperor'.[236] That self-perception of loneliness persisted until the very end of his life. It is discernible even in his epitaph where he depicts himself as a solitary figure endlessly striving to guard the Children of the New Rome.[237] Yet, the character of the emperor's loneliness changed. When he conversed with Ibn Shahram, it was as an isolated and frustrated character who longed to take power, but who was surrounded by advisers determined to exclude him from important decisions. As Basil gradually beat off his rivals for power, he developed his rhetoric of personal control. Whether Basil continued to feel isolated personally is difficult to know. He looked for his truest friends, if we are to believe the verses and illustrations in his Psalter, from among the military saints.[238] But behind Basil's rhetoric of absolute power and isolated splendour grew a significant reality of co-operation and loyalty to the

---

[236] al-Rudhrawari, *Eclipse*, vi. 33.
[237] See above 8.3.
[238] Ibid.

emperor within Byzantium and among the empire's neighbours. At the height of his powers Basil could campaign deep into the Balkans at the head of the army, confident that the rest of the empire and his position as emperor were safe. It was only at the end of his life that true political loneliness returned. Basil came back to Constantinople in the summer of 1023 from his rather mixed final campaign in the east. Riding around the capital city he found the citizens ran from him into their houses.[239] He continued to plan campaigns, seeing the vanguard of the Sicilian expedition leave under the command of Orestes, one of his most loyal commanders.[240] But he was not to journey west. He died in Constantinople on 6 December 1025.[241] During his fifty-year reign he had withstood deadly dangers. At times he had inflicted deadly punishments on others. His is not a reign to warm the heart. But as an exercise in the preservation of emperor and empire it is unparalleled in Byzantine history.

[239] Aristakes of Lastivert, *Récit des malheurs*, 25.

[240] Skylitzes, *Synopsis*, 368.

[241] The precise date is given by Yahya; Skylitzes confirms that Basil died in December but does not cite the exact day (Yayha, *PO* 47, p. 481; Skylitzes, *Synopsis*, 369).

Appendix A: Coverage of Basil's reign in John Skylitzes' Synopsis Historion

Chapter	General subject-matter	Notable narratives
1	Skleros Revolt	Skleros' decision to rebel
2	Skleros Revolt	Skleros' eastern allies
3	Skleros Revolt	Negotiations with Skleros Exploits of Alyates
4	Skleros Revolt	Skleros' victory at Lapara
5	Skleros Revolt	Court bribes Skleros supporters Bourtzes' defeat in the Anti Taurus
6	Skleros Revolt	Skleros' victory at Rhageai
7	Skleros Revolt	Erotikos' defence of Nikaia
8	Skleros Revolt	Skleros defeats Phokas Exploits of Constantine Gauras
9	Skleros Revolt	Phokas defeats Skleros
10	Skleros Revolt	Skleros' captivity in Baghdad
11	Bulgaria: summary chapter	Rise of Kometopouloi
12	Bulgaria	Byzantine invasion of 986 and defeat

13	Earthquake in Constantinople	
14	Phokas Revolt	Phokas' decision to rebel
15	Phokas Revolt	Skleros' escape from Baghdad
16	Phokas Revolt	Skleros' decision to ally with Phokas
17	Phokas Revolt	Phokas imprisons Skleros Phokas' defeat at Chrysopolis
18	Phokas Revolt	Phokas' defeat at Abydos
19	Phokas Revolt	Skleros surrenders
20	Eastern Frontier: summary chapter	Events in the east 990–1001 Iberians enter Byzantine service [Pakourianos, Pherses, Phebdatus]
21	Internal affairs: summary chapter	Arrest of Eusthathios Maleinos Novel against the Powerful
22	Patriarch of Constantinople	Turnover of patriarchs— 990s
23	Bulgaria	Capture of Taronitai Ouranos victory at Spercheios
24	Bulgaria: summary chapter	Dyrrachion: including surrender of Chryselioi

25	Bulgaria: summary chapter	Rebels [Bobos, Malakeinos, Glabas, Vatatzes] Venetian alliance
26	Bulgaria	Invasion of eastern Bulgaria (1000) [Theodorokan, Xiphias]
27	Bulgaria: summary chapter	Defectors [Dobromeros, Nikolitzas]
28	Bulgaria	Defectors continued [Draxanos]
29	Eastern Frontier: summary chapter	Ouranos at Antioch
30	Bulgaria: summary chapter	Basil's campaign to Vidin (1001) Samuel attacks Adrianople
31	Bulgaria	Unsuccessful siege against Krakras
32	Taxation	*Allelengyon*
33	Eastern Frontier	Destruction of Holy Sepulchre
34	General summary chapter	Natural disasters Revolt of Meles in southern Italy
35	Bulgaria	Victory at Kleidion (1014) Death of Samuel
36	Bulgaria	Defeat for Botaneiates
37	Bulgaria	Byzantine raids
38	Bulgaria	Byzantine raids Bulgarian defections

		Death of Gabriel Romanos
39	Peripheries: summary chapter	Fleet sent to Khazaria (1016)
		Capture of Tzoulas
		Surrender of Vaspurakan
40	Bulgaria	Byzantine raids
41	Bulgaria	Death of John Vladislav
42	Bulgaria	Daphnomeles captures Ibatzes
43	Bulgaria	Bulgarian surrenders
		Basil's triumphs (Athens, Constantinople)
44	Bulgaria	Diogenes captures Sermon of Sirmion
45	Domestic revolt	Phokas–Xiphias revolt
	Eastern Frontier	War in Iberia
46	Northern affairs	Attacks by Rus ships
47	Western affairs	Orestes sent to Sicily
		Basil's death

Appendix B: Translation of the Prooimion to John Skylitzes' Synopsis Historion

Synopsis of histories beginning from the slaying of the Emperor Nikephoros, the former *Logothete* of the *Genikon*, up to the reign of Isaac Komnenos, composed by John Skylitzes, *kouropalates* and former *megas droungarios* of the *bigla*

First the monk George, who also served the most holy Patriarch Tarasios as *synkellos*, and after him the *homologetes* Theophanes, the *hegoumenos* of the Agros [monastery], made an *epitome* of history excellently in the style of the ancients, having very persistently pursued historical books, and having summed them up in a language which was simple and uncontrived, indeed being concerned only with the essence itself of what happened. One of them, that is George, began from the Creation and reached the usurpers, I mean Maximianos and his son Maximinos. The other, that is Theophanes, having made George's end point his beginning, abridged the rest of the chronography, and having arrived at the death of the emperor Nikephoros, the former *Logothete* of the *Genikon*, stopped his account. After him no one else has dedicated himself to such an enterprise. For some have tried, such as the *didaskalos* Sikeliotes, and the *hypertimos* Psellos, *hypatos* of the philosophers in our own time, and others in addition to them. But having undertaken the task in a desultory way, they both lack accuracy; for they disregard very many of the more important events, and they are of no use to their successors, since they have made merely an enumeration of the emperors and indicated who took imperial office after whom, and nothing more. For even if they seem to mention certain actions, even then, since they have narrated them without accuracy, they hinder those who chance upon them [i.e. later readers] and have not helped. For Theodore Daphnopates, Niketas the Paphlagonian, Joseph Genesios and Manuel, [that is] Byzantines [i.e. Constantinopolitans], and Nikephoros the deacon of Phrygia, and Leo the Asian, and Theodore of Side who became *proedros* [i.e. archbishop], and his nephew and namesake [Theodore] archbishop of the church in Sebasteia, and in addition Demetrios of Kyzikos, and the monk John the Lydian, each has had his own agenda, the one proclaiming praise of the emperor, the other a *psogos* of the patriarch, another an encomium of a friend; but while each one fulfils his own purpose in the guise of history, each has fallen short of the intention of those aforesaid men inspired by God [i.e. George and Theophanes]. For they wrote histories at length of the things which happened during their times and shortly before: one sympathetically, another with hostility, another in search of approval, another as he had been ordered. Each one composing his own history, and differing from one another in their narrations, they have filled the listeners with dizziness and confusion. Having found pleasure in the labour of the aforesaid men [i.e. George and Theophanes], we have hoped that a synopsis would be of not inconsiderable profit for those who love history and most of all for those who prefer that which is very easy to that which is more wearisome; [a synopsis which] gives a very shortened account of the events in different times, which is free from the weight of documentation. We have read the histories of the writers mentioned above carefully, and have removed that which was written in a state of emotion or in search of approval, and have disregarded differences and disagreements, and have shaved off whatever we have found which is too close to legend, and have gathered that which is suitable and whatever does not result from rhetoric, and have also added whatever we have learnt from old men by oral testimony. Having put them together into one [unit] rapidly, we have left behind for posterity nourishment which is soft and finely ground in language, so that on the one hand those who are acquainted with the books of the aforesaid historians [Theodore Daphnopates etc.] may have a record by using and approaching this book as a travelling companion—for reading can foster recollection, and recollection can nourish and increase memory, just as in contrast neglect and idleness foster forgetfulness, which Lethe follows, dimming and confusing the memory of deeds completely. [We have also left this nourishment] on the other hand so that those not yet acquainted with histories may have this *epitome* as a guide, and by examining that which is written with a wide perspective may receive a more complete knowledge of what happened. But let me now begin.

Bibliography

Primary sources

Greek

Actes d'Iviron I: Des origines au milieu du XIe siècle, eds. J. Lefort, N. Oikonomides, and D. Papachryssanthou, Archives de l'Athos XIV (Paris, 1985).

Actes de Lavra I: Des origines à 1204, eds. P. Lemerle, A. Guillou, D. Papachryssanthou and N. Svoronos, Archives de l'Athos V (Paris, 1970).

Actes du Prôtaton, ed. D. Papachryssanthou, Archives de l'Athos VII (Paris, 1975).

Actes de Xénophon, ed. D. Papachryssanthou, Archives de l'Athos XV (Paris, 1986).

ATTALEIATES, MICHAEL: *Michael Attaleiates, Historia,* ed. I. Bekker, CSHB (Bonn, 1853).

BRYENNIOS, Nikephoros: *Nicephori Bryennii, Historiarum Libri Quattuor,* ed. and trans. P. Gautier, CFHB 9 (Brussels, 1975).

'Campaign Organisation and Tactics': G. T. Dennis, *Three Byzantine Military* Treatises, CFHB 25 (Washington DC, 1985).

CHONIATES, MICHAEL: *Michaelis Choniatae Epistulae,* ed. F. Kolovou, CFHB 41 (Berlin, 2001).

Constantini Porphyrogeniti Imperatoris De Cerimoniis Aulae Byzantinae, ed. J. Reiske, CSHB (Bonn, 1829–30).

DAPHNOPATES, THEODORE, *Correspondance,* eds. J. Darrouzès and G. Westerink (Paris, 1978).

De Administrando Imperio, ed. G. Moravcsik and trans. R. J. H. Jenkins, CFHB 1 (Washington DC, 1967).

Die byzantinischen Kleinchroniken, ed. P. Schreiner, CFHB 12, 3 vols. (Vienna, 1975–9).

DIGENES AKRITES: *Digenis Akritis: The Grottaferrata and Escorial Versions,* ed. E. Jeffreys (Cambridge, 1998).

GEOMETRES, JOHN, *Anecdota Graeca, E Codd. Manuscriptis Bibliothecae Regiae Parisiensis,* ed. J. A. Cramer, 4 vols. (Oxford, 1839–41).

GEORGE THE MONK: *Georgius Monachus Chronicon,* ed. C. de Boor (and P. Wirth), 2 vols. (Stuttgart, 1904, repr. 1978).

GEORGE THE MONK CONTINUATUS: *Theophanes Continuatus,* ed. I. Bekker, CSHB (Bonn, 1838).

GLYKAS, MICHAEL, *Annales (Biblos Chronike),* ed. I. Bekker, CSHB (Bonn, 1836).

KEDRENOS: *Georgius Cedrenus,* ed. I. Bekker, CSHB, 2 vols. (Bonn, 1938–9).

KEKAUMENOS: *Cecaumeni Consilia et Narrationes,* ed. and trans. G. Litavrin (Moscow, 1972).

KOMNENE, ANNA: *Anne Comnène, Alexiade,* ed. B. Leib, 3 vols., 2nd edn. (Paris, 1967).

LEO VI, *Tactica, PG* 107, cols. 669–1120.

LEO THE DEACON: *Leonis Diaconi Caloënsis Historiae Libri Decem,* ed. C. B. Hase, CSHB (Bonn, 1828).

—— (speeches): I. Sykutres, Λέοντος τοῦ Διακόνου ἀνέκδοτον ἐγκώμιον Βασιλείου Β, *EEBS* 10 (1932), 425–34.

LEO OF SYNADA: *The Correspondence of Leo, Metropolitan of Synada and Syncellus,* ed. M. P. Vinson, CFHB 23 (Washington DC, 1985).

Les Listes de préséance byzantines des IXe et Xe siècles, ed. N. Oikonomides (Paris, 1972).

MANASSES, CONSTANTINE: *Constantini Manassis Breviarum Chronicum*, ed. O. Lampsidis, CFHB 36 (Athens, 1996).

Miracles of St Eugenios: N. M. Panagiotakes, 'Fragments of a Lost Eleventh-Century Byzantine Historical Work', in C. Constantinides, N. M. Panagiotakes, E. Jeffreys, and A. D. Angelou (eds.), Φιλέλλην, *Studies in Honour of Robert Browning* (Venice, 1996), 321–57.

Miracles of Sampson: PG 115, cols. 277–308.

OURANOS, NIKEPHOROS, *Épistoliers byzantins du Xe siècle*, ed. J. Darrouzès (Paris, 1960), 217–48.

Ouranos Taktika (a): J. A. de Foucault, 'Douze chapitres inédits de la "Tactique" de Nicéphore Ouranos', *TM* 5 (1973), 281–310.

Ouranos Taktika (b): E. McGeer, *Sowing the Dragon's Teeth: Byzantine Warfare in the 10th Century* (Washington DC, 1995), 88–162.

PACHYMERES, GEORGE: *Georges Pachymérès: Relations historiques*, ed. A. Failler and trans. V. Laurent, CFHB 24 (Paris, 1984).

Patria: T. Preger, *Scriptores Originum Constantinopolitanarum*, 2 vols. (Leipzig, 1901–7; repr. 1989).

Praecepta Militum: E. McGeer, *Sowing the Dragon's Teeth: Byzantine Warfare in the 10th Century* (Washington DC, 1995), 12–58.

PSELLOS, MICHAEL: *Michele Psello Imperatori di Bisanzio (Cronografia)*, ed. S. Impellizzeri and trans. S. Ronchey, 2 vols. (Rome, 1984).

—— *Michaelis Pselli Scripta Minora*, eds. E. Kurtz and F. Drexl, 2 vols. (Milan, 1937–41).

PSEUDO-PSELLOS: *Michaeli Pselli Historia Syntomos*, ed. and trans. W. Aerts, CFHB 30 (Berlin, 1990).

Regesten: F. Dölger, *Regesten der Kaiserurkunden des öströmischen Reiches von 565–1453*, 3 vols. (Munich, 1925).

Régestes: V. Grumel, *Les Régestes des actes du patriarcat de Constantinople Régestes*, vol. I, fascs. II–III, *Les Régestes de 715–1206*, 2nd edn., J. Darrouzès (Paris, 1989).

St Athanasios: *Vitae Duae Antiquae Sancti Athanasii Athonitae,* ed. J. Noret, CCSG 9 (Brepols, 1982).

St Lazaros of Mount Galesion: *AASS,* Nov. 3:508–88 (Brussels, 1910), 508–88 (*BHG* 979); trans. R. P. H. Greenfield, *The Life of Lazaros of Mt. Galesion: An Eleventh-Century Pillar Saint* (Washington DC, 2000).

St Neilos the Younger: G. Giovanelli, *Bios kai politeia tou hosiou patros hemon Neilou tou Neou,* ed. G. Giovanelli (Grottaferrata, 1972).

St Nikon: *The Life of St Nikon,* ed. and trans. D. F. Sullivan (Brookline, Mass., 1987).

St Phantinos: *La vita di San Fantino il Giovane,* ed. and trans. E. Follieri (Brussels, 1993).

St Sabas: *Historia et laudes SS. Sabae et Macarii iuniorum e Sicilia auctore Oreste patriarcha Hieroslymitani,* ed. G. Cozza Luzi (Rome, 1893).

St Symeon the New Theologian: *Vie de Syméon le Nouveau Théologien (949–1022) par Nicétas Stéthatos,* ed. and trans. P. I. Hausherr (Rome, 1928).

'Skirmishing': G. Dagron and H. Mihăescu, *Le Traité sur la guérilla (De velitatione) de l'empereur Nicéphore Phocas* (Paris, 1986), 32–135.

Skylitzes, John: *Ioannis Skylitzae Synopsis Historiarum,* ed. I. Thurn, CFHB 5 (Berlin, 1973); trans. (French) B. Flusin and J.-C. Cheynet, *Jean Skylitzès: Empereurs de Constantinople* (Paris, 2003).

Skylitzes Continuatus: ʽΗ Συνέχεια τῆς χρονογραφίας τοῦ Ἰωάννου Σκυλίτζη, ed. E. T. Tsolakes (Thessalonika, 1968).

Souda: Suidae Lexicon, ed. A. Adler, 5 vols. (Leipzig, 1928–38).

Svoronos, N., *Les Novelles des empereurs macédoniens concernant la terre et les stratiotes* (Athens, 1994); trans. (English)

E. McGeer, *The Land Legislation of the Macedonian Emperors* (Toronto, 2000).

SYNADENOS, PHILETOS, *Épistoliers byzantins du Xe siècle*, ed. J. Darrouzès (Paris, 1960), 249–59.

THEOPHANES, *Chronographia*, ed. C. de Boor, 2 vols. (Leipzig, 1883–5).

Theophanes Continuatus, ed. I. Bekker, CSHB (Bonn, 1838).

THEOPHYLACT OF OCHRID: *Théophylacte d'Achrida Lettres*, ed. and trans. P. Gautier, CFHB 16/2 (Thessalonika, 1986).

Traité: 'Le Traité des transferts', ed. J. Darrouzès, *REB* 42 (1984).

Typikon (Pakourianos): P. Gautier, 'Le Typikon du sébaste Grégoire Pakourianos', *REB* 42 (1984), 5–145.

ZEPOS, J., and ZEPOS, P., (eds.), *Ius Graecoromanum*, 8 vols. (Athens, 1931).

ZONARAS: *Ioannis Zonarae Annales*, ed. M. Pinder, CSHB, 2 vols. (Bonn, 1841).

—— *Ioannis Zonarae Epitomae Historiarum Libri XIII–XVIII*, CSHB, ed. T. Büttner-Wobst (Bonn, 1897).

Armenian, Georgian, and Syrian

ARISTAKES OF LASTIVERT, *Récit des malheurs de la nation arménienne*, trans. M. Canard and H. Berbérian according to the edn. and trans. (Russian) by K.Yuzbashian, Bibliothèque de Byzantion, 5 (Brussels, 1973).

BAR HEBRAEUS: *The Chronography of Gregory Abu'l Faraj, the Son of Aaron, the Hebrew Physician, Commonly Known as Bar Hebreus*, ed. and trans. E. A. Wallis Budge (London, 1932).

ELIAS OF NISIBIS: *La Chronographie de Mar Elie bar Sinaya, Métropolitain de Nisibe*, ed. and trans. L. J. Delaporte (Paris, 1910).

Georgian Royal Annals: *Rewriting Caucasian History: The Georgian Chronicles*, trans. R. Thomson (Oxford, 1996).

Life of John and Euthymios: B. Martin-Hisard, 'La Vie de Jean et Euthyme: Le Statut du monastère des Ibères sur l'Athos', *REB* 49 (1991), 67–142.

MATTHEW OF EDESSA: *Armenia and the Crusades in the Tenth to Twelfth Centuries: The Chronicle of Matthew of Edessa*, trans. A. E. Dostourian (Lanham and London, 1993).

MICHAEL THE SYRIAN: *Chronique de Michel le Syrien, Patriarche Jacobite d'Antioche (1169–99)*, ed. and trans. J. B. Chabot (Paris, 1905–10).

STEPHEN OF TARON: *Des Stephanos von Taron armenische Geschichte*, trans. H. Gelzer and A. Burckhardt (Leipzig, 1909).

THOMAS ARTSRUNI: *History of the House of the Artsrunik'*, trans. R. W. Thomson (Detroit, 1985).

Arabic and Persian

ADUD AL-DAULA: *Die Hofkorrespondenz Adud ad-Daulas*, ed. J. C. Bürgel (Wiesbaden, 1965).

CANARD, M., 'Deux documents arabes sur Bardas Sklèros', *Studi bizantini e neoellenici*, 5 (1939), 55–69.

IBN BUTLAN: *The Medico-Philosophical Controversy between Ibn Butlan of Baghdad and Ibn Ridwan of Cairo*, ed. and trans. J. Schlacht and M. Meyerhof (Cairo, 1937).

IBN HAWKAL, *La Configuration de la terre*, trans. J. H. Kramers and G.Wiet, 2 vols. (Beirut and Paris, 1964).

IBN AL-KARDABUS, *Historia de al-Andalus (Kitab al-Iktifa)*, trans. F. Maíllo Salgado (Madrid, 1986).

IBN MISKAWAYH, *Eclipse of the Abbasid Caliphate*, ed. and trans. H. Amedroz and D. Margoliouth, 6 vols. (Oxford, 1920–1), vol. v.

AL-RUDHRAWARI, *Eclipse of the Abbasid Caliphate*, ed. and trans. H. Amedroz and D. Margoliouth, 6 vols. (Oxford, 1920–1), vol. vi.

AL-TANUKHI: *Table Talk of a Mesopotamian Judge*, trans. D. Margoliouth (London, 1922).

VASILIEV, A. A., *Byzance et les Arabes*, 3 vols. (Brussels, 1950).

YAHYA IBN SA'ID AL-ANTAKI, 'Histoire', ed. and trans. (French) I. Kratchkovsky and A. Vasiliev, *PO* 18 (1924), 699–832 and *PO* 23 (1932), 349–520; 'Histoire de Yahya ibn Sa'id d'Antioche', ed. I. Kratochkovsky, trans. (French) F. Micheau and G. Troupeau, *PO* 47 (1997), 373–559; trans. (Italian) B. Pirone, *Yahya al-Antaki Cronache dell'Egitto fatimide e dell'impero Bizantino 937–1033* (Bari, 1998).

Western and Northern

ADEMAR OF CHABANNES: *Ademari Cabannensis Chronicon*, ed. P. Bourgain, R. Landes, and G. Pons, CCCM 129 (Brepols, 1999).

AMATUS OF MONTE CASSINO: *Storia de' Normanni di Amato di Montecassino volgarizzata in antico francese*, ed. V. de Bartholomaeis (Rome, 1935).

Annals of Bari: *Annales Barenses*, ed. G. H. Pertz, *MGH ss* 5 (Hanover, 1844).

Annals of Benevento: *Annales Beneventani 788–1130*, ed. G. H. Pertz, *MGH ss* 3 (Hanover, 1839).

Annals of Quedlingburg: Annales Quedlingburgenses, ed. G. H. Pertz, *MGH ss* 3 (Hanover, 1839).

Chronicles of Hungary: *Scriptores rerum Hungaricarum tempore ducum regumque stirpis arpadienae gestarum*, ed. E. Szentpétery (Budapest, 1937–8).

Chronicon Venetum quod vulgo dicunt Altinate, ed. H. Simonsfeld, *MGH ss* 14 (Hanover, 1883).

Chronicon Salernitanum: A Critical Edition with Studies on Literary and Historical Sources and on Language, ed. U. Westerbergh (Stockholm, 1956).

Codex Diplomaticus Cavensis, eds. M. Morcaldi, M. Schiani, S. De Stephano, R. Gaetani d'Aragona, S. Leone and G. Vitolo, 8 vols. (Naples, Milan, and Pisa, 1873–93).

Codex Diplomaticus Regni Croatiae, Dalmatiae et Slavoniae, 1, ed. M. Kostrenčic (Zagreb, 1967).

Codice Diplomatico Amalfitano, i, ed. R. Filangieri di Candida (Naples, 1917).

DANDOLO, ANDREA: *Chronicon Venetum: Andreae Danduli ducis Venetiarum chronica per extensum descriptum aa. 46–1280*, ed. E. Pastorello (Bologna, 1938).

FULBERT OF CHARTRES: *The Letters and Poems of Fulbert of Chartres*, ed. and trans. F. Behrends, OMT (Oxford, 1976).

GERBERT OF AURILLAC: *Correspondance: Gerbert d'Aurillac*, eds. P. Riché and J.-P. Callu, 2 vols. (Paris, 1993).

Gesta Normannorum Ducum, ed. and trans. E. M. C. van Houts, OMT, 2 vols. (Oxford, 1992–5).

GLABER, RALPH: *Rodulfi Glaber Historiarum Libri Quinque*, ed. and trans. J. France, OMT (Oxford, 1989).

JOHN THE DEACON, 'La cronaca Veneziana del Giovanni Diacono', in G. Monticolo (ed)., *Chronache Veneziane* (Rome, 1890).

LEO MARSICANUS: *Chronica Monasterii Casinensis (Die Chronik von Montecassino)*, ed. H. Hoffmann, *MGH ss* 34 (Hanover, 1980).

LIUDPRAND OF CREMONA, *Relatio de Legatione Constantinopolitana*, ed. and trans. B Scott (London, 1993).

LUPUS PROTOSPATHARIUS: *Lupus Protospatharius*, ed. G. H. Pertz, *MGH ss* 5 (Hanover, 1844).

ORDERIC VITALIS: *The Ecclesiastical History of Orderic Vitalis*, ed. M. Chibnall, OMT, 6 vols. (Oxford, 1969–80).

Priest of Diokleia: *Letopis Popa Dukljanina*, ed. F. Šišić (Belgrade and Zagreb, 1928).

Russian Primary Chronicle, Laurentian Text, ed. and trans. S. H. Cross and O. P. Sherbowitz-Wetzor (Cambridge, Mass., 1953).

THIETMAR OF MERSEBURG: *Thietmar Merseburgensis Episcopi Chronicon,* ed. R. Holtzmann, *MGH* SrG NS 9 (Berlin, 1935).

THOMAS OF SPLIT, *Thomae Archidiaconi Spalatensis: Historia Salonitanorum pontificum atque Spalatensium a S. Domnis usque ad Rogerium (d.1266),* ed. Fr. Rački (Zagreb, 1894).

WILLIAM OF APULIA: *Guillaume de Pouille, La Geste de Robert Guiscard,* ed. and trans. M. Mathieu (Palermo, 1961).

Secondary literature

ADONTZ, N., 'Les Taronites en Arménie et à Byzance', *B* 9 (1934), 715–38.

—— 'Les Taronites en Arménie et à Byzance', *B* 10 (1935), 531–51.

—— 'Les Taronites en Arménie et à Byzance', *B* 11 (1936), 21–42.

—— 'Tornik le moine', *B* 13 (1938), 143–64.

—— 'Samuel l'Arménien roi des Bulgares', reprinted in his *Études arméno-byzantines* (Lisbon, 1965), 347–407.

—— 'Observations sur la généalogie des Taronites', reprinted in *Études arméno-byzantines* (Lisbon, 1965), 339–45.

AHRWEILER, H., 'Recherches sur l'administration de l'empire byzantin aux IXè–XIè siècles', *BCH* 84 (1960), 1–109.

—— 'La Frontière et les frontières de Byzance en Orient', *Acts of the 14th International Congress 1971,* 3 vols. (Bucharest, 1974), i. 209–30.

—— 'Recherches sur la société byzantine au XIe siècle: Nouvelles hiérarchies et nouvelles solidarités', *TM* 6 (1976), 99–124.

ANGOLD, M., *The Byzantine Empire 1025–1204,* 2nd edn. (New York, 1997).

ANGOLD, M., 'The Autobiographical Impulse in Byzantium', *DOP* 52 (1998), 225–57.

—— 'Autobiography and Identity: The Case of the Later Byzantine Empire', *Byz Slav* 60 (1999), 36–59.

—— (ed.), *Byzantine Aristocracy* (Oxford, 1984).

ANTOLJAK, S., 'Wer könnte eigentlich Joannes Skylitzes sein?', *Acts of the 14th International Congress 1971* (Bucharest, 1974), 677–82.

ARBAGI, M., 'The Celibacy of Basil II', *Byzantine Studies (Études byzantines)* 2(1) (1975), 41–5.

ARUTJUNOVA-FIDANJAN, V. A., 'Sur le problème des provinces byzantines orientales', *REArm* 14 (1980), 157–69.

—— 'The Social Administrative Structures in the East of the Byzantine Empire', *JÖB* 32.3 (1982), 21–34.

—— 'Some Aspects of Military Administrative Districts in Armenia during the Eleventh Century', *REArm* 20 (1986–7), 309–20.

—— 'The New Socio-Administrative Structures in the East of Byzantium', *Byz Forsch* 19 (1993), 79–86.

ASHDRACHA, C., 'Inscriptions Byzantines de la Thrace orientale (VIIIe–XI siècles)', *Αρχαιολογικὸν Δελτίον*, 44–6 (1989–91) (Athens, 1996), 239–334.

ASTRUC, C., 'L'Inventaire dressé en septembre 1200 du trésor et de la bibliothèque de Patmos, édition diplomatique', *TM* 8 (1981), 15–30.

AVALICHVILI, Z., 'La Succession du curopalate David d'Ibérie, dynaste de Tao', *B* 8 (1933), 177–202.

BAUN, J., *Tales from Another Byzantium: Celestial Journey and Local Community in the Medieval Greek Apocrypha* (Cambridge, forthcoming).

BEATON, R., 'Cappadocians at Court: Digenes and Timarion', in M. Mullett and D. Smythe (eds.), *Alexios I Komnenos* (Belfast, 1996), 329–38.

—— *The Medieval Greek Romance,* 2nd edn. (London, 1996).

BECK, H. G., 'Zur byzantinischen "Mönchskronik"', in *Speculum Historiale: Geschichte im Spiegel von Geschichtsschreibung und Geschichtsdeutung (Festschrift K. Adler)* (Freiburg and Munich, 1965), 188–97.

BEIHAMMER, A., 'Der harte Sturz des Bardas Skleros. Eine Fallstudie zu zwischenstaatliche Kommunikation und Konfliktführung in der byzantinisch-arabischen Diplomatie des 10. Jahrhunderts', in R. Bösel and H. Fillitz (eds.), *Römische Historische Mitteilungen,* 45 (Vienna, 2003), 21–57.

BELKE, K., and MERSICH, N., *TIB, Phrygien und Pisidien* (Vienna, 1990).

—— and RESTLE, M., *TIB, Galatien und Lykaonien* (Vienna, 1984).

BIANQUIS, T., *Damas sous la domination fatimide (359–468/969–1076): Essai d'interprétation de chroniques arabes médievales,* 2 vols. (Damascus, 1986–9).

BIDDLE, M., *The Tomb of Christ* (Stroud, 1999).

BIKHAZI, R. J., 'The Hamdanid Dynasty of Mesopotamia and North Syria 254–404/868–1014', Ph.D. Thesis (Michigan, 1981).

BIVAR, A. D. H., 'Bardes Skleros, the Buwayids and the Marwanids at Hisn Ziyad in the Light of an Unnoticed Arab Inscription', in S. Freeman and H. Kennedy (eds.), *Defence of the Roman and Byzantine Frontiers* (Oxford, 1986), 9–21.

BLONDAL, S., and BENEDIKZ, B. S., *The Varangians of Byzantium* (Cambridge, 1978).

DE BOOR, C., 'Zu Johannes Skylitzes', *BZ* 13 (1904), 356–69.

—— 'Weiteres zur Chronik des Skylitzes', *BZ* 14 (1905), 409–67.

BRETT, M., *The Rise of the Fatimids: The World of the Mediterranean and the Middle East in the Fourth Century of the Hijra, Tenth Century C.E.* (Leiden, 2001).

BROKKAAR, W. G., 'Basil Lacapenos: Byzantium in the Tenth Century', *Studia Byzantina et Neohellenica Neerlandica*, 3 (Leiden, 1972), 199–234.

BROWNING, R., 'Byzantine Scholarship', *PP* 28 (1964), 3–20.

—— 'Byzantine Literature', *DMA*, ii. 505–21.

BRYER, A., and WINFIELD, D., *The Byzantine Monuments and Topography of the Pontus*, 2 vols. (Washington DC, 1985).

CAHEN, C., 'Une correspondance buyide inédite', *Studi orientalistici in onore di G. Levi della Vida*, 2 vols. (Rome, 1956), i. 87–97.

—— *Pre-Ottoman Turkey: A General Survey of the Material and Spiritual Culture and History* (trans. J. Jones Williams) (London, 1968).

CAMERON, A., *Procopius and the Sixth Century* (London and New York, 1996).

CANARD, M., 'Quelques noms de personnages byzantins dans une pièce du poète Abu Firas', *B* 11 (1936), 451–60.

—— 'Deux documents arabes sur Bardas Sklèros', *Studi bizantini e neoellenici* 5 (1939), 55–69.

—— 'Deux episodes des relations diplomatiques arabo-byzantines au Xe siècle', *Bulletin des Études Orientales de l'Institut Français de Damas* (1949–50), 51–69.

—— 'La Date des expéditions mésopotamiennes de Jean Tzimiscès', *Mélanges Henri Grégoire, Ann. de l'Inst. de Phil. et d'Hist. Or. et Slav.* 10 (1950), 99–108.

—— 'Une vie du patriarch melkite d'Antioche, Christophore', review of H. Zayyat, 'Vie du patriarche melkite d'Antioche, Christophore (967) par le protospathaire Ibrahim b. Yuhanna, document inedit du Xe siècle', *B* 18 (1953), 561–9.

—— 'La Destruction de l'Église de la Resurrection par le Calife Hakim et l'histoire de la descent du feu sacré', *B* 25 (1955), 16–43.

—— 'Quelques "à côté" de l'histoire des relations entre Byzance et les Arabes', *Studi medievali in onore di G. Levi della Vida*, 2 vols. (Rome, 1956), i. 98–119.

—— 'Les Sources arabes de l'histoire byzantine aux confins des Xe et XIe siècles', *REB* 19 (1961), 284–314.

—— 'Les Relations politiques et sociales entre Byzance et les Arabes', *DOP* 18 (1964), 35–56.

CHEYNET, J.-C., 'Du Stratège de thème au duc: Chronologie de l'évolution au cours du XI siècle', *TM* 9 (1985), 181–94.

—— 'Du Prénom au patronyme: les étrangers à Byzance', in N. Oikonomides (ed.), *SBS* 1 (Washington DC, 1987), 57–65.

—— *Pouvoir et contestations à Byzance* (Paris, 1990).

—— 'Fortune et puisssance de l'aristocratie', in V. Kravari, J. Lefort, and C. Morrisson (eds.), *Hommes et richesses dans l'empire byzantin*, 2 vols. (Paris, 1989–91), ii. 199–213.

—— 'Sceaux byzantins des musées d'Antioche et de Tarse', *TM* 12 (1994), 391–479.

—— 'L'Apport arabe à l'aristocratie byzantine des Xe–XIe siècles', *Byz Slav* 61 (1995), 137–46.

—— 'L'Aristocratie byzantine (VIIIe–XIIIe s.)', *Journal de Savants* (2000), 281–322.

—— 'La Patricienne à ceinture: Une femme de qualité', in P. Henriet and A.-M. Legras (eds.), *Au Cloître et dans le monde: Femmes, hommes et sociétés (IXe-XVe siècle). Mélanges en l'honneur de Paulette L'Hermit-Leclerq* (Paris, 2000), 179–87.

—— *Sceaux de la collection de Zacos (Bibliothèque Nationale de France) se rapportant aux provinces orientales de l'Empire byzantin* (Paris, 2001).

—— 'Épiskeptitai et autre gestionnaires de biens publics (d'après les sceaux de l'IFEB)', in W. Seibt (ed.), *SBS* 7 (Washington DC, 2002), 87–117.

—— 'Par Saint Georges, Par Saint Michel', *TM* 14 (2002), 115–34.

CHEYNET, J.-C., 'Basil II and Asia Minor', in P. Magdalino (ed.), *Byzantium in the Year 1000* (Leiden, 2002), 71–108.

—— 'Les Limites du pouvoir à Byzance: une forme de tolerance?' in *Toleration and Repression in the Middle Ages. In Memory of Lenos Mavromatis* (Athens, 2002), 15–28.

—— 'Grandeur et decadence des Diogénai', in V. N. Vlyssidou (ed.), *The Empire in Crisis (?): Byzantium in the 11th Century (1025–1081)* (Athens, 2003), 119–37.

—— and MORRISSON, C., 'Lieux de trouvaille et circulation des sceaux', in N. Oikonomides (ed.), *SBS* 2 (Washington DC, 1990), 105–31.

—— —— and SEIBT, W., *Sceaux byzantins de la collection Henri Seyrig* (Paris, 1991).

—— and Vannier, J.-F., *Études prosopographiques* (Paris, 1986).

CIGGAAR, K., *Western Travellers to Constantinople: The West and Byzantium, 962–1204* (Leiden, 1996).

CROKE, B., 'City Chronicles of Late Antiquity', in *Christian Chronicles and Byzantine History, 5–6th Centuries* (Aldershot, 1992), no. IV.

CROSTINI, B., 'The Emperor Basil II's Cultural Life', *B* 64 (1996), 53–80.

CUTLER, A., 'The Psalter of Basil II', in *Imagery and Ideology in Byzantine Art* (Aldershot, 1992), no. III.

DAGRON, G., 'Minorités ethniques et religieuses dans l'Orient byzantin à la fin du Xe et au XIe siècles: L'Immigration syrienne', *TM* 6 (1976), 177–216.

—— *Constantinople imaginaire* (Paris, 1984).

—— and MIHĂESCU, H., *Le Traité sur la guérilla (De velitatione) de l'empereur Nicéphore Phocas* (Paris, 1986).

DAIN, A., *La 'Tactique' de Nicéphore Ouranos* (Paris, 1937).

DARROUZES, J., *Épistoliers byzantins du Xe siècle* (Paris, 1960).

—— 'Sur la chronologie du patriarche Antoine III Stoudite', *REB* 46 (1988), 55–60.

DAVIDS, A., *The Empress Theophano: Byzantium and the West at the Turn of the First Millennium* (Cambridge, 1995).

DÉDÉYAN, G., 'Les Arméniens en Cappadoce aux Xe et XIe siècles', in C. D. Fonseca (ed.), *Le aree omogenee della civiltà rupestre nell'ambito dell'impero bizantino: la Cappadocia* (Lecce, 1981), 75–95.

—— 'Mleh le grand, stratège de Lykandos', *REArm* 15 (1981), 73–102.

DENNIS, G. T., *Three Byzantine Military Treatises* (Washington DC, 1985).

DIEHL, C., 'Le Trésor et la bibliothèque de Patmos au commencement du 13e siècle', *BZ* 1 (1892), 488–525.

DJOBADZE, W. Z., *Materials for the Study of Georgian Monasteries in the Western Environs of Antioch-on-the-Orontes* (Louvain, 1976).

—— *Archaeological Investigations in the Region West of Antioch-on-the-Orontes* (Stuttgart, 1986).

—— W. Z., *Early Medieval Georgian Monasteries in Historic Tao, Klarjet'i and Šavšeti* (Stuttgart, 1992).

DOIMI DE FRANKOPAN, P., 'The Numismatic Evidence from the Danube Region, 971–1092', *BMGS* 21 (1997), 30–9.

—— 'The Workings of the Byzantine Provincial Administration in the 10th–12th Centuries: the Example of Preslav', *B* 71 (2001), 73–97.

DURIĆ, I., 'Theophylacte d'Achrida sous la tente d'Aaron', *ZRVI* 27 (1988), 89–91.

EBERSOLT, J., *Musées impériaux ottomans: Catalogues des sceaux byzantins* (Paris, 1922).

ESTAPANAN, J. C., *Skylitzes matritensis, i: reproducciones y miniaturas* (Madrid, 1965).

Evans, H. C., and Wixom, W. D., *The Glory of Byzantium: Art and Culture of the Middle Byzantine Era, A.D. 843–1261* (New York, 1997).

von Falkenhausen, V., *Untersuchungen über die byzantinische Herrschaft in Süditalien vom 9. bis ins 11. Jahrhundert* (Wiesbaden, 1967).

—— 'Zur byzantinischen Verwaltung Luceras am Ende des 10. Jahrhunderts', *Quellen und Forschungen aus italienischen Archiven und Bibliotheken*, 53 (1973), 395–406.

—— 'A Provincial Aristocracy: The Byzantine Provinces in Southern Italy' in M. Angold (ed.), *Byzantine Aristocracy* (Oxford, 1984), 211–35.

—— 'Between Two Empires: Byzantine Italy in the Reign of Basil II' in P. Magdalino (ed.), *Byzantium in the Year 1000* (Leiden, 2002), 135–59.

Farag, W. A., 'The Truce of Safar A.H. 359', Paper from the Eleventh Spring Symposium at Birmingham University (Centre for Byzantine Studies, Birmingham, 1977).

—— 'Byzantium and its Muslim Neighbours during the Reign of Basil II (976–1025)', Ph.D. Thesis (Birmingham, 1979).

—— 'The Aleppo Question: A Byzantine–Fatimid Conflict of Interest in Northern Syria in the Later Tenth Century', *BMGS* 14 (1990), 44–60.

Featherstone, J., 'Olga's Visit to Constantinople', *HUS* 14 (1990), 293–312.

—— 'Olga's Visit to Constantinople in *De Cerimoniis*', *REB* (forthcoming).

Felix, W., *Byzanz und die islamische Welt im früheren 11. Jahrhundert* (Vienna, 1981).

Ferluga, J., 'John Scylitzes and Michael of Devol', *ZRVI* 10 (1967), 163–70.

—— 'Die Chronik des Priesters von Diokleia als Quelle für byzantinische Geschichte', *Vyzantina*, 10 (1980), 431–60.

FINE, J. V. A., *The Early Medieval Balkans: A Critical Survey from the Sixth to the Late Twelfth Century* (Ann Arbor, 1983).

—— 'Basil II and the Decline of the Theme System', *Studia Slavico-Byzantina et Medievalia Europensia* 1 (Sofia, 1989), 44–7.

FORSYTH, J. H., 'The Chronicle of Yahya ibn Sa'id al-Antaki', Ph.D. Thesis (Michigan, 1977).

FLUSIN, B., and CHEYNET, J.-C., *Jean Skylitzès: Empereurs de Constantinople* (Paris, 2003).

FRANKLIN, S., and SHEPARD, J., *The Emergence of Rus 750–1200* (Cambridge, 1996).

FREI, P., 'Das Geschichtswerk des Theodoros Daphnopates als Quelle der *Synopsis Historiarum* des Johannes Skylitzes', in E. Plockinger (ed.), *Lebendige Altertumswissenschaft: Festgabe zur Vollendung des 70. Lebensjahres von Herman Vetters* (Vienna, 1985) 348–53.

GARLAND, L., 'Basil II as Humorist', *B* 67 (1999), 321–43.

GARSOÏAN, N. G., 'Armenian Integration into the Byzantine Empire', in H. Ahrweiler and A. E. Laiou (eds.), *Studies on the Internal Diaspora of the Byzantine Empire* (Washington DC, 1998), 53–124.

GAUTIER, P., 'Monodie inédite de Michel Psellos sur le basileus Andronic Doucas', *REB* 24 (1966), 153–64.

—— 'Le Dossier d'un haut fonctionnaire d'Alexis Ier Comnène, Manuel Straboromanos', *REB* 23 (1965), 168–204.

GAY, J., *L'Italie méridionale et l'empire byzantin depuis l'avènement de Basil I jusqu'à la prise de Bari par les Normands (867–1071)*, (Paris, 1904).

GELZER, H., 'Ungedruckte und wenig bekannte Bistumsverzeichnisse der orientalischen Kirche', *BZ* 1 (1892), 245–82; 2 (1893), 22–72.

GRABAR, A. and MANOUSACAS, M. I., *L'Illustration du manuscrit de Skylitzès de la Bibliothèque Nationale de Madrid* (Venice, 1979).

GRÉGOIRE, H., 'Du Nouveau sur l'histoire bulgaro-byzantine. Nicétas Pegonitès, vainqueur du roi bulgare, Jean Vladislav', *B* 12 (1937), 289–91.

—— and ADONTZ, N., 'Nicéphore au col roide', *B* 8 (1935), 203–12.

GRIERSON, P., 'Tombs and Obits of Byzantine Emperors', *DOP* 16 (1962), 1–62.

—— and BELLINGER, A. R., *Catalogue of the Byzantine Coins in the Dumbarton Oaks Collection and in the Whittemore Collection*, 5 vols. (Washington DC, 1966–99).

GRIGORIADIS, I., 'A Study of the *Prooimion* of Zonaras' Chronicle in Relation to Other 12th-Century Historical *Prooimia*', *BZ* 91 (1998), 327–44.

GRIGORIOU-IOANNIDES, M., '*Themata* et *tagmata*. Un problème de l'institution de thèmes pendant les Xe et XIe siècles', *Byz Forsch* 19 (1993), 35–41.

GROUSSET, R., *Histoire de l'Arménie* (Paris, 1947).

GUILLAND, R. G., *Recherches sur les institutions byzantines,* 2 vols. (Amsterdam, 1967).

—— 'Curopalate', in *Titres et fonctions de l'empire byzantin* (London: Variorum, 1976), no. III.

GUILLOU, A., 'La Lucanie Byzantine: Étude de géographie historique', *B* 35 (1965), 119–49.

—— 'Production and Profits in Southern Italy (9th to 11th century)', *DOP* 38 (1974), 91–109.

HALDON, J., 'The Organisation and Support of an Expeditionary Force: Manpower and Logistics in the Middle Byzantine Period', in K. Tsiknakes (ed.), *Byzantium at War (9th to 12th c.)* (Athens, 1997), 111–51.

—— *Warfare, State and Society in the Byzantine World 565–1204* (London, 1999).

—— 'Approaches to an Alternative Military History of the Period ca. 1025–1071' in V. N. Vlyssidou (ed.), *The Empire in Crisis (?) Byzantium in the 11th Century (1025–81)*, (Athens, 2003), 45–74.

—— and KENNEDY, H., 'The Arabo-Byzantine Frontier in the Eighth and Ninth Centuries: Military and Society in the Borderlands', *ZRVI* 19 (1980), 79–116.

HAMIDULLAH, M., 'Nouveaux documents sur les rapports de l'Europe avec l'Orient musulman au moyen âge', *Arabica*, 7 (1960), 281–98.

HARVEY, A. *Economic Expansion in the Byzantine Empire 900–1200* (Cambridge, 1989).

HENDY, M. F., *Studies in the Byzantine Monetary Economy c.300–1450* (Cambridge, 1985).

HICKS, M., 'The Life and Historical Writings of Michael Attaleiates', M. Litt. Thesis (Oxford, 1987).

HILD, F., *Das byzantinische Strassensystem in Kappadokien* (Vienna, 1977).

—— and RESTLE, M., *TIB, Kappadokien* (Vienna, 1981).

HINTERBERGER, M., *Autobiographische Traditionen in Byzanz* (Vienna, 1999).

HIRSCH, F., *Byzantinische Studien* (Leipzig, 1876).

HØGEL, C., 'Hagiography under the Macedonians: The Two Recensions of the Metaphrastic Menologion', in P. Magdalino (ed.), *Byzantium in the Year 1000* (Leiden, 2002), 217–32.

HOLMES, C., 'Basil II and the Government of Empire (976–1025)', D.Phil. Thesis (Oxford, 1999).

—— ' "How the East was Won" in the Reign of Basil II', in A. Eastmond (ed.), *Eastern Approaches to Byzantium* (Aldershot, 2001), 41–56.

—— 'Byzantium's Eastern Frontier in the Tenth and Eleventh Centuries', in D. Abulafia and N. Berend (eds.), *Medieval Frontiers: Concepts and Practices* (Aldershot, 2002), 82–104.

—— 'Political Elites in the Reign of Basil II', in P. Magdalino, *Byzantium in the Year 1000* (Leiden, 2002), 35–69.

—— 'The Rhetorical Structures of John Skylitzes' *Synopsis Historion*, in E. Jeffreys (ed.), *Rhetoric in Byzantium* (Aldershot, 2003), 187–99.

HONIGMANN, E., *Die Ostgrenze des byzantinischen Reiches von 363 bis 1071, nach griechischen, arabischen, syrischen und armenischen Quellen* (Brussels, 1935).

HOWARD-JOHNSTON, J. D., 'Byzantine Anzitene', in S. Mitchell (ed.), *Armies and Frontiers in Anatolia* (Oxford, 1983), 239–90.

—— 'Procopius, Roman Defences North of the Taurus and the New Fortress of Citharizon', in D. H. French and C. S. Lightfoot (eds.), *The Eastern Frontier of the Roman Empire* (Oxford, 1989), 203–29.

—— 'Crown Lands and the Defence of Imperial Authority in the Tenth and Eleventh Centuries', *Byz Forsch* 21 (1995), 76–99.

—— 'Anna Komnene and the *Alexiad*', in M. Mullett and D. Smythe (eds.), *Alexios I Komnenos* (Belfast, 1996), 260–302.

HUNGER, H., *Die hochsprachliche profane Literatur der Byzantiner*, 2 vols. (Munich, 1978).

IVANISEVIČ, V., 'Interpretations and Dating of the Folles of Basil II and Constantine VIII—the Class of A2', *ZRVI* 27 (1989), 37–9.

JANIN, R., *La Géographie ecclésiastique de l'empire byzantin*, i. *Les Églises et les monastères*, 3 vols., 2nd edn. (Paris, 1969).

JANSSENS, F., 'Le Lac de Van et la stratégie byzantine', *B* 42 *(1972),* 388–404.

JEFFREYS, E., 'The Attitudes of Byzantine Chroniclers towards Ancient History', *B* 49 (1979), 199–238.

—— 'Malalas' Sources', in E. Jeffreys, B. Croke, and R. Scott (eds.), *Studies in John Malalas* (Sydney, 1990), 208–13.

—— JEFFREYS, M., and SCOTT, R. (trans.), *The Chronicle of John Malalas* (Melbourne, 1986).

—— CROKE, B., and SCOTT, R. (eds.), *Studies in John Malalas* (Sydney, 1990).

JONES, L., 'The Visual Expression of Power and Piety in Medieval Armenia: The Palace and Palace Church at Aghtamar', in A. Eastmond (ed.), *Eastern Approaches to Byzantium* (Aldershot, 2001), 221–41.

JORDANOV, I., 'Les Sceaux de deux chefs militaire byzantins trouvés à Préslav: Le Magistros Leo Mélissenos et le patrice Théodorokan', *Byzantinobulgarica* (1986), 183–9.

—— 'La Stratégie de Preslav aux Xe–XIe siècles selon les données de la sigillographie', in N.Oikonomides (ed.), *SBS* 1 (Washington DC, 1987), 89–96.

—— 'Molybdobulles de domestiques des scholes du dernier quart du Xe siècle trouvés dans la stratégie de Preslav', in N. Oikonomides (ed.), *SBS* 2 (Washington DC, 1990), 203–11.

—— *Pechatite ot strategiiata v Preslav, 971–1088* (Sofia, 1993).

—— 'Medieval Plovdiv According to the Sphragistic Data', in N. Oikonomides (ed.), *SBS* 4 (Washington DC, 1995), 111–39.

KALDELLIS, A., *The Argument of Psellos' Chronographia* (Leiden, 1999).

KAPLAN, M., 'Les Grands Propriétaires de Cappadoce', in C. D. Fonseca (ed.), *Le aree omogenee della civiltà rupestre nell'ambito dell'impero bizantino: la Cappdocia* (Lecce, 1981),125–58.

KAPLAN, M., *Les Hommes et la terre à Byzance du VIe au XIe siècle* (Paris, 1992).

KARAGIANNOPOULOS, I., and WEISS, G., *Quellenkunde zur Geschichte von Byzanz (324–1453)*, 2 vols. (Weisbaden, 1982).

KARPOZELOS, A., Βυζαντινοὶ ἱστορικαὶ χρονογράφοι (Athens, 1997).

KAŽDAN, A. P., 'Der Mensch in der byzantinischen Literaturgeschichte', *JÖB 29* (1979), 1–21.

—— 'An Attempt at Hagio-Autobiography: The Pseudo-Life of "Saint" Psellos"', *B* 53 (1983), 546–56.

—— 'Approaches to the History of Byzantine Civilisation from Krause to Beck and Mango', in A. P. Každan and S. Franklin (eds.), *Studies on Byzantine Literature of the Eleventh and Twelfth Centuries* (Cambridge, 1984), 11–22.

—— 'The Social Views of Michael Attaleiates', in A. P. Každan and S. Franklin (eds.), *Studies on Byzantine Literature of the Eleventh and Twelfth Centuries* (Paris, 1984), 23–86.

—— 'Aristocracy and the Imperial Ideal', in M. Angold (ed.), *Byzantine Aristocracy* (Oxford, 1984), 43–58.

—— 'The Formation of Byzantine Family Names in the Ninth and Tenth Centuries', *Byz Slav* 58 (1997), 90–105.

—— and RONCHEY, S., *L'aristocrazia bizantina del principo del XI alla fine del XII secolo* (Palermo, 1997).

—— and WHARTON-EPSTEIN, A., *Change in Byzantine Culture in the Eleventh and Twelfth Centuries* (Berkeley, 1985).

KENNEDY, H., *The Prophet and the Age of the Caliphates* (London, 1986).

KIRMEIER, J., *Kaiser Heinrich II. 1002–1024* (Augsburg, 2002).

KONSTANTOPOULOS, K. M. Βυζαντιακὰ μολυβδόβουλλα τοῦ ἐν Ἀθήναις Ἐθνικοῦ Νομισματικοῦ Μουσείου (Athens, 1917).

KREUTZ, B., *Before the Normans* (Philadelphia, 1991).

Krivocheine, B., *Symeon the New Theologian (949–1022)* (New York, 1986).

Krumbacher, K., *Geschichte der byzantinischen Literatur von Justinien bis zum Ende des oströmischen Reiches, (527–1453)*, 2 vols. (New York, repr. 1970 of 1897 edn.).

Kühn, H. J., *Die byzantinische Armee im 10. und 11: Jahrhundert. Studien zur Organisation der Tagmata* (Vienna, 1991).

Laiou, A., 'Imperial Marriages and their Critics in the Eleventh Century: The Case of Skylitzes', *DOP* 46 (1992), 165–76.

Laurent, V., *Les Sceaux byzantins du Médailler Vatican* (Vatican, 1962).

—— 'La Chronologie des gouveneurs d'Antioche sous la seconde domination byzantine', *Mélanges de l'Université St Joseph de Beyrouth* 38 (1962), 221–54.

—— *Le Corpus des sceaux de l'empire byzantin*, v. *L'Église* (Paris, 1963–72).

—— *Le Corpus des sceaux de l'empire byzantin*, ii. *L'Administration centrale* (Paris, 1981).

Lauxtermann, M. D., 'John Geometres—Poet and Scholar', *B* 58 (1999), 356–80.

—— 'Byzantine Poetry and the Paradox of Basil II's Reign', in P. Magdalino (ed.), *Byzantium in the Year 1000* (Leiden, 2002), 199–216.

—— *Byzantine Poetry from Pisides to Geometres: Texts and Contexts* (Vienna, 2003).

Lemerle, P., *Prolégomènes à une édition critique et commentée des 'Conseils et Récits' de Kékauménos* (Brussels, 1960).

—— *Cinq études sur le XIe siècle byzantin* (Paris, 1970).

—— *Le Premier Humanisme byzantin: Notes et remarques sur enseignement et culture à Byzance des origins au Xe siècle* (Paris, 1971).

LEMERLE, P., *The Agrarian History of Byzantium from the Origins to the Twelfth Century: The Sources and Problems* (Galway, 1979).

LEYSER, K., 'Ritual, Ceremony and Gesture: Ottonian Germany', in T. Reuter (ed.), *Communications and Power in Medieval Europe: The Carolingian and Ottonian Centuries* (London and Rio Grande, 1994), 189–213.

LIDDELL, H. G. and SCOTT, R. *A Greek–English Lexicon*, updated by H. S. Jones and R. McKenzie, 2nd edn. (Oxford, 1968).

LJUBARSKIJ, J. N., 'Man in Byzantine Historiography from John Malalas to Michael Psellos', *DOP* 46 (1992), 177–86.

—— 'New Trends in the Study of Byzantine Historiography', *DOP* 47 (1993), 131–8.

—— 'Some Notes on the Newly Discovered Historical Work by Psellos', in J. S. Langdon and S. W. Reinert (eds.), *To Hellenikon: Studies in Honor of Speros Vryonis Jr.*, 2 vols. (New Rochelle and New York, 1993), i. 213–28.

—— 'Concerning the Literary Technique of Theophanes Confessor', *Byz Slav* 56 (1995), 317–22.

—— 'Quellenforschung and/or Literary Criticism: Narrative Structures in Byzantine Historical Writings', *Symbolae Osloensis*, 73 (1998), 5–78.

LOUD, G., 'Byzantine Italy and the Normans', in J. D. Howard-Johnston (ed.), *Byzantium and the West* (Amsterdam, 1988).

MCGEER, E., 'Tradition and Reality in the *Taktika* of Nikephoros Ouranos', *DOP* 45 (1991), 129–40.

—— *Sowing the Dragon's Teeth: Byzantine Warfare in the 10th Century* (Washington DC, 1995).

MCGRATH, S., 'The Battles of Dorostolon (971): Rhetoric and Reality', in T. S. Miller and J. Nesbitt (eds.), *Peace and War in Byzantium: Essays in Honor of George T. Dennis* (Washington DC, 1995), 152–64.

—— 'A Study of the Social Structure of the Byzantine Aristocracy as seen through Ioannis Skylitzes' 'Synopsis Historiarum', Ph.D. Thesis (Washington: Catholic University of America, 1996).

McGuckin, J., 'Symeon the New Theologian and Byzantine Monasticism', in A. Bryer and M. Cunningham (eds.), *Mount Athos and Byzantine Monasticism* (Aldershot, 1996), 17–35.

Macrides, R., 'The Historian in the History', in C. Constantinides, N. M. Panagiotakes, E. Jeffreys, and A. D. Angelou (eds.), Φιλέλλην, *Studies in Honour of Robert Browning* (London, 1996), 205–24.

—— and Magdalino, P., 'The Fourth Kingdom and the Rhetoric of Hellenism', in P. Magdalino (ed.), *The Perception of the Past in Twelfth-Century Europe* (1992, London), 117–56.

Magdalino, P., 'Byzantine Snobbery', in M. Angold (ed.), *Byzantine Aristocracy* (Oxford, 1984), 92–111.

—— 'Honour among the Romaioi: The Framework of Social Values in the World of Digenes Akrites and Kekaumenos', *BMGS* 13 (1989), 183–218.

—— *The Empire of Manuel I Komnenos (1143–1180)*, (Cambridge, 1993).

—— '*Digenes Akrites* and Byzantine Literature: The Twelfth-Century Background to the Grottaferrata Version', in R. Beaton and D. Ricks (eds.), *Digenes Akrites: New Approaches to Byzantine Heroic Poetry* (London, 1993), 1–14.

—— 'The Year 1000 in Byzantium', in P. Magdalino (ed.), *Byzantium in the Year 1000* (Leiden, 2002), 233–70.

—— 'The Medieval Empire (780–1204)', in C. A. Mango (ed.), *The Oxford History of Byzantium* (Oxford, 2002).

—— (ed.), *Byzantium in the Year 1000* (Leiden, 2002).

MAGUIRE, H., 'The Beauty of Castles: A Tenth-Century Description of a Tower at Constantinople', Δελτιον της Χριστιανικης Αρχαιολογικης Εταιρειας, 17 (1993–4), 21–4.

MAHÉ, J.-P., 'Basile II et Byzance vus par Grigor Narekac'i', *TM* 11(1991), 555–72.

DI MAIO, M., 'Smoke in the Wind: Zonaras' use of Philostorgius, Zosimos, John of Antioch and John of Rhodes in his Narrative of the Neo-Flavian Emperors', *B* 48 (1988), 230–55.

MAKSIMOVIC, L., and POPOVIC, M., 'Les Sceaux byzantins de la région danubienne en Serbie', in N. Okonomides (ed.), *SBS* 3 (Washington DC, 1993), 113–42.

MALAMUT, E., *Sur la route des saints byzantins* (Paris, 1993).

MANANDIAN, H. A., *The Trade and Cities of Armenia in Relation to Ancient World Trade*, trans. N. G. Garsoïan (Lisbon, 1965).

MANGO, C. A., 'A Byzantine Inscription Relating to Dyrrachium', *Archaëologischer Anzeiger*, 3 (1966), 410–14.

—— Review article of I. Thurn, *Ioannis Skylitzae Synopsis Historiarum*, in *JHS* 95 (1975).

—— *Byzantine Literature as a Distorting Mirror* (Oxford, 1975).

—— *Empire of the New Rome* (London, 1980).

—— *The Art of the Byzantine Empire* (Toronto, 1986).

—— *Byzantine Architecture* (London, 1986).

—— 'The Tradition of Byzantine Chronography', *HUS* 12 (1988), 360–72.

—— 'The Palace of the Boukeleon', *Cah Arch* 45 (1997), 41–50.

—— and ŠEVČENKO, I. (eds.), 'Byzantine Books and Bookmen' (Washington DC, 1975).

—— and SCOTT, R. (trans)., *The Chronicle of Theophanes Confessor* (Oxford, 1997).

MANOUKIAN, A. (ed.), *Documents of Armenian Architecture (Documenti di Architettura Armena)*, 19 vols. (Milan, 1969–98).

Markopoulos, A., 'Théodore Daphnopatès et la Continuation de Théophane', *JÖB* 35 (1985), 171–82.

—— 'Byzantine History Writing at the End of the First Millennium', in P. Magdalino (ed.), *Byzantium in the Year 1000* (Leiden, 2002).

Martin, J-M., 'Une frontière artificielle: la Capitanate italienne', *Acts of the 14th International Congress 1971*, 3 vols. (Bucharest, 1974), ii. 379–85.

—— *La Pouille du VIe au XIIe siècle* (Rome, 1993).

—— 'Les Problèmes de la frontière en Italie méridionale (VIe–XIIe siècles): L'Approche historique', *Castrum*, 4 (1992), 259–76.

—— and Noyé, G. , *La Capitanata nella del storia Mezzogiorno medievale* (Bari, 1991).

—— 'Les Façades de l'Italie du sud', *Castrum*, 7 (1995), 467–512.

Mercati, S. G., 'Sull'epigrafio di Basilio II Bulgaroctonos', *Collecteana Bizantina*, 2 vols. (Rome, 1970).

Minorsky, V., 'New Light on the Shadaddids of Ganja (951–1075)', *Studies in Caucasian History* (London, 1953).

Miquel, A., *La Géographie humaine du monde musulman jusqu'au milieu du 11e siècle*, 3 vols. (Paris, 1967).

Moravcsik, G., *Byzantinoturcica, Die byzantinischen Quellen der Geschichte der Türkvölker*, 2nd edn. (Berlin, 1958).

Morris, R., 'The Poor and the Powerful in Tenth-Century Byzantium: Law and Reality', *PP* 73 (1976), 3–27.

—— 'The Two Faces of Nikephoros Phokas', *BMGS* 12 (1988), 83–115.

—— 'Succession and Usurpation: Politics and Rhetoric in the late Tenth Century', in P. Magdalino (ed.), *New Constantines: The Rhythms of Imperial Renewal in Byzantium* (Aldershot, 1994), 199–214.

MULLETT, M., 'Aristocracy and Patronage in the Literary Circles of Comnenian Constantinople', in M. Angold (ed.), *Byzantine Aristocracy* (Oxford, 1984), 173–201.

—— 'Writing in Early Medieval Byzantium', in R. McKitterick (ed.), *The Uses of Literacy in Early Medieval Europe* (Cambridge, 1990), 156–84.

—— 'The Madness of Genre', *DOP* 46 (1992), 233–43.

—— *Theophylact of Ochrid: Reading the Letters of a Byzantine Archbishop* (Aldershot, 1997).

MUTHESIUS, A., *Byzantine Silk Weaving AD 400 to AD 1200* (Vienna, 1997).

DER NERSESSIAN, S., 'Remarks on the Date of the Menologium and the Psalter written for Basil II', *B* 15 (1940–1), 104–25.

NERSESSIAN, V., *Treasures from the Ark: 1700 Years of Armenian Christian Art* (London, 2001).

NESBITT, J., and OIKONOMIDES, N., *Catalogue of Byzantine Seals at Dumbarton Oaks and in the Fogg Museum of Art*, 4 vols. (Washington DC, 1991–2001).

—— and BRAUNLIN, M., 'Selections from a Private Collection of Byzantine Bullae', *B* 68(1998), 157–82.

NICOL, D. M., *Byzantium and Venice: A Study in Diplomatic and Cultural Relations* (Cambridge, 1988).

OBOLENSKY, D., *The Byzantine Commonwealth: Eastern Europe, 500–1453* (London, 1971).

—— 'Cherson and the Conversion of the Rus: An Anti-Revision-ist View', *BMGS* 13 (1983), 244–56.

—— 'Ol'ga's Conversion: The Evidence Reconsidered', *HUS* 12–13 (1988–9), 145–58.

OIKONOMIDES, N., 'Recherches sur l'histoire du Bas-Danube au Xe–XIIe siècles: Mésopotamie d'Occident,' *RESEE* 3 (1965), 57–79.

—— *Les Listes de préséance byzantines des IXe et Xe siècles* (Paris, 1972).

—— 'L'Organisation de la frontière orientale de Byzance aux Xe–XIe siècles et le taktikon de l'Escorial', *Acts of the 14th International Congress 1971*, 3 vols. (Bucharest, 1974), i. 285–302.

—— 'L'Évolution de l'organisation administrative de l'empire byzantin au XIe siècle', *TM* 6 (1976), 125–52.

—— 'Le Dédoublement de Saint Théodore et les villes d'Euchaïta et d'Euchaina', *AB* 104 (1986), 327–35.

—— *A Collection of Dated Byzantine Lead Seals* (Washington DC, 1986).

—— *Studies in Byzantine Sigillography*, 6 vols. (Washington DC, 1987–95).

—— 'Tax Exemptions for the Secular Clergy under Basil II', in J. Chrysostomides (ed.), Καθηγήτρια: *Essays presented to Joan Hussey for her Eightieth Birthday* (Camberley, 1988), 317–26.

—— 'Terres du fisc et revenu de la terre aux Xe et XIe siècles', in V. Kravari, J. Lefort, and C. Morrisson (eds.), *Hommes et richesses*, 2 vols. (1989–91, Paris), ii. 321–37.

OLIVIER, J. M., 'Le "Scylitzès" d'Ochrid retrouvé', *BZ* 89 (1996), 417–19.

OSTROGORSKY, G., 'Une ambassade serbe auprès de l'empereur Basile II', *B* 19 (1949), 187–94.

—— 'Agrarian Conditions in the Byzantine Empire in the Middle Ages', in M. Postan (ed.), *Cambridge Economic History of Europe, i. The Agrarian Life of the Middle Ages*, 2nd edn. (Cambridge, 1966), 204–34.

—— *History of the Byzantine State*, trans. J. Hussey, 2nd English edn. (Oxford, 1968).

—— 'Observations on the Aristocracy in Byzantium', *DOP* 25 (1971), 3–32.

PANAGIOTAKES, N. M., 'Fragments of a Lost Eleventh-Century Byzantine Historical Work', in C. Constantinides, N. M. Panagiotakes, E. Jeffreys, and A. D. Angelou (eds.), Φιλελλην, *Studies in Honour of Robert Browning* (Venice, 1996), 321–57.

PAPACOSTAS, T. C., 'A Tenth-Century Inscription from Syngrasis, Cyprus', *BMGS* 26 (2002), 42–64.

PERTUSI, A., 'Venezia e Bisanzio nel secolo XI', rpr. in V. Branca (ed.), *Storia della civiltà veneziana*, 3 vols. (Florence, 1979), i. 175–98.

POLEMIS, D., 'Some Cases of Erroneous Identification in the Chronicle of Scylitzes', *Byz Slav* 26 (1975), 74–81.

POPPE, A., 'The Political Background to the Baptism of the Rus', *DOP* 30 (1976), 196–244.

—— 'Once Again Concerning the Baptism of Olga, Archontissa of Rus', *DOP* 46 (1992), 271–7.

PRINZING, G., 'Entstehung und Rezeption der Justiana-Prima-Theorie im Mittelalter, *Byzantinobulgarica*, 5 (1978), 269–87.

—— 'Die Bamberger Guntertuch in neuer Sicht', *Byz Slav* 54 (1993), 218–31.

PROKIC, B., *Die Zusätze des Johannes Skylitzes* (Munich, 1906).

RAPP, S. H., 'Imagining History at the Crossroads: Persia, Byzantium and the Architects of the Written Georgian Past', Ph.D. Thesis (Michigan, 1997).

REUTER, T., *Germany in the Early Middle Ages 800–1056* (London, 1991).

RICKS, D., and MAGDALINO, P., (eds.), *Byzantium and the Modern Greek Identity* (Aldershot, 1998).

RIPPER, T., *Die Marwaniden von Diyar Bakr: Eine kurdische Dynastie im islamischen Mittelalter* (Würzburg, 2000).

ROBERT, L., 'Sur les lettres d'un métropolite de Phrygie au Xe siècle', *Journal des Savants* (1961), 97–166; (1962), 1–74.

RODLEY, L., 'The Pigeon House Church at Çavuşin', *JÖB* 33 (1983), 301–39.

ROUECHE, C., 'Byzantine Writers and Readers: Story Telling in the Eleventh Century', in R. Beaton (ed.), *The Greek Novel* (London and Sydney, 1988), 123–32.

ROZEN, V. R., *Imperator Vasilij Bolgarobojca: Izvlechenija iz letopisi Jach-i Antiochijskago* (St Petersburg, 1883; repr. London, 1972).

RUNCIMAN, S., *History of the First Bulgarian Empire* (London, 1930).

—— 'The Country and Suburban Palaces of the Emperors', in *Essays in Honor of Peter Charanis*, ed. A. E. Laiou-Thomadakis (Rutgers, NJ, 1980), 219–28.

SALAMON, M., 'Some Notes on an Inscription from Medieval Silistra', *RESEE* 9 (1971), 487–96.

SAUNDERS, W. B. R., 'The Aachen Reliquary of Eustathius Maleinus 969–970', *DOP* 36 (1982), 211–19.

—— 'Qalat Siman: A Frontier Fort of the Tenth and Eleventh Centuries', in S. Freeman and H. Kennedy (eds.), *Defence of the Roman and Byzantine Frontiers* (Oxford, 1986), 291–305.

SCHLUMBERGER, G., *Sigillographie de l'empire byzantin* (Paris, 1884).

—— *Un empereur au dixième siècle: Nicéphore Phocas* (Paris, 1890).

—— *L'Épopée byzantine à la fin du dixième siècle*, 3 vols. (Paris, 1896–1905).

SCOTT, R., 'The Classical Tradition in Byzantine Historiography', in M. Mullett and R. Scott (eds.), *Byzantium and the Classical Tradition* (Birmingham, 1981), 61–73.

—— 'Malalas and his Contemporaries', in E. Jeffreys, B. Croke, and R. Scott (eds.), *Studies in John Malalas* (Sydney, 1990), 67–85.

SEIBT, W., 'Untersuchungen zur Vor- und Frühgeschichte der "bulgarischen" Kometopulen', *HA*, 89 (1975), 65–98.

—— 'Ioannes Skylitzes: Zur Person des Chronisten', *JÖB* 25 (1976), 81–6.

—— *Die Skleroi* (Vienna, 1976).

—— *Die byzantinischen Bleisiegel in Österreich, i. Kaiserhof* (Vienna, 1978).

—— 'Die Eingliederung von Vaspurakan in das byzantinische Reich (etwa Anfang 1019 brz. Anfang 1022)', *HA* 92 (1978), 49–66.

SEURE, G., 'Antiquités thraces de la Propontide', *BCH* 36 (1912), 543–641.

ŠEVČENKO, I., 'The Illuminators of the Menologium of Basil II', *DOP* 16 (1962), 243–76.

—— 'A Byzantine Inscription from Silistra Reinterpreted', *RESEE* 7 (1969), 591–98.

—— 'Poems on the Deaths of Leo VI and Constantine VII in the Madrid Manuscript of Skylitzes', *DOP* 23–4 (1969–70), 185–228.

—— 'Levels of Style in Byzantine Prose', *JÖB* 31.1 (1981), 289–312.

—— 'Some Additional Remarks to the Report on Levels of Style', *JÖB* 32.1–2 (1982), 220–38.

—— 'The Madrid Manuscript of the Chronicle of Scylitzes in the Light of its New Dating', in I. Hütter (ed.), *Byzanz und der Westen* (Vienna, 1984), 117–30.

SEWTER, E. R. A., *Michael Psellus: Fourteen Byzantine Rulers* (London, 1966).

SHEPARD, J., 'John Mauropous, Leo Tornices and an Alleged Russian Army: The Chronology of the Pecheneg Crisis of 1048–9', *JÖB* 24 (1975), 61–79.

—— 'Byzantinorussica', *REB 33* (1975), 211–25.

—— 'Scylitzes on Armenia in the 1040s and the Role of Catacalon Cecaumenus', *REArm* (1975–6), 296–311.

—— 'Isaac Comnenus' Coronation Day', *Byz Slav* 38 (1977), 22–30.

—— 'Byzantium's Last Sicilian Expedition: Skylitzes' Testimony', *Rivista di studi bizantini e neoellenici, 14–16* (1977–9), 145–59.

—— 'A Suspected Source of Scylitzes' *Synopsis Historiarum*: The Great Catacalon Cecaumenus', *BMGS* 16 (1992), 171–81.

—— 'Some Remarks on the Sources for the Conversion of Rus', in S. W. Swierkosz-Lenart (ed.), *Le origini e lo sviluppo della cristianità slavo-bizantina* (Rome, 1992), 59–95.

—— 'Byzantium in Equilibrium', in T. Reuter (ed.), *NCMH* iii (Cambridge, 1999), 553–66.

—— 'Byzantium Expanding', in T. Reuter (ed.), *NCMH* iii (Cambridge, 1999), 586–604.

Sifonas, C. S., 'Basile II et l'aristocratie byzantine', *B* 64 (1994), 118–33.

Sinclair, T., *Eastern Turkey: An Architectural and Archaeological Survey*, 4 vols. (London, 1987–90).

Siuziumov, M., 'Ob istochnikakh Leva Dialona i Skilitsii', *Vizantiiskoe Obozrenie*, 2 (1916), 106–66.

Skoulatos, B., *Les Personnages byzantins de l'Alexiade* (Louvain, 1980).

Snipes, K., 'A Newly Discovered History of the Roman Emperors by Michael Psellos', *JÖB* 32.2 (1982), 53–61.

—— 'The "Chronographia" of Michael Psellos and the Textual Tradition and Transmission of the Byzantine Historians of the Eleventh and Twelfth Centuries', *ZRVI* 27–8 (1989), 43–61.

Sokolova, I. V., 'Les Sceaux byzantins de Cherson', in N. Oikonomides (ed.), *SBS* 3 (Washington, DC, 1993), 99–111.

Speck, P., 'Der "Zweite Theophanes" Eine These zur Chronographie des Theophanes', Ποικίλα Βυζαντινα, 13 (1975), 431–75.

Speck, P., *Byzantinische Bleisiegel in Berlin* (Bonn, 1986).

Spieser, J.-M., 'Inventaires en vue d'un recueil des inscriptions historiques à Byzance, i. Les inscriptions de Thessalonique', *TM* 5 (1973), 145–80.

Stephenson, P., 'A Development in Nomenclature on the Seals of the Byzantine Provincial Aristocracy in the Late Tenth Century', *REB* 52 (1994), 187–211.

—— 'The Byzantine Frontier in the Balkans in the Eleventh and Twelfth Centuries', Ph.D. Thesis (Cambridge 1995)

—— 'Byzantine Policy towards Paristrion in the Mid-Eleventh Century: Another Interpretation', *BMGS* 23 (1999), 43–66.

—— 'The Byzantine Frontier at the Lower Danube in the Late Tenth and Eleventh Century', in D. Power and N. Standen (eds.), *Frontiers in Question: Eurasian Borderlands, 700–1700* (Basingstoke and London, 1999), 80–104.

—— *Byzantium's Balkan Frontier* (Cambridge, 2000).

—— 'The Legend of Basil the Bulgar-slayer', *BMGS* 24 (2000), 102–32.

—— 'The Byzantine Frontier in Macedonia', *Dialogos*, 7 (2000), 23–40.

—— 'The Balkan Frontier in the Year 1000', in P. Magdalino (ed.), *Byzantium in the Year 1000* (Leiden, 2002), 109–33.

—— 'Images of the Bulgar-slayer: Three Art Historical Notes', *BMGS* 25 (2001), 44–68.

—— *The Legend of Basil the Bulgar-Slayer* (Cambridge, 2003).

Svoronos, N., 'Remarques sur la tradition du texte de la novelle de Basile II concernant les puissants', *Recueil des Travaux de l'Inst. d'Ét. byz, Mélanges G. Ostrogorsky* II, 2 vols. (Belgrade, 1964), 427–34.

—— *Les Novelles des empereurs macédoniens concernant la terre et les stratiotes* (Athens, 1994).

Szemioth, A., and Wasilewski, T., *Sceaux byzantins de Musée National de Varsovie* (Warsaw, 1966).

Tarchnishvili, P. M., 'Le Soulèvement de Bardas Sklèros', *BK* 17–18 (1964), 95–7.

Teall, J. T., 'The Grain Supply of the Byzantine Empire', *DOP* 13 (1959), 89–139.

Ter Ghevondyan, A., *The Arab Emirates in Bagratid Armenia* (Lisbon, 1976).

Theodoridis, D., 'Theognostos Melissenos, Katepan von Mesopotamia', *BZ* 78 (1985), 363–4.

Thierry, M., 'Données archéologiques sur les principautés arméniennes de Cappadoce orientale au XI siècle', *REArm* 26 (1996–7), 119–72.

Thierry, N., *Haut Moyen-âge en Cappadoce: Les Églises de Çavusin*, 2 vols. (Paris, 1994).

Tiftixoglu, V., 'Zur Genese der Kommentare des Balsamon', in N. Oikonomides (ed.), *Byzantium in the Twelfth Century* (Athens, 1991), 438–532.

Tinnefeld, F., 'Die Stadt Melitene in ihrer späteren byzantinischen Epoche (934–1101)', *Acts of the 14th International Congress* 1971, 3 vols. (Bucharest, 1974), ii. 435–43.

Todt, K.-P., 'Region in Griechisch-Orthodoxes Patriarchat von Antiocheia in mittelbyzantinischer Zeit (969–1084)', *BZ* 94 (2001), 239–67.

Tougher, S., *The Reign of Leo VI (886–912): Politics and People* (Leiden, 1997).

Toumanoff, C., 'Armenia and Georgia', in J. Hussey (ed.), *The Cambridge Medieval History*, iv. *The Byzantine Empire: Byzantium and its Neighbours* (Cambridge, 1967), 593–637.

Toumanoff, C., 'The Bagratids of Iberia from the Eighth to the Eleventh Centuries', *Le Muséon*, 74 (1961), 5–42.

TREADGOLD, W., *Byzantium and its Army 284–1081* (Stanford, Calif., 1995).

—— *A History of the Byzantine State and Society* (Stanford, Calif., 1997).

TSAMAKDA, V., *The Illustrated Chronicle of Ioannes Skylitzes in Madrid* (Leiden, 2002).

VASILIEV, A. A., *Byzance et les Arabes*, 3 vols. (Brussels, 1950–68).

VINSON, M. P., *The Correspondence of Leo, Metropolitan of Synada and Syncellus* (Washington DC, 1985).

VRYONIS, S., *The Decline of Medieval Hellenism in Asia Minor and the Process of Islamization from the Eleventh through the Fifteenth Century* (Berkeley, Calif., 1971).

—— 'Byzantium: The Social Basis of Decline in the Eleventh Century', in *Byzantium: Its Internal History and Relations with the Muslim World* (London, 1971), no. II.

WALKER, P. E., 'A Byzantine Victory over the Fatimids at Alexandretta (971)', *B* 42 (1972), 431–40.

—— 'The "Crusade" of John Tzimisces in the Light of New Arabic Evidence', *B* 47 (1977), 301–27.

—— *Exploring an Islamic Empire: Fatimid History and its Sources* (London, 2002).

WALTER, C., *The Warrior Saints in Byzantine Art and Tradition* (Aldershot, 2001).

WASSERSTEIN, D., *The Rise and Fall of the Party Kings* (Princeton, 1985).

WHARTON-EPSTEIN, A., *The Art of Empire: Painting and Architecture of the Byzantine Periphery: A Comparative Study of Four Provinces* (Pennsylvania State University, 1988).

WHITTOW, M., *The Making of Orthodox Byzantium* (London, 1996).

WILSON, N., 'The Madrid Scylitzes', *Scrittura e Civiltà*, 2 (1978), 209–19.

WINKELMANN, F., *Byzantinische Rang- und Ämterstruktur im. 8. und 9. Jahrhundert* (Berlin, 1985).

YUZBASHIAN, K. N., 'L'Administration byzantine en Arménie aux Xe et XIe siècles', *REArm* 10 (1973–4), 139–83.

ZACOS, G., *Byzantine Lead Seals II*, compiled by John Nesbitt (Berne, 1985).

(*The George*) *Zacos Collection of Byzantine Lead Seals*, 1 (Auction 127, Spinks catalogue, 7 October 1998).

(*The George*) *Zacos Collection of Byzantine Lead Seals*, 2 (Auction 132, Spinks catalogue, 25 May 1999).

(*The George*) *Zacos Collection of Byzantine Lead Seals*, 3 (Auction 135, Spinks catalogue, 6 October 1999).

ZACOS, G., and VEGLERY, A., *Byzantine Lead Seals*, 3 vols. (Basel, 1972).

ZEPOS, J., and ZEPOS, P., *Ius Graecoromanum*, 8 vols. (Athens, 1931).

Index

Aaron, son of John Vladislav 213, 366

Aaron Kometopoulos 212, 489–91

Aaron Radomir 214–15

Abara 373

Abasgia 40 n. 44, 53, 311–12, 322, 360, 367, 482 n. 94, 484

Abbasid caliphate 303, 448

Abu al-Hayja 354

Abu Sahl Senacherim 210 n. 93

Abu Shudja al-Rudhrawari 41, 47, 241, 253–4, 277, 288 n. 100, 289–90, 498

Abu Taghlib 262, 265–6, 451, 457, 479

Abydos: Phokas revolt 218, 232 n. 139, 246, 248, 256 n. 34, 258, 266, 270–1, 287, 345, 460–1, 522, 545; Rus attack 512; Skleros revolt 248, 263, 452, 456 n. 27

adab 253 n. 32, 254 n. 33

Adana 371 n. 165

Ademar of Chabannes 45, 498, 528

Adrian Komnenos 219

Adrianople: Armenian Gospel Book 63, 404; Bulgarian attack in Romanos I's reign 151; Bulgarian attack (1002) 414, 496, 546; defectors 107–8, 495; *doux* of 302, 396, 404–5, 413–17

Adud al-Daula: size of empire 308–9, 479; and Hamdanids 262, 265, 479; Skleros revolt 242, 245, 248–9, 253, 265, 289–90, 308–9, 378, 385, 457, 479–80; death 328, 480

Aegean Sea theme 296 n. 118

Agapios, patriarch of Antioch 96, 345, 382–3

Agatha Lekapene 127, 138

Agathias 174 n. 6

Agtht'amar 310 n. 16

Ajtony 418

Akhaltzikhe 242

Akşehir Gölü 263

al-Acfar 268, 349, 352, 477–8
al-Aziz, Fatimid caliph 58 n.
  99, 307
al-Hakim, Fatimid caliph:
  appraisal by Yahya ibn
  Sa'id 50, 352 n. 121;
  negotiations with Basil
  II 58 n. 99, 64, 307, 352,
  476; attack on Holy
  Sepulchre 45, 50, 477;
  persecutions by 38, 352 n.
  121; Nikephoros Xiphias
  revolt (1021–2) 517
al-Kalkashandi 252, 277
al-Makrizi 477 n. 83
al-Rudhrawari, *see* Abu Shudja
  al-Rudhrawari
al-Shirazi 242
al-Tabari 254 n. 33
al-Tanukhi 262
Aleppo: bishop of 382;
  Byzantine client 47–8, 52,
  245, 307, 309, 321, 332, 377–
  8, 407, 456–7, 467, 470, 475–
  8, 493, 524, 526–7; emirs
  of 132 n. 23, 334, 354;
  Fatimid occupation 355,
  478; Mirsadid occupation
  355–6; trade embargo
  478 n. 88
Alexandria, patriarch
  of 382 n. 186

Alexios I Komnenos:
  usurpation of 209, 541;
  pedigree 452; seals 219;
  Balkan campaigns 220–1,
  224, 492; political
  inclusivity 217–8, 541;
  political unrest 208, 220,
  222, 541; Treaty of
  Devol 360; literary
  production during
  reign 175–239; associate of
  John Skylitzes 81, 85–9,
  216, 492, 541–2; criticized by
  John Zonaras 175, 180
Alexios, *droungarios* 126
allelengyon 27, 70–1, 535–7,
  546
Alousianos, son of John
  Vladislav 213, 366
Alyates family 206
Amanos Mountains 332 n. 67,
  359, 376, 444
Amatus of Montecassino 43
Amida 308, 326, 479
Amorion 117, 264, 453; *see
  also* Pankaleia
Anatolia: administration of, 13,
  25, 314–15, 370, 371–2,
  532–4; Alexios
  Komnenos 221; economy
  of 58 n. 97; aristocratic
  estates 22, 25, 27, 32, 232,

235–6, 462–5, 518; lack
of written evidence
for 13, 54, 533–4; literature
from 177; refugees
from 177–8; troops
from 364, 405
Anatolikon 264, 295, 520
Anazarbos 335
Andrea Dandolo 44, 49–52
Andronikos Doukas 191,
199, 257
Andronikos Doukas,
domestikos of the
scholai 254 n. 33
Andronikos Lydos, *see*
Andronikos Doukas
Andronikos Skleros 293–4
Anemas: in Byzantine
military service 207, 221,
223; from Crete 207;
family 207–8, 294
Ani 53, 101, 310 n. 16, 312,
340 n. 85, 361, 366
n. 157, 483
Anna Komnene: content of
Alexiad 207–8, 210,
214–15, 220; structure of
Alexiad 115 n. 108;
criticism of 179
Anna Porphyrogenita,
sister of Basil II 4,
71, 246, 460, 511, 514

Annals of Bari 42, 51, 429
Annals of Benevento 42 n. 52
Anthes Alyates 191, 199,
204–5, 256, 544
Antigone 128
Antioch: annals of 112 n. 102;
basilikos of 377–81;
Byzantine capture of
(969) 304, 332, 355, 359,
375–6, 448;
Basil II relieves 194, 307;
Comes Orientalis 186; *doux*
of 160, 194, 257, 295,
301, 313, 330–60, 362,
370 n. 161, 389–90, 396,
424, 451, 458, 466 n. 58,
476–7, 481, 486;
earthquake 338; Fatimid
attacks 160, 194, 268, 307;
Ibn Butlan 356–7; *katepano*
of 353, 389; *kommerkiarios*
of 371 n. 165; *kourator*
of 373 n. 167; *krites* of 370;
monasteries 444–5;
monophysite settlers 444,
531; patriarchs of 96, 337 n.
78, 345, 382–3; Phokas
revolt 246, 344–5; Skleros
revolts 248, 263, 265, 341,
451; *strategos* of A. and
Lykandos 333–4; Yahya
ibn Sa'id 38, 330–60

Ashot III of Ani 340 n. 85
Ashot Taronites: capture by
Samuel Kometopoulos 103,
165, 194, 221, 406, 494;
marriage to Samuel's
daughter 103, 196; governor
of Dyrrachion 103;
defection to Byzantium 104
astrology 62
Athens 60 n. 107, 421, 501,
547
Athos: documentary evidence
from 50, 56, 108–9, 396,
404–6, 408–9, 493, 495;
Georgians 251–2; Iviron
252, 404, 408; Lavra 56,
384; Vatopedi 409;
Xenophon 210
Attaleia 117, 257, 451, 456
n. 27
Attica 163
Atzupotheodore 267, 465
Azerbaijan 193 n. 53, 311,
312 n. 21, 444, 484

Bačkovo monastery 209–10
Bad ibn Dustuk 250, 309–10,
329, 480
Baghras 376
Bagrat III of Abasgia and
Iberia 311–12, 322, 481–2
Bagrat of Taron 316

Bagrat, son of George of
Abasgia and Iberia 362–3 n.
148, 483
Bagrat, cousin of Bagrat
III 482 n. 94
Bagrat, *patrikios* and
magistros 320
Bagratids of Ani 310 n. 16
Balanias 301 n. 1, 307, 340,
342
Balasitzes (Mount) 166
Balsamon 85
Bamburg 60 n. 108
Banu Abu Imran 444
Banu Kilab 349
Banu Noumeir 349
Bar Hebreus: appraisal of Basil
II's reign 41, 379 n. 177
Bardas Boilas 134 n. 31, 141,
145, 314 n. 25
Bardas Kouleïb 379
Bardas Moungos 191, 199
Bardas Parsakoutenos 456
Bardas Phokas, father of
Nikephoros II 145, 148
Bardas Phokas: nephew of
Nikephoros II 243, 452;
doux of Chaldia and
Koloneia 315–16, 330, 432;
revolt against John Tzimiskes
(971) 232 n. 139, 315 n. 27,
464; *domestikos* of the *scholai*

Bardas Phokas (*cont.*):
(978–9) 116–17, 343, 378,
452–6, 464; *doux* (?) of
Antioch (986–7) 343–4,
458, 475; revolt (987–9) 3,
12, 25, 27, 30–2, 46, 54, 59,
68–9, 71, 97–8, 115–16, 118,
159, 191, 218, 240–1, 246,
258, 260, 266–8, 281, 306,
309, 311, 344–5, 458–61,
464–5, 467, 510–11, 528,
545; death 4, 232 n. 139,
246, 267–8, 270–1, 287, 345,
460–1, 465, 528; father of
Nikephoros (rebel of
1021–2) 35
Bardas Phokas, son of Bardas
Phokas 465
Bardas Skleros: defence of
Arkadioupolis (971) 272–6,
291; revolt against John
Tzimikes (?) 325 n. 51;
stratelates 324; *doux* of
Mesopotamia 156, 243, 261,
324–8, 338–9, 389, 450, 478–
9; revolt, first (976–9) 3,
12, 46, 54, 61, 68, 96, 110,
115–17, 157–9, 188–9, 191,
193 n. 53, 199, 204–5, 240–5,
255–9, 261–6, 270, 283, 306,
308–9, 311, 341, 377–80,
382–3, 450–7, 485, 544;
captivity in Baghdad 156,
241, 245, 265, 276, 283, 290,
308–9, 328, 351, 378, 385,
457, 544; release from
Baghdad 110, 116, 252–4,
276–80, 282, 285, 458, 464,
545; revolt, second (987) 12,
69, 114, 159, 191, 246, 260,
279–80, 344, 458–9, 464,
480, 545; capture by Bardas
Phokas (987–9) 246, 283;
revolt, third (989) 4, 12, 32,
191, 246, 279–80; surrender
4, 69, 267, 278, 282–8, 459–
61, 545; *kouropalates* 465;
death 288; encomium used
by Skylitzes 99, 111, 153,
272–98, 450–60, 479; sources
about his career 40 n. 44
Bari 42, 51, 72, 433,
437–8, 440, 442
n. 104, 504–5, 507
Barzouyah 304, 377
Basean plain 313, 320 n. 39,
480
Basil I 448
Basil II Porphyrogenitus:
accession 3, 243, 449–50;
Basil Lekapenos, the
Parakoimomenos 34, 46–7,
118, 245, 342, 457–8, 469–74,
523, 526–7; centralization

of power and administration 24–9, 59, 381–9, 440, 473–4, 525–7; contemporary descriptions of 2–7, 30–1, 45, 470–4, 516, 528–9; as godfather 235–6; image of 3, 6–7, 12, 15, 59, 237, 470–4, 528–9, 542–3; legislation 5–6, 15, 21–3, 26–7, 33, 59, 70, 102, 462–75, 526–7, 545; marital status 28, 45 n. 60, 519–20; use of plenipotentiaries 529; the 'Powerful' 5–6, 15, 18, 21–6, 33, 35, 59, 70, 101, 461–75, 517–22, 527–8, 535–6, 545; psalter 15, 64–5, 220 n. 118, 472, 528, 542; victory triumphs 60 n. 107, 112, 421, 501, 522, 536, 543, 547; taxation 2, 27, 51–2, 70–1, 368–91, 427, 440–7, 456, 462–3, 474, 486, 502, 531–7, 546; wealth 2–3, 30–1, 534–5; death, epitaph, and tomb 44 n. 56, 113, 450 n. 3, 472, 506, 515, 524–5, 542–3; legend of the 'Bulgar-slayer' 3, 19; political legacy and long-term significance of reign 4–5, 20–9, 525–43;

for external relations, cam-paigns, and annexations see Armenia; Armenians; Bulgaria; Bulgarians; Buyids; Fatimids; Georgians; Ottonians; Rus; Samuel Kometopoulos; Sicily; southern Italy; Syria; Umayyads; Venice; *for revolts see* Bardas Phokas, revolt (987–9); Nikephoros Phokas, revolt (1021–2); Nikephoros Xiphias revolt (1021–2); Bardas Skleros, first to third revolts (976–89)

Basil, *doux* of Chaldia and Trebizond 318

Basil, the *Parakoimomenos,* *see* Basil Lekapenos

Basil Argyros: *katepano* of Vaspurakan 363, 365, 367; *strategos* of Samos 190, 365, 505

Basil Boiannes: *katepano* of Italy, 426 n. 70; suppression of Meles' revolt 53, 422, 435, 439, 505–6, 513 n. 176; fortification construction 437, 441–3, 506–7

Basil Glabas 107, 546

Basil Lekapenos: son of
Romanos I 469; alliance
with Nikephoros II 449,
469; Skleros revolt 156, 324–
5, 452; relations with Basil
II 46–7, 245, 342, 457–8,
469–74, 523, 526–7;
deposition of 34, 118, 245,
457–8, 470; clients of 251 n.
27, 469–74
Basil Melias 336 n. 76
Basil Mesardonites 190 n. 47,
439, 446–7, 505, 507
Basil Skleros 295
Basilika Therma, battle of 264,
453
basilikos 265, 341, 376–81, 428
Batatzes 107, 545
Bathn Hanzit 326
Beirut 307, 340
Belgrade 425
Benjamin, son of Symeon of
Bulgaria 143
Beroe 398
Berroia 105, 114, 195, 200,
398, 420, 497
Bingöl Dağı 358 n. 137
Bighas, *see* Pegasios
Bithynia 148
Bitlis Pass 326
Bitola 56, 500

Blachernai church 137;
ikon 460; synod of 84, 87,
293
Bodin, *archon* of the Serbs 91
Bodina 105, 114, 420
Boetia 163
Bohemond of Antioch 214 n.
106, 360
Boleslav, king of Poland 514
Boris II of Bulgaria 49, 102,
169, 399, 488–90
Botaneiates family 203, 541
Boukellarion 405
Bovino 507
Braničevo 425
Bryennios family 203, 217
Bulgaria: annexation by Basil
II 2, 17, 40 n. 43, 42, 52, 57,
60 n. 107, 110–12, 198, 212,
321, 419–20, 500–2;
campaigning by Basil II 5,
13–14, 38–9, 48–51, 55–6,
68–9, 104–11, 114, 154–5,
162–70, 193–9, 212, 224–33,
407–17, 487–500, 526;
church 428; governance by
Byzantines 13, 27, 48–9, 57,
392–428, 449, 500–2; *doux*
of 423; *katepano* of 302,
422 n. 62, 423 n. 64;
patriarch of 428; *see also*

Bulgarians; Kometopouloi;
Rus; Samuel Kometopoulos
Bulgarians: relations with
Romanos I 126, 135–8,
141–2, 149, 151, 155 n. 83;
defeat of Basil II (986) 4, 36,
47, 68, 102, 110, 163, 167,
188, 224–8, 246, 250, 344,
402, 458, 490–2, 544; troops
in Byzantine armies 422; *see
also* Symeon of Bulgaria;
Peter of Bulgaria; Boris II of
Bulgaria; Kometopouloi;
Samuel Kometopoulos
Burgundy 50
Buyids: diplomatic and
military relations with
Byzantium 32, 64, 156, 242,
245, 248–9, 277–8, 308–10,
344, 351, 385, 450, 457, 470,
479–80, 523, 526

Cairo 38
Calabria 43, 56 n. 93, 432,
435–47, 504
Capetians 72; *see also* Hugh
Capet
Cappadocia 102, 193 n. 53,
257, 280, 336 n. 76, 364, 375,
452, 483, 517, 521
Capua-Benevento 432, 505–6

Capitanata 441–3, 446, 506–8,
531
Catherine, wife of Isaac I 214
Çavuşin, Great Pigeon House
Church 336 n. 77
Ceyhan River 323
Chalcedon 267 n. 50
Chaldia: *artoklines* of 317 n.
32; *chartoularios* of 317 n.
32; Basil II winters
(1021–2) 98 n. 70, 322;
doux of 301, 312–22, 324,
330, 362, 396; *katepano*
of 317, 330; *krites* of 317;
kourator of 373 n. 167;
protonotarios of 317;
strategos of 134 n. 31, 141,
145, 152, 314, 318–19; *see
also* Derxene; Koloneia
Charpete 261, 265–6
Charsianon 213, 258, 264–5,
378, 453, 456
Chauzizion, *see* Hafdjidj
Cherson: Rus sack 71, 511,
514–15; Tzoulas family 515;
11th-c. refortification 206
Chliat 250
chorion 22–3
Chortzine 336 n. 77
Chosnis, *basilikos* of
Tarsos 380

Christopher: *katepano* of
Longobardia 423 n. 64;
katepano of Thessalonika
and Bulgaria 423 n. 64,
424 n. 65
Christopher, patriarch of
Antioch 337 n. 78
Christopher Epeiktes 191, 199
Christopher Lekapenos 136
Chronicle of Salerno 432
Chronicon Paschale 112 n. 102
Chronicon Venetum 44
Chryselios family 104, 365–6,
496–8, 545
Chrysocheir 512
Chrysopolis 246, 258, 266–7,
460, 545
Chutur 242, 277–8
Cilicia 303–4, 335, 336 n. 77,
337, 365, 371 n. 165, 448
Civitate 441
Constantine VII
Porphyrogenitus: histori-
ography of reign 93–4, 190,
202; legislation 21, 467;
trade 482 n. 94, 513;
usurpation of 144 n. 53, 469
Constantine VIII
Porphyrogenitus:
Ardanoutzin 482 n. 94; co-
emperor and heir to Basil
II 3, 28, 60 nn. 106, 107,

240, 243, 290, 421, 424, 448–
50, 519–24; death of Bardas
Phokas 460–1, 522;
daughters 28, 520; plots
against 213, 367;
propaganda 113 n. 105
Constantine IX
Monomachos 101, 111,
295–6, 435 n. 91, 538
Constantine X Doukas 203,
360
Constantine Bourtzes 353
Constantine Dalassenos 353,
355–6
Constantine Diogenes 199,
222, 233–5, 414 n. 16, 419,
421, 423–5, 502, 547
Constantine Gauras 191, 199,
269–70, 544
Constantine Lekapenos 125 n. 6
Constantine Maleinos 334
Constantine Manasses:
career 175–6;
historian 77 n. 25, 175–6,
179; connection to John
Skylitzes 67 n. 1
Constantine Skleros 267 n. 51,
273–4, 288
Constantinople: annals
of 112–13; Basil II's absence
from 411; blockade during
Skleros revolt 263, 452;

blockade during Phokas revolt 256; buildings 59–60, 70, 127; centre of government 24–6; centre of literary production 172–85; earthquake (989) 37, 70, 545; *eparch* of 82, 84 n. 43, 87–8; Great Palace 302, 384, 466 n. 58; officials dispatched from 43, 303, 369–91, 428–9, 463, 486–7, 504; *Patria* 61; patriarchs 59, 70, 81 n. 37, 126, 128, 189, 449, 535, 545; prisoners and hostages sent to 108, 192, 234, 425, 426 n. 70, 465, 489, 500–1; relics 94; Rus attack (941) 129, 134, 140, 145–6, 148–9; St Sophia 37 n. 37, 70, 133; sources of evidence for 50, 54, 59–62, 70; triumphs and processions 112, 421, 488, 501, 522, 536, 543, 547

Conversano 437

Cordoba 505

Corinth 164

Cosenza 437

Crescenti 509

Crete: Byzantine attack (949) 513; Byzantine annexation (961) 132 n. 23, 207; 11-c. governance 222; John Xenos 57

Croats 63, 426, 497

Cyprus 243, 248

Dalmatia 63, 426, 496

Damascus 47, 340

Damian Dalassenos 160, 347–9, 364, 409–10, 476

David Areianites 222, 411, 419, 422–5, 435

David Kometopoulos 489

David Nestoritzes 412, 499

David Senacherim 209–10 n. 92, 484

David of Tao: Skleros revolt (976–9) 245, 251–2, 265–6, 311, 315 n. 27, 319–20; death 321, 405 n. 19, 480–1; regional authority 311–12, 319–20, 361, 390, 439, 480–1; Phokas revolt (987–9) 311, 320, 406 n. 21, 480; legacy 311–12, 361, 480–2

De Administrando Imperio 144, 314 n. 26, 513

De Cerimoniis 44 n. 56, 513

Demetrios, cousin of Bagrat III 482 n. 94

Demetrios of Kyzikos 113 n. 105, 549

Derkos 60 n. 107

Derxene 320;
    artiklines of 317 n. 32;
    chartoularios of 317 n. 32;
    kourator of 373 n. 167;
    krites of 317; *protonotarios*
    of 317; *strategos* of 317–18;
    see also Chaldia; Taron

Devol 229; Treaty of 359–60;
    see also Michael of D.

Digenes Akrites 177–8

Dio Cassios 178

Diogenes family 203, 222

Diogenes Philomates 424 n.
    65

Diokleia 41–2, 196, 419, 493

Dipotamon 263

Diyar Bakr 265, 277 n. 72,
    308–9, 321, 326, 329, 479,
    484, 518

Diyar Mudar 349, 478

Djazira 266, 308, 325, 327,
    478

Djabala 340

Djubayl 340

Dniepr River 513–14

Dobromeros 105, 197,
    200, 546

Doge, *see* Venice

Dometianos Kaukanos 422 n.
    60

Doukas family 92, 203, 217

doukate, see *doux*

doux 301–67, 392–427; of
    Adrianople 302, 396, 404,
    413–17; of Ani and Iberia
    366 n. 157; of Antioch 160,
    194, 257, 295, 301, 313,
    330–60, 362, 370 n. 161,
    389–90, 396, 424, 451, 458,
    466 n. 58, 476–7, 481, 486; of
    Bulgaria, Thessalonika and
    Serbia 423; of Chaldia 301,
    312–22, 324, 362, 396, 432;
    of Chaldia and Koloneia
    315–16; of Chaldia and
    Trebizond 318; of Dalmatia
    496; of the East 321, 329, 347;
    of Mesopotamia 156, 243,
    261, 301, 312, 322–30, 338,
    362, 396, 450, 478; of
    Philippoupolis 224; of
    Skopje 208 of
    Thessalonika 165, 194,
    302, 396, 403–18, 494, 499;
    of the West 409

Draxanos 105–7, 197, 546

Dristra: inscription 56;
    seals 409 n. 31; siege of
    (971) 110, 207, 218, 223,
    325 n. 51, 332, 449; *strategos*
    of 192, 398, 400, 415, 418,
    496–7; *see also*
    Ioannoupolis; Thrace

Drougoubiteia 108, 398
Dvin 484
dynatoi, see 'Powerful'
dynastai 191, 232
Dyrrachion: Ashot
   Taronites 103–5; bishop
   of 428; Chryselioi 104–5,
   365–6, 496, 545; competition
   between Byzantines and
   Bulgarians 42, 103–5,
   496–8; Eustathios
   Daphnomeles 104–5, 233,
   498; inscription 56; John
   Vladislav (death) 212,
   500, 547; *strategos* of 366 n.
   156, 399, 418, 498; surrender
   in 1005 (?) 42, 104–5, 496–8

eastern frontier: *basilikos* of
   376–81; *doux* 313–67;
   economy 356–7, 443–5,
   486–7, 531; *episkeptites*
   of 373–4; evidence for 38–55;
   governance 13, 304–91,
   475–87; *katepano* of 313–67;
   krites 370–91; *krites* of the
   east 386; *kommerkiarios* of
   371; *kourator* of 373–6;
   see also Fatimids; Buyids
Ecloga Basilicorum 88
economy: contraction under
   Basil II (?) 27–8, 525;
   expansion on eastern
   frontier 356–7, 373–4,
   444–5, 531–2; expansion in
   southern Italy 443, 531;
   trade with Rus 513–14
Edessa (Macedonia) 398
Edessa (Mesopotamia) 325
Eirene Komnene 175, 179
Elias of Nisibis: appraisal of
   Basil II's reign 40, 498
Elitzes 422 n. 60
epigraphical evidence 56,
   59–60, 242–3, 248, 333,
   363 n. 148, 424 n. 65,
   453, 500
episkeptites 373–4
Epiphanios Katakalos 373 n.
   167
Escorial Taktikon 59, 301–2,
   323, 357–9, 396–9, 403,
   430, 488
Euchaneia 218
Eugenios, *patrikios* 432
Euphrosyne, daughter of John
   Kourkouas 131 n. 22
Euros River 166
Eustathios Daphnomeles:
   capture of Ibatzes 52, 105,
   111, 191 n. 50, 199–200,
   228–33, 270 n. 57, 292, 421,
   498, 502, 547; *strategos* of
   Dyrrachion 104–5, 233, 498;

Eustathios Daphnomeles (*cont.*):
    John Skylitzes' use of
    encomium of 99, 153–4, 419
Eustathios Maleinos: *strategos*
    of Antioch and Lykandos
    333–4, 336–7, 365; *strategos*
    of Tarsos 337, 341; Skleros
    revolt 205, 257, 341, 451;
    Phokas revolt 258, 465;
    imprisonment 70, 101–2,
    465, 466 n. 57, 545
Euthymios Karabitziotes
    373 n. 167
Eutykios, *patrikios,*
    see Kouleïb
exkoubitores 141, 434

Fars 308
Fatimids: Byzantine relations
    with 32, 47–8, 52, 64, 194,
    248, 252 n. 29, 268, 287,
    306–8, 323, 337–42, 346–51,
    390, 407, 410, 417, 433, 450,
    458, 466 n. 58, 468, 475–8,
    494, 512 n. 176, 524, 526; *see
    also* al-Aziz; al-Hakim
Florentino 441
Fulbert of Chartres 63

Gabriel Romanos, tsar of
    Bulgaria 212, 500; son of
    Samuel Kometopoulos

167–8, 170, 419; defeat at the
    Battle of Spercheios 167–8;
    death 419–20, 547
Gabriel Kaukanos 422 n. 60
Gagic of Ani 101
Ganja 311
gastald 440
Genesios 92, 124, 182, 549
Genizah 478 n. 88
genos 187–239
George of Abasgia and
    Iberia 53, 318 n. 35, 322, 360,
    362–3 n. 148, 367, 482–4, 517
George the Monk 178
George the Monk Continuatus
    125 n. 6
George the *Synkellos* 122,
    179, 548
George Akropolites 204 n. 79
George Kedrenos 66–7 n. 1,
    75, 79–80, 82–6
George Maniakes: revolt
    of 111, 435, 538;
    encomium used by John
    Skylitzes 111, 113, 292–3
George Melias 335–6, 365; *see
    also* Melias, *domestikos* of the
    scholai
George Soussouboule 143
George Tzoulas 515, 547
Georgians: alliances with Basil
    II 193 n. 53, 245, 251–2,

265–6, 287, 311, 453, 480–1;
annexations by Basil II 1, 5,
13, 312, 360–2, 481–3;
Byzantine campaigns
against 39, 53–4, 97–8,
112–13, 312, 318 n. 35,
320–2, 444, 517, 528, 535–7;
Byzantine governance of 27,
360–2, 481–3; monasteries in
Antioch 444–5; troops in
Byzantine armies 192,
211 n. 95, 405 n. 19, 415 n.
44, 545; *see also* Athos;
Iberia; Tao
Georgian Royal Annals 40 n.
44, 252 n. 28
Gerace 437
Gerbert of Aurillac 62, 508
Germanikeia 209, 323, 334
Great Chronographer 112
n. 102
Gregory V, Pope 509
Gregory Kourkouas 224
Gregory Pahlawuni 330
Gregory Pakourianos, *megas
domestikos* 208, 210
Gregory Pakourianos, son-in-
law of Nikephoros
Komnenos 209
Gregory Tarchaneiotes 434 n.
89, 439
Gregory of Taron 316

Gregory Taronites: Phokas
revolt 98 n. 69, 320, 406,
460; *doux* of Thessalonika
165, 194, 196, 221, 403,
406–7, 409, 494; death 165,
406–7
Grigor Narekac'i 241, 485
Gurgen of Iberia 349, 477, 481
Gurgen of Vaspurakan 485
Gymnopelagisia 406

Hafdjidj 357–8, 373 n. 167
hagiographical sources 54–62
Hagiozacharites brothers 191,
199, 265
Haimos Mountains 197, 400,
402, 414
Halys River 259, 453–5
Hamdanids 262, 307–8, 325 n.
51, 326–8, 333, 339, 354,
377–8, 381, 451, 457,
475–8, 524
Harkh 320 n. 39
Harput, *see* Charpete
Hebdomon 525
Helen Lekapene 469 n. 63
Hellas: Bulgarian attacks
on 163, 490, 495; *strategos*
of 107
Henry II, emperor of
Germany 437, 506, 508–9
Her, Plain of 484–5

Herakleios 4, 525

Hierissos 493

Hilal al-Sabi 348

Himerios Solomon 373 n. 167

Hims 47 n. 65, 512 n. 176

Hisn Ziyad, *see* Charpete

Historia Syntomos 87

historiography 77, 112 n. 102,
　129–30, 172–83, 289–98,
　548–50

Holy Sepulchre, Jerusalem 45,
　50, 69 n. 10, 164, 352 n. 121,
　477, 546

Hugh Capet, king of
　France 62, 509

Hungary 42 n. 51, 62

Humbertopoulos 88 n. 50

Ibatzes 52, 111, 191 n. 50, 199,
　228–33, 421, 498, 547

Iberia: *doux* of 366 n. 157;
　katepano of 301, 313, 319,
　360–2, 390; *kourator* of
　373 n. 167; *krites* of 370,
　371 n. 163; *see also* Ani;
　Bagrat III; Georgians;
　Mesopotamia; Tao

Ibn al-Kalanisi 47, 349

Ibn al-Kardabus 63

Ibn Baghil 380

Ibn Bassam 63

Ibn Butlan 356–7, 445 n. 114

Ibn Haldun 254 n. 33

Ibn Hawqal 262, 376 n. 171,
　463

Ibn Marwan, *see* Muhhamid al-
　Daula

Ibn Miskawayh: appraisal of
　Basil II's reign 40, 241,
　248–9, 262

Ibn Shahram: embassy to
　Constantinople 46–7, 242,
　245, 253, 262, 277 n. 72, 289,
　378, 385, 457, 464 n. 51, 467,
　470, 474, 523, 526, 542

idiostata 22

Ikonion 264

Ikhshidids 252 n. 29

Imm 357, 359

Ioannoupolis 398, 400

Isaac Brachamios 191, 199

Isaac I Komnenos: Basil II as
　guardian of 235; coup
　of 110, 213–14, 359,
　548; abdication and
　death 83, 294

Isaac Komnenos, brother of
　Alexios I 219

Italy: *katepano* of 53, 190, 302,
　422, 426, 430–40, 505–7; *see
　also* southern Italy

Iviron monastery 252,
　404, 408

Izz al-Daula 308

Jarrahids 531

Jericho 399

Jerusalem: patriarch of 58, 96 n. 66; pilgrimage 45, 50, 509; St Mark's monastery 379 n. 11; *see also* Holy Sepulchre

John I Tzimiskes: family 139, 314; as *domestikos* of the *scholai* 336 n. 77; usurpation 316, 332–3, 449, 467; coronation 134; Balkan campaign against the Rus 95, 110, 207, 218, 221, 223, 272–4, 332, 399, 448–9, 488; annexation of Bulgaria 17, 60 n. 107, 95, 221, 399–400; military campaigns 3, 95, 218, 249, 277 n. 72, 301, 304, 325–7, 336 n. 77, 339–40, 377–8, 479; frontier governance 301–2, 323–4, 327–8, 337–8, 430–3, 449, 486, 488–9; revolts against 232 n. 139, 315 n. 27, 325 n. 51, 464; image 537; eulogy 80; death 115, 243, 338, 389, 489; Leo the Deacon's appraisal 36, 490; John Skylitzes' coverage 95, 103, 139, 207, 218, 272–4, 292

John II Komnenos 237

John, son of Symeon of Bulgaria 136 n. 38, 143

John Smbat of Ani 312, 483

John Vladimir, *see* Vladimir of Diokleia

John Vladislav, tsar of Bulgaria 212; negotiations with Basil II 52, 170, 418 n. 51, 419, 500; fortifications 56; death 212, 366, 419, 500

John, *basilikos* of Melitene and *Armeniaka themata* 380–1

John, the Deacon: appraisal of Basil II's reign 43, 49–52, 497

John, *kourator* of Antioch 373 n. 167

John, patriarch of Antioch, *chartophylax* of Haghia Sophia 383

John, patriarch of Bulgaria 428

John, the *Protonotarios* 524

John, the *Rector* 126, 143–4

John Alakasseus 273–5

John Amiropoulos 434 n. 89, 439

John Chaldos 404–5, 407 n. 22, 408–9, 494

John Geometres: career 251 n. 27; comments about Basil II 60–1, 250, 411, 469 n. 63, 493

John Hexamilites 373 n. 167

John Italos 123 n. 2

John Kinnamos 115 n. 108

John Komnenos, father of
  Alexios I 235

John Kourkouas, *domestikos* of
  the *scholai*: career and
  campaigns 131, 133, 135–6,
  146, 148, 313–14, 323;
  eulogy of 135–6, 139;
  dismissal by Romanos I 131

John Kourkouas 223, 505

John Lazaropoulos 97–8

John the Lydian 549

John Malalas 77, 112 n. 102,
  174 n. 6, 186

John of Melitene 250, 251
  n. 27

John Orsoleo 52, 504 n. 152

John the Oxite 88 n. 50

John Radenos 131 n. 21

John Sikeliotes 59 n. 104, 122,
  123 n. 2, 548

John Skylitzes: relations with
  Alexios Komnenos 81–90,
  216–17, 541–2; Basil II's
  reign in the *Synopsis
  Historion* 11–12, 33, 37,
  46–54, 66–72, 96–9,
  101–19, 152–70, 188–99,
  204–16, 224–39, 247–98,
  324–8, 338–9, 348–9, 353 n.
  124, 363–4, 401–24, 434–5,
  450–547; career 80–91,
  216–17; chronological
  scope of the *S.H.* 66–8;
  contexts of the *S.H.* 12,
  171–239, 291–8, 300–1;
  Continuation of the
  S.H. 67–8, 75, 80, 83, 85,
  427 n. 74; dating of the
  S.H. 80–91, 203; edn. by I.
  Thurn 68, 75–80, 129; use of
  encomia (*see also* Bardas
  Skleros; Eustathios
  Daphnomeles; George
  Maniakes; Katakalon
  Kekaumenos) in the
  S.H. 99, 110–12, 157–8,
  272–98, 324–6, 338–9,
  450–60, 479; entertainment
  in the *S.H.* 148–9, 168–70,
  177, 225–6, 230, 455;
  extended narratives in the
  S.H. 110–12, 115–16;
  J. Ljubarskij, analysis of
  author and text 114–19;
  manuscript tradition of
  the *S.H.* 76–80; Madrid
  manuscript of the *S.H.* 77–
  9, 184; manuscript
  [U] 68 n. 2, 76–7, 79–80,
  97 n. 67, 196, 212–13 n. 101,
  267 n. 50, 422 n. 62; 'mega

episode' narratives in the *S.H.* 114–19, 159; Michael of Devol 76–7, 89, 196, 211–12 n. 97, 267 n. 50, 422 n. 62, 429 n. 77, 491; author as critic of Michael Psellos 90, 112, 200, 548; military clichés 146–52, 162, 167–8, 223–5, 259, 269–74, 348, 353 n. 124, 454–6, 487–502; modern analyses of author and text 75–119; preface to the *S.H.* 121–5, 182–3, 200, 548–50; problems with interpreting the *S.H.* 66–72, 125–70, 324–5, 338–9, 363–4, 395–6, 401–2, 405 n. 19, 424 n. 65, 487–90; prosopography in the *S.H.* 92, 144, 161, 185–239, 293–4, 291–4, 412, 419, 494, 541; Romanos I's reign in the *S.H.* 121, 125–52, 454–5; J. Shepard, analysis of author and text 72, 75, 99–102, 109–14, 126 n. 8; treatment of rhetoric 134–9, 157, 185, 548–50; source materials for the *S.H.* 12, 91–119, 124–5, 153–4, 223–4, 255–98, 548–50; syntax of the *S.H.* 131–4,

155–6, 185; telescoping in the *S.H.* 100–10, 118–19, 159, 163–4, 169, 190 n. 47, 212 n. 97, 435 n. 91, 483, 487; thematic organization and summary chapters in the *S.H.* 100–10, 118–19, 163–4, 487–91, 497–8, 535–6, 545–7; translation of the *S.H.* 78; author's working methods 83 n. 41, 91–119, 124–70, 292–4, 454–6, 496–8, 549–50

John Xenos, *see* Crete

John Xeros 446

John Zonaras: career 175; in relation to John Skylitzes 66–7 n. 1, 77 n. 25, 82, 83 n. 41, 97–8, 175–9, 199–200, 237; working methods 129, 178–80, 199–200

John and Euthymios, Life of 40 n. 44, 241, 251, 453

Joseph Genesios, *see* Genesios

justice, administration of 368–91

Justinian I 186

Kaisareia 256, 264, 452

Kakhetia 481

Kalbids 505

Kalokyros Delphinas 246, 258, 267, 287, 439, 460–1, 464, 507 n. 162

Kaloudia 326 n. 56

Karin, *see* Theodosioupolis

K'art'li, Chronicle of 40 n. 44

Kasogians 515

Katakalon Kekaumenos 91, 111, 292–3

katepanate, see *katepano* and *doux*

katepano 312–13; of Antioch 353, 389; of Bulgaria 302, 422 n. 62; of Bulgaria and Thessalonika 423 n. 64; of Chaldia and Mesopotamia 317, 330; of Iberia 301, 313, 318, 360–2, 390; of Italy 53, 190, 302, 422, 426, 430–40, 505–7; of Italy and Calabria 435 of Italy Longobardia, and Calabria 435; of Longobardia 423 n. 64; of Mesopotamia 329; of Mesopotamia, Taron, and Vaspurakan 330; of Mesopotamia of the West 398; of Thessalonika 424 n. 65; of Vaspurakan 313, 363–7, 390; see also *doux*

Katotikos, *megas kourator* of Antioch 373 n. 167

Kekaumenos: advice book 55, 177, 219 n. 115, 283 n. 88, 395, 533 n. 220; parallels with John Skylitzes' testimony 107, 155, 401, 419–20, 499

Kemal al-Din 353

Kephalonia 435

Khachik, Armenian *katholikos* 444

Khalidiyat 326

Khazaria 515, 547

Khoy, *see* Her

Kiaba Longos 166

Kibyrrhaiotai 258, 451

Kiev 511–15, *see also* Rus; Vladimir

Kitab al Daha'ir wa-l-tuhaf 252 n. 29

Kleidion, Battle of 52, 69, 110, 154–5, 166, 168, 197–8, 211, 412, 499, 528, 546

Kleterologion of Philotheos 302 n. 3, 408 n. 28

Klimen, son of John Vladislav 213 n. 101

Koloneia: *doux* of 315–16, 330; *krites* of 317

Kometopouloi 17, 32, 47, 49, 102–3, 114, 97 n. 67,

163, 169, 249, 401, 433, 489, 544

kommerkiarios 371

Komnenos family 203, 213, 217, 222, 541

Kontoleo Tornikios 435, 505

Kontostephanos family 217

Kotyaion 264

Koukoulithos 205, 257

Kouleïb *basilikos*: at Melitene 378; at Antioch 341, 377–80, 384, 388, 464 n. 51

kourator 192, 373–6, 445–6

Kourkouas family 125 n. 6, 151, 189, 315–16

Krakras 164, 419, 546

Kresimir III of Croatia 426 n. 70

krites, see Bulgaria; eastern frontier; southern Italy

Laodikeia 301 n. 1, 307, 356–7, 531

Lapara, Battle of 257, 261, 263, 451–2, 544

Larissa (Cappadocia) 280

Larissa (Thessaly) 428; Bulgarian attacks on 103, 163, 402

lead seals, as evidence 8, 13, 59, 219, 300, 302, 316–91, 394–447, 532–3

legislation: novel against the 'Powerful' of Romanos I 20, 462, 471; of Constantine VII 21; of Nikephoros II 21; of 988 against new monastic foundations 59; (996) of Basil II 5–6, 15, 21–3, 26–7, 32, 59, 70, 102, 462–75, 526–7, 545; significance of the anti-'Powerful' novels 21–3, 26, 461–75

Lekapenos family: estates 314–15; pedigree 520; treatment by John Skylitzes 125 n. 6, 127, 133, 136–9, 144–5, 188–9

Lemnos 512

Leo VI 530

Leo, *katepano* of Antioch 353

Leo the Deacon: court rhetorician 59, 250; entertainment 177 n. 12; historian of John Tzimiskes' reign 274–5, 490; historian of Basil II's reign 36–7, 46, 117, 226–7, 241, 250, 411 n. 35, 451–3, 456 n. 27, 492, 511 n. 171, 549; sources 95 n. 62, 223

Leo, Metropolitan of Ochrid 429 n. 77

Leo, Metropolitan of Synada: embassy to Ottonians 57, 410 n. 32, 508; letters 57, 410, 495, 508
Leo, the *Protovestiarios* 61, 116–17, 264–5, 452
Leo, *strategos* of Derxene and Taron 317–18
Leo Aichmalotos 191, 199
Leo Alyates 206
Leo Areianites 223
Leo Argyros 127, 190
Leo the Asian, *see* Leo the Deacon
Leo Maleinos 334
Leo Marsicanus 42 n. 52, 441 n. 103
Leo Melissenos: *doux* of Antioch (985) 342, 409, 457, 475; service in the Balkans (986) 225–7, 343–4, 492; rehabilitation 287, 347, 466
Leo Moroleo 151
Leo of Ostia, *see* Leo Marsicanus
Leo Phokas, brother of Nikephoros II 334
Leo Phokas, son of Bardas 246, 345–6, 461
Leo Sarakenopoulos 400
Leo Tornikios 100–1, 538
Leo of Tripoli 131 n. 21

Letopis Popa Dukljanina, *see* Priest of Diokleia
Levounion, Battle of (1091–2) 88 n. 50, 215, 224
literacy 183–4
Little Preslav 198, 414
Logothete 92, 125 n. 6
Lombard: law 440–1; princes 43–4, 63, 393, 429, 505–8; settlers 442–3
Longobardia 429, 432, 440; *katepano* of 435–8; *kourator* of 446; *strategos* of 436; *see also* Calabria; Italy
Lucera 507 n. 162
Liudprand of Cremona 533 n. 222
Lupus Protospatharius 51, 429
Lykandos 257, 263, 336 *krites* of 370–1; *strategos* of 333–5; *see also* Antioch; Melitene; Sebasteia

Macedonia: centre of Kometopoulos power 49, 105–6, 114, 170, 249, 396, 398–428, 490–501; *praitor* of 84 n. 43
Maghreb 32, 306, 393
Magyar 418
Malakenos, *see* Malakeinos
Malakeinos 107–8, 546

Maleinos family 333–4, 468
Mamistra 335
Mamlan, emir of
  Azerbaijan 312
Manganeios Prodromos
  176 n. 10
Mansour ibn Loulou 354–5,
  478 n. 88
Manuel I Komnenos 175–6,
  236–7
Manuel, historian 133, 549
Manuel Erotikos 110, 116, 189,
  452, 544
Manuel Straboromanos 185
Manzikert: Battle of (1071)
  206; controlled by David of
  Tao 312 n. 21; *kourator*
  of 373 n. 167
Marash, *see* Germanikeia
Margum 425
Maria, wife of John
  Vladislav 210 n. 92, 212,
  213 n. 101, 501
Maria Argyrina 52, 504
Maria Lekapene of Bulgaria
  136, 140
Maria Skleraine, mistress of
  Constantine IX 295
Marianos Argyros 190
Marwanids 309, 321, 329, 354,
  390, 439, 480, 484–5
Masudi 254 n. 33

Matthew of Edessa: appraisal of
  Basil II's reign 40–1, 340 n.
  85, 484
Mauron Oros 332 n. 67,
  359, 376
Mayafariqin 265, 308, 479
Megale Gephyra, Thessaly 56,
  424 n. 65
megistanes 191–2
Meles: tax revolt in Apulia 51–
  3, 72, 190, 365, 433–5, 440,
  505–7, 512 n. 176, 516, 546
Melias: foundation of *tourmai*
  (later themes) of Lykandos
  and Tzamandos 336, 519;
  attack on Melitene (934)
  145
Melias, *domestikos* of the *scholai*
  (972) 308, 325 n. 51, 326–7
Melitene: Bar Gagai mon-
  astery 379; Basil II winters
  there (1022–3) 444, 484 n.
  101; *basilikos* of 378–81;
  local chronicle 379; emirs
  of 127–8, 135; fortifications
  357, 360; *krites* of 370–1;
  kourator of 373 n. 167;
  kouratoria 374–5; military
  action against during 920s-
  30s 147, 323; resettlement
  (after 934) 444; siege of
  (934) 127–8, 140, 145, 147,

Melitene (*cont.*):
304, 374–5, 448; Skleros
revolts 262, 279, 326 n. 56,
378, 450,
458; attacks by Turks
359–60; *see also* Lykandos;
Mesopotamia
Menologion of Basil II 65
Mesopotamia: *doux* of 156,
261, 301, 312–13, 322–30,
338, 362, 389, 478;
episkeptites of 373; *katepano*
of 317, 329–30; *kourator*
of 373 n. 167; *krites* of
370–1; *strategos* of 152,
323–4; *see also* Chaldia;
Iberia; Melitene; Taron;
Vaspurakan
Mesopotamia of the West 398
Messina: landing at (1024)
506; Madrid Skylitzes 79
n. 31; siege of (1040s) 110
Michael II 123 n. 2
Michael IV the Paph-
lagonian 76, 113 n. 105,
213, 427 n. 74, 429 n. 77
Michael VI 91, 213–14, 295,
359
Michael VII Doukas 203, 206,
295 n. 113
Michael VIII Palaiologos
204 n. 79

Michael, son of Symeon of
Bulgaria 125 n. 6, 143
Michael, *doux* of Antioch 352
Michael Anemas 208 n. 87
Michael Attaleiates: connection
to John Skylitzes 83 n. 41,
122 n. 1, 174, 185, 206–7;
encomium of the
Botaneiatai 203, 235
Michael Botaneiates 222, 235
Michael Bourtzes: *strategos* of
Mauron Oros 332 n. 67,
359, 376; assassination of
Nikephoros Phokas 332–3;
in Antioch (969–71) 332,
337–8; *tagma* of *stratelatai*
338; *doux* of Antioch
(976–7?) 338–41, 451;
Skleros revolt 158, 191, 199,
257, 341, 451, 544; *doux* of
Antioch during 990s warfare
against Fatimids 194, 288,
345–7, 364, 367, 389–90,
409–10, 466 n. 58, 468,
475–6, 493; fortification at
Imm 357
Michael of Devol, *see* John
Skylitzes
Michael Glykas: career 176;
connection to John
Skylitzes 67 n. 1, 77 n. 25,
237

Michael Kontostephanos 353
Michael Kourtikios 117, 258, 451, 456 n. 27
Michael Maleinos 333 n. 70
Michael Psellos: career 90; *Chronographia* 123 n. 2, 180, 203, 214, 294–5, 474; coverage of Basil II's reign 3, 6–7, 12, 15, 19, 29–35, 37, 46, 241, 247, 268, 281–6, 303, 462, 470–5, 499, 511 n. 171, 516–17, 522–3, 528, 534; use of encomium of Bardas Skleros 281–3, 291–8; encomia of Constantine X and Michael VII 203, 295 n. 113; *Historia Syntomos* 123 n. 2; modern historians' reading of 11, 19, 31–5, 462–75, 516; contemporary of John Skylitzes 90, 122, 200, 548
Michael Skleros 293
Michael the Syrian: appraisal of Basil II's reign 41, 379
Miracles of St Eugenios of Trebizond: as a history of Basil II's reign 54, 97–9, 241, 318, 422 n. 62
Mirdasids 354, 439, 478 n. 88
Miroslava Kometopoulos 196
Moglena 422 n. 60

Mokh 262, 466 n. 58, 485
Mokios, monastery of 237
Monopoli 442 n. 104
Montecorvino 441
Mopsuestia, *see* Mamistra
Moses Kometopoulos 489
Mosul 262, 265, 266 n. 48, 308–9, 325 n. 51, 326–8, 334, 339, 379 n. 177, 444, 451, 457, 479
Mouselai 468 n. 62
Mstislav 515
Muhhamid al-Daula 321, 329, 480–1
Muş 250, 309, 336 n. 77
Muslims in Byzantium 304, 345, 356–7, 487

Naupaktos 175, 428
Nicholas the eunuch (commander of eastern field army 970–1) 337
Nicholas, *katepano* of Chaldia and Mesopotamia 317, 330
Nicholas, *krites* of Thessalonika, Strymon and Drougoubiteia 108
Nicholas Anemas, *doux* of Skopje (?) 208
Nicholas Chryselios 365, 367
Nicholas Mermentoulos 84

Nicholas Skleros 82, 296 n. 118
Nikaia: defence of by Manuel
    Erotikos 110, 116, 189, 248,
    544; controlled by Skleros
    268, 452; residence of
    Constantine VIII 522; death
    of Isaac Komnenos 83;
    during First Crusade 215;
    Empire of 204 n. 79
Nikephoros I 124, 548
Nikephoros II Phokas:
    usurpation 449, 467, 469;
    coronation of 134; image
    537; legislation 21; frontier
    governance 314–16, 324,
    327–8, 331–6, 355, 365,
    432–3, 444, 486–7; military
    campaigns 3, 132, 207, 335,
    336 n. 77, 355, 359, 376;
    military manuals associated
    with 285, 372 n. 165;
    taxation 533; assassination
    332–3, 449; eulogy 251;
    nephew Bardas 243, 314–16;
    Leo the Deacon's
    account 36, 315, 376;
    Skylitzes' coverage of 94–5,
    103, 132, 134, 533 n. 222
Nikephoros III Botaneiates
    203, 209, 222, 235
Nikephoros Botaneiates 404 n.
    14, 412–13, 419, 546

Nikephoros Bryennios 177,
    179, 235
Nikephoros Diogenes 88 n.
    50, 222
Nikephoros Kabasilas 403 n.
    14
Nikephoros Komnenos 363–5,
    367
Nikephoros Komnenos,
    brother of Alexios I 209
Nikephoros Ouranos: keeper of
    the imperial inkstand 384,
    457, 523–4; embassy to
    Baghdad during Skleros
    revolt 156, 351, 385, 457;
    epitropos of the Lavra 384;
    in the Balkans as *domestikos*
    of the *scholai* 194, 200, 349,
    409–11, 417, 422, 529; defeat
    of Samuel at River
    Spercheios 48, 69, 103, 105,
    107–10, 163–8, 196, 349,
    409–10, 413, 495, 545; at
    Antioch as *kraton* of the
    East 321, 349–52, 383–9,
    409, 422, 435, 477, 481, 529,
    546; letters 54–5, 387;
    military manual 55, 351
    n. 120
Nikephoros Phokas, son
    of Bardas: revolt of Bardas
    Phokas (987–9) 465;

revolt of (1021–2) 32–5,
53, 70, 192, 318, 322, 373
n. 167, 416–17, 484, 517–22,
547
Nikephoros of Phrygia 549
Nikephoros Xiphias: in
Bulgaria 198, 200, 221,
414–17, 419, 521–2, 546;
strategos of Philippoupolis
416; at Battle of Kleidion
166, 168, 198, 200, 416,
499; revolt of (1021–2)
32–5, 53, 70, 192, 318, 322,
373 n. 167, 416–17, 484,
517–22, 547
Niketas, *doux* of
Chaldia 318 n. 35
Niketas Choniates 132 n. 24,
172
Niketas of Mistheia 353
Niketas the Paphlagonian 549
Niketas Pegonites 366, 419
Niketas of Pisidia 362
Nikolitzas 105–6, 188, 197,
200, 546
Nis 426
Nisibis 325
Normans: attacks on
Byzantium during reign
of Alexios Komnenos
88 n. 50, 220, 222, 538;
11th-c. attacks on

Byzantine southern Italy 4,
43, 45, 435, 505–6, 538–9;
12th-c. kingdom 184
numismatic evidence 8, 59,
394, 415 n. 44, 425, 444 n.
114

Obeïdallah *basilikos*: at
Antioch 265, 341, 379–84,
388; at Melitene 379
Ochrid 84 n. 43, 208–10, 212,
423, 427–8, 429 n. 77, 534
oikeiakon, epi ton 371
Olga 513
Optimatoi 223, 363
Orestes, eunuch: in
Bulgaria 419; invasion of
Sicily 72, 112, 432, 506,
543, 547
Orestes, patriarch of
Jersualem 58
Oria 442 n. 104
Orontes River 349, 476
Otto I, emperor of Germany
44, 432–3
Otto II, emperor of Germany:
invasion of southern Italy
45, 47, 435, 437, 503–4,
507 n. 162, 508; marriage to
Theophano 44, 433
Otto III, emperor of Germany:
negotiations with Basil

Otto III (*cont.*):
　II　57–8, 508; rivalry with
　　Byzantium in Rome　57–8
Ottonians　2, 32, 43–4, 72, 393,
　432–3, 508–9

Pakourianos　192, 208–9, 545
Pakourianos, *archon* of the
　archontes　210
Palagiano　446–7
Palermo　79 n. 31
Pandulf, prince of Capua　506
Pankaleia, Battle of　264, 452
Pankratios, *katepano* of
　Antioch　353
Paphlagonia　218
Paristrion　426
Paspalas, *topoteretes*　405
Patmos, monastery of St
　John　36 n. 36, 184 n. 30
Paul, *manglabites* at court of
　Romanos I　127, 143
Paul Bobos　107–9, 495, 546
Pechenegs: during John
　Tzimiskes' reign　273; during
　Basil II's reign　192, 415 n.
　44, 418, 425; 11th-c.
　invasions across Danube
　110, 538–9; defeat by
　Byzantines at Levounion
　(1091–2)　88 n. 50, 215,
　222, 224

Pecs　63
Pegai　126, 135, 149
Pegasios　191, 199, 268
　466 n. 58
Pelagonia　170
Peloponnese　163, 249,
　446, 490
Peri Metatheseon　96, 99
Perkri　367
Pernikos　164
Peter, emperor of
　Bulgaria　102–3, 489;
　son of Symeon of
　Bulgaria　143; marriage to
　Maria Lekapene　136, 140;
　revolts by brother
　Michael　125 n. 6; father of
　Boris II　169, 489
Peter, the *Stratopedarches*　116,
　257, 263–4, 325, 332
Peter Deljan　213, 219,
　427 n. 74
Peter Orsoleo, Doge of Venice
　52, 504
Phebdatos　192, 202, 415, 545
Pherses　192, 193 n. 53, 202,
　545; *see also* Tzotzikios, his
　father
Philagathos, tutor to Otto
　III　509
Philetos Synadenos　54, 350,
　383–8, 477

Philippoupolis: Byzantine
stronghold 164, 170, 224–5,
343 n. 90; *strategos* of 405,
413, 415–17
Philokales, *protovestiarios*
471 n. 71
Philomelion 537
Phokaia 456 n. 27
Phokas family: estates 25,
462–6, 518; historiography
of 94, 269–71, 520 n. 192;
pedigree 203, 519–20; threat
to Basil II 5, 30–2, 461–75,
517–22
Photeinos 126
Photios, patriarch of
Constantinople 189
Phrygia 452
Pikridion, monastery
of 123 n. 2
pilgrims 45, 63, 509
Pindos Mountains 103
Pisa 438, 504
Platypodos 126
Pliska 198, 200, 402, 414, 495
Podandos 373
Poland 44, 514
Polyeuktos, patriarch of
Constantinople 449
'Poor' 20–2, 27
'Powerful': identity of 20;
legislation against 5–6, 15,

20–3, 26–7, 59, 70, 461–75;
Basil II's treatment of 101,
461–75, 517–22, 535–6,
545
Praecepta Militum 285
praitor, see *krites*
Preslav: seat of Bulgarian
royal power 49; attacked
by Byzantium 198, 200, 218,
399, 402, 414, 449, 495;
seals 107–8 n. 90, 343–4 n.
90, 399–400, 404, 409 n. 31,
488; *see also* Ioannoupolis
Prespa, Lake, 421
Priest of Diokleia: appraisal of
Basil II's reign 41, 57, 196,
395, 419–20, 499–500
Prokopios of Kaisareia 174 n. 6
Prousianos, son of John
Vladislav 213
Pyramos River, *see* Ceyhan

Qalat Siman 355

Raban 267 n. 51
Rachab, *see* Rachais
Rachais 373 n. 167
Radomir, son of John Vladislav
213 n. 101
Ralph Glaber 45, 50, 63
Rawwaddids 312 n. 22, 484
Reggio 504

Rhageai, Battle of 264–5, 452, 544

Rheims, *see* Gerbert of Aurillac

Rhodope Mountains 166

Robert, son of Hugh Capet 62

Robert Guiscard 88 n. 50, 435 n. 93

Rodandos 373

Rodomir, *see* Aaron Radomir

Romanos I Lekapenos: eulogy of 136–8; Italian expedition (935) 513; legislation 20, 462, 471; Myrelaion 137; coverage of John Skylitzes 125–52, 188, 202; trade 482 n. 94

Romanos II Porphyrogenitus 93, 132, 243, 290, 449

Romanos III Argyros 28, 38, 113 n. 105, 190, 213, 424, 440, 520, 527, 538

Romanos IV Diogenes 206, 222, 359

Romanos of Bulgaria, son of Peter of Bulgaria 49, 102, 489

Romanos, son of Samuel Kometopoulos of Bulgaria, *see* Gabriel Romanos

Romanos Argyros 127

Romanos Dalassenos 362–3 n. 148

Romanos Kourkouas, son of Theophilos 139

Romanos Kourkouas, brother-in-law of Prousianos 213

Romanos Lekapenos, grandson of Romanos I 131–2 n. 22

Romanos Skleros: first Skleros revolt 204, 452; defection to Basil II during the second Skleros revolt 261, 279, 288, 459–60; service in Syria (after 989) 268, 346, 466 n. 58

Romanos Skleros, *doux* of Antioch (1054) 295–6, 358

Rome: Byzantine jurisdictional dispute with 45–6; object of Byzantine–Ottonian rivalry 57–8, 509

Rossano, Calabria, *see* St Neilos of

Rozen, V. R. 16

Ruj valley 346

Rus: attack on Abydos 512; alliances with Basil II 4, 27, 44, 71, 102, 112, 246, 250, 251 n. 27, 267, 415 n. 44, 460, 483; attack on Bulgaria (968–71) 95, 207, 218, 223, 272–6, 291, 325 n. 51, 332, 337, 399–400, 448–9, 488; attack on Constantinople

(941) 129, 134, 140, 145–6,
148–9; conversion 4, 17, 71,
246, 510–15; troops in
Byzantine armies 422 n. 61,
512–14
Russian Primary Chronicle 41,
510, 513

Sachakios Brachamios 188, 380
Sahak of Handzith 195 n. 59
St Athanasios of the Lavra 56
St Demetrios, *see* Thessalonika
St Eugenios, *see* Miracles of St
Eugenios
St George 218–19
St John the Baptist 94
St John the Evangelist,
monastery in
Constantinople 525
St John and St Euthymios, *see*
John and Euthymios, Life of
St Lazarus of Mount
Galesion 55
St Neilos of Rossano 58
St Nikon Metanoeite of
Sparta 56, 107–8, 241, 498
St Phantinos the Younger 56
St Photios, *see* Thessalonika
St Sabas the Younger 58
St Symeon the New
Theologian 61, 267 n. 50
St Symeon of Sinai 425

St Symeon Stylitzes the
Younger, Monastery of 445
St Theodore *Stratelates* 218–19
St Theodore Tiron 218 n. 113
St Vladimir, *see* Vladimir of
Diokleia
Saktikios 141–2
Salamis 248
Salians 43
Salerno 432
Salibas, *katepano* of
Antioch 389
Samos 190, 435 n. 91, 505
Samosata 323
Samuel Kometopoulos,
emperor of Bulgaria: rise
of 42, 49, 102, 103 n. 81,
159, 163, 195, 401–2, 489–
93; victory over Basil II at
Gates of Trajan (986) 68,
163, 167, 225, 491–2; as
emperor 411 n. 35; dealings
with Taronitai 103, 165,
196, 406–7; defeated by
Nikephoros Ouranos at
River Spercheios 48, 103,
110, 163–4, 166–8, 409–10,
495; peace of 1005 with Basil
II (?) 51, 104–5,
411–12, 496–8; defeated at
Skopje 197; defeated at
Kleidion (1014) 168, 499;

Samuel Kometopoulos (*cont.*):
  palace at Ochrid 427, 534–5;
  death 52, 168, 211–12, 499,
  546
Saoune 304, 377
Sardica 36, 166–7, 225–6, 246,
  402, 413, 491
Sarudj 349
Sarvenisni 265
Sayf al-Daula 334
Schlumberger, G. 5, 9, 16,
  32, 48
Sebasteia 359, 370
Second Sophistic 172
Seleukeia 373, 386
Seleukeia Pieria 96
Senacherim, prince of
  Vaspurakan 209–10, 312,
  483–5, 518
Serbs: diplomatic contacts with
  Byzantium 50, 63, 406, 493;
  doux of Bulgaria, Thes-
  salonika and Serbia 423; *see
  also* Diokleia; Sirmion
Sergios, patriarch of
  Constantinople 71, 189,
  535
Sermon 192, 199, 233–5, 421,
  425, 547
Serres 398
Servia 105–6, 114, 188, 200,
  420, 497

Seyrig lead seal collection 354,
  359, 370 n. 161
Shadaddids 484
Sicily: diplomatic relations
  with 64, 252 n. 29; Basil
  II's campaign against 2, 72,
  112, 433, 506, 512 n. 176,
  535, 543, 547; George
  Maniakes' campaign
  against 113; siege of
  Messina 110; threat
  from 32, 437, 503, 505
Sikeliotes, *see* John Sikeliotes
Sirmion 192, 233–4, 421, 423,
  425, 547
Sisinnios, patriarch of
  Constantinople 81 n. 37,
  189
'Skirmishing' 372 n. 165, 463
Skleraine (anon.), wife of
  Constantine IX 295–6
Skleros family: estates 25, 267,
  462–6; history after Basil
  II 293–7
Skopje 197, 208, 422–3, 426,
  496, 502
Skylitzes Continuatus, see John
  Skylitzes, Continuation
Sofia 36
Solomon *basilikos* of
  Melitene 381
Souda 61

southern Italy: external threats to 4, 32, 44–5, 47, 51, 432–7, 503–5, 508; Byzantine governance of 13, 428–47; internal revolt 51, 72, 363, 505–6, 516, 546

Spaneas 176 n. 10

Sparta 56

Spercheios River, Battle of 48, 69, 103, 105, 107–10, 163–8, 196–7, 349, 409–10, 413, 495, 545

Sphengos 512, 515

Stara Zagora, *see* Beroe

Stephen, king of Hungary 63

Stephen, *magistros* 128

Stephen, Metropolitan of Nikomedia 157, 451

Stephen Kontostephanos 188, 225–7, 343 n. 90, 492

Stephen Lekapenos 144 n. 53

Stephen of Taron: appraisal of Basil II's reign 33, 38, 47–8, 50, 73, 160, 194–5, 227–8, 241, 248–9, 256 n. 34, 320 n. 39, 346, 348, 350, 401, 407, 492–4, 512 n. 176

Stilo, Battle of 437, 504, 507 n. 162

Stoponion 166

Strymon 108, 398

Sumbat Davit'isdze 40 n. 44

Svyatopluk 514

Svyatoslav, prince of Kiev 207, 223

Sylvester II, Pope, *see* Gerbert of Aurillac

Symeon, emperor of Bulgaria 135, 137–8, 142–3, 149, 155 n. 83, 399

Symeon Metaphrastes 62

Synada 58 n. 97; *see also* Leo of S.

Syngrasis 248

Synopsis Historion, *see* John Skylitzes

Syria: Byzantine–Fatimid hostility 47–54, 307–8, 323, 339–41, 346–56, 390, 407, 458, 466 n. 58, 475–8, 512 n. 176; Byzantine governance 338–56, 369–91

Syrian monophysites 28, 304, 335 n. 74, 382–3, 444, 487, 531

Taktikon Vári 55, 227, 492

Tao: Skleros revolt 193 n. 53, 245, 251–2, 265–6, 287, 311, 319–20, 453, 480; annexations of 2, 18, 48, 192, 302, 312, 322, 349, 360–2, 405 n. 19, 481, 484, 512 n. 176,

Tao (*cont.*):
  517; support for Phokas
  revolt 98, 266, 311, 320, 460
Taranto 446–7, 506–8
Tarasios, patriarch of
  Constantinople 548
Taron 195, 309, 313, 316, 320,
  336 n. 77; *katepano* of 330;
  kourator of 373 n. 167;
  strategos of 317–18; *see also*
  Derxene; Mesopotamia;
  Vaspurakan
Taronites family: migration to
  Byzantium 519; in the
  Balkans 165, 194–6, 200,
  222, 466 n. 58, 545
Tarsos: Armenian
  monophyites 444; emir
  of 132 n. 23; *basilikos*
  of 380; *kourator* of 373 n.
  167; *krites* of 54, 350, 383–8,
  477; *strategos* of 337, 341
taxation: administration
  of 368–91, 440–7, 474, 486;
  customs revenue 463,
  482 n. 94; increase in 24, 27,
  70–1, 462–3; in kind
  (Bulgaria) 427, 502, 532;
  remission of 2, 28, 531–2;
  tribute 375–91, 446–7, 456,
  534–5; *see also allenlengyon*
Tephrike 373

Tertiveri 441
Thatoul Pakourianos 209
Theodora Porphyrogenita 203,
  216, 540
Theodore, patriarch of
  Antioch 382
Theodore Alyates 206
Theodore Chryselios 366 n. 155
Theodore Daphnopates: letters
  of 155 n. 83; source of John
  Skylitzes 93–6, 124, 182, 549
Theodore Karantenos 456
Theodore Melias 336 n. 76
Theodore Prodromos 176 n.
  10
Theodore of Sebasteia 36 n.
  36, 96–9, 124, 154, 182, 549
Theodore Senacherim 89 n.
  51, 210
Theodore of Side 549
Theodorokan 198, 200, 404–5,
  413–16, 546
Theodoroupolis 218, 400
Theodosioupolis: location
  of 315–17; emirate of 313;
  capture of (949) 152, 314,
  357–8; controlled by David
  of Tao 320, 480; refor-
  tification (1018) 322, 482;
  strategos of 314 n. 26, 366
  n. 157; inscription 362–3
  n. 148

Theognostes, historian, 123
n. 2
Theognostes Melissenos 329
n. 60
Theophanes the Confessor 77,
122–4, 130 n. 20, 179–80,
548
Theophanes Continuatus:
coverage of the 9th c. 123 n.
2; coverage of Romanos I's
reign 121, 125–52, 314 n.
26, 373–4, 454;
entertainment 177 n. 6;
relationship to John
Skylitzes' *Synopsis* 92–3,
121, 125–52, 157, 188
Theophanes, the
Parakoimomenos 135
Thephano, regent for Basil II
and Constantine VIII, wife
of Romanos II and
Nikephoros II 336 n. 77,
401, 449, 489
Theophano, wife of Otto II
of Germany 44, 433, 508
Theophano Mamantos, wife of
Constantine Lekapenos
125 n. 6
Theophilos Kourkouas 139,
151–2, 314
Theophylact Botaneiates 154,
222, 424 n. 65, 499

Theophylact Dalassenos
353–4, 363 n. 148, 521
Theophylact Lekapenos,
patriarch of Constantinople
128, 136
Theophylact of Ochrid:
complaints of 210 n. 93;
correspondent of Nicholas
Mermentoulos 84 n. 43; of
Nicholas Anemas 208;
Gregory Pakourianos 209;
eulogies to Aaron 214–15
Thermopylae 349
Thessalonika: Bulgarian
attack 163, 165, 412–13,
490; Bulgarian commanders
settled 105–7; defectors to
the Bulgarians 107–9; *doux*
of 165, 194, 196, 302, 396,
403–18, 494, 495, 499;
katepano of 423–4; *krites*
of 108; *strategos* of 404 n.
16, 408–9; metropolitan
428; Panaghia ton
Chalkeon 423 n. 64; St
Demetrios 195, 218–19,
220 n. 118; St Photios 56,
214 n. 114; St Phantinos
56 n. 93
Thessaly, Plain of 163, 490
Thietmar of Merseburg 44,
514

Thomas Artsruni Con-tinuatus 41
Thomas of Split 42 n. 51
Thrace: Long Walls of 60 n. 107; *praitor* of 84 n. 43; *strategos* of 398–400; *see also* Dristra; Ioannoupolis
Thrakesion 108
Tiflis 481
Tikrit 444
Tmutokoran 515
Tornik 251, 320
toupha 501
Traianos, son of John Vladislav 213 n. 101
Trajan's Gates, Basil II's defeat in (986) 36, 68, 491
Trani 442 n. 104
Trebizond: Basil II winters there (1021–2) 98, 322, 535; customs revenue 463, 482 n. 94; *doux* of Chaldia 313; *doux* of Chaldia and T. 318; Phokas revolt (988–9) 98; Miracles of St Eugenios 54
Triaditza, *see* Sardica
tribute, *see* taxation
Tripoli 307, 339–40, 349, 476; emir of 132 n. 23
Troia 441
Turks 4, 110, 215, 538–9

Tryphon, patriarch of Constantinople 126, 128
Tyre 307
Tzamandos 257, 335–6
Tzotzikios, father of Pherses 193 n. 53
Tzotzikios, son of Phebdatus 192, 415, 418
Tzoulas family 515

Umayyads of Spain 63, 505
Uqalids 40 n. 43, 309
Urmiah, Lake 484

Van, Lake 250, 262, 302, 309–12, 316, 320 n. 39, 321, 360, 363, 367, 480–6
Varangians 27
Vaspurakan: annexation 2, 18, 53, 71, 102, 190, 209, 302, 310 n. 16, 312, 328–9, 360–1, 422 n. 60, 547; *katepano* of 313, 330, 363–7, 390, 483–6, 518; *see also* Mesopotamia; Taron
Venice: alliance with Byzantines in Basil II's reign 49–52, 190, 438, 493, 496, 504, 546; alliance with Byzantines in Alexios Komnenos' reign 86–7; Doge of 52, 86–7, 190;

doux of Dalmatia 496;
historiography of 43, 51;
location of Basil II's
psalter 64–5, 472
Vidin 197, 414, 418, 496, 546
Vieste 507
Vladimir, prince of Diokleia
41–2, 196, 419, 493, 500
Vladimir, prince of Kiev:
family 512; alliance with
Basil II (988) 4, 71, 246, 266,
460, 511–15; conversion 17,
246, 510–15

William of Apulia 43, 435 n. 91

Yahya ibn Sa'id: appraisal of
Basil II's reign 16, 33, 38,
46–54, 67 n. 1, 73, 98 nn.
69–70, 104, 160, 193, 241,
249, 254 n. 34, 279–80,
326, 330–60, 395, 401, 407,
416, 419, 423, 426, 428, 453,
456, 459, 472–3, 477, 483–4,
493, 500, 519, 534, 537, 543
n. 241

Zan Patrik 320
Zaphranik 466 n. 58, 485
Zarzma 242, 453
Zoe Porphyrogenita 520

Anzitene 261, 323, 325–6, 450
Apahunikh 320 n. 39
Apameia 346, 348, 478 n. 88
Aparank 485
Apocalpyse of Anastasia 61
Apochaps, *see* Melitene, siege
 (934)
Aposalath, *see* Melitene, siege
 (934)
Apulia, *see* Longobardia
Aquae Saravenae, *see*
 Saravenisni
Aqueduct of Valens 70
Arabissos 373
Araxes River 358 n. 138
Ardanoutzin 481–2
Argyros family 92, 125 n. 6,
 138, 189–90, 202, 520
Aristakes of Lastivert: appraisal
 of Basil II's reign 2, 39, 98 n.
 70, 318 n. 35, 361, 364–5,
 422 n. 60, 466 n. 57, 484,
 522, 528, 535
Aristandros and Kallithea 176
Arkadioupolis 272–6, 285, 291
Armenia: annexations by Basil
 II 1–2, 13, 53, 71, 312, 329,
 362–6, 483–6; *see also* Ani;
 Vaspurakan
Armeniaka themata 327, 371,
 381
Armeniakon 405 n. 18

Armenians: Gospel Book
 (Adrianople) 63; brigands
 360; *katholikos* 444;
 monophysites 28; settlers in
 Byzantine east 304, 380,
 444, 487, 518–19; settlers in
 Bulgaria 427; soldiers in
 Byzantine armies 49, 63,
 145, 210, 262 n. 42, 345, 427,
 451, 519
army: cause of tensions within
 the state 15, 466–8, 521–5,
 527; military threats after
 Basil II 538–40; organization
 in the Balkans 396–428;
 organization in the east
 299–368; organization in
 southern Italy 429–440;
 Skylitzes' (mis)interpretation
 of 146–52; tactics and
 strategy 55, 226–8, 272–4,
 285–6, 375–6, 538–9; theme
 army decline 27–8, 533 n.
 220; theme army survival
 407–9, 436–7
Arsenios 127, 143, 145
Artach 373 n. 167
Artah 357, 359
Artsruni 310 n. 16, 360,
 483–5, 518
Artze 373 n. 167, 405
Ascoli 507 n. 162